When Governments Collide

When
Governments
Collide

When Governments Collide

Coercion and Diplomacy in the Vietnam Conflict 1964-1968

Wallace J. Thies

University of California Press

Berkeley Los Angeles London

University of California Press
Berkeley and Los Angeles, California

University of California Press, Ltd.
London, England

© 1980
The Regents of the University of California

First Paperback Printing 1982
ISBN 0-520-04646-3

Printed in the United States of America

1 2 3 4 5 6 7 8 9

Thies, Wallace J
    When governments collide: Coercion and diplomacy in
    the Vietnam conflict, 1964–1968
  Based on the author's thesis, Yale.
  Bibliography: p.
  Includes index.
    1. Vietnamese Conflict, 1961–1975. 2. Vietnamese
  Conflict, 1961–1975—Diplomatic history. I. Title.
  DS557.7.T46   959.704'32   74-64659

Contents

Tables

Acknowledgments

Anyone who undertakes a project of this magnitude inevitably incurs numerous debts to those individuals and organizations that assist in the process of researching and compiling the manuscript. The International Studies Association and Yale University's Institution of Social and Policy Studies provided grants that enabled me to do much of the preliminary research for this project. Leonard Boudin graciously allowed me to examine the trial transcript from *U.S. vs. Ellsberg and Russo* in his office, while Thomas J. Miller of the U.S. Department of State helped me gain access to the Appendices to the Department's "Working Paper on the North Vietnamese Role in the War in South Vietnam." Congressman Robert Giaimo was instrumental in helping me acquire copies of the "negotiating volumes" of *The Pentagon Papers* when portions of them were first declassified, while Morton Halperin and Monica Andres of the Center for National Security Studies provided me with additional sections of those volumes as they became available. Joe Leitmann helped xerox the declassified material and made sure that the pages that I needed got to me safely. Nicholas Knorr generously provided me with his set of the *Vietnam Documents and Research Notes* series.

I owe special thanks to William P. Bundy, Garry Brewer, John Steinbruner, Paul Seabury, Alexander George, William S. Turley, and King C. Chen, who read all or part of the manuscript and offered many helpful comments and suggestions. The Committee on Research and the Department of Political Science at the University of California, Berkeley, provided grants that enabled me to complete the research and have the manuscript typed, while Chalmers Johnson arranged time off from my teaching duties so that I could work full-time on the project.

I am especially grateful for the advice and encouragement provided by H. Bradford Westerfield, who supervised this project when it took the form of my doctoral thesis at Yale. Not only did he give generously of his time, helping me gain access to sources which otherwise might have remained closed and plowing through innumerable chapter drafts, but he continually brought to my attention issues that I had overlooked or taken for granted, all the while urging me to rethink and reformulate passages that were unclear or otherwise in need of improvement. His influence was felt on virtually every page. Needless to say, though, responsibility for the final product is mine alone.

I owe my greatest debt, however, to my wife, Arlene, who shared both the burdens and the joys of this project with me from its inception, and who supplied patience and understanding even as it grew to consume more hours than either of us ever dreamed possible. For the past five years, this book has been a major part of our lives, and I will always be grateful both for her encouragement and for her ability to smooth the way with a gentle "Shhh! Daddy's trying to write."

Concord, California
January 20, 1979

Abbreviations Used in the Footnotes

The most important documentary material used in this study is drawn from the four so-called "negotiating volumes" of *The Pentagon Papers* (U.S. Department of Defense, *U.S.-Vietnam Relations, 1945-1967* [Washington, D.C.: U.S. Government Printing Office, 1971], VI. C. 1–4). Because those volumes were the last to be compiled and were thus put together hastily, they present serious problems for the analyst attempting to identify his sources carefully and completely. Each volume is divided into numerous sections and subsections, often with separate pagination for each subsection. As a result, establishing the exact location of a cable or memo cited in those volumes requires the identification of both the volume and the section (or subsection) in which the item appears. Without the use of some system of abbreviations, providing full citations for each cable or memo drawn from the "negotiating volumes" would have made the footnotes prohibitively long; but since the "negotiating volumes" contain several dozen subsections, the following list of abbreviations is provided as an aid for those readers who wish to follow the notes closely:

Volume	Sections and Subsections	Abbreviations Used in the Notes
VI. Settlement of the Conflict	The Seaborn Mission to Hanoi, June 1964–	
C. History of Contacts	June 1965	
1. Negotiations, 1965–1966	Discussion	Seaborn Discussion
	Summary	Seaborn Summary
	Chronology	Seaborn Chronology
	Project MAY-FLOWER—The First Bombing Pause	(not cited—duplicates material in the Gravel edition of *The Pentagon Papers* [see below])

Volume	Sections and Subsections	Abbreviations Used in the Notes
	XYZ (Mai Van Bo Contacts), May 1965–February 1966	
	Summary and Analysis	XYZ Summary and Analysis
	Chronology	XYZ Chronology
	Pinta: The Rangoon Contact	
	Summary and Analysis	Pinta Summary and Analysis
	Principal Events in the Rangoon Contact	(not cited)
	Chronology	Pinta Chronology
	The Ronning Missions: March and June 1966	
	Summary and Analysis	Ronning Summary and Analysis
	Chronology	Ronning Chronology
VI. Settlement of the Conflict	Summary	(not cited)
C. History of Contacts	Discussion	Marigold Discussion
2. Marigold	Chronology	Marigold Chronology
VI. Settlement of the Conflict	Principal Dates During Sunflower	(not cited)
C. History of Contacts	Discussion	Sunflower Discussion
3. Sunflower	Chronology	Sunflower Chronology
VI. Settlement of the Conflict	The Setting	The Setting
C. History of Contacts	The U.S. and DRV Conditions for "Talks" Converge	Conditions for Talks
4. Negotiations, 1967–1968	Settlement Terms	Settlement Terms

Volume	Sections and Subsections	Abbreviations Used in the Notes
	Settlement Terms—Extracts	Settlement Terms—Extracts
	Aspen [The Swedish Channel]	Aspen
	Pennsylvania [Aubrac-Marcovich]	Pennsylvania
	Rumanian–North Vietnamese Contacts, October 1966–November 1967	Rumanian Chronology
	Packers (Rumanian-NVN Track): November 1967–February 1968	Packers
	Killy: Italian–North Vietnamese Track, February–March 1968	Killy
	Ohio [Norwegian Channel]	Ohio

Because of the large number of books and articles cited in this study, the full citation for each is given the first time each appears; thereafter, sources are identified only by the last name of the author(s) (in the case of multiple works by the same author, the date of publication is included to identify the specific work being cited). A complete list of the books and articles cited in the notes can be found in the bibliography.

In addition, the following abbreviations are used in the notes:

Full Citation	Abbreviation
"Experiences of the South Vietnamese Revolutionary Movement During the Past Several Years"; a history of the Viet Cong movement written by a Communist cadre sometime around 1963; captured by U.S. troops in South Vietnam during Operation CRIMP in January 1966	The CRIMP Document

Full Citation	*Abbreviation*
Department of State Bulletin	DOSB
Courtroom transcript of *U.S. vs. Ellsberg and Russo*, U.S. District Court, Los Angeles, 1971	Ellsberg Trial Transcript
Foreign Broadcast Information Service	FBIS
The Pentagon Papers, The Senator Gravel Edition, 5 volumes (Boston: Beacon Press, 1971)	I, II, III, IV, V Gravel
Public Papers of the President: Lyndon B. Johnson (published annually)	Johnson Papers
National Security Study Memorandum No. 1, 1969 (an interagency study of U.S. options in the Vietnam conflict, commissioned by President Nixon for his use in reviewing U.S. policy toward the war)	NSSM-1
U.S. Department of Defense, *U.S.-Vietnam Relations, 1945-1967* (Washington, D.C.: U.S. Government Printing Office, 1971) (the official U.S. Government edition of *The Pentagon Papers*)	U.S.-Vietnam Relations
U.S. Department of State, "Working Paper on the North Vietnamese Role in the War in South Vietnam," reprinted in *Vietnam Documents and Research Notes*, no. 37, May 1968	Working Paper

Abbreviations Used in the Text

AFP Agence France Presse
AP Associated Press
ARVN Army of the Republic of (South) Vietnam

BOQ Bachelor Officers' Quarters

CAS Controlled American Source (CIA Station, Saigon)
Chicom Chinese Communist
CIA Central Intelligence Agency
CINCPAC Commander-in-Chief, Pacific
CJCS Chairman, Joint Chiefs of Staff
COMUSMACV Commander, U.S. Military Assistance Command, Vietnam
COSVN Central Office for South Vietnam

DCM Deputy Chief of Mission
DIA Defense Intelligence Agency
DMZ Demilitarized Zone
DOSB Department of State Bulletin
DPM Draft Presidential Memorandum
DRV Democratic Republic of (North) Vietnam

ExComm Executive Committee

FBIS Foreign Broadcast Information Service
FYI For Your Information

GCI Ground Controlled Intercept
GVN Government of (South) Vietnam

ICC International Control Commission
ISA International Security Affairs

JCS Joint Chiefs of Staff

LOC Lines of Communication

MACV Military Assistance Command, Vietnam
MAROPS Maritime Operations

NLF National Liberation Front
NSAM National Security Action Memorandum
NSC National Security Council
NSSM National Security Study Memorandum
NVA North Vietnamese Army
NVN North Vietnam

OPLAN Operations Plan
OSD Office of the Secretary of Defense

PAVN People's Army of (North) Vietnam
POL Petroleum, Oil, Lubricants
POW Prisoner of War

RLAF Royal Laotian Air Force
ROK Republic of (South) Korea

SAM Surface-to-Air Missile
SEATO Southeast Asia Treaty Organization
SNIE Special National Intelligence Estimate
SOP Standard Operating Procedure
SVN South Vietnam

UPI United Press International
USAF United States Air Force
USG United States Government
USIS United States Information Service
USN United States Navy

VC Viet Cong
VNAF (South) Vietnamese Air Force
VPA (North) Vietnam People's Army
VWP Vietnam Workers' Party

Glossary of Code Names

ARC LIGHT Program of air strikes by U.S. B-52 aircraft on Communist-held targets in South Vietnam.

ASPEN Secret negotiating channel between the U.S. and North Vietnam, involving Swedish diplomats as intermediaries.

BARREL ROLL Covert program of air strikes by U.S. planes flown by U.S. pilots on infiltration targets in Laos, begun mid-December 1964.

BUTTERCUP Abortive diplomatic contact between U.S. Embassy officials in Saigon and agents purportedly representing the National Liberation Front.

DE SOTO PATROLS Intelligence-gathering patrols conducted by U.S. Navy destroyers in the Gulf of Tonkin.

FARMGATE Covert program of air strikes against Communist-held targets in South Vietnam by VNAF aircraft flown by USAF pilots.

FLAMING DART I & II Air strikes on North Vietnam by U.S. planes and pilots in February 1965 in reprisal for Viet Cong attacks on U.S. installations at Pleiku and Qui Nhon.

KILLY Secret negotiating channel between the U.S. and North Vietnam, involving Italian officials as intermediaries.

MARIGOLD Secret negotiating channel between the U.S. and North Vietnam, involving Polish and Italian officials as intermediaries.

MAYFLOWER U.S. diplomatic initiative involving a brief pause in the bombing of North Vietnam in May 1965 combined with efforts to open talks through the DRV Embassy in Moscow.

OHIO Secret negotiating channel between the U.S. and North Vietnam, involving Norwegian diplomats as intermediaries.

OPLAN 34A Three-phase program of covert operations against North Vietnam, begun February 1, 1964.

PACKERS Secret negotiating channel between the U.S. and North Vietnam, involving Rumanian diplomats as intermediaries.

PENNSYLVANIA Secret negotiating channel between the U.S. and North Vietnam, involving two French citizens (Raymond Aubrac and Herbert Marcovich) as intermediaries.

PINTA Direct diplomatic contact between the U.S. and North Vietnam, conducted through the U.S. Embassy and DRV Consulate in Rangoon, Burma.

ROLLING THUNDER Program of overt air strikes by U.S. aircraft against North Vietnam, begun March 2, 1965.

SUNFLOWER Secret negotiating channel between the U.S. and North Vietnam, involving both the use of intermediaries (British and Soviet officials during Prime Minister Kosygin's February 1967 visit to London) and direct contacts between U.S. and DRV diplomats in Moscow.

XYZ Direct diplomatic contact between the U.S. and North Vietnam, involving two retired

Foreign Service Officers (Edmund Gullion
and Paul Sturm) and DRV diplomats in
Paris.

YANKEE TEAM Program of low-level reconnaissance flights
by U.S. aircraft over Communist-held areas
in Laos, begun May 1964 and later
expanded to allow for suppressive fire by
escort aircraft if fired upon first.

1

Introduction

IN THE MONTHS following the coup
that ousted the regime of President Ngo Dinh Diem, officials of the U.S.
Government responsible for the American aid program to South Vietnam watched with growing dismay as the continuing political turmoil in
Saigon and the increasing strength and boldness of the Viet Cong
guerrillas resulted in a steady deterioration of the position of the anti-
communist forces in South Vietnam. Frustrated by the failure of suc-
cessive Saigon governments to conduct the war effort effectively,
American officials began more and more to look outside South Vietnam for possible solutions. In particular, the focus of planning in
Washington shifted steadily away from programs internal to South
Vietnam and toward the option of using American military force in an
attempt to induce the government of North Vietnam to cease its
support and direction of the insurgency in the South. While this effort
centered initially on developing a program of covert operations aimed at
exerting "progressively escalating pressures" on the North Vietnamese,
the continuing decline in the South soon led to explicit consideration of
overt pressures against the North.[1]

The first serious proposals for overt pressures against North Vietnam
were apparently raised by the Joint Chiefs of Staff in January 1964; by
the end of February, those proposals were receiving serious study within
the government.[2] As the Pentagon analyst notes:

there was considerable theorizing during this period about the best manner of
persuading North Vietnam to cease aid to the NLF/VC by forceful but

1. For details on the planning for covert pressures against the North, see III Gravel, pp. 149–152.
On the shift toward explicit consideration of overt pressures, see III Gravel, p. 152 ff.
2. The JCS proposal is reprinted as Document no. 157 in III Gravel, pp. 496–499. For additional
details on the studies of possible overt pressures against the North, see III Gravel, pp. 154–157;
David Halberstam, *The Best and the Brightest* (Greenwich, Conn.: Fawcett, 1972), pp. 434–439; and
Chapter 2, below.

restrained pressures which would convey the threat of greater force if the North Vietnamese did not end their support of the insurgency in South Vietnam. In certain circles in Washington, at least, there was what appears now to have been an amazing level of confidence that we could induce the North Vietnamese to abandon their support of the SVN insurgency if only we could convince them that we meant business, and that we would indeed bomb them if they did not stop their infiltration of men and supplies to the South.[3]

This line of reasoning dominated the planning for pressures against the North that continued throughout 1964 and into 1965. While overt pressures were initially rejected in the hope that the threat of such pressures, conveyed by third-country emissaries and reinforced by the covert program along with a well-publicized buildup of American forces in Southeast Asia and the Western Pacific, would suffice to end North Vietnamese aid to the insurgents in the South, it was apparent by September 1964 that more drastic measures would be required.[4] By November 1964, preparations for overt pressures were under way in earnest under the aegis of an interagency working group chaired by William Bundy. The February 1965 attacks on the American installations at Pleiku and Qui Nhon served to trigger those preparations, resulting in the initiation on March 2, 1965 of a campaign of sustained bombing against North Vietnam code-named ROLLING THUNDER. But while the nature of the actions under consideration shifted steadily in the direction of increasingly severe pressures, culminating in ROLLING THUNDER, the concepts and assumptions underlying the planning for pressures against the North remained largely the same. ROLLING THUNDER, much like the covert program that preceded it, was seen by civilian officials as a program of gradually intensifying pressures designed to erode North Vietnamese will to continue by holding out the prospect of progressively mounting levels of destruction unless they complied with American demands to end their role in the war in the South.[5] While expectations concerning North Vietnamese suscepti-

3. III Gravel, pp. 64–65.

4. On the hope that threats would suffice, see III Gravel, pp. 65, 170; and Halberstam, pp. 486–487. See also the account of the Seaborn missions to Hanoi in Chapter 2, below. On the publicity given the U.S. buildup, see III Gravel, pp. 177, 182; and Chapter 2, below. On the emerging consensus that overt pressures would at some point be required, see III Gravel, pp. 192–202.

5. American perceptions of the way in which the bombing was to influence North Vietnamese decision-making are discussed extensively in III Gravel; see, for example, pp. 153, 198–200, 289–290, 312–321. See also Ambassador Taylor's remarks in a CBS interview on February 14, 1965, cited by William Simons, "The Vietnam Intervention, 1964–1965," in Alexander George, David Hall, and William Simons, *The Limits of Coercive Diplomacy* (Boston: Little, Brown, 1971), pp. 145–146. However, as we shall see in Chapters 2–4, below, the bombing program that was implemented by the Johnson Administration differed significantly from the program envisioned in the plans drawn up during 1964 and the first few months of 1965.

bility to such pressures varied within the U.S. Government, there appears to have been a consensus by February 1965, albeit a fragile one, that a program of restrained but gradually rising pressures would at some point induce the North Vietnamese to seek a settlement on terms favorable to the United States.[6]

In line with this belief, a related focus of the planning during 1964–1965 centered on the way in which military pressures would mesh with diplomatic initiatives to produce an acceptable settlement. The problems confronting American planners in this respect were seen as essentially twofold. On the one hand, while it was generally assumed that some kind of international conference on Vietnam was inevitable, the shaky situation in the South meant that much of the work done in anticipation of such a conference focused, ironically, on the possibility of having to stall off international pressures for negotiations until the bombing had had time to improve the American bargaining position.[7] On the other hand, both during the period leading up to the expected talks and then once the talks had begun, it would be necessary to "orchestrate" military pressures with diplomatic communications so as to enable the U.S., in John McNaughton's words, to "'negotiate' by an optimum combination of words and deeds."[8] The bombing, in this respect, was seen as an American "blue chip," the halting of which could be traded for an end to the North Vietnamese role in the insurgency; hence, a corollary theme in the Administration's planning was the necessity of keeping up the pressure for as long as it took to secure North Vietnamese compliance with American demands, regardless of any talks or negotiations that might be under way.[9]

And yet, despite the extensive preparations and optimistic expectations, it soon became apparent that the North Vietnamese were not collapsing under the weight of the bombing. Indeed, by March 1968,

6. For examples of the differing estimates of North Vietnamese susceptibility to overt pressures, see III Gravel, pp. 155–157, 212–215, 294–297. For a superb account of both the emergence of the consensus on bombing and also the fragility of that consensus, see Halberstam, pp. 585–645. See also James C. Thomson, "How Could Vietnam Happen?" *The Atlantic*, April 1968, p. 51; "Bill Moyers Talks About LBJ, Power, Poverty, War, and the Young," *The Atlantic*, July 1968, pp. 29–30; and William Simons, "The Vietnam Intervention, 1964–1965," in George, Hall, and Simons, pp. 148–149.

7. On the belief that a negotiated settlement was inevitable, see III Gravel, pp. 204–205, 225–228. On the possibility of having to stall off negotiations until the bombing had improved the American bargaining position, see III Gravel, pp. 204–205, 221–228, 247–248, 331–332.

8. Document no. 209 in III Gravel, p. 581. See also (all in III Gravel): Document no. 171, p. 526; Document no. 223, p. 602; Document no. 226, pp. 610–611, 615; Document no. 241, p. 665; and Document no. 246, p. 678.

9. On these points, see III Gravel, pp. 167, 247–248; Halberstam, pp. 691–692; and Maxwell Taylor, *Swords and Ploughshares* (New York: W. W. Norton, 1972), pp. 352–353.

despite three years of ROLLING THUNDER and the presence of over
500,000 American troops in South Vietnam, the U.S. was no closer to a
satisfactory settlement than it had been at the start of 1965. How can we
account for this failure of the plans for pressuring North Vietnam to
work out as expected? Why did it take so long just to begin formal negotiations on a settlement (begun in Paris in May 1968)? What was it that
went wrong?

Beliefs about the "persuasive force" of "sustained pressure," to use
McGeorge Bundy's words,[10] were not the only ones called into question
by the Johnson Administration's experiences in Vietnam. Implicit in
the plans for pressuring North Vietnam were two additional assumptions that were rarely subjected to serious scrutiny: first, that the leadership of the Administration would be able to exert close control over the
Administration's actions, thus enabling it to "orchestrate" military pressures with diplomatic communications to Hanoi and to convey certain
messages to Hanoi by the actions that it took (e.g., the spectre of inevitable destruction unless the North complied with American demands—
a signal that was to be conveyed by the pattern of gradually rising pressures against the North); and, second, that the U.S. was not irrevocably
committing itself by going ahead with ROLLING THUNDER, that the
bombing could be turned on or off, up or down at will, and that if it did
not work it could always be stopped.[11] And yet, the experience of three
years of pressuring the North was such as to call both of these assumptions into question. Concerning the first, not only did the Administration find it difficult to convey clear "signals" to Hanoi, but in addition,
at numerous points in the war, Administration officials found themselves in the awkward position of saying one thing and doing another.[12]
Concerning the second, as indicated by the bitterly divisive intragovernmental struggles during 1967 and 1968 over stabilizing and ultimately halting the bombing, it was considerably harder to turn the
bombing off than would have been expected on the basis of the studies

10. See Document no. 250 in III Gravel, p. 689.

11. For examples of the belief that the U.S. could "orchestrate" words and deeds, see the references in note 8, above. On the belief that the U.S. was not irrevocably committing itself by going
ahead with the bombing, see (all in III Gravel): Document no. 188, pp. 557–558; Document no.
220, p. 595; Document no. 223, p. 602; Document no. 224, p. 605; Document no. 246, p. 678. See
also III Gravel, p. 316; and Halberstam, pp. 624–626. The only major challenge to the latter
assumption came from George Ball, although Halberstam reports that John McNaughton was
privately skeptical of the Administration's ability to control events in Vietnam. On this, see the
October 5, 1964 memo by Ball, reprinted in The Atlantic, July 1972, p. 41; and Halberstam, pp.
447–449.

12. The Administration's difficulties in these respects will be discussed in more detail in Chapters 6–8, below.

prepared during 1964 and 1965.[13] Why should this have been the case? Why weren't the Administration's expectations concerning "signalling" and "orchestrating" borne out, and how did its difficulties in these areas affect efforts to reach a satisfactory settlement? Why weren't expectations about the controllability of the bombing borne out? What factors intervened to upset those expectations, and what effect did they have on efforts to end the war?

In attempting to answer questions such as these, however, it will be important to realize that the problem confronting us is not quite as one-sided as the discussion to this point might suggest. As we shall see, at three points in the war, the North Vietnamese indicated a willingness to begin direct talks with the U.S. without a prior cessation of the bombing, even to the point of engaging in talks with an authorized representative of the U.S. in Paris in August and September of 1965.[14] How can we account for this apparent departure by the North Vietnamese from their frequently stated insistence on a bombing cessation as the price for talks? Did these episodes signal tacit acceptance of the bombing as an American "blue chip," or were there other reasons for this apparent North Vietnamese willingness to engage in "unconditional discussions"?

In addition to questions concerning specific aspects of the Vietnam conflict, there is a second and more general set of questions that we wish to consider here. The theorizing within the Johnson Administration during 1964–1965 on the subject of pressuring North Vietnam was not original; rather, it was to a large extent a reflection of a particular set of ideas on the role of force in foreign policy—ideas that originated in the mid-1950s in response to the Eisenhower Administration's "New Look" in defense.[15] As presented in Secretary Dulles's famous speech on "massive retaliation," the "New Look" incorporated the "basic

13. On these points, see IV Gravel, pp. 107–276; and Halberstam, pp. 776–770, 782–784.

14. The U.S. representative was Edmund Gullion, who met four times with the senior DRV diplomat in Paris, Mai Van Bo, as part of the initiative code-named XYZ. The other two instances occurred during the initiatives code-named PINTA and MARIGOLD. In addition, the American chargé d'affaires in Moscow met several times with his DRV counterpart during January and February 1967, although the DRV representative was unwilling to discuss substantive issues without a bombing halt. On these contacts, see Chapters 3–4, below.

15. On this point, see Bernard Brodie, "Learning to Fight a Limited War," in William Gerberding and Bernard Brodie, The Political Dimension in National Strategy: Five Papers, Security Studies Project, University of California, Los Angeles, 1968, pp. 26–32; Robert Osgood, "The Reappraisal of Limited War," Adelphi Papers, 54 (February 1969), 43–44; Colin Gray, "What RAND Hath Wrought," Foreign Policy, 4 (Fall 1971), 112–115; and Alexander George, "The Development of Doctrine and Strategy," in George, Hall, and Simons, pp. 5–11.

decision" to "deter aggression" by depending primarily on a "great capacity to retaliate, instantly, by means and at places of our choosing." Such an approach, Dulles argued, would enable the U.S. to "get, and share, more basic security at less cost."[16]

The "New Look," however, provoked widespread criticism and a major controversy over strategy. With the growth of Soviet nuclear capabilities and the emergence of the balance of terror, critics of the "New Look" argued that the most likely form of future conflict would be local attacks conducted for limited objectives along the Sino-Soviet periphery.[17] Furthermore, the critics argued, with American cities vulnerable to Soviet nuclear forces, not only would threats of "massive retaliation" in response to local attacks lack credibility, but reliance on such a doctrine would, in the event an attack occurred, put the U.S. in the position of having to "put up or shut up."[18] "There is no escaping the conclusion," Kaufmann argued, "that the doctrine of massive retaliation would be likely to confront us continually with having to choose between one or the other of these two most distasteful alternatives."[19]

To escape that dilemma, the critics urged the Administration to maintain a capability to respond to local attacks with sizable conventional forces and, if necessary, to use those forces to deny victory to an aggressor while keeping the conflict geographically confined and limited with respect to the objectives sought and the weapons employed. The objective during wartime would not be to annihilate an opponent's forces but rather to "convince" him to break off the conflict short of obtaining his objectives but without resorting to nuclear war. "To accomplish these ends," Kaufmann argued,

the enemy would have to be persuaded of a number of things. He would have to be persuaded that he could not achieve his objectives by the means currently being employed. He would also have to be convinced that he could not attain them by expanding the war in scope or in weapons. At the same time, . . . he

16. Quoted in DOSB, January 25, 1954, p. 108. Useful overviews of the "New Look" can be found in Samuel Huntington, *The Common Defense* (New York: Columbia University Press, 1961), pp. 64–88; and Glenn Snyder, "The New Look," in Warner Schilling, Paul Hammond, and Glenn Snyder, *Strategy, Politics, and Defense Budgets* (New York: Columbia University Press, 1962).

17. See Bernard Brodie, "Unlimited Weapons and Limited War," *The Reporter*, November 18, 1954, pp. 19–20; William Kaufmann, "Limited Warfare," in Kaufmann (ed.), *Military Policy and National Security* (Princeton, N.J.: Princeton University Press, 1956), p. 103; Robert Osgood, *Limited War: The Challenge to American Strategy* (Chicago: University of Chicago Press, 1957), pp. 5, 126, 158–159; and Henry Kissinger, *Nuclear Weapons and Foreign Policy* (Garden City, N.Y.: Doubleday, 1958), pp. 14–15, 23–24, 41–42.

18. William Kaufmann, "The Requirements of Deterrence," in Kaufmann (ed.), p. 24.

19. Ibid., pp. 24–25. See also Brodie (1954), pp. 18–19; Osgood (1957), pp. 1, 5–6, 159–161; and Kissinger (1958), pp. 115, 130–131.

would have to have it demonstrated that the costs of fighting to him out-weighed the costs to the United States, and consequently that the advantages of terminating the conflict were greater than the advantages of continuing it.[20]

In the years that followed, the ideas first developed by Kaufmann, Brodie, Osgood, and Kissinger were the subject of continuing study and refinement, culminating in the mid-1960s with the appearance of Schelling's *Arms and Influence* and Kahn's *On Escalation*.[21] In the process, however, some subtle but significant changes were introduced, changes perhaps best symbolized by Schelling's distinction between "deterrence" and "compellence."[22] Theorists such as Kaufmann, that is, writing in the context of a Cold War dominated by the spectre of future Koreas, were primarily interested in strengthening deterrence by knocking down the belief that threats of nuclear retaliation could provide a cheap substitute for the conventional forces necessary to fight Korea-style conflicts. By the mid-1960s, however, the controversies over "massive retaliation" and "limited war" had been largely resolved by the Kennedy Administration's commitment to "flexible response" and subsequent upgrading of American conventional forces. In addition, the memory of Korea no longer dominated limited war thinking; instead, Schelling identified three types of "limited war"—"wars of the battlefield" (Korea), "wars of risk" (nuclear crises), and "wars of pain and destruction" (the American bombing of North Vietnam).[23]

As a result of these changes in the strategic environment, theorists such as Schelling and Kahn began to explore the possibility of using force and threats of force not only to deter an opponent from taking some undesirable action but also to induce an opponent to stop doing something he was already engaged in or even to undo something he had already accomplished. Furthermore, while the writings of the limited

20. William Kaufmann, "Limited Warfare," in Kaufmann (ed.), p. 113. See also Kaufmann, "The Requirements of Deterrence" and "Limited Warfare," pp. 24–25 and 116–122 in Kaufmann (ed.); Osgood (1957), pp. 1, 5; Kissinger (1958), pp. 125, 130–139; and Bernard Brodie, *Strategy in the Missile Age* (Princeton, N.J.: Princeton University Press, 1959), pp. 313–314.

21. Thomas Schelling, *Arms and Influence* (New Haven, Conn.: Yale University Press, 1966); Herman Kahn, *On Escalation* (Baltimore: Penguin Books, 1965). See also Daniel Ellsberg, "The Theory and Practice of Blackmail," in Oran Young (ed.), *Bargaining: Formal Theories of Negotiation* (Urbana: University of Illinois Press, 1975), pp. 343–363; Maxwell Taylor, *The Uncertain Trumpet* (New York: Harper & Bros., 1960); Henry Kissinger, *The Necessity for Choice* (New York: Harper & Bros., 1960); Thomas Schelling, *The Strategy of Conflict* (Cambridge, Mass.: Harvard University Press, 1960); Klaus Knorr and Thornton Read (eds.), *Limited Strategic War* (New York: Praeger, 1962); Morton Halperin, *Limited War in the Nuclear Age* (New York: John Wiley, 1963); and Bernard Brodie, *Escalation and the Nuclear Option* (Princeton, N.J.: Princeton University Press, 1966).

22. Schelling (1966), pp. 69–78.

23. Ibid., pp. 166–176.

war theorists had been marked by an implicit belief that the only way to "convince" an expansionist opponent of the futility of Korea-style attacks was by slugging it out on the battlefield for as long as it took to "persuade" the opponent to quit, Schelling and Kahn focused on techniques for using force and/or threats of force to induce an opponent's withdrawal or compliance by communicating the threat of greater destruction to follow unless or until the opponent backed down. Schelling and Kahn, in short, were primarily interested in what might be called the "articulate" or "expressive" use of force. For them, military actions were important not so much for the damage they caused as for the messages they conveyed to an opponent.[24]

Perhaps the best illustration of this approach can be found in a chapter by Schelling suggestively titled "The Idiom of Military Action."[25] Starting from the premise that "war is always a bargaining process, one in which threats and proposals, counterproposals and counterthreats, offers and assurances, concessions and demonstrations, take the form of actions rather than words, or actions accompanied by words,"[26] Schelling attempted to explore the nature of this bargaining process, with special emphasis on the ways in which states may use actions to communicate with their opponents. In this respect, Schelling's discussion of "wars of pain and destruction" (which he also refers to as "coercive wars") is especially instructive.

In particular, Schelling argues that the distinguishing feature of coercive war is "the direct exercise of the power to hurt, applied as coercive pressure, intended to create for the enemy the prospect of cumulative losses that were more than the local war was worth, more unattractive than concession, compromise, or limited capitulation." What is important here is the way in which the pressure is to be exerted:

24. See, for example, Schelling (1966), pp. 79–90; and Kahn, pp. 205–210, 246–252. One should not exaggerate the differences between the "limited war" theorists (Kaufmann, Brodie, Osgood, Kissinger) and Schelling and Kahn. Both groups sought to devise techniques to use military force to "persuade" an opponent to back down; the major difference had to do with the techniques identified by each group. While analysts such as Kaufmann and Brodie emphasized the use of conventional forces to block an opponent's advance and simultaneously inflict costs high enough to induce the opponent's withdrawal, Schelling and Kahn suggested that the necessary costs could be imposed in a theater other than the one opened up by the attacker's hostile action. That is, if the opponent undertook some undesirable action (e.g., attempting to seize a piece of territory), the defender could seek to induce the opponent's withdrawal by implementing or threatening to implement coercive measures in another theater of battle (e.g., bombing the opponent's cities) unless or until the opponent complied with the coercer's demands. The efficacy of these strategies will be discussed in more detail in Chapter 5, below.

25. Chapter 4 in Schelling (1966), pp. 126–189.

26. Ibid., p. 142.

the hurting does no good directly, it can only work indirectly. Coercion depends more on the threat of what is yet to come than on damage already done. The pace of diplomacy, not the pace of battle, would govern the action; and while diplomacy may not require that it go slowly, it does require that an impressive unspent capacity for damage be kept in reserve. Unless the object is to shock the enemy into sudden submission, *the military action must communicate a continued threat*. . . . To use the threat of further violence against somebody requires that you keep something in reserve—that the enemy still have something to lose. This is why coercive warfare . . . is likely to look restrained. The object is to exact good behavior or to oblige discontinuance of mischief, not to destroy the subject altogether.[27]

And yet, despite the efforts of Schelling and Kahn and their predecessors, our understanding of the role of coercion in international politics is relatively limited.[28] Perhaps the most serious problem in this respect has been the absence of any extended critical examination of the assumptions underlying the theorizing on military force as an instrument of coercion. As we saw earlier, the Johnson Administration's strategy for coercing North Vietnam rested on three main assumptions:

1. That a program of gradually rising military pressures would induce the government in Hanoi to end its support for the insurgency in South Vietnam.

2. That the leadership would be able to "fine-tune" the Administration's actions so as to enable it to "orchestrate" words and deeds and "signal" by deed as well as by word.

3. That the use of force would be controllable—i.e., that the pressures against the North could be turned on or off, up or down at will.

27. Ibid., pp. 167, 172–173 (emphasis added).

28. This point is conceded by Schelling (1966), p. 167. By "coercion" we mean (following Ellsberg): "the art of influencing the behavior of others by threats" ("The Theory and Practice of Blackmail," in Young [ed.], p. 344). At times, the threats may be purely verbal; at other times, they may take the form of actions intended to convey the prospect of more forceful actions to follow if compliance is not forthcoming; while at still other times, coercive pressures may take the form of actions intended to impose serious costs on an opponent, thus tacitly threatening a high level of continuing costs until the opponent complies. In addition, it will be helpful to distinguish between two types of coercive threats—i.e., "compellent threats," intended to induce an opponent to stop doing something the latter is *already* engaged in and/or to undo something the latter has *already* accomplished; and "deterrent threats," intended to *prevent* an opponent from taking some action by posing for him a prospect of cost and risk outweighing his potential gain. For additional discussion of the nature of coercion, see Schelling (1966), pp. 1–34; and Alexander George, "The Development of Doctrine and Strategy," in George, Hall, and Simons, pp. 22–23. On the distinction between deterrent and compellent threats, see Schelling (1966), pp. 69–86; and Alexander George, "The Development of Doctrine and Strategy," in George, Hall, and Simons, pp. 23–24.

Not surprisingly, the work of virtually all the theorists considered above, from Kaufmann up to and including Schelling and Kahn, was based on a substantially similar set of assumptions. That is, implicit in the work of almost all of those theorists was the belief that an opponent would back down in the face of American military pressure.[29] Equally striking was their tendency to assume that it would be possible for an American Administration to "orchestrate" words and deeds and shape its actions in a way that communicated precise and specific messages to an opponent.[30] Finally, as Brodie himself noted in a retrospective analysis of limited war thinking, "scenarios on limited war have almost universally assumed that the United States would be free to escalate or deescalate or make whatever adjustments in policy that the President and his advisers might think desirable."[31]

Despite the importance of these assumptions, their validity was rarely challenged in the writings of the theorists under consideration.[32] The years since the mid-1960s, moreover, have seen relatively little in the way

29. Thus, for example, Schelling's (1966, p. 175) analysis of American efforts to coerce North Vietnam points out the "hard choice" between "being clear so that he [the enemy] knows what we want or vague so that he does not seem too submissive when he complies" and neglects the harder choice that would arise if the enemy failed to comply as expected. Kahn's discussion is more restrained, recognizing that either the U.S. or the Soviet Union might wish to back down in some future crisis (Kahn, pp. 248–250); while Kaufmann, likewise, concedes at one point that the U.S. might find it necessary to "cut losses and bow out as gracefully as possible from difficult and unprofitable conflicts" ("Force and Foreign Policy," in Kaufmann [ed.], p. 248). Despite that qualifier, virtually all of Kaufmann's work was marked by confidence in American ability to wage limited war successfully.

30. See, for example, William Kaufmann, "Limited Warfare," in Kaufmann (ed.), pp. 113–114, 122–123; Osgood (1957), pp. 24, 239; Kissinger (1958), pp. 140–142, 189; Halperin (1963), pp. 126–128; Kahn, p. 55; and Schelling (1966), pp. 142–151. Kahn (pp. 221–224) did suggest that adversaries involved in an escalating conflict might have difficulty comprehending each other's intentions; while Schelling (1966, p. 151) qualified his analysis by noting that problems such as background noise and misinterpretation might complicate attempts to embody specific messages in the actions taken by governments. Still, the work of both Schelling and Kahn was characterized by a relatively high degree of confidence in the ability of governments to "orchestrate" words and deeds and "signal" by deed as well as by word.

31. Brodie (1968), p. 30. For an optimistic appraisal of the prospects for controlling violence during crisis situations, see Albert and Roberta Wohlstetter, "Controlling the Risks in Cuba," *Adelphi Papers*, 17 (April 1965), especially pp. 18–19. Kahn (pp. 231–234) did recognize that it might be harder to go down the escalation ladder than up; while Schelling (1966, pp. 93–94) conceded that "accidents" might result in uncontrolled escalation, although the manipulation of that risk, in his view, opened up additional possibilities for coercion. Similarly, Osgood (1957, pp. 25–26) recognized that the "controllability" of violence might decrease as the level of violence increased. That was one reason why, in his view, statesmen should make strenuous efforts to minimize the amount of force used in wartime.

32. The only exceptions are Brodie (1968); and Schelling (1966), pp. 85–86. Schelling's views will be discussed in more detail in Chapter 5, below.

of efforts to remedy this situation. While several analysts have published essays critical of the doctrines of limited/coercive war, those essays have, on the whole, been content to emphasize the failure of those doctrines as applied during the Vietnam conflict without exploring in detail the reasons for that failure.[33] Similarly, while there have been several valuable studies of bargaining and coercive tactics during crisis situations, those studies have been primarily concerned with the impact of crises on state behavior and only secondarily with issues such as the ability of governments to "orchestrate" words and deeds and to "signal" by deed as well as by word.[34] Even the one book-length study of "coercive diplomacy" that is available is less helpful than its title might suggest, primarily because of the restrictive conceptual framework within which its authors have chosen to develop their ideas.[35] It will be helpful to elaborate on this last point in order to introduce some of the theoretical perspectives to be developed in the present study.

As presented by George and his colleagues, success at "coercive diplomacy" depends primarily on two factors: "first, what is demanded of the opponent and, second, how strongly disinclined the opponent is to comply," although George notes elsewhere that "the coercing power's own motivation is also an important factor that must enter into the calculus of a coercive strategy."[36] These factors are not independent

33. Andrew Pierre, "America Down, Russia Up: The Changing Political Role of Military Power," *Foreign Policy*, 4 (Fall 1971), 168–176; Raymond Aron, "The Evolution of Modern Strategic Thought," *Adelphi Papers*, 54 (February 1969), 9–11; Melvin Gurtov and Konrad Kellen, "Vietnam: Lessons and Mislessons," P-4084, RAND Corp., June 1969, pp. 13–15; Osgood (1969), pp. 49–51; and Gray, pp. 122–125. An important exception is Ernest May's study of bombing as an instrument of coercion, *"Lessons" of the Past* (New York: Oxford University Press, 1973), chap. 5.

34. See, for example, Oran Young, *The Politics of Force* (Princeton, N.J.: Princeton University Press, 1968); Glenn Snyder, "Crisis Bargaining," in Charles Hermann (ed.), *International Crises: Insights from Behavioral Research* (New York: Free Press, 1972); and Phil Williams, *Crisis Management* (London: Martin Robertson, 1976). While these authors were sensitive to the constraints that governments face in using military force as an instrument of coercion (Young, chap. 6, provides an important analysis of Schelling's concept of the "idiom" of military action), their primary concern was with "crisis" as an independent variable, with the result that none of these studies constitutes the full-fledged reappraisal of coercion in international politics being called for here. Indeed, much of their work was based on the "model" of coercive bargaining developed by Schelling in order to refine and extend the "model," as opposed to challenging the validity of the model itself.

35. George, Hall, and Simons (cited in note 5, above). Also of less help than its title might suggest is the volume on *Coercion* (Nomos XIV) edited by J. Roland Pennock and John W. Chapman (Chicago: Aldine Atherton, 1972). Of the book's fifteen essays, only three (those by McIntosh, Jervis, and Chapman) deal with coercion in international politics, none of which challenge the Johnson Administration's assumptions listed above.

36. Alexander George, "The Development of Doctrine and Strategy," in George, Hall, and Simons, pp. 22, 26. A similar approach is developed in Williams, pp. 160 ff. See also the "credibility-critical risk" model developed by Snyder, "Crisis Bargaining," in Hermann (ed.).

of each other, since, as George points out, "the strength of the opponent's motivation not to comply is highly dependent on what is demanded of him"; similarly, "the chances that coercive diplomacy will
be successful will be appreciably greater if the objective selected—and
the demand made—by the coercing power reflects only the most important of its interests that are at stake, for this is more likely to create an
asymmetry of motivation favoring the coercing power."[37] Finally,
practitioners of "coercive diplomacy" are enjoined to use the least
amount of force necessary to attain their goals. In contrast to what
George describes as "traditional military strategy," coercive diplomacy

focusses upon affecting the enemy's will rather than negating his capabilities. It
does not rely on ample or quick use of force to achieve political objectives.
Rather, if threats alone do not suffice and force is actually used, it is employed
in a more limited, selective manner than in the quick, decisive strategy. That is,
force is used in an exemplary, demonstrative manner, in discrete and controlled increments, to induce the opponent to revise his calculations and agree
to a mutually acceptable termination of the conflict.[38]

One problem with this approach, however, is that, much like the
approaches used both by the theorists of limited/coercive war and by
the planners in the Johnson Administration, it implicitly assumes that
governments involved in coercion can be best conceptualized as single,
calculating actors that attempt to increase their chances of success by
manipulating the demands they make of an opponent.[39] But while there

37. George, "The Development of Doctrine and Strategy," in George, Hall, and Simons, pp. 22, 26.
38. George, "The Development of Doctrine and Strategy," in George, Hall, and Simons, p. 18.
In effect, the approach developed by George and his colleagues did not seek to challenge the
Johnson Administration's assumptions listed above, although George did suggest that coercive
diplomacy "is viable only under special conditions and, moreover, is quite difficult to implement
successfully" ("The Development of Doctrine and Strategy," in George, Hall, and Simons, p. 19).
The essay by Simons ("The Vietnam Intervention, 1964–1965") was more sensitive to the problems
involved in "signalling" and "orchestrating," although it was handicapped by the fact that it
appeared prior to the publication of The Pentagon Papers' "negotiating volumes" with their account
of the Seaborn missions to Hanoi (discussed in Chapters 2–3, below). Omission of the Seaborn
missions leads both Simons and George (in the book's final chapter) to a number of erroneous conclusions, especially as to whether the U.S. was transmitting ultimatums to Hanoi.
39. This is not to suggest that George and his colleagues were unaware of the differences between
a government and a unitary actor—see, for example, George's comment ("Comparisons and
Lessons," in George, Hall, and Simons, p. 234) on the importance of exploiting splits among officials in the target state's government. But while they have acknowledged these differences, neither
George and his colleagues nor the theorists of limited/coercive war have explored in detail the
differences between coercing an individual and coercing the individuals who collectively comprise
another government (the sole exception here is Schelling [1966], pp. 85–86). As a result, while
George and his colleagues have exhorted policymakers to seek out detailed information on their
opponents in another government, they have to some extent disregarded their own advice, as ex-
emplified by George's analysis of the interaction between "Washington," "Moscow," "Peking," and

may appear to be a relationship between changes in the demands made of an opponent (for the sake of creating an asymmetry of motivation) and success at coercive diplomacy, such a relationship conceals at least as much as it reveals. On the one hand, since governments are essentially coalitions of numerous individual decision-makers, virtually all of whom occupy positions within large, semi-autonomous, bureaucratic organizations, any government involved in an attempt at coercion is likely to speak with many voices at once.[40] As a result, senior officials may find it difficult to improve their chances of coercing another government by reducing the demands being made of their opponent for the simple reason that they can never be certain which voices their opponents are listening to and what inferences their opponents are drawing from the "signals" being sent their way.[41] On the other hand, since a decision to yield in the face of coercive pressures must often be made by the very officials who argued (often long and hard) for going ahead with whatever action brought on the coercive pressures to begin with (and then imposed on subordinates who will very likely have built up a sizable stake in terms of careers, promotions, and budgets in a continuation of the previous policy), the decision to yield is one that may be fraught with peril for the careers and at times the lives of the officials who must make it, a point that can easily be concealed by dispassionate references to "affecting the enemy's will."[42] For officials involved in an attempt at coercion, then, the problems that they must confront include not only deciding what demands they should make of an opponent but also learning *who* on the other side must do *what* if the attempt at

---

"Hanoi" in the Laotian and Vietnamese cases ("Comparisons and Lessons," in George, Hall, Simons, pp. 236–237). One of the goals of the present study will be to suggest that the necessary information about the workings of other governments often is available, provided analysts and officials are diligent in seeking it out and know what to look for (this point is discussed in more detail in Chapters 5–8, below).

40. For a discussion of the impact of organizational and job perspectives on governmental performance, see Graham Allison, *Essence of Decision* (Boston: Little, Brown, 1971), chaps. 3 and 5; and Morton Halperin, *Bureaucratic Politics and Foreign Policy* (Washington, D.C.: The Brookings Institution, 1974), chaps. 3, 5, and 14. For a critique of the arguments by Allison and Halperin, see Stephen Krasner, "Are Bureaucracies Important?" *Foreign Policy*, 7 (Summer 1972); and Robert Art, "Bureaucratic Politics and Foreign Policy: A Critique," *Policy Sciences*, 4:4 (December 1973); see also the rebuttal to the views of Krasner and Art, presented in Robert Gallucci, *Neither Peace Nor Honor* (Baltimore: Johns Hopkins University Press, 1975), chap. 6.

41. Although senior officials generally assume that their opponents will notice immediately any statements or action(s) aimed at them and correctly discern their meaning, such is often not the case. This problem is discussed in more detail in Chapters 7 and 8, below.

42. On this point, see the discussion of DRV decision-making in Chapters 5 and 6, below. See also Adam Ulam's assessment of the effect of the collapse of the scheme to put missiles in Cuba on Khrushchev's position at the top of the Soviet government, in *Expansion and Coexistence* (New York: Praeger, 1968), p. 675.

coercion is to succeed and *how* can the coercer's actions be manipulated, if at all,[43] to strengthen the position of those in the target state willing to pursue the policies being demanded by the coercer. Further, since a prerequisite of successful manipulation is an awareness of which of the coercer's actions officials in the target state are paying close attention to and what "messages" are being inferred from those actions, officials on the side doing the coercing will have to accumulate considerable information about the interests and preferences of their opposite numbers and the constraints under which the latter must operate.

All of this, in turn, suggests the second set of questions to be considered here. In particular, how valid were the assumptions identified earlier as implicit in the theorizing on coercion in international politics? Considering that many of the most innovative ideas concerning strategy and tactics were drawn from the level of interpersonal relations —e.g., between buyer and seller, employer and employee, landlord and tenant, criminal and victim[44]—how relevant would those observations be when the parties involved in an attempt at coercion were not individuals but rather governments? To what extent and under what circumstances are governments motivated by and thus responsive to "pain"? Could a government successfully engage in the "orchestrating" and "signalling" required to "communicate a continued threat"?[45] Would it be possible to reverse the escalatory process, or would a government involved in an attempt at coercion find itself committed to an indefinite expansion of the conflict?

This chapter, in short, has suggested two reasons for attempting a reappraisal of the role of coercion in international politics: not only should such a reappraisal contribute to a better understanding of the causes of the American frustration in Vietnam but it should also help in filling in an important gap identified earlier in the literature on limited/coercive war—namely, an evaluation of the validity of the assumptions implicit in much of the theorizing on that subject. The importance of such a reappraisal should not be underestimated. There is no guarantee that the U.S. will not find itself engaged in another coercive conflict in the future. If such a conflict should occur, it will be crucial to understand

43. As we shall see in Chapters 6 and 8, below, senior officials are likely to encounter serious difficulties in attempting to control the actions of their own government in accordance with their policy preferences.

44. This tendency was especially noteworthy in the works of Ellsberg and Schelling. For additional discussion of this point, see Allison, pp. 15–20.

45. On this point, see the description of the coercive process in Schelling (1966), p. 172.

both the possibilities as well as the limitations on using force and threats of force to induce another government to comply with American demands. While the Vietnam conflict possessed certain unique features (the fragmentation of Southern society, the confidence and determination of the leadership in the North), it should still be possible to acquire at least some understanding of the utility of force and threats of force for purposes of coercion from a careful examination of the Johnson Administration's efforts to coerce North Vietnam.

Consequently, in Chapters 2 to 4, below, we look closely at the historical record of the Vietnam conflict between 1964 and 1968 in order to gather the "data" on which our reappraisal will be based.[46] As we shall see, the experience of the Johnson Administration in that conflict was such as to call into question the validity of each of the three assumptions discussed above. As a result, in Chapters 5 to 7, we attempt to explain why this should have been the case.[47]

46. As should be evident from our discussion to this point, the period 1964–1968 was chosen because of the strong parallels between the Johnson Administration's strategy for coercing North Vietnam and the ideas developed by theorists such as Schelling and Kahn. While it would have been interesting to extend our discussion of Vietnam policymaking beyond 1968, such an extension is unnecessary for our purposes and beyond the scope of the present study. Although attempts to coerce Hanoi played an important role in the Nixon Administration's handling of the Vietnam conflict, the Nixon Administration made use of a number of strategies in pursuing its goals in Southeast Asia, including building up the South Vietnamese armed forces ("Vietnamization") and use of brute force to destroy North Vietnamese capabilities for sustained conflict (the Cambodian and Laotian incursions). To do justice to the development of Vietnam strategy under Nixon would thus have required a separate book-length project over and above the present study.

47. It should be noted that the first two of the three assumptions listed earlier are really two sides of the same coin—i.e., in trying to explain why the North did not back down, it may have been that the Administration's strategy was inherently flawed or that the strategy was basically sound but the Administration's implementation was flawed (i.e., the "orchestration" was faulty). Alternatively, the failure of the Administration's efforts to coerce Hanoi may have been a product of both of these factors. In any event, while we consider assumptions 1 and 2 separately in Chapters 5 and 6, below, it should be kept in mind that they are in fact closely related.

PART I

Coercing Hanoi

2

Pressures Against the North: Preparation and Experimentation

For MOST AMERICAN policymakers, the aftermath of the Diem coup was a deeply frustrating period. Those who had hoped that Diem's removal would usher in an era of government stability and progress in the war were instead subjected to a series of disheartening revelations, the effect of which was increasingly to undermine the optimistic assumptions on which American policy toward South Vietnam had been based. The coup, as Mecklin reports, "released an avalanche of new information on the true state of the struggle against the Viet Cong, all of it bad. It was a story of decay that had been underway for months, or years."[1] More importantly, evidence of the deterioration began to penetrate the screen of optimism that had previously cloaked reports to Washington. In December 1963, Ambassador Lodge forwarded a report describing the Saigon Government's tenuous hold on Long An province, which apparently made a strong impression on Secretary McNamara, then preparing for another visit to South Vietnam. Thus forewarned, McNamara returned from his trip impressed with the gravity of the situation, reporting to the President that "Viet Cong progress has been great during the period since the coup with my best guess being that the situation has in fact been deteriorating in the countryside since July to a far greater extent than we had realized." Still, he conceded that his appraisal may have been overly pessimistic, pointing out that both Lodge and General Harkins (COMUSMACV) felt that January would bring a significant improvement.[2]

1. John Mecklin, *Mission in Torment* (Garden City, N.Y.: Doubleday, 1965), p. 282.
2. On the Long An report, see III Gravel, pp. 28–32. McNamara's report is reprinted as Document no. 156 in III Gravel, pp. 494–496.

The hopes of Lodge and Harkins notwithstanding, the situation in the South was destined to get worse before it got better. On January 30, General Nguyen Khanh staged a coup ousting the ruling triumvirate of generals and shattering, in the process, whatever hopes might have remained for a stable and effective government in Saigon. Contributing further to the pessimistic climate was a series of reports issued in February 1964 by a special CIA team sent to check on the quality of Vietnamese intelligence. The team's reports were uniformly negative, finding the Strategic Hamlet program to be at a "virtual standstill" and even going so far as to suggest that the "tide of the insurgency in all four corps areas appears to be going against the GVN."[3]

It was in this atmosphere of deepening gloom that proposals for directly pressuring North Vietnam began receiving serious consideration in Washington. As suggested in Chapter 1, those proposals were based on three largely implicit assumptions: (1) that the North Vietnamese would be responsive to a program of gradually rising military pressures; (2) that the U.S. would be able to "orchestrate" words and deeds and "signal" by deed as well as by word in a way that would lead to a satisfactory settlement; and (3) that the U.S. would be free to escalate or de-escalate the pressures at will. But before we can attempt to judge the validity of those assumptions, there are a number of specific questions that must first be explored. For example, what expectations did American planners hold concerning the impact of military pressures on the North? How were those pressures expected to influence North Vietnamese decision-making? In what way were the North Vietnamese to become convinced that it was in their interest to end their support for the Viet Cong?

Of greater importance is the question of how the plans for pressuring North Vietnam were drawn up and then translated into action. As we shall see, there was a strong desire among civilian officials, the President included, to "experiment" in an attempt to see what could be accomplished by measures short of the overt use of force against the North— e.g., by threats, threatening deployments, and covert operations. To a large extent, this was the result of the President's refusal to give serious consideration to overt pressures until after the Presidential election,

3. Quoted in II Gravel, p. 194. For additional details on the CIA team's reports, see III Gravel, pp. 32–35; and Halberstam, pp. 374–375. The significance of the team's reports can be seen by contrasting them with earlier estimates that had stated that, while the situation might have been deteriorating in the Delta, satisfactory progress was being made in the northern part of South Vietnam. For examples of this judgment, see III Gravel, pp. 20, 25, 495. For a summary of other pessimistic reports reaching Washington at this time, see III Gravel, pp. 39–42.

although it also reflected serious disagreements between civilian and military planners over the nature and severity of the pressures that would be required. As a result, the Johnson Administration had under consideration during 1964 several approaches to the problem of pressuring North Vietnam, no one of which was ever completely accepted or rejected. Instead, responsibility for both the planning and execution of policy was fragmented among a multiplicity of agencies that had few incentives to coordinate their activities with each other (especially since the President was also unwilling to give more than sporadic attention to Vietnam prior to the election). Consequently, the actions that were taken by the U.S. during 1964 were the product not of a single, integrated plan but rather of several distinct planning efforts, the implementation of which happened to overlap. This outcome suggests several additional questions. In particular, what combinations of military pressures and diplomatic communications were envisioned by different groups in the Administration as offering the greatest potential for influencing North Vietnamese decision-making, and how did these compare with the combination of words and deeds actually transmitted to Hanoi? Could a fragmented and disjointed planning effort produce an "orchestrated" set of words and deeds that would have the desired effect on decision-making in Hanoi? More importantly, how would this multi-track effort appear to the North Vietnamese? What impact, if any, did it have on their calculations?

I. First Proposals for Pressuring the North
(December 1963-March 1964)

While planning for South Vietnamese "hit and run" operations against the North had been underway since May 1963, it was not until the Vietnam Policy Conference in Honolulu on November 20, 1963 that proposals for carrying the war to North Vietnam were seriously considered by American policymakers. At that conference, it was decided to develop a combined MACV-CAS/Saigon plan for a 12-month program of covert operations against the North. Plans for these operations were reviewed by Secretary McNamara during his December 1963 trip to Saigon and forwarded to the White House on December 19. Two days later, the President directed that an interdepartmental committee headed by Major-General Krulak should study the MACV-CAS plan to select from it the operations involving the least risk.[4]

4. On these points, see III Gravel, p. 151.

The Krulak Committee's report, submitted on January 2, 1964, recommended a variety of covert operations to be carried out in three phases over a 12-month period and intended to "inflict increasing punishment upon North Vietnam and to create pressures, which may convince the North Vietnamese leadership, in its own self-interest, to desist from its aggressive policies."[5] The Committee's recommendations were approved by the President on January 16, with implementation of the initial phase to begin on February 1. As described by the Pentagon analyst:

The first phase (February through May) called for intelligence collection through U-2 and communications intelligence missions and psychological operations involving leaflet drops, propaganda kit deliveries, and radio broadcasts. It also provided for about "20 destructive undertakings . . . designed to result in substantial destruction, economic loss and harassment." The second and third phases involved the same categories of action, but of increased tempo and magnitude, and with the destructive operations extending to "targets identified with North Vietnam's economic and industrial well-being."[6]

The Committee's report was noteworthy in two respects. On the one hand, implicit in its recommendations was the belief, apparently shared by high-level civilian officials, that there was some level of damage to the North's economy that would cause it to abandon its support for the Viet Cong. Underlying this was the explicit assumption that current North Vietnamese strategy was to support the Viet Cong

at little cost to itself and at little risk to its industrial complex, while counting for victory upon United States and South Vietnamese war weariness. . . . The importance attached by Hanoi's leaders to the development of North Vietnam's economy suggests that progressive damage of its industrial projects, attrition of its resources and dislocation of its economy might induce a decision to call off its support of the Viet Cong. This reaction might be intensified by the traditional Vietnamese fear of Chinese domination, where expanded operations by our side could arouse concern in Hanoi over the likelihood of direct Chinese Communist intervention in North Vietnamese affairs.[7]

On the other hand, with respect to the level of damage required to end the North's participation in the war, the report was curiously ambivalent. While the assumption that the North sought victory at little cost to itself would seem to imply that relatively low levels of damage would suffice to end its role in the insurgency, the committee took the position that

5. Quoted in III Gravel, p. 151.
6. Ibid., p. 150.
7. Quoted in III Gravel, p. 152.

it is far from clear whether even the successful conduct of the operations . . . would induce Hanoi's leaders to cease and desist. . . . Toughened, as they have been, by long years of hardship and struggle, they will not easily be persuaded by a punitive program to halt their support of the Viet Cong insurgency unless the *damage* visited upon them is of great magnitude.[8]

The committee, in short, recommended that the U.S. commit itself to a program of pressures against the North even while doubting that the operations recommended would suffice to accomplish the goal of ending the North's role in the insurgency. The effect was thus to reinforce the belief that it would be possible to "convince" the North Vietnamese while simultaneously focusing attention on the need for harsher measures that seemed to offer greater potential for influencing Hanoi's calculations.[9] This theme was promptly picked up by the Joint Chiefs of Staff (JCS) in a pair of memos to Secretary McNamara, both of which argued that "victory" could not be achieved unless the U.S. was "prepared fully to undertake a much higher level of activity" which, they suggested, should include preparations for an increased American role in the war in the South as well as preparations for committing American forces directly against the North, specifically air bombing of selected targets.[10]

Probably in response to proposals of this type (in addition to the JCS, both Ambassador Lodge and Walt Rostow were advocating increased pressures against the North), the President directed on February 20 that "contingency planning for pressures against North Vietnam should be speeded up. Particular attention should be given to shaping such pressures so as to produce the maximum credible deterrent effect on Hanoi."[11] And yet, despite the emphasis on "maximum credible deterrent effect," American actions and public statements were in fact conveying a somewhat ambiguous picture to Hanoi. The operations carried out under Phase I of the covert program (which had been formally designated OPLAN 34A) came nowhere near achieving the Krulak Committee's goal of inflicting "substantial destruction, economic loss, and harassment" on the North.[12] For one thing, the program experienced what the JCS would later term a "slow beginning,"

8. Quoted in III Gravel, pp. 151, 153 (emphasis in original).

9. On this point, see III Gravel, pp. 152–153.

10. The JCS memo quoted here, dated January 22, 1964, is reprinted as Document no. 157 in III Gravel, pp. 496–499. See also the JCS memo to Secretary McNamara, dated February 18, 1964, discussed in III Gravel, pp. 44–46.

11. Quoted in III Gravel, p. 154. Ambassador Lodge had cabled the White House on February 15, arguing for his preferred "carrot and stick" approach, discussed in greater detail below. On Rostow's views, see II Gravel, pp. 310–311.

12. See III Gravel, p. 150.

with few operations carried out successfully during Phase I (February-May).[13] In addition, the nature of the operations attempted was such that it is doubtful the North Vietnamese felt themselves under any new and/or more serious pressures. The CIA had been air-dropping sabotage teams into North Vietnam ever since 1961, although, as Goulden reports, those operations had "an *ad hoc* quality, their object [being] random harassment rather than accomplishment of long-range war goals."[14] Under OPLAN 34A, the frequency of those operations was increased, but the North Vietnamese apparently viewed them as an extension of the old, random harassment program rather than as a new and threatening development.[15] In any event, the outcome of the operations under OPLAN 34A remained the same as under the old program —in almost every case, the teams were promptly captured as soon as they set foot in North Vietnam.[16]

Similarly, public statements by American officials during this period were noteworthy primarily for the ambiguous image they created concerning future American policy in Vietnam. On February 21, the day after his directive concerning contingency planning for pressures against the North, the President himself engaged in a not-very-subtle attempt to play on North Vietnamese fears of wider war. In a prepared speech at the University of California, Los Angeles, the President described the war in the South as "first and foremost a contest to be won by the Government and people of that country for themselves" but added that "those engaged in external direction and supply would do well to be reminded that this type of aggression is a deeply dangerous game." To insure there was no mistaking his message, the President instructed his press secretary to inform newsmen that the speech constituted a deliberate warning to Hanoi that the U.S. might feel compelled to carry the war to the North, a theme that was dutifully disseminated by the press in the days that followed.[17]

13. See V Gravel, p. 322.

14. Joseph C. Goulden, *Truth Is the First Casualty* (Chicago: Rand, McNally, 1969), p. 86. See also William Westmoreland, *A Soldier Reports* (Garden City, N.Y.: Doubleday, 1976), p. 106.

15. On this point, see the DRV's "Memorandum Regarding the U.S. War Acts Against the Democratic Republic of Viet Nam in the First Days of August 1964," which notes that "in recent years, U.S. and South Vietnamese air and naval craft have repeatedly intruded into the airspace and the territorial waters of the Democratic Republic of Viet Nam, threatened the security of the population of the coastal regions, and smuggled in many commando groups for espionage and sabotage activities—all these groups have been, however, captured by the army and people of the Democratic Republic of Viet Nam. *But since July 30, 1964,* the United States and its stooges have made a new and more serious step forward." For the text of this memo, see John Galloway, *The Gulf of Tonkin Resolution* (Rutherford, N.J.: Fairleigh-Dickenson University Press, 1970), p. 498 (emphasis added).

16. On this point, see Halberstam, p. 499; III Gravel, p. 72; and Westmoreland, p. 107.

17. For the President's remarks, see DOSB, March 16, 1964, p. 399. On the President's instruc-

Whatever coercive effect the President's statement may have had, however, was almost certainly dissipated by the events of the next three weeks. The President's remarks, as Geyelin reports, "immediately kicked up reaction from those opposed to deeper involvement in the Vietnamese war."[18] As a result, on February 27, partly to dispel fears that the U.S. was about to escalate the war, Secretary Rusk stressed at a news conference that "the central problem, as far as the pacification of South Vietnam is concerned, is in South Vietnam, . . . and no miracle in the north is going to suddenly transform or eliminate the problem in South Vietnam."[19] Two days later, the President himself told reporters that "the plans [for extending the war] that have been discussed in the papers are not plans that have come to my attention or that I have approved." To complete the turnabout, on March 14, the President himself denied, in a nationally televised interview, that his UCLA speech had contained any hint that the war might be extended to North Vietnam.[20]

The outcome of this episode appears to have been principally twofold. On the one hand, as Wicker has argued, it is quite possible that officials in Hanoi interpreted the events of February and March as evidence that the President would talk harshly but would not actually commit American forces against North Vietnam, and that he would have little domestic support if he did try to enlarge the war. There was certainly no evidence of any decline in North Vietnamese support for the Viet Cong in the weeks following the UCLA speech; if anything, that support increased. Some regular units of the North Vietnamese army began preparing for infiltration into South Vietnam as early as April 1964. Furthermore:

Starting in early 1964, Hanoi began to develop its infiltration trails through Laos into an army-scale supply route, capable of handling continuous truck traffic to South Vietnam. A large group of North Vietnamese army construction battalions . . . was deployed in the area by 1964 to oversee the development of this road net.[21]

tions to his press secretary, see Philip Geyelin, *Lyndon B. Johnson and the World* (New York: Praeger, 1966), p. 188; and Tom Wicker, *JFK and LBJ* (Baltimore: Penguin, 1968), pp. 217–222. For an example of the press's handling of the President's warning, see Max Frankel, "Washington Hints at Saigon Raids on North Vietnam," *New York Times*, February 23, 1964, p. 1.

18. Geyelin, p. 188.

19. The Secretary's remarks can be found in DOSB, March 16, 1964, p. 408. See also Geyelin, p. 188; and Wicker, p. 218.

20. For the President's news conference of February 29, see Johnson Papers, 1963–1964, p. 324. At that same news conference, the President also noted that "we must rely on [the South Vietnamese] for such action as is taken to defend themselves" (Johnson Papers, 1963–1964, p. 323). For the President's March 14 interview, see DOSB, April 6, 1964, p. 526.

21. On these points, see Wicker, p. 238; and Working Paper, p. 12. See also Thomas Latimer,

On the other hand, public reaction to his UCLA speech apparently impressed the President with the need for careful preparation prior to any major changes in the American role in the war. Sometime near the end of February 1964, he asked Secretary McNamara and General Maxwell Taylor (CJCS) to make another trip to South Vietnam, the purpose of which would be twofold. First, as Halberstam reports, the President was irritated and nervous as a result of the Khanh coup, and he was less than enthusiastic about the prospect of further instability in Saigon:

It would, he said, kill him with the Congress and with the newspapers. He couldn't sell this war if they [the South Vietnamese] were going to play musical chairs. And he wanted this message brought to them: he wanted them to shape up and cool it. . . . [Thus,] McNamara arrived with presidential orders that there were to be no more coups, and the embassy was ordered to get McNamara and Khanh on the front pages everywhere, to make it clear that Khanh was our man.[22]

Second, McNamara was also to examine the possibility of bombing as a way of increasing the pressure on the North. Particular emphasis in this respect was placed on reviewing the evidence bearing on Hanoi's control of the Viet Cong, including data on the infiltration of men and materiel from North Vietnam. As noted in the cable informing the Saigon Embassy of the McNamara-Taylor mission: "One of our basic projects here is preparing strongest possible material on this subject for use as appropriate to support stronger measures. We need to be sure your intelligence effort is geared to furnish such information promptly in usable form."[23]

And so, on arriving in South Vietnam, McNamara and Taylor went through the motions of touring the provinces with Khanh, showing the Vietnamese that Khanh was indeed the "American boy." In addition, they attended an extensive series of briefings and conferences, intended to provide a comprehensive review of the situation. The results of that review, however, were uniformly negative. Despite Khanh's pledge to prosecute the war more vigorously, his seizure of power had not reversed the deterioration in South Vietnam. If anything, the deterioration had accelerated after the coup as a result of the debilitating effect of the continued turmoil in Saigon. Even Taylor, normally able to see a

---

"Hanoi's Leaders and Their South Vietnam Policies," unpublished Ph.D. thesis, Georgetown University, 1972, pp. 172–173; and Chester Cooper, *The Lost Crusade*, rev. ed. (Greenwich, Conn.: Fawcett, 1972), p. 279.

22. Halberstam, p. 430.
23. Quoted in III Gravel, p. 47. See also Halberstam, p. 431.

silver lining in even the darkest cloud, was forced to concede the seriousness of the situation:

The enemy was clearly making the most out of the political turbulence and reduced military effectiveness resulting from the November and January coups. The political structure linking the central government with the provinces had virtually disappeared. Thirty-five of the 41 province chiefs were new appointees, and most of the senior military commands had changed hands twice since the previous October. The desertion rate in the South Vietnamese forces was high and increasing. . . .[24]

On returning to Washington, McNamara first reported orally to the President on March 13 and then formally to the National Security Council (NSC) on March 16. His report was approved by the President and issued as NSAM-288 on March 17, with the directive for all agencies "to proceed energetically" in implementing its recommendations. While the report counseled against initiating direct pressures against the North (the President had informed McNamara that he wanted to make no major decisions about bombing at the time) and concentrated instead on measures to improve the performance of the South Vietnamese government and armed forces, the last two of its twelve recommendations nonetheless formally endorsed preparations for extending the war outside the borders of South Vietnam. Specifically, those recommendations were:

11. To authorize continued high-level U.S. overflights of South Vietnam's borders and to authorize "hot pursuit" and South Vietnamese ground operations over the Laotian line for the purpose of border control. More ambitious operations into Laos involving units beyond battalion size should be authorized only with the approval of Souvanna Phouma. Operations across the Cambodian border should depend on the state of relations with Cambodia.

12. To prepare immediately to be in a position on 72 hours' notice to initiate the full range of Laotian and Cambodian "Border Control" actions (beyond those authorized in paragraph 11, above) and the "Retaliatory Actions" against North Vietnam, and to be in a position on 30 days' notice to initiate the program of "Graduated Overt Military Pressure" against North Vietnam.[25]

Although the Pentagon analyst reported an "official consensus" that the program outlined in NSAM-288 was a "prescription suited to the illness as we diagnosed it," not everyone shared the belief that

24. Taylor (1972), p. 310; see also Halberstam, p. 430.
25. For the President's directive, see III Gravel, p. 157. For the NSAM-288 recommendations, see Document no. 158 in III Gravel, pp. 509–510.

McNamara's recommendations would suffice to turn the situation around. In a March 14 memo commenting on the Secretary's draft report to the President, General Taylor voiced JCS disapproval of the decision to defer overt military action against the North, stating that the Chiefs "did not believe that the recommended program in itself will be sufficient to turn the tide against the Viet Cong in South Vietnam without positive action being taken against the Hanoi government at an early date."[26]

Nor were the JCS alone in their dissent. On March 15, Ambassador Lodge cabled his comments on McNamara's report, in which he argued for an alternative approach to the problem of ending North Vietnamese support for the insurgency. As described by the Pentagon analyst, Lodge's approach

envisioned a secret contact with Hanoi at which an ultimatum would be delivered demanding the DRV's cessation of support for the VC insurgency. Rewards for compliance would include our making available food imports to help alleviate the known shortages affecting North Vietnam in late 1963 (and early '64). In the case of non-compliance, we would undertake previously threatened punitive strikes to which we would not admit publicly.[27]

On March 17, the same day that he signed NSAM-288, the President cabled a reply indicating favor for Lodge's "carrot and stick" approach and reserving judgment on overt pressures against the North. Three days later, the President sent a second cable to Lodge, confirming that overt pressures were being considered on a contingency basis only and stressing that "the immediate problem in this area is to develop the strongest possible military and political base [in the South] for possible later action."[28]

But at the same time that the JCS and Lodge were calling for stronger measures against the North, some disturbing pieces of information were emerging that cast doubt on the utility of overt pressures as a tool for influencing North Vietnamese policy. In March 1964, a small study group drawn from State's Policy Planning Staff completed a study of possible pressures against the North. The group's approach was substantially similar to that taken by the Krulak Committee, in that it was

26. For the Pentagon analyst's comment, see III Gravel, p. 57. Taylor's memo is quoted in III Gravel, p. 56.

27. III Gravel, p. 163.

28. This cable is reproduced as Document no. 160 in III Gravel, p. 511. The President's cable of March 17 is discussed in III Gravel, p. 161.

based on a concept of exploiting "North Vietnamese concern that their industrialization achievements might be wiped out or could be defended (if at all) only at the price of Chicom control" and of demonstrating "that their more powerful communist allies would not risk their own interests for the sake of North Vietnam."[29]

But while the Krulak Committee argued that the North would be responsive to direct pressures, provided they were of sufficient magnitude, the Johnson Group concluded that it was "not likely that North Vietnam would (if it could) call off the war in the South even though U.S. actions would in time have a serious economic and political impact."[30] Instead, as summarized by Halberstam, the group suggested that

the bombing would fail because the North was motivated by factors which were not affected by physical change and physical damage. The North Vietnamese were not hooked on the idea of economic growth determination . . . but were determined to extend their regime's control to the entire country rather than maintain their industrialization. That was what motivated them and that was what they considered their unfinished business. They had invested a great deal in it and would continue to invest in it; no North Vietnamese government could afford to do less.[31]

Adding credence to this line of argument were the results of two sets of war games (known as the "Sigma Games") played in the winter of 1963 and the spring of 1964, both of which attempted to simulate an American bombing campaign against the North. While the results of the second set proved more favorable to the American side than the first, the real lesson of the games, as Halberstam argues, "was not how vulnerable the North was to U.S. bombing but rather how invulnerable it was. . . . For every American move, there seemed to be a ready countermove for Hanoi."[32]

In contrast to the Krulak Committee's report, however, neither the Johnson Group's report nor the results of the Sigma Games had much impact on the planning for increased pressures against the North. Instead, the results of both seem to have been largely ignored by senior American policymakers. As one participant in the Sigma Games noted, it was simply inconceivable to those officials that the "persistence with

29. III Gravel, p. 155. The group's chairman was Robert Johnson.
30. Quoted in III Gravel, p. 156.
31. Halberstam, p. 435.
32. Halberstam, pp. 561, 559.

which Hanoi's simulated representatives countered U.S. strategies could correspond with the real course of events."[33]

II. The Question of Further Pressures:
Covert, Overt, or "Carrot and Stick"
(March-June 1964)

By mid-March, then, preparations for greater pressures against the North were moving forward on three tracks at once—the covert program (OPLAN 34A), planning for overt pressures as specified in NSAM-288, and Lodge's "carrot and stick" approach—with one of the three, i.e., the covert program, in the process of being implemented. Still, it was not at all clear how far the Administration was prepared to go in exerting pressure on the North or whether more drastic measures, such as those advocated by the JCS, would in fact be necessary. As the Pentagon analyst points out, "there were many inhibitions that discouraged doing more than the bare necessity to get the job done," the most important of which centered on fears of Communist escalation, perhaps involving the Soviets and/or the Chinese, in response to overt American pressures against the North.[34]

As a result, from March to August, "we tried to make a go of it with the program approved in NSAM-288, in the hope that the program would carry us toward our objective by increasing the amount of aid and advice we gave to the South Vietnamese to enable them to help themselves."[35] Almost from the start, however, the implementation of that program ran behind schedule, with the GVN unwilling and/or unable to carry its share of the load. As these failings became apparent, the focus of attention within the U.S. Government was inevitably drawn back to the more drastic actions against the North considered but temporarily deferred by NSAM-288.[36]

But while a consensus was slowly emerging on the eventual need for greater pressures on the North, there was no consensus over how to exert those pressures. The inhibitions on the direct use of American power mentioned above were by no means shared by all government agencies, with the result that the planning effort specified by Recom-

---

33. Allen Whiting, "The Scholar and the Policy-Maker," *World Politics*, 24 (Spring 1972), 232. For a discussion of why the Johnson Group's report was ignored, see Halberstam, pp. 436–437.

34. III Gravel, p. 57.

35. Ibid.

36. For a discussion of GVN failures and the effect these had on U.S. policy, see III Gravel, pp. 59–83.

mendation 12 of NSAM-288 was marked by serious disagreements among the agencies involved.

Evidence of these disagreements became apparent even before the end of March. As the Pentagon analyst notes: "The principal planning agencies responding to the President's directive regarding Recommendations 11 and 12 were the JCS and the Department of State together with OSD/ISA, and the two efforts took rather different approaches."[37] The JCS responded by directing CINCPAC to prepare the detailed plans called for by Recommendation 12, an effort resulting in CINCPAC OPLAN 37-64, approved by the JCS on April 17, 1964. That JCS preparations in this respect went beyond the usual contingency planning can be seen from their instruction that CINCPAC's planning should permit "sequential implementation" of Recommendation 12's three categories of action. More than anything, the JCS wanted to carry out those actions, beginning with border control operations in Laos and Cambodia, in order to impress the North Vietnamese with American resolve to deny the insurgents a sanctuary, and they pressed repeatedly for authorization to go ahead.[38]

The State/ISA effort, in contrast, reflected skepticism about the need for immediate implementation of the actions outlined in Recommendation 12. State's initial comments in this respect not only argued against operations in Laos and Cambodia before going ahead with increased pressures on the North but also questioned the utility of retaliatory actions against the North on the grounds that it would be difficult to respond in kind to Viet Cong terrorism and that retaliatory actions were inappropriate for conveying "the picture of concerted and steadily rising pressures that reflect complete U.S. determination to finish the job." Instead, the State/ISA effort focused on developing a set of political scenarios intended to accommodate only the program of graduated overt military pressures mentioned in Recommendation 12. Among the actions envisioned by the State/ISA scenarios were: a speech by General Khanh stating GVN war aims, Presidential consultations with Congressional leaders, consultations with allied nations, release of a new White Paper on the North Vietnamese role in the insurgency, and initiatives leading to a Geneva conference on Vietnam.[39]

37. Ibid., p. 157.

38. On these points, see III Gravel, pp. 157, 159, 161-162; see also Document no. 159 in III Gravel, p. 510.

39. On these points, see III Gravel, pp. 157-161. The State Department comment is quoted on p. 158.

These efforts at scenario development continued into April and formed the basis for a high-level policy review in Saigon on April 19–20, attended by Rusk, Lodge, Harkins, Wheeler, and William Bundy, among others. At that meeting, Lodge "questioned the wisdom of both massive publicity [the State/ISA scenarios] and of massive destruction actions [the JCS approach] before a well-planned and well-executed diplomatic attempt had been made to persuade North Vietnam to call off the VC."[40] Lodge then went on to repeat the arguments for his "carrot and stick" approach, but this time adding two new points to his earlier proposals. First, he suggested using the new Canadian representative to the International Control Commission (ICC), J. Blair Seaborn, to communicate to the North Vietnamese both the threat of air strikes if they did not call off the Viet Cong (the "stick") as well as a pledge of assistance if they did (the "carrot"). Second, Lodge proposed that an added element of the "carrot" might be a pledge to withdraw some American personnel from South Vietnam on the grounds that "it would be very hard indeed for Ho Chi Minh to provide a salable package for his own people and for other communist nations unless we can do something that Hanoi can point to, even though it would not be a real concession on our part."[41]

The major immediate outcome of the Saigon policy review was a decision to go ahead with the Lodge approach. On April 30, Rusk visited Ottawa, where he reached agreement with the Canadian Government on using Seaborn as an interlocutor between Washington and Hanoi as well as on the general nature of the message Seaborn was to carry. Lodge, however, was still not satisfied with the way the contact was shaping up. In a May 15 cable to the President, he suggested an air strike against the North as a way of adding credibility to Seaborn's message and hinted at his dismay over JCS proposals for a massive effort against the North:

3. If prior to the Canadian's trip to Hanoi there has been a terroristic act of the proper magnitude, then I suggest that a specific target in North Vietnam be considered as a prelude to his arrival. The Vietnamese Air Force must be capable of doing this, and they should undertake this type of action.

4. I much prefer a selective use of Vietnamese air power to an overt U.S. effort perhaps involving the total annihilation of all that has been built in North Vietnam since 1954, because this would surely bring in the Chinese communists, and might well bring in the Russians. Moreover, if you lay the whole country to waste, it is quite likely that you will induce a mood of fatalism

40. III Gravel, p. 162.
41. Ibid., p. 163.

in the Viet Cong. Also there will be nobody left in North Vietnam on whom to put pressure. Furthermore, South Vietnam's infrastructure might well be destroyed. What we are interested in here is not destroying Ho Chi Minh (as his successor would probably be worse than he is), but getting him to change his behavior. This is what President Kennedy was trying to do in October with Diem and with considerable success.[42]

Lodge had good reason to be concerned. The JCS had argued throughout April and May for prompt implementation of the "massive destruction actions" that he opposed. Adding urgency to their arguments was the offensive launched by the Pathet Lao on May 17, which resulted in Communist control over much of the Plaine des Jarres. In response, on May 21, U.S. aircraft began flying low-level reconnaissance missions over Communist-held territory in Laos. Two days later, the JCS again pressed for authority to step up preparations for the actions outlined in Recommendation 12 of NSAM-288.[43]

The JCS, moreover, "were not the only Presidential advisers to sense the urgency created by the situation in Laos."[44] Explaining that the fragile political situation in Saigon was seen in Washington as an obstacle to an expanded American role in the war, Secretary Rusk cabled Lodge seeking suggestions for ways to achieve greater solidarity in the South as a prelude to increased pressures on the North. Lodge, in turn, replied that we could not expect a much better performance from the GVN unless some new action against the North was brought into the picture, a view that was by now widely shared among the President's top advisers.[45]

This belief, combined with the ongoing Pathet Lao offensive, led to a resumption of scenario development. This time, however, given the crisis atmosphere generated by events in Laos, the new scenario was prepared as a draft memorandum for the President and reviewed by the President's top military and civilian advisers meeting as an Executive Committee of the National Security Council. The new scenario was completed on May 23 and discussed by the ExComm on May 24–25.[46]

The ExComm, however, decided not to retain the scenario approach in its recommendations to the President. While the reasons for this decision are not entirely clear, it appears, as the Pentagon analyst points

---

42. For Lodge's cable, see Seaborn Chronology, p. 2. On the Rusk visit to Ottawa, see III Gravel, pp. 163–164.
43. On these points, see III Gravel, pp. 164–166.
44. Ibid., p. 166.
45. On these points, see III Gravel, p. 166; and Seaborn Chronology, p. 4.
46. For the May 23 scenario, see III Gravel, pp. 167–168.

out, that "the potential for entering into an escalating conflict in which our limited objectives might become obscured weighed heavily in the decision." Instead, the ExComm recommended a number of specific actions, the most important of which was that the President decide

that the U.S. will use selected and carefully graduated military force against North Vietnam, under the following conditions: (1) after appropriate diplomatic and political warning and preparation, (2) and unless such warning and preparation—in combination with other efforts—should produce a sufficient improvement of non-Communist prospects in South Vietnam and in Laos to make military action against North Vietnam unnecessary.

Underlying this recommendation was the explicit assumption that "a decision to use force if necessary, backed by resolute and extensive deployment, and conveyed by every possible means to our adversaries, gives the best present chance of avoiding the actual use of force."[47]

In addition, the ExComm recommended: (1) communicating U.S. resolve and limited objectives to Hanoi through Seaborn; (2) conducting a high-level strategy conference in Honolulu; (3) diplomatic initiatives at the UN; (4) consultation with SEATO allies; (5) seeking a Congressional resolution in support of Administration policies; (6) periodic force deployments throughout Southeast Asia; and (7) an initial air strike against North Vietnam coupled with a diplomatic offensive to restore peace in the area.[48]

Most of the recommended actions, however, did not receive immediate Presidential approval. On May 28, the President met with Canadian Prime Minister Pearson to secure Pearson's agreement to the use of the Seaborn channel, although this appears to have been largely a formality in light of Secretary Rusk's April 30 trip to Ottawa. Similarly, the President approved the convening of a high-level conference in Honolulu, scheduled for June 1–2. Decisions on the other recommendations, however, were apparently deferred. Most importantly, "it was abundantly clear that the President had *not* made the decision to use force if necessary, at this time."[49]

While the purpose of the Honolulu Conference was ostensibly to review for the President's final approval a series of plans for effective action in Vietnam, the outcome of the conference was actually to defer decisions on the issues facing the government. Prior to the conference,

---

47. On these points, see III Gravel, pp. 169–170.
48. See III Gravel, p. 170.
49. William Bundy, personal communication, September 26, 1977 (emphasis in original). See also III Gravel, p. 170.

the differences within the government over how best to exert pressure on the North had come to a head. While the May 23 scenario had envisioned a series of air strikes, aimed first at transport facilities and then at targets having "maximum psychological effect on the North's willingness to stop [the] insurgency," the ExComm had been unwilling to go that far and had instead recommended a series of lesser measures—i.e., threats of force, conveyed via Seaborn and backed up by force deployments and leaks to the press. Underlying this approach, as we saw, was the hope that if the Administration could convince the North Vietnamese that it really would bomb them unless they called off the Viet Cong, they would choose to do so rather than risk the loss of their industrial complex.[50]

The JCS, however, in a memo submitted prior to the Honolulu Conference, were sharply critical of such an approach. Drawing a distinction between measures designed to influence North Vietnamese *will* to support the insurgency and measures aimed at the destruction of North Vietnamese military *capabilities*, the Chiefs left no doubt of their preference for the latter. They were, however, willing to embark on the former course as an "initial measure," and they proposed in this respect a pair of sustained attacks on the facilities at Vinh and Dien Bien Phu, both of which were associated with North Vietnamese support for the Pathet Lao and the Viet Cong. Above all, the Chiefs wanted to begin attacking the North *now*, and they denounced the approach recommended by the ExComm as unnecessarily timid:

We should not waste critical time and more resources in another protracted series of "messages," but rather we should take positive, prompt, and meaningful military action to underscore our meaning that after more than two years of tolerating this North Vietnamese support we are now determined that it will stop.[51]

The Honolulu Conference, however, did not attempt to resolve the conflict between these competing approaches to the problem of pressuring the North. While the conferees apparently agreed that overt pressures would at some point be necessary, the consensus was that those pressures should be delayed for some time yet. The subject of increased

50. The purpose of the Honolulu Conference was set forth in a May 26 cable from the President to Lodge, quoted in III Gravel, p. 72. On the May 23 scenario, see III Gravel, p. 168.

51. For a summary of the JCS memo, see III Gravel, pp. 172–173. General Taylor did not subscribe to the views presented in this memo. For a summary of his views, see III Gravel, p. 179. See also III Gravel, pp. 165–166, for a summary of JCS arguments on how the destruction of North Vietnamese capabilities would, in their view, be a relatively simple task.

pressures, as the conferees were well aware, was politically explosive, especially in an election year; and the conferees accordingly concentrated on the preliminary steps necessary to prepare for an expanded American role in the war—i.e., consultations with allies and the need for a Congressional resolution. In the process, they simply papered over the differences within the government over how best to pressure the North, advising the President of the need for "more refined targeting and a clearer definition of just what should be hit and how thoroughly, and above all, for what objective." In addition, the conferees proposed an "urgent U.S. information effort" to reduce public doubts about the importance of the American stake in Southeast Asia.[52]

These recommendations, as the Pentagon analyst notes, "apparently struck a responsive chord at the White House." On the one hand, noncommitting actions designed to improve the U.S. image of resolve to stand firm in Southeast Asia were given immediate approval by the President. These actions, which included augmenting Army supplies stored in Thailand and on Okinawa, were given extensive press coverage, as a tacit warning to the North Vietnamese.[53] On the other hand, the White House apparently shared the consensus at Honolulu that overt pressures could be deferred for the time being. Indicative of White House thinking in this respect was a memo distributed by McGeorge Bundy prior to a June 15 meeting on the subject of a Congressional resolution. This memo, cited by the Pentagon analyst as providing a clear picture of the President's preferences, concentrated on the measures open to the U.S. in the event a Congressional resolution was not sought and concluded that "defense of U.S. interests is possible, within these limits, over the next six months" (i.e., until after the Presidential election).[54]

The President's decision, in short, was to hold off on major pressures against the North while going ahead with actions that would hopefully bolster the American image of determination to continue resisting North Vietnamese efforts to take over South Vietnam. One of those actions occurred three days after the June 15 meeting mentioned above, when Seaborn met with the North Vietnamese Premier, Pham Van Dong. Seaborn's instructions for this meeting encompassed 13 specific

---

52. On these points, see III Gravel, pp. 77, 174–177. The quoted excerpts are from Assistant Secretary Bundy's memo to Secretary Rusk prior to Rusk's meeting with the President to report on the Honolulu Conference; quoted in III Gravel, pp. 176–177.

53. For the Pentagon analyst's comment, see III Gravel, p. 177. For an example of the press coverage given the American buildup in Thailand, see Jack Raymond, "U.S. Reinforcing Arms Stockpile at Thailand Base," New York Times, June 21, 1964, p. 1.

54. Quoted in III Gravel, p. 181.

points, most of which fell into two categories—the message he was to convey and a list of topics on which the U.S. desired his evaluation. Among the points he was to convey were the following: that, while U.S. objectives were limited, the U.S. was determined to contain the DRV within the territory allocated to it by the 1954 Geneva Accords; that the U.S. sought neither bases in South Vietnam nor the overthrow of the DRV; that the U.S. was fully aware of Hanoi's control over the Viet Cong and that the U.S. held Hanoi responsible for the war in the South; that the U.S. stake in resisting North Vietnamese efforts to overthrow the GVN had a significance of worldwide proportions; that there were many examples of peaceful coexistence between the U.S. and other Communist states and that economic benefits might accrue to the DRV if it confined itself to the development of its own national territory; that U.S. patience with the DRV was growing thin; and that U.S. military strength was vastly superior to that of North Vietnam and China. In addition, Seaborn was to attempt an evaluation of the North Vietnamese outlook on the war, probing for evidence of differences of opinion with respect to the Sino-Soviet conflict, indications of North Vietnamese desires for contacts with the West, evidence of factionalism within the Party and/or the Government, and evidence of civil-military strife.[55]

On June 18, Seaborn met with Pham Van Dong, at which time he conveyed the U.S. message, adding the explicit threat that if the conflict should escalate, the "greatest devastation" would result for the North.[56] When he had finished, Seaborn offered to convey Pham Van Dong's reply to the U.S. Government; the Premier, however, stated that he had no specific message at this time, but that he would elaborate on the North Vietnamese view of the situation. He began by outlining the DRV view on a settlement of the conflict:

President Ho Chi Minh has explained what we mean by a just solution. First, it requires an American withdrawal from Indochina. Secondly, it means that the affairs of the south must be arranged by the people of the south. It must provide for the participation of the Liberation Front. No other group represents the broad wishes of the people. The program of the Front is the best one possible. There must be peace and neutrality for South Vietnam—neutrality in the Cambodian manner.

Thirdly, a just solution means reunification of the country. . . . But we want peaceful reunification, without military pressures. We want negotiation around a table. There must be sincere satisfaction with the arrangement for it to be

55. On these points, see Seaborn Chronology, pp. 5–9.
56. On this point, see Seaborn Discussion, p. 1.

viable. We are in no hurry. We are willing to talk but we shall wait until South Vietnam is ready. . . .[57]

It would appear from these remarks, which, according to Seaborn, were delivered without truculence or belligerency, that Pham Van Dong was attempting to present a "salable package" of his own to the United States. Under questioning, the Premier told Seaborn that he had not referred to neutrality for South Vietnam as only a first step, but that whether South Vietnam remained neutral or not depended on the South Vietnamese people. Furthermore, he conceded that the NLF did not represent the entire South Vietnamese people, claiming that there was no reason to fear an NLF takeover of a coalition government. Hinting that he expected a U.S. counterproposal, the Premier told Seaborn that he was looking forward to further conversation during Seaborn's next visit and that Seaborn would meet Ho Chi Minh at that time.[58]

But while Pham Van Dong was apparently trying to sketch out a solution allowing the U.S. a face-saving exit from the war, he was adamant with respect to the North's determination to fight on and its confidence in final victory:

. . . our people are determined to struggle. It is impossible, quite impossible (excuse me for saying this) for you Westerners to understand the force of the people's will to resist and to continue. The struggle of the people exceeds the imagination. It has astonished us too.

Since the fall of the Ngo brothers, it has been a *cascade*. The prospect for the USA and its friends in South Vietnam is *sans issu*. Reinforcing the Khanh army doesn't count. The people have had enough. The South Vietnamese mercenaries have sacrificed themselves without honor. The Americans are not loved, for they commit atrocities. How can the people suffer such exactions and terror?

. . . To return to Vietnam, it is a question of a *guerre à outrance* which the USA won't win in any event, or neutrality.

. . . The USA is in a difficult position, because Khanh's troops will no longer fight. If the war gets worse, we shall suffer greatly but we shall win. If we win in the south, the people of the world will turn against the USA. Our people will accept the sacrifices whatever they may be. But the DRVN will not enter the war. If the war is pushed to the north, *nous sommes un pays socialiste, vous savez et le peuple se dressera*. But we shall not force the USA, we shall not provoke the USA.[59]

---

57. For Pham Van Dong's reply, see Settlement Terms—Extracts, p. 3.
58. On these points, see Seaborn Discussion, pp. 1–2, 4; and Seaborn Summary, pp. 1–2.
59. Quoted in Settlement Terms—Extracts, pp. 3–4.

On returning from Hanoi, Seaborn transmitted two messages to Ottawa which were then passed to Washington. The first described his meeting with Pham Van Dong and the Premier's reply to the U.S. message; the second presented his answers to the questions on which he had been asked to gather information. From the American point of view, Seaborn's evaluation was uniformly negative. While cautioning that it was difficult to form meaningful judgments on the basis of a short visit to Hanoi, he nonetheless reported that he had found no evidence of civil-military splits nor did he have any new information on factional line-ups within the Party and Government. In addition, he had found no evidence of frustration or war weariness, and he further stated that he did not believe that the prospect of material gain (Lodge's "carrot") would induce the North Vietnamese to seek a settlement with the United States. Most importantly, Seaborn reported that the North Vietnamese leadership was unconvinced the U.S. really would carry the war to the North, but even if it did, he pointed out, the North Vietnamese were confident they would win in the end.[60]

Although Seaborn's report probably understated the extent of disagreements over policy within the DRV leadership,[61] he was very likely correct in reporting that the leadership was unconvinced that the U.S. would carry the war to the North. In this respect, it is important to consider the context in which Seaborn conveyed his message to Hanoi. As we saw earlier, U.S. public statements during the first quarter of 1964 had presented an ambiguous picture concerning American willingness to carry the war to the North. This ambiguity was by no means resolved during the period March–June 1964, despite the repeated emphasis in internal policy statements on the importance of convincing the North Vietnamese of American determination to do whatever was necessary to defend South Vietnam. Instead, American public statements continued to follow an erratic course, oscillating between hints of an expanded war and denials that plans to carry the war to the North were under consideration.

Thus, in contrast to the President's UCLA speech, the speeches and news conferences of the President and Secretaries Rusk and McNamara during March, April, May, and early June were generally restrained in that, while pledging continued and/or expanded aid for South

---

60. This summary of Seaborn's report is based on Seaborn Summary, p. 1; and on confidential interviews (hereafter referred to as "Interview Data").

61. Factional splits within the DRV leadership will be discussed in more detail in Chapters 5 and 6, below.

Vietnam, they largely avoided any suggestion that the war might be carried to the North.[62] On June 2, the same day that his top advisers were meeting in Honolulu to consider plans for increased pressures against the North, the President himself asserted at a news conference that he knew of no plans within the Administration for carrying the war to North Vietnam.[63] On June 18, however, the day Seaborn met with Pham Van Dong in Hanoi, the Administration launched a press campaign coupling threats of wider war with demonstrations of American strength in Southeast Asia. In an obvious attempt to lend credibility to Seaborn's message, the Administration on June 18 released testimony by Assistant Secretary of State William Bundy before a Congressional subcommittee, which included Bundy's assertion that the U.S. was determined to drive the Communists out of South Vietnam, even if that meant "attacking countries to the North."[64] The next day, Secretary Rusk advised newsmen during a background luncheon that the American commitment to South Vietnam was unlimited and comparable to the commitment to West Berlin.[65] In addition, Pentagon officials publicized the American buildup in Thailand and South Vietnam, while repeatedly calling attention to the warning contained in Bundy's Congressional testimony.[66] On July 1, however, Secretary Rusk seemingly reversed field, stating at a news conference that "peace" was the Administration's goal in Southeast Asia and that "peace, obviously, is not obtained by going out and looking for war. . . ." When asked about the Administration's tendency to "blow hot and cold" on the issue of Southeast Asia, Rusk blamed the press,

62. See, for example, the President's news conferences of April 4, 11, 16, 21, 23, and 25 and the President's speech before the Associated Press in New York on April 20 (texts for all of these can be found in Johnson Papers, 1963-1964). See also Secretary Rusk's April 25 speech at Valparaiso University, reprinted in DOSB, May 11, 1964, pp. 732-737. Speeches by Secretary McNamara and Secretary Rusk on March 26 and May 22, respectively, left open the possibility that the war might be expanded, but both were generally restrained in tone. For McNamara's speech, see DOSB, April 13, 1964, p. 569; for Rusk's, see DOSB, June 8, 1964, p. 891.

63. Johnson Papers, 1963-1964, p. 739. Similarly, speeches by Walt Rostow and Secretary Rusk on June 5 and June 14, respectively, were devoid of hints that the war would be expanded outside the borders of South Vietnam. For both speeches, see DOSB, June 22, 1964, pp. 963-964 (Rostow's); and July 6, 1964, pp. 3-5 (Rusk's).

64. "Congress Told U.S. Would Fight in Laos," New York Times, June 19, 1964, p. 5. See also General Westmoreland's refusal to rule out attacks on North Vietnam, in "U.S. General Ready to Challenge Hanoi," New York Times, June 18, 1964, p. 6.

65. Max Frankel, "U.S. Stressing It Would Fight to Defend Asia," New York Times, June 20, 1964, p. 1.

66. See Jack Raymond, "U.S. Reinforcing Arms Stockpiles at Thailand Bases," New York Times, June 21, 1964, p. 1; and Peter Grose, "Net of U.S. Bases Widened in Asia to Counter China," New York Times, June 22, 1964, p. 1. See also Tom Wicker, "Johnson Affirms U.S. Would Fight to Protect Asia," New York Times, June 29, 1964, p. 1.

ascribing the inconsistency in Administration statements to "changing fads . . . in the way in which the entire speeches are reported."[67] The Secretary's comments notwithstanding, it seems likely that the obvious inconsistencies in the Administration's public statements contributed to a conviction in Hanoi (reported by Seaborn) that the U.S. would not attack the North.

Thus, by the end of June, the stage was set for the test of wills that would eventually follow. The U.S., through Seaborn, had explicitly threatened the North with the "greatest devastation" unless it acted to restrain the Viet Cong; the North, for its part, had indicated a willingness to resist and confidence in final victory. The struggle would soon be joined in the Gulf of Tonkin, in a fashion that would be both dramatic and significant.

III. Confrontation in the Gulf (July-August 1964)

Throughout July, the situation in the South more or less "jogged along" in the fashion predicted by Ambassador Lodge at the Honolulu Conference in June. Lodge himself resigned as Ambassador at the end of June and was replaced by the team of Maxwell Taylor as Ambassador and U. Alexis Johnson as Deputy Ambassador, a selection intended to underscore the importance attached to South Vietnam by the United States. Shortly after arriving in Saigon, however, the new Ambassador was greeted by a GVN campaign to force the hand of the U.S. on the issue of carrying the war to the North, with both Generals Khanh and Ky lobbying publicly for an extension of the war. Taylor, for his part, tried to discourage these efforts while at the same time arguing for patience in American dealings with the GVN. To avoid a head-on collision, he suggested that the U.S. express a willingness to engage in joint planning with the GVN for expanding the war.[68]

But even as Taylor was urging restraint on the issue of widening the war, the U.S. was moving cautiously to expand its activities outside the borders of South Vietnam aimed at "convincing" the North Vietnamese to "leave their neighbors alone." One of the most important of these activities was the ongoing campaign of public warnings and leaks to the press, supplemented by explicit threats of wider war conveyed privately to Hanoi.

67. DOSB, July 20, 1964, pp. 84, 87.

68. For Lodge's comment at the Honolulu Conference, see II Gravel, p. 323. On the GVN campaign to extend the war to the North, see II Gravel, pp. 328–329; and III Gravel, p. 81. For Taylor's suggestion, see Document no. 162 in III Gravel, pp. 512–513. See also II Gravel, p. 328; and III Gravel, p. 81.

As we saw in the preceding sections, public statements intended to raise the spectre of American military action against the North had begun in February 1964, when President Johnson warned the North Vietnamese that support for the Viet Cong constituted a "deeply dangerous game." But while the Administration took a hawkish stance in mid-June in an attempt to add credibility to the warnings conveyed privately by Seaborn, its position had softened considerably by the time of Secretary Rusk's July 1 news conference. By mid-July, however, the Administration had reverted to its hawkish stance. On July 10, the U.S. and South Vietnam staged a well-publicized display of air power at DaNang under the guise of South Vietnam's first Air Force Day. Three days later, William Bundy told an interviewer from the French broadcasting corporation that the U.S. had "not excluded the possibility of action against North Vietnam itself'; more ominously, Bundy refused to rule out the use of nuclear weapons against the North, saying only that the matter had been studied carefully and that "I do not think it is appropriate to discuss the measures that might be employed in a case that has not yet arisen."[69]

And yet, even before the end of July, U.S. public statements would again veer sharply, this time in the direction of restraint on the issue of carrying the war to the North. In response to statements by Generals Khanh and Ky on "Marching North," "qualified sources" in Saigon let it be known that Ambassador Taylor had told Khanh that an extension of the war would be contrary to U.S. policy. At the same time, officials in Washington asserted that the Administration still believed that the war should be confined to the South, telling reporters that the President himself had ordered American officials to avoid threatening statements so as not to arouse undue concern in Peking. Soon thereafter, Administration officials announced that the U.S. would send 5,000 more troops to South Vietnam—a decision, they emphasized, intended to signify both Washington's commitment to Saigon and Washington's belief that additional resources could best be used in the South rather than against the North.[70]

69. On these points, see Seymour Topping, "Ceremony Shows Saigon Air Power," *New York Times*, July 11, 1964, p. 2; and the AP dispatch, "U.S. Action on Hanoi Still Not Ruled Out," *New York Times*, July 14, 1964, p. 3. See also General Ky's comment that he had thirty pilots trained on jet fighter-bombers and ready to fly against the North, cited in the AP dispatch, "Jet Pilots Reported Ready," *New York Times*, July 14, 1964, p. 3.

70. On these points, see Peter Grose, "Khanh and Taylor Clash Over Extension of War," *New York Times*, July 24, 1964, p. 1; Max Frankel, "Demands Puzzle U.S.," *New York Times*, July 24, 1964, pp. 1, 3; Edwin L. Dale, Jr., "U.S. to Enlarge Vietnam Force by 5000 Advisers," *New York Times*, July 28, 1964, pp. 1, 5; and Max Frankel, "U.S. Finds Saigon Modifying Stand," *New York Times*, July 29, 1964, pp. 1, 3.

A second set of activities involved air operations in Laos. These, as we saw earlier, had begun on May 21, when, in response to a Pathet Lao offensive, U.S. aircraft began flying low-level reconnaissance missions over Communist-held areas in Laos and the U.S. gave several T-28 aircraft to the Royal Laotian Government for use against the Pathet Lao. On June 7, after one of the reconnaissance planes had been shot down, the U.S. added armed escorts to the reconnaissance flights, authorizing them to return hostile ground fire. On June 9, after one of the escorts had been shot down, U.S. jets attacked two Pathet Lao installations in retaliation, including an antiaircraft gun site.[71] These flights were supplemented at the end of June by transport and night reconnaissance missions and by the furnishing of additional T-28 aircraft and munitions to support a Royal Laotian counteroffensive. In addition, a number of T-28 strikes were aimed at harassing North Vietnamese forces stationed in Laos along the Ho Chi Minh Trail. As part of that effort, on August 1 and again on August 2, Laotian T-28s bombed and strafed two North Vietnamese villages in Nghe An province near the Laotian border.[72]

A third set of activities involved operations under the covert program (OPLAN 34A), which, by the summer of 1964, was in Phase II of implementation. Despite the higher levels of activity implied by Phase II, however, the program had as yet achieved little in the way of meaningful results—in fact, over 80 percent of the sabotage teams infiltrated into the North were captured before they could make any progress on their mission.[73] In addition to these operations, U.S. destroyers conducted infrequent intelligence-gathering patrols along the North Vietnamese coastline, code-named DE SOTO patrols.

Perhaps the most significant aspect of these activities, however, stemmed from the fact that each was the responsibility of a separate

71. Like virtually everything else done by the U.S. in Indochina, the June 9 attack did not come off quite as planned. While the attack was intended to silence the offending antiaircraft battery in retaliation for the shooting down of two American planes, U.S. Air Force jets, flying in poor weather, attacked a Pathet Lao installation, but not the one intended. To rectify that error, another flight of Air Force jets attacked the "correct" target later on June 9. On this point, see Max Frankel, "U.S. Will Keep Up Pressure in Laos Until Crisis Ends," *New York Times*, June 18, 1964, pp. 1, 5; and Arthur Dommen, *Conflict in Laos*, rev. ed. (New York: Praeger, 1971), pp. 274–275.

72. On these points, see V Gravel, p. 320; the untitled Reuters dispatch in the *New York Times*, June 25, 1964, p. 3; and the DRV's "Memorandum Regarding the U.S. War Acts Against the Democratic Republic of Viet Nam in the First Days of August 1964," in Galloway, pp. 498–499. North Vietnamese claims concerning the attacks of August 1–2 were later admitted to be "probably accurate" by American officials; see Document no. 225 in III Gravel, p. 609.

73. See Peter Grose, "Sabotage Raids on North Confirmed by Saigon Aide," *New York Times*, July 23, 1964, p. 1.

agency of the government, with little or no coordination among them.[74] As a result, when three of these activities unexpectedly coincided during a five-day period (July 31–August 4, 1964), the outcome was an unforeseen but not unwelcome (from the Administration's point of view) confrontation between the U.S. and North Vietnam.

The unfolding of this critically important sequence of events began at approximately 12:20 A.M. on July 31 (Tonkin Gulf time), when South Vietnamese naval units began a new series of operations under OPLAN 34A, bombarding North Vietnamese installations on the islands of Hon Me and Hon Hgu.[75] Less than twelve hours later, the destroyer U.S.S. *Maddox* commenced a DE SOTO patrol, during which it cruised up and down the North Vietnamese coastline, approaching to within eight nautical miles of the mainland and four nautical miles of offshore islands, all the while gathering photographic and electronic intelligence. In the early morning of August 2, the *Maddox*'s pre-assigned patrol track brought it into the vicinity of Hon Mat island, several kilometers east of Hon Ngu. Suspecting hostile action by North Vietnamese junks massing near it, the *Maddox* put out to sea but later, after the patrol commander's request to terminate the patrol had been overruled, resumed its patrol track, heading toward a predetermined check point north of Hon Me.[76] To further complicate matters, at the same time the

74. The planning and execution of OPLAN 34A missions were controlled by the Studies and Operations Group (SOG), which, while a MACV component, was supervised by a special office within the JCS. Requests for DE SOTO patrols were coordinated by the DIA, which had primary responsibility for drafting the mission plan, while the timing of the mission and ship selection were handled through the Navy chain of command. The documents available do not make clear which agency, if any, controlled target-selection for the Laotian T-28 strikes, although it appears that both the U.S. Embassy in Vientiane and the CIA (which recruited a number of Thai pilots to help fly the missions) were involved. The evidence available also suggests that the strikes on DRV border posts were not intended by U.S. officials, resulting instead from pilot error. For more details on the handling of 34A raids and DE SOTO patrols, see V Gravel, p. 328; Westmoreland, pp. 106–107; Goulden, pp. 122–123; Anthony Austin, *The President's War* (Philadelphia: J.B. Lippincott, 1971), p. 230; and Eugene Windchy, *Tonkin Gulf* (Garden City, N.Y.: Doubleday, 1971), pp. 59, 68. On the T-28 strikes, see Document no. 225 in III Gravel, pp. 608–609; and Austin, p. 238.

75. Detailed accounts of the August 1964 events in the Gulf of Tonkin can be found in V Gravel, pp. 320–341; Halberstam, pp. 500–503; Goulden, pp. 23–37, 122–160; Galloway, pp. 48–66; Windchy, pp. 54–220; and Austin, pp. 242–315. For details on the July 31 34A raid, see Goulden, pp. 127–128; Galloway, p. 49; Windchy, pp. 75–76; and Austin, p. 251.

76. For details on the *Maddox*'s mission and patrol track, see Goulden, pp. 121–131; Galloway, pp. 49–50; Windchy, pp. 55–108; Austin, pp. 247–256; and V Gravel, p. 322. It has been alleged that the *Maddox* "repeatedly simulated attacks by jabbing in toward the shore with its fire-control radars turned on" (Peter Dale Scott, *The War Conspiracy* [Indianapolis, Ind.: Bobbs-Merrill, 1972], p. 53), but this appears to be an exaggeration. As Windchy (p. 82) notes, the *Maddox* was a "short legged" destroyer with a relatively small fuel capacity; consequently, to save fuel, it spent the opening days of the patrol cruising at 5–10 knots, sauntering in and out of North Vietnam's coastal waters. In addition, Windchy (p. 101) raises some interesting questions about the *Maddox*'s ability to electronically provoke the North Vietnamese.

Maddox was poking around in the vicinity of the July 31 34A raid, there occurred the attacks by Laotian aircraft on the North Vietnamese border posts mentioned above.

While the 34A raid, the DE SOTO patrol, and the Laotian T-28 strikes were ostensibly separate and unrelated operations, the coincidence of all three within the space of a few days apparently was more than the North Vietnamese could take. On the afternoon of August 2, after it had swung back into the vicinity of Hon Me, the *Maddox* was pursued at high speed by three North Vietnamese torpedo boats. Evaluating their intent as hostile, the *Maddox* opened fire, after which the North Vietnamese launched torpedoes at it and attempted to return its fire.[77] The *Maddox*, however, assisted by aircraft from the carrier *Ticonderoga*, was able to drive off the North Vietnamese boats, sinking one and damaging the other two in the process. After the engagement, the *Maddox* proceeded to Yankee Station off the coast of South Vietnam, where it refueled and was joined by a second destroyer, the *C. Turner Joy*.

Back in Washington, the President's initial reaction to the incident was that an American ship had been fired on in an area where it had a right to be, and he immediately ordered the *Maddox*, along with the *Turner Joy*, to resume the patrol. While he was unwilling to go along with suggestions for a retaliatory air strike, he did consent to a note of protest, which warned that "The United States Government expects that the authorities in Hanoi will be under no misapprehension as to the grave consequences which would inevitably result from any further unprovoked offensive military actions against United States forces."[78]

As a result of the President's orders, the *Maddox* and the *Turner Joy* resumed the patrol on August 3, cruising again in the vicinity of Hon Me and Hon Ngu before turning out to sea for the evening.[79] At approximately 12:30 A.M. on August 4 (Tonkin Gulf time), however, South Vietnamese forces conducted another 34A raid, shelling North Vietnamese installations at Cua Ron and Vinh Son. Radio communications intercepted by the destroyers indicated that the North

77. Apparently, the patrol commander, Captain John Herrick, and the *Maddox*'s skipper, Commander Herbert Ogier, intended the *Maddox*'s first shots to be "warning shots." The *Maddox*'s gunnery officer, Lieutenant Raymond Connell, however, has been quoted as saying the first shots were aimed to hit the North Vietnamese boats. On this point, see Goulden, p. 132; Galloway, p. 51; Windchy, pp. 120–121, 136; and Austin, pp. 259–260. There is no doubt, however, that it was the *Maddox* that fired first.

78. On the President's reaction, see Halberstam, pp. 500–501; Goulden, pp. 134–136; Galloway, pp. 52–53; and Austin, pp. 264–265. The warning to Hanoi is quoted in V Gravel, p. 324.

79. On the destroyers' whereabouts during August 3–4, see Goulden, pp. 137–142; Galloway, p. 55; Windchy, pp. 171–172, 178–179, 182–184; and Austin, pp. 271–275.

Vietnamese were in an uproar over the raid, leading the patrol commander, Captain John Herrick, to cable his superiors that "Evaluation of information from various sources indicates DRV considers patrol directly involved with 34A ops [sic]. DRV considers U.S. ships present as enemies because of these ops and have already indicated readiness to treat us in that category."[80]

As if to bear out Herrick's warning, at 7:40 P.M. on August 4 (Tonkin Gulf time), the destroyers observed surface radar contacts thirty-six miles to the northeast and reported that they had received information indicating an attack by North Vietnamese torpedo boats was imminent. Two hours later, having picked up new radar contacts evaluated as hostile, the destroyers opened fire while aircraft from the *Ticonderoga* conducted rocket and strafing attacks in the area where the North Vietnamese boats were thought to be. While there would later be serious doubts as to whether an attack had in fact taken place, the destroyers reported at the time that they were under continuous torpedo attack and that they had sunk two of the attackers during the engagement.[81]

On the basis of those reports, alert orders to prepare for reprisal strikes against North Vietnam were sent to the *Ticonderoga* and to the carrier *Constellation*, then steaming south from Hong Kong. In all, sixty-four sorties would be flown against North Vietnamese torpedo boat bases and an oil storage depot near Vinh, an action characterized by the President as "limited and fitting."[82] In addition to the air strikes, the Tonkin incidents provided the Administration with an opportunity to carry out a number of other actions under consideration ever since the Honolulu Conference in June. Most importantly, the Administration took advantage of the incidents to secure passage of a Congressional Resolution approving the President's handling of the incidents and pledging that "the United States is . . . prepared, as the President determines, to take all necessary steps, including the use of armed force, to assist any member or protocol state of the Southeast Asia Collective Defense Treaty requesting assistance in defense of its freedom."[83]

Second, selected forces from CINCPAC OPLAN 37-64 were moved to bases in South Vietnam, Thailand, and the Western Pacific, both to deter hostile responses to the reprisals and to reinforce the signal of

80. Quoted in Austin, p. 275. See also Goulden, p. 141. This cable was sent at approximately 6:30 A.M. on August 4 (Tonkin Gulf time).

81. For details on the August 4 incident, see V Gravel, pp. 325-326; Goulden, pp. 142-147; Galloway, pp. 56-58; Windchy, pp. 186-210; and Austin, pp. 278-287.

82. On the reaction in Washington, see V Gravel, pp. 326-327; Goulden, pp. 147-157; Windchy, pp. 211-220; and Austin, pp. 287-290. For the President's comment, see Johnson Papers, 1963-1964, pp. 927-928. For a detailed description of the air strikes, see Windchy, pp. 221-242.

83. Quoted in V Gravel, p. 341.

resolve to stand firm in Southeast Asia hopefully conveyed by the air strikes. In the aftermath of the crisis, virtually all of these forces, whose movements had been widely publicized, remained in the area of their August deployments, available for future use against the North.[84]

Finally, to insure that no one in Hanoi misunderstood the meaning of these actions, Seaborn was asked to carry another message during his next visit to Hanoi, scheduled to begin on August 10. Among the points he was to convey to Pham Van Dong, whom he saw on August 13, were the following. First, he was to present the American view of the Tonkin incidents, emphasizing that the *Maddox* was in no way connected with the raids on Hon Me and Hon Ngu and stating that "the Americans were and are at a complete loss to understand the DRV motive" for the August 4 attack on the *Maddox* and the *Turner Joy*. In addition, he was to stress that the American response was aimed solely at the offending patrol craft and their supporting installations, and he was to characterize the deployment of additional American forces as "precautionary."[85]

Second, Seaborn was to reiterate several of the points conveyed during his first trip, including that the U.S. goal was to preserve South Vietnam's territorial integrity and that the U.S. held Hanoi "directly responsible" for Viet Cong actions in the South. In addition, he was to refer again to the "economic and other benefits" which might accrue if the North called off the insurgency.

Finally, Seaborn was to present a number of new points, the most important of which was that the reprisals added credibility to his earlier warning that American patience with the DRV was growing thin. In addition, he was to point out that the U.S. had "ways and means of measuring the DRV's participation in, and direction and control of, the war in South Vietnam and Laos," and that the U.S. would be "carefully watching" the DRV's response to his message. "If the DRV persists in its present course," he was to warn, "it can expect to continue to suffer the consequences."[86]

The immediate effect of Seaborn's message, however, was to produce

84. On these points, see "More U.S. Forces Sent to Asia," *New York Times*, August 6, 1964, pp. 1, 6, 7; Peter Grose, "Saigon Chief Visits Alerted Troops on Border," *New York Times*, August 9, 1964, p. 34; and Westmoreland, p. 109.

85. For Seaborn's message, see Document no. 168 in III Gravel, pp. 521–522, with all excerpts quoted here taken from those pages. Surprisingly, Seaborn made no mention of the 34A raid on August 4 when referring to DRV motivation for the alleged second attack. Apaprently, senior officials in Washington were not aware of that raid when they ordered the reprisal and drafted the new message for Seaborn. On this point, see the account of Secretary McNamara's 1968 testimony on the Tonkin incidents in Goulden, p. 220; and Austin, p. 310.

86. In a flash cable on August 9, the State Department instructed the American Embassy in Saigon to ask Seaborn to delete the words *to continue* from that sentence, but the documents available do not indicate whether that request reached Seaborn in time. See Seaborn Chronology, p. 19.

anger on Pham Van Dong's part. Blaming the reprisals on President Johnson's need to outbid the Republican candidate in the upcoming election, the Premier indicated that he fully expected further "acts of aggression" by the U.S. but warned that the other Socialist countries would come to North Vietnam's aid if it was attacked. Pham Van Dong, moreover, was not without threats of his own, telling Seaborn that, "Up to now we have tried to avoid serious trouble; but it now becomes more difficult because the war has been carried to our territory. . . . If war comes to North Vietnam, it will come to the whole of Southeast Asia. . . ."[87]

Despite his initial angry reaction, Pham Van Dong did drop two hints near the end of the conversation suggesting he remained interested in negotiating a settlement with the United States. In contrast to the three-point stance he had outlined during their meeting in June, he now told Seaborn that a solution was to be found in a return to the Geneva Agreements—a statement noteworthy in that on July 24, President Johnson told a news conference that "until there is demonstrated upon the part of those who are ignoring the agreements reached at the conference table [i.e., the 1954 Agreements] some desire to carry out their agreement, we expect to continue our efforts in Vietnam."[88] Furthermore, at the close of their talk, Pham Van Dong again hinted at his hope for an American counterproposal, telling Seaborn that he should continue to bear messages from the U.S., no matter how unpleasant they might be.

Further evidence of North Vietnamese interest in negotiating with the U.S. appeared shortly after Seaborn's return from Hanoi. On August 6, UN Secretary General U Thant visited Washington, at which time he apparently told both Secretary Rusk and President Johnson of his interest in arranging private talks between the U.S. and North Vietnam. While specific arrangements were not discussed, Thant left Washington convinced that he had received an American go-ahead. Consequently he transmitted a message to Hanoi through the Soviets, asking whether North Vietnam would be interested in talking with the United States. While the North Vietnamese reply (which apparently reached Thant sometime in September) expressed interest in his proposal, no

87. This account of Pham Van Dong's reply to Seaborn is based on Seaborn Discussion, p. 2; Seaborn Summary, p. 2; and Interview Data.

88. Johnson Papers, 1963–1964, p. 889. Similarly, on August 12, the President told the American Bar Association in New York that "For 10 years, . . . we have had one consistent aim—observance of the 1954 Agreements which guaranteed the independence of South Vietnam" (Johnson Papers, 1963–1964, p. 953).

such favorable response was forthcoming from Washington. Instead, with the Presidential campaign in full swing and the Republican candidate chiding the Administration on its alleged softness in opposing Communist expansion in Vietnam, it appears that Thant's proposal was simply shelved until after the election.[89]

While Thant's initiative would never get off the ground, due to Washington's disinterest, the North Vietnamese response raises an intriguing question. The arrival of Thant's message in Hanoi coincided roughly with the August 13 meeting between Seaborn and Pham Van Dong, during which, as we saw, Seaborn presented a harsh and uncompromising statement of the American position. Furthermore, Thant's message arrived at a time when American officials were publicly deprecating the prospects for a negotiated settlement and portraying American objectives in terms every bit as uncompromising as those presented by Seaborn.[90] Nor was this a situation in which the North Vietnamese had "nothing to lose" by going along with Thant. Coming, as it did, in the context of the Tonkin reprisals and the explicit threat conveyed by Seaborn, an expression of interest in Thant's proposal carried with it the risk that it would be interpreted in Washington as a sign that the North Vietnamese were having second thoughts about Seaborn's warning and were sufficiently worried about the possibility of future reprisals that they were now seeking a way out.[91] In view of the risks involved and the slim chances for success, why did the North Vietnamese express interest in the proposed talks?

89. The full story of Thant's efforts will probably never be known, since neither of the two principal actors involved, Thant and Adlai Stevenson (then U.S. ambassador to the UN), ever committed the full story to paper. Furthermore, Thant and Stevenson both appear to have inspired conflicting accounts of the episode. The most authoritative account has been provided by John Bartlow Martin, *Adlai Stevenson and the World* (Garden City, N.Y.: Doubleday, 1977), pp. 803–804, 809–811, 827–831. In addition, detailed accounts have been pieced together by David Kraslow and Stuart Loory, *The Secret Search for Peace in Vietnam* (New York: Vintage, 1968), pp. 91–109; and by Geyelin, pp. 202–210. See also Cooper (1972), pp. 392–394; Henry Brandon, *Anatomy of Error* (Boston: Gambit, 1969), pp. 43–45; Mario Rossi, "U Thant and Vietnam: The Untold Story," *New York Review of Books*, November 17, 1966, pp. 8–10; and Norman Cousins, "Vietnam: The Spurned Peace," *Saturday Review*, July 26, 1969, pp. 12–13.

90. See, for example, Secretary Rusk's comments on "Meet the Press" on August 30, in DOSB, September 21, 1964, p. 397; Assistant Secretary Bundy's comments over the Voice of America, in DOSB, September 7, 1964, pp. 335–336; and the comments of Henry Cabot Lodge (then serving as special envoy to the NATO governments), in the *New York Times*, August 25, 1964, p. 10.

91. Apparently, no one in Washington drew this connection between the Seaborn and Thant initiatives, probably as a result of the closeness with which knowledge of Thant's proposal was held in the Administration. Stevenson apparently discussed the matter only with Rusk, and over the phone at that. Rusk, in turn, apparently kept the matter to himself, not even informing William Bundy until it was too late to salvage the initiative. On these points, see Martin, pp. 827–831; Kraslow and Loory, pp. 98–105; and Halberstam, p. 754.

While it is impossible to argue with certainty on this matter, it may well be that they simply discounted both Seaborn's warning and the disparaging public comments about the prospects for negotiations. As we saw earlier, Seaborn reported, on returning from his first visit to Hanoi, that the North Vietnamese were unconvinced that the U.S. really would carry the war to the North, and we suggested that one factor contributing to their disbelief was the inconsistency in Administration statements on future U.S. policy in Vietnam. Significantly, in this respect, while Administration statements stiffened temporarily in the aftermath of the Tonkin incidents, on August 22, the Administration released a paper by Willard Matthias, a member of the CIA's Board of National Estimates, which urged that the U.S. consider "some kind of negotiated settlement based upon neutralization" for South Vietnam. While Administration officials were quick to point out that the Matthias paper was not a policy document, "qualified sources" indicated that Matthias's views were "widely held in the government and the subject of recurrent official discussions."[92]

Furthermore, Matthias's paper was released at a time of mounting turmoil in South Vietnam. On August 7, in an attempt to use the heightened tensions brought on by the Tonkin incidents to shore up his own position, General Khanh proclaimed a nationwide state of emergency; on August 16, he promulgated a new constitution through which he became President with greatly expanded powers. This maneuver, however, touched off a weeklong series of riots and demonstrations, leading Khanh to resign on August 25. Between August 25 and September 4, when Khanh returned to office, this time as Premier, South Vietnam slipped into near-anarchy. Simultaneously, hints began appearing in the American press that the U.S. was reconsidering its role and might even cut off aid if Khanh was not restored to power.[93] The effect of these events may well have been to convince the North Vietnamese

92. See Jack Raymond, "CIA Aide Suggests Saigon 'Settlement,'" New York Times, August 23, 1964, pp. 1, 3. In fact, the motive for the release of the Matthias paper, as Raymond notes, was Presidential politics. A copy of the paper had been obtained by the Chicago Tribune, which stated its intention to publish portions of the document, apparently to publicize a possible "sell-out" in Southeast Asia. To guard against that kind of publicity, the Administration released the entire study, carefully labeling it the work of a single official and not a policy document. To the North Vietnamese, however, this could well have appeared as a tacit signal of interest in a negotiated settlement.

93. See Jack Langguth, "U.S. Said to Issue Saigon a Warning," New York Times, September 2, 1964, p. 1; and "U.S. Is Apprehensive," New York Times, September 3, 1964, p. 2. For details on South Vietnam's government crisis, see Robert Shaplen, The Lost Revolution, rev. ed. (New York: Harper & Row, 1966), pp. 270 ff.; Taylor (1972), pp. 310 ff.; III Gravel, pp. 83–87; and Westmoreland, pp. 71–72.

that, far from preparing to carry the war to the North, the U.S. was thinking of abandoning South Vietnam, leading them to go along with Thant's proposal in the hope that a convenient forum for talks might help speed the American decision to withdraw.

The North Vietnamese, however, were by no means restricting themselves to a single option. While leaving the door open to a negotiated settlement, they were at the same time actively preparing for a decisive military push aimed at toppling the regime in Saigon, should the diplomatic initiatives fail. Sometime in 1964, Nguyen Chi Thanh, member of the Vietnam Workers' Party (VWP) Politburo and four-star general in the North Vietnamese Army (NVA), was dispatched to the South to take command of the Party's military and political assets there. In addition, during 1964, infiltration into the South increased significantly, to a rate roughly double that of previous years, accompanied by preparations for an expansion of the trails through Laos, which would begin at the end of the rainy season in November. The most ominous development, however, occurred in October, when the 95th Regiment of the NVA's 325th Division departed for South Vietnam—the first complete NVA unit to be infiltrated into the South.[94]

The North Vietnamese were not the only ones preparing for an escalation of the war. In the aftermath of the Tonkin reprisals, American policy entered a "holding phase" that lasted into September 1964. As announced in a Department of State strategy paper of August 14, nothing was to be done over the next few weeks to take the onus for escalation off the North Vietnamese. DE SOTO patrols and 34A operations were temporarily suspended (except for resupply of air-dropped teams and leaflet missions over North Vietnam) and no new military moves were made in Laos, although reconnaissance and T-28 missions continued.[95] Despite these restraints, several important developments took place during the "holding phase," all of which portended a higher level of conflict in the near future.

First, impediments to an expanded American role in the war were gradually cleared away. On August 15, new rules of engagement were put into effect, authorizing American forces to pursue attacking ships and aircraft into North Vietnamese territorial waters and airspace,

94. On these points, see Latimer, p. 187; III Gravel, pp. 207–208; Peter Grose, "Vietnam Outlook Bleaker a Year After Diem's Fall," *New York Times*, November 2, 1964, p. 18; Dommen, p. 280; and Working Paper, pp. 12, 19. See also the analysis of North Vietnamese decision-making in Chapter 5, below. Because of the time required to move an entire regiment down the Ho Chi Minh Trail to South Vietnam, Washington would not become aware of the 95th Regiment's departure until several months after the fact.

95. Document no. 175, in III Gravel, pp. 533–534.

although pursuit into Chinese waters and airspace was still forbidden. In addition, planning for cross-border operations in Laos continued, resulting in an August 16 recommendation by General Westmoreland to go ahead with the first phase of the program even though it was, in Westmoreland's words, an "overly ambitious scheme."[96]

Second, as we saw earlier, August 1964 was a month of political turmoil in the South, the principal effect of which was to destroy any remaining hopes on the American side that the GVN on its own could defeat the Viet Cong. As described by the Pentagon analyst, the central perception in Washington during this period was one of "impending chaos and possible failure in South Vietnam. Among several agencies, the emerging mood was that some kind of action was urgently needed. . . ."[97]

Third, the Tonkin reprisals exerted a significant influence on the thinking of American officials. On the one hand, the ease with which the reprisals had been carried out, the Congressional Resolution secured, and the North Vietnamese seemingly put in their place, all of which was accomplished in the context of widespread praise at home for the Administration's handling of the incidents, induced a sense of optimism concerning the possibilities for applying American power directly against the North. On the other hand, "officials developed mixed feelings regarding the effect of the Tonkin reprisals for signalling firm U.S. commitments in Southeast Asia." While the reprisals were seen as the most forceful expression of American resolve to date, there was a feeling that the U.S. could not afford to "rest on [its] laurels." Instead, it was felt that the "signal" sent by the reprisals would have to be continually reinforced if the U.S. was to succeed in "convincing" the North Vietnamese to yield. Failure to follow through with new pressures against the North, so the argument went, might be interpreted as a sign of uncertainty and irresolution on the part of the U.S.[98]

But even as a consensus was emerging on the need for new pressures against the North, there was still no consensus over how to go about exerting those pressures. During the period of the "holding phase," the dispute between military and civilian planners over fast- versus slow-paced pressures that had first erupted in May 1964 flared up again, as American policymakers debated the nature of future pressures against the North. It is to those policy debates that we now turn.

96. On the new rules of engagement, see Document no. 176 in III Gravel, pp. 537–538; and V Gravel, p. 337. For Westmoreland's comment, see Document no. 177 in III Gravel, p. 540; and V Gravel, p. 338.
97. V Gravel, p. 339.
98. On these points, see V Gravel, pp. 335–336.

IV. Post-Tonkin Policy Assessments
(September-October 1964)

In the aftermath of the Tonkin reprisals, virtually all senior American officials involved in Vietnam planning agreed on the eventual need for additional pressures against the North. Where these officials disagreed was on the nature and tempo of the actions to be taken. Civilian planners continued to advocate relatively restrained measures that would, in the words of State's August 14 strategy paper, "maintain our initiative and [the] morale of [the] GVN and Khanh, but that would not involve major risks of escalation." Among the actions favored by civilian planners were 34A operations, cross-border operations in Laos, DE SOTO Patrols, reprisals for "special" DRV/VC activity, and possible withdrawal of American dependents from South Vietnam. While it was conceded that those measures "would not in themselves go far to change Hanoi's basic actions," they were seen as "foreshadowing systematic military action against [the] DRV," with January 1, 1965 serving as a contingency date for planning purposes for the start of heavier pressures. Underlying this approach was the belief that, since more drastic measures carried a higher risk of Communist counterescalation, those actions should be deferred until the GVN had had time to stabilize itself.[99]

The JCS, in contrast, adamantly opposed the idea of deferring overt pressures against the North, arguing that the situation in the South would only get worse and not better. Reiterating their earlier claim that "the military course of action which offers the best chance of success remains the destruction of DRV will and capabilities as necessary to compel the DRV to cease providing support to the insurgencies in South Vietnam and Laos," the Chiefs called for both the immediate deployment of the remaining OPLAN 37-64 forces and the initiation of a program of air strikes against the North.[100]

These conflicting recommendations formed the basis for a high-level policy review in Washington in early September, attended by Rusk, McNamara, Wheeler, Taylor, and McCone. Following the precedent set at Honolulu in June, the conferees took a cautious approach to the problem of pressuring the North, rejecting both JCS suggestions for an immediate bombing campaign as well as suggestions that the U.S.

99. On these points, see Document no. 175 in III Gravel, pp. 535–537; and Document no. 181 in III Gravel, p. 546.

100. JCSM-746-64, August 26, 1964, reprinted as Document no. 183 in III Gravel, pp. 551–552. For CINCPAC's views, see Document no. 179 in III Gravel, pp. 542–545. See also III Gravel, p. 193.

undertake actions intended to provoke a North Vietnamese response which could then be used to legitimize a campaign of overt pressures against the North. In effect, the conferees opted for the slow-paced approach favored by civilian planners, although they were careful not to rule out the possibility of deliberately provoking the DRV, stating that they might be ready to recommend such a course by early October, "depending on GVN progress and Communist reaction in the meantime." For the immediate future, however, the conferees recommended that the U.S. take only limited actions designed to "assist morale in South Vietnam and show the Communists we still mean business, while at the same time seeking to keep the risks low and under our control at each stage." Among the actions recommended were a resumption of DE SOTO patrols and 34A operations, limited GVN air and ground operations in the corridor area of Laos, and preparations for reprisals "in the event of any attack on U.S. units or any *special* DRV/VC action against South Vietnam."[101] These recommendations were approved by the President and issued as NSAM-314 on September 10, 1964.[102]

Much like earlier efforts to put pressure on the North, however, implementing actions for NSAM-314 did not proceed quite as planned. DE SOTO patrols in the Gulf of Tonkin were resumed in mid-September, but on the night of September 18, the destroyers *Morton* and *Edwards* picked up surface radar contacts that continued closing despite evasive action by the destroyers. After firing warning shots, both destroyers opened fire in earnest, with radar indicating hits for both vessels. However, no rounds or torpedoes were reported from any of the contacts,

---

101. On these points, see III Gravel, p. 193; and Document no. 191 in III Gravel, pp. 561–562. The quoted excerpts are all from Document no. 191 in III Gravel, p. 562 (emphasis in original). See also Document no. 188 in III Gravel, pp. 556–559 for John McNaughton's suggestion that the U.S. might deliberately attempt to provoke the DRV. In addition, on September 4, Pentagon officials announced that the U.S. military buildup in South Vietnam would continue despite the recent political turbulence there. On this point, see John W. Finney, "U.S. to Continue Saigon Build-Up; Khanh Stirs Hope," *New York Times*, September 5, 1964, p. 1.

102. NSAM-314 is reprinted as Document no. 195 in III Gravel, pp. 565–566. NSAM-314's slow and cautious approach to pressuring North Vietnam was reflected in the public statements of Administration officials at the time. See, for example, Tad Szulc, "Top Officials Seek Saigon Plan," *New York Times*, September 8, 1964, pp. 1, 11; Tad Szulc, "U.S. Officials See No Quick Defeat of Vietnam Reds," *New York Times*, September 11, 1964, pp. 1, 3; Max Frankel, "No Shift Due Now in Vietnam Policy," *New York Times*, September 12, 1964, p. 1; and Tom Wicker, "Uprising Creates New GOP Issue," *New York Times*, September 14, 1964, pp. 1, 14. See also Ambassador Taylor's September 10 press conference, during which he said that he knew of "no special interest" in air operations along the Ho Chi Minh Trail in Laos (DOSB, September 28, 1964, p. 434); and Secretary Rusk's assertion that "we do not intend to strike out rashly into a major war" in Southeast Asia (Speech before the Economic Club of Detroit, September 14, 1964, DOSB, October 5, 1964, p. 466).

and reconnaissance flights the next day were unable to locate any debris from the incident. After reviewing reports of the incident, President Johnson suspended the patrol, and there would be no further patrols scheduled until February 1965. In the aftermath of the incident, moreover, maritime operations under OPLAN 34A were not resumed until October 1964.[103]

Operations in Laos proceeded in similar halting fashion. On September 11, representatives from the American embassies in South Vietnam, Laos, and Thailand met in Saigon to discuss the implementation of NSAM-314's provision for operations in Laos. With respect to air operations, the Embassy representatives

agreed that if their primary objective was military in nature, "sharp, heavy" and concentrated attacks would be needed and that U.S. and/or VNAF/ FARMGATE forces would be required. If their impact was intended to be primarily psychological (presumably affecting both communists and the GVN), they believed that the operations could be more widely spaced, relying primarily on Laotian T-28's with some U.S. strikes on harder targets. In view of Souvanna Phouma's reported opposition to VNAF strikes in the Panhandle, the representatives conceded that the slower-paced operation with RLAF aircraft offered the best course.

In terms of ground operations, the representatives recommended company-size penetrations by South Vietnamese forces of up to 20 kilometers into Laos.[104]

These recommendations, however, were not cabled to Washington until September 19, and it was not until October 6 that Washington transmitted its reply—an interval that, significantly, encompassed the President's September 28 speech in Manchester, New Hampshire, in which he derided suggestions for "going north in Vietnam" and announced that he wanted to be "very cautious and careful, and use [bombing] only as a last resort." While Washington's reply authorized the embassy in Vientianne to urge the Laotian government to begin strikes in the corridor area "as soon as possible," authorization was withheld on both U.S. strikes on the harder targets and GVN ground

103. For details on this incident, see III Gravel, pp. 194–195; Max Frankel, "U.S. Maintaining Forces on Alert in Gulf of Tonkin," *New York Times*, September 20, 1964, pp. 1, 3; Max Frankel, "Johnson Barred Reprisal Attack," *New York Times*, September 22, 1964, p. 3; and John W. Finney, "U.S. Believes Destroyers Scored Hits in Tonkin Gulf," *New York Times*, September 23, 1964, p. 1. On GVN maritime operations during August and September, see III Gravel, p. 195; and Document no. 225 in III Gravel, p. 606.

104. On these points, see III Gravel, p. 195. FARMGATE was a covert program whereby American pilots flew planes with VNAF markings.

operations in Laos.[105] But since T-28 strikes against North Vietnamese forces in Laos had been under way since at least June 1964, the T-28 corridor strikes amounted to little more than a continuation of an ongoing program rather than an intensification of the pressures being applied outside South Vietnam.

More importantly, though, NSAM-314 reflected the judgment prevalent among civilian planners that overt pressures against the North could be deferred while efforts were made to stabilize the situation in the South. That judgment, however, came under serious challenge during October 1964. On October 14, Ambassador Taylor cabled a deeply pessimistic appraisal of the situation in the South:

[September] and October thus far have seen little or no progress in the overall situation . . . and some deterioration. . . . It has been a period characterized by government instability, civil disorders (now quieting), indications of increased infiltration from the north, and a high level of military activity on the part of the Viet Cong and the Government forces. . . . A recent analysis suggests that if the present rate of infiltration is maintained the annual figure for 1964 will be on the order of 10,000. Furthermore, . . . we are finding more and more "bona fide" North Vietnamese soldiers among the infiltrees. I feel sure that we must soon adopt new and more drastic methods to reduce and eventually end such infiltration if we are ever to succeed in South Vietnam.[106]

Picking up the theme of Taylor's cable, the JCS on October 21 and again on October 27 submitted proposals for an immediate extension of the war to the North, arguing that the Viet Cong could not be defeated until they were isolated from their source of direction and supply in the North.[107] Arguments such as these took on added urgency after November 1, when the Viet Cong launched a surprise attack on the Bien Hoa airbase, killing five Americans and destroying or seriously damaging thirteen B-57 jet bombers. Although both Taylor and the JCS urged a retaliatory air strike—not an unreasonable proposal in light of NSAM-314's provision on reprisals—the President was unwilling to

105. The conference's recommendations are reprinted as Document no. 196 in III Gravel, pp. 566–567; Washington's reply is reprinted as Document no. 204 in III Gravel, pp. 576–577. See also III Gravel, p. 196. For the President's Manchester speech, in which he also announced that "just for the moment I have not thought that we were ready for American boys to do the fighting for Asian boys," see Johnson Papers, 1963–1964, p. 1164. That theme had also been developed by the President on September 25 in remarks at the dedication of the Eufala Dam in Oklahoma (Johnson Papers, 1963–1964, p. 1126).

106 Document no. 210 in III Gravel, p. 583; see also III Gravel, p. 207.

107. For a summary of JCS proposals, see III Gravel, p. 208. See also John McNaughton's October 13 memo, Document no. 209 in III Gravel, pp. 580–583; and Taylor's comments on the JCS proposals, Document no. 217 in III Gravel, pp. 590–591.

respond with the election only two days away, and thus no action was taken.[108]

The decision not to respond, however, when viewed in the context of the events of August through October, appears to have been a particularly fateful one with respect to the Administration's efforts to "convince" the North Vietnamese of its resolve to defend South Vietnam. As we saw earlier, at a time when infiltration from the North was rising dramatically, American actions were restrained first by the "holding phase" and then by the cautious approach to implementing NSAM-314. Furthermore, there had been no shortage of warnings about what the U.S. would do in the event of an attack like the one on Bien Hoa. In June and again in August, Seaborn told Pham Van Dong that the U.S. held Hanoi "directly responsible" for Viet Cong actions in the South; in addition, during their August meeting, he cited the Congressional Resolution as a sign of U.S. determination to resist attacks on American forces. Similarly, in the aftermath of the September incident in the Gulf of Tonkin, Secretary McNamara stated emphatically that U.S. air and sea forces were "prepared to respond immediately to any attack." And yet, when the attack came, the Administration not only failed to respond, it also quietly withdrew most of the remaining B-57s from Bien Hoa, hardly the type of precedent to discourage future terrorist attacks.[109]

Still, it was in the aftermath of Bien Hoa that preparations for an expanded American role in the war began in earnest. Sometime on November 1 or 2, the President ordered the formation of an interagency task force, chaired by William Bundy and charged with studying "immediately and intensively" all the options open to the U.S. in Vietnam,

108. While this decision was rationalized on the grounds that the attack came in the course of a war in which the U.S. was aiding one of the belligerents (i.e., the GVN), as opposed to the Tonkin incidents, when U.S. ships "on U.S. business" were attacked in international waters, it is possible that the magnitude of the JCS-proposed air strike was a factor in the President's decision. What the Chiefs proposed was not a reprisal but rather an all-out air assault, including air strikes in Laos, a B-52 strike on Phuc Yen airfield near Hanoi, and fighter-bomber strikes on other DRV airfields, the Hanoi-Haiphong POL facilities, and other military and industrial targets in the DRV. On the public handling of the Bien Hoa attack, see Tad Szulc, "U.S. Rushes Jets to Replace B-57's Hit by Viet Cong," *New York Times*, November 2, 1964, pp. 1, 18. On the JCS proposals, see Document no. 230 in III Gravel, pp. 628-629. See also III Gravel, pp. 209-210, 288-289; and Geyelin, pp. 200-201.

109. For Seaborn's comments, see Seaborn Chronology, p. 7; and Document no. 168 in III Gravel, pp. 521-522. McNamara's warning is quoted in Max Frankel, "U.S. Maintaining Forces on Alert in Gulf of Tonkin," *New York Times*, September 20, 1964, p. 3. On the removal of the B-57s from Bien Hoa, see the UPI dispatch, "B-57's at Bien Hoa Reported Shifted," *New York Times*, November 5, 1964, p. 3; the UPI dispatch, "A-Capable Bombers Leave Viet Bases; Cabinet Gets Reins," *Washington Post*, November 5, 1964, p. A17; and III Gravel, p. 209.

including, by implication at least, that of withdrawal.[110] The "options" produced by the Bundy Working Group, however, were in fact all choices for wider war, although it would not be until February 1965 that the Administration would be prepared to implement the Working Group's proposals.

V. Planning for Wider War
(November-December 1964)

The Bundy Working Group began its deliberations in an atmosphere of urgency. There was, as the Pentagon analyst put it, "an awareness that another Bien Hoa could occur at any time. . . . Moreover, the news services were reporting the threat of civil protest against the new Saigon government, and the increased level of guerrilla infiltration from the North was being publicly aired."[111] To reverse the deterioration in the South and compel the North Vietnamese to end their role in the war, the Working Group identified three options open to the U.S., which it labeled "A," "B," and "C." While all three combined efforts to improve the situation in the South with military measures against the North, there were important differences between them with respect to the nature and tempo of the actions to be taken.

Option A was essentially a status quo proposal, providing for "intensified efforts to improve the situation in South Vietnam and for somewhat intensified military action [outside South Vietnam] in line with current policy."[112] Basic to Option A was "continued rejection of negotiation in the hope that the situation will improve," although it was conceded that the GVN itself might open talks with the North Vietnamese or the National Liberation Front.[113] In that event, the U.S. response would be either to "stand aside" or to "seek to cover a retreat by accepting negotiations" which could hopefully be used to buy time.[114]

Option B, also known as the "fast/full squeeze," "provided for everything in A plus a program of U.S. military pressures against North Viet-

---

110. III Gravel, p. 210.

111. Ibid., p. 211. The new government referred to was that of Premier Tran Van Huong, installed on November 1. For details on South Vietnamese politics during this period, see Shaplen (1966), pp. 283-298.

112. III Gravel, p. 223.

113. William Bundy, "The Broad Options," Document no. 224 in III Gravel, p. 605. See also III Gravel, p. 224.

114. William Bundy and John McNaughton, "Courses of Action in Southeast Asia," Document no. 241 in III Gravel, p. 661. See also III Gravel, p. 224.

nam. These were to continue 'at a fairly rapid pace and without inter-
ruption' until the DRV agreed to stop supporting and directing the war
in South Vietnam." Negotiations would "occur simultaneously with a
continuation of the pressures and would be based on 'inflexible insistence on our present objectives.'"[115]

Option C ("progressive squeeze-and-talk") provided for "every military action included in A plus 'graduated military moves against infiltration targets first in Laos and then in the DRV, and then against other
targets in North Vietnam.'" These would be accompanied by

"communications with Hanoi and/or Peiping" indicating . . . "a willingness to
negotiate in an affirmative sense." From the outset, "we would be accepting the
possibility that we might not achieve our full objectives." Accordingly, the
concept for C included provision for an initial bargaining position that added
"certain bargaining elements" to the basic U.S. objectives. Once negotiations
started, the military pressures would cease.[116]

Despite three weeks of intensive effort, the Working Group's final
product, which was to serve as the basis for still another high-level
review, reflected the same lack of consensus on the question of
pressuring the North that had hampered earlier policy reviews.
Nowhere was this more apparent than in the case of the recurrent
controversy over the proper target for American military pressures—i.e.,
DRV will or capabilities. As indicated by the description of the options,
all three envisioned some sort of negotiations as the probable outcome
of American actions; and for civilian members of the Working Group,
bargaining strength during those negotiations would result not so much
from the damage done by American actions as from carrying them out
in a way that foreshadowed increasingly severe pressures against the
North, thus exploiting North Vietnamese fears of wider war. As
explained by the Pentagon analyst:

Under A, emphasis was placed on obtaining maximum leverage from exploiting the threat of further escalation—to be demonstrated primarily through
reprisal actions and deployments. Under B, a similar kind of psychological
leverage was to be achieved through the clearly ascending nature of the actions.

115. III Gravel, p. 224. In these passages, the Pentagon analyst is apparently quoting from the
Bundy memo on "The Broad Options," Document no. 224 in III Gravel, p. 605. See also Document no. 223 in III Gravel, p. 602, for McNaughton's characterization of Option B.

116. III Gravel, p. 224. The internal quotes were apparently taken by the Pentagon analyst from
Bundy's memo on "The Broad Options," Document no. 224 in III Gravel, p. 605; from the Bundy/
McNaughton memo, Document no. 241 in III Gravel, pp. 659–660; and from Bundy's "Analysis of
Option C," Document no. 225 in III Gravel, p. 614. See also Document no. 223 in III Gravel, p.
602, for McNaughton's characterization of Option C.

. . . Under C, the effect was to be achieved by the combined effects of (1) maximizing the threat of impending escalation after each graduated and carefully paced step and (2) minimizing the communist governments' problems of "face" as they moved toward negotiations.[117]

And yet, even though William Bundy would state on the eve of the high-level review that "we all accept the *will* of the DRV as the real target," a reading of the inputs prepared by military planners indicates that they continued to insist on the destruction of North Vietnamese capabilities—a focus that resulted in a considerably different rationale for progressively escalating pressures. In the view of the Joint Staff:

> The actual U.S. requirement with respect to the DRV is reduction of the *rate of delivery* of support to the Viet Cong, to levels below their minimum sustaining action. After that is accomplished, effective corollary actions in South Vietnam can end the insurgency, which is the U.S. objective.
>
> In the present unstable situation something far less than total destruction may be all that is required to accomplish the above. A very modest change in the government's favor . . . may be enough to turn the tide and lead to a successful solution. Of course it is not possible to predict in advance with complete assurance the precise level of measures which will be required to achieve the above. This is the reason for designing a program of progressively increasing squeeze.[118]

To further confuse things, the JCS, despite the Joint Staff's emphasis on reducing the rate of delivery to the Viet Cong, seemed primarily interested in attacking "capabilities" only indirectly related to the infiltration problem, such as DRV airfields, the Hanoi-Haiphong POL facilities, and other military and industrial targets on the "94-target list"—targets that one might expect to be associated with "will-breaking" strikes aimed at making the cost of the war prohibitively high for the DRV.[119] In contrast, civilian advocates of Option C, despite their emphasis on eroding DRV will, envisioned early military actions under C as aimed at infiltration targets in Laos and the southern DRV, with

117. III Gravel, pp. 225–226.

118. Bundy's comment can be found in Document no. 239 in III Gravel, p. 649 (emphasis in original). For the Joint Staff's comments, see Document no. 227 in III Gravel, p. 620 (emphasis in original).

119. For a description of JCS targetting plans, see Document no. 230 in III Gravel, pp. 628–629. For a description of the "94-target list," see III Gravel, p. 288. While JCS plans did provide for strikes at infiltration targets in Laos and the southern DRV, it is interesting to note their rationale for those strikes: "Attacking targets in Laos and conducting low-level reconnaissance in the southern DRV will provide militarily useful operations within the immediate capabilities of forces in place and, at the same time, will serve to *divert notice from the preparations and force deployments necessary for the ensuing stronger actions* [i.e., the strikes on DRV airfields, POL, and industrial targets]." Document no. 230, III Gravel, p. 629 (emphasis added).

strikes against industrial targets relegated to a second phase of military pressures.[120]

Furthermore, while most Working Group members favored Option C on the ground that it held more promise of achieving U.S. objectives than Option A while being more "controllable" than Option B, it was far from clear just what could be expected of C. Even Bundy and McNaughton, two of the staunchest advocates of C, conceded that the most likely DRV response to C would be to "hold firm while stimulating condemnation of [the] U.S. by world opinion," in which case the expected South Vietnamese elation over the attacks on the North would wane and the deterioration in the South would resume, forcing the U.S. to decide whether to "intensify our military actions, modify our negotiating positions, or both." Overall, according to Bundy and McNaughton:

The variable factors are too great to permit a confident evaluation of how the Option C course of action might come out. *At best*: to avoid heavy risk and punishment, the DRV might feign compliance and settle for an opportunity to subvert the South another day. That is, a respite might be gained. *At worst*: South Vietnam might come apart while we were pursuing the course of action. *In between*: we might be faced with no improvement in the internal South Vietnam situation and with the difficult decision whether to escalate on up to major conflict with China.[121]

Despite these uncertainties, there appears to have been a widely shared belief (at least among civilian officials) that the actions included in Option C offered a reasonable chance of achieving an acceptable settlement before the escalatory process got out of hand. As envisioned by the advocates of Option C, the role of military pressures against the North was to strengthen the U.S./GVN bargaining position by providing something that could be halted in return for an end to the DRV's role in the insurgency. While the Group's final report recognized that the DRV might respond militarily to Option C (air attacks against the South or an offensive in Laos were the two possibilities mentioned, although these were characterized as "initially unlikely"), implicit in the report was the belief that at some point the North Vietnamese would halt their efforts, apparently as a result of their fear of wider war. But why the North Vietnamese should have been any more afraid of wider war than their American counterparts was never made clear by the

120. See, for example, the Bundy/McNaughton memo, Document no. 241 in III Gravel, p. 664.

121. Document no. 241 in III Gravel, pp. 665–666. On the preferences of the members of the Working Group, see III Gravel, p. 223. On the views of William Bundy and John McNaughton, see Daniel Ellsberg, *Papers on the War* (New York: Pocket Books, 1972), p. 93.

Working Group. Furthermore, little if any consideration was given to the possibility that the North Vietnamese might attempt to match American escalation by stepping up the rate of infiltration to the South, despite a warning from the intelligence community that the North Vietnamese were "intensely committed" to the success of their effort in the South.[122]

These inconsistencies were, if anything, compounded in the meetings held by the Principals (Rusk, Ball, McNamara, Wheeler, McGeorge Bundy, and McCone, along with William Bundy and McNaughton) to review the Working Group's findings. At their initial meeting on November 24, the group was able to reach a consensus on several points, the most important of which, from our point of view, was that "the situation in South Vietnam would deteriorate further under Option A even with reprisals, but that there was a 'significant chance' that the actions proposed under B or C would result in an improved GVN performance and 'make possible' an improved security situation. . . ."[123]

On November 27, the Principals met again, this time joined by Ambassador Taylor and Michael Forrestal (from the Bundy Working Group). Opening the meeting with a prepared briefing, Taylor described the situation in South Vietnam as bleak and characterized U.S. involvement there as a "losing game." "To change the situation," he argued,

we need to do three things: first, establish an adequate government in South Vietnam; second, improve the conduct of the counterinsurgency campaign; and, finally, persuade or force the DRV to stop its aid to the Viet Cong and to use its directive powers to make the Viet Cong desist from their efforts to overthrow the government of South Vietnam.

Of these, it was clear that Taylor saw the third as the most important—as he stated later in the briefing, even if progress were to be made on the first two, "we will not succeed in the end until we drive the DRV out of its reinforcing role and obtain its cooperation in bringing an end to the Viet Cong insurgency."[124]

Despite the importance attached to ending the DRV's role in the war, the actions proposed by Taylor for this purpose were relatively restrained. As outlined in his "Suggested Scenario for Controlled Escalation,"

122. For a discussion of DRV reactions to Option C, see Document no. 241 in III Gravel, p. 665. For the intelligence community's comment, see Document no. 240 in III Gravel, p. 653.

123. III Gravel, p. 237. Ball, however, expressed doubt on this point. For the other points on which there was a consensus, see III Gravel, p. 237.

124. For Taylor's briefing, see Document no. 242 in III Gravel, pp. 668–673. See also III Gravel, p. 240.

these included discussions with friendly governments, alerting selected U.S. troop units, private communications with Hanoi, air strikes in Laos, a Laotian air attack on the Mu Gia pass inside the DRV with U.S. air cover, a Vietnamese Air Force attack on an infiltration target in the DRV just north of the Demilitarized Zone (DMZ), a "significant" maritime operation with U.S. air cover, and a joint U.S./GVN air strike on an infiltration target just north of the DMZ. Military actions were to be continued "sequentially with not more than a few days gap between each"; at the same time, the U.S. would be prepared to make "higher level responses to attacks from [North Vietnamese] MIGs or VC spectaculars in South Vietnam."[125]

The restrained nature of these actions becomes even more remarkable when viewed in light of the terms for a cessation of the attacks that Taylor wished to be communicated to Hanoi. In return for a halt to infiltration and an end to the insurgency in the South, the U.S. and the GVN would halt their air attacks, the U.S. would reduce its military presence in the South to the level specified by the 1954 Geneva Accords, the GVN would begin trade talks with the DRV, the U.S. and the GVN would give assurances not to use force or support the use of force to overthrow the 1954 Accords with respect to the DRV, and the GVN would permit Viet Cong desiring to return to the North to do so without their weapons or would grant amnesty to Viet Cong peacefully laying down their arms and desiring to remain in the South.[126] In effect, Taylor was proposing the unconditional surrender of the Viet Cong, even though the GVN was literally on the brink of collapse under the strain of the war.

At the conclusion of Taylor's briefing, there was an extended discussion of his report and of future courses of action in South Vietnam. As the Pentagon analyst notes, not only did the Principals not challenge Taylor's proposed settlement terms, but they also apparently accepted his suggestion that "over the next two months we adopt a program of Option A plus the first stages of Option C," despite the earlier consensus that the situation in the South would deteriorate further under Option A even with reprisals.[127]

This "softening" on the issue of additional military pressures continued in the days that followed. On November 28 and again on

125. See Document no. 242 in III Gravel, p. 672.

126. See Document no. 242 in III Gravel, p. 673. Under the 1954 Accords, the U.S. was restricted to 685 military personnel in South Vietnam. On this point, see II Gravel, pp. 431, 438.

127. See III Gravel, pp. 243, 247; and Document no. 244 in III Gravel, p. 675. The Principals did agree, however, that to get any improvement in the GVN, it would be necessary to move into parts of Option C very quickly.

November 30, the Principals met with Taylor to continue their review of American policy. At the November 30 meeting, the discussion focused on a draft NSAM prepared by William Bundy for review by the Principals prior to being submitted to the President. As outlined by Bundy, military pressures against the North would be undertaken in two phases. During an initial 30-day phase, the U.S. would undertake intensified forms of actions already under way plus armed reconnaissance operations in Laos and reprisals for any "major or spectacular Viet Cong action in the South." After that,

first phase actions may be continued without change, or additional military measures may be taken, including the withdrawal of dependents and the possible initiation of strikes a short distance across the border against the infiltration routes from the DRV. In the latter case this would become a transitional phase. Thereafter, if the GVN improves its effectiveness to an acceptable degree and Hanoi does not yield on acceptable terms, or if the GVN can only be kept going by stronger actions, the U.S. is prepared . . . to enter into a second phase program . . . of graduated military pressures directed systematically against the DRV. Such a program would consist principally of progressively more serious air strikes, of a weight and tempo adjusted to the situation as it develops (possibly running from two to six months). Targets in the DRV would start with infiltration targets south of the 19th Parallel and work up to targets north of that point. . . . The whole sequence of military actions would be designed to give the impression of a steady, deliberate approach and to give the U.S. the option at any time (subject to enemy reaction) to proceed or not, to escalate or not, and to quicken the pace or not. Concurrently, the U.S. would be alert to any sign of yielding by Hanoi, and would be prepared to explore negotiated solutions that attain U.S. objectives in an acceptable manner.[128]

During their discussion, the Principals made several changes in the Bundy paper, resulting in further softening on the issue of additional pressures. In effect, as the Pentagon analyst notes, "Option A along with the lowest order of Option C actions were being recommended . . . in a manner that would represent the least possible additional commitment."[129]

On December 1, the Principals and Taylor met with the President at the White House. While the President apparently accepted the strategic concept for actions against the North set forth in the Bundy paper, he approved the implementation of the first phase only. Furthermore, "the

128. Document no. 246 in III Gravel, p. 678. For a description of Phase One actions, see Document no. 246 in III Gravel, pp. 682–683.

129. III Gravel, p. 246. For a list of the changes made, see III Gravel, p. 246.

President made it clear that he considered that pulling the South Vietnamese together was basic to anything else the U.S. might do." Toward this end, he approved a draft statement to be presented by Taylor to the South Vietnamese, in which a U.S. decision to move into Phase Two operations was made contingent on first securing certain reforms from the GVN.[130]

Thus, the November policy review produced only a slight change in the American commitment to South Vietnam. In addition, the implementation of Phase One pressures proceeded in such a way as to further minimize whatever impact they might have had on the North Vietnamese. Included in Phase One were three sets of actions, only two of which were military in nature. First, GVN maritime operations, while nothing new in themselves, were to be intensified as part of Phase One. On December 12, the JCS submitted a two-package proposal for these operations. As described by the Pentagon analyst:

Included in their first 30-day package were coastal bombardment of radar sites, barracks, and PT-boat bases plus a maritime equivalent of aerial armed reconnaissance. Patrol boats would make "fire sweeps" along the coast against "targets of opportunity." In addition, upon their return from bombardment missions, it was proposed that the GVN PT-boats attempt the capture of NVN junks and SWATOW craft.

To these operations, Package Two added air cover from U.S. aircraft and included missions against North Vietnamese targets north of the 19th Parallel.[131]

The operations actually carried out, however, resulted in little, if any, new pressure on the DRV. With the exception of the coastal "fire sweeps," all of the Package One operations were approved, while decisions on Package Two were deferred. However, as General Johnson, acting Chairman of the JCS, pointed out at a December 19 meeting of the Principals, with the disapproval of the fire sweeps, the only new element in the package, "the 34A program was, in effect, not intensified at all." Furthermore, as the discussion at that meeting revealed, "seasonal sea conditions were now so severe that no maritime operation had been completed successfully during the previous three weeks."[132]

130. On these points, see III Gravel, pp. 249–250. The draft statement had originally been included in Bundy's draft NSAM, Document no. 246 in III Gravel, pp. 679–680.

131. On these points, see III Gravel, p. 252. SWATOWs were North Vietnamese gunboats, designed in Russia and built in China, armed with 37-mm. cannon (see Windchy, p. 110).

132. On these points, see III Gravel, p. 253. The Pentagon analyst also points out that "there was little additional MAROPS activity during January 1965; the normal documentary sources indicate very little for this period" (III Gravel, p. 253).

A similar pattern held for the second category of military operations—armed reconnaissance missions in Laos. As we saw earlier, U.S. aircraft (under the code name YANKEE TEAM) had been flying reconnaissance and escort missions over Communist-held territory in Laos since May 1964, although the rules of engagement for those flights prohibited attacking ground targets except in response to hostile ground fire. As part of Phase One, the JCS developed a program of armed reconnaissance missions code-named BARREL ROLL. As described by the Pentagon analyst:

The first mission was flown [on December 14] by USAF jet aircraft along Route 8. It was followed on the 17th by carrier-based A-1 and jet aircraft, striking along Routes 121 and 12. On the 18th, this pattern of two missions by four aircraft each was determined . . . to be the weekly standard—at least through the third week.[133]

Once again, however, it is doubtful that the North Vietnamese felt themselves under any new or intensified pressures. Responding to a query as to "why neither the DRV nor the Communist Chinese had made any public mention of or appeared to have taken cognizance of our BARREL ROLL operations," the Defense Intelligence Agency reported that the Communists apparently made no

distinction between BARREL ROLL missions on the one hand and the Laotian T-28 strikes and YANKEE TEAM missions on the other. . . . [It] would be most difficult to distinguish between YANKEE TEAM with its flak suppression aircraft [and] BARREL ROLL missions. . . . BARREL ROLL strikes have followed T-28 strikes by varying periods of time and have been of lesser intensity. They probably appear to be a continuation of the Laotian program. . . . [While] the Communists are apparently aware of some increased use of U.S. aircraft, they probably have not considered the BARREL ROLL strikes to date as a significant change in the pattern or representing a new threat to their activities.[134]

A third aspect of Phase One involved the publicizing of evidence of increased infiltration from the North, with Chester Cooper, a member of McGeorge Bundy's staff, selected to compile a public version of the available data on infiltration. Cooper's report, however, was never made public, apparently because of objections raised by Secretary McNamara, despite Ambassador Taylor's recommendation that the

133. III Gravel, p. 254.
134. Quoted in III Gravel, p. 254. See also Westmoreland, p. 110.

GVN release the report, along with press briefings and public statements, during the week of December 10–17.[135]

It was probably not by chance that Taylor wanted the infiltration report released during December 10–17. Not only was that the week that BARREL ROLL strikes began in Laos; it also coincided with Seaborn's third visit to Hanoi. Seaborn's trip had originally been scheduled for November, but he had been asked to delay it to allow the U.S. time to prepare a new message for Hanoi. In contrast to the two previous messages, with their less-than-subtle threats of direct U.S. military action against the DRV, the December message was quite restrained. Seaborn was to take the position that

The United States has nothing to add to the points made by Seaborn on his last visit. . . . All the recent indications from Washington, however, point to a continued and increasing determination on the part of the U.S. to *assist the South Vietnamese in their struggle.* Although he has no specific message on this trip, Seaborn has noted from its public statements increased U.S. concern at DRV role in direct support of Viet Cong, and this together with reported high-level meetings [in] Washington makes him feel that time is ripe for any new message Hanoi may wish to convey.

In addition, Seaborn was to "convey attitude of real personal concern over the growing possibility of direct confrontation between GVN and DRV," although such a statement could hardly be expected to strike fear into the hearts of the leaders in Hanoi, given the shaky status of the regime in Saigon.[136]

The outcome of Seaborn's visit, however, like everything else associated with Phase One, turned out to be something of a disappointment.

135. On these points, see III Gravel, pp. 255–256; and Document no. 246 in III Gravel, p. 681. Not only was the Cooper report not released, but in a December 15 interview the President rejected suggestions for carrying the war to the North and argued that the "wisest course" remained the line of policy the Administration was then following—i.e., helping the South Vietnamese to help themselves. See Tom Wicker, "President Charts Soft Approach on Basic Policies," *New York Times,* December 16, 1964, pp. 1, 14.

136. Seaborn Chronology, p. 22 (emphasis added). See also the 1971 report on the Seaborn missions by Secretary of State for External Affairs Mitchell Sharp, which notes that Seaborn was instructed by his government to "deliver passively so passive a message" (Canadian House of Commons, *Proceedings,* June 17, 1971, p. 6804). In addition, in contrast to Seaborn's reference to recent U.S. public statements, American officials were, at the time the note was drafted (a copy of the message was passed to the Canadian Embassy in Washington on December 3), publicly discouraging speculation that the high-level review then under way would produce a drastic change in the U.S. role in the war. See, for example, Jack Raymond, "U.S. Discourages Talk of Widening Vietnamese War," *New York Times,* November 28, 1964, p. 1; and President Johnson's November 28 news conference, in Johnson Papers, 1963–1964, pp. 1615–1616.

Seaborn did not get an appointment with Pham Van Dong; instead, he passed his message to Colonel Ha Van Lau, the DRV official in charge of liaison with the ICC. While Ha Van Lau did take notes during his meeting with Seaborn, he made no response to the suggestion that the time was ripe for a new message from Hanoi.[137]

More ominous than Ha Van Lau's silence, however, were North Vietnamese actions on the military front. With the end of the rainy season in Laos in November, they undertook a "massive effort" to improve the network of trails leading to the South: "Existing paths were widened, river crossings strengthened, and new sections of road constructed so that trucks and other heavy vehicles could ply many parts of the Trail system from the Mu Gia Pass to the tri-border junction of Laos, Cambodia, and South Vietnam." In addition, two more NVA regiments had departed for the South by December 1964, signalling the start of the steady buildup that would continually frustrate American efforts to bring the insurgency to an end.[138]

More importantly, whatever inclination the North Vietnamese might have had to heed Seaborn's latest warning was almost certainly dispelled by the events of late December. On December 20, South Vietnamese military leaders purged the civilian High National Council, originally installed after the disorders of August to draft a new constitution and establish new national institutions for South Vietnam. This move, which flew in the face of pledges of government stability given Ambassador Taylor earlier in the month, precipitated a new round of turmoil in Saigon, accompanied by the inevitable hints in the American press that the U.S. was reconsidering its role in the war.[139] This time, however, there was an element of bitterness involved that had been absent in previous spats. General Khanh, for example, reportedly urged that American policy be openly criticized, and he even went so far as to

137. These points are based on Seaborn Summary, p. 3; and on Interview Data. Seaborn was instructed not to actively seek an appointment with any ranking DRV leaders, but he was to make it clear that he was available if anyone he had seen earlier wished to see him again. He did see Pham Van Dong informally at a social gathering, but the latter did not attempt to discuss substantive issues with him or seek a further appointment. On these points, see Seaborn Summary, p. 3.

138. On the improvement of the roads in Laos, see Dommen, p. 280. On the departure of the NVA regiments, see Working Paper, p. 12.

139. See, for example, Peter Grose, "Saigon Military Uprising Denounced by U.S. Aides," New York Times, December 21, 1964, p. 1; John W. Finney, "U.S. Warns Vietnamese Military Help Is Based on Free Civil Rule," New York Times, December 23, 1964, pp. 1, 5; Peter Grose, "U.S. Orders Halt in Advance Plans for Vietnam War," New York Times, December 27, 1964, p. 1; and Tad Szulc, "Aid Rise to Saigon May Be Withheld," New York Times, December 28, 1964, p. 1. For details on the GVN crisis, see Shaplen (1966), pp. 249 ff.; Taylor (1972), pp. 329–330; II Gravel, pp. 345–350; and III Gravel, pp. 259–262.

propose that the military assist in the preparation of anti-American street demonstrations in Saigon. The U.S., for its part, ordered American advisers to withdraw from all advance planning for nonroutine military and civilian operations, while letting it be known that it was considering reversing a decision to send additional aid to Saigon.[140]

Then, on December 24, at the height of the GVN crisis, Viet Cong agents exploded a bomb at the Brink Bachelor Officers' Quarters in Saigon, killing two Americans and wounding thirty-eight others. The Administration, however, declined to retaliate, despite a provision in the Bundy paper approved on December 1 for prompt reprisals in response to Viet Cong "spectaculars" such as an attack on Saigon or "major attacks on U.S. citizens." The President, Halberstam reports,

was still hesitant, particularly about bombing during the Christmas season. He cabled Taylor that he did not want to move against the North unless he was sure that American security was faultless. . . . Then he pointed out that he wanted the American mission in greater "fighting trim." He wanted dependents out. And Johnson, the man who felt he could reason with anyone, was unhappy about the political situation in Saigon. Why couldn't we line them up better, and get them on the team? Why did we have this "lack of progress in communicating sensitively and persuasively. I don't believe we are making the all-out effort for political persuasion which is called for. I don't know if we are making full use of the kind of Americans who have the knack for this kind of communication" (which of course infuriated Taylor, who was already fed up with trying to deal with Vietnamese politicians).[141]

The effect of this pattern of events on Hanoi was probably twofold. On the one hand, if, as suggested earlier, the North Vietnamese did believe the U.S. was thinking about abandoning South Vietnam, the combination of continued turmoil in Saigon and increasingly tense relations between the U.S. and the GVN could only have reinforced that belief. On the other hand, the American failure to respond to the Bien Hoa and Brink BOQ attacks, combined with the restrained American actions during the last four months of 1964, may well have encouraged the North Vietnamese to attempt additional "spectaculars" in the hope that such attacks, by eroding both the morale of the Americans in South Vietnam and public support in the U.S. for the American presence there, would hasten the decision that South Vietnam was not

140. On Khanh's role, see Peter Grose, "Vietnam Defies U.S. Insistence on Unified Rule," *New York Times*, December 24, 1964, pp. 1, 3. For the U.S. response, see the articles cited in note 139, above.

141. On these points, see Document no. 246 in III Gravel, p. 682; and Halberstam, pp. 619–620. See also III Gravel, pp. 292–293; and Westmoreland, pp. 113–114.

worth the cost in American lives. If that was the case, however, it would
have been a most fateful choice. For when the next "spectacular" came
along in February 1965, the Administration would be anything but
reluctant to respond. Instead, the hesitation and uncertainty that had
characterized its handling of the Bien Hoa and Brink BOQ attacks
would be gone, with consequences of the most profound nature.

3

The Perils of Escalation

As THE NEW YEAR opened, a sense of impending disaster in South Vietnam had become increasingly widespread among the agencies responsible for the American effort there. Militarily, the year began with a disastrous GVN defeat in the battle of Binh Gia, in which ARVN units suffered over 400 casualties as well as "enormous" equipment losses. In Saigon, General Khanh, Premier Huong, and Chief of State Suu issued a communique on January 9 in which the generals promised to abide by their August 1964 pledge to establish civilian rule. Within days, however, student and Buddhist riots swept South Vietnam's major cities, leading the Armed Forces Council to oust Huong and appoint General Khanh to deal with the situation. Khanh, in turn, named Nguyen Xuan Oanh as Acting Premier while the search for "permanent" leadership acceptable to all factions got under way.[1]

These developments, however, had a curious effect on the views of American policymakers. Despite the President's insistence at the December 1 policy review that a move to "Phase II" pressures be contingent on the establishment of a stable and effective GVN, the continuing turmoil in Saigon did not result in a questioning of the American commitment by U.S. officials. Instead, there was a willingness to go ahead with intensified pressures despite the obvious weakness of the GVN. Characteristic of this line of thought was an important cable from Ambassador Taylor and Alex Johnson, in which General Westmoreland concurred, redefining the conditions under which Phase II pressures could be undertaken:

1. On the battle of Binh Gia, see the UPI dispatch, "Six-Day Battle at Binh Gia Ends in Defeat for Saigon," *New York Times*, January 3, 1965, p. 1. For additional details on South Vietnamese politics during this period, see Shaplen (1966), pp. 297–303; Taylor (1972), pp. 330–335; II Gravel, pp. 352–353; and III Gravel, pp. 261–262.

A. In association with the GVN after the latter had proved itself as a reasonably stable government able to control its armed forces.

B. Under a situation such as now as an emergency stimulant hopefully to create unity at home and restore failing morale.

C. As a unilateral U.S. action to compensate for a reduced in country U.S. presence.

In other words, as the Pentagon analyst notes, "under any conceivable alliance condition short of complete U.S. abandonment of South Vietnam, Ambassador Taylor and his top-level associates in Saigon saw the graduated air strikes of Phase II as an appropriate course of action." Without them, they concluded, "we see slight chance of moving toward a successful solution."[2]

And yet, even as the Administration was edging toward a program of overt pressures against the North, it still had not resolved a number of key issues about the nature and timing of the proposed pressures—issues that, as we saw in Chapter 2, had been largely papered over during 1964. For one thing, the Administration remained deeply divided on the question of whether the overall goal of the pressures should be to erode DRV will (the approach favored by civilian planners) or to destroy DRV capabilities for supporting the insurgency (the military's preferred approach), with a further possibility being to concentrate on the infiltration routes in the southern DRV and Laos in an attempt to impede the flow of men and supplies to the insurgents in the South.[3] Second, while the draft NSAM prepared by William Bundy for the December 1 policy review had specified that air strikes during "Phase II" would begin with "infiltration-related targets south of the 19th Parallel"

2. The Taylor/Johnson cable is quoted in III Gravel, pp. 264–265. For the Pentagon analyst's comment, see III Gravel, p. 265. For the views of officials in Washington, see the January 4, 1965 and January 27, 1965 memos by John McNaughton, Documents no. 247 and no. 249 in III Gravel, pp. 683–684, 686–687; the January 6 and February 18 memos by William Bundy, Documents no. 248 and no. 252 in III Gravel, pp. 684–686, 692–693; and the January 27 memo to the President from Robert McNamara and McGeorge Bundy, quoted in Lyndon B. Johnson, The Vantage Point (New York: Popular Library, 1971), pp. 122–123. Also on the views of McNamara and McGeorge Bundy (who were considerably more optimistic concerning the possibilities for relieving the situation in the South by striking at the North than were McNaughton and William Bundy), see Halberstam, pp. 622–631; and Martin, p. 827.

3. Although there would seem to be a strong resemblance between the military's preference for destroying DRV military capabilities and interdicting infiltration routes, the resemblance is superficial at best. As we suggested in Chapter 2, the JCS were primarily interested in attacking "capabilities" only indirectly related to the infiltration problem, such as airfields, POL, and industrial targets. In addition, they proposed to use attacks on infiltration routes in Laos and the southern DRV as a diversionary tactic prior to the massive strikes that they advocated (on this point, see Document no. 230 in III Gravel, p. 629).

and then "work up to targets north of that point," the President, as we saw, had deferred a decision on Phase II so that, as of January 1965, there was still no consensus concerning which targets should be struck and in what order. Third, 1964 had been marked by a persistent and as yet unresolved dispute between civilian and military planners over the tempo of the proposed program, with civilian officials generally in favor of a slower rate of escalation than was advocated by their military counterparts.

Fourth and most importantly, there was the question of how the Administration would integrate its strategy for coercing the North with its efforts to contain the spread of the insurgency in the South. Implicit in the preparations for the air war during 1964 was the assumption that South Vietnamese forces, stiffened by U.S. aid and advisers, would be able to hold their own against the Viet Cong while the bombing "persuaded" the North Vietnamese to "call off" the insurgency or at least halt the flow of men and supplies to the South. (In the latter case, it was felt, the insurgency would be reduced to dimensions manageable by the South Vietnamese themselves.) As early as March 1965, however, evidence began to accumulate indicating that this belief was no longer valid and that a much greater American effort in the ground war would be required. In addition, by April 1965 most American officials were convinced that the North Vietnamese were unlikely to be "persuaded" by the bombing as long as they felt they were winning in the South. As a result, Administration officials were forced to consider several additional thorny questions concerning the relationship of the air war over the North to the ground war in the South—e.g., what priorities should be attached to the goals of eroding DRV will, destroying DRV capabilities, impeding infiltration, and providing air support for Allied forces in the South, and how should resources be allocated among them?

In analyzing the efforts of Administration officials to deal with issues such as these, it must be kept in mind that while there were several options open to the Administration, it also faced some important trade-offs and constraints. For example, a program intended to erode DRV will would not necessarily have to begin by attacking "lucrative" industrial targets. Instead, such a program could begin by attacking infiltration routes and staging areas (thus "signalling" the Administration's willingness to widen the war), followed by attacks on "valuable" but still infiltration-related targets (e.g., costly bridges, railroad yards), thus tacitly threatening to strike industrial targets next if compliance was not forthcoming. Furthermore, since the number of "lucrative" targets was

Table 1
Pressures Against the North: Goals, Constraints, and Tradeoffs

Objective(s) to be pursued through the bombing	Type of target	Targeting Options Advantages/Disadvantages	Pace of Pressures
Erode DRV will	1. Infiltration targets (roads, staging areas, barracks, military bases)	1. Useful for impeding infiltration; useful for signalling willingness to widen war (thus indirectly affecting DRV will); however, not useful for eroding DRV will if strikes confined to these targets for prolonged period.	Slow
Destroy DRV capabilities	2. Non-infiltration military targets (airfields, radar stations, antiaircraft defenses)	2. Useful for signalling willingness to widen war; useful for removing obstacles to "will-breaking" strikes—i.e., antiaircraft defenses.	Medium
Impede infiltration into South Vietnam	3. "Valuable," infiltration-related targets (costly bridges, rail lines or yards, harbors)	3. Useful for impeding infiltration; useful for eroding DRV will; however, effect on DRV will likely to wear off if program does not at some point move off to high-value targets (category no. 4).	Fast
	4. High-value targets (industrial facilities, power plants)	4. Useful for eroding DRV will; however, not useful for impeding infiltration; high risk of Soviet/Chinese intervention if done rashly; once targets destroyed, opponent has little incentive to comply.	

small[4] and since most civilian planners believed that it was the *threat* of future pressures that would exert the greatest influence over the DRV, Administration officials would have to take care not to let the air war escalate too rapidly, lest the momentum inherent in the "graduated pressures" approach result in industrial targets being destroyed before DRV policy could be reoriented to comply with U.S. demands. (Decisions on the timing of escalatory moves would also hinge on judgments of what could be done without provoking a violent response from the Soviets and/or the Chinese.) However, while there would be no incompatibility during the early weeks of the air war between the goals of eroding DRV will and impeding infiltration, the Administration would find it progressively more difficult to strike a balance between those two goals as the war dragged on. A program that lingered indefinitely in the southern DRV and Laos in order to concentrate on the infiltration routes could not be expected to have much impact on the will of the leadership in Hanoi. Conversely, to the extent that Administration officials chose to undertake "will-breaking" strikes against industrial targets (most of which were in the northern DRV and, more importantly, were only marginally relevant to the North's ability to infiltrate men and supplies into the South[5]), they would have to divert planes and pilots away from strikes against infiltration targets closer to South Vietnam.

In short, then, Administration officials faced a number of critical choices in their effort to develop both a plausible rationale for a program of overt pressures against the North and a bombing program consistent with that rationale. At the risk of some oversimplification, those choices are summarized in Table 1. How the Administration would deal with those choices would have a significant impact on its ability to transmit the proper "signals" to Hanoi. Unfortunately, however, the Administration's efforts in this respect during 1965 continued to be plagued by the same problems that had hampered it during 1964.

4. As the Pentagon analyst noted (IV Gravel, pp. 56–57): "When North Vietnam was first targetted the JCS found only 8 industrial installations worth listing on a par with airfields, military supply dumps, barracks complexes, port facilities, bridges, and oil tanks. Even by the end of 1965, after the JCS had lowered the standards and more than doubled the number of important targets, the list included only 24 industrial installations, 18 of them power plants which were as important for such humble uses as lighting streets and pumping water as for operating any real factories."

5. As Admiral Sharp (CINCPAC) noted in his report on the air war, virtually all of the war materiel expended by DRV/VC forces in both the North and the South plus the road-building, maintenance, and transportation equipment needed to keep the supplies moving were imported into North Vietnam rather than produced locally (Admiral U. S. G. Sharp and General William Westmoreland, *Report on the War in Vietnam* [Washington: U.S. Government Printing Office, 1968], p. 4). See also IV Gravel, pp. 31–32, 56–58.

I. Prelude to ROLLING THUNDER
(January-February 1965)

At the same time that officials in Washington and Saigon were redefining the conditions under which overt pressures against the North
might be attempted, other developments were taking place that insured
that no other option would be available. On the one hand, it was
during January 1965 that Adlai Stevenson informed U Thant that
under no circumstances would the U.S. participate in private talks with
the DRV, thus effectively eliminating the negotiating option. On the
other hand, January was also a month of intensified preparations for
carrying the war to the North. In the aftermath of the August and
September incidents in the Gulf of Tonkin, the JCS ordered CINCPAC
to prepare contingency plans for use with future DE SOTO patrols that
would include a "prepackaged set of reprisal targets that might be politically acceptable, with preassigned forces that would be in a high state of
readiness to strike these targets, and with a detailed strike plan that
would provide a range of retaliatory options." In addition, since the
high-alert status envisioned in connection with the DE SOTO patrols
could be maintained only for short periods of time, CINCPAC was to
draw up plans for limited reprisals with forces already in place and from
a normal readiness posture.[6]

These preparations, as the Pentagon analyst notes, "came to a head at
the end of January, when a tentative decision had evidently been
reached in Washington to authorize resumption of the DE SOTO
patrols on or about February 3." The patrol, however, was postponed
until February 7; in the meantime, the JCS asked CINCPAC to modify
his reprisal plans to allow for three attack options, involving three, five,
or seven targets, and to be prepared to conduct air strikes against them
in any combination.[7]

Despite the extensive preparations, the eventual execution of the air
strikes did not come off quite as planned. On February 4, the DE SOTO
patrol was canceled in deference to Soviet Premier Kosygin's visit to

---

6. On the demise of Thant's proposal, see Martin, pp. 829–830; Kraslow and Loory, pp. 99–101;
and Geyelin, pp. 205–207. Interestingly, Washington's final refusal to participate in the proposed
talks came just as it was receiving additional indications of DRV interest in a negotiated settlement.
On January 29, the American Embassy in Paris passed to Washington a French report of conversations between French officials and the ranking DRV diplomat in Paris, Mai Van Bo, in which Bo
supposedly showed interest in negotiating a settlement along the lines of the 1954 Geneva Accords
(Interview Data). On CINCPAC's contingency plans, see III Gravel, p. 298.

7. On these points, see III Gravel, p. 299.

Hanoi, which began on February 6. On February 7, Viet Cong guerrillas launched a 2:00 A.M. (Saigon time) mortar attack on the U.S. advisory compound and airfield at Pleiku, killing eight Americans and wounding 109 others. This time, there was no hesitation on the Administration's part:

The decision to strike back was reached in a 75-minute meeting of the NSC on the evening of February 6 (Washington time) in the Cabinet Room of the White House, and in the presence of Senate Majority Leader Mike Mansfield and House Speaker John McCormack. McGeorge Bundy, on his mission to Saigon at the time, had joined Ambassador Taylor and General Westmoreland in recommending prompt retaliation. . . .[8]

Militarily, however, the reprisals proved to be "something of a fizzle." With the cancellation of the DE SOTO patrol, only one attack carrier was on station off South Vietnam; two others had left for the Philippines and had to be recalled to participate in the strike. The mildest attack option (three targets) was selected, but bad weather forced many sorties to abort, with the result that only one target (the Dong Hoi barracks) was struck in force. To stiffen the reprisal, and also to make it appear as a joint U.S./GVN response, the next day (February 8) twenty-four VNAF A-1H aircraft (supported by U.S. flak suppression) struck the barracks at Chap Le.[9]

In Washington, meanwhile, the NSC convened again on the morning of February 7 (Washington time) to discuss the text of a White House statement on the reprisals and the handling of a press briefing scheduled for later that day, both of which would be crucial in conveying to Hanoi the implications of the reprisals for the future U.S. role in the war. Toward this end, Administration statements not only stressed North Vietnamese responsibility for the Pleiku attack, thus implying that future attacks would trigger a retaliatory response, but also left open the possibility that the air strikes might be expanded to include reprisals for attacks on South Vietnamese forces or even to encompass a program of continuous air strikes against the North. To reinforce the signal of U.S. resolve that had hopefully been conveyed by the reprisals, the President

8. Ibid., p. 302. See also Halberstam, pp. 632–633; and Johnson, pp. 124–125.

9. On these points, see III Gravel, pp. 302–303; and Sharp and Westmoreland, pp. 14–15. There was also an attack of sorts by American planes on Dong Hoi on February 8, when U.S. aircraft expended "suppressive fire" on antiaircraft batteries that fired on U.S. reconnaissance flights. Administration officials denied that this constituted a raid, but it could easily have appeared otherwise from the ground. On this, see Max Frankel, "U.S. Stops Raids to Assess Effects," *New York Times*, February 9, 1965, pp. 1, 13.

on February 7 ordered the withdrawal of American dependents from South Vietnam.[10]

In the days that followed, however, these "flashing red warning signals" went unheeded. On February 10, the Viet Cong launched another attack aimed directly at U.S. forces, killing twenty-three Americans in an assault on the enlisted men's barracks in Qui Nhon. In response, 160 U.S. and VNAF planes struck the barracks at Chanh Hoa and Vit Thu Lu. These strikes, however,

were not characterized as a reprisal linked to the immediate incident. Instead, the White House release of February 11 listed a long series of Viet Cong incidents and attacks that had occurred since February 8, most of which were not "spectacular" but quite normal features of the Vietnam war. The statements moreover characterized the U.S. air strikes as a response to these "further direct provocations by the Hanoi regime," and to these "continued acts of aggression." The words "retaliation" and "reprisal" were carefully avoided. . . . The change in terminology . . . was clearly deliberate . . . [and] reflected a conscious U.S. decision to broaden the reprisal concept as gradually and as imperceptibly as possible to accommodate a much wider policy of sustained, steadily intensifying air attacks against North Vietnam. . . .[11]

The attacks on Pleiku and Qui Nhon and the subsequent reprisals marked a clear turning point in the Administration's tortuous advance toward overt military pressures on the DRV. Gone forever were any hopes of using the *promise* of "Phase II" pressures to extract reforms from the GVN. Instead, there was a willingness to plunge ahead despite the "Alice-in-Wonderland atmosphere" in Saigon.[12]

Nowhere was this tendency more apparent than in the spate of recommendations received by the President in the aftermath of the Pleiku attack, all of which called for sustained air attacks on North Vietnam. On the way home from Saigon, for example, the McGeorge Bundy group (Bundy, McNaughton, Leonard Unger, Chester Cooper, and General Andrew Goodpaster) drafted a report recommending a policy of "sustained reprisal," which, they argued, offered "the best available way of increasing our chance of success in Vietnam. . . ." On February 9

10. The White House statements and the text of Secretary McNamara's opening statement at his briefing of the press are reprinted in DOSB, February 22, 1965, pp. 238–240. See also III Gravel, pp. 304–305; and Charles Mohr, "Bundy Gives Optimistic Report on Vietnam," *New York Times*, February 9, 1965, p. 12.

11. On these points, see III Gravel, p. 306; and Sharp and Westmoreland, p. 15.

12. III Gravel, p. 323. At the time of the Pleiku and Qui Nhon attacks, South Vietnam possessed little more than a facade of legitimate government, since the search for a replacement for ex-Premier Huong was still under way and the GVN was being run by Acting Premier Oanh.

and 12, Ambassador Taylor weighed in from Saigon with cables advocating a "measured, controlled sequence of actions against the DRV taken in reprisal for DRV-inspired actions in South Vietnam. . . ." Meanwhile, in response to a February 8 request from Secretary McNamara, the JCS prepared an eight-week program of air strikes against infiltration targets in the southern DRV, which they on February 11 predictably urged their superiors to approve.[13]

But while the President's advisers were virtually unanimous in recommending more forceful measures against the North, their impressive-sounding prose (e.g., Bundy's assertion that "once such a policy is put in force, we shall be able to speak in Vietnam on many topics and in many ways, with growing force and effectiveness") served to conceal important disagreements with respect to the goals of the proposed pressures and the manner in which they were to be applied. In contrast to earlier proposals aimed at influencing the will of the DRV leadership, the Bundy group had announced that their "primary target in advocating a reprisal policy is the improvement of the situation in South Vietnam" (eroding DRV will was relegated to the category of an "important but longer-range purpose").[14] Ambassador Taylor, however, recommended exactly the opposite approach in his cable of February 12:

In review of the rationale for concept of graduated reprisals we are of the opinion that, in order of importance, it should have the following objectives: (a) the will of Hanoi leaders; (b) GVN morale; and (c) physical destruction to reduce the DRV ability to support the VC. Of these three, the first appears to us [as] by far the most important, since our effectiveness in influencing Hanoi leadership will, in the long run, determine the success or failure of our efforts in both North and South Vietnam.

In addition, Taylor in his February 9 cable (probably in an attempt to

13. For the recommendations of the McGeorge Bundy group, see III Gravel, pp. 309–315. Ambassador Taylor's recommendations are discussed in III Gravel, pp. 315–317. For McNamara's request and the JCS eight-week program (which also provided for actions such as naval gunfire and 34A operations), see III Gravel, pp. 306, 318–321. It was Secretary McNamara who ordered the program confined to infiltration targets in the southern DRV; consequently, the JCS program did not fully reflect their preferences, although they were, as always, eager to begin attacking the North.

14. Striking the North, the Bundy group argued, would improve morale in the South, increase U.S. leverage over the GVN (which could then be used to press for a more effective pacification program), and depress the morale of VC cadres in the South. How the proposed raids would have increased U.S. leverage—which was minimal despite the presence of 20,000 U.S. troops in the South—was left unclear by the group; similarly, how air strikes in the North would affect the morale of VC cadres in the South (especially with the GVN on the brink of collapse) was never persuasively established. On these points, see III Gravel, pp. 311–314.

make the proposal more palatable to the President) specified that the air strikes should be directed "solely at DRV military targets and infiltration routes."[15]

Somewhat surprisingly, though, there does not appear to have been a serious effort to reconcile these divergent proposals in the days leading up to the President's decision to go ahead with a program of continuous air strikes against the North (code-named ROLLING THUNDER). Instead, the White House cable to Ambassador Taylor on February 13 announcing the new policy referred only to a "program of measured and limited air action jointly with GVN against selected military targets in DRV remaining south of 19th Parallel until further notice." Similarly, a February 18 cable to nine U.S. Embassies in the Far East noted only that

policy on Vietnam adopted today calls for following: Joint program with GVN of continuing air and naval action against North Vietnam whenever and wherever necessary. Such action to be against selected military targets and to be limited and fitting and adequate as response to continuous aggression in South Vietnam directed in Hanoi.[16]

Perhaps the most significant aspect of these two cables was what they did *not* state: the objective(s) to be pursued through the new policy, how long the air strikes would remain south of the 19th Parallel, and how the targets to be struck and the pace of escalation were to be related to the objective(s) being pursued and the "signals" supposedly being conveyed to Hanoi.

As things turned out, though, the ad hoc approach preferred by the White House was no more immune to being overtaken by events than were the carefully prepared contingency plans drawn up by CINCPAC prior to Pleiku. On February 17, the British Ambassador in Washington informed Secretary Rusk of a Soviet hint that the British-Soviet Co-chairmanship of the 1954 Geneva Conference might be reactivated. With Rusk's consent, London instructed its ambassador in Moscow to propose to the Soviets that the two Co-chairmen request that the governments represented at the 1954 Conference and those on the ICC "furnish the Co-chairmen without delay with a statement of their views on Vietnam and, in particular, on the circumstances in which they consider that a peaceful settlement could be reached."[17] While the

15. For Taylor's cables, see III Gravel, pp. 315–316. Interestingly, the Bundy group did not address the question of which targets should be hit and in what order.

16. For these two cables, see III Gravel, pp. 321, 324.

17. "Recent Exchanges Concerning Attempts to Promote a Negotiated Settlement of the Conflict in Vietnam," Cmnd. 2756 (London: Her Majesty's Stationery Office, 1965), p. 20. See also III Gravel, pp. 325–326.

British proposal offered the Administration an opportunity to stake out a tough negotiating position while avoiding the need for a presentation to the UN Security Council which "might require the Soviets to act as defense counsel for Hanoi," it posed a problem with respect to the timing of the air strikes, since the date set for ROLLING THUNDER 1, February 20, was also the date on which the British Ambassador in Moscow was to approach the Soviets.[18] To complicate matters further, Colonel Pham Ngoc Thao launched a semi-coup on February 19 aimed at ousting General Khanh, and, with VNAF energies suddenly diverted to buzzing Saigon and threatening to bomb coup forces, Ambassador Taylor recommended cancellation of the air strike, a suggestion that was promptly accepted by Washington.[19]

Although the coup forces were quickly defeated, the coup nonetheless resulted in Khanh's ouster, as a majority of the Armed Forces Council on February 20 voted "no confidence" in their Commander-in-Chief and exiled him to the post of Ambassador-at-large. In Moscow, meanwhile, the Soviets made no immediate reply to the British proposal, leaving the Administration in something of an awkward position. On February 16, GVN forces had captured an armed, oceangoing North Vietnamese vessel attempting to unload a huge quantity of arms and ammunition for the Viet Cong in Vungro Bay, South Vietnam. As explained by the Pentagon analyst:

Throughout this time, Secretary Rusk was visibly torn on the question of whether or not to proceed with the air strikes. He wanted very much to push ahead immediately, in order to exploit promptly the DRV arms ship incident, which seemed to beg for some response. But he hesitated to launch a strike on behalf of and in concert with a government that was teetering and whose Commander-in-Chief was in the process of being deposed; he also wished to avoid angering the Soviets, thus possibly sabotaging their Co-Chairmen effort. On the other hand, he wanted to make it clear that the U.S. would not indefinitely accept a "unilateral cease-fire" while the Co-Chairman effort dragged on.[20]

By February 24, with no word from Moscow and Khanh's departure set for the next day, a decision was made to go ahead with the initial ROLLING THUNDER strike on February 26. But that mission, too, was aborted, this time as a result of bad weather over the North. As it turned out, it was not until March 2 that the first ROLLING

18. The White House cables of February 13 and 18 announcing the start of the air war had both envisioned taking the Administration's case to the Security Council. The "defense counsel" remark is from a Rusk cable to Taylor, quoted in III Gravel, p. 326. See also III Gravel, p. 328.

19. On these points, see III Gravel, pp. 325, 327; and Shaplen (1966), pp. 310–312.

20. III Gravel, p. 329.

THUNDER strike was finally executed. By then, the Co-Chairmen initiative would be all but dead, although it was not until mid-March that the Soviets formally rejected the British initiative.[21]

II. The Air War Begins (March-May 1965)

Although twice forced to postpone the start of ROLLING THUNDER, the Administration attempted to put the delay to good use by launching a campaign of threats and warnings reminiscent of the one that accompanied the first Seaborn mission to Hanoi in June 1964. On February 24, during their regularly scheduled meeting in Warsaw, U.S. Ambassador John Moors Cabot informed Chinese Ambassador Wang Kuo-chuan that he had been instructed to "restate" American policy toward Vietnam:

So long as the Viet Cong, directed and supported by North Vietnam and encouraged by your side, continues its attacks in South Vietnam, the U.S. will find it necessary to afford the GVN such help as it desires and needs to restore peace. The pressures being mounted by the North Vietnamese across the frontiers of South Vietnam are intolerable. We must and will take action to stop them. . . . If there is any doubt in Hanoi as to this U.S. position, I hope that you will convey it to them.[22]

Adding credence to Cabot's warning was a sequence of events that unfolded in rapid-fire succession. On the day of the meeting in Warsaw, the State Department announced that U.S. planes manned by U.S. crews were being used to attack Viet Cong forces in South Vietnam, while a Pentagon spokesman briefed reporters on the bomb loads carried by U.S. jets based in the Far East in a pointed effort to dramatize the firepower available for use against the North.[23] At a news conference the next day, Secretary Rusk warned that the North·Vietnamese would have to end the infiltration of men and supplies into the South and rejected the idea of a negotiated settlement in the absence of "any indication that Hanoi is prepared to stop doing what it is doing against its neighbors."[24] On February 26, the Administration leaked the

21. On these points, see III Gravel, pp. 329–330, 346–347; and "Recent Exchanges," pp. 27–28.
22. Seaborn Chronology, pp. 24–25.
23. On these points, see Jack Langguth, "U.S. Jet Bombers Attack Viet Cong; First Such Strike," New York Times, February 25, 1965, pp. 1, 3; Max Frankel, "U.S. Admits Shift in Vietnam Stand," New York Times, February 25, 1965, p. 1; and Jack Raymond, "Deadly U.S. Jets in Asian Arsenal," New York Times, February 25, 1965, p. 3.
24. DOSB, March 15, 1965, p. 364.

contents of a "White Paper" on North Vietnamese "aggression," making no secret of the fact that it was intended to justify a program of air strikes against the North. The next day, the White Paper itself was formally released, accompanied by warnings that the U.S. would abandon its policy of "restraint" if the DRV did not halt its "aggression" in the South.[25] On February 28, the "highest American and South Vietnamese officials" in Saigon told reporters that they were "virtually certain" that President Johnson had decided on a limited but continuous air war against the North; in addition, reports that air strikes had been planned for February 20 and February 26 were leaked to newsmen in Saigon.[26]

On March 2, the long-awaited air strikes were finally launched, as 104 U.S. aircraft struck the Xom Bang Ammunition Depot while nineteen VNAF A-1H's (with U.S. flak suppression) struck the naval base at Quang Khe.[27] Conveniently for the U.S., the air strikes coincided with Seaborn's fourth visit to Hanoi, and the Administration took advantage of this by asking him to convey directly to Pham Van Dong that portion of Ambassador Cabot's February 24 statement that dealt with Vietnam. Pham Van Dong, however, was unavailable, and Seaborn was again forced to settle for Ha Van Lau, whom he saw on March 4. While Ha Van Lau agreed to pass the message on to Pham Van Dong, he dismissed it as nothing new, pointing out that his government had already received a report on the Warsaw talks from the Chinese.[28]

Four days later, in a move described to reporters as further evidence of the Administration's resolve to stand firm, the first of two battalions of U.S. Marines landed at DaNang to strengthen the defenses of the air base there. At the same time, the Administration continued to take a tough stance on the issue of negotiations. On March 8, a widely circulated report quoted the President as saying that "we are not going to negotiate at this time and certainly not so long as the Communists continue to violate the Geneva Accords." Adding credibility to the report (which the White House made no effort to deny) were the

25. See Max Frankel, "U.S. White Paper Brands Hanoi as an 'Aggressor' and Hints at Air Strikes," *New York Times*, February 27, 1965, p. 1; and John W. Finney, "Hanoi Aggression Detailed by U.S. in White Paper," *New York Times*, February 28, 1965, p. 1.

26. On these points, see Robert Kleiman, "U.S. Said to Plan Limited Air War as Lever on Hanoi," *New York Times*, March 1, 1965, pp. 1, 9; and Jack Langguth, "Saigon Rules Out Peace Until Reds Drop Their Role," *New York Times*, March 2, 1965, p. 1.

27. Extreme caution must be used in interpreting gross sortie totals; in this case, not all of the 104 aircraft involved actually dropped bombs on the target—some were tankers, for example. In addition, large fixed-target strikes of this sort included pathfinder aircraft, a combat air patrol (to guard against hostile aircraft), search and rescue aircraft, and flak suppression aircraft.

28. On these points, see Seaborn Discussion, p. 3; and Seaborn Summary, pp. 3-4.

Administration's rejections on March 9 and March 12 of appeals for talks from U Thant and the French, respectively.[29]

The Administration's tough talk, however, was somewhat at variance with its actions over North Vietnam. The ROLLING THUNDER strike on March 2 was followed on March 3 by a 30-plane BARREL ROLL strike in Laos, but the next ROLLING THUNDER strike did not occur until March 14, when VNAF planes hit the barracks on Tiger Island, followed the next day by a U.S. strike on the ammunition depot at Phuqui.[30] The long delay between strikes, combined with British and French efforts to promote a negotiated settlement, was a source of constant irritation to Ambassador Taylor. "It appears to me," he cabled Washington on March 8,

that to date DRV leaders believe air strikes at present levels on their territory are meaningless and that we are more susceptible to international pressure for negotiations than are they. Their estimate may be based in part on activities of "our friends" to which we seem to be an active party.

In a separate cable, Taylor called for a multi-week program that would convey the correct "signals" to Hanoi:

What seems to be lacking is an agreed program covering several weeks which will combine the factors, frequency, weight, and location of attack into a rational pattern which will convince the leaders in Hanoi that we are on a dynamic schedule which will not remain static in narrow zone far removed from them and the sources of their power but which is a moving growing threat which cannot be ignored. . . . In formulating a more effective program of future attacks, I would be inclined to keep the rate as indicated [once or twice a week involving two or three targets on each day], maintain the weight on target as for recent strikes, but begin at once a progression of U.S. strikes North of 19th Parallel in a slow but steadily ascending movement.[31]

Taylor had good reason to be concerned. Although some Administration officials apparently expected a quick North Vietnamese capitula-

29. On these points, see Max Frankel, "U.S. Turns Down Thant Proposal on Truce Parley," New York Times, March 10, 1965, pp. 1, 2; "Johnson Reported to Say He Can't Halt Coups," New York Times, March 8, 1965, p. 3; and the AP dispatch, "Rusk Informs French Envoy of Coolness to Asia Parley," New York Times, March 13, 1965, p. 3.

30. On the BARREL ROLL strike, see the AP dispatch, "U.S. Bombing Raid on Red Route in Laos Reported," New York Times, March 4, 1965, p. 1. On the basis of public sources (i.e., reporters watching U.S. planes take off and land from DaNang), the next BARREL ROLL strike did not occur until March 10, although it is possible that one or more strikes were flown by carrier-based jets. See Jack Langguth, "U.S. Officers Report Recent Gains in Vietnam War," New York Times, March 11, 1965, p. 2. The ROLLING THUNDER strikes of March 14–15 were originally scheduled for March 13 but delayed as a result of bad weather. See III Gravel, p. 336.

31. For Taylor's cables, see III Gravel, pp. 334–335.

tion—one estimate being that it would take two to three months of strikes for the U.S. to reach a "position of strength" from which "meaningful negotiations" would be possible[32]—it appears that DRV policy was actually moving in the opposite direction. On returning from Hanoi, Seaborn reported that the North Vietnamese were not especially worried by the air strikes, which they saw as a last-ditch effort to improve the U.S. bargaining position prior to an international conference which the U.S. sought in order to extricate itself from a lost cause in the South. Since the air strikes to that point had not been particularly damaging, Seaborn believed that the North Vietnamese felt it in their interest to hold back on a conference, since such a conference could only deprive them of the victory they expected, as had happened in 1954.[33]

In addition, despite Taylor's call for a "rational pattern" to the bombing, the Administration's planning for the conduct of the air war was evolving in a manner that was hardly conducive to conveying the kinds of "signals" that Taylor had in mind. As we saw in Chapter 2, Administration officials had been unable to reach agreement during 1964 on the question of how to pursue the goal of ending the North's role in the insurgency, with civilian officials generally in favor of using a gradually escalating bombing campaign to erode the will of the DRV leadership to continue their role in the war in the South and military officials in favor of a high-intensity program that would physically destroy DRV capabilities for supporting the insurgency. Nor had the President shown an inclination to resolve the dispute by means of a firm decision committing the Administration to one or the other of these courses of action. As a result, beginning in late 1964, the attention of both civilian and military planners apparently gravitated to a third course of action—

32. For this estimate, see Peter Grose, "'Two Wars' in Vietnam," *New York Times*, March 4, 1965, p. 10. See also Raphael Littauer and Norman Uphoff (eds.), *The Air War in Indochina*, rev. ed. (Boston: Beacon Press, 1972), p. 34. This optimism was not shared by all Administration officials, however; see, for example, the February 18, 1965 memo by William Bundy, Document no. 252 in III Gravel, pp. 692–693.

33. For Seaborn's report, see Seaborn Discussion, p. 3; and Interview Data. Seaborn presented these observations to Taylor on March 7, and they formed the basis for the latter's cables of March 8. Adding credence to Seaborn's analysis was the fact that on March 3, Mai Van Bo told French officials that, while the DRV had previously been willing to negotiate (possibly a reference to the U Thant initiative discussed earlier), American actions had changed the situation, so that negotiations could not be considered at that time (Seaborn Discussion, p. 3). In addition, it appears that the early air strikes were not very damaging at all. As Secretary McNamara noted in an analysis of the Pleiku and Qui Nhon reprisal strikes, "with a total of 267 sorties (including flak suppression, etc.) directed against 491 buildings, we destroyed 47 buildings and damaged 22" (III Gravel, p. 333). In addition, at least four U.S. aircraft were lost in those strikes; four more were lost in the March 2 strike on Xom Bang (Sharp and Westmoreland, pp. 14–15; III Gravel, p. 333).

namely, directing the initial air strikes against infiltration-related targets in the southern DRV. From the point of view of civilian officials, such strikes offered a convenient way to *begin* the air war, since they could be justified publicly as a response to DRV "aggression," and since they also minimized the risks of escalation by avoiding more sensitive targets in the northern DRV. (Both arguments, moreover, would be important in persuading the President to agree to the air strikes.) Further, while attacks on infiltration-related targets did not fully reflect the preferences of military officials, they were nonetheless willing to go along with such an approach because of their overriding concern to begin attacking the DRV as soon as possible.[34]

But while both civilian and military planners apparently viewed attacks on infiltration-related targets in the southern DRV as an initial step, the White House, as evidenced by the above-quoted cables announcing the start of the air war, was unwilling to commit itself to a long-term program, preferring instead an ad hoc approach in which targeting decisions were made on a week-to-week basis. As a result, the planning that was being conducted during February and March for future strikes continued to center on infiltration-related targets in the southern DRV. As we saw earlier, in response to Secretary McNamara's February 8 request, the JCS on February 11 forwarded to their superiors an eight-week program for strikes against infiltration targets south of the 19th Parallel. While this particular program was never adopted, by February 13 the Chiefs were urging on Secretary McNamara the advantages of attacking the DRV railway system south of the 20th Parallel, with special emphasis on five bridges of over 300 feet in length and the railway yards at Vinh. In response, on February 27, McNamara invited the Chiefs to draw up the detailed plans required for such a program, a planning effort that coincided with one begun independently at Pacific Command headquarters in Hawaii for an interdiction campaign aimed at all DRV lines of communication (LOCs) south of the 20th Parallel. Both of these planning efforts were completed by the end of March.[35]

34. Thus, for example, the Bundy/McNaughton version of "Option C," Taylor's "Suggested Scenario For Controlled Escalation," and William Bundy's draft NSAM for the December 1 policy review all suggested beginning the air strikes with attacks on infiltration targets; in addition, both "Option C" and the draft NSAM referred to attacks on "other targets" after the initial attacks had been completed. On these points, see (all in III Gravel): Document no. 241, p. 659; Document no. 242, p. 672; and Document no. 246, p. 678. See also III Gravel, pp. 318–321, 340–344; and the JCS comments on the importance of attacking the DRV without further delay, quoted in III Gravel, p. 173.

35. On these points, see III Gravel, pp. 318–321, 340–344.

And yet, despite the repeated calls for a "systematic," "orchestrated" approach that would result in a "rational pattern which will convince the leaders in Hanoi that we are on a dynamic schedule," the outcome of these various planning efforts was an air war that transmitted to Hanoi what can only be characterized as ambiguous signals. By mid-March, much of the hesitation that had characterized the Administration's handling of the initial air strikes was wearing off. Beginning with ROLLING THUNDER 7 (March 19–25), targets were released in weekly batches, with the precise timing of the strikes left to field commanders; in addition, the requirement for concurrent U.S./VNAF strikes was dropped. Furthermore, in addition to two fixed target strikes (one U.S. and one VNAF), ROLLING THUNDER 7 provided for three armed reconnaissance missions (one U.S. and two VNAF), during which the attackers could search for locomotives, rolling stock, and vehicles along specified route segments, as well as attack three radar stations (one on each route segment).[36] As a result, the air war almost immediately took on a new character—air strikes were launched on an almost daily basis; in addition, the strikes began to creep gradually north in the direction of Hanoi and Haiphong. As part of ROLLING THUNDER 8 (March 26–April 1), U.S. jets struck at targets north of the 20th Parallel for the first time in the war, hitting the Bachlong Island Radar Station on March 26 and again on March 29.[37] These strikes were followed on April 3 (as part of ROLLING THUNDER 9) by an attack by over one hundred Air Force and Navy jets on the Dong Phuong and Thanh Hoa highway and railway bridges (the first nonmilitary targets to be struck), just 65 and 72 miles south of Hanoi. On April 4, the Thanh Hoa bridge was struck again, along with a nearby thermal power plant.[38] Significantly, as Simons notes, the press briefing describing these attacks "stressed that it had taken several years for the

36. For more details on ROLLING THUNDER 7, see III Gravel, pp. 284–285, 339.

37. For more details on ROLLING THUNDER 8, see III Gravel, pp. 284–285. See also Jack Langguth, "U.S. Strikes Deep in North Vietnam," New York Times, March 27, 1965, pp. 1, 2; and Jack Langguth, "U.S. Bombers Hit Radar Post Again," New York Times, March 30, 1965, p. 1.

38. On the bridge raids of April 3–4, see William Simons, "The Vietnam Intervention, 1964–1965," in George, Hall, and Simons, p. 180; and "U.S. Fliers Bomb Two Bridges Linking Hanoi with Bases," New York Times, April 4, 1965, p. 1. Along with the attacks on the Dong Phuong and Thanh Hoa bridges, VNAF planes supported by U.S. flak suppression struck the Ho Chi Minh bridge south of Dong Hoi (near the DMZ) on April 4, while forty-five U.S. Navy planes flew an armed reconnaissance mission along Route 1 from the DMZ to Thanh Hoa. On these attacks, see Tad Szulc, "U.S. Says Bombing Cut Vital Routes," New York Times, April 5, 1965, p. 1; and Jack Langguth, "Hanoi MIGs Down Two American Jets in First Air Clash," New York Times, April 5, 1965, p. 1.

Vietnamese to rebuild one of these bridges and that 'the present regime has taken great pride in its restoration.'"[39] Attacks of this sort not only suggested a willingness to destroy highly valued targets but could also have been construed, especially in light of the President's April 7 speech at Johns Hopkins offering "unconditional discussions," as a tacit ultimatum to Hanoi to negotiate a settlement acceptable to the U.S. or else risk the loss of industrial facilities as the next step in the air war.[40]

But then, just as it appeared that the bombing was taking on the appearance of a "moving growing threat that cannot be ignored," the conduct of the air war changed noticeably. As Simons notes, in the aftermath of the bridge raids of April 3–4,

the daily attacks employed significantly fewer sorties, allocated among a variety of military targets and armed reconnaissance missions farther south. Only on April 9, 16, and 23 and on May 4 and 8 did the attacks involve total numbers of aircraft as large or larger than the first bridge raid. Even on these occasions, the attacks against comparable targets were carried out by smaller groups of aircraft in widely scattered areas. Only rarely did any of the sorties of April and May venture to within 100 miles of the Hanoi-Haiphong complex.[41]

This apparent turnabout in the conduct of the air war is especially puzzling in light of the importance attached by various Administration officials to a program of relentlessly mounting pressures on the North. Ambassador Taylor, for example, had repeatedly called for a steady movement northward in the air strikes, warning that "If we tarry too long in the [southern DRV], we will give Hanoi a weak and misleading signal which will work against our ultimate purpose."[42] Further, Administration officials had made no secret of the fact that they hoped to increase the pressure on the North; in this respect, they had repeatedly informed reporters in Washington that the air strikes would be moved northward in an attempt to erode DRV will.[43] And yet, "tarrying in the

39. Simons, "The Vietnam Intervention, 1964–1965," in George, Hall, and Simons, p. 180.

40. For the President's April 7 speech, see U.S. Senate, Committee on Foreign Relations, *Background Information Relating to Southeast Asia and Vietnam*, 6th rev. ed. (Washington, D.C.: U.S. Government Printing Office, 1970), pp. 224–229. See also the Administration's reply on April 8 to an appeal from seventeen nonaligned nations for negotiations without preconditions, in which the Administration set forth for the first time its terms for a settlement of the conflict (in *Background Information*, pp. 229–231).

41. Simons, "The Vietnam Intervention, 1964–1965," in George, Hall, and Simons, p. 190.

42. On this point, see Taylor's cables of March 8 and 13, quoted in III Gravel, p. 336.

43. See, for example, the following articles, all by Max Frankel in the *New York Times*: "More U.S. Strikes Likely in Attempt to Deter Hanoi," March 3, 1965, pp. 1, 10; "U.S. Goals in Asia," March 12, 1965, p. 3; and "Administration Steps Up Pressure to Force Aid Cut to Guerrillas," March 16, 1965, pp. 1, 3.

South" was very likely the impression conveyed to Hanoi by the conduct of the air war during April and early May.

While it is difficult to speak with certainty on these matters, it appears
that the turnabout in the air war was essentially an unintended by-
product of the procedures used to identify potential targets for the air
strikes. By the end of March 1965, most officials in Washington were
convinced that the optimism that accompanied the start of the air war
was unwarranted and that a regular and continuous program of air
strikes, probably stretching over several months, would be required.[44]
This realization, however, coincided with the completion of the planning efforts by the JCS and CINCPAC for multi-week campaigns aimed
at interdicting the infiltration routes of the southern DRV. In addition,
because of the preoccupation on the part of both civilian and military
officials with attacking infiltration-related targets, it appears that these
were the only detailed planning efforts available for consideration by
senior officials.[45] Finally, since the JCS had been careful to describe the
DRV railway bridges as an "attractive, vulnerable, and remunerative
target system which would hurt the North Vietnamese psychologically,
economically, and militarily," and since infiltration-related targets had
the extra advantage of being closely related to DRV "aggression,"
which, after all, was the principal legal justification for the bombing in
the first place, it should not be surprising that the JCS/CINCPAC proposals formed the basis for the extended air campaign decided upon by
civilian officials in late March.[46]

As a result, ROLLING THUNDER 9 (April 2–8) "inaugurated a
planned LOC interdiction campaign against North Vietnam south of
latitude 20°." What this meant, though, was that the bridge raids of
April 3–4 were *not* intended as the harbinger of relentlessly increasing,
"will-breaking" strikes against high-value targets. Instead, in keeping
with standard military practice, they were directed toward the much
more mundane goal of trapping as much rolling stock as possible south

44. On this change of attitude, see III Gravel, pp. 338–340, 346.

45. In this respect, John McNaughton noted in a March 24, 1965 memo that "will-breaking
strikes on [the] DRV" was one course of action that had been rejected "for one reason or another"
(the other rejected courses were "large troop deployments" and "exit by negotiations"). In an annex
to that memo, McNaughton went on to note that "will-breaking strikes on the North are balked (1)
by flash-point limits [i.e., fears of uncontrollable escalation], (2) by doubts that the DRV will cave
and (3) by doubts that the VC will obey a caving DRV. (Leaving strikes only a political and anti-
infiltration nuisance.)" On this, see Document no. 253 in III Gravel, pp. 694, 696.

46. On these points, see General Wheeler's memo to Secretary McNamara, quoted in III Gravel,
pp. 340–341; and the Pentagon analyst's comments on the preferences of civilian officials, III
Gravel, p. 341.

of the 20th Parallel, where it could later be destroyed by the (widely scattered) air raids that constituted the rest of the campaign.[47] But while such an approach may have been the most effective way to attack the DRV railway system, no one in Washington appears to have been paying much attention to the "signal" that this particular set of targetting decisions would convey to Hanoi, nor does there appear to have been any attempt to reconcile the interdiction campaign with the previously asserted goal of eroding DRV will.[48]

This latter omission, however, did not necessarily represent a serious flaw in the Administration's handling of the air war. At the same time that the interdiction campaign was getting under way, Administration officials were becoming increasingly preoccupied with developments in South Vietnam. On March 24, John McNaughton characterized the situation there as "bad and deteriorating"; while on April 1, McGeorge Bundy speculated that

A key question for Hanoi is whether they continue to make real headway in the South, or whether the conflict there starts to move against them or at least appear increasingly tough. If the former, even a major stepup in our air attacks would probably not cause them to become much more reasonable; if the latter, the situation might begin to move on a political track—but again in not less than 2–3 months. . . .

In addition, the deterioration in the South was prompting persistent calls from the military for additional American ground forces.[49]

It was in this context that senior American officials gathered in Washington at the start of April for yet another high-level policy review. Although the President told reporters just prior to an April 1 meeting with Ambassador Taylor and the NSC that he knew of "no far-reaching strategy that is being suggested or promulgated," he was, as the Pentagon analyst notes, "being less than candid."[50] In line with the belief that the North Vietnamese would not "become much more reasonable" until they were convinced they could not win in the South, the Administration was seriously considering a greatly expanded American role in the ground war. However, primarily as a result of

47. For the description of ROLLING THUNDER 9, see III Gravel, p. 285. For JCS preferences with respect to the bridge raids, see III Gravel, pp. 341, 343.

48. The reasons for the neglect of these seemingly vital issues will be explored in more detail in Chapter 6, below.

49. For McNaughton's comment, see Document no. 253 in III Gravel, p. 695; Bundy's assessment is quoted in III Gravel, p. 346. For the various troop proposals being advanced by the military at this time, see III Gravel, pp. 406, 438–440, 445–452, 462–472.

50. See Johnson Papers, 1965, p. 370; and III Gravel, p. 348.

Ambassador Taylor's strenuous opposition to any large buildup of American forces, the President agreed only to two additional battalions of Marines, along with an "18–20,000 man increase in U.S. military support forces." But while Taylor succeeded in slowing the troop juggernaut, he was forced to concede something on the troops' mission. No longer would they be confined to providing security for American bases; instead, they would now be available for "more active use under conditions to be established and approved by the Secretary of Defense in consultation with the Secretary of State."[51]

In addition to the troop decision, the April policy review resulted in Presidential approval for a whole smorgasbord of programs designed to improve the situation in the South: a 21-point program drawn up by the Army Chief of Staff, a 41-point program of nonmilitary actions submitted by Ambassador Taylor, a 16-point USIS program, and a 12-point program of covert operations presented by the CIA. In addition, the President approved a "general framework" for the air war which effectively committed the Administration to an interdiction-oriented strategy for the foreseeable future. As announced in NSAM-328:

> We should continue roughly the present slowly ascending tempo of ROLLING THUNDER operations, being prepared to add strikes in response to a higher rate of VC operations, or conceivably to slow the pace in the unlikely event [the] VC slacked off sharply for what appeared to be more than a temporary operational lull.
>
> The target systems should continue to avoid the effective GCI range of MIGs. We should continue to vary the types of targets, stepping up attacks on lines of communication in the near future, and possibly moving in a few weeks to attacks on the rail lines north and northeast of Hanoi. . . .
>
> Air operations in Laos, particularly route blocking operations in the Panhandle area, should be stepped up to the maximum remunerative rate.[52]

NSAM-328 proved to be but the first in a series of major policy initiatives. The JCS, for example, with Secretary McNamara's consent, continued to plan for the earliest possible introduction of a three-division force (two U.S., one ROK) into South Vietnam. In conjunction

---

51. NSAM-328, Document no. 254 in III Gravel, p. 703. In other words, the Marines would now be available for counterinsurgency operations within fifty miles of their bases. For additional details on the April policy review, see Halberstam, pp. 686–692; and III Gravel, p. 448.

52. NSAM-328, Document no. 254 in III Gravel, p. 703. The 21-point Army program had been drawn up during a visit to South Vietnam by the Army Chief of Staff between March 5 and 12 and initially approved by the President on March 15 (on these points, see III Gravel, pp. 95–96, 338–339). For a description of Taylor's 41-point program, see III Gravel, pp. 98–99.

with this planning, CINCPAC convened a staff conference in Honolulu on April 9–10, which recommended deploying the 173rd Airborne Brigade to Bien Hoa/Vung Tau and another Army brigade to Qui Nhon— a request that was eagerly seconded by Westmoreland on April 11. On April 13, McNamara, with Presidential sanction, approved deployment of the 173rd but not the second brigade. At that point, however, Ambassador Taylor, who first learned of this decision from a copy of the directive ordering CINCPAC to move the 173rd from Okinawa to South Vietnam, moved to block the deployment on the grounds that it had come as a "complete surprise" in view of the understanding reached in Washington at the April policy review.[53]

In response, John McNaughton informed Taylor on April 15 that "highest authority believes the situation in South Vietnam has been deteriorating and that, in addition to actions against the North, something new must be added in the South to achieve victory." The "something new" turned out to be seven additional programs to be undertaken by the U.S., including the deployment of an Army brigade to Bien Hoa/Vung Tau. This explanation, however, infuriated Taylor, leading him to cable McGeorge Bundy that he was "greatly troubled" by the tone of McNaughton's message:

First, it shows no consideration for the fact that . . . this mission is charged with securing implementation by the two-month-old Quat government of a 21-point military program, a 41-point nonmilitary program, a 16-point Rowan USIS program and a 12-point CIA program. Now this new cable opens up new vistas of further points as if we can win here somehow on a point score. We are going to stall the machine of government if we do not declare a moratorium on new programs for at least six months. Next, it shows a far greater willingness to get into the ground war than I had discerned in Washington during my recent trip. . . .[54]

On April 17, Taylor played his trump card, informing Washington that he would not seek GVN concurrence for the measures listed in McNaughton's message until he had received clear guidance on U.S. purposes and objectives in South Vietnam.[55]

In order to soothe Taylor's ire and reestablish a consensus on the

53. Taylor's cable is quoted in III Gravel, p. 451. For additional details on troop deployments, see III Gravel, pp. 408, 450–451.

54. McNaughton's cable is quoted in III Gravel, p. 451. The other six measures in the McNaughton cable are listed on pp. 455–456 of III Gravel. For Taylor's reply, see III Gravel, pp. 103–104.

55. See Document no. 255 in III Gravel, pp. 704–705. See also Halberstam, p. 697.

American role in the war, Secretary McNamara convened a hastily called conference at Honolulu on April 20, a meeting that proved to be significant in several respects.[56] For one thing, the conferees endorsed the turnabout of the air war begun by ROLLING THUNDER 9, telling the President that the "present tempo" of the air war was "about right" and that "sufficient increasing pressure" would be provided by "repetition and continuation" (the contrast with earlier proposals for relentlessly increasing the pressure on Hanoi could hardly have been greater). Further, the conferees legitimized the revised concept for the conduct of the air war by redefining the conditions under which an acceptable settlement would emerge. Picking up on the thread put forth by McGeorge Bundy on April 1, the conferees concluded that a "settlement will come as much or more from VC failure in the South as from DRV pain in the North." The strategy for "victory," consequently, was to "break the will of the DRV/VC by depriving them of victory." To support the new strategy, the conferees recommended that the U.S. commit nine additional maneuver battalions plus support troops, along with one Australian and three Korean battalions; additional forces were considered but not specifically recommended. Significantly, in this respect, tasks in the South were now to have first call on air assets in the area; the bombing in the North, while considered "essential to our campaign," was to be relegated to secondary importance.[57]

Most importantly, though, the Honolulu Conference marked the explicit abandonment of the earlier optimism about the length of the war. In contrast to the estimate that two to three months of bombing would enable the U.S. to attain a "position of strength," the conferees agreed that the DRV could not be expected to come to a position acceptable to the U.S. in less than six months; conceivably, it might take "more than six months, perhaps a year or two, to demonstrate VC failure in the South."[58] Still, the conferees were not inclined to question the ultimate success of the American effort in Vietnam, only that it might take longer than previously expected.

56. Present at the conference were McNamara, McNaughton, William Bundy, Taylor, Wheeler, Westmoreland, and Sharp.

57. The excerpts quoted here are all from Secretary McNamara's report to the President, Document no. 256 in III Gravel, pp. 705–706. On the change in strategy, see III Gravel, pp. 469, 479; on the allocation of air assets, see III Gravel, pp. 358–359; and on the troop recommendations, see III Gravel, pp. 456–457. Not all of the recommended deployments were immediately approved by the President: five battalions were approved by April 30, the rest by June 1 (see III Gravel, pp. 458–461).

58. Secretary McNamara's report, Document no. 256 in III Gravel, p. 706. See also Halberstam, pp. 700–701.

III. Project MAYFLOWER:
The First Pause in the Bombing (May-June 1965)

With his top advisers now convinced that considerably more time and effort than had previously been thought necessary would be required to bring the war to a successful conclusion, the President decided on a dramatic move. On May 10, he informed Ambassador Taylor that he was considering a brief pause in the bombing of the North, and he asked Taylor to clear the move with Premier Quat as quickly as possible. "You should understand," he explained to Taylor,

that my purpose in this plan is to begin to clear a path either toward restoration of peace or toward increased military action, depending upon the reaction of the Communists. We have amply demonstrated our determination and our commitment in the last two months and I now wish to gain some flexibility.[59]

While the President spoke of clearing a path either toward "restoration of peace" or "increased military action," it appears that the latter was foremost in his thoughts. All of the evidence available at the time indicated that the North Vietnamese were not interested in negotiating on terms acceptable to the Administration. In response to the President's April 7 offer of "unconditional discussions," Pham Van Dong had announced that "the unswerving policy of the DRV Government is to respect strictly the 1954 Geneva Agreements on Vietnam and to implement correctly their basic provisions" which, he claimed, were "embodied" in the so-called "Four Points" (see Appendix I). These, in turn, constituted the "basis" for the

soundest political settlement of the Vietnam problem. If this basis is recognized, favorable conditions will be created for the peaceful settlement of the Vietnam problem, and it will be possible to consider the reconvening of an international conference along the pattern of the 1954 Geneva Conference on Vietnam.[60]

In addition, intelligence estimates available to the President were unanimous in their judgment that the North Vietnamese were unlikely

---

59. Quoted in III Gravel, p. 366.

60. Excerpts from Pham Van Dong's speech are reprinted in *U.S.-Vietnam Relations*, VI. B. 2., pp. 136–141. In addition, on April 9, Hanoi Radio broadcast the text of an interview given by Ho Chi Minh to a correspondent from *Akahata* (the newspaper of the Japanese Communist Party), in which Ho took a somewhat harder line than Pham Van Dong, stating that: "To settle the South Vietnam question, first of all the U.S. must withdraw from South Vietnam, let the South Vietnamese people themselves settle their own affairs, and stop its provocative attacks against the DRV. The *carrying out* of these basic points will bring about favorable conditions for a conference along the pattern of the 1954 Geneva Conference" (quoted from *U.S.-Vietnam Relations*, VI. B. 2., p. 112, emphasis added).

to engage in "meaningful discussions" unless and until they were sub-jected to much higher levels of military pressure. Faced with the pro-spect of having to expand the war, a pause offered the President a con-venient tool for defusing the criticism that would inevitably accompany any escalation, since if a pause were held and the North Vietnamese failed to respond, the President would be free to claim that it was they who were blocking the path to peace and that he had no choice but to step up the pressure.[61]

And so, after learning from Taylor of Quat's concurrence, the Presi-dent decided to go ahead with the pause, which was code-named MAY-FLOWER and scheduled to begin at noon on Wednesday, May 12 (Washington time).[62] Although the pause was not announced publicly, privately the Administration made two moves to call it to the attention of Moscow and Hanoi and to suggest that the North Vietnamese might wish to reciprocate. On the evening of May 11, Secretary Rusk cabled Ambassador Foy Kohler in Moscow, instructing him to contact the DRV Embassy there and inform the North Vietnamese Ambassador of the Administration's hope that "this first pause in the air attacks may meet with a response which will permit further and more extended sus-pension of this form of military action in the expectation of equally con-structive actions by the other side in the future." In addition, Rusk summoned Soviet Ambassador Dobrynin to the State Department and orally conveyed the same message to him, confirmed by a written text.[63]

Contacting the North Vietnamese in Moscow, however, proved to be easier said than done. On the morning of May 12, Kohler had his Deputy Chief of Mission (DCM) telephone the DRV Embassy to re-quest an appointment for him with the North Vietnamese Ambassador. The North Vietnamese, however, refused to receive Kohler, citing the lack of diplomatic relations between the two countries, and suggested that he send his message to the Soviet Government in its capacity as Co-Chairman of the 1954 Geneva Conference. After checking with Washington, Kohler decided to have a written version of the message hand-delivered to the DRV Embassy; in addition, he sought an urgent appointment with Soviet Acting Foreign Minister Kuznetsov.[64]

61. On these points, see III Gravel, pp. 363–365.

62. The pause was timed to allow the completion of all of that week's ROLLING THUNDER missions. During the pause, U.S. planes were diverted to targets in the South. On these points, see III Gravel, pp. 366, 368.

63. For the full text of the Administration's message, see III Gravel, p. 369. Kohler was to convey the message orally and confirm it with a written text. See also III Gravel, p. 370, for Rusk's account of his meeting with Dobrynin.

64. On these points, see III Gravel, p. 371.

The new plan ran into snags right from the start. The message delivered to the DRV Embassy was returned the next day, ostensibly unopened; Kuznetsov, meanwhile, was unavailable, and Kohler was forced to settle for Deputy Foreign Minister Firyubin. Firyubin, however, not only lectured Kohler about the misconceptions underlying American policy in South Vietnam but also refused his request that the Soviets pass the message to the North Vietnamese. Still, Firyubin made no effort to return the written text of the message given him by Kohler.[65]

While Kohler was grappling with the problem of making contact, the President was engaged in a none-too-subtle effort to drive a wedge between the North Vietnamese and their Chinese allies. In a speech timed to coincide with the start of the pause, he suggested that the Chinese goal was domination of all Southeast Asia and that the Chinese were prepared to fight to the last North Vietnamese in pursuit of that end. Since the U.S. would never abandon its commitment to South Vietnam, he continued, "it would clearly be in the interest of North Vietnam to now come to the conference table."[66]

These efforts to coax a response from Hanoi all proved to be of no avail, to no one's great surprise. On May 15, Hanoi Radio accused "U.S. ruling circles" of spreading "deceptive news about a cessation of the bombing" and described reports of a pause as a "worn out trick of deceit and threat, especially since [they were] unleashed simultaneously with Johnson's May 13 speech harping again on his 'peace' and 'unconditional discussions' swindle." The next day, Hanoi Radio broadcast a commentary on the President's May 13 speech, accusing him of slandering China and dismissing the speech as a "contemptible trick." The Soviets, meanwhile, were effectively removing themselves from the picture. On May 15, Foreign Minister Gromyko met with Secretary Rusk in Vienna and told him that the Soviets would not negotiate over Vietnam and that the U.S. would have to find a way to establish contact directly with the North Vietnamese.[67] As a result of these negative responses, the President decided to resume the bombing, beginning at 8:00 A.M. on May 18 (Saigon time).

65. On these points, see III Gravel, pp. 371–374; and Kraslow and Loory, p. 122. There is no doubt that the North Vietnamese were aware of the message, since Hanoi Radio broadcast a verbatim text on December 10, 1965 (see the UPI dispatch, "Hanoi Broadcasts U.S. Note of May," *New York Times*, December 12, 1965, p. 2).

66. For the President's speech, see Johnson Papers, 1965, pp. 522–526. See also Max Frankel, "Driving a Wedge," *New York Times*, May 14, 1965, p. 13.

67. The May 15 broadcast is quoted in an AP dispatch, "Hanoi Charges U.S. 'Deceit' in Talk of Lull in Bombing," *New York Times*, May 16, 1965, p. 4. For the May 16 broadcast, see "Johnson Speech Derided by Hanoi," *New York Times*, May 17, 1965, pp. 1, 3. On the Rusk-Gromyko meeting, see III Gravel, p. 377.

The resumption of the bombing, however, signalled not the end but rather the beginning of one of the more tantalizing and mysterious episodes of the entire conflict. On the morning the bombing resumed, the ranking DRV diplomat in Paris, Mai Van Bo, called on the Asian Director of the Quai d'Orsay, Etienne Manac'h, ostensibly to explain Hanoi's rejection of an Indian proposal for a cease-fire along the 17th Parallel, policed by an Afro-Asian force. As conveyed informally by Manac'h to the Political Counsellor of the U.S. Embassy in Paris on May 19, Bo took advantage of the meeting to comment on the Four Points, explaining that they "were to be considered not as prior conditions but rather as working principles for a negotiation which should, in DRVN view, represent ultimate goals of a settlement in Vietnam."[68]

Bo's message touched on an important aspect of the DRV's position on negotiations. While Pham Van Dong had described the Four Points as the "basis for the soundest political *settlement*," the Administration, as the Pentagon analyst notes, had focused on the sentence that followed—i.e., "If this basis is recognized, favorable conditions will be created for the peaceful settlement of the Vietnam problem and it will be possible to consider the reconvening of an international conference along the pattern of the 1954 Geneva Conference on Vietnam." If Manac'h was reporting accurately, it would appear that the North Vietnamese were softening their position, possibly to the point of no longer demanding "recognition" of the Four Points as a precondition for negotiations.[69]

There were, however, two factors that cast doubt on the reliability of Manac'h's report. For one thing, Manac'h insisted that Bo's approach preceded the resumption of the bombing, even though, as the Pentagon analyst notes, "the earliest that Bo saw the French was probably 9:00 A.M., Paris time. The bombings had resumed at 8:00 A.M., Saigon time—in other words, eight hours earlier." Second, the "official" version of Bo's message was passed to the DCM of the Paris Embassy on May 20 by the Quai's Director of Political Affairs, Charles Lucet, and it differed significantly from the version passed by Manac'h. According to the Embassy's summary of Lucet's version:

68. American Embassy Paris cable no. 6582, May 19, 1965, quoted in XYZ Chronology, p. 1. Unfortunately, third-hand accounts (i.e., the Paris Embassy's summary of Manac'h's version of Bo's message) are all that are available at present. For additional details on this episode, see III Gravel, pp. 379–380.

69. On this point, see XYZ Summary and Analysis, p. 1. See also III Gravel, p. 380, which notes that Manac'h's report came to the U.S. Embassy in the form of a "highly glossed version" that made it "appear that the DRV was clearly responding to the bombing pause by a significant softening of its position on 'prior conditions.'"

Bo stressed that the Four Points should not be "isolated" from "declaration" which followed. . . . The Four Points constituted "best base" from which to find "most just" solution. Recognition [of] these "principles" would create favorable conditions for solution [of the] problem and would "open" possibility of convocation conference like Geneva, 1954.

Under questioning, Lucet's version continued, Bo had added a bonus, stating that an American withdrawal from South Vietnam would not be a precondition for negotiations but would instead depend on the outcome of the negotiations: "If there were agreement on the 'basis,' then a 'ways and means' of application of 'principles' would be found and in a peaceful manner; . . . 'our suggestion humiliates no one.'"[70]

While the messages passed by Manac'h and Lucet were deemed worthy of further exploration by officials in Washington, those officials were deeply distrustful of the French (who had, after all, been among the severest critics of American policy in Vietnam) and were unwilling to rely on them as intermediaries. Since Seaborn was scheduled to begin his fifth visit to Hanoi on May 31, Lucet was given only a polite "thank you" and a request that the U.S. be kept informed of further developments; in the meantime, the Administration concentrated on preparing a new message for Seaborn.[71]

This new message, which Seaborn was instructed to present to a "senior DRV official if and only if his first contacts with his normal liaison contact, in which he would inquire about availability [of] senior officials, meet with forthcoming response and DRV initiative for appointment," consisted largely of a rehash of previous U.S. statements, including Seaborn's March message, the President's Johns Hopkins speech, and the message transmitted via Moscow during the May bombing pause. The crux of the message, however, centered on the Four Points and in particular on the ambiguity in Bo's May 18 approach to the French. According to Seaborn's instructions:

If but only if senior DRV representative gets on to Pham Van Dong Four Points of April 8, Seaborn would reply that he has no message from USG on this subject. However, his study of four points would indicate that some might be acceptable to USG but that others would clearly be unacceptable. It has also not been clear whether DRV statements should be taken to mean that the recognition of these points was required as, in effect, a condition for any discussions. He would say that the USG appears to have made its position clear, that it would

70. On these points, see XYZ Summary and Analysis, p. 1; and American Embassy Paris cable no. 6612, May 20, 1965, quoted in XYZ Chronology, p. 1. The troop withdrawal "bonus" should be viewed in light of Ho's *Akahata* interview, cited in note 60, above. See also III Gravel, p. 379.

71. On these points, see XYZ Chronology, p. 2; and III Gravel, pp. 380–381.

accept unconditional discussions in the full sense, with either side free to bring up any matter, and that he would be personally interested in whether the DRV representative wished to clarify the question of whether their recognition is regarded by the DRV as a condition to any discussions.[72]

In contrast to his two previous visits, Seaborn did receive an appointment with a "senior DRV official"—Foreign Minister Nguyen Duy Trinh, whom he saw on June 3. However, when Seaborn asked Trinh whether the Four Points were preconditions for negotiations or ultimate goals of a negotiation, "Trinh's reaction to the [U.S.] message was totally negative, and in the exchange preceding its recitation he studiously avoided going beyond the vague statement that Pham Van Dong's four points were the 'basis for solution of the Vietnam question.'" As a result, Seaborn returned from Hanoi convinced that the North Vietnamese were not interested in negotiating with the United States.[73]

The evidence available, however, suggests that Seaborn's conclusion was at least partially incorrect. The North Vietnamese, that is, probably were interested in negotiating, although only on terms acceptable to them. For one thing, the fact that Seaborn received an appointment with the Foreign Minister suggests that the North Vietnamese were expecting something more than another restatement of the American position. In fact, assuming that Seaborn's March 1965 report was correct (i.e., that the North Vietnamese believed that the U.S. was anxiously seeking negotiations to extricate itself from a losing cause), it is quite possible that they were expecting Seaborn to respond to Mai Van Bo's May 18 message with a U.S. offer to "recognize" the Four Points in return for a settlement offering a face-saving exit from the conflict.

Furthermore, despite the disappointing (from Hanoi's perspective) message carried by Seaborn, the North Vietnamese retained their interest in a negotiated settlement. The events of the first two weeks of June 1965 were especially important in this respect. By then, the Viet Cong summer offensive was in full stride, with generally disastrous results for GVN forces. On June 9, for example, Viet Cong forces in division strength attacked the Special Forces camp at Dongxoai; in the ensuing four-day battle, two ARVN battalions were destroyed and GVN forces suffered more than 650 casualties. Total ARVN casualties during the second week of June were twice as high as for any previous week in the

72. On these points, see Seaborn Chronology, pp. 27–28 (emphasis in original); III Gravel, p. 380; and Canadian House of Commons, *Proceedings*, June 17, 1971, p. 6804.

73. On these points, see III Gravel, p. 380; XYZ Summary and Analysis, p. 2; and Canadian House of Commons, *Proceedings*, June 17, 1971, p. 6804.

war. To cap things off, the South Vietnamese military forced Premier Quat to resign on June 12, a move that seemed to augur a return to the chaotic situation that existed at the start of the year.[74]

In Washington, meanwhile, the Administration appeared to be on the brink of a major foreign policy decision. Throughout early June, the President had been preoccupied with the theme of "peace" in his speeches; on several occasions he appeared to be hinting at a readiness to end the American role in the war. At the same time, there were signs that the Administration was considering a major expansion of the American war effort. On June 7, Ambassador Taylor arrived in Washington for another high-level policy review, prompting James Reston to comment that the President faced the "painful decision" of either sending as many as 300,000 American troops to South Vietnam or returning to the "original American position that the war had to be won by the South Vietnamese, . . . [which] in the present circumstances is tantamount to accepting defeat."[75]

As things stood in mid-June, then, the Viet Cong were running wild, the GVN appeared to be coming apart at the seams, and the Administration was seemingly on the brink of either pulling out or greatly expanding the American role in the war. Given the coincidence of these factors, it was probably not by chance that Mai Van Bo called on Manac'h on June 14 to inquire if there had been any response from the Americans to his May 18 message. Once again, it would appear that the North Vietnamese were attempting to influence the Administration's decision by holding out the prospect of a face-saving ("our suggestion humiliates no one") exit from the South. This time, however, the Administration did not follow up on Bo's approach, having opted instead for a continuation of the American buildup in South Vietnam.[76]

IV. Probing for Weakness (July-September 1965)

As the Viet Cong summer offensive gained momentum and an ARVN collapse became a distinct possibility, the response of the U.S. military command in Saigon was, not surprisingly, to request a substantial

---

74. On these points, see II Gravel, p. 473; III Gravel, p. 440; and Shaplen (1966), pp. 345-347.

75. On these points, see Robert Semple, Jr., "Johnson Says U.S. Awaits Peace Bid," *New York Times*, June 9, 1965, p. 11 (all of the speeches referred to by Semple can be found in Johnson Papers, 1965, pp. 630-651); and James Reston, "Washington: A Critical Review of Vietnam," *New York Times*, June 11, 1965, p. 30.

76. On the June 14 Bo-Manac'h meeting, see XYZ Chronology, p. 2. Two days later, Secretary McNamara announced that the U.S. would send six additional maneuver battalions plus support troops to South Vietnam (see DOSB, July 5, 1965, pp. 12-19).

increase in American ground combat forces. On June 7, General West-moreland cabled Admiral Sharp that recent ARVN losses had made it impossible to continue the planned expansion of GVN forces, since trainees would be needed to fill the gaps in existing battalions. With Viet Cong forces growing in strength, he continued, "I can see no course of action open to us except to reinforce our efforts in South Vietnam with additional U.S. or Third Country forces as rapidly as is practical during the critical weeks ahead." He concluded by enumerat-ing the forces necessary to reverse the deterioration—forces which, if approved in their entirety, would have brought the total number of U.S. and Third Country maneuver battalions in South Vietnam to forty-four.[77]

Westmoreland's request touched off a major debate within the Ad-ministration—a debate fueled largely by his admission that the 44-battalion force would suffice only to establish a favorable balance of forces by the end of 1965 and that additional forces would be required in 1966 if the U.S. was to seize the initiative from the Viet Cong. Making the case for the 44-battalion force was Secretary McNamara, who argued in a July 1 Draft Presidential Memorandum (DPM) that the U.S. should not only go ahead with the troop buildup but also that the mission of American forces in South Vietnam be changed from the conservative "denial of victory" strategy sanctioned at Honolulu in April to an aggressive strategy that soon became known as "search and destroy." In addition, to support the buildup and change of strategy in the South, the DPM proposed that the air war over North Vietnam be greatly intensified. As described by the Pentagon analyst:

The July 1 version of his memorandum recommended a total quarantine of the movement of war supplies into North Vietnam, by sea, rail, and road, through the mining of Haiphong and all other harbors and the destruction of rail and road bridges leading from China to Hanoi; the Secretary also urged the destruc-tion of fighter airfields and SAM sites "as necessary" to accomplish these objectives.

Underpinning these recommendations was a rationale borrowed from a CIA assessment which McNamara quoted approvingly in concluding the DPM:

Over the longer term we doubt if the Communists are likely to change their basic strategy in Vietnam (i.e., aggressive and steadily mounting insurgency)

---

77. For Westmoreland's cable, see III Gravel, pp. 438–440. For details on the 44-battalion force, see III Gravel, p. 467. At the time, there were one Australian and fifteen American battalions in South Vietnam.

unless and until two conditions prevail: (1) they are forced to accept a situation in the war in the South which offers them no prospect of an early victory and no ground for hope that they can simply outlast the U.S. and (2) North Vietnam itself is under continuing and increasingly damaging punitive attack. So long as the Communists think they scent the possibility of early victory (which is probably now the case), we believe that they will persevere and accept extremely severe damage to the North. Conversely, if North Vietnam itself is not hurting, Hanoi's doctrinaire leaders will probably be ready to carry on the Southern struggle almost indefinitely. If, however, both of the conditions outlined above should be brought to pass, we believe Hanoi probably would, at least for a period of time, alter its basic strategy and course of action in South Vietnam.[78]

Whatever the substantive merits of McNamara's recommendations, the July 1 DPM at least presented a strategy that was both coherent and internally consistent, in the sense of identifying the conditions that would have to be met to achieve an acceptable settlement—i.e., reversing the decline in the South and imposing costs on the North—and proposing actions that were directly relevant to those conditions—namely, a troop buildup in the South and an interdiction campaign intended to impose costs on the North (by destroying bridges and rail lines) while contributing to the weakening of DRV/VC forces in the South.[79] However, it was one thing to put down on paper a strategy to guide the war effort; it was another matter entirely for McNamara to persuade his colleagues in the Administration to accept the DPM's ideas as their own.

To the right of McNamara in the July escalation debate were the JCS, who, while supporting the escalatory moves proposed by the DPM, sought to go even further in striking the North. The military view, as the Pentagon analyst notes, was that the war should be intensified on all fronts, in the North as well as in the South, and in this respect it appears that the Chiefs' recommendations were guided not so much by a desire to identify a strategy that would make the most efficient use of scarce resources (e.g., by focusing the air war on targets that would both make the war costly for the North and contribute to the war effort in

78. For Westmoreland's admission, see III Gravel, pp. 471, 482. On the July 1 DPM, see IV Gravel, pp. 24–26. For the CIA assessment, see IV Gravel, p. 26.

79. This is not to imply that it would have been possible to cut off completely or even reduce drastically the flow of men and supplies to the South, nor does our discussion here imply approval of the measures recommended by the DPM. All we are concerned with here is the ability of the Administration to identify and reach agreement on a coherent and internally consistent strategy for prosecuting the war. The efficacy of the strategies pursued by the Administration will be considered in Chapters 5, 6, and 8, below.

the South by impeding infiltration) as by a desire to strike anything and everything of value in the North, no matter how tenuous its relationship to the war in the South.[80]

At the same time that the Chiefs were complaining that the air war wasn't being escalated rapidly enough, George Ball was making the reverse argument on the issue of American troop deployments in the South. In a July 1 memo, he warned the President:

Once large numbers of U.S. troops are committed to direct combat, they will begin to take heavy casualties in a war they are ill-equipped to fight in a non-cooperative if not downright hostile countryside. Once we suffer large casualties, we will have started a well-nigh irreversible process. Our involvement will be so great that we cannot—without national humiliation—stop short of achieving our complete objectives. *Of the two possibilities I think humiliation would be more likely than the achievement of our objectives—even after we have paid terrible costs.*

Ball then argued forcefully for holding the line at 15 battalions and 72,000 men and for beginning exploratory contacts with the North Vietnamese about the possibility of a negotiated settlement.[81]

With the bureaucracy thus divided, the President asked Secretary McNamara to make another fact-finding visit to South Vietnam, although it appears that the purpose of this trip was not so much to consider the merits of the 44-battalion request as to nail down the nagging question of what would be required over and above the 44-battalion force.[82] On returning to Washington, McNamara gave the President a revised version of the DPM in which the recommended deployments to be made during 1965 were unchanged—34 battalions (175,000 men)—with an additional 27 battalions (100,000 men) to be deployed during 1966. The recommendation on the air war, however, changed significantly. As described by the Pentagon analyst, the

80. On these points, see IV Gravel, pp. 21, 24.

81. Document no. 260 in IV Gravel, pp. 615–616 (emphasis in original). See also III Gravel, pp. 472–473; IV Gravel, p. 22; and Document no. 258 in IV Gravel, pp. 609–610. In between Ball and McNamara was William Bundy, who argued for a "middle way" course of action (18 battalions, 85,000 troops, preparations to send two additional divisions to Vietnam, and intensified efforts to arrange a negotiated settlement). On Bundy's views, see III Gravel, pp. 415, 473; IV Gravel, pp. 23–24; and Document no. 259 in IV Gravel, pp. 610–615.

82. In the July 1 DPM, McNamara had stated that Westmoreland was uncertain of his troop needs for 1966; in addition, on July 17, while he was in Vietnam, McNamara received a cable from Deputy Secretary Vance informing him that the President had decided to go ahead with the 44-battalion force, thus suggesting that that question had been largely decided before McNamara left for Saigon. On these points, see IV Gravel, p. 296; III Gravel, pp. 475–476; and Westmoreland, pp. 142–143.

July 20 memorandum backed off from the July 1 recommendations—
perhaps, although it is impossible to tell from the available materials—
because of intimations that such drastic escalation would be unacceptable to
the President. Instead of mining North Vietnam's harbors as a quarantine
measure, the Secretary recommended it as a possible "severe reprisal should the
VC or DRV commit a particularly damaging or horrendous act" such as
"interdiction of the Saigon river." But he recommended a gradual increase in
the number of strike sorties against North Vietnam from the existing 2,500 per
month to 4,000 "or more," still "avoiding striking population and industrial
targets not closely related to the DRV's supply of war material to the VC."[83]

Despite the more moderate tone of the revised version of the DPM,
the underlying strategic concepts remained the same, as evidenced by
McNamara's emphasis on building up U.S. forces in the South, avoiding strikes on "population or industrial targets," and increasing the
number of strike sorties over the North in order to impede infiltration
and make the war costly for the North Vietnamese. But while the President engaged in an elaborate series of consultations designed to elicit
affirmations of support for the proposed policy from senior officials at
State, Defense, Treasury, the military, and the Congress, the resulting
consensus was more apparent than real. The JCS, for example, continued to press "for permission to expand the bombing virtually into a
program of strategic bombing aimed at all industrial and economic
resources as well as at all interdiction targets." Secretary McNamara,
however,

refused to approve an overall JCS concept for fighting the Vietnam War which
included much heavier ROLLING THUNDER strikes against key military and
economic targets coordinated with a blockade and mining attack on North
Vietnam ports, and he also continued to veto JCS proposals for dramatic
attacks on major POL depots, power plants, airfields, and other "lucrative"
targets.[84]

While the President apparently supported his Defense Secretary's
refusal to transform the air war along the lines suggested by the JCS, he
appears to have been sensitive to the risks inherent in allowing so
important a set of members of his Administration as the JCS to become
too disgruntled. As a result, the actual conduct of the air war reflected
not so much an agreed-on strategy subordinating military operations to

---

83. IV Gravel, p. 26.

84. For a description of the consultations engaged in by the President, see Johnson, pp. 146–151.
On JCS preferences concerning the air war, see IV Gravel, p. 38. On Secretary McNamara's views,
see IV Gravel, p. 29.

the ultimate goal of ending the insurgency in South Vietnam as a Presidential desire to keep as many members of his Administration as possible reasonably satisfied with the course the Administration was following. Despite Secretary McNamara's opposition to JCS proposals for attacks on "lucrative" targets such as POL depots, power plants, and airfields, the President did approve limited attacks on such targets, although authorization for such attacks was doled out at the rate of a few targets per new ROLLING THUNDER series (which, by mid-1965, had shifted from a one-week to a two-week approval cycle). By the end of the year, the policy of "incremental escalation" had resulted in attacks on six power plants (only two of which were in the main power grid), four POL storage installations (17 percent of total bulk storage capacity), two manufacturing plants (one explosives plant and one textile factory, the latter hit by mistake), and two small ports, as well as the usual assortment of bridges, military barracks, and supply depots. In addition, the policy resulted in a certain amount of embarrassment for the Administration, since attacks on "lucrative" targets "seemed inconsistent with a purely interdiction rationale, while failure to attack the most important of them did not satisfy a strategic bombing rationale."[85]

Nor was the President insensitive to suggestions that the Administration undertake a more vigorous effort to achieve a negotiated settlement, suggestions that originated not only from those, like George Ball, who felt the war unwinnable and that the U.S. should cut its losses and get out, but also from those, like Secretary McNamara, who had been in favor of expanding the American role in the war.[86] In this respect, the

85. On the incremental nature of the Administration's policy, see IV Gravel, p. 29; and Andrew H. Baggs, "Bombing, Bargaining, and Limited War: North Vietnam, 1965–1968," Unpublished Ph.D. thesis, University of North Carolina, Chapel Hill, 1972, pp. 60–65, 119–122. The summary of targets struck is provided in IV Gravel, pp. 55–56. On the inconsistencies in the Administration's policies, see IV Gravel, p. 30. The distinction between "lucrative" and "interdiction" targets is certainly not an easy one to maintain, especially since certain of the targets assigned by both the Pentagon analyst and the JCS to the "lucrative" category (e.g., POL and ports) could also be justified under an interdiction rationale (although this would not be the case for targets such as MIG airfields and industrial facilities, especially since any output lost from the latter was simply replaced by imports). In any event, the point to be stressed here is that Administration decisions on which targets to hit and when resulted not from a careful effort to classify targets and then strike only targets in a certain category but rather from a continuous struggle between military and civilian officials during which strategic considerations were effectively lost sight of and the resulting "signals" to Hanoi were, to say the least, confusing.

86. The July 20 version of the DPM recommended that the Administration launch a "vigorous effort on the political side to lay the groundwork for a favorable outcome by clarifying our objectives and establishing channels of communication" (quoted in Johnson, p. 145). See also IV Gravel, p. 27.

debate over the 44-battalion force had been accompanied by an emerging consensus within the Administration that once the U.S. was clearly committed to preventing a DRV/VC victory in the South (which it would be, it was felt, if the decision should be to go ahead with the 44-battalion force), the North Vietnamese might well reconsider whether they wished to take on American units (as opposed to ARVN) and thus become more amenable to a negotiated settlement on terms acceptable to the United States.[87] Since the President was clearly concerned about the political risks associated with a decision to increase the size of the American force in South Vietnam to 175,000 men, he apparently shared the view that the summer of 1965 would be an opportune time to probe DRV willingness to continue the struggle, especially if the probe could be completed before American troops began fighting and dying in large numbers.[88]

What gave these considerations special significance was a fortuitous event that took place in Paris on July 16. On that date, an American businessman, Urah Arkas-Duntov, met with Mai Van Bo—a meeting Duntov arranged on his own initiative, with the help of two French journalists. Although Bo told Duntov that the Four Points provided the proper "basis" for any negotiations between the U.S. and North Vietnam, he apparently did not insist on U.S. "recognition" of the Four Points as a precondition for negotiations. In addition, he characterized the withdrawal of American forces from South Vietnam as a technical problem, stating that it could be worked out as it had been with the French in 1954, and that it could take place over a two-to-three year period. Furthermore, he said very little about the bombing of the North and gave no indication that it would have to be stopped prior to any negotiations.[89]

For some reason, though, Duntov did not inform the State Department of this meeting until July 29. Still, upon learning of the meeting, the Administration seized on it as a means of establishing the contact recommended by both Ball and McNamara. Ball promptly phoned Edmund Gullion, a retired Foreign Service Officer who was then Dean of the Fletcher School at Tufts, and asked him to take over the contact.[90]

---

87. Interview with William Bundy (July 28, 1975). See also Richard Dudman, "Military Policy in Vietnam," *Current History*, 50:294 (February 1966), 94.

88. Indicative of the President's concern was the artfully worded announcement at his July 28 news conference that the U.S. would increase its forces in South Vietnam from 75,000 to 125,000 troops "almost immediately" and that "additional forces will be needed later and they will be sent as requested" (Johnson Papers, 1965, p. 795).

89. On these points, see XYZ Chronology, pp. 2–3.

90. On the date of Duntov's report, see XYZ Chronology, p. 3. The delay was apparently the

Gullion flew immediately to Washington, where he was briefed on the contact and on the message he was to carry. Gullion's message was itself noteworthy in a number of respects. For one thing, in contrast to the messages carried by Seaborn, with their bellicose warnings that the DRV would have to contain itself to the territory assigned it by the 1954 agreements or else suffer the consequences, Gullion was to "show desire for peace, and a free, independent, and *unified* Vietnam." Second, he was to continue the probe of the meaning of the Four Points begun by Seaborn in May—specifically, he was to announce that the U.S. was ready to discuss the Four Points, which "in some measure" paralleled Administration thinking on a settlement, and to inquire whether other points could be introduced into any formal negotiations. Third, although Gullion's message was couched in terms somewhat more conciliatory than the messages carried by Seaborn, the Administration's goal remained unchanged. As the Pentagon analyst notes, the Administration sent Gullion "with the intention of seeking peace from a position of U.S. strength." In this respect, he was to warn that a "prolongation of the conflict is bound to lead to progressively larger U.S. pressures and long-term China control in North Vietnam," and that "pressures in the U.S. [for] a wider war were growing and that it would be increasingly harder to exercise restraint."[91]

On August 6, Gullion held his first meeting with Bo,[92] at which time

result of Duntov's insistence on reporting the contact directly to George Ball. Gullion, who had come to Ball's attention while serving as U.S. Ambassador to the Congo during 1960–1964, was an obvious choice—an experienced negotiator, fluent in French, with a background in Vietnam (he had served in the U.S. mission in Saigon from December 1949 to September 1952), but who, as a private citizen, could be disowned if necessary. These points are based on interviews with William Bundy (July 28, 1975) and Edmund Gullion (February 20, 1975).

91. For Gullion's message, see XYZ Chronology, pp. 7–8 (emphasis added). For the Pentagon analyst's comment, see XYZ Summary and Analysis, p. 3. To help preserve the secrecy of the contact, Gullion was given the code name "X"; Mai Van Bo was code-named "R"; and the contact was named "XYZ." "Y" was Paul Sturm, another retired Foreign Service Officer, who entered the contact in November 1965. Since there never was a "Z", however, the name "XYZ" was something of a misnomer. As a further precaution, Gullion did not use the Paris Embassy's cipher facilities in communicating with Washington; instead, his reports and instructions were hand-carried between Washington and Paris by pouch. The XYZ Chronology section thus consists almost entirely of summaries of these hand-carried messages—summaries apparently prepared by the Pentagon analyst (in contrast to the chronology sections for the other contacts, which consist largely of verbatim excerpts from the actual cables, etc.). These points are based on interviews with Edmund Gullion (February 20, 1975) and William Bundy (July 28, 1975).

92. Gullion had left for Paris on August 1 or 2; he made his initial contact by simply knocking on the door of Bo's residence. Bo, however, was not immediately available, and a delay of "two or three days" ensued before their first meeting, on August 6 (interview with Edmund Gullion, February 20, 1975). But before that meeting could be held, Duntov reentered the picture, meeting with Bo on August 5, despite a State Department request that he hold off. The meeting proved to

Bo continued to take a very forthcoming stance, making no mention of the bombing and telling Gullion that, while reunification could take place over a long or a short time, it could only be done on the basis of a free decision by the Vietnamese people. Gullion, for his part, accepted in principle DRV demands for a U.S. troop withdrawal, while stipulating that any withdrawal provisions would also have to apply to North Vietnamese troops in the South, a stipulation that Bo did not explicitly reject. The first meeting did, however, produce a number of troublesome points, among them Bo's claim that the NLF alone was qualified to speak for the South in any peace conference. In addition, Bo distinguished between "discussion" and a "settlement," telling Gullion that there could be no settlement without U.S. "recognition" of the "principles" in the Four Points. Again, however, the DRV position remained vague, as Bo did not specify what he meant by "recognition." Bo did state that he wanted to know the U.S. reaction to a number of questions, but Gullion cut him off by launching into a preplanned discussion of a U.S. version of the Four Points (see Appendix II). Bo, in turn, told Gullion that he wanted to insure an understanding of the DRV position and took the initiative in arranging a second meeting.[93]

At their second meeting, on August 13, Gullion concentrated on the issue of convening a no-preconditions Geneva conference. However, while he and Bo were able to agree on Geneva as the site for any peace conference, the issue of preconditions was left unsettled. Bo, for example, continued to take a vague position on whether the U.S. would have to "recognize" the Four Points prior to any conference; similarly, he seemed to reject the U.S. version of the Four Points but not "definitively or finally." Gullion tabled a draft statement in which it was proposed that a reconvened Geneva Conference would take up the DRV's Four Points and "other propositions" as well; Bo, however, agreed with the first part but not the second. When Gullion threatened to break off the contact, Bo insisted on another meeting "in case there should be some change in the points of confrontation." On a more positive note, Bo appeared to agree with Gullion's statement that any troop withdrawals would have to be phased and balanced and include both North Vietnamese and American forces then in South Vietnam.[94]

---

be uneventful, although Bo did make explicit his willingness to receive an authorized American representative for the purpose of explaining the American position. On these points, see XYZ Chronology, pp. 4–5, 8.

93. On these points, see XYZ Chronology, pp. 8–10; and XYZ Summary and Analysis, pp. 3, 7. Gullion cut Bo off because he had memorized his presentation and was anxious to present it in its entirety (interview with Edmund Gullion, February 20, 1975).

94. Gullion's instructions for the second meeting can be found on p. 10 of XYZ Chronology; a summary of the meeting is given on pp. 12–13. The Pentagon analyst puts the date for the second

On August 18, Gullion saw Bo for the third time, a session that proved to be quite productive, despite fears in Washington that the North Vietnamese were about to renege on their earlier concessions. On August 13, *Le Monde* published an interview given by Ho Chi Minh to Philippe Devillers, in which Ho demanded that the U.S. give

tangible proofs that it accepts the four-point stand of the Government of the DRV which conforms to the essential political and military clauses of the 1954 Geneva Agreement on Vietnam; it must immediately stop the air attacks against DRV territory, stop forthwith the aggressive war against the south of our country, and withdraw from there all U.S. troops and weapons. That is peace with honor; there is no other way out.[95]

At their August 18 meeting, Bo identified a halt in the bombing of the North as the "tangible proof" demanded by Ho; but on several other issues, Bo took a position more conciliatory than that taken by Ho. On the troop withdrawal issue, Bo did not deny the presence of NVA troops in South Vietnam and insisted that his statements on phased and balanced withdrawals represented the official DRV position. Similarly, despite Ho's claim that the NLF was the "sole authentic representative of the South Vietnamese people," Bo did not reject the idea that a mutually acceptable formula on South Vietnamese representation at a peace conference could be worked out, provided other obstacles to a conference were removed. In addition, Bo expressed interest in the meaning of the U.S. version of the Four Points and again stressed the desirability of another meeting.[96]

At this point, then, it appeared as if Gullion and Bo were making substantial progress toward a reconvened Geneva Conference, and Gullion was instructed to use his next meeting with Bo, scheduled for September 3, to attempt to clear away the remaining obstacles to such a conference. In particular, he was to probe for DRV reciprocity on the issue of a bombing halt (specifically, he was to suggest a reduction in Viet Cong incidents in the South) and to attempt to resolve the representation issue by indicating that "groups" would be allowed to attend a peace conference and express their views.[97]

---

meeting at August 15, but this is probably a misprint. As the summary of the meeting indicates, Bo asked Gullion if he had seen the text of an interview given by Ho Chi Minh to Philippe Devillers, which appeared in *Le Monde* on the morning of their second meeting. The *Le Monde* interview actually appeared on August 13; the basis for the confusion is probably that the text was broadcast over Hanoi Radio on August 15—two days after it appeared in *Le Monde*.

95. Quoted in XYZ Chronology, p. 11.

96. On the third Bo-Gullion meeting, see XYZ Chronology, pp. 13–14.

97. For Gullion's instructions, see XYZ Chronology, pp. 14–15. In the meantime, Administration officials in Washington were making a concerted effort to raise DRV interest in a negotiated

Contributing to the Administration's hopes that a breakthrough might be possible was the arrival of a high-level DRV delegation led by VWP Politburo member Le Duc Tho in Paris on August 25.[98] Unfortunately, though, these hopes proved to be illusory. During their initial meeting, Bo had told Gullion that there was a difference between "discussion and settlement"—i.e., "There could not be [a] settlement without [U.S.] recognition of the principles within the four points."[99] Significantly in this respect, on September 2, Radio Hanoi broadcast the text of a speech delivered by Pham Van Dong on August 31, and, while the speech did not imply that U.S. "recognition" of the Four Points was a precondition for negotiations (which would have made little sense, since talks were already under way between Bo and Gullion in Paris), the Premier emphasized that:

The purpose of the Vietnamese people's bold struggle has been fully embodied in the four-point stand of the DRV Government.

This is the sole correct stand of peace which has been recognized by world public opinion as the only basis for a *settlement* of the Vietnam problem. This four-point stand fully conforms to the most important political and military provisions of the 1954 Geneva agreements on Vietnam, and the whole world is now of the view that these agreements must be correctly implemented. *This four-point stand must be solemnly accepted by the U.S. Government before a political settlement of the Vietnam problem can be contemplated.*

The warning was clear: while talks (along the lines of the Bo-Gullion meeting in Paris) would be possible without U.S. "recognition" of the Four Points, a *settlement* could not be "contemplated" until the U.S. had "accepted" the Four Points.[100]

---

solution by hinting at a readiness to be flexible in arranging a settlement. See, for example, the comments by Secretary Rusk, McGeorge Bundy, and Arthur Goldberg cited in DOSB, September 13, 1965, pp. 431, 441, 443. See also "U.S. Aides Explain Position on Truce," New York Times, August 24, 1965, p. 11; Max Frankel, "U.S. Diplomacy by TV," New York Times, August 25, 1965, p. 4; and Secretary Rusk's news conference of August 27, DOSB, September 20, 1965, pp. 481–483.

98. Tho left Hanoi on July 14 accompanied by Tran Quang Huy, alternate member of the VWP Central Committee, and Hoang Tu, DRV Ambassador to Rumania, to attend the Rumanian Party Congress in Bucharest. When the Congress ended on July 24, however, the DRV delegation apparently remained in Rumania, since there was no announcement of its departure over Radio Bucharest, as there was for all the other delegations. On August 13, a DRV delegation led by Tho turned up in East Berlin, where it apparently stayed until departing for Paris. The delegation that visited Paris included, in addition to Tho and Huy, Nguyen Van Tran, secretary of the VWP Central Committee, and Nguyen Thanh Le, deputy editor-in-chief of *Nhan Dan*. It is difficult to resist the inference that Le and Tran joined the delegation in order to brief Tho on the latest thinking in Hanoi on how the contact with Gullion should be handled. These points are based on FBIS Daily Reports for July 15, August 16, and September 21, 1965.

99. On this point, see XYZ Chronology, p. 9.

100. Pham Van Dong's speech is quoted in XYZ Chronology, p. 18 (emphasis added). See also

This hard-line element in the DRV stance was very much in evidence during the final Bo-Gullion meeting on September 3. During that meeting, Bo took a harsh and uncompromising stance, reneging on two crucial issues: first, he insisted that U.S. troops would have to be withdrawn before any elections in South Vietnam; and, second, he accused the U.S. of escalating both the air war over the North and the ground war in the South in an attempt to force negotiations on the DRV, and he demanded that the bombing be stopped "unilaterally, immediately, totally, and definitively." When Gullion pointed out that Bo's position was inconsistent with his earlier statements, Bo became "obviously agitated" and demanded that Gullion agree that he (Bo) had always taken a consistent line in their talks, something that Gullion refused to do.[101]

The ill-fated meeting on September 3 proved to be the effective end of the contact. Gullion returned to the DRV mission for a prearranged fifth meeting on September 7; Bo, however, did not show up, and Gullion was told only that he was "sick." After that, Gullion remained in Paris for some time in the hope that the contact might be renewed; but, with the North Vietnamese showing no interest in continuing the talks, he decided to return to his position at Tufts.[102]

In the months that followed, the Administration made one last effort to renew the contact. Before bowing out, Gullion suggested that another representative might have better luck with Bo, and he recommended Paul Sturm, another retired Foreign Service Officer, who had served in Vietnam between 1952 and 1955. On November 18, Sturm held his first meeting with Bo, at which time he presented a message virtually identical to that conveyed by Gullion during his first meeting with Bo. Given the absence of anything new in Sturm's instructions, it is not surprising that the meeting produced nothing of substance. On December

the DRV Foreign Ministry memorandum of September 23, 1965, which used a formula identical to that used by Pham Van Dong on August 31 (for the relevant portion of the memo, see XYZ Chronology, p. 21). Significantly, an article in Vietnam Courier on September 27, 1965 by Nguyen Van Vinh seemed to suggest that acceptance of the Four Points was a precondition for negotiations: "If the U.S. accepts the above four-point stand, we shall be ready to come to the conference table and talk with them at any time and in any place" (cited in Donald Zagoria, Vietnam Triangle [New York: Pegasus, 1967], p. 123). The discrepancy between these two formulations suggests that there was considerable disagreement in Hanoi on the question of whether and when to begin negotiations with the United States. On this point, see the discussion of DRV policymaking in Chapters 5–6, below.

101. On these points, see XYZ Chronology, pp. 18–19.

102. These points are based on XYZ Chronology, p. 19; and on an interview with Edmund Gullion (February 20, 1975). The reasons for the breakdown of the contact and for the DRV decision to enter into the contact will be discussed in more detail in Chapter 6, below.

29 and again on January 3, 1966, Sturm met with Bo's deputy, Vo Van Sung, but again nothing of substance ensued. By then, the Administration's (and the DRV's) attention was focused on a new channel via Rangoon, with the meetings in Paris relegated to a distinctly secondary role.[103]

V. Contact in Rangoon (October 1965-February 1966)

With the collapse of Gullion's mission to Paris, the attention of Administration officials was inevitably drawn back to the unpleasant issues of troops and bombing. Although the President had decided in July to go ahead with the full 44-battalion force (known as the "Phase I" force), he had deferred a decision on additional forces for 1966 (the "Phase II" force). Throughout the summer and fall of 1965, the U.S. military commands in Saigon, Honolulu, and Washington concentrated on refining their estimates of the forces necessary for Phase II. By November, with Phase I deployments scheduled to be completed by the end of the year, a decision on Phase II could not be put off much longer.[104]

In similar fashion, the Administration faced a critical decision concerning the future of the air war. As explained by the Pentagon analyst:

It was clear by November that even the gradual rate of escalation of 1965 was approaching a point at which any further increase would be possible only by attacking the sensitive targets in the Hanoi/Haiphong sanctuaries and the China buffer zone. As of the end of October, 126 of the 240 existing JCS targets had been struck; and of the remaining 114, two-thirds (75) were in the off-limits areas, and 29 of the other 39 remaining were in the touchy northeast quadrant.[105]

It was precisely to issues such as these that Secretary McNamara addressed an early-November Draft Presidential Memorandum (DPM). In McNamara's view, the Administration had but two options: "One is to go now for a compromise solution and hold further deployments to a minimum. The other is to stick with our stated objectives and with the war, and provide what it takes in men and materiel." Since the "compromise solution," as the Pentagon analyst notes, was expected to be "unstable, difficult to sell domestically, and damaging to 'U.S. political

103. These points are based on XYZ Chronology, pp. 21–22; and on interviews with Edmund Gullion (February 20, 1975) and William Bundy (July 28, 1975).

104. On these points, see IV Gravel, pp. 299–302. The terms "Phase I" and "Phase II" were first used in General Westmoreland's July 1965 "Concept of Operations" for South Vietnam (see III Gravel, pp. 481–483).

105. IV Gravel, p. 59.

effectiveness on the world scene,'" McNamara recommended that the Administration pursue the second course by going ahead with the Phase II deployments and intensifying the bombing of the North. But before those actions were taken, McNamara suggested, there should be a pause in the bombing of the North on the grounds that:

1. It would offer the DRV and VC a chance to move toward a solution if they should be so inclined. . . .
2. It would demonstrate to domestic and international critics that our efforts to settle the war are genuine.
3. It would probably tend to reduce the dangers of escalation after we resumed the bombing. . . .
4. It would set the stage for another pause perhaps in late 1966, which might produce a settlement.[106]

McNamara's DPM was discussed at the White House on November 7; in the meantime, the proposal for a bombing pause had, predictably, stirred up strong opposition from the military services. The JCS were, at the time, pressing for a "sharply accelerated [bombing] program which will leave no doubt that the U.S. intended to win and achieve a level of destruction which [the North Vietnamese] will not be able to overcome." Nor were the Chiefs alone in opposing a pause—in a November 9 memo for the President that reflected the views of Secretary Rusk, the State Department recommended against a pause "at the present time."[107]

While these deliberations were under way in Washington, ominous developments were taking place in South Vietnam. Throughout the summer and fall of 1965, the North Vietnamese had greatly increased the rate of infiltration into the South. In addition, the Viet Cong had intensified their recruiting and were consolidating many of their smaller units into units of regimental size. By mid-November,

six confirmed, two probable, and one possible PAVN regiments had been identified in South Vietnam. The Viet Cong regimental-size units had increased from five in July of 1965 to 12. The total strength of the PAVN/VC army was estimated at 27 PAVN infantry battalions and a total of 110 PAVN/VC battalions.

And, as the bloody fighting in the region of the Ia Drang Valley illustrated, the PAVN units in the South were no longer being held in

---

106. On these points, see IV Gravel, pp. 49, 303.

107. For the JCS arguments, see IV Gravel, pp. 60–62. For the State Department memo, see IV Gravel, pp. 33–34.

reserve but were now being committed against U.S. forces in pitched battles.[108]

In response to these developments, General Westmoreland informed Washington on November 23 that

the VC/PAVN buildup rate is predicted to be double that of U.S. Phase II forces. Whereas we will add an average of seven maneuver battalions per quarter the enemy will add 15. This development has already reduced the November battalion equivalent ratio from an anticipated 3.2 to 1, to 2.8 to 1, and it will be further reduced to 2.5 to 1 by the end of the year. If the trend continues, the December battalion equivalent ratio, even with the addition of Phase II, will be 2.1 to 1.

As a result, Westmoreland argued, additional U.S. forces would be required over and above the projected Phase II buildup. At a minimum, 48,000 additional troops would be needed (23,000 of which would be South Koreans), although Westmoreland's preferred course of action called for 64,500 additional troops.[109]

Westmoreland's request resulted in a hastily planned change of itinerary for Secretary McNamara. After attending a NATO conference in Paris, McNamara flew to Saigon, where, in the course of a two-day visit, he and Westmoreland worked out a revised troop deployment schedule for 1966, dubbed Phase IIA (add-on). On returning to Washington, McNamara submitted a new version of the November 7 DPM, in which he again characterized the choice facing the Administration as one of either going for a "compromise solution" or sticking with the Administration's "stated objectives" and providing what it takes in men and materiel. But while the options remained the same, the costs of pursuing the latter course were now seen to have risen dramatically. In view of the increased infiltration from the North, McNamara estimated that even with the "contemplated Phase II addition of 28 U.S. battalions, we would only be able to hold our present geographical positions." As a result, he continued, if the decision should be to "provide what it takes," the U.S. would have to increase its Phase II deployment from 28 to 40 battalions. Simultaneously, the bombing of the North in the sensitive northeast quadrant would be expanded to include "'controlled' reconnaissance of lines of communication throughout the area,

108. On these points, see IV Gravel, pp. 303–304; Westmoreland, pp. 156–157; and Halberstam, pp. 743–744. Up to and through the XYZ contact, regular PAVN units, although in South Vietnam, had been held in a reserve role away from the fighting.

109. On these points, see IV Gravel, pp. 306–307. The 64,500-man force would also contain 23,000 South Koreans.

bombing of petroleum storage facilities and power plants, and mining of harbors." Even so, McNamara concluded, "we should be aware that deployments of the kind I have recommended will not guarantee success. U.S. killed-in-action can be expected to reach 1000 a month, and the odds are even that we will be faced in early 1967 with a 'no decision' at an even higher level," perhaps requiring the deployment of as many as 200,000 more Americans.[110]

Despite the gloomy prognosis, McNamara was not yet ready to come out in favor of the "compromise" option. Instead, he recommended that the Administration proceed with both the additional deployments and the intensification of the bombing, although he again suggested that these actions be taken after a bombing pause. This time, McNamara's suggestions for a pause met with a more favorable reaction within the bureaucracy—on December 6, William Bundy and Alex Johnson prepared a new memo for the President, reversing the State Department's position and recommending that the President "approve a pause as soon as possible this month."[111]

But while the "top civilian echelons of the State and Defense Departments" were, by the start of December, "solidly in favor of McNamara's proposal," the President remained undecided for several more weeks.[112] In fact, as late as December 24, no final decision had been made on a pause, either for or against. On that date, U.S. and South Vietnamese forces began a 30-hour truce in the South; included in the truce was a temporary suspension of bombing raids over the North. Although ground operations in the South resumed on December 26, the bombing of the North did not. On December 27, having learned from Mc-George Bundy that no definite time had been set for a resumption of the

110. The November 30 DPM is reprinted as Document no. 262 in IV Gravel, pp. 622–623. On the troop deployments, see also IV Gravel, p. 309.

111. For McNamara's recommendation, see Document no. 262 in IV Gravel, p. 623. For the State Department memo, see IV Gravel, p. 36. It appears that one reason for the more favorable attitude toward a pause was a spate of unfavorable publicity, suggesting that the Administration had been less than vigorous in its pursuit of peace. In a story that broke on November 15, Eric Sevareid revealed enough of the details of the Thant/Stevenson initiative to necessitate a reluctant confirmation by the State Department that the North Vietnamese had agreed to talk and that Washington had turned the offer down. On November 17, a State Department spokesman confirmed reports that Mai Van Bo had approached the French after the May 1965 pause, although he denied that the approach constituted a genuine peace initiative. For the Sevareid article, see "The Final Troubled Hours of Adlai Stevenson," Look, November 30, 1965, p. 84. See also E. W. Kenworthy, "Hanoi Offer in 1964 to Discuss Peace Rejected by U.S.," New York Times, November 16, 1965, p. 1. On the Mai Van Bo story, see Max Frankel, "U.S. Confirms Bid by Paris on Hanoi," New York Times, November 18, 1965, p. 1.

112. Johnson, p. 235.

bombing, the President decided to prolong the two-day-old pause for several more days—at least until January 1.[113]

Once the pause was under way, Administration officials moved quickly in an effort to induce a favorable response from Hanoi. Although the start of the pause was not announced publicly, officials did not hesitate to admit that a pause was under way and that the Administration was using it in an effort to begin talks with the North Vietnamese. More importantly, the President made an all-out effort to impress both foreign and domestic audiences with the Administration's interest in negotiations by dispatching high-level emissaries to all points of the globe.[114] At the same time, Administration spokesmen made an effort to project an image of reasonableness in the hope of convincing the North Vietnamese to accept the Administration's offer of negotiations. In an interview broadcast over Canadian television on December 29, Secretary Rusk indicated that the U.S. could accept all but the third of Hanoi's Four Points. Ten days later, the White House released a new 14-point statement of the American position (see Appendix III). While each of the points had already been stated publicly in one form or another, "this was the first time they had been stripped of smothering rhetoric and assembled in one document."[115]

While the "peace offensive" was gathering momentum, the Administration also made use of more traditional channels to call the pause to the attention of the North Vietnamese and invite a response. The most serious effort in this respect was made in Rangoon, although American diplomats in Paris and Moscow also made contact with DRV representatives in the hope that at least one of the channels would bear fruit.

113. These points are based on Johnson, p. 237; Cooper (1972), p. 351; and on an interview with William Bundy (July 28, 1975). The factor that tipped the balance in the President's mind was probably further unfavorable publicity, this time over a "peace feeler" conveyed by two Italian emissaries, La Pira and Primicerio. On the La Pira initiative, see Kraslow and Loory, pp. 126–135. See also Evans and Novak, who report that embarrassment over leaks to the press was the primary factor in the President's decision to go ahead with a pause (Rowland Evans and Robert Novak, *Lyndon B. Johnson: The Exercise of Power* [New York: Signet, 1966], pp. 580–581).

114. The Administration's willingness to admit that a pause was under way stood in contrast to the May 1965 pause, when officials attempted to camouflage the political basis for the pause by claiming that it was due to "operational reasons"—i.e., to permit reconnaissance and bomb damage assessment. On the May 1965 pause, see III Gravel, p. 368; and Max Frankel, "U.S. Orders Pause in Bombing Raids on North Vietnam," *New York Times*, May 15, 1965, p. 1. For details on the peace offensive, see Cooper (1972), pp. 352–353; and Kraslow and Loory, pp. 137–145.

115. Cooper (1972), p. 353. For Rusk's interview, see DOSB, January 17, 1966, pp. 86–89. Twelve of the 14 Points were mentioned in the Rusk interview; all 14 were released by the White House on January 7, 1966 (reprinted in DOSB, February 14, 1966, p. 225). See also Max Frankel, "Elusive Peace Keys," *New York Times*, January 1, 1966, p. 3.

On December 29, the State Department instructed the American Ambassador in Rangoon, Henry Byroade, to convey the following message to the North Vietnamese Consul General, Vu Huu Binh:

> As you are no doubt aware, there has been no bombing in North Vietnam since December 24, although some reconnaissance flights have continued. No decision has been made regarding a resumption of bombings and unless there is a major provocation we would hope that the present stand-down, which is in its fifth day, could extend beyond New Year. If your government will now reciprocate by making a serious contribution toward peace, it would obviously have a favorable effect on the possibility of further extending the suspension.
>
> I and other members of my Embassy staff stand available at any time to receive any communication you may wish to address to me or us.[116]

In contrast to Foy Kohler's frustrating experience during the May 1965 pause, Byroade had no difficulty getting an appointment with Vu Huu Binh, whom he saw at the DRV Consulate on the afternoon of December 29 (Rangoon time). Binh, for his part, accepted the aide memoire, promising Byroade that he would transmit it to his government. Despite this assurance, however, there was no immediate response to Byroade's message. Although the DRV Foreign Ministry broadcast a statement on January 4 which denounced the pause as a "trick," the statement did not foreclose the possibility of further contacts between the two sides. Significantly, following the line staked out by Pham Van Dong on August 31, 1965 (see Section IV, above), the statement did not demand U.S. "recognition" of the Four Points as a precondition for negotiations, although it insisted that

a political *settlement* of the Vietnam problem can be envisaged only when the U.S. Government has accepted the four-point stand of the Government of the Democratic Republic of Vietnam, has proved this by actual deeds, has stopped unconditionally and for good its air raids and all other acts of war against the Democratic Republic of Vietnam.[117]

116. Pinta Chronology, p. 1b. The same message, along with a French translation of the Four Points given by Gullion to Bo on August 6, 1965, was passed by Sturm to Vo Van Sung in Paris on January 3, 1966, although nothing came of the meeting. On January 24, Foy Kohler met with the DRV Chargé in Moscow; the latter, however, had nothing new to say and told Kohler that any further contacts should be made in Rangoon. On these points, see XYZ Chronology, p. 22; and Pinta Chronology, p. 11.

117. Pinta Chronology, p. 5 (emphasis added). The fact that this statement was not released until the pause was in its second week suggests that there may have been some disagreement in Hanoi on the issue of how to respond. On this point, see Richard Eder, "Red's Line Stirs Hope on Vietnam," *New York Times*, January 3, 1966, p. 4; and the discussion in Chapter 6, below. On the Byroade-Vu Huu Binh meeting, see Pinta Chronology, pp. 1b–2; and Kraslow and Loory, p. 139.

In Washington, meanwhile, Administration officials let it be known that they were watching the ground war in the South for some sign of restraint by the DRV/VC forces there. But while there appears to have been a modest decline in the level of NVA/VC activity while the pause was under way, Administration spokesmen brushed it aside, arguing that such a modest reduction did not in itself merit a continuation of the pause.[118] During this same period, however, the ground war was being pushed ahead full throttle by the U.S. military command in Saigon. On January 9, 1966, U.S. and Australian forces launched the "biggest attack" of the war to that point in an effort to drive the Viet Cong from the Hobo Forest near Saigon. Nine days later, an additional 8,500 U.S. troops began landing at Vungtau and Chulai to bolster the American effort. On January 30, four thousand U.S. Marines undertook the "largest amphibious operation" since Inchon as part of a search and destroy operation in Quangnai Province.[119]

As the pause entered its fourth week with still no word from Hanoi, Administration sources in Washington informed newsmen that if the North Vietnamese did not respond positively within a short period of time, the U.S. would have no choice but to increase its military effort. In addition, on January 20, Byroade was instructed to seek another appointment with Vu Huu Binh to inquire if there had been any reply from Hanoi to the December 29 message. When Byroade arrived at Binh's residence the next day, however, Binh did not wait for him to open the conversation but instead told Byroade that, while he had transmitted the message as requested, "in his own personal opinion the tone and content . . . were such that he considered it an ultimatum." When Byroade asked about a reply, Binh stated that he had not yet received any instructions but that "in the meantime his government had issued public statements which indicated its position." As Byroade was about to leave, Binh announced that he was ready to listen if Byroade had anything further to say. Byroade, however, did not pursue

118. On the decline in enemy activity, see Franz Schurmann, Peter Dale Scott, and Reginald Zelnik, *The Politics of Escalation in Vietnam* (Greenwich, Conn.: Fawcett, 1966), p. 117. See also Max Frankel, "U.S. Scans Combat for Sign from Foe," *New York Times*, January 2, 1966, p. 1; Hedrick Smith, "U.S. Is Reported Offering to Extend Vietnam Lull," *New York Times*, January 6, 1966, p. 1; Richard Eder, "U.S. Is Reported to Set Deadline for Peace Drive," *New York Times*, January 17, 1966, p. 1; and Max Frankel, "Rusk Asserts All But Communists Hail U.S. Peace Bid," *New York Times*, January 22, 1966, p. 1.

119. On these points, see the UPI dispatch, "8000 GI's Open Biggest Attack of War," *New York Times*, January 9, 1966, p. 1; the AP dispatch, "Second Brigade Arrives," *New York Times*, January 18, 1966, p. 3; and the UPI dispatch, "4000 Marines Go Ashore in Search for VC," *New York Times*, January 30, 1966, p. 1.

Binh's comments about "public statements" or willingness to listen but instead turned the conversation in the direction of continued infiltration into the South while the pause was under way.[120]

As January drew to a close with still no word from Hanoi, the President decided that he could wait no longer. The bombing resumed on the morning of January 31 (Saigon time); that very afternoon, however, Vu Huu Binh's interpreter called at the American Embassy, requesting that Byroade meet with Binh that evening.[121]

When Byroade arrived, Binh informed him that the North Vietnamese message was still being typed, so the two men had a "rather pleasant 20 minutes of small talk not touching on Vietnam." The message, however, proved to be something of a letdown. While it took note of the U.S. 14 Points, it accused the U.S. of refusing to recognize the "fundamental national rights of the Vietnamese people, namely peace, independence, sovereignty, unity and territorial integrity . . . as stipulated by the 1954 Geneva Agreements on Vietnam." Furthermore, it rejected the U.S. demand that the Viet Cong lay down their arms and accept amnesty and argued that the American refusal to accept the third of the Four Points amounted to rejection of all four. The message concluded by quoting the paragraph cited above from the Foreign Ministry's statement of January 4, which, as we saw, insisted that a *settlement* could be envisaged only after the U.S. had accepted the Four Points and proved this with deeds. After orally presenting the DRV message, Binh stated that he was "ready to listen to what the Ambassador may wish to expound on the U.S. position."[122]

Vu Huu Binh's performance during this meeting was in many respects the most intriguing aspect of the entire Rangoon contact. On the surface, at least, it would appear that his presentation was designed to signal a readiness to open substantive negotiations with the U.S., since he had explicitly mentioned the major elements of the American position (the 14 Points, amnesty for the Viet Cong, and U.S. willingness to accept all but the third of the Four Points), presented the DRV's rebuttal, and then offered to hear the American reply. To insure that

120. On these points, see Richard Eder, "U.S. Is Reported to Set Deadline for Peace Drive," *New York Times*, January 17, 1966, p. 1; "Issue Studied Day-to-Day," *New York Times*, January 18, 1966, p. 1; and Pinta Chronology, pp. 8–9. Binh obviously *had* received instructions, since it is highly unlikely that he would have characterized the American message an an "ultimatum" on his own authority.

121. On these points, see IV Gravel, pp. 67–68; and Pinta Chronology, p. 13.

122. On these points, see Pinta Chronology, pp. 12–14. A written copy of the DRV message accompanied Vu Huu Binh's oral presentation; in addition, a copy of the Foreign Ministry memorandum of January 4 was given to Byroade at this meeting.

the Americans did not miss the point, the DRV message repeated verbatim the key paragraph from the January 4 statement, which, as we saw, did not insist on U.S. "recognition" of the Four Points as a precondition for negotiations.[123]

Unfortunately, however, whether the DRV message was in fact intended to signal a readiness to begin negotiations with the U.S. and, if so, whether that readiness entailed a willingness to compromise on substantive issues were questions that were left unclear by the subsequent discussion. In his reply, Byroade did not follow up on the substantive aspects of the DRV message but instead turned the conversation to procedural matters, asking whether it would be possible to arrange a meeting of U.S. and DRV representatives to discuss both the DRV's Four Points as well as the U.S.'s 14 Points. In response, Binh appeared to contradict himself by telling Byroade that

there was no possibility for negotiations unless we accepted their Four Points. He said their position was the embodiment of their national rights. If we proved our acceptance of the Geneva Agreements by actual deeds there could be a basis for a political settlement. If we rejected the Geneva Agreements, which embody their rights, there could be no negotiations.

Despite Binh's rejection of Byroade's suggestion for a no-preconditions conference, the meeting ended on a hopeful note, with Binh assuring Byroade he would communicate to Hanoi anything further that Byroade might have to say.[124]

On February 2, Byroade was instructed to probe North Vietnamese willingness to continue the contact despite the resumption of the bombing. Toward that end, he arranged to deliver a short note to the DRV

123. On these points, see Pinta Summary and Analysis, p. 2; and Pinta Chronology, pp. 12–14. Viewed from this perspective, Binh's performance during his January 21 meeting with Byroade—i.e., his allusion to "public statements" indicating the DRV's position and his announcement of readiness to listen to whatever Byroade had to say—becomes much more understandable. That is, Binh was hinting at a readiness to begin substantive negotiations, but the hint was too subtle and went unnoticed. Hence the more elaborate signal transmitted during the January 31 meeting.

124. On these points, see Pinta Chronology, pp. 13–14. While Binh's statement would appear to contradict the "signal" seemingly contained in the written version of the DRV message, there is reason to believe the reversal may not have been intentional. Neither Byroade nor Binh had been privy to the earlier contacts between the two sides; as a result, Binh probably did not realize the significance of the January 4 memorandum and thus inadvertently claimed that there could be no negotiations without prior U.S. acceptance of the Four Points. Alternatively, Byroade's summary of the meeting may not have captured Binh's words precisely; Byroade did mention that there was "some confusion" over "faulty interpretation" (Pinta Chronology, p. 14). In Byroade's defense, it would have been unrealistic to have expected him to detect immediately the differences between Pham Van Dong's April 8, 1965 speech and the DRV message of January 31. He had, after all, been preoccupied with U.S.-Burmese relations and not with Vietnam.

consulate informing Vu Huu Binh that the DRV message was being given "careful study" in Washington and that a "detailed response" could be expected "within a few days time." But before the American reply was completed, U.S. and South Vietnamese leaders met in Honolulu for two days of talks, during which they pledged to continue their "defense against aggression," defined specifically as the "defeat" of the "Viet Cong and those illegally fighting on [South Vietnamese] soil." In a news conference on February 8, Premier Ky and Chief of State Thieu not only branded the Viet Cong as "criminals" and "assassins" but insisted that they would neither recognize nor engage in negotiations with the Viet Cong, much less form a coalition government.[125]

On February 16, Byroade finally received the American reply to the DRV message of January 31, which he delivered to Vu Huu Binh on February 19. Although the message offered nothing new in the way of concessions, it did attempt to rebut the DRV message by asserting that the U.S. did in fact respect the basic rights of the Vietnamese people. In addition, the message probed for soft spots in the DRV position. In a letter broadcast on January 28, Ho Chi Minh had described the program of the NLF as seeking to "achieve independence, democracy, peace and neutrality in South Vietnam and to advance toward peaceful reunification." "If this is all that is intended when it is stated that the affairs of the South Vietnamese be settled 'in accordance with the program of the NLF,'" the U.S. message noted, then the third of Hanoi's Four Points "would not be an obstacle to negotiations." But if the DRV expected that the NLF "arbitrarily be accorded integral participation in a coalition government or be accepted as the 'sole genuine representative of the entire South Vietnamese people' prior to, and without regard to, an election," such an outcome could not be accepted by the United States. The question of the future political structure in the South, the message continued, should be determined by the South Vietnamese themselves through "truly free elections," the results of which the U.S. was "categorically prepared to accept."[126]

By February 19, however, whatever interest the North Vietnamese might have had in substantive negotiations had disappeared. Although

125. For Byroade's instructions and his message to Vu Huu Binh, see Pinta Chronology, pp. 21, 25. For the Honolulu Declaration, see DOSB, February 28, 1966, pp. 305–307; see also Charles Mohr, "Ky Rejects Talks With Insurgents," New York Times, February 9, 1966, pp. 1, 14.

126. Ho's letter was reprinted in the New York Times, January 29, 1966, p. 2. The letter conformed to the formula presented in the Foreign Ministry memorandum of January 4, stating that "if the United States Government really wants a peaceful settlement, it must accept the Four Point stand of the DRV government and prove this by actual deeds." For the U.S. message, see Pinta Chronology, pp. 26–27.

Vu Huu Binh agreed to transmit the American message to Hanoi, he noted that there had been many developments since his last meeting with Byroade, including the resumption of the bombing of the North and the intensification of the war in the South. As a result, Binh stated, "I consider it inappropriate to continue the contacts made at your request between you and myself."[127] With that, the Rangoon contact came to an abrupt end. Not for another eleven months would an American official engage in face-to-face talks with a representative of the DRV.

VI. The Ronning Missions to Hanoi
(February-June 1966)

Despite the sudden and unexpected demise of the Rangoon contact, it soon became clear that Vu Huu Binh's brush-off of Byroade was by no means the end of the matter. While the North Vietnamese were unwilling to resume direct contacts with American officials, they continued to express an interest in negotiations, although their statements to this effect remained cloaked in a veil of ambiguity that made it virtually impossible to determine what price, if any, they were willing to pay for a settlement.

The channel through which these equivocal signals were passed was a Canadian one, involving Chester Ronning, a retired Sinologist and former Canadian High Commissioner in New Delhi. On January 27, 1966, while the Rangoon contact was still under way, Ronning met with William Bundy in Washington to discuss his forthcoming mission as Canada's "special representative" to Saigon and Hanoi, who would offer Canada's "good offices" for the purpose of getting peace talks started. Although Bundy had no choice but to cooperate, privately American officials expressed dismay over Ronning's highly critical attitudes concerning U.S. policy and over the possibility that his mission was intended to sound out the prospects for Chinese admission to the UN.[128]

127. On these points, see Pinta Chronology, pp. 28–30. Although Binh cited military factors during his meeting with Byroade, an aide memoire recounting his remarks that was delivered two days later also mentioned the Honolulu Conference as one of the reasons for breaking off the contact. As we shall see in Chapter 6, it was probably the rejection of a coalition government at Honolulu, and not the resumption of the bombing, that was the real reason for the breakdown of the contact.

128. On these points, see Chester Ronning, A Memoir of China in Revolution (New York: Pantheon, 1974), pp. 255–256; and Ronning Chronology, pp. 1–8. Ronning would be carrying the Canadian reply to Ho's letter, and it was hoped that this would enable him to obtain a visa to Hanoi. In addition, Ronning hoped to take advantage of a long-standing invitation from Chinese Foreign Minister Chen Yi to stop in Peking.

Although Ronning's mission was temporarily delayed by problems of visas and travel schedules, by March 3 he was in Saigon and on March 7 he reached Hanoi, where he spent the next few days climbing the hierarchy of North Vietnamese officialdom. In the course of these talks, the North Vietnamese not only expressed complete confidence in their ultimate victory but also remained totally unwilling to budge from the Four Points as the basis for a settlement.[129] Finally, however, Ronning was granted an interview with Pham Van Dong, at which time the ambiguity in the DRV position reappeared. For the first part of the interview, the Premier revealed the same obdurate attitudes held by his subordinates; but then, toward the end of the meeting, he interjected a new element into the discussion. In response to a suggestion by Ronning that some arrangement should be found to allow direct contacts between the U.S. and the DRV, Pham Van Dong replied: "All this depends on one thing only—that our Canadian friends should persuade their American friends to adopt the Four Points and the Foreign Ministry statement of January 4." Ronning, however, countered by saying that Canada had no desire to mediate—could not the Premier make a specific proposal that could be conveyed to the U.S.? At that point, according to Ronning's account:

Pham Van Dong repeated that the four principles [sic] were essential, but that the January 4 statement had opened the way for a new step. He insisted that "the U.S. unconditionally stop all air raids against North Vietnam."

I immediately intervened to obtain clarification on this point. Was he implying that the U.S. need only stop the bombing for informal talks to begin?

He replied: "I shall answer you. If the United States Government declares that it will stop all military action and attacks against the Democratic Republic for good, and unconditionally, we will talk."

Under questioning, Pham Van Dong continued to manifest a conciliatory attitude (in contrast to his earlier intransigence), telling Ronning that he was prepared to "negotiate" on all of the Four Points and hinting that he expected an American response—"For our part," the Premier noted, "we will look into the attitude of the U.S.A. and with all understanding."[130]

Pham Van Dong's performance during this meeting, much like Vu Huu Binh's performance on January 31, raises a number of intriguing questions. As we saw in the preceding section, the Foreign Ministry

129. On these points, see Ronning Chronology, pp. 9–11; and Ronning, pp. 256–259. Ronning never did receive a visa for Peking.

130. These points are based on Ronning, pp. 260–265; Ronning Chronology, pp. 13–15; and Interview Data.

memorandum of January 4 had apparently been intended to signal DRV readiness for negotiations without prior American "recognition" of the Four Points. Where the DRV position was ambiguous, though, was on the question of whether this apparent readiness to negotiate also signified a willingness to compromise on substantive issues—an ambiguity that Byroade had failed to probe. In his conversation with Ronning, Pham Van Dong referred to the January 4 statement at least three times, even going so far as to state that: "The Americans have paid no heed to our January 4 statement. They have ignored Ho Chi Minh's letter. We are prepared [to negotiate] but, because of this attitude, what can we do?"[131] Still, the DRV position remained ambiguous. The officials with whom Ronning spoke, including Pham Van Dong himself, all insisted that the DRV would win and that the U.S. would eventually have to "accept" the Four Points as part of a settlement. In addition, the Premier had drawn a distinction between "talks" and "negotiations"—a bombing halt would bring only informal "talks" (apparently, this was intended to refer to a resumption of Rangoon-style contacts); "negotiations" would come later. Even here, though, there was some uncertainty over what the Premier was offering, since, as we saw earlier, the North Vietnamese had apparently been ready to discuss substantive issues during the "talks" between Byroade and Vu Huu Binh.

The DRV position, in short, was clouded in ambiguity—an ambiguity that was so well contrived that it is difficult to believe that it might have been accidental.[132] Once again, though, the subtleties of the DRV position went unappreciated in Washington. After stopping off in Ottawa to discuss his mission with Prime Minister Pearson and Secretary of State for External Affairs Paul Martin, Ronning proceeded to Washington, where he met with William Bundy on March 20. The American reaction to Ronning's report was twofold. On the one hand, Bundy speculated that the North Vietnamese were engaged in what seemed to be a clever ploy—since they had in the past demanded that the U.S. "accept" the Four Points and prove this by "actual deeds" (a bombing halt), Bundy suggested that acceptance of Pham Van Dong's offer would be viewed as tacit American acceptance of the Four Points (although, as we have seen, it appears that the North Vietnamese were trying to

131. Ronning, p. 263; see also Ronning Chronology, pp. 13–15. As we saw in note 126, above, Ho's letter adhered to the formula linking the Four Points to a settlement that was presented in the January 4 memorandum. Ronning himself mentioned the January 4 memo and Ho's letter first, but it was Pham Van Dong who, later in the conversation, steered the discussion back to the January 4 memo (see Ronning, p. 264).

132. On the importance of ambiguity in offers to negotiate, see Robert Jervis, *The Logic of Images in International Relations* (Princeton, N.J.: Princeton University Press, 1970), pp. 113–138.

signal something quite different—specifically, a willingness to open discussions without prior U.S. acceptance of the Four Points). On the other hand, even if Pham Van Dong's references to the January 4 memorandum had been correctly understood, there was still no willingness to make the concession he demanded. Instead, the consensus in Washington was that "we could hardly respond positively to this; we could at best only seek further information."[133]

The reason for Washington's unwillingness to make any concessions at this point is not difficult to fathom. At the same time that Ronning was in Hanoi, the South Vietnamese were facing their gravest political crisis since the Diem coup. On March 10, the head of the ruling military junta, Marshall Ky, persuaded his colleagues to demand the resignation of the I Corps Commander, General Nguyen Chanh Thi. Thi's removal, however, sparked a series of Buddhist-led, anti-Government demonstrations that began on March 12 in DaNang and Hue and then spread through all the central Vietnamese coastal cities, as well as to Saigon itself. "What most alarmed the resident American officials," as Fitzgerald notes,

was that neither the police nor the army moved against the demonstrators except in Nha Trang. In DaNang, the headquarters of the First Corps, thousands of soldiers and civil servants marched with the dock workers shouting anti-government and occasionally anti-American slogans. Most of the regular army operations stopped and the port of DaNang closed down. The entire government appeared to be falling—to be replaced by no one.[134]

With South Vietnam teetering on the brink of anarchy, the Ronning initiative, not surprisingly, was temporarily sidetracked while American officials concentrated on the crisis in Saigon. Although Bundy had told Ronning on March 20 that Pham Van Dong's remarks merited careful consideration, it soon became clear that the Americans were in no hurry to draft a reply. The delay, however, proved to be more than the Canadians could take. On April 22, Martin phoned Bundy to ask why there had been no response to the North Vietnamese message. Apparently, the Canadians were not the only ones growing impatient—Martin mentioned that they had had some word from "Asia" to the effect that they, too, were concerned about the time lapse since Ronning's visit. By

133. On the Bundy-Ronning meeting, see Ronning Chronology, pp. 11–15; on the Washington consensus, see Harold Jacobsen's March 31 memo to Bundy in Ronning Chronology, p. 15. There is no evidence of any disagreement with Jacobsen's conclusion.

134. Frances Fitzgerald, *Fire in the Lake* (New York: Vintage, 1972), p. 370. For details on the Buddhist "Struggle Movement," see Fitzgerald, pp. 368–388; II Gravel, pp. 369–378; IV Gravel, pp. 82–92; and Westmoreland, pp. 168–176.

this time, though, things were settling down somewhat in South Vietnam, and Bundy was able to assure Martin that a reply would soon be forthcoming.[135]

When it came, however, on April 26, the formal American response proved to be something of a disappointment, at least from the Canadian point of view. The text of the oral message that was to be carried by Ronning stated bluntly that the United States "could not accept the apparent suggestion that the U.S. Government must agree to a permanent cessation of the bombing of North Vietnam as a unilateral and non-reciprocated pre-condition to the holding of talks." Instead, the message reiterated the standing American offer of "discussions or negotiations without any preconditions whatever," as well as indicating a readiness to consider a "reciprocal reduction in hostilities in Vietnam, which could include the question of the bombing of North Vietnam."[136]

Perhaps the most interesting feature of the American reply, though, came in a Memorandum to the Government of Canada which accompanied the oral message to be carried by Ronning. Noting that a direct channel had been opened recently in Rangoon and that the North Vietnamese had chosen to break off the contact, the Memorandum argued that

Against this background, and in light of repeated North Vietnamese statements insisting upon the acceptance of the so-called "Four Points" before any discussions or negotiations—and insisting that the U.S. demonstrate such acceptance by "concrete acts" such as the unequivocal and permanent cessation of bombing of the North—the U.S. Government is unable to evaluate the message conveyed to Mr. Ronning as indicating any real "give" in Hanoi's position. We understand that Prime Minister Pham Van Dong reiterated the DRV's "four points," but at the close of the conversation suggested or hinted that Hanoi might be prepared to enter into discussions if the U.S. would declare a permanent cessation of bombing attacks on the North. It seems most probable that this was still intended to be linked with acceptance of the "four points," although a contrary interpretation is conceivable. In any event, it should of course be clear that the U.S.G. could not accept a unilateral cessation of this form of military activity without some reciprocal action of the North Vietnamese side. . . .[137]

135. On Bundy's March 20 comment to Ronning, see Ronning Chronology, p. 15. On the Martin-Bundy phone call, see Ronning Chronology, p. 16. "Asia" almost certainly referred to the North Vietnamese, who were probably making inquiries through the Canadian ICC mission in Hanoi. In South Vietnam, the military junta had given in to Buddhist demands by promising elections for a constituent assembly in three to five months; in response, the Buddhists called off further demonstrations. On these points, see II Gravel, p. 373; and Fitzgerald, p. 377.

136. Ronning Chronology, p. 18.

137. Ibid., p. 17.

What this paragraph suggests is that the Administration remained un-aware of the significance of the DRV's January 4 memorandum and the repeated references to it by both Vu Huu Binh and Pham Van Dong. Although, as we saw earlier, the North Vietnamese apparently were no longer demanding acceptance of the Four Points as a precondition for discussions with the U.S., the Administration chose to interpret Pham Van Dong's remarks not in the context of the January 4 memo but rather in terms of a ploy to mousetrap the U.S. into tacit acceptance of the Four Points.

And yet, as the final sentence in the paragraph cited above should indicate, even if the significance of the January 4 memo and Pham Van Dong's remarks had been correctly understood, it remains highly unlikely that Washington would have been prepared to respond any differently than it did. At the same time that the Canadians were plan-ning and executing the Ronning initiative, the Administration was going through a prolonged period of soul-searching concerning the air war over the North, much as it had during the yearlong debate that pre-ceded the start of ROLLING THUNDER. The immediate cause of this new debate was the 37-day bombing pause, as Administration officials grappled with the question of when and how the bombing should be resumed. On a deeper level, though, the renewed debate was largely the product of an awareness that the bombing had not "worked," in the sense of inducing the North Vietnamese to accept a settlement on terms favorable to the United States. As a result, the debate over the mechanics of resuming the bombing was simultaneously a debate over the whole philosophy of the air war and especially over the goals to be pursued by the bombing. In many respects, the bombing controversy of early 1966 bore a striking resemblance to that of 1964, both with respect to the participants involved and the issues addressed.[138]

Perhaps the most interesting feature of the renewed debate, however, was the way in which it highlighted the inconsistencies that had plagued the air war ever since its inception. As we saw earlier, the 1964

138. On the one hand, the military were still arguing that the air war should be reoriented in the direction of physically destroying DRV capabilities to carry on the war in the South. See, for example, the proposals by Admiral Sharp on January 12 and by the JCS on January 18, in IV Gravel, pp. 41–42, 59–62, 67. On the other hand, on January 25, 1966, George Ball sent the Presi-dent a memo strongly implying that the bombing should not be resumed, on the grounds that it was likely to lead to war with China and possibly the Soviet Union (see IV Gravel, pp. 51–53). Caught in the middle, as they had been in the past, were William Bundy and John McNaughton, both of whom felt that the bombing should be resumed but that, contrary to the arguments of the JCS, the resumption should take place at a level equal to or below the pre-pause level, with any escalation deferred until some time after the resumption. For their views, see IV Gravel, pp. 37–38, 67–68.

debate had resulted in general acceptance, at least among civilian officials, of a rationale emphasizing the impact of a program of gradually
rising pressures on the *will* of the DRV leadership to continue their
support for the war in the South (although the military, as we saw, had
persistently opposed such an approach, arguing instead for an all-out
effort aimed at destroying DRV *capabilities*). But while a campaign
aimed at eroding DRV will would, at the very least, require actions
designed to convey a credible threat of attack on highly valued targets
such as industrial facilities (and quite possibly at least some "demonstra-
tion" strikes), the air war, as we saw, was initially restricted to military
installations related to the infiltration of men and supplies into South
Vietnam—an approach that was chosen largely because it was felt to be
easier to justify both at home and abroad but which very likely conveyed confusing "signals" to Hanoi (see Section II, above). This
initial inconsistency was then compounded by decisions taken later in
the summer of 1965. Although it had been decided at the Honolulu
Conference in April 1965 that the war could not be won until DRV/
VC forces had been denied victory in the South—a judgment that
would seem to require an all-out effort against the infiltration routes in
order to reduce as much as possible DRV/VC military strength in the
South—it was in the aftermath of that conference that the bombing
began to move northward in the direction of Hanoi and Haiphong and
that sporadic attacks were launched against "lucrative" targets—
outcomes that would seem to be more compatible with a program aimed
at eroding DRV will. But while there was considerable confusion over
the goal(s) that the Administration was pursuing through the bombing,[139] there was no denying the fact that the air war was not having the
desired effect on either DRV will or on its ability to infiltrate men and
supplies into South Vietnam. Not only were the North Vietnamese not
buckling under the weight of the bombing, but the rate of infiltration
had climbed steadily throughout 1965, reaching approximately 4,500
men per month by early 1966.[140]

139. Indeed, it was left to one of the foremost opponents of the air war—George Ball—to provide
perhaps the most accurate appraisal of the motives underlying the bombing: "Admittedly, we have
never had a generally agreed rationale for bombing North Vietnam. But the inarticulate major
premise has always been that bombing will somehow, some day, and in some manner, create
pressure on Hanoi to stop the war. This is accepted as an article of faith, not only by the military
who have planning and operational responsibilities but also by most civilian advocates of bombing
in the Administration." (Memorandum to the President, January 25, 1966, quoted in IV Gravel, p.
51.)

140. On the conduct of the air war during 1965, see IV Gravel, pp. 29, 56–58; and Baggs, pp.
60–65, 119–122. On the rate of infiltration, see the AP dispatch, "U.S. Aide Says North Vietnam
Steps Up Infiltration Into South," *New York Times*, April 4, 1966, p. 2; and Cooper (1972), p. 365.

By January 1966, though, the flaws inherent in the Administration's handling of the air war were painfully apparent, at least to John McNaughton. "There is a conflict," he wrote,

> between the objective of "persuading Hanoi," which would dictate a program of painful surgical strikes separated by fairly long gaps, and the objective of interdiction, which would benefit from continuous heavy bombings. No program can be designed which optimizes the chances of achieving both objectives at the same time.

Furthermore, since the program "probably cannot be expected directly or indirectly to *persuade* Hanoi to come to the table or to settle either (1) while Le Duan and other militants are in ascendance in the politburo or (2) while the North thinks it can win in the South," McNaughton proposed a three-point "compromise program" that emphasized sparing non-interdiction targets, interdicting DRV lines of communication as much as possible, and searching for politically cheaper methods (such as an anti-infiltration barrier) that would end North Vietnamese support for the insurgency.[141]

Despite McNaughton's efforts, it is doubtful whether these considerations had much impact on his superiors. On January 24, less than a week after McNaughton's effort to devise a "compromise" program, Secretary McNamara gave the President the final draft of the November 1965 DPM, which reflected decisions made by the President in the aftermath of the Secretary's late-November trip to Vietnam. Once again, McNamara perceived only two available options: going for a "compromise," or sticking with our "stated objectives" and providing what it takes in men and materiel. Once again, the Secretary opted for the latter course. In the South, U.S. maneuver battalions would rise from 34 to 74; meanwhile, attack sorties against the North would rise

from a level of roughly 3000 per month—the rate for the last half of 1965—to a level of at least 4000 per month to be reached gradually and then maintained throughout 1966. The sortie rate against targets in Laos, which had risen from 511 per month in June 1965 to 3,047 in December, would rise to a steady 4500 and those against targets in South Vietnam, having risen from 7,234 in June to 13,114 in December, would drop back to 12,000 in June 1966, but then climb to 15,000 in December.[142]

The failure of the bombing to affect DRV will was explicitly conceded by the Administration in April 1966; see Max Frankel, "U.S. Alters Bombing Plan," *New York Times*, April 21, 1966, p. 2.

141. McNaughton's memo is reproduced in IV Gravel, pp. 42–46 (emphasis in original).

142. See IV Gravel, p. 49. The number of South Korean and Australian battalions would rise from nine to twenty-one and from one to two, respectively.

In essence, this was a prescription for "more of the same," including more of the same inconsistencies that had characterized the American effort since the start of the buildup in 1965.

In the weeks that followed, the Administration pursued a path disturbingly similar to that taken in 1965. The JCS continued to advocate rapid escalation, while civilian officials continued to dole out authority to escalate on an incremental basis. As described by the Pentagon analyst:

[the] routine continued, with CINCPAC recommending programs 13 days prior to the start of a month and the JCS acting on these recommendations two days later. In consequence, McNamara received from the Chiefs on 19 February the same advice that had been given during the pause. He and the President responded much as before, though now permitting armed reconnaissance within the geographical limits fixed just before the pause and authorizing a significant increase—to above 5000—in numbers of sorties.[143]

By March 1966, however, the pendulum began to swing in the direction of more rapid escalation, especially with respect to a JCS proposal to attack the North's POL system. Although a special intelligence estimate produced in February 1966 had discounted the impact of POL strikes on DRV capabilities, in March the CIA produced an "apparently very influential report" that took the "bold step, for an intelligence document, of explicitly recommending a preferred bombing program of greater intensity, redirected largely against 'the will of the regime as a target system.'"[144] The effect of this report was to strengthen greatly JCS proposals for escalation; in particular, "the report gave a substantial boost to the proposal to hit the POL targets." With the CIA report in hand, Secretary McNamara began to reconsider his earlier opposition to the POL strikes. Finally, in late March, McNamara reversed his position and, in an April memorandum for the President, endorsed most of the JCS recommendations:

McNamara proposed authorizing attacks on seven of nine POL storage facilities in the Hanoi-Haiphong area. . . . In addition, McNamara recommended attacks on the Haiphong cement plant and on roads, bridges, and railroads connecting Haiphong and Hanoi and leading from the two cities to the Chinese border, and asked that the military commanders be permitted to run up to 900 sorties into the northeast quadrant, at their discretion.[145]

143. IV Gravel, p. 75. For the JCS proposals, see IV Gravel, pp. 60–61, 70–71.
144. IV Gravel, p. 71. For a summary of the March CIA report, see IV Gravel, pp. 71–74. On the February SNIE, see IV Gravel, pp. 68–70.
145. On these points, see IV Gravel, pp. 74–77.

McNamara's recommendations were discussed at the White House on March 28; that meeting, however, resulted in continued incremental escalation. With the South Vietnamese political crisis raging at full force, the President chose, as he always had in the past, to defer a decision on major escalatory actions until the situation had stabilized somewhat in South Vietnam. "As for McNamara's proposals," the Pentagon analyst noted,

the President approved only giving commanders discretion to launch 900 sorties into the northeast quadrant during April and permission to strike roads, railroads, and bridges outside or just on the fringe of the prohibited circles around Hanoi and Haiphong. He did not consent to measures involving more visible escalation of the air war.

At the same time, though, CINCPAC was ordered to be prepared to execute attacks during April on the targets on which the President had deferred a decision.[146]

Interestingly enough, these decisions came just eight days after Ronning reported to Bundy on his conversation with Pham Van Dong. At this point, then, the significance of the early-1966 bombing debate for the Ronning initiative should be clear. Even if the Administration had grasped the significance of Pham Van Dong's message, and even if there had been no South Vietnamese political crisis, it still seems highly improbable that the North Vietnamese offer of "talks" in exchange for a bombing halt would have been accepted. The reason is simply that the Administration was at the time engaged in the process of hammering out a limited and fragile consensus on the issue of escalating the air war. In view of the difficulty involved in fashioning that consensus, it seems highly unlikely that the Administration would under any circumstances have executed an abrupt about-face and accepted the North Vietnamese offer. Furthermore, acceptance would have jeopardized the one aspect of the air war on which virtually all Administration officials could agree—i.e., that the bombing constituted an American "blue chip" that should be traded for some reciprocal reduction in North Vietnamese military activity. Since acceptance of Pham Van Dong's proposal would have jeopardized not only the tenuous consensus then emerging on the POL strikes but also the more fundamental consensus on negotiating strategy, it should not be surprising that the Administration regarded that offer as completely out of the question.[147]

146. See IV Gravel, p. 79.
147. On the difficulty in fashioning the consensus, see IV Gravel, pp. 58–81. On the belief in the bombing as a "blue chip," see the memos on negotiating strategy produced in April 1966 by Maxwell Taylor and by William Bundy, discussed in IV Gravel, pp. 95-97.

Perhaps the most unfortunate aspect of this period, though, was the way in which the Administration's preoccupation with the POL question joined with the subtleties of DRV diplomacy to blur certain aspects of the relationship between Washington and Hanoi. In this respect, one cannot help feeling that Pham Van Dong's "offer" of "talks" in exchange for a bombing cessation was made more for the benefit of the Canadians than for officials in Washington. If the DRV had been seriously concerned with obtaining a bombing cessation in exchange for talks, it could have had it during the 37-day pause simply by responding somewhat more vigorously to the American initiative in Rangoon while allowing word of the contact to leak out (which would, as most Administration officials conceded in pre-pause memoranda, have made it extremely difficult for the U.S. to resume bombing).[148] If anything, the DRV's handling of both the Rangoon contact and the earlier contact in Paris suggests that it was quite willing to "talk" while the bombing continued (indeed, as William Bundy noted at the time, the formal DRV response in Rangoon was probably deliberately timed to come *after* the bombing resumed, thus demonstrating a lack of fear about the possibility that it would be resumed).[149] What this meant, though, was that the Administration's options were *not* confined solely to accepting or rejecting the "offer" of "talks" for a bombing cessation. Instead, the Administration might well have found it advisable to attempt to probe the substantive aspects of the DRV position (as opposed to procedural issues such as when and how to "talk") by means of quiet diplomacy along the lines of the Rangoon contact.[150]

Unfortunately, though, not all of this was clear at the time, so that in the aftermath of the March 28 decisions, three main developments took place. First, military officials continued to press the President for authority to attack the DRV POL system. The President, however, continued to withhold authorization for the attacks, a reluctance that probably stemmed from the second development taking place at the time—namely, a renewal of the South Vietnamese political crisis. Although the crisis had seemingly been defused by a mid-April promise by the ruling military junta to hold elections within three to five months, new disturbances broke out in early May in response to some indiscreet comments by Marshall Ky to the effect that the junta had promised elections for a constituent assembly, not a legislature, and that he intended

148. On this point, see IV Gravel, pp. 32–36. This line of argument was suggested by William Bundy in a personal communication, September 26, 1977.

149. For Bundy's memo on this point, see Pinta Chronology, p. 22.

150. The issues that would have had to be addressed during such a probe will be discussed in more detail in Chapter 6, below.

to stay in power for at least another year. On May 14, the Ky Government airlifted troops to DaNang and then to Hue in an attempt to regain control of those cities by force. With dissident ARVN troops dropping shells on the American base at DaNang (where Ky's troops were stationed), and with U.S. General Walt threatening to use U.S. jets to shoot down Ky's planes if they attacked the rebels, the President once again decided to hold off on the POL attacks until the dust had cleared in South Vietnam.[151]

By May 22, the Ky Government had completed the capture of DaNang, and with that the backbone of the Buddhist revolt was broken. There would still be further unpleasantness ahead, such as the burning of the American consulate in Hue on May 31, but in general the fall of DaNang suggested that Ky would ultimately be successful in reasserting his authority. Apparently, this modicum of stability was sufficient for the President. On May 31, he authorized attacks on six minor POL storage areas; in addition, he informed British Prime Minister Wilson of his decision to authorize attacks on the main storage areas near Hanoi and Haiphong. While the strikes were originally to have been carried out on June 10, they were again deferred, this time on account of the third main development taking place during this period. On June 3, the Canadian Government learned that Ronning would be allowed to fly to Hanoi on the ICC flight scheduled for June 14. With this information in hand, Secretary Rusk (who was then in Europe) intervened, cabling a recommendation to the President on June 7 and to McNamara on June 8 that the strikes be deferred until after Ronning had been able to learn whether "there is any change in the thus far harsh and unyielding attitude of Hanoi."[152]

Although Rusk's intervention was sufficient to have the strikes deferred, the Administration was clearly growing impatient, as evidenced by the attempt to get a report from Ronning at the earliest possible moment (the American Embassy in Vientiane, Laos, was to contact him during his stopover there on the return flight from Hanoi). This time, however, the Canadians refused to cooperate: Ronning was ordered to speak to no one until he could report personally to Martin in Ottawa. Martin, moreover, decided that the Americans would have to come to Ottawa to hear Ronning's report.[153]

With no choice but to comply, Bundy flew to Ottawa, where, on June

151. On these points, see II Gravel, pp. 374–375; and Fitzgerald, pp. 383–384.
152. The quoted excerpt is from Rusk's June 7 cable, IV Gravel, p. 104. For the June 8 cable, see Ronning Chronology, p. 24; and IV Gravel, p. 104. On the POL strikes, see IV Gravel, pp. 102–103. On Ronning's second visit to Hanoi, see Ronning Chronology, p. 23.
153. On these points, see Ronning Chronology, pp. 26–28.

21, he met with Ronning and Martin. While the North Vietnamese had rejected the American offer of negotiations without preconditions and/or a bombing halt in exchange for some reduction in the level of their own military activity, there were nonetheless elements of interest in Ronning's report. For one thing, Ronning had clarified with both Nguyen Co Thach (the Deputy Foreign Minister) and Nguyen Duy Trinh (the Foreign Minister) that acceptance of the Four Points was not a precondition for U.S.-DRV "talks." In addition, despite professing disappointment over the American reply, DRV officials on at least two occasions told Ronning that they wished to keep the Canadian channel open.[154]

Despite the clarification on the issue of the Four Points, the Administration interpreted Ronning's report as being completely negative, and, although Bundy promised that the report would be given careful consideration, it appears that the Administration was not especially disappointed. Plans for the POL strikes had been in the works ever since April, and, with the military champing at the bit, senior officials were apparently relieved that the way was now clear to carry out the attacks. On June 22, the day after the Ottawa meeting, the "execute" message was released, although, once again, the Administration's plans did not work out quite as expected. The strikes were twice scheduled, only to be postponed on account of bad weather; then, on June 24, word that the strikes were planned leaked out to the press, forcing another cancellation. It was not until June 29, after several more delays due to bad weather, that the POL strikes were actually carried out. Although the Administration was at first euphoric in its claims regarding the results of the strikes, those claims, as we shall see, proved to be greatly exaggerated.[155]

VII. Searching for an Exit (July-November 1966)

In many respects the weeks following the POL strikes on June 29 constituted a turning point in the evolution of American strategy for the war. The strikes themselves kicked off a flurry of activity that had the effect of greatly enlarging the American role in the war. On July 2, for example, in response to a Presidential directive to accelerate the flow of troops to General Westmoreland, Secretary McNamara announced

154. On these points, see Ronning Chronology, pp. 29–38, especially pp. 30–33.
155. For Washington's reaction to the POL strikes, see IV Gravel, pp. 106–107; and Cooper (1972), p. 370.

that the latest revision of the troop deployment schedule had been approved as "Program #3"—a decision that would bring authorized American troop strength in South Vietnam to 391,000 at the end of 1966 and 431,000 by June 1967. On July 8, McNamara informed Admiral Sharp (CINCPAC) that "the President wished that first priority in the air war be given to the complete 'strangulation' of North Vietnam's POL system, and he [Admiral Sharp] must not feel there were any sortie limitations for this purpose." The very next day, a new ROLLING THUNDER program (#51) went into effect; as part of the "strangulation" campaign, the ceiling for attack sorties on North Vietnam and Laos was raised from 8,100 to 10,100 per month.[156]

And yet, within two months, the sense of optimism that had fueled the July escalation would be replaced by a growing sense of frustration over the inability of the bombing to accomplish American objectives in the war. The POL strikes, as the Pentagon analyst notes, proved to be "the last major escalation of the air war recommended by Secretary McNamara." By October 1966, McNamara would be advocating stabilization and eventual reduction in the number of attack sorties over North Vietnam. Similarly, attitudes on the question of ground troops were also undergoing an important transformation in the face of the insatiable appetite of the war in the South. "By the fall of 1966, when Program #4 was under consideration," wrote the Pentagon analyst, "the President would no longer be instructing McNamara to honor all of General Westmoreland's troop requests as fully and rapidly as possible."[157]

The basis for this reversal of attitudes is not difficult to fathom. In the aftermath of the POL strikes, the intelligence community attempted to keep very close tabs on the progress of the "strangulation" campaign. As part of this effort, by the end of July 1966, DIA was reporting that 70 percent of North Vietnam's large bulk storage capacity had been destroyed, along with 7 percent of the capacity of known dispersed sites. And yet:

What became clearer and clearer as the summer wore on was that while we had destroyed a major portion of North Vietnam's storage capacity, she retained enough dispersed capacity, supplemented by continuing imports . . . to meet her ongoing requirements. The greater invulnerability of dispersed POL meant an ever-mounting U.S. cost in munitions, fuel, aircraft losses, and men. By August we were reaching the point at which these costs were prohibitive.

156. On these points, see IV Gravel, pp. 108–109, 320–324.
157. IV Gravel, pp. 107–108.

As a result, on September 4, the "strangulation" campaign was abandoned and the primary emphasis of the air war shifted back to the "attrition of men, supplies, equipment, and . . . POL."[158]

The failure of the POL campaign had a powerful impact on Secretary McNamara, who "made no effort to conceal his dissatisfaction and disappointment at the failure of the POL attacks." The impact, moreover, was magnified because the failure of the POL campaign coincided with what was known as the "JASON Summer Study"—an analysis of the American war effort by a group of distinguished scientists working through the Institute for Defense Analyses' JASON Division. The reports submitted by the group added up to a devastating critique of the air war that concluded in no uncertain terms that neither the will nor the capability of the North Vietnamese to continue had been significantly affected by the bombing.[159]

The combined effect of these two developments was sufficient to convert McNamara from a proponent of escalation to a forceful advocate of de-escalation leading to a negotiated settlement. This change of heart, though, put him in direct conflict with his ostensible subordinates, the professional military, who were at the time renewing their requests for rapid escalation. On September 13, for example, Admiral Sharp called for a "relentless application of force . . . designed progressively to curtail North Vietnam's warmaking capacity." The JCS, meanwhile, were suggesting a course of action that would have added 688,500 reservists to the armed forces in order to meet U.S. needs both in Vietnam and worldwide.[160]

By now, however, about the only thing that was being progressively curtailed was McNamara's tolerance for suggestions such as the ones the military were bombarding him with. Dissatisfied with Administration policies, he decided to go to Vietnam for a firsthand look at the situation. In the course of three days in Vietnam, all of his doubts were apparently confirmed. On returning to Washington, he presented the President with a starkly pessimistic report of his findings and recommendations. Although McNamara was able to inform the President that "we have by and large blunted the communist military initiative," he was nonetheless concerned for the simple reason that he could see

no reasonable way to bring the war to an end soon. . . . There is no sign of an impending break in enemy morale and it appears that he can more than

---

158. On these points, see IV Gravel, pp. 109–110. For an analysis of the reasons underlying the failure of the POL campaign, see IV Gravel, pp. 110–112.

159. On these points, see IV Gravel, pp. 112–113.

160. On these points, see IV Gravel, pp. 123–124, 346–347.

replace his losses by infiltration from North Vietnam and recruitment in South Vietnam. . . . Pacification has if anything gone backward. . . . Nor has the ROLLING THUNDER program of bombing the North either significantly affected infiltration or cracked the morale of Hanoi.[161]

The most significant part of McNamara's report, however, dealt with the change in strategy that he recommended for the U.S. in Vietnam. Arguing that the North Vietnamese had adjusted to the blunting of their victory drive and that they had shifted to a strategy of "keeping us busy and waiting us out," McNamara argued that we must "improve our position by getting ourselves into a military posture that we credibly would maintain indefinitely—a posture that makes trying to 'wait us out' less attractive." Toward that end, he proposed a five-point program that would stabilize American ground forces in Vietnam at 470,000 men; involve construction of an anti-infiltration barrier along the 17th Parallel; stabilize the air war over the North; pursue a vigorous pacification effort in the South; and, most importantly, seek a negotiated settlement. Although McNamara was not optimistic on the possibility of starting negotiations, he did suggest steps that could be taken to improve the chances of getting talks started, including a halt in the bombing of North Vietnam or, at the least, a shift in the bombing away from the Hanoi/Haiphong area.[162]

McNamara's recommendations, predictably, stirred up a violent reaction from the JCS—the only point they agreed with in McNamara's entire report was his prognosis that the U.S. was in for a long war. In this respect, the Chiefs were especially disturbed by McNamara's suggestions concerning negotiations. They "seemed to sense," as the Pentagon analyst noted, "that a significant turn in our views about Vietnam had been taken in the high policy circles of our government." In an obvious attempt to deflect the turn toward negotiations, the Chiefs argued that "the war has reached a stage where decisions taken over the next 60 days can determine the outcome of the war and, consequently, can affect the over-all security interests of the U.S. for years to come." As a result, they argued, not only would further overt actions in search of negotiations be "nonproductive," they would be "counterproductive," since they would cast doubt on the Administration's resolve to pursue the war to a successful conclusion. In addition, the JCS once again dusted off the bombing program prepared in November 1964,

161. Quoted in IV Gravel, p. 348 (emphasis omitted). The text of McNamara's report is presented in full in IV Gravel, pp. 348–355.

162. On these points, see IV Gravel, pp. 348–353 (emphasis omitted). For the President's reaction to McNamara's memo, see IV Gravel, pp. 130–133.

requesting that the President be informed that it was not too late to gain the military benefits that would accrue if that program were put into operation.[163]

The JCS were right about one thing—the war had in fact reached a stage where decisions taken over the next sixty days would be of crucial significance for the outcome of the war. What made this exchange between McNamara and the JCS so important was a chain of events that had been unfolding in Saigon and Hanoi ever since the end of June. On June 27, Janusz Lewandowski, the Polish representative on the ICC, met with Giovanni D'Orlandi, the Italian Ambassador to South Vietnam, at which time Lewandowski announced that he had just returned from Hanoi with a "very specific peace offer." According to Lewandowski, the North Vietnamese had been deeply disappointed by the proposal carried by Ronning on his second visit (which they viewed as tantamount to asking for their unconditional surrender). Still, they were open to a "political compromise" settling the whole Vietnam conflict once and for all, and they were willing to go "quite a long way" in order to achieve one.[164]

On June 29, D'Orlandi conveyed this message to Ambassador Lodge in Saigon; meanwhile, the Italian Ambassador in Washington informed the State Department directly. Although Administration officials at first dismissed the message as containing little that was new, there were two aspects to Lewandowski's report that were intriguing enough to merit further probing by the Italians. First, there was the list of items that Lewandowski claimed were *not* being demanded by Hanoi as part of a settlement. Specifically, the North Vietnamese were not demanding immediate reunification, the establishment of a socialist system in the South, a change in South Vietnamese foreign policy, neutralization of South Vietnam, immediate U.S. withdrawal (although a "reasonable calendar" for withdrawal would be sought), and the right to interfere in the GVN (although they would prefer it to be headed by someone other than Ky). Second, there were the conditions set by the North Vietnamese for entering into negotiations. According to Lewandowski, while the North Vietnamese would insist that the NLF "take part" in the negotiations, they were no longer demanding that the NLF be considered as *the* representative for South Vietnam; there was no question, as

163. For the Pentagon analyst's comment, see IV Gravel, p. 357. For the JCS memo, see IV Gravel, pp. 127–129, 356–358. See also IV Gravel, pp. 131–132, for a summary of various proposals for escalating the conflict being pushed by the military at this time. These proposals were, for the time being at least, rejected by the President.

164. On these points, see Marigold Chronology, pp. 1–3.

D'Orlandi told Lodge, of the Front having a monopoly on representa-tion for the South. In addition, the North Vietnamese insisted on a suspension (not cessation) of bombing. These conditions, as mentioned above, were intriguing enough to merit a request for further probing by the Italians. In particular, Washington wished to know whether they in fact represented a softening of the DRV position or simply an accident of translation.[165]

In the weeks that followed, the contact seemingly made real progress on a number of fronts. On July 9, Lodge met with Lewandowski and D'Orlandi, at which time he informed them that the U.S., too, sought an overall settlement, and he probed for further details on Hanoi's ideas on reaching a settlement. Meanwhile, in Rome, Italian officials gave Arthur Goldberg a written account of the contact to that point, which contained three points of special interest: (1) the North Vietnamese were in fact seeking only a "suspension" of the bombing and not a cessation; (2) the North Vietnamese were no longer demanding that the NLF be recognized as the sole representative of the South Vietnamese people and were willing to allow GVN participation in the negotiations so long as the NLF also participated; and (3) the POL strikes had not prejudiced the Polish initiative.[166]

After what seemed to be a promising beginning, however, the initia-tive suddenly ran into a brick wall. On July 24, Lewandowski, speaking under instructions from Warsaw, replied to the questions posed by Lodge on July 9; the harsh and uncompromising nature of his reply seemed to suggest that any "progress" to that point had been strictly illusory. Accusing the U.S. of escalating both the air war over the North and the ground war in the South, Lewandowski stated that dis-cussions under such conditions "could be looked upon as a maneuver to force the DRV to negotiate under American conditions." Furthermore, Lewandowski suggested that no negotiations could be possible without a bombing cessation, and that "if the U.S. desires a peaceful solution, it must recognize the Four Points proposed by the DRV and prove it in practice. The U.S. must stop bombing and other military activity against North Vietnam. Only then can a political solution be expected."

165. On these points, see Marigold Chronology, pp. 1–4; and Settlement Terms, p. 7.
166. During their July 9 meeting, Lodge asked Lewandowski when, where, and with whom the North Vietnamese contemplated negotiating, what actions Hanoi proposed to take or not take during a bombing suspension, and whether the negotiations could realistically be kept secret if the bombing were suspended (see Marigold Chronology, pp. 8–9). For the written report passed to Goldberg by the Italians, see Marigold Chronology, pp. 9–11. The Italian report did mention a North Vietnamese suggestion that Ky might be replaced by a less extremist personality once the negotiations were under way.

This was, as D'Orlandi put it, "definitely a step backward."[167] Still, by using the wording of the January 4 memo, Lewandowski (and presumably the North Vietnamese) carefully left the door open to further contacts in the future.

As things turned out, though, the whole affair was left in limbo for the next six weeks. Lewandowski made another visit to Hanoi and returned profoundly discouraged, telling D'Orlandi in early September that he could find no evidence of a desire to stop the war. Significantly, Lewandowski attributed Hanoi's intransigence at least partly to the absence, during his most recent visit, of Pham Van Dong and Vo Nguyen Giap, "the only two in the whole place who talk sense and understand the real situation in the South." Despite this, Lewandowski and D'Orlandi resolved on their own initiative to try once again to work out a compromise formula—an effort that was subsequently (if unenthusiastically) endorsed by Washington.[168]

Almost from the start, however, the renewed effort ran into a new snag. Lewandowski insisted that the effort should be aimed at a total settlement, involving some unspecified change in the personnel of the GVN, and not just at mutual de-escalation, which would have had the effect of preserving the status quo in Saigon. This, though, was precisely the approach that was hardest for Washington to contemplate. Consequently, even in the process of giving its qualified approval to the Lewandowski-D'Orlandi effort, Washington again attempted to steer the initiative in the direction of finding a formula for a mutual U.S.-DRV withdrawal from the war.[169]

In the weeks that followed, the contact consisted largely of a three-way sparring match over the issue of what kind of settlement to pursue. Lewandowski told D'Orlandi that Hanoi was not trying to ram the Viet Cong down the Americans' throats and that the U.S. should consider a coalition government, the bulk of which would consist of "sensible South Vietnamese politicians," with one or two men each from the "right" and from the NLF in "unimportant ministries." Washington, for its part, continued to push the initiative in the direction of working out a formula for mutual de-escalation that would leave the GVN in place untouched. D'Orlandi, meanwhile, was caught in the middle, telling Lewandowski that he could not possibly sell such a scheme to the Americans while telling the Americans that Lewandowski was totally uninterested in the mutual de-escalation approach.[170]

167. See Marigold Chronology, pp. 12–13.
168. See Marigold Chronology, pp. 13–15.
169. On these points, see Marigold Chronology, pp. 14–17.
170. On these points, see Marigold Chronology, pp. 17–23.

This three-sided contest suddenly took on added importance in mid-November. On November 13, two days before Lewandowski was scheduled to depart for Hanoi, Washington made a major effort to clarify his role and to move the contact forward in a manner favorable to the United States. Specifically, Lodge was to query Lewandowski on his role as seen by himself and by Hanoi and also on the way in which he proposed to move from discussions to a final settlement. In addition, in an attempt to get the contact on the "right track" (from Washington's point of view), the Administration introduced a new concept into the bargaining—the so-called "Phase A–Phase B" plan. "We understand," Lodge was told by Washington,

that considerations of face inevitably play a role in Hanoi's thinking. Does this perhaps explain, in Lewandowski's view, why we are unable to get any meaningful response to the question "what would happen if the bombing of North Vietnam stopped?" Does Lewandowski see any way around this? Could some package deal be worked out which *in its totality* represented what both we and Hanoi would agree to as a reasonable measure of mutual deescalation, but which would have two separate phases in its execution. Phase A would be a bombing suspension, while Phase B, which would follow after some adequate period, would see the execution of all the other agreed deescalatory actions. Hanoi's actions taken in Phase B would appear to be in response to our actions in Phase B rather than to the bombing suspension.

At the same time, an identical proposal was passed to British Foreign Secretary George Brown for transmission to the Soviets during his forthcoming visit to Moscow.[171]

Lewandowski, however, refused to be pinned down. Meeting with Lodge and D'Orlandi on November 14, he dismissed the American question on how to achieve a final settlement as "very theoretical" and

171. For Washington's November 13 cable to Lodge, see Marigold Chronology, pp. 27–28 (emphasis in original). The Phase A–Phase B proposal was transmitted to London on November 16; see Marigold Chronology, pp. 34–35. On the origins of the Phase A–Phase B proposal, see Cooper (1972), pp. 374, 387–389, 399–400; and Kraslow and Loory, pp. 20–22, 25–26. See also Kraslow and Loory, p. 32, who report that Ambassador Harriman saw the President on November 11 in order to bring him up to date on the MARIGOLD contact, which may account for the timing of the Washington initiative. Both the Cooper and the Kraslow/Loory accounts attribute the decision to try out the Phase A–Phase B plan to a November 2 meeting in Rome involving Cooper (then accompanying Ambassador Harriman on a round-the-world swing) and D'Orlandi. Further, both accounts state that the proposal was not passed to Lodge until November 15, after a November 14 meeting involving Lodge, Lewandowski, and D'Orlandi. The Marigold Chronology section, however, clearly indicates that the proposal was transmitted in a November 13 cable and given to Lewandowski on November 14. The November 15 meeting dealt with questions about a possible coalition government in the South, something that does not come out in the Cooper and Kraslow/Loory accounts.

neatly reversed the Phase A–Phase B proposal by stating that it "recognizes that you can't trade [a] bombing suspension for something else." Lewandowski, moreover, had some questions of his own, which, taken together, added up to a less-than-subtle inquiry as to whether Washington would acquiesce in the formation of a new government in the South. Washington, however, proved equally adept at dodging questions, telling Lewandowski (through Lodge, in a meeting on November 15) only that "We support the emerging constitutional process in South Vietnam. The orderly formation of a responsive and representative government based on free elections will receive our support."[172]

This, then, was where the matter stood on the eve of Lewandowski's departure for Hanoi. Prodded from within by McNamara's forceful advocacy and fearful of embarrassing leaks to the press if it did not cooperate with the Lewandowski/D'Orlandi initiative, the Administration had begun a tentative search for an exit, although it clung to the hope of forcing the DRV to accept a settlement involving mutual de-escalation that would leave the GVN intact. Hanoi, for its part, had given some tantalizing hints of a willingness to make concessions on substantive issues, provided the final settlement included at least some changes in the South Vietnamese status quo and not just mutual de-escalation. The next three months would witness intensive efforts to narrow the remaining gap between the two sides. Unfortunately, as Cooper notes, the effort "would not always be whole-hearted and would more often than not be marked by groping and fumbling. It would be accompanied by Byzantine-like conspiracies, bitter—if muted—in-fighting, and soul-searing phases of euphoric hope and deep despair."[173] Ultimately, it would be an effort characterized by failure.

172. On the November 14 meeting, see Marigold Chronology, pp. 30–31. On the November 15 meeting, see Marigold Chronology, pp. 32–34.
173. Cooper (1972), p. 389.

4

Negotiating While Fighting

JUST AS LEWANDOWSKI'S mid-November trip to Hanoi marked the start of the final and most intense phase of the MARIGOLD contact, so too did the Johnson Administration's reluctant acceptance of his attempted mediation signify the start of a new and deeply frustrating phase of the war. With the failure of the air war to win for the Administration a "position of strength," and with the failure of the American troop buildup to "convince" DRV/VC forces that they could not win the ground war in the South, Administration officials were confronted with a situation in which an ability to coordinate military moves with diplomatic initiatives would be of the greatest importance if an acceptable settlement was to be coaxed from the North Vietnamese. Admittedly, those officials had long anticipated the need to integrate military strategy with diplomacy, as evidenced by John McNaughton's October 1964 comment that "words across any conference table should be orchestrated with continuing military pressures."[1] What was not anticipated, however, was how difficult the task of "orchestration" would prove to be.

In fairness to the Administration, it must be conceded that many of the problems that it encountered during this period of "negotiating while fighting" were the result of the complexity inherent in any attempt at coercion on the scale of the effort made by the Johnson Administration and thus largely beyond the control of any group of officials, no matter how well-intentioned. During the period November 1966–March 1968, both sides, as we shall see, pursued a dual-track strategy involving both military and diplomatic components. On the American side, the watchwords continued to be "incremental escalation" and "mutual de-escalation," whereby a policy of doling out

1. Document no. 209 in III Gravel, p. 381. See also the references in Chapter 1, note 8, above.

bits and pieces of escalatory authority was combined with a single-minded focus on the goal of a mutual U.S.-DRV exit from the war—an outcome that would have the not unwelcome effect of preserving the GVN as the sole governmental authority in South Vietnam. The North Vietnamese, meanwhile, were following a dual-track strategy of their own: as the rate of infiltration climbed, North Vietnamese Army units shouldered an increasing share of the fighting in the South; at the same time, though, the DRV leadership, or at least that segment of it headed by Pham Van Dong, continued its efforts to negotiate the U.S. out of Vietnam and establish a coalition government in Saigon.

Further complicating the Administration's efforts to achieve an acceptable settlement was the fact that during the period November 1966–March 1968 the parties exchanged messages through eight major diplomatic channels, with the usual pattern involving simultaneous exchanges through several channels.[2] As a result of this combination of factors—i.e., the simultaneous pursuit by both sides of a dual-track strategy involving multiple diplomatic channels—this period was by far the most complex of the war and the most difficult for the outside analyst to deal with. But at least the analyst has the benefit of hindsight. The situation was far more difficult for the officials involved, who had to wrestle with events one day at a time, never quite certain what their opponents were up to or which message or action might someday prove decisive.

I. Three Exercises in Futility
(December 1966-July 1967)

A. Failure in Warsaw

On November 30, Lewandowski returned from Hanoi with perhaps the most significant message carried by an intermediary during the entire

2. The eight main channels were: Lewandowski and the Government of Poland (code-named MARIGOLD); the British and Soviet governments during the February 1967 Wilson/Kosygin meetings in London (code-named SUNFLOWER); a direct channel involving the U.S. and DRV missions in Moscow (also code-named SUNFLOWER); two French citizens, Raymond Aubrac and Herbert Marcovich (code-named PENNSYLVANIA); the Government of Sweden (code-named ASPEN); the Government of Norway (code-named OHIO); the Government of Rumania (code-named PACKERS); and the Government of Italy (code-named KILLY). There were also numerous soundings by various private individuals and government officials, of which the most important were Harry Ashmore and William C. Baggs, Harrison Salisbury, U Thant, and Charles Collingwood. On these, see Ashmore and Baggs, *Mission to Hanoi* (New York: G. P. Putnam's Sons, 1968), pp. 100–196; Salisbury, *Behind the Lines—Hanoi* (New York: Harper & Row, 1967); and *U.S.-Vietnam Relations*, VI. A. 1., pp. 94–97. There was also a mysterious late-1967 contact between the U.S. and the NLF (code-named BUTTERCUP); on this, see Don Oberdorfer, *Tet!* (New York: Avon, 1971), pp. 80–82.

conflict. On the basis of his conversations with Lodge, he had formulated a 10-point statement of the American position (see Appendix IV), which he had discussed with the North Vietnamese while in Hanoi. There was sufficient interest in his formulation, he told Lodge, that "I am authorized to say that if the U.S. are really of the views which I have presented, it would be advisable to confirm them directly by conversation with the North Vietnamese Ambassador in Warsaw." Under questioning, Lewandowski revealed that his source in Hanoi was Pham Van Dong, who had the "Presidium behind him."[3]

Despite Lewandowski's insistence that speed was of the utmost importance—he told Lodge that delay would give those in Hanoi "working against a solution" time to "put down the clamps on talks"—Lodge refused to commit himself to acceptance of Lewandowski's formulation. The matter was of such importance, Lodge insisted, that it would have to be referred to Washington. In addition, there were a number of problems, from the American point of view, with the wording of Lewandowski's draft. Of these, the most important centered on the second point—a thinly veiled reference to the creation of a coalition government in the South. Lodge told Lewandowski outright during their meeting on November 30 that the wording of Point 2 would have to be changed, and he suggested for openers that *would* be substituted for *must*.[4]

In Washington, the reaction to Lodge's report of his meeting with Lewandowski was threefold. First, Lewandowski made no mention of a bombing halt prior to the opening of talks, and this aspect of the contact exerted a powerful attraction on Washington's thinking. Second, however, the attractiveness of Lewandowski's proposal was diminished by his failure to include an explicit reference to the Phase A–Phase B plan in the 10 Points, although Washington was reassured somewhat when Lodge reported that Lewandowski had strongly implied on November 30 that he had presented the plan orally while in Hanoi.[5] Third, despite these misgivings, Washington was willing to go ahead with the contact, telling Lodge (who then told Lewandowski on December 3) that the 10 Points broadly reflected the U.S. position, although

3. On these points, see Marigold Chronology, pp. 36–37. Lewandowski's 10 Points were apparently based on the responses to his questions provided by Lodge on November 15. On this point, see Marigold Chronology, pp. 32–34; and Kraslow and Loory, p. 26.

4. On these points, see Marigold Chronology, p. 37.

5. Whether Lewandowski actually presented the Phase A–Phase B proposal while in Hanoi is one of the more intriguing aspects of the whole affair. This was clearly a central concern of Washington's; yet when Washington queried Lodge on what Lewandowski said while in Hanoi, Lodge replied that Lewandowski "merely cited 'your Phase A and Phase B,' with clear implication that [he] had given his presentation in Hanoi in accordance with your [Washington's] formulation." On this point, see Marigold Chronology, pp. 37–38.

"several specific points are subject to important differences of interpretation." Also on December 3, Lodge told Lewandowski that the American Embassy in Warsaw would contact the DRV Embassy there on December 6 or soon thereafter.[6]

And yet, even before Lewandowski was informed of Washington's approval of the Warsaw contact (code-named MARIGOLD), things began to come apart. On December 2, U.S. jets struck the Van Dien vehicle depot and the Ha Gia POL facility, 6.7 and 16 nautical miles, respectively, from the center of Hanoi. As things turned out, these and subsequent attacks would play a key role in undermining the initiative, and in this respect the timing of the attacks was especially important. As the Pentagon analyst notes:

Beginning in June 1966, there was a marked increase in the amount of ordnance expended against North Vietnam. This was true for the country as a whole, for Route Package VI, and for the areas within 10 miles of the center of Hanoi and five miles of the center of Haiphong. During the last two weeks of November, probably on account of weather, air strikes against the North were at their lowest level since June, rising markedly again during the first and second weeks of December.[7]

As a result, while the targets struck on December 2 had been authorized on November 10, the strikes were not executed until almost three weeks later, due to bad weather over the target area. Unfortunately, however, the period of bad weather ("the last two weeks in November") coincided with Lewandowski's stay in Hanoi (he left Saigon on November 15 and returned on November 30). As was subsequently reported by D'Orlandi, Lewandowski believed that the reduced bombing during his stay in Hanoi was interpreted by the North Vietnamese as a signal of tacit American support for his initiative. If the North Vietnamese were in fact seeking a deeper meaning to the pattern of bombing, the timing of

6. On these points, see Marigold Chronology, pp. 37–38; and Kraslow and Loory, pp. 40–41. The delay between December 3 and December 6 was necessary to give the U.S. Ambassador in Warsaw, John Gronouski, time to read up on the contact to that point. It should also be noted that Lodge's reply hardly conveyed the full flavor of Washington's reaction to the 10 Points. William Bundy, for example, subsequently characterized them as a "rather bizarre concoction" containing "enough concessions to titillate anyone" (interview with the author, March 4, 1977). Furthermore, Bundy recalls that Lodge had not reported fully on his conversations with Lewandowski and D'Orlandi, so that officials in Washington felt somewhat in the dark on the discussions in Saigon. Despite this, the U.S. gave what Bundy described as a "measured and correct" response to Lewandowski's proposal for talks in Warsaw, which (in Bundy's view) was the product of careful thought and much hard work (especially by Lewellyn Thompson).

7. Marigold Discussion, p. 16. On the December 2 strike, see Marigold Chronology, p. 38.

the attacks could have been construed as a none-too-subtle effort to soften them up prior to the Warsaw meeting.[8]

At their meeting on December 3, then, Lewandowski dutifully informed Lodge that the bombing was jeopardizing the contact. The warning, however, had no effect: on December 4, the Ha Gia facility was bombed again, along with the Yen Vien railroad yard, 5.5 nautical miles from the center of Hanoi.[9]

Despite the ill-timed raids, there was still a reasonable chance of salvaging the contact. On December 5, the American Ambassador in Warsaw, John Gronouski, was summoned by Foreign Minister Adam Rapacki to hear the Polish version of the contact to that point. Significantly, Rapacki told Gronouski that Polish support for the initiative had been extended after Lodge had "confirmed" Lewandowski's formulation on November 30, a remark that strongly implied that Lodge's December 3 reference to "important differences of interpretation" was a U.S. attempt to renege on its original position. As a result, Rapacki pressed Gronouski to clarify the U.S. position, telling him it would be better if the Poles could transmit to Hanoi a statement defining the differences Washington had in mind rather than a vague reference to "differences of interpretation." As Gronouski noted in his report to Washington, "Rapacki said such a statement might have a significant effect on Hanoi's attitude toward both a meeting in Warsaw and the whole problem."[10]

8. On the November 10 decision, see Marigold Chronology, pp. 25–26; Sharp and Westmoreland, p. 25; and Cooper (1972), p. 405. On Lewandowski's view of the DRV's thinking on the bombing, see Marigold Chronology, pp. 54 ff., especially p. 56; and Cooper (1972), p. 405. It could be argued that the North Vietnamese could see that the weather was bad and thus would not jump to the conclusion that the reduced bombing was linked to Lewandowski's diplomacy. However, as Gallucci (p. 83) notes: "The way in which targets were released, that is, in groups or 'packages' every two weeks also meant that . . . much strike and restrike was done in adverse weather to guard against the loss of targets should authorization be revoked, as well as to keep up the sortie rate. This was admitted quite clearly by Major General Gilbert L. Meyers, former deputy commander of the 7th Air Force in Vietnam during Senate testimony in 1967: 'If the weather was bad, we were always concerned about the repercussions as a result of not flying the sorties that had been allocated to us.'" As a result, it is possible that the North Vietnamese actually did overlook the connection between the weather and the bombing.

9. On these points, see Marigold Chronology, p. 38; Cooper (1972), p. 405; and Kraslow and Loory, p. 40.

10. On the Rapacki-Gronouski meeting of December 5, see Marigold Chronology, pp. 39–40. It would appear from Rapacki's remarks that the Poles had not as yet transmitted the "important differences of interpretation" statement to Hanoi. This inference is strengthened by a Rapacki comment to Gronouski on December 6 that Lodge's original position (expressed during the November 30 meeting with Lewandowski) had been conveyed to Hanoi and that it remained to be seen how the U.S. statement on "differences of interpretation" would be received in Hanoi. All this suggests that the Poles jumped the gun in informing Hanoi of U.S. "acceptance" of Lewandowski's proposal. On these points, see Marigold Discussion, p. 4; and Marigold Chronology, p. 43.

Although Administration officials would repeatedly express skepticism over whether the Poles had in fact secured Hanoi's consent to go through with the meeting in Warsaw, it appears that Rapacki was speaking sincerely when he urged Gronouski to clarify the U.S. position.[11] As suggested by Lewandowski's reference to opponents of talks in Hanoi, the veiled reference to a coalition government in Point 2 was probably the minimum condition required for Pham Van Dong to secure the backing of a Politburo majority.[12] If this was so, the importance of the "differences of interpretation" statement becomes clear: Washington, from the viewpoint of both Hanoi and Warsaw, was hedging on its "agreement" (as expressed by Lodge's "confirmation" of Lewandowski's formulation) to discuss a change in the South Vietnamese status quo. Since the North Vietnamese apparently were ready to talk only on the condition that those talks consider a coalition government for the South, Rapacki's attempt to pressure Gronouski into producing a detailed statement of the American position becomes readily understandable.[13]

Clarification, however, was the one thing that Washington did not wish to provide. As was later explained to Gronouski:

While we are entirely prepared to have Lewandowski's formulation stand as "presenting a general statement of the U.S. position," we are anxious to avoid a restatement of our position in our own words because (a) this would oblige us to take some harder positions than those put forward by Lewandowski which

11. On Washington's skepticism, see Marigold Chronology, pp. 64, 69, 83. It seems likely that the North Vietnamese did agree to go through with the Warsaw talks, even though we have only Polish assurances in this respect. The Poles, after all, would only have looked foolish by stretching the truth on this matter, especially since the Italians (and very likely the Soviets) had been informed of the initiative from the start. On December 22, the Soviet Chargé in Washington, Alexander Zinchuk, told William Bundy that the Polish effort had been a serious one which the Soviets had fully supported and that it was his opinion that some elements in Hanoi had been seriously interested in negotiating. On February 17, 1967, Zinchuk told Bundy that the Soviets had reviewed the contact with the North Vietnamese and had determined that the North Vietnamese were prepared to go through with the talks in Warsaw. This position was later reiterated by Soviet Ambassador Dobrynin in remarks to Secretary Rusk and William Bundy on February 23 and March 23, respectively. On these points, see Marigold Discussion, pp. 1–2, 4–5; Marigold Chronology, pp. 78–79; Sunflower Discussion, p. 24; and Sunflower Chronology, pp. 75, 87.

12. Decision-making in Hanoi will be discussed in more detail in Chapters 5–6, below.

13. This line of argument would be valid even if the Poles did not immediately transmit the "differences of interpretation" statement to Hanoi as suggested in note 10, above. The Poles presumably were sensitive to Hanoi's interest in the coalition government issue. Lewandowski, after all, had been in touch with DRV leaders, and he had persistently rejected the mutual de-escalation approach in favor of a total settlement package, including some change in the South Vietnamese status quo; in addition, it seems reasonable to assume that the coalition government issue would be discussed in his reports to Warsaw. Hence, even if the Poles delayed transmitting the "differences of interpretation" statement to Hanoi, they probably knew the importance of nailing down Washington's "commitment" to discuss a coalition government.

apparently have gone far enough to make the North Vietnamese ready to consider talking with us and (b) any formulation which can be attributed directly to us could be used to embarrass the GVN or to embarrass us in our relations with them.[14]

This unwillingness to clarify the American position was especially pronounced with respect to Lewandowski's Point 2, which, Gronouski was told, "is obviously most troublesome."[15] As a result, Gronouski was to adhere to the formula presented by Lodge on December 3; that is:

Lewandowski's formulation broadly reflects the position of the U.S. Government on the issues covered and we would be prepared to accept it as the basis for direct discussions with the North Vietnamese if they are in fact interested in pursuing the matter, and if they were informed that latitude for interpretation of such general language is inevitable.[16]

On December 6, Gronouski met with Rapacki to convey this nonclarification of the American position; Rapacki, for his part, stated that the matter could be delayed no longer and that the American position would now be transmitted to Hanoi. Still, Rapacki continued to press for a precise statement of the American position, although this time he told Gronouski that the statement should be presented at Gronouski's first meeting with the DRV Ambassador, "in the event it takes place."[17]

That meeting, however, never did take place, and it appears that this was due at least in part to the Administration's failure to heed the warnings being provided by the Poles. In this respect, Polish representatives in both Warsaw and Saigon repeatedly emphasized that the recent stepup in the bombing along with American evasiveness on the "differences of interpretation" clause were jeopardizing the contact, and they urged that the U.S. both refrain from *escalating* the bombing and clarify its position.[18]

If anything, however, the effect of these warnings was exactly the opposite of the one intended. Not only was Gronouski instructed, as we saw earlier, to avoid clarifying the American position, but he was also told to stress, with respect to the bombing, that mutual de-escalation

14. This point was made in a December 7 cable to Gronouski; see Marigold Chronology, p. 51.

15. This point was made in a separate cable to Gronouski, also dated December 7; see Marigold Chronology, p. 48.

16. These instructions were given to Gronouski in a cable on December 5, which Gronouski received *after* his December 5 meeting with Rapacki; see Marigold Chronology, p. 41.

17. On the December 6 meeting, see Marigold Chronology, pp. 42–43.

18. For the Polish warnings, see Marigold Chronology, pp. 44–46, 53–59, 60–61. The Poles never did press for a bombing cessation.

was one of the topics the U.S. was prepared to discuss.[19] More importantly, Polish warnings on the bombing resulted in a stiffening of the
Administration's resolve *not* to cancel any of the strikes authorized on
November 10 as part of ROLLING THUNDER 52. On December 6,
the President, after meeting with Rostow, McNamara, Vance, and the
JCS at his Texas ranch, decided to leave ROLLING THUNDER 52
unchanged, despite the arrival on the previous day of a Gronouski cable
conveying Rapacki's initial warning on the bombing.[20] On December
10, Gronouski was told:

You should be aware that for the immediate future the bombing pattern will
remain unchanged from what it has been over the past several weeks. This may
well involve some targets which Rapacki will insist represent further escalation,
just as in the past he took to be escalation certain variations in our bombing
pattern which in fact represented no real new departures in the pattern as a
whole. With foregoing in mind you should avoid giving Poles any slight indications which they might take to mean that we are escalating or deescalating at
present. Present bombing pattern has been authorized for some time and we do
not wish to withdraw this authorization at this time.[21]

As a result, on December 13 and again on December 14, the Yen
Vien and Van Dien targets were both struck. Although Gronouski was
told by Washington on December 15 that "there is no basis for charging
us with escalation of conflict," the strikes could easily have been viewed
in a much different light by the North Vietnamese. As the Pentagon
analyst notes:

19. Gronouski was to try to steer any conversations with the North Vietnamese in the direction
of mutual de-escalation by interpreting Lewandowski's Point 8 as the Phase A–Phase B proposal
(even though this would seem somewhat implausible, given Lewandowski's wording). On these
points, see Marigold Chronology, pp. 46–53.

20. Kraslow and Loory, pp. 64–65, report that Gronouski's cable conveying Rapacki's warning
was considered at the December 6 meeting at the Texas ranch. See also Brandon, p. 80; and
Cooper (1972), p. 406, both of whom mention a determination to go ahead with the bombing
despite the Polish warnings (Lewandowski had also warned Lodge on December 3 about the bombing; see Marigold Chronology, p. 38). The decision to leave ROLLING THUNDER 52 unchanged
becomes more understandable when one considers the background to the November 10 decision
on ROLLING THUNDER 52. The targets approved on November 10, William Bundy recalls
(interview with the author, March 4, 1977), were the "residue" of a much longer list suggested by
the military. The original list had struck officials in the State Department as too extensive, and
there had been considerable debate over the composition of the list, with the result that a number
of targets were dropped. The military, as a result, attached more importance than usual to attacking
the remaining targets, and any effort to delete those targets would have "sent a tremor through the
whole military structure." The final outcome of the debate (at least as perceived from the State
Department) was a tacit agreement that the Hanoi-area targets would be hit once and then quietly
dropped from the authorized list. The attacks of December 2 and 4, however, did not destroy the
targets, so the President decided not to call off further strikes against the Hanoi-area targets.

21. Marigold Chronology, p. 60.

The most sensitive area of all, that within five miles of the center of Hanoi, was struck (with about 25 tons of ordnance) for the first time in the war during the last week of June as part of a general attack on POL facilities. About three tons more were expended in this area in mid-August. It was not hit again until the first week of December (the 2nd and 4th) when almost 50 tons were expended, then hit yet again during the second week in December (the 13th and 14th) with over 100 tons. The intended targets in all of the December attacks were the Yen Vien railroad yard and the Van Dien vehicle depot, but apparently there was collateral damage in all cases. In particular, during the December 13-14 attacks, the Chinese and Rumanian Embassies seem to have been hit, along with some residential structures in central Hanoi. *From the ground, then, there might appear to have been an increase in the intensity of attack, measured both in tons of ordnance expended and type of target, commencing December 2, i.e., immediately following Hanoi's assent to some form of U.S.-DRV meeting in Warsaw.*[22]

The outcome of these ill-timed strikes was predictable enough. On December 13, before he knew of the renewed bombing of Hanoi, Rapacki warned Gronouski that "we should realize that leadership of DRNVN does not want to and cannot yield under pressure." On December 14, Rapacki summoned Gronouski to inform him of a DRV request that all conversations with the U.S. be ended. The raids on Hanoi, Rapacki noted, were conducted "precisely at the moment when the U.S. Government knew that the matter of a Warsaw contact with Hanoi was actively being considered. This was the last drop that spilled over the cup [*sic*]."[23]

All this left Gronouski in an unenviable position. Washington had interpreted Rapacki's December 13 warning as a last-ditch effort to extract concessions from the U.S. prior to the start of talks with the North Vietnamese and had instructed Gronouski to press for direct contacts with the North Vietnamese (preferably along the lines of the Phase A–Phase B plan) and to warn Rapacki that the Poles would bear the responsibility if the contact broke down. But before he received these instructions, Gronouski was hit by Rapacki's broadside announcing that the talks were off. At that point, Gronouski abandoned all thoughts of a counterattack and opted instead for retreat, recommending that the

22. For the December 15 cable, see Marigold Chronology, p. 62. For the Pentagon analyst's comment, see Marigold Discussion, p. 16 (emphasis added). See also Kraslow and Loory, pp. 67–70; and Cooper (1972), p. 406. Harrison Salisbury, who visited the Van Dien target while in North Vietnam between December 23, 1966 and January 7, 1967, reported that a nearby Polish-built high school was also destroyed in one of the raids (see Salisbury, pp. 68, 131–133). The importance attached by the military to striking these targets (see note 20, above) probably accounts for the heavy expenditure of ordnance during the attacks on December 13–14.

23. For Rapacki's December 13 warning and Washington's reaction, see Marigold Chronology, pp. 60, 63–64. On the Rapacki-Gronouski meeting of December 14, see Marigold Chronology, p. 67.

U.S. try to reopen the contact by promising not to bomb in the vicinity of Hanoi and Haiphong while the U.S.-DRV talks were under way.[24]

This suggestion, however, was received with something less than enthusiasm by an Administration already under siege both by "doves" who wanted the bombing halted entirely and "hawks" who wanted to obliterate everything of value in North Vietnam, beginning with Hanoi and Haiphong. Gronouski was politely but firmly told that "on the basis of the overall picture as we can see it from Washington, the Polish case, except for some fairly superficial and transitory matters, is a weak one and we wonder whether they will try to sell it to world opinion." Consequently, Gronouski was to reject Rapacki's arguments and attempt to put the onus on the Poles for "changing the signals and then seeking to put the blame on us." Still, he was also to express a deep desire to meet with the North Vietnamese; in addition, the Yen Vien and Van Dien targets were quietly removed from the authorized list, although neither Gronouski nor the Poles were told of this.[25]

Gronouski's efforts, however, proved to be in vain; Rapacki simply refused to try to reopen the Warsaw contact. On December 22, Gronouski informed the Poles that there would be no bombing within a 10-mile circle around Hanoi, although the Administration still clung to the hope of "appropriate reciprocal action with respect to bombs, mortar, and similar terrorist activities" around Saigon—a hope that was abandoned on December 24. This gesture, however, came too late to be of any use. As was later explained to Gronouski by the Poles:

Michalowski opened his reply by observing that at one point in my discussions with Rapacki I had expressed the hope that someone was putting as much pressure on Hanoi as Poles were placing on us to get negotiations started. He said with some feeling that he could assure me that Poles put heavy pressure on Hanoi and in fact put prestige of [Government of Poland] on line in getting Hanoi to agree at outset to idea of having talks in Warsaw. He added that he personally knew how much pressure was brought to bear because he was engaged in exercising some of it. He went on to say that leadership in Hanoi is by no means a monolithic group and that from the beginning, when Poles got agreement from Hanoi to initiate talks in Warsaw, it was a very close decision with many of the Hanoi leadership strongly opposed. He said they obtained such agreement after exerting strong pressure and putting Poland's prestige on the line; but it was a delicate matter in Hanoi implying that agreement was by a narrow margin among the leadership. He said at this point the Poles have been

24. On the "counterattack-retreat" point, see the Pentagon analyst's comment, Marigold Chronology, p. 64. For Washington's instructions to Gronouski, see Marigold Chronology, pp. 64–66. For Gronouski's suggestion of a partial bombing halt, see Marigold Chronology, p. 68.

25. For Gronouski's instructions, see Marigold Chronology, pp. 69–70.

able to convince Hanoi to have at least a small degree of confidence in intentions of U.S. He added that bombing of December 3 [sic] had given a weapon to those in Hanoi who had not wanted to agree to negotiations in the first place. He said it was for this reason that Poles had repeatedly conveyed to Lodge and me their fear of negative effects of a repetition of December 3 bombing. But he said even after December 3 . . . Poles were able to prevail in Hanoi to keep possibility of talks open, and "believe me we talked to them several times a day to keep pressure on them and convince them." But he said the bombing of December 13 and 14 "undercut our whole argument, destroyed that little bit of confidence that existed in Hanoi about intentions of U.S., and left us wide open to charges of being completely naive." He said with bombing of December 13 and 14, those who had initially been skeptical about negotiations were given a powerful tool to support their case and in fact prevailed. He added that even with the December 3 bombing, if we had been able to interval [sic] between December 3 and 13 to come in with the message we did on the 24th, that part of leadership in Hanoi which wanted negotiations would have prevailed and he is confident that talks would have happened. But he said by December 24 a whole new condition existed: "We were accused of being naive and had lost our effectiveness and those who on December 3 had been able to control situation and move toward negotiations were by this time discredited." Thus he said situation by December 26 in Hanoi had so changed that it was impossible to go back to December 1 or the post–December 3 period.[26]

As indicated by the Polish postmortem, by January 1967 the MARIGOLD contact was effectively dead. By then, the interest of American policymakers had shifted to an attempt to open a direct channel to Hanoi via Moscow (see Section I-B, below); what little interest remained in MARIGOLD centered on heading off embarrassing leaks to the press. In this respect, it is unfortunately true that the Administration was more concerned with preempting the Poles and getting its version of the story out first than with insuring that the conditions that led to the breakdown of the contact would not be repeated. Lewandowski was to make one last effort to revive the contact before the end of his tour in March 1967, but by then the Administration would be preoccupied with escalation and his efforts again proved abortive.[27]

B. Failure in Moscow and London

Although the collapse of the Polish initiative meant the loss of an important opportunity for direct U.S.-DRV talks without a bombing halt,

26. On the Hanoi-area bombing halt, see Marigold Chronology, pp. 76–78, 81. The Polish postmortem was provided by Jerzy Michalowski, one of two Directors-General of the Polish Foreign Ministry. For Michalowski's remarks, see Marigold Chronology, pp. 94–95.

27. On the Administration's fear of leaks to the press, see Marigold Chronology, pp. 71–133. On Lewandowski's efforts to revive the contact, see Marigold Chronology, pp. 125–134.

it by no means signified the end to the sparring over whether and how to open negotiations. While the North Vietnamese were unwilling to go through with the Warsaw talks, they were willing to receive an American representative in Moscow, although this extended only to accepting messages from the American side. This time, the North Vietnamese would want to make sure of American "good will" prior to the opening of substantive talks.

The catalyst for this renewed effort to open direct talks took the form of a visit to North Vietnam by Harrison Salisbury between December 23 and January 7. While in Hanoi, Salisbury had a lengthy interview with Pham Van Dong, during which the Premier again projected an image of utmost confidence, stressing repeatedly that the DRV would win. Still, he was willing to consider a negotiated settlement, and in this respect he followed a path similar to that taken during his talk with Ronning in March 1966. Specifically, he tried once again to make clear that the Four Points were not preconditions for negotiations, although this time he told that to Salisbury directly rather than following the indirect approach used with Ronning.[28] More importantly, although Pham Van Dong again insisted that only after the bombing stopped would the DRV be willing to begin talks on a settlement, he continued to keep DRV intentions shrouded in ambiguity, especially with respect to two key issues. On the persistent U.S. demand for military reciprocity as the price of a bombing halt, the Premier insisted that "this was a matter of principle," that "Vietnam should not be compelled to pay a price to get the U.S. to halt something which it had no right to do in the first place." Still, he hinted at reciprocity:

If the U.S. really wants a settlement the first thing is to have good will. Of course we know what we should do if the U.S. shows good will. If they stop the whole war, we know what we should do. If they stop doing harm to the North, we know what we should do.[29]

Second, on the question of whether DRV readiness to enter into talks without prior American recognition of the Four Points signalled a willingness to make concessions on substantive issues, Pham Van Dong used his interview with Salisbury to throw out some tantalizing but still ambiguous hints. For example, Salisbury quoted him as saying, "The

28. On these points, see Salisbury, pp. 194–199.
29. The "matter of principle" and "not . . . pay a price" quotations are paraphrases of Pham Van Dong's remarks by Salisbury; see Salisbury, p. 201. The "we know what we should do" statement, however, is a direct quote; see Sunflower Chronology, p. 7. At another point, Salisbury (in his report to the State Department) quoted Pham Van Dong as saying that once the U.S. halts air attacks on the North, "as far as we are concerned we will take an appropriate stand" (Sunflower Chronology, p. 7).

moment the U.S. puts an end to the war, we will respect each other and settle every question." At another point, the Premier noted that, once hostilities had ended, "we can speak about other things. After this, there will be no lack of generosity on our part."[30]

While Administration officials would later dismiss these remarks as "interesting mood music" that "do not get us very far," Salisbury felt certain he was on to something important.[31] Just before his appointment with Pham Van Dong, he stopped at the British Consulate in Hanoi to ask for advice in the event the Premier suggested clandestine talks with the United States. The British Consul, J. H. R. Colvin, reported this to London, which passed it on to Washington. In response, the British were asked to pass a message to Salisbury authorizing him to state, in the event Pham Van Dong did suggest clandestine talks, that the U.S. placed the highest priority on finding a mutually agreeable arrangement for exchanging ideas and that it would attempt to meet any suggestions the North Vietnamese might offer.[32]

The message, however, arrived too late for Salisbury to use during his interview with Pham Van Dong; meanwhile, Salisbury told Colvin that

(a) he will report the essence of his four-hour conversation with Pham Van Dong only to the Secretary; (b) the Prime Minister had treated him as an actual or potential emissary; (c) he would not use the British cipher facilities; (d) when asked if clandestine discussions had been suggested, he said this subject must be reserved for the Secretary; (e) his articles will not include references to negotiations, etc.; (f) he thought that the NVN Government "had gone further than even [sic] before, and if there were any receptivity in the U.S. Administration there were grounds for further exploration."[33]

Following the mix-up with Salisbury in Hanoi, the Administration decided to contact the North Vietnamese directly. The U.S. Chargé in Moscow, John Guthrie, was instructed on January 5 to inform the DRV ambassador (who was then scheduled to leave shortly for Hanoi) that:

Although the U.S. Government has attempted to deliver the following message to the North Vietnamese authorities indirectly in the last few days, we would appreciate it if he would make sure that those authorities are informed

30. On these points, see Sunflower Chronology, p. 7; and Salisbury, p. 198.

31. See Sunflower Chronology, p. 7, for a report on Salisbury's briefing of Secretary Rusk concerning his talk with Pham Van Dong. The Premier's hints of reciprocity were viewed as "replays of earlier statements" given to other emissaries (i.e., Jean Sainteny, a retired French official who visited Hanoi in July 1966; and the Swedish Ambassador to Peking), while his statements on "no lack of generosity" were shrugged off on the grounds that they "appear to be without substance."

32. On these points, see Sunflower Chronology, pp. 3–4.

33. This summary of Salisbury's remarks is provided by the Pentagon analyst, Sunflower Chronology, p. 5.

directly by him upon his return to Hanoi as follows: The U.S. Government places the highest priority in finding a mutually agreeable, completely secure arrangements [sic] for exchanging communications with the government of the DRV about the possibilities of achieving a peaceful settlement of the Vietnamese dispute. If the DRV is willing to explore such possibilities with us we will attempt to meet any such suggestion they have to offer regarding the time and place of such discussions and we will be prepared to receive such information directly from the North Vietnamese through diplomatic contacts at any capital where we both maintain posts or otherwise.[34]

The DRV response to Guthrie's request for an appointment was a mixture of caution and curiosity. It was not until January 10 that Guthrie was able to meet with DRV Minister-Counselor Le Chang (the delay was apparently necessary to allow a check with Hanoi on whether to grant Guthrie an appointment). On January 17, Guthrie met again with Le Chang at the latter's request, at which time Le Chang sought to clarify two aspects of the American message. Specifically, the North Vietnamese wanted an explanation of the phrase "completely secure arrangements"; more importantly, they wanted more information on the kind of settlement envisioned by the United States.[35]

The significance of this request can best be understood in light of Pham Van Dong's "no lack of generosity" comment to Salisbury. Taken together, these messages suggest that some North Vietnamese leaders were still interested in negotiating with the U.S. despite the collapse of the Polish initiative. Their interest, in this respect, was probably heightened by the U.S. message of January 10, which, as we saw, made no mention of mutual de-escalation and instead referred only to "achieving a peaceful settlement of the Vietnamese dispute." Coming, as it did, in the aftermath of Salisbury's second stop at the British Consulate (how could the North Vietnamese know that Salisbury would refuse to use the British cipher facilities[36]), the North Vietnamese may well have

34. Sunflower Chronology, p. 6. Guthrie was the senior Embassy official pending the arrival of Ambassador Lewellyn Thompson. Cooper (1972), p. 414, traces the origins of the Moscow contact not to Salisbury but to a Soviet message that the North Vietnamese would be receptive to a contact in Moscow. Kraslow and Loory, p. 164, state that the indications of receptivity came from the North Vietnamese themselves. However, as the first sentence of the U.S. message suggests (especially the reference to indirect means of delivery), the Salisbury interview with Pham Van Dong was in fact the catalyst for the Moscow contact.

35. On these points, see Sunflower Chronology, pp. 7–8; Cooper (1972), pp. 414–415; and Kraslow and Loory, pp. 167–168. The fact that these meetings were even held suggests that DRV demands for a bombing halt as the price for "talks" were not to be taken literally.

36. It seems highly improbable that the North Vietnamese had the ability to break the British cipher, although they may have tried. They obviously knew that Salisbury visited the British Consulate shortly after his meeting with Pham Van Dong, and they may well have assumed that Salisbury did so in order to transmit a summary of the Premier's remarks.

interpreted the American message as indicating a willingness to return to the spirit, if not the letter, of the Lewandowski approach with its stress on working out new governing arrangements for South Vietnam. Still, having been burned once in Warsaw, the North Vietnamese would want to be sure—hence Le Chang's cautious probe.

If the North Vietnamese were in fact probing to see whether the U.S. was ready to discuss a coalition government for South Vietnam, they were to be deeply disappointed. On January 20, Guthrie delivered the American reply to Le Chang's inquiries—a reply that was not exactly responsive to DRV concerns. On the central issue of the American vision of a settlement, Guthrie was to tell Le Chang that

we believe DRV already has considerable information, by both public and private means, of U.S. position on settlement of Vietnam problem, and has also received formulations from others in contact with U.S. Government. . . . We believe discussions should seek to establish whether common ground now exists for an acceptable settlement.

In addition, Guthrie was to present a list of topics that the U.S. was prepared to discuss:

1. Arrangements for the reduction or the cessation of hostilities.
2. Essential elements of the Geneva Accords of 1954 and 1962, including withdrawal of any forces coming from outside South Vietnam and now present there.
3. Arrangements for a free determination by North Vietnam and South Vietnam on the issue of reunification.
4. Recognition of the independence and territorial integrity of North and South Vietnam, or of all Vietnam if the people should choose reunification.
5. The international posture of South Vietnam, including relationships with other nations.
6. Appropriate provisions relating to the internal political structure of South Vietnam, including freedom from reprisals and free political participation.
7. Appropriate objective means for insuring the integrity of all provisions agreed to.[37]

This list, however, was little more than a rehash of earlier U.S. position statements: the first two points were the oft-rejected mutual de-escalation approach, and the remaining five had appeared at one time or another in the XYZ Four Points (see Appendix II), the 14 Points (see Appendix III), and the U.S. message delivered in Rangoon on February 19, 1966. While the sixth point did touch on the central issue of South

37. For the U.S. message of January 20, see Sunflower Chronology, pp. 9–10.

Vietnam's internal politics, it would appear from the references to "free-dom from reprisal" and "free political participation" that this was the standard American position of amnesty for the Viet Cong, and it was apparently interpreted as such by the North Vietnamese.

Not surprisingly, on January 27, Le Chang completely rejected the American proposal for immediate talks. Not only did he accuse the U.S. of escalating the war and demanding that the Vietnamese people accept conditions that were "absurd and arrogant," but he also demanded an "unconditional" cessation of the bombing. Once that step had been taken, the DRV "could then exchange views with the U.S. concerning the place or date for contact between the two parties as the Government of the United States proposed in its message handed over on January 10, 1967." The next day, DRV Foreign Minister Trinh pub-licized the DRV negotiating position in an interview broadcast by Radio Hanoi.[38]

In many respects, the "Trinh formula," as it came to be known, was a stop backward from the apparent DRV willingness to negotiate as part of the MARIGOLD contact without a prior suspension of the bombing. Still, the North Vietnamese did not close the door completely. During their meeting on January 27, Le Chang told Guthrie that the DRV message was a response to the U.S. message of January 10; his govern-ment would comment on the January 20 message "at [an] appropriate time."[39] The Administration, in turn, seized on this slight opening in an attempt to continue the Moscow contact and press for its preferred ap-proach involving mutual de-escalation.

On January 31, Guthrie was instructed to call on Le Chang and make the following points: the U.S. is prepared for "direct and private talks covering any elements that either side believes should be considered in reaching a peaceful solution"; the U.S. is prepared to implement further measures of de-escalation in addition to the Hanoi-area bombing halt (still in effect) and "would be impressed with similar acts of restraint on the part of the DRV"; the U.S. was prepared to stop the bombing "as a prior and ostensibly unilateral action," although "before doing this we would want a private understanding with the DRV that additional sub-sequent steps would be taken that would amount in the aggregate to an equitable and reciprocal reduction of hostile action" (the Phase A–

---

38. On the January 27 meeting between Guthrie and Le Chang, see Sunflower Chronology, pp. 12–13. The words used by Trinh (as broadcast in English by Radio Hanoi) were as follows: "It is only after the unconditional cessation of U.S. bombing and all other acts of war against the DRV that there could be talks between the DRV and the U.S." (Sunflower Chronology, p. 17).

39. See Sunflower Chronology, p. 13.

Phase B plan); and, finally, the approaching Tet truce would be "particularly appropriate for discussions along the lines suggested above."[40]

Since Guthrie was able to deliver this message to Le Chang on February 2 despite the latter's earlier insistence on a bombing halt as the price for talks, it appears that the DRV leadership retained at least some interest in continued contacts along with a readiness to be flexible on the conditions under which "talks" could be held. This point was not lost on everyone in the Administration—Arthur Goldberg, for example, who had been deeply involved in trying to refute Polish charges of U.S. bad faith during MARIGOLD, proposed on February 2 that, so long as the Moscow contacts continued, the U.S. should refrain from attacking new targets in North Vietnam and that non-infiltration targets (involving approximately 5 percent of total sorties) should be suspended once the Tet cease-fire had ended.[41]

The President, however, was unwilling to go along with suggestions such as these. The military had strenuously opposed any reduction in U.S. military activity over Tet and were at the time seeking authority to mine DRV ports. In response to these pressures, the President characteristically staked out the middle ground and refused to budge. While unwilling to escalate the bombing, he also refused to de-escalate it unless the North Vietnamese reduced their own military activity. Thus, on January 28, he approved ROLLING THUNDER 53, which was essentially a continuation of previous bombing guidelines. That program, in turn, would stand unchanged until late February, despite the arguments of Goldberg and other Administration "doves."[42]

With the approach of the four-day Tet truce, which began on February 8 and coincided with a visit to London by Soviet Premier Kosygin, both sides engaged in a flurry of activity. On February 6, Guthrie met again with Le Chang, although their discussion centered on preserving the secrecy of the contact rather than on substantive issues. On the same day, Kosygin arrived in London, and, while the British were encouraged by his willingness to discuss Vietnam, he began his talks with Prime Minister Wilson by taking the not-very-promising line (from

40. On these points, see Sunflower Chronology, pp. 18–20.

41. For Goldberg's proposal, see Sunflower Chronology, pp. 21–22. For other proposals for U.S. de-escalation, see IV Gravel, pp. 142–143.

42. For the JCS proposals, see IV Gravel, pp. 141, 144–145. On ROLLING THUNDER 53, see IV Gravel, pp. 140–141. ROLLING THUNDER 53 did include authorization to strike the Thai Nguyen steel plant and the Haiphong cement plant, but these were not struck until ROLLING THUNDER 54 was in effect, probably because of bad weather (see IV Gravel, pp. 148–149). On the President's demand for reciprocity—"just almost any step," as he put it in a February 3 news conference—see Sunflower Discussion, p. 8.

Washington's point of view) that the Trinh formula indicated genuine
DRV willingness to talk, and he urged Wilson to use the Washington-
London "hot line" in an effort to persuade the President to stop the
bombing.[43]

From that point on, however, the Moscow-London initiative (dubbed
SUNFLOWER) began to unravel, and whatever chance there might
have been to open substantive talks with the North Vietnamese was
effectively lost in the ensuing confusion. On February 7, the American
Embassy in Moscow was given a personal letter from President Johnson
for Ho Chi Minh, which Guthrie gave to Le Chang on February 8. In
the letter, the President outlined a new formula for mutual de-escalation:

I am prepared to order a cessation of the bombing against your country and the
stopping of further augmentation of U.S. forces in South Vietnam as soon as I
am assured that infiltration into South Vietnam by land and by sea *has stopped.*
These acts of restraint on both sides would, I believe, make it possible for us to
conduct serious and private discussions leading to an early peace.[44]

What this did was to reverse the formula presented by Guthrie on February 2, which, as we saw, offered a bombing halt in exchange for a
prior understanding as to what the DRV would do *after* the bombing
stopped.

A similar reversal was at the heart of what came to be known as the
"battle of the tenses," which resulted in the worst misunderstanding
between the U.S. and Britain since the cancellation of the Skybolt
missile program in 1962. The British, as we saw earlier, had been given
the original Phase A–Phase B plan in November 1966, and they assumed that it remained U.S. policy—an assumption supported both by
briefings given to Wilson and Brown by Chester Cooper and by an am-
biguously worded message from the President to Wilson that arrived on
February 7.[45] Not surprisingly, Wilson spent virtually the entire week

43. On the Guthrie/Le Chang meeting on February 6, see Sunflower Chronology, p. 26. On the
Wilson/Kosygin meeting, see Sunflower Discussion, pp. 27–28; Harold Wilson, *A Personal Record:
The Labour Government, 1964-1970* (Boston: Little, Brown, 1971), pp. 347–349; and Kraslow and
Loory, p. 189. Wilson used this meeting to spell out the Phase A–Phase B plan in detail but got "no
flicker of interest" from Kosygin (Sunflower Chronology, p. 27).
44. Sunflower Chronology, p. 34 (emphasis added). Again, the fact that Guthrie was able to
deliver this letter suggests that the North Vietnamese were prepared to be flexible on the issue of a
bombing cessation as the price for "talks."
45. On the "battle of the tenses," see Sunflower Discussion, pp. 15–17. For Cooper's briefings,
see Cooper (1972), pp. 423–425; and Sunflower Chronology, pp. 23–24. For the President's message
to Wilson, which noted that the U.S. was "prepared . . . to inform Hanoi that if they will agree to
an assured stoppage of infiltration into South Vietnam, we will stop the bombing of North Vietnam and stop further augmentation of U.S. forces in South Vietnam," see Sunflower Chronology,
p. 30.

trying to interest Kosygin in the Phase A–Phase B plan. Although Kosygin at first shrugged it off and instead pressed the Trinh formula, by February 10 he was sufficiently interested to request a copy of the proposal in writing. A draft was quickly prepared by Cooper and given to Kosygin by Wilson that evening. Cooper's draft, as might be expected, reflected the original proposal given to the Poles and the British in November 1966.[46]

When a copy of Cooper's draft arrived in Washington, however, it caused consternation among officials there who were preoccupied with a considerably different problem. The North Vietnamese had taken advantage of the Tet bombing pause to make an all-out effort to move men and supplies into the South. More ominously, as William Bundy informed Cooper on February 9, "intelligence sources reveal that the North Vietnamese have been moving during the past two weeks an additional division from central North Vietnam southward, presumably to reinforce the two North Vietnamese divisions which are already within or just north of the DMZ." These efforts appeared, to Washington at least, as a deliberate attempt to take advantage of a "loophole" in the Phase A–Phase B plan. That plan had always envisioned a gap of between one and three weeks between the phases—i.e., the bombing would end, followed a few weeks later by an end to infiltration and by further U.S. acts of de-escalation, with the length of the gap to be negotiated between the U.S. and the DRV. DRV troop movements, however, now raised the spectre that this gap would be used for a southward dash by the three divisions mentioned by Bundy.[47]

46. For Wilson's efforts to press the Phase A–Phase B plan, see Wilson, pp. 347–356; Sunflower Discussion, pp. 15–16; and Sunflower Chronology, pp. 27–38. For a time, Wilson sought to incorporate the plan in the text of a joint U.K.-USSR statement as Co-Chairmen of the 1954 Geneva Conference calling for a reconvening of the Conference. But since the Soviets were never enthusiastic about such an approach (apparently because of the problems such a proposal would create with respect to Chinese participation), Wilson focused most of his efforts on the Phase A–Phase B plan itself (i.e., the version given to Lewandowski and Foreign Secretary George Brown in November 1966). Although a British draft of the proposal was given to Kosygin in writing on February 7, it was not until Wilson told Kosygin on February 10 that he was authorized to state that the U.S. would move first to stop the bombing if it was assured that infiltration would stop that Kosygin expressed serious interest in the proposal, asking Wilson for a written version that could be cabled to Hanoi. On the Geneva Conference proposal and Soviet reaction, see Sunflower Discussion, pp. 16, 18–21; Sunflower Chronology, pp. 31–32, 36–38. On the February 7 meeting and proposal, see Sunflower Discussion, pp. 15–16; Sunflower Chronology, pp. 31–32; and Wilson, pp. 350–351. On the version given Kosygin on February 10, see Sunflower Discussion, pp. 16–17; Sunflower Chronology, pp. 46–47; and Wilson, pp. 355–356.

47. For Bundy's message, see Sunflower Chronology, p. 40. On the DRV resupply effort, see IV Gravel, pp. 143–144. On the gap between Phase A and Phase B, see Cooper (1972), pp. 429–430. For a discussion of U.S. fears of a southward dash by the DRV divisions in or near the DMZ, see Sunflower Discussion, pp. 12–13; and Sunflower Chronology, p. 52.

As a result, American policymakers decided to scrap the old Phase A–Phase B plan and emphasize instead a different formula. The revised formula, which had already been incorporated into the President's letter to Ho Chi Minh, now made a bombing halt (combined with an end to the American buildup in the South) contingent on the actual stopping of infiltration. This new version was cabled to the British late in the evening of February 10 (*after* Wilson had already passed Cooper's draft to Kosygin) and was given to Kosygin just as he was boarding a train for a one-day excursion to Scotland.[48]

As a result of Washington's abrupt about-face, "the atmosphere at Downing Street that night," as Cooper notes in a classic understatement, "was gloomy and hostile." Wilson, at last, could restrain himself no longer and, in the early morning hours of February 11, sent two messages over the "hot line" describing the "hell of a situation" that he had been put in for his last day of talks with Kosygin, scheduled for February 12.[49] Within an hour, the White House responded, telling Wilson bluntly that the matter did not hang

on the tense of verbs. Moscow had from George Brown in November the Phase A–Phase B formulation. Hanoi had it from the Poles. Hanoi has shown no flicker of interest for more than two months. Meanwhile, their buildup continues and they have used three periods of no bombing (Christmas, New Year's, and Tet) for large-scale movement and preparation of their forces for further military action.

In addition, the White House emphasized once again that the U.S. could not "stop the bombing while three (possibly four) divisions dash south from the DMZ before—underline word their rpt their—promise is to take effect."[50]

The White House was right about one thing—the matter did not hang on "the tense of verbs"—although for the wrong reasons. Part of the problem, as we have seen, was that Washington was simply insensitive

48. On these points, see Cooper (1972), pp. 430–433; Wilson, pp. 356–358; Sunflower Discussion, p. 9; and Sunflower Chronology, pp. 47, 50, 53–57.

49. See Cooper (1972), p. 433; Wilson, pp. 358–359; and Sunflower Chronology, p. 53. For some reason, the Pentagon analyst dates Wilson's messages to the early morning of February 12, even though the accounts of Wilson and Cooper leave no doubt that they were actually sent early on February 11 (i.e., a few hours after the mix-up at the train station). As Wilson's memoirs make clear, numerous messages were exchanged between Washington and London during February 11–12. It is possible that the dates on some were confused during the process of compiling the "Sunflower" volume of the Pentagon Papers.

50. Sunflower Chronology, pp. 54–56; see also Sunflower Discussion, p. 16. Again, the Pentagon analyst dates this message to February 12, while Wilson (p. 360) indicates that it was actually sent on February 11. See also Cooper (1972), pp. 433–434.

to the main concerns of the North Vietnamese. The North Vietnamese had in fact shown a "flicker of interest," but this had been directed not toward proposals for mutual de-escalation but instead toward proposals that held out the prospect of some type of coalition government for South Vietnam.

In addition, Washington's stress on an end to infiltration stemmed not just from a concern for the safety of American forces stationed south of the DMZ but also from an awareness that an end to infiltration would give the U.S. an enormous military advantage. As William Bundy explained to Lodge:

we believe British will have made clear that our stopping "augmenting" would still permit rotation and continued supply. Stoppage of infiltration defined as meaning that men and arms cannot move from DRV into South Vietnam. . . . Deprived of additional men and of urgently needed equipment from the North, we believe NVA/VC forces would be significantly weakened in concrete terms and would probably suffer serious adverse effects on their morale. If infiltration in fact ceases and this word can be picked up by South Vietnam and allied psychological warfare units, we believe there are big chances that Chieu Hoi and reconciliation programs would produce substantially larger returns. In short, we think proposal is defensible and forthcoming, if it should ever be surfaced, but at the same time clearly favorable in terms of its effect on the military and morale situation.

The North Vietnamese may have been stubborn, but they certainly were not stupid; to have expected them to accept a proposal that would put their forces at such a clear disadvantage can only be described as naive.[51]

All this, however, wasn't clear at the time, with the result that the British continued to search for a de-escalatory formula that would be acceptable to both sides. On the afternoon of February 12, Cooper and

51. For Bundy's cable to Lodge, see Sunflower Chronology, p. 45; see also Sunflower Chronology, p. 39. It may be that the charge of naivete is unwarranted, since no one in Washington expected the North Vietnamese to accept the proposal. If that was the case, though, it would hardly make sense to go through with the whole exercise of passing the proposal via the British. As the Pentagon analyst notes (Sunflower Discussion, p. 14), the Administration clearly had a stake in maintaining good relations with the British and in persuading Kosygin to use Soviet influence in Hanoi for the purpose of opening direct U.S.-DRV negotiations. Hence, if no one expected the North Vietnamese to accept, it would have made more sense to disown Cooper's draft rather than go through with the switch of proposals at the train station—a process that irritated Kosygin and infuriated Wilson. On the other hand, going through with the exercise would have made sense if the Administration's proposals were to be surfaced eventually as evidence of its "reasonableness." Yet the Administration went to great lengths to keep its proposals secret. The Administration's behavior was, to say the least, puzzling.

Secretary to the Cabinet Burke Trend "sketched out a new proposition involving a commitment by Hanoi to keep its forces in place north of the 17th Parallel in exchange for an extension of the Tet bombing pause." Cooper and Trend checked with Wilson, who liked the idea, but all hands agreed on the importance of obtaining Washington's blessing before presenting the idea to Kosygin.[52]

That approval, however, was not immediately forthcoming. Despite prodding phone calls from Cooper, the White House would not be rushed, leaving Wilson in the uncomfortable position of having to stall for time in the hope that White House approval would arrive before the end of his final session with Kosygin (which was being held at Chequers). By 11:00 P.M. (London time), with Kosygin growing impatient to leave and still no word from Washington, Cooper "in utter desperation . . . called Rostow and dangled the telephone as far out the window as [he] could get it so that [Rostow] could hear the sound of the roaring motors [of Kosygin's police escort]. That did it. By about midnight, [Rostow] thought, the Washington version of the new proposition would be ready."[53]

The whole exercise, however, was doomed to fail, Cooper's acrobatics notwithstanding. Five minutes after Kosygin left, a message came through from Washington stating that the text of the "new" U.S. proposal would arrive shortly. The message, however, proved to be another disappointment. As described by Wilson:

If I could get a North Vietnamese assurance, either direct to the U.S., or through us, "before 10:00 A.M. British time tomorrow" (Monday) that all movements of troops and supplies into South Vietnam would stop at that time, I could promise an assurance from the U.S. that they would not resume bombing from that time. The U.S. buildup would stop within a matter of days. All of us concerned with the week's operations could then build on these acts to promote "further balanced measures of deescalation." There could then be a prompt move "to a neutral spot" to engage in unconditional discussions to bring peace.[54]

As should be evident, the proposal passed to Wilson was anything but "new"; it was in fact none other than the proposal presented in the

52. See Cooper (1972), p. 436. It appears that this proposal was aimed solely at the PAVN divisions near the DMZ and that "normal" infiltration would have been permitted (although Cooper's account is ambiguous on this point). Washington, however, was still aiming for a complete end to infiltration, as will be clear below.

53. Cooper (1972), pp. 436–437; see also Wilson, pp. 362–364.

54. Wilson, pp. 363–364. For the text of this cable, see Sunflower Chronology, p. 60. See also Cooper (1972), pp. 437–438; and Sunflower Chronology, p. 55.

President's letter to Ho Chi Minh. The 10:00 A.M. deadline, moreover, all but assured that the proposal would be rejected, suggesting that the White House was more concerned with undermining Wilson's efforts than with reaching agreement with the North Vietnamese. That failure, while inevitable, was not from lack of effort on the British and Soviet sides. Wilson, as Cooper notes, "dashed off for Claridges where he spent an hour with Kosygin discussing the new proposal." After complaining about the lack of time and the ultimatum–like character of the message, Kosygin agreed to transmit it to Moscow. True to his word, three priority cables were sent from London to Moscow shortly after Wilson departed; in addition, Kosygin called Brezhnev to urge that the North Vietnamese accept the offer. Meanwhile, Wilson managed to squeeze out a six-hour extension of the bombing pause.[55]

Despite these efforts, the "new" proposal was no more successful than its predecessors. As the Pentagon analyst notes:

At 3:32 P.M. British time, February 13, just 28 minutes before the expiration of the deadline on the U.S. proposal for using the Tet truce to begin deescalation, Hanoi broadcast a letter from Ho to the Pope. Ho was sharp in tone, denouncing U.S. aggression and demanding an unconditional and definitive cessation of all attacks on the DRV, U.S. withdrawal from South Vietnam and recognition of the NLF as the conditions for "peace." Ho did not refer to conditions for "talks." Carefully read, therefore, the letter did not address the question of mutual deescalation as a first step toward negotiations. However, its timing and tone gave the impression of a rebuff to U.S. proposals.[56]

Two days later, Le Chang presented Guthrie with Ho's reply to the President's letter of February 8. Ho was harsh and uncompromising, accusing the U.S. of "war crimes" and insisting on an "unconditional cessation" of the bombing as a precondition for talks. Consistent with this formula (something that DRV policy had not been up to that point) was Le Chang's announcement to Guthrie that he could no longer meet with him.[57] Failure in Warsaw had now been matched by failures in London and Moscow.

C. Failure in Washington

At the same time that the events described above were taking place, certain other intermediaries were also involved in the effort to promote

55. On these points, see Cooper (1972), pp. 438–439; Wilson, pp. 364–365; Allen Whiting's testimony in Ellsberg Trial Transcript, pp. 15,833–15,834; Sunflower Discussion, pp. 18–20; and Interview Data.

56. Sunflower Discussion, p. 12. For the text of Ho's letter, see Sunflower Chronology, pp. 66–67.

57. Sunflower Chronology, pp. 69–70, 71–72.

a negotiated settlement. In January 1967, for example, a pair of private American citizens, Harry Ashmore and William Baggs, traveled to Hanoi, where they met with Ho Chi Minh. Although Ho insisted that there could be no productive talks until the bombing stopped, he did take a conciliatory line on the Four Points, letting it be known they were negotiable and adding that: "If the U.S. wants to talk about a halt to the buildup of fighting forces in the South, let it first stop building up its own side. If that were done and the bombing stopped there would be much to talk about."[58]

On returning to Washington, Ashmore and Baggs reported to the State Department; a few weeks later, they drafted in collaboration with William Bundy and Averill Harriman a letter to Ho stating that the U.S. "remains prepared for secret discussions at any time, without conditions, and that such discussions might cover the whole range of topics relevant to a peaceful settlement." This letter was mailed to the DRV legation in Phnom Penh, Cambodia, on February 5; three days later, as we saw earlier, Guthrie passed to Le Chang the text of the President's letter to Ho which took a somewhat harder line, demanding an end to infiltration in exchange for a bombing halt and an end to the U.S. buildup. The coincidence of these two letters eventually led to a minor furor, triggered by charges from Ashmore and Baggs that the Administration had engaged in "double-dealing" that "effectively and brutally" canceled a "conciliatory feeler."[59]

A much more extensive effort was undertaken by the Government of Sweden. On November 11, 1966, Swedish Foreign Minister Nilsson met with Secretary Rusk in Washington, at which time Nilsson described two recent conversations between Swedish and DRV representatives in Warsaw and Hanoi. The more important of these took place in Hanoi, involving DRV Foreign Minister Trinh and the Swedish Ambassador to Peking; in the course of their talk, Trinh took a position similar to that being conveyed at the time via Lewandowski. Specifically, Trinh emphasized that the DRV sought a political rather than a military solution and added that, if the U.S. unconditionally and definitively ended the bombing and recognized the NLF as one of the spokesmen for the South Vietnamese people (albeit the most valid one), then the North Vietnamese "knew what they had to do." In response, Rusk urged that the Swedes seek clarification, especially on the issue of reciprocity for a

58. Ashmore and Baggs, pp. 46–48.

59. Ibid., pp. 79–80. For the Administration's reply, see *U.S.-Vietnam Relations*, VI. B. 4., pp. 237–271; and Sunflower Chronology, pp. 106–109.

bombing halt, and this the Swedes undertook with a vengeance. In the months that followed, Swedish diplomats met repeatedly with representatives of the U.S., the DRV, and the NLF, although, as the Pentagon analyst notes, "the Swedes were more active over time than any other intermediary [but they] produced the least amount of information."[60]

The most audacious effort of all, however, was undertaken by the Rumanians. On October 22, 1966, Ambassador Goldberg met with Rumanian Foreign Minister Corneliu Manescu, at which time Goldberg noted that the U.S. required some "indication as to what North Vietnam would do in response to a prior cessation of the bombing." Three months later, Manescu brazenly informed the American Ambassador in Bucharest that "you always say you must have signal as to what would happen [if the bombing stopped]. What I tell you is the signal." Unfortunately, Manescu could not be more specific concerning the content of the "signal," aside from insisting that the Rumanians had been in continuous contact with Hanoi and that the "signal" was an accurate one. Nor were the Rumanians ever able to state precisely what would happen if the bombing stopped, despite repeated prodding from Washington.[61]

Despite the time and effort invested in these negotiating tracks by the participants, it is clear with the benefit of hindsight that they were all sideshows compared to the main events unfolding in Warsaw, Moscow, and London. In fact, these efforts were, if anything, counterproductive, in that they distracted busy officials in Washington and Hanoi and forced them to deal with essentially irrelevant issues. For this, the intermediaries must themselves share much of the blame. Ashmore and Baggs, for example, not realizing that everything the North Vietnamese said to them had already been passed to the U.S. through other channels, clearly had an inflated sense of their own importance and were unwilling to concede that the Administration might have preferred to deal with Hanoi through what it felt to be a more reliable channel (i.e. Moscow). Similarly, the Swedish role was motivated largely by considerations of Swedish domestic politics—specifically, a desire to pacify the Swedish Left by playing an active and "constructive" role in arranging

60. The Swedish role is detailed in Aspen, pp. 1–60 (for the November 11 Rusk-Nilsson meeting, see Aspen, pp. 1–7). The Pentagon analyst's comment is cited in Jack Anderson's column in the *Washington Post*, June 14, 1972, p. C27.

61. On these points, see Rumanian Chronology, pp. 1–7. Manescu's announcement that he was giving the "signal" came on January 23, 1967; on January 28, however, he was forced to admit that he had no specific knowledge of what Hanoi would do but that he had based his statements on various information and developments which the Rumanian Government had noted.

negotiations. The Rumanians, on the other hand, were simply "very poor reporters. They did not pick up distinctions such as talks, negotiations, and settlement terms. . . . It is likely that Hanoi did not take the Rumanians seriously."[62]

By far the most important "distraction," though, was the renewed interest in escalation that surfaced in Washington immediately after the collapse of the Moscow talks. All through January and February 1967, the military had pressed for rapid escalation, and, although the President resisted these pressures while the Moscow and London contacts were under way, once those contacts broke off the whole range of escalatory options came under review. An interagency effort produced a "shopping list" of options that went to the President on February 21. The next day, Presidential approval was granted for a number of measures, although, true to form, the President approved "only a limited number of the measures presented to him, by and large those that would incur little risk of counterescalation."[63] Implementation began almost immediately: on February 24, U.S. artillery units began firing over the DMZ at targets in North Vietnam; on February 27, U.S. planes began mining internal waterways and coastal estuaries in North Vietnam south of the 20th Parallel; and on March 10, the Thai Nguyen Iron and Steel plant was bombed for the first time. As the Pentagon analyst notes, "the slow squeeze was once more the order of the day with the emphasis on progressively destroying North Vietnam's embryonic industrial capability."[64]

Interestingly enough, this mid-February shift of emphasis from diplomacy to escalation kicked off a cyclical pattern that was to dominate the conduct of the war over the next three months. With the decisions on escalation out of the way, the attention of senior officials quickly reverted to the question of diplomatic contacts with the North Vietnamese. On March 11, Lewellyn Thompson, the American Ambassador in Moscow, was instructed to seek an appointment with his DRV counterpart to inform him that the U.S. was convinced that the "shortest road" to a settlement was through "direct talks between our repre-

62. The Pentagon analyst's comment on the Rumanian role can be found in Jack Anderson's column in the *Washington Post*, June 14, 1972, p. C27. On the Swedish role, see The Setting, p. 3.

63. On the military's proposals for escalation, see IV Gravel, pp. 139, 144–145, 415. On the post-Tet review, see IV Gravel, p. 145. On the "shopping list," see IV Gravel, pp. 145–147, 421–424. On the President's decision, see IV Gravel, p. 148.

64. On these points, see IV Gravel, pp. 148–149. All these actions were approved by the President on February 22. The President also approved strikes on power plants in the DRV (except those in the Hanoi and Haiphong areas) and on the Haiphong cement plant. For additional details on the conduct of the air war, see Baggs, p. 184.

sentatives. [It] would not appear from record that we and DRV disagree on this point but that we have been unable to find way of moving toward talks."[65]

Thompson, however, was less than enthusiastic about these instructions, replying on March 13 that, in view of the recent escalation of the bombing,

> this strikes me as a singularly inappropriate time to make this approach. It will almost certainly be rebuffed by DRV who will not wish to give appearance of submitting to increased military pressure. More importantly, . . . our approach at this time will be interpreted by Soviets as cynically timed to insure refusal and merely build up our record of peace efforts.

In response, Secretary Rusk personally urged Thompson to go ahead, telling him somewhat cryptically that, "given the potentialities which lie ahead, we are not indifferent to establishing a record if that is all that Hanoi will permit."[66]

Thompson, of course, was right all along. If there was one lesson that should have been apparent from the MARIGOLD fiasco, it was the danger of coupling peace initiatives with attacks on sensitive targets (like the Thai Nguyen plant). To make matters worse, on March 14, two days before an Embassy official phoned the DRV Embassy to seek an appointment for Thompson, U.S. jets conducted extremely heavy attacks on the North (128 missions involving approximately 450 planes). Thus, it should not have been surprising when, after some temporizing by both sides, the North Vietnamese refused to grant Thompson an appointment.[67]

With the collapse of this latest effort to begin talks with the DRV, questions of escalation once again came to the fore. On March 18,

65. On these points, see Sunflower Chronology, pp. 91–92. The timing of this initiative was based at least in part on comments by a member of the Soviet UN delegation, who had suggested that this was a good time for U.S.-DRV talks and that these could take place without a bombing halt. In addition, with the recent arrival of both Ambassador Thompson and DRV Ambassador Nguyen Tho Chan, it was hoped that ambassadorial-level talks (which had been the goal of the Guthrie–Le Chang talks) could now begin.

66. On these points, see Sunflower Chronology, pp. 92–93.

67. On the March 14 air strikes, see IV Gravel, p. 455. In response to the American Embassy's initial request for an appointment for Thompson, made by phone on March 16, the DRV Embassy had been noncommital. They obviously had to check first with Hanoi, and they thus requested that the U.S. Embassy call back on March 18. On March 17, however, the Embassy was told to delay to gain time to assess an initiative put forward by U Thant on March 14. Hence, the Embassy did not call back until March 21, at which time the North Vietnamese refused to receive Thompson, citing as their reason the "new steps of escalation" which the U.S. was carrying out "every day." On these points, see Sunflower Chronology, pp. 93–94; and U.S.-Vietnam Relations, VI. A. 1., p. 57.

General Westmoreland dropped a bombshell in the form of a troop request totaling 201,250 more Americans. Although Westmoreland had accepted the Program #4 ceiling of 470,000 Americans on the grounds that more troops would have strained both the Vietnamese economy and the military services' capabilities, he now argued that the ceiling did not "permit sustained operations of the scope and intensity required to avoid an unreasonably protracted war." Consequently, 100,000 more troops (the "minimum essential force") would be needed "as soon as possible but no later than July 1, 1968"; beyond that, an additional 100,000 men (the "optimum force") might well be needed during fiscal 1969. In the meantime, the air war over the North was escalated another notch with the addition on March 22 of two significant new targets: the Haiphong power plants.[68]

Although the JCS would not formally endorse Westmoreland's request until April 20, the President almost certainly knew that a troop request was in the works, and it is difficult to resist the inference that this was a factor in driving the escalation-diplomacy cycle forward.[69] On April 5, the American Embassy in Moscow was instructed to deliver to the DRV Embassy a new letter from the President for Ho Chi Minh. While conciliatory in tone, the new letter was essentially another rehash of previous American position statements, and it was treated as such by the North Vietnamese. On April 6, the day it was delivered, it was returned to the U.S. Embassy marked "Unacceptable: Return to sender."[70]

With the failure of this latest diplomatic move, the attention of senior officials swung back to questions of escalation. On April 8, ROLLING THUNDER 55 was approved, which added a number of targets to the authorized list, among them

the Kep airfield, the Hanoi power transformer near the center of town, and the Haiphong cement plant, POL storage, and ammunition dump . . . along with

68. For Westmoreland's request, see IV Gravel, pp. 427–431; and Westmoreland, p. 227. On the air war, see IV Gravel, pp. 150–151. Bad weather over the North caused the cancellation of many of the strikes that the military had hoped to launch against industrial targets there.

69. The delay between the request and the JCS endorsement was necessary to allow detailed studies on the "validity" of the request. Concerning the President's knowledge of the request, the President and Westmoreland were both present at the Guam Conference on March 20–21, 1967; the Pentagon analyst suggests that Westmoreland probably did indicate that he needed more troops. See IV Gravel, pp. 150, 424–427, especially p. 426.

70. For the text of the letter, see Johnson, p. 596. See also Sunflower Chronology, p. 97. As part of this effort, the Administration apparently tried to persuade the Soviets to mediate: see IV Gravel, p. 446, for a William Bundy memo that refers to "pressing [the Soviets] hard" in "early April."

more bridges, railroad yards and vehicle parks elsewhere in the country. The restrictions on the Hanoi and Haiphong perimeters were relaxed to permit the destruction of these new targets.[71]

Still, the Administration did not abandon its hopes for enticing the DRV into some type of arrangement for mutual de-escalation (or, at the least, building a record that could be used to good effect with public opinion at home and abroad). In April 1967, the Canadians suggested that "both sides agree to respect once again the Demilitarized Zone along the 17th Parallel. This could be a first step toward restoring the terms of the 1954 Agreement and might lead to further deescalation." The State Department, in turn, expanded on this suggestion, proposing on April 19 a U.S.-DRV withdrawal to lines ten miles south and north, respectively, of the DMZ. In addition, American representatives "contacted the Canadians and suggested that they meet soon with their Indian and Polish partners in the ICC to explore the implications of an ICC 'peacekeeping force,' as opposed to a mere monitoring force, in the expanded Zone." The next day, however, the Haiphong power plants were struck for the first time, leading the Soviets (who had been urged to sell the DMZ plan to Hanoi) to question American sincerity. The North Vietnamese rejected the proposal on April 22.[72]

With the demise of the DMZ proposal, the attention of Administration officials was inevitably forced back to questions of escalation. This time, though, the Administration embarked on a searching reappraisal of American strategy in the war, an effort undertaken largely in response to the JCS endorsement of Westmoreland's troop request on April 20 but also in response to the continued escalation of the air war. While the reappraisal was under way, the air assault on jet airfields and power plants in the DRV continued unabated, culminating on May 19 with an attack on the Hanoi power plant. The failure of these attacks, despite the destruction of the targets involved, to have any measurable effect on the DRV's ability to support the war in the South added an element of urgency to the efforts of civilian policymakers to reorient the

71. IV Gravel, p. 151. The Haiphong cement plant had been authorized as part of ROLLING THUNDER 53 and 54 (see note 64, above). According to Admiral Sharp, the "execute" message for ROLLING THUNDER 55 was not sent until April 23 (Sharp and Westmoreland, p. 32).

72. On these points, see Cooper (1972), pp. 444–446. In addition, on April 10, Ambassador Thompson in Moscow was instructed to contact Soviet Foreign Minister Gromyko (whom he saw on April 13) to inform him of U.S. readiness to contact Pham Van Dong during the Premier's forthcoming trip to Moscow, although nothing ever came of this initiative (see Sunflower Chronology, pp. 98–99).

air war in the direction of (hopefully) more productive attacks on the infiltration routes in the southern DRV.[73]

The immediate cause of the reappraisal, as already noted, was a JCS memo on April 20 endorsing the Westmoreland troop request and arguing for a Reserve call-up and involuntary extension of tours of duty in order to allow the services to meet Westmoreland's needs. These recommendations, as the Pentagon analyst notes,

promised to spawn significant political and economic repercussions and they stimulated a plethora of inter-agency reviews and studies. . . . The first of these reviews originated in the State Department, in the office of Undersecretary Nicholas deB. Katzenbach. In a memorandum, he listed three jobs which he felt had to be done in Vietnam:

1. Assess the current situation in Vietnam and the various political and military actions which could be taken to bring this to a successful conclusion.

2. Review the possibilities for negotiation, including an assessment of the ultimate U.S. position in relationship to the DRV and NLF.

3. Assess the military and political effects of intensification of the war in South Vietnam and in North Vietnam.

In addition, Katzenbach requested that the agencies involved undertake an assessment of two alternative courses of action: Course A, which provided the 200,000 men sought by Westmoreland and greatly intensified actions against the North; and Course B, which limited troop increases to "those that could be generated without calling up the Reserves"—i.e., nine battalions (10,000 men).[74]

Katzenbach's priorities were indicative of the thinking prevalent among civilian officials. By April 1967, the overriding concern of the civilians was to find some way to end the war, preferably through negotiations (Katzenbach's points 1 and 2); escalation (Katzenbach's point 3) was the preferred alternative only among the military and the Congressional "hawks." The civilians, moreover, had good reason to be thinking about an exit. On April 27, General Westmoreland met with the President in Washington; as described by the Pentagon analyst:

When asked about the influence of increased infiltration upon his operations, Westmoreland replied that as he saw it "this war is action and counteraction. Anytime we take an action we expect a reaction." The President replied: "When we add divisions can't the enemy add divisions? If so, where does it all

73. On the air war, see IV Gravel, pp. 152–154; Cooper (1972), pp. 447–449; and Sharp and Westmoreland, pp. 32–40.

74. See IV Gravel, pp. 154, 436–439. (The "material missing" from Gravel can be found in U.S.-Vietnam Relations, IV. C. 6. b., p. 76.)

end?" Westmoreland answered: "The VC and DRV strength in South Vietnam now totals 285,000 men. It appears that last month we reached the crossover point *in areas excluding the two northern provinces.* Attritions will be greater than additions to the force. . . . The enemy has eight divisions in South Vietnam. He has the capability of deploying 12 divisions although he would have difficulty supporting all of these. He would be hard pressed to support more than 12 divisions. If we add 2½ divisions, it is likely the enemy will react by adding more troops." The President then asked "At what point does the enemy ask for volunteers?" Westmoreland's only reply was, "That is a good question."

Even more disturbing were Westmoreland's estimates of how long the war would last—estimates that stood in sharp contrast to the optimism of 1964 and 1965. According to Westmoreland, "unless the will of the enemy is broken or unless there was an unraveling of the VC infra-structure the war could go on for five years." With the minimum essential force (100,000 more men), the war could go on for three years; and even with the optimum force (200,000 more men), Westmoreland felt the war could go on for two more years.[75]

Of greater importance, though, was the way in which the Spring 1967 reappraisal repudiated the strategy of "graduated pressures." As we saw earlier, the strategy advocated by most civilian officials during 1964 assumed that the spectre of mounting destruction would eventually erode DRV will to continue the war in the South. Although this approach had never been formally endorsed by the President, neither had it been definitively rejected; if anything, after nearly two years of squabbling over an appropriate focus for the air war, the "slow squeeze" had finally begun in earnest in February 1967 with the Presi-dent's authorization of attacks on targets such as the Thai Nguyen Iron and Steel Plant and the Haiphong Cement Plant. By then, however, most civilian officials had come to the conclusion that increasing pres-sures were counterproductive, in that they only strengthened DRV will to continue. Consequently, as the reappraisal proceeded, virtually all of the original proponents of the "graduated pressures" approach put themselves on record as favoring restrictions on both the air war over the North and on the number of American troops committed to the ground war in the South.

On May 1, for example, William Bundy weighed in with a paper argu-ing against both mining Haiphong's harbor and attacking any more major targets in North Vietnam (with the exception of the already

75. IV Gravel, p. 442 (emphasis in original); see also Westmoreland, pp. 227–228.

approved Hanoi power station), an argument "based essentially on the belief that these actions will not change Hanoi's position or affect Hanoi's capabilities in ways that counterbalance the risk and adverse reaction in China and with the Soviets alone." The timing and suddenness of American moves since December 1966 (MARIGOLD, SUN-FLOWER, and the bombing of Hanoi) had, in Bundy's view, given the North Vietnamese the impression that "we wish to get the war over by 1968 at all costs." Hence, he argued for a "steady firm course" that would "persuade them that we are prepared to stick it if necessary."[76]

Although Bundy did not come right out and say it, his paper implied that escalation would be counterproductive by leading the North Vietnamese to think the U.S. was looking for a quick way out, thus increasing their determination to fight on. John McNaughton, however, was more direct. On May 5, in a "rough draft" of a DPM on the air war, he argued that

the military gain from destruction of additional military targets north of 20° will be slight. If we believed that air attacks in that area would change Hanoi's will, they might be worth the added loss of American life and the risks of expansion of the war. However, there is no evidence that this will be the case, while there is considerable evidence that *such bombing will strengthen Hanoi's will*. In this connection, Consul-General Rice . . . said what we believe to be the case—that we cannot by bombing reach the critical level of pain in North Vietnam and that, "below that level, pain only increases the will to fight." Sir Robert Thompson . . . said . . . that our bombing, particularly in the Red River basin, "is unifying North Vietnam."

Consequently, McNaughton recommended that the bombing be reoriented toward attacks on the infiltration routes through the southern DRV (a suggestion that was seconded in memos by Rostow on May 6 and William Bundy on May 8).[77]

At the same time that these proposals were being aired, a similar reappraisal was taking place on the question of troops for the ground war in the South. In this respect the most extensive critique of the Westmoreland strategy came from the Systems Analysis Office, and it, too, represented a repudiation of the rationale under which American troops had

76. For Bundy's memo, see IV Gravel, pp. 155–156, 444–447. A similar argument was made by McGeorge Bundy in an unsolicited letter to the President, cited in IV Gravel, pp. 157–159.

77. For McNaughton's memo, see IV Gravel, pp. 160–162, 474–476 (emphasis added). For Rostow's memo, see IV Gravel, pp. 163–165, 476–477. For William Bundy's memo of May 8, see IV Gravel, pp. 165–168.

originally been sent to South Vietnam. As we saw in Chapter 3, the basing of Marines at DaNang had been justified at least in part by a belief that such a move would deter further DRV involvement by demonstrating American readiness to "do what was necessary" to save South Vietnam. The Systems Analysis critique, however, argued that "Hanoi is willing to wait. We have hurt them some, and we can even hurt them some more, but not so badly as to destroy their society or their hope for regaining in the future the material things they sacrifice today." Consequently:

Additional forces, added burdens on the U.S. economy, and the calling of the reserves will only serve to increase [the] DRV's belief that the U.S. will not remain in South Vietnam for the long pull. Additional forces make it appear that we are trying for the quick kill. Hanoi knows that we cannot achieve it and that the American public will be bitter and divided unless we do. We should be looking for ways to ease the burden for the years ahead, rather than making the war more costly.[78]

All of these strains of thought came together on May 19 in a DPM prepared by McNaughton for McNamara's signature. The DPM was a comprehensive document covering both the air war over the North and the ground war in the South, drawing heavily on the memos summarized above. Still, there were a number of distinctive features about the DPM. Most importantly, it constituted an all-out effort to set a ceiling, once and for all, on the American role in the war. McNaughton had been deeply disturbed by the trend in U.S. policy; in an earlier memo to McNamara commenting on the May 5 "rough draft," he noted that

there is [a] fatal flaw in the strategy in the draft. It is that the strategy falls into the trap that has ensnared us for the past three years. It actually *gives* the troops while only *praying* for their proper use and for constructive diplomatic action. Limiting the present decision to an 80,000 add-on does the very important business of postponing the issue of a Reserve call-up (and all of its horrible baggage), but postpone it is all that it does—probably to a worse time, 1968. Providing the 80,000 troops is tantamount to acceding to the whole Westmoreland-Sharp request. This being the case, they will "accept" the 80,000. But six months from now, in will come messages like the "470,000-570,000" messages, saying that the requirement remains at 201,000 (or more). Since no pressure will have been put on anyone, the military war will have gone on as before and

78. IV Gravel, p. 457. See also IV Gravel, pp. 456–459, for the rest of the Systems Analysis critique.

no diplomatic progress will have been made. It follows that the "philosophy" of the war should be fought out now so everyone will not be proceeding on their own major premises, and getting us in deeper and deeper; at the least, the President should give General Westmoreland his limit. . . . That is, if General Westmoreland is to get 550,000 men, he should be told "that will be all and we mean it."

Consistently with this advice, the DPM argued strenuously for rejecting Course A (the 200,000-man increase) and for adopting Course B (now defined as providing 30,000 more troops while cutting back on the bombing of the North). In addition, the DPM advised issuing a NSAM "nailing down U.S. policy as described herein"—i.e., Course B.[79]

Second, in line with the attempt to put a ceiling on the American role, the DPM proposed a far-reaching redefinition of American objectives in the war. According to McNaughton:

Our commitment is only to see that the people of South Vietnam are permitted to determine their own future. This commitment ceases if the country ceases to help itself. It follows that no matter how much we might hope for some things, our *commitment* is *not*:

to expel from South Vietnam regroupees, who are South Vietnamese (though we do not like them),

to ensure that a particular person or group remains in power, nor that the power runs to every corner of the land (though we prefer certain types and hope their writ will run throughout South Vietnam),

to guarantee that the self-chosen government is non-Communist (though we believe and strongly hope it will be), and

to insist that the independent South Vietnam remain separate from North Vietnam (though in the short-run, we would prefer it that way).[80]

Third and finally, McNaughton went further than ever before in suggesting some type of accommodation between the NLF and the GVN. As part of the timetable for implementing the DPM's proposals, McNaughton suggested that, in September, the U.S. should attempt to

move the newly-elected Saigon government well beyond its National Reconciliation program to seek a political settlement with the non-Communist members of the NLF—to explore a ceasefire and to reach an accommodation with the non-Communist South Vietnamese who are under the Viet Cong banner; to accept them as members of an opposition political party, and, if necessary, *to accept their individual participation in the national government*—in sum, a settle-

79. For the "fatal flaw" comment, see IV Gravel, p. 478 (emphasis in original). For McNaughton's DPM, see IV Gravel, pp. 169–177, 479–489.

80. IV Gravel, p. 175 (emphasis in original).

ment to transform the members of the Viet Cong from military opponents to political opponents.[81]

McNaughton's DPM, however, proved to be no more successful in redefining and reorienting the American role in the war than were the frantic diplomatic efforts discussed earlier in getting the U.S. out of the war. Secretary McNamara showed the DPM to the President on May 19; his reaction, however, was apparently a cool one, leading McNamara to request on May 20 that various agencies undertake a study of a number of alternative bombing programs. Although "the Washington papermill must have broken all previous production records" in responding to McNamara's request, the result of the intensified paper-shuffling was predictable enough.[82] The JCS "literally bombarded" McNamara with memos, all of which argued for escalation in one form or another; the CIA continued to produce estimates arguing that meaningful interdiction was impossible; and caught in the middle were the civilians—McNamara, Vance, McNaughton, Harold Brown (Secretary of the Air Force), Paul Nitze (Secretary of the Navy), and William Bundy—all of whom opposed escalation but still hoped that reorienting the bombing would result in more effective interdiction of infiltration.[83]

In an attempt to reconcile these various points of view, McNaughton once again undertook to prepare a DPM, this time on the air war alone. In the new memo, completed on June 12, McNaughton examined three alternatives: intensified attacks on the Hanoi-Haiphong area; emphasis on the infiltration routes south of the 20th Parallel; and extension of the current program (dubbed "A," "B," and "C," respectively). Once again, McNaughton made the case for reorienting the bombing toward the infiltration routes (Alternative B); and once again, his efforts proved to be in vain.[84]

There is, as the Pentagon analyst notes, no evidence that the President even saw the new DPM. With the Six Day War in the Middle East and the June 23 summit with Soviet Premier Kosygin at Glassboro,

81. Ibid., p. 176 (emphasis added).

82. On the President's reaction, see IV Gravel, pp. 177, 183. The President did, however, order a halt to bombing within ten miles of Hanoi. The ban went into effect on May 22 and remained in effect, except for one attack in mid-June, until August 9. The President later described this as a "course midway between the proposal of those who wanted to cut back our air action and the plan advanced by those who believed we should step up strikes in the North" (see Johnson, p. 368). For McNamara's "bombing options" request, see IV Gravel, p. 183.

83. For the views of the participants in the bombing options debate, see IV Gravel, pp. 117–118, 192–195, 489–508.

84. For the June 12 DPM, see IV Gravel, pp. 189–191, 509–510.

there were plenty of distractions to keep Presidential attention focused elsewhere. In any event, the President's eventual decision was to adopt Alternative C—i.e., "continuing the bit-by-bit expansion of armed reconnaissance and striking a few new fixed targets in each ROLLING THUNDER series, but still holding back from closing the ports. . . ."[85]

Nowhere was the preference for continued incremental escalation better illustrated than in the President's decision on ROLLING THUNDER 57, approved on July 20. As described by the Pentagon analyst, "16 fixed targets were selected, including one airfield, one rail yard, two bridges, and 12 barracks and supply areas. . . ." In addition, "armed reconnaissance was expanded along 23 road, rail, and waterway segments between the 30-mile and the 10-mile circles around Hanoi." ROLLING THUNDER 57 was, in short, "a decision to postpone the issue, insuring that the partisans would continue their fight."[86]

A similar decision for incremental escalation was the eventual outcome of the Westmoreland troop request. The President had been in no hurry to confront a decision of that magnitude, and it was not until early July that the troop request began to receive serious consideration. Shortly before he left on July 5 for another visit to South Vietnam, McNamara received a Systems Analysis memo suggesting that the number of troops that could be provided without a Reserve call-up or NATO drawdown was three-and-two-thirds division equivalents, somewhat more than previously expected. McNamara, in turn, apparently was "given the green light by the President to negotiate anywhere below this level but not to exceed it, that is, not to bump up against the crucial mobilization line."[87]

As things turned out, the actual troop decision proved to be something of an anticlimax. On McNamara's last night in Saigon, he and Westmoreland worked out the basis for further deployments by simply taking the forces available (the three-and-two-thirds divisions) and subtracting from that the number of spaces that could be filled by Vietnamese civilians—approximately 14,400. This worked out to a 45,000-man increase, or an overall ceiling of 525,000. Although it would require another month of bargaining to work out which units would be sent to Vietnam, the 525,000-man ceiling was maintained and eventually published within the Pentagon on August 14 as Program #5.[88]

85. IV Gravel, pp. 191, 196.

86. See IV Gravel, p. 196.

87. See IV Gravel, pp. 513–514.

88. See IV Gravel, pp. 523–527. For additional details on the troop decision, see Johnson, p. 370; and Westmoreland, p. 230.

The President, in short, had once again opted for "more of the same," both for the air war over the North and the ground war in the South, even though "more of the same" had, to this point at least, produced little in the way of progress toward a settlement of the conflict. As a result, it would take another nine months of at times Byzantine intrigue, not to mention enormous human suffering in North and South Vietnam, before American and North Vietnamese representatives would finally sit down together in Paris.

II. End of a Policy (June 1967–May 1968)

The period separating the ROLLING THUNDER 57/Program #5 decisions and the opening of the Paris peace talks was at once substantially similar to and yet noticeably different from preceding periods. On the one hand, similarities abounded, especially with respect to the negotiating positions staked out by the parties and the tenacity with which they clung to those positions. On the other hand, however, this period differed sharply from the recent past in at least one critical respect—a difference that can be traced largely to the decision sometime in 1967 by officials in Hanoi to abandon their own version of "incremental escalation" and to launch an all-out offensive during the 1968 Tet holiday. This "Tet Offensive," as it came to be known, would have a decisive effect on the course of the war, although not the one intended. In the U.S., the offensive would lead the Johnson Administration to abandon once and for all its own escalatory strategy, while the failure of the offensive to produce a general uprising in the South would play a major role in leading the DRV to respond positively to President Johnson's dramatic offer of March 31, 1968.

A. "The More Things Change. . . ."

The "sameness" in American and DRV policy referred to above became evident very early in the period under consideration. On June 1, 1967, the Norwegian Ambassador in Peking, Ole Algard, had an interesting talk with his DRV counterpart, Ngo Loan, the substance of which was reported to Washington on June 14. During their talk, Loan stressed a number of points that had already been made by Pham Van Dong in his meetings with Ronning, Lewandowski, and Salisbury. Among other things, Loan told Algard that, while the DRV was strongly disposed toward negotiations, it was deeply distrustful of American intentions, viewing the escalation of the bombing and the American buildup in the South as evidence that the U.S. intended to stay permanently in South

Vietnam. In addition, Loan noted that whenever the DRV had shown interest in negotiations, the U.S. had taken this as a sign of weakness and escalated the bombing. As a result, the DRV imposed one condition for negotiations—namely, an "unconditional" end to the bombing—although Loan stressed that this was the only condition and that speeches from "other quarters" (Peking) did not reflect DRV thinking. Furthermore, according to Loan, once negotiations were under way, the DRV position would be "very flexible"—"we are," as he put it, "ready for very far-reaching compromises to get an end to the war."[89]

Just as Loan's remarks were a replay of previous DRV position statements, so too was the American response a replay of previous American appeals for reciprocity for a bombing halt. Although Algard was asked to probe whether Loan's failure to demand a "permanent" as well as "unconditional" cessation represented any softening of the DRV position, the U.S. reply noted that the American position remained unchanged—a cessation without "at least some private assurance of appropriate reciprocal action by North Vietnam" would give the DRV a military advantage and would not be conducive to further talks. In addition, while Algard could assure Loan that the U.S. meant what it said about a six-month withdrawal deadline at the Manila Conference, the U.S. reply noted that this withdrawal was to be coupled with the withdrawal not just of regular DRV forces in the South but also with the removal of the "regroupees"—i.e., the native southerners who went north after 1954 but who were later sent back to the South.[90]

Algard, however, was unable to see Loan until August 5. In the meantime, the locus for efforts to open direct U.S.-DRV talks shifted to another channel, this one involving two Frenchmen, Raymond Aubrac and Herbert Marcovich, and Henry Kissinger, then professor of government at Harvard. Marcovich and Kissinger had met for a private talk in Paris in June 1967, during which Marcovich mentioned that he had a friend (Aubrac) who had opened his home to Ho Chi Minh in 1946 when Ho was in Paris for negotiations with the French. The two had grown quite fond of each other, and Marcovich wondered whether it would be possible to build on their friendship to promote a political settlement.[91]

89. These points are based on Ohio, pp. 1-3; and on Interview Data. Algard's report was passed to the U.S. Embassy in Oslo by Norwegian Foreign Minister Lyng and thence to Washington.

90. For the U.S. response, see Ohio, pp. 2-5. In addition, Algard was asked to probe for details on Loan's suggestion that the DRV position was flexible and open to compromise.

91. For background on the Aubrac/Marcovich channel, see Pennsylvania, pp. 1-3; Cooper (1972), pp. 450-451; and Kraslow and Loory, pp. 219-220. The reason for the delay between Algard's first and second meeting with Loan was a Hanoi decision to recall all DRV Ambassadors for consultations during the summer of 1967 (see Oberdorfer [1971], p. 63; and Ohio, p. 5).

With the consent of the State Department and the French Government, Aubrac and Marcovich visited Hanoi between July 21 and 26. While there, they met twice with Pham Van Dong and once with Ho Chi Minh (although the meeting with Ho was noteworthy mainly for its revelation of how little Ho was involved in the day-to-day business of governing).[92] Nor was much new ground covered in the meetings with Pham Van Dong. During the first meeting, held on the morning of July 24, Marcovich outlined "as a private idea" a proposal involving an end to the bombing coupled with a DRV assurance that the cessation would not be used to gain a military advantage.[93] Although the Premier replied with the by now familiar stand that "We want an unconditional end of bombing and if that happens there will be no further obstacle to negotiations," it appears that he was intrigued by Marcovich's proposal.

For one thing, Pham Van Dong used this first meeting with Aubrac and Marcovich to soften the DRV position slightly by indicating that no formal announcement of a bombing halt would be required—a de facto cessation would be satisfactory. In addition, he closed the meeting by telling Aubrac and Marcovich: "You see, dear friends, that the problem is very complicated. You may think that your travels are useless. In fact you have given us much to think about. I will see you again and we will talk again." Perhaps even more important, however, was what Pham Van Dong did *not* say during this first meeting. In contrast to his meetings with Seaborn, Ronning, and Salisbury, there were no expressions of confidence in an eventual DRV victory. Instead, the Premier was sober and restrained, even expressing concern that the next step in the bombing would be an attack on the dikes and appealing to Aubrac and Marcovich to help turn world opinion against such a move. Pham Van Dong, then, was apparently speaking sincerely when he told Aubrac and Marcovich that they had given him "much to think about."[94]

92. Ho admitted to Aubrac that the details of the negotiations were in Pham Van Dong's hands; in addition, after the meeting with Ho, Pham Van Dong told Aubrac that "we try to spare President Ho as many details as we can. He is an old man; we want him to live to see his country unified" (Pennsylvania, p. 6).

93. This was a variant of a proposal given by President Johnson to Soviet Premier Kosygin during the Glassboro Summit in June 1967, whereby the U.S. would halt the bombing if the North Vietnamese would agree that their forces near the DMZ would not advance southward (which was itself a variant of the proposal developed by Cooper and the British during SUNFLOWER). On the Glassboro meeting, see Johnson, p. 257. On the first meeting with Pham Van Dong, see Pennsylvania, pp. 4–5. One suspects that the "private proposal" was passed to Marcovich by Washington via Kissinger, but the "Pennsylvania" section of *The Pentagon Papers* is silent on this point. So, too, are all public accounts of the negotiations, with the exception of Kraslow and Loory, p. 222, who report that Kissinger told Aubrac and Marcovich what the U.S. wanted said to the North Vietnamese.

94. On this meeting, see Pennsylvania, pp. 4–5. Pham Van Dong's concern over the bombing

Unfortunately, however, the DRV leadership was by no means of one mind on the issue of negotiating with the United States. On July 22, the day after Aubrac and Marcovich arrived in Hanoi, the Army newspaper *Quan Doi Nhan Dan* published an article by General Le Quang Dao, deputy chief of the Army's Political Directorate, which insisted that the war in the South could be won only by waging a protracted and extremely violent struggle there. That sort of argument, as Latimer notes, when used by one of the top leadership, usually meant that someone was suggesting the opposite course—namely, negotiations—something that General Dao adamantly opposed.[95] It would appear, moreover, that the effect of this vehement opposition to negotiations by at least part of the leadership was to set a limit on just how far Pham Van Dong could go in his reply to Aubrac and Marcovich. In effect, the Premier could do no more than reiterate earlier DRV position statements, although he did stress the DRV's desire for negotiations.

Still, there were a number of points worth noting about the Premier's reply (see Appendix V), delivered during his second meeting with Aubrac and Marcovich on July 25. For one thing, there was his stress on "economizing" in the war in the South ("We could easily step up our action inside [Saigon]. But we take only those actions which have political meaning and which economize human lives"). Similarly, Pham Van Dong hinted at his distaste for a military solution ("We do not want to humiliate the U.S. Lenin did not like war but fought when necessary. As Lenin we are Communists"). Viewed in the context of Le Quang Dao's stress on violent struggle as the only route to achieving the DRV's objectives in the South, the Premier's remarks are suggestive of the cleavages in the DRV leadership.[96]

In addition, in contrast to the first meeting, there was a touch of the old ebullience in the Premier's remarks ("We have defeated the Mongols three times . . ."). Still, following the approach used with Ronning and Salisbury, he was willing to consider a negotiated settlement. Once again, the precondition for negotiations was a de facto cessation of the

---

was apparently well-founded, since there were numerous news reports during July 1967 of attacks on the dikes. See, for example, the AP dispatch, "Hanoi Charges U.S. Bombing Killed Many Villagers on July 13," *New York Times*, July 21, 1967, p. 3; the AFP dispatch, "Big Crater in Dike Near Hanoi Is Laid to U.S. Bombing," *New York Times*, July 22, 1967, p. 4; the UPI dispatch, "Dam in North Vietnam Hit Four Days in a Row, Hanoi Says," *New York Times*, July 27, 1967, p. 6; and the AFP dispatch, "Newsmen in Hanoi See Damaged Dikes," *New York Times*, August 1, 1967, p. 3. According to these reports, attacks on the dikes occurred on July 7–10, July 13, July 19, and July 29. See also note 107, below.

95. Latimer, pp. 299–301.

96. In all probability, planning for the Tet Offensive had already begun—Oberdorfer (1971), pp. 63, 72, dates the decision to launch the Offensive to July 1967—and it is possible that the Premier's remarks indicated his opposition to such a costly venture.

bombing, and the goal of the negotiations was a coalition government for South Vietnam. Even so, the Premier attempted to make this as easy as possible for the U.S. to accept:

As for the South, our goals are national independence, democracy, peace and neutrality. Some people think we want to impose Socialism on the South. We are convinced that the NLF will not make such an error. The NLF envisages a broad coalition government, including *all* significant groups and religions *without consideration of past activities including members du gouvernement fantoche et cadres d'armée fantoche.* (He repeated the underlined words.) The essential thing is to forget the past.[97]

As in the case of the MARIGOLD contact, it appears that the goal of a coalition government for the South was the minimum condition necessary to gain Politburo acquiescence to negotiations with the United States. To make sure that no one in Washington missed this point, Loan used his second meeting with Algard, on August 5, to stake out a position virtually identical to that outlined by Pham Van Dong in his July 25 meeting with Aubrac and Marcovich. In particular, Loan took an optimistic view of the DRV's situation, telling Algard there was no reason why the DRV should let itself be forced into negotiations by American escalation—"Sooner or later we will win this war," as he put it. Still, he was willing to discuss negotiations (despite his telling Algard again that each time the DRV had shown interest in negotiations, it had been interpreted by the U.S. as a sign of weakness and had been followed by escalation), and he again stressed that a bombing cessation was an absolute condition for negotiations. Furthermore, Loan indicated once again that the DRV would be flexible in the event negotiations began, although he claimed that he did not possess detailed information on the specific points on which the DRV was ready to compromise. However, he did call attention to the DRV's attitude on the demarcation line at the 1954 Geneva Conference as an example of DRV flexibility. In addition, Loan noted that the 1954 Accords had stipulated reunification within two years, and he told Algard that the DRV objective was now considerably lower: reunification would be postponed until an indefinite point in the future. Nor would American troops have to be withdrawn before the negotiations were completed (in this respect, he cited the precedent of the French withdrawal in 1956). Loan refused, however, to budge on the all-important issue of a coalition government—the Americans, he told Algard, would have to

97. Pennsylvania, p. 9 (emphasis in original). The comment in parentheses was supplied by Kissinger, who prepared the report on the Aubrac/Marcovich meetings with Pham Van Dong.

accept the political situation in the South as it was, just as de Gaulle had accepted it in Algeria.[98]

In Washington, the reaction to Loan's review of the DRV position was to dismiss it as just another recital of the standard DRV line (which it was, although Washington did not understand that this was the *minimum* the DRV could settle for rather than a maximum bid for bargaining purposes). Even so, the Administration decided to pursue the matter further. Loan had told Algard that negotiations that failed would be worse than no negotiations at all, and he suggested that some type of preliminary contact might be useful to insure that the negotiations would in fact succeed. The Administration seized on this suggestion, asking the Norwegians to inquire whether secret preliminary U.S.-DRV contacts would be possible. In addition, the Norwegians were to raise once again the idea of mutual de-escalation, indicating that the U.S. would be "flexible" on the nature and form of the DRV's restraint. Finally, Loan had told Algard that the coalition government would not be Communist-dominated, even though the NLF would participate, and the Norwegians were asked to seek clarification on the safeguards that the DRV would agree to against a Communist takeover.[99]

The Norwegian channel, however, was destined to be overshadowed by events elsewhere. In early August, before a report on the second Algard-Loan meeting reached Washington (the report did not arrive until August 16), the President made two fateful decisions. On August 9, Senator Stennis's Preparedness Subcommittee began hearings on the conduct of the air war over North Vietnam. Since the subcommittee members were all well-known "hawks" intent on discrediting the McNamara policy of restrained bombing, it was surely no coincidence that

the very day the Stennis hearings opened, an addendum to ROLLING THUNDER 57 was issued authorizing an additional 16 fixed targets and an

---

98. These points are based on Ohio, pp. 5-6; and on Interview Data. As suggested earlier (see notes 35 and 44, above), one probably should not make too much of the insistence by Loan and Pham Van Dong on a bombing cessation as the price for talks. As indicated by DRV behavior during the SUNFLOWER (Moscow) contact and also by DRV willingness to exchange messages with the U.S. via Aubrac and Marcovich in Paris (see below), whenever DRV officials found it convenient, they were willing to be flexible on the conditions under which informal "talks" could be held. However, probably because of the Hanoi-area strikes during MARIGOLD and U.S. evasiveness (from the DRV's point of view) during SUNFLOWER, the year of 1967 would witness a gardual stiffening of the DRV position on the issue of a bombing cessation, a process that was probably accelerated by the August–September air assault on Hanoi and Haiphong (see below).

99. On these points, see Ohio, pp. 5-6, 8-9.

expansion of armed reconnaissance. Significantly, six of the targets were within the sacred 10-mile Hanoi inner circle. They included the thermal power plant, three rail yards, and two bridges. Nine targets were located on the northeast rail line in the China buffer zone, the closest one eight miles from the border . . . ; the tenth was a naval base, also within the China buffer zone. Armed reconnaissance was authorized along eight road, rail, and waterway segments between the 10-mile and 4-mile circle around Haiphong, and attacks were permitted against railroad rolling stock within the China buffer zone up to within eight miles of the border.[100]

Implementation of this decision began almost immediately. On August 11-12, U.S. jets for the first time in the war attacked the Doumer Bridge, located near the center of Hanoi; in those attacks, according to a DRV Foreign Ministry statement, "more than 100 persons were killed or wounded and numerous homes were destroyed."[101] On August 20-23, after a week of bad weather diverted the attacks to the China buffer zone and the southern DRV, Hanoi was pounded by some of the heaviest raids of the war. Interestingly enough, among the targets struck during the latter series of raids (in which the DRV claimed "more than 100" persons were killed) were the Yen Vien railroad yard and the Van Dien supply depot—the same targets involved in the MARIGOLD snafu.[102]

The timing of these attacks (which, if anything, served to confirm Loan's assertion that DRV interest in negotiations was always followed by escalation) was especially important in light of the President's second early-August decision. On August 11, the President approved the text of a message that was to be passed to Pham Van Dong via Aubrac, Marcovich, and Kissinger. While the message contained nothing new, it did put the official seal of approval on the "private proposal" given to Pham Van Dong by Marcovich on July 24:

The United States is willing to stop the aerial and naval bombardment of North Vietnam if this will lead promptly to productive discussions between representatives of the U.S. and the DRV looking toward a resolution of the issues

100. IV Gravel, p. 198. On the Stennis hearings, see IV Gravel, p. 197.

101. On these points, see IV Gravel, p. 198; and the AFP dispatch, "Hanoi Asks Action Against Bombings," *New York Times*, August 13, 1967, pp. 1, 8. In a later dispatch by Reuters, the DRV modified its casualty report on the August 11-12 raids to 8 killed, 13 wounded, and 352 left homeless ("Hanoi Says Raids Killed Eight," *New York Times*, August 17, 1967, p. 10). DRV claims should be viewed with some skepticism, but see also the discussion of bombing accuracy (or the lack of it) in Townsend Hoopes, *The Limits of Intervention* (New York: David McKay, 1969), pp. 77-79.

102. These points are based on the *New York Times'* coverage of the air war between August 22 and August 25, 1967.

between them. We would assume that, while discussions proceed either with public knowledge or secretly, the DRV would not take advantage of the bombing cessation or limitation. Any such move on their part would obviously be inconsistent with the movement toward resolution of the issues between the U.S. and the DRV which the negotiations are intended to achieve.[103]

On August 17, Kissinger met with Aubrac and Marcovich in Paris and gave them a written draft of the Administration's message, noting that it reflected the views of the Secretaries of State and Defense and that it had been approved by the President. In addition, he made a number of points orally, among them that the phrase "take advantage" referred to "any increase in the movement of men and supplies into the south," and that the decision to add new targets to the air war had been made before a report on Aubrac and Marcovich's visit to Hanoi had reached Washington (although the latter claim was patently false, since a memo on the visit was circulated by Chester Cooper on August 2, while the bombing decision was not made until August 9). Finally, Kissinger added the not-very-subtle warning that in the absence of meaningful negotiations, the level of violence was likely to rise.[104]

After some quibbling over the wording of the message, Aubrac and Marcovich agreed to carry it to Hanoi, and they asked if there could be some restriction on the bombing to assure their personal safety. While Kissinger took these points up with Washington, Aubrac and Marcovich sought an appointment with Vo Van Sung (the number two man in the DRV mission in Paris), which was granted on 20-minutes notice. Sung, however, had no instructions to grant them visas to Hanoi, although he had been told to transmit any messages they might wish to send. As a result, on August 18, after meeting twice with Kissinger and also with Chester Cooper (who was introduced to leave no doubt that Kissinger spoke for the Administration), Aubrac and Marcovich sent a message to Hanoi requesting visas. On August 19, they learned from Kissinger that, "effective August 24 there would be a noticeable change in the bombing pattern in the vicinity of Hanoi to guarantee their personal safety and as a token of good will." This change, Kissinger told them during a second meeting on August 19, would be in effect until September 4.[105]

103. Pennsylvania, p. 10.
104. On these points, see Pennsylvania, pp. 11–12. For the Cooper memo, see Pennsylvania, pp. 1–3. Kissinger also told Aubrac and Marcovich that the phrase "productive discussions" referred to a desire to avoid Korea-style protracted talks while military operations continued unabated.
105. On these points, see Pennsylvania, pp. 12–13; and Cooper (1972), p. 452. Aubrac and Marcovich suggested that the phrase "with the understanding that" be substituted for "if" in the first sentence of the U.S. message; Washington accepted their suggestion.

The visa request, however, was turned down on August 21, which also happened to be the date of the third Algard-Loan meeting in Peking. Algard had only slightly more success than Aubrac and Marcovich. Loan gave no direct reply on the points the U.S. was interested in; instead, he stuck to the familiar formula of no talks without a bombing halt and no settlement without a coalition government. However, he did express some interest in the idea of U.S. "flexibility" on DRV reciprocity, and he also asked whether Algard would be interested in accepting an invitation to visit Hanoi. Algard promised an early reply.[106]

Back in Paris, meanwhile, getting to Hanoi was precisely what Aubrac and Marcovich were trying to do, although without much success. On August 21, they transmitted a second appeal for visas. Four days later, however, Mai Van Bo told them that, in view of the recent escalation of the bombing of Hanoi, it would be too dangerous for them to travel there, despite the assurances given to them by Kissinger. At that point, Aubrac and Marcovich gave Bo a written version (see Appendix VI) of the message passed to them by Kissinger on August 17 and asked him to transmit it to Hanoi.[107]

In the days that followed, however, neither channel produced much in the way of results. In Paris, Aubrac and/or Marcovich visited Bo almost daily between August 29 and September 9, although without much success. On August 31, for example, Bo told Aubrac that their second appeal for visas had also been rejected, noting that his government was unfavorably impressed by the coincidence of the appeal and the escalation of the bombing of Hanoi. On September 2, Bo repeated that comment to Marcovich, although he asked him to make sure nothing "happened to Hanoi in the next few days." The next day, Aubrac and Marcovich informed Bo that the Hanoi-area suspension had been extended for 72 hours—i.e., through September 7. On September 7, however, with still no word from Hanoi on the U.S. message, the suspension was indefinitely prolonged.[108]

On September 8, Kissinger returned to Paris after a brief stop in Washington; the same day, Marcovich met with Bo to inform him of Kissinger's arrival. At this point, it looked as if something might yet be salvaged from the contact. Bo had told Marcovich on September 7 that he would seek authority to meet with Kissinger; and on the 8th he told

---

106. These points are based on Ohio, p. 9; and on Interview Data.

107. On these points, see Pennsylvania, pp. 14–16. During this meeting, Aubrac and Marcovich also passed to Bo the comment by Kissinger that the attacks on the dikes (see note 94, above) were accidental.

108. On these points, see Pennsylvania, pp. 17–19; and IV Gravel, p. 205.

Marcovich that if there was no bombing in the Hanoi area, "something could well happen" during the ten days that Kissinger planned to be in Paris.[109]

Something did happen, but it wasn't what Aubrac and Marcovich were hoping for. On September 9, after meeting with Kissinger, they saw Bo and told him that Washington was "growing impatient with the absence of any response from Hanoi." Bo, in turn, told them the U.S. message was being studied in Hanoi but they must realize the situation there was quite complex. After hedging on the question of meeting Kissinger, Bo told Aubrac and Marcovich that "what I really want to know is whether the August 25 message is still valid." Aubrac and Marcovich assured him that it was, but they also repeated Kissinger's warning about U.S. impatience over the absence of a reply from Hanoi.[110]

As things turned out, a reply was not long in coming. On September 10, Bo invited Marcovich (Aubrac had returned to his home in Rome) to meet with him the next day; at that meeting, Bo handed over the DRV's reply:

> The essence of the American propositions is the stopping of bombing under conditions. The American bombing of the DRV is illegal. The U.S. should put an end to the bombing and cannot pose conditions.
>
> The American message has been communicated after an escalation of the attacks against Hanoi and under the threat of continuation of the attacks against Hanoi. It is clear that this constitutes an ultimatum to the Vietnamese people.
>
> The Government of the DRV energetically rejects the American propositions.
>
> The position of the Government of the DRV is that the U.S. should cease definitely and without conditions the bombing and all other acts of war against the DRV. It should withdraw American troops and satellites from South Vietnam, recognize the NLF of South Vietnam and let the Vietnamese people themselves regulate their internal affairs. It is only after the unconditional stopping by the U.S. of the bombing and all other acts of war against the DRV that it would be possible to engage in conversations.[111]

Perhaps the most interesting feature of the DRV message was what it did *not* say—specifically, it did not insist that the U.S. recognize the NLF as the sole legitimate representative of the South Vietnamese people. Instead, the message simply called on the U.S. to "recognize" the NLF and "let the Vietnamese people themselves regulate their

109. Pennsylvania, pp. 18–20.
110. Ibid., pp. 20–21.
111. Ibid., pp. 21–22.

internal affairs." Viewed in the context of Pham Van Dong's statement to Aubrac and Marcovich that the coalition government would include representatives of *all* groupings within South Vietnam, including members of the "puppet" government and army, it would appear that the message was intended, once again, to make the idea of a coalition government as easy as possible for the U.S. to accept. Furthermore, the North Vietnamese clearly did not expect the matter to end then and there (despite their "energetic rejection" of the American propositions). Bo told Marcovich to pass the message to Kissinger and to contact him (Bo) "as soon as there is a reply." When Marcovich urged Bo to meet with Kissinger, Bo told him to "give the message to Kissinger and when the reply is here we shall see about the meeting."[112]

Kissinger, however, never did get to meet with Bo, although this was not for lack of trying on the part of Aubrac and Marcovich. Their efforts, though, were probably not helped by the conduct of the air war over the North. On September 10, the dock area of the port of Campha was struck for the first time in the war. Two days later, American jets began a sustained effort to isolate the port of Haiphong from the rest of the country by attacking railroad yards, warehouses, and bridges in the heart of the city along with bridges in the suburbs. Indicative of the White House attitude at this time was a September 12 meeting during which the President requested that the Joint Staff develop recommendations, within present policy guidelines, for increasing the pressure on North Vietnam—this despite the unfortunate outcomes during the MARIGOLD and SUNFLOWER initiatives that resulted from attempting to couple escalation and diplomacy.[113]

The result of this attempt to "squeeze" Hanoi to the conference table was a continued deadlock. On September 13, Marcovich gave Bo a message from Kissinger stating that he (Kissinger) had a reply to the DRV's September 11 message which he had been instructed to deliver personally. Bo, however, refused to see Kissinger, telling Marcovich that "because of the continued threat of bombing Hanoi which has the character of an ultimatum, the direct meeting with Kissinger cannot take place." Bo also mentioned the bombing of Haiphong, accusing the U.S. of striking populated areas (which was probably true, since the targets hit were in the center of the city). Still, when asked whether the

112. Ibid., pp. 21–22.

113. These points are based on the *New York Times'* coverage of the air war during September and October 1967 (see especially the *Times'* coverage on September 11, 13, 18, and 19, 1967); on IV Gravel, p. 205; and on Baggs, p. 209. On the White House meeting of September 12, see IV Gravel, p. 529.

contact should continue, Bo replied "definitely yes. . . . We want to keep this channel open."[114]

As a result, Marcovich saw Bo the next day and handed him another message from Kissinger, which characterized Hanoi's attitude as "baffling":

> If we bomb near Hanoi we are accused of bringing pressure. If we voluntarily and without any suggestion from Hanoi impose a restraint on our actions and keep this up without time limit we are accused of an ultimatum. In fact, the American proposal contained neither threats nor conditions and should not be rejected on these grounds.

Reading from his notes, Marcovich added Kissinger's "official" comment that "Washington does not consider the attacks on September 11 as escalation. The attacks closest to the center of Haiphong were in an area which had been attacked three times previously, most recently on June 26. Mr. Kissinger is prepared to give more detailed clarifications." Finally, Marcovich gave Kissinger's "personal" comment:

> A. Bo should remember that the number of officials aware of the current exchange of views is very small. This makes it very difficult to reverse decisions taken prior repeat prior to the decision to send the message of August 25 and maintain secrecy.
>
> B. It seems more useful to seek a solution to the present situation than to debate about how we got there. Hanoi should remember that the U.S. message of August 25 offered to end the bombing and all other acts of war against the DRV in circumstances which the U.S. Government considers not to involve conditions but which rather repeat statements made by Hanoi. If Bo wants clarification, I stand ready to give it.[115]

While Bo was sufficiently interested to ask Marcovich to leave his notes for him to study, he refused to do any more than that. As a result, on September 16, Kissinger gave Aubrac and Marcovich the text of Washington's official reply (dated September 13) to the DRV message of September 11, which they passed to Bo later in the day. The message, however, contained nothing new—it simply asserted that the American offer contained "neither threats nor conditions" and asked the DRV to reconsider its position.[116]

The DRV reply, however, would not be ready until September 23, despite prodding messages from Kissinger and frequent inquiries by

114. Pennsylvania, pp. 23–24.
115. Ibid., pp. 24–25.
116. Ibid., pp. 27–28.

Aubrac and Marcovich. When it came, it proved to be a major disappointment. As dicated by Bo to Marcovich, the message accused the U.S. of following a "two-faced policy" and rejected Kissinger's suggestion that the Hanoi-area bomb halt represented an act of restraint by the United States. While the bombing had been halted near Hanoi, the message noted, it had been intensified elsewhere, as in Campha, Haiphong, and Vinh Linh province (near the DMZ), "where the bombing has had the character of extermination and systematic destruction."[117]

Interestingly enough, however, the DRV reply did not reject outright the U.S. message of August 25; instead, it simply reiterated the DRV view that "the essence of the U.S. position is to offer to stop bombing with conditions." Then, after taking note of the U.S. message of September 13, Bo closed with a clear signal that the DRV wished to keep the channel open for further bargaining:

As far as you [Marcovich] and Aubrac are concerned, I have received you at any time you have requested. I listen to you. I accept messages from you. I call you when I have something to say. I believe that this demonstrates our good will sufficiently. However, as I have pointed out earlier, we have no illusions about American policy. What do you think of all this?[118]

Kissinger was quick to pick up the hint. On September 25, Marcovich carried another message from Kissinger to Bo, in which Kissinger repeated his earlier argument that the attacks on Hanoi, Campha, and Haiphong were not the result of a "two-faced policy" but rather the outcome of the "extreme secrecy" with which the details of the initiative were held in Washington. In an attempt to smooth the way to talks, Kissinger summarized the positions of the two sides in a way that minimized the gap between them:

Washington has indicated its readiness to stop bombing and has only asked to confirm its understanding of Hanoi's view that this would lead promptly to productive negotiations. Hanoi has implied that an end of bombing would in fact have this result. If this is indeed the view of both governments, the remaining obstacles to direct talks can be overcome. I am certain that the above reflects U.S. views. Could Bo confirm that it also reflects the view of Hanoi?

To this, Bo replied by dodging the question—there could be no formal talks as long as the bombing continued; however, he seemed to hint at flexibility in the DRV position by adding that preliminary talks between

117. Ibid., pp. 31–35.
118. Ibid., p. 35.

himself and Kissinger might not fall under such a prohibition, and he told Marcovich he would let him know whether such preliminary talks would be possible.[119]

Bo's suggestion, however, proved to be just another blind alley. On September 30, the day after the President publicly aired the "no advantage" formula in a speech at San Antonio, Aubrac and Marcovich called on Bo to ask if there had been any word from Hanoi concerning preliminary talks. Bo, however, replied that he could not talk directly to anyone representing the U.S. Government, because "too much had happened since July." Still, he did not break off the contact, telling Aubrac and Marcovich that he was available to talk with them at any time and that he would continue to report to Hanoi on his discussions with them.[120]

Bo's refusal to see Kissinger was the effective end of the Paris contact, although Aubrac and Marcovich pursued their futile quest for another three weeks. On October 2, Marcovich saw Bo on his own initiative to impress upon him information he had received from Kissinger (who by now had returned to Cambridge) indicating growing impatience in Washington. At that meeting, Marcovich and Bo decided to send a message to Kissinger, which was drafted by Marcovich on the basis of his notes and mailed to Kissinger that day. While the message contained little that was new, it did refer to the "Trinh formula" as a "solemn engagement [by the DRV] to talk after the unconditional end of bombing." Since this was one of the points that Washington had been trying to nail down all along, there was some concern in Washington when Bo told Marcovich on October 4 that he had never used the words "solemn engagement"—a retraction that Marcovich hotly disputed.[121]

Marcovich was nothing if not persistent. Late in the evening of October 4, he saw Bo again, and while Bo refused to discuss his reneging on the term "solemn engagement," he did collaborate with Marcovich on another message to Kissinger. The message, however, simply repeated the DRV demand for an unconditional bombing halt as the price for talks, while spelling out in some detail the "scenario" for announcing the halt to the DRV.[122]

119. Ibid., pp. 37–38.

120. Ibid., pp. 38–40.

121. Ibid., pp. 41–42. In essence, the message argued that the DRV position remained unchanged—i.e., there could be no talks without a bombing cessation—and it then spelled out the ways in which the U.S. could inform the DRV of a cessation. Marcovich saw Bo on October 4 at Kissinger's request to confirm the text of the message.

122. Pennsylvania, pp. 43–44.

Four days later, Aubrac and Marcovich were back to see Bo with the U.S. reply:

> The U.S. Government understands the position of the DRV to be as follows: That upon the cessation by the U.S. of all forms of bombardment of the DRV, without expression of condition, the DRV would enter promptly into productive discussions with the U.S. The purpose of these discussions would be to resolve the issues between the U.S. and the DRV.
>
> Assuming the correctness of this understanding of the position of the DRV, the U.S. Government is prepared, in accordance with its proposal of August 25, to transmit in advance to the DRV the precise date upon which the bombardment of the DRV would cease and to suggest a date and a place for the commencement of discussions.

What is clear, however, is that Washington was not "assuming" anything. What it wanted was an assurance from Bo, delivered in advance of a bombing cessation, that the cessation would lead "promptly" to "productive" discussions. Bo, not surprisingly, told Aubrac and Marcovich that the U.S. was still posing conditions, although he agreed to send the message on to Hanoi.[123]

The new message proved to be no more successful than its predecessors. On October 9, Marcovich saw Bo in order to emphasize both the importance of the U.S. message as well as Washington's impatience over the absence of a meaningful reply from Hanoi. While expressing surprise that Marcovich saw anything new in the U.S. message, Bo did say that if Kissinger came to Paris over the weekend he would be available to see Aubrac and Marcovich at any time.[124]

Kissinger, however, did not come to Paris until October 20. In the meantime, the Norwegian channel continued to plug along, although in much more leisurely fashion. Washington had been sufficiently intrigued by the first three Algard-Loan meetings to send Chester Cooper to Oslo, where he met with Algard on September 8 and 13. On September 12, however, State announced that it wished to hold off on further messages via the Norwegians in order to concentrate on developments in Paris. As a result, for the next four weeks, the Norwegians were kept on "hold." Algard, in particular, was asked to stay in Oslo while awaiting further information on a visa to Hanoi. The information that came in, though, was not what Algard was hoping for. Loan saw the Norwegian Chargé in Peking on October 10 (at the latter's request) and,

123. Ibid., pp. 45–48.
124. Ibid., pp. 48–49.

in response to a question concerning Algard's visa, announced that the situation had totally changed as a result of the escalation of the air war. American peace probes were now viewed as attempts to lure Hanoi into a trap, so a visit by Algard was not desirable at that time. In addition, Loan mentioned somewhat cryptically that further exchanges in Peking were insecure for both parties and that Hanoi had other channels (specifically, the Soviet Foreign Ministry in Moscow) if further contact was desired.[125]

The breakdown in Peking obviously boded ill for the channel in Paris. Marcovich saw Bo on October 17, at which time Bo accused the U.S. of

following a policy of escalation of an extremely serious nature. In these conditions the U.S. proposals of peace are double-faced. At a time when the U.S. is pursuing a policy of escalation we cannot receive Kissinger, nor comment on the American proposals transmitted through this channel. The position of the government of the DRV is perfectly clear: it is only when the U.S. has ended without condition the bombardment that discussions *can* take place.[126]

Washington, of course, reacted negatively to all this. Kissinger stopped there on October 19 on his way to Paris and was told he should impress on Aubrac and Marcovich Washington's discouragement not just over the DRV message of October 17 but also over the renewed DRV military activity near the DMZ. Aubrac and Marcovich, however, were undaunted. After meeting with Kissinger on October 20, they called Bo to request an urgent appointment. This time, however, Bo told them bluntly that "the situation was worsening. There is no reason to talk again." After some further pleading by Aubrac, Bo broke off the conversation, telling them: "Our position is perfectly clear. We stand on the Trinh interview . . . of January 28. There is nothing new to say."[127]

B. *Through the Maze to Paris*

With the collapse of the Peking and Paris contacts, the attention of Administration officials was inexorably drawn back to questions of escalation. The Hanoi-area suspension had been imposed on the military without any explanation as to its purpose, with the result that the military commanders lobbied persistently to have the restriction lifted. In addition, the military were pressing for authority to hit Phuc Yen air-

125. These points are based on Ohio, pp. 10–16; Cooper (1972), pp. 455–457; and Interview Data.
126. Pennsylvania, p. 50 (emphasis in original).
127. On these points, see Pennsylvania, pp. 51–53; and Johnson, p. 268.

field, the largest unstruck MIG airfield and the center for much of North Vietnam's air defense activity. To make matters worse, bad weather had impeded the air war during September: only 8,540 attack sorties were flown that month compared to 11,634 in August. That, plus the Hanoi-area sanctuary, had allowed a considerable amount of damage recovery in North Vietnam.[128]

By October, the pressures for escalation were becoming harder to resist. Six new targets were approved by the President on October 6, including five in or near Haiphong. On October 24, just after Bo's refusal to see Aubrac and Marcovich, the White House authorized attacks on Phuc Yen and the Hanoi power plant along with a temporary lifting of the Hanoi-area ban. Both Phuc Yen and Hanoi were hit the next day, and the attacks on Hanoi continued for five straight days. In the meantime, planning continued throughout October for an accelerated deployment of the Program #5 forces for South Vietnam.[129]

Despite the escalation of the air war, the military continued to press for authority to execute actions that had already been repeatedly rejected by the President—e.g., mining DRV ports and shrinking the Hanoi and Haiphong restricted zones to 3 and 1.5 nautical miles, respectively. Meanwhile, the "doves" were also active. On October 12, thirty Congressmen sent the President an open letter suggesting that he end the bombing and open negotiations with Hanoi. This was followed on October 21 by a massive anti-war protest in Washington (involving some 50,000 demonstrators). To cap things off, on November 1, Secretary McNamara submitted a lengthy memo to the President calling for a stabilization of the American effort in the South and, significantly, a complete bombing halt over the North by the end of 1967.[130]

Still, the result of these various pressures was predictable enough. Following the by now familiar pattern, the President attempted to stake out the middle ground, which, in operational terms, resulted in further incremental escalation. While not accepting JCS proposals for rapid escalation, the President did consent to an attack on the Haiphong shipyard area, which was hit on November 16 for the first time in the war. The next day, the Bac Mai airfield near the center of Hanoi was struck, also for the first time in the war. On December 14–15, the Doumer Bridge was hit again, while ten new targets were approved on December

128. On these points, see IV Gravel, pp. 207–208.
129. On these points, see IV Gravel, pp. 208, 529–532.
130. On the proposals for escalation and the "dovish" protests, see IV Gravel, pp. 215–217. On the McNamara memo, see Johnson, pp. 372–373; and Oberdorfer (1971), p. 115.

16, including seven within the 10-mile circle around Hanoi and two within the 4-mile circle around Haiphong.[131]

By the end of the year, however, the President was running out of bits of escalation to dole out to the military. As the Pentagon analyst notes:

> By the end of October, six of the seven MIG-capable airfields which Secretary McNarama had taken a strong stand against in the Stennis hearings had been hit, and only five of the August list of 57 [JCS] recommended targets (which had meanwhile grown to 70 as new recommendations were made) remained unstruck. Thus, except for the port of Haiphong and a few others, virtually all of the economic and military targets in North Vietnam that could be considered even remotely significant had been hit. Except for keeping it up, almost everything bombing could do to pressure North Vietnam had been done.[132]

With the air war thus coming to the end of the line, the focus of attention within the Administration once again swung back to negotiations in late 1967. The impetus for this shift came from a rather unlikely source—the Rumanians, who had lost none of their audacity despite their earlier ill-fated venture into Vietnam diplomacy. On October 25, the Rumanian Prime Minister, Ion Gheorghe Maurer, called in Ambassador Richard H. Davis to discuss Maurer's late-September visit to Hanoi. According to Maurer, he had told the North Vietnamese that the Rumanians sought an immediate, permanent, and unconditional end to the bombing along with a DRV declaration of readiness to negotiate with the United States. Furthermore, Maurer claimed, the North Vietnamese had agreed that that was the correct approach (although when Davis asked if the DRV declaration would precede or follow the bombing cessation, Maurer cavalierly replied that he had not discussed such details while in Hanoi—that would be up to the North Vietnamese).[133]

The American response to Maurer's initiative was twofold. On November 1, State sent Davis a lengthy set of questions that it hoped Maurer could answer. Three days later, State indicated that the indefatigable Averill Harriman could stop off in Bucharest later in the month to pursue the matter directly if the Rumanian Government so wished (which it did). As things turned out, it was the latter step that proved to be significant.[134]

131. On these points, see IV Gravel, pp. 14–15, 216; and Hoopes (1969), p. 103.

132. IV Gravel, p. 216.

133. On these points, see Rumanian Chronology, pp. 8–12; and Cooper (1972), p. 457.

134. Rumanian Chronology, pp. 14–20. Maurer was in Moscow when the November 1 cable arrived, and thus he did not see Davis until November 15. When he did respond to the American inquiries, his replies were either evasive or disdainful of details such as the distinction between "talks," "contacts," and "negotiations."

On November 29, Harriman saw Maurer in Bucharest; during their talk, he was able to elicit some additional details about Maurer's visit to Hanoi and meetings with Pham Van Dong. Maurer's account, however, revealed, if anything, a hardening of the DRV position. Pham Van Dong was no longer willing to settle for a de facto cessation; instead, he told Maurer that North Vietnam would declare itself ready for discussions if the U.S. ended the bombing unconditionally and permanently and declared that it would never resume. In addition, Hanoi would want a delay between the cessation and the opening of talks in order to test American sincerity.[135]

Still, it was in the aftermath of the Harriman-Maurer talk that the question of negotiations in general and the Rumanian track in particular began receiving sustained high-level attention in Washington. Harriman, as the Pentagon analyst notes, had explained the "no advantage" formula to Maurer in a way that gave the appearance of some softening of the American position:

"The North could," Harriman indicated, "continue supplying its forces to the extent that it does now but . . . it must not increase." Harriman expressed the hope [that the Rumanians] would take appropriate steps with Hanoi to explain this. Maurer said that he would take such steps under consideration. Harriman concluded that what was lacking was any "indication" or "impression" or "message" that Hanoi wanted serious negotiations.[136]

The Rumanians were quick to follow up on Harriman's suggestion. On December 12, two Rumanian diplomats, Macovescu and Iliescu, left Bucharest for Hanoi, arriving on December 14. Their schedule in Hanoi was interesting, to say the least:

(a) dinner on Friday, the 15th, with Foreign Minister Trinh, (b) a meeting with Trinh on the morning of December 16, (c) Sunday afternoon meeting with Pham Van Dong, (d) on the *morning of the 18th* there was a DRV Politburo meeting, (e) another meeting with Trinh after the Politburo session in which Trinh spoke to Macovescu and Iliescu from a written text. [The] Rumanians left Hanoi on the evening of the 18th.[137]

The results of the Rumanian mission, however, were not immediately passed to Washington. Macovescu and Iliescu stopped in Peking on

---

135. Rumanian Chronology, pp. 22–28. Despite this hardening of the DRV position, the North Vietnamese were not closing off any options. In early November, Loan met Algard at a Soviet Embassy reception and told him he wished to continue discreet contacts while meeting "accidentally" at receptions (Ohio, pp. 18–19; and Interview Data).

136. Packers, p. 1; see also Rumanian Chronology, p. 33.

137. Packers, p. 1 (emphasis in original).

their way home and did not reach Bucharest until Christmas Eve. Two days later, the Rumanian Ambassador in Washington, Corneliu Bogdan, advised Harriman that his government wished to send an emissary to the U.S.; Harriman naturally accepted. But before the emissary arrived, some significant developments took place elsewhere. On December 29, Trinh spoke at the Mongolian Embassy in Hanoi and in the process modified the "Trinh formula" of January 28, 1967. Specifically, he changed the DRV stance on opening talks with the U.S. after a bombing cessation from "could" to "will"; in addition, he omitted any reference to a "permanent" cessation:

> The stand of the Vietnamese people is quite clear. That is the Four Point stand of the DRV Government and the political program of the NLFSV. That is the basis for the settlement of the Vietnam question.
>
> The U.S. Government has unceasingly claimed that it wants to talk with Hanoi but has received no response. If the U.S. Government truly wants to talk, it must, as was made clear in our statement on 28 January 1967, first of all stop unconditionally the bombing and all other acts of war against the DRV. After the U.S. has ended the bombing and all other acts of war against the DRV, the DRV will hold talks with the U.S. on questions concerned.

Trinh's remarks were broadcast by Radio Hanoi on January 1, 1968. Two days later, the U.S. military commands were ordered to suspend bombing within five miles of the center of Hanoi.[138]

On January 5, Macovescu and Iliescu (along with Bogdan and Celack, another Rumanian diplomat) met with Harriman in Washington to discuss their visit to Hanoi. As they described it, they had presented the U.S. view as outlined by Harriman on November 29; in response, Trinh read to them on December 18 a statement similar to the one he would make publicly on December 29, although Trinh appeared somewhat more forthcoming in the version given to the Rumanians. As quoted by Macovescu, Trinh had told them that:

> The basis for [a] settlement of the Vietnamese issue is provided by the Four Points of April 8, 1965; the Ministry of Foreign Affairs subsequently issued its January 28, 1967 statement. This is our position of principles on which no concession is possible.
>
> We are not against discussions but any discussions should take place according to principle. As soon as discussion engaged in [sic], our attitude will be *serious and responsible* but it depends on attitude of the U.S. whether such discussions are fruitful.

138. For Trinh's remarks, see Packers, p. 2; on the Hanoi-area suspension, see IV Gravel, p. 15.

We affirm the following. If the U.S. Government really wants discussions with the Government of the DRV it should first unconditionally cease bombing and any other act of war against the DRV. After the unconditional cessation of all bombing and any other U.S. act of war against the DRV and at the end of an appropriate period of time the government of the DRV will enter into *serious* discussions with the U.S. Government.[139]

Although Macovescu argued that Trinh's comments (both public and private) constituted the "sign" that Harriman had requested on November 29, the Administration was still not satisfied. Harriman, in particular, raised the question of whether Trinh was trying to make U.S. acceptance of the Four Points a precondition for discussions. To this, Macovescu responded that:

In the public statement it says the basis for negotiations is the Four Points but in private conversations they say we will come with this basis but the U.S. side, we expect, will come with its own point of view. They especially said this.[140]

In addition, there was also a question over the interval between the bombing cessation and the opening of talks. Although Trinh's private comments referred to "an appropriate period of time" between the cessation and the opening of talks, the Rumanians managed to interject an element of confusion into the contact. At a January 6 meeting with Rusk and Harriman, Macovescu read from a document which purported to describe the DRV position:

As long as the U.S. acts of war go on we [the North Vietnamese] cannot have any contacts with them. *As soon as* they cease the bombings and discontinue the acts of aggression we shall be prepared to receive any person, even a representative of the U.Ș. who may wish to make known to us the American point of view or to get informed on our viewpoint. We shall regard these future contacts as normal diplomatic activity. The American representatives will be received by our representatives at the former's suggestion.[141]

On January 11, Rusk, Bundy, and Harriman met twice with Macovescu and Iliescu and gave the Rumanians a seven-point written

139. For Trinh's statement, see Packers, pp. 3–4 (emphasis added). When Macovescu asked whether Trinh had intentionally omitted the adjective "permanent" concerning a bombing cessation, Trinh confirmed that he had. This change in the DRV position was also called to Algard's attention in Peking on January 2 and relayed to Washington on January 9 (Interview Data).

140. Packers, p. 5. On the U.S. reaction to the Rumanian report, see Johnson (p. 268), who claimed that "we could discover nothing new in Hanoi's stand, nothing different from what they had often said before. . . ."

141. Packers, p. 6 (emphasis added).

statement of the U.S. position, along with a number of points which were made orally. The written points were essentially an elaborate explanation of the "no advantage" formula, along with an attempt to smoke out the DRV position on the interval between a bombing cessation and the start of talks. Picking up on Macovescu's suggestion that the DRV was prepared to receive an American representative "as soon as" the bombing ended, the U.S. statement noted that "the first contacts should take place almost immediately, perhaps one or two days after the cessation of bombing."[142]

Armed with this further statement of the American position, Macovescu and Iliescu, accompanied by Celack, returned to Hanoi via Bucharest, arriving on January 22. Meanwhile, the seriousness with which the Administration viewed the Rumanian initiative was indicated by a January 16 decision to extend the Hanoi-area bombing halt to include the area within five nautical miles of the center of Haiphong. The Rumanians left Hanoi on January 28, but for some unknown reason a report on their talks was not transmitted to Washington until February 12. By then, the Rumanian channel would be largely overshadowed by events elsewhere.[143]

In particular, during January 1968, the attention of both the U.S. and the DRV came to focus on a new diplomatic channel—this one involving an old hand at Vietnam diplomacy, Giovanni D'Orlandi, who by now had returned from Saigon to become Inspector General of the Italian Foreign Ministry. Although D'Orlandi had been meeting irregularly with the DRV Ambassador in Prague since September 1967, it was not until January 1968 that the channel began to gather momentum. During that month, D'Orlandi flew to Prague, where he held his third meeting with Ambassador Su (the first two had been held in September and November 1967). Interestingly, Su (who had just recently been in Hanoi) now told D'Orlandi that there was general approval of the idea of negotiations and that he had been authorized to meet with Italian Foreign Minister Fanfani. It was arranged that Su would travel to Rome on February 4.[144]

142. Ibid., p. 7. For the U.S. written points, see Packers, pp. 7–9. For the oral points, see Packers, p. 9. For various other points made orally by Rusk and others and intended to clarify the U.S. position, see Packers, pp. 9–12. Kraslow and Loory (p. 229) report that the Rumanians were given a rehash of the points already passed via Aubrac and Marcovich because the Rumanians did not know of the Paris channel and it was hoped they would do a selling job on Hanoi.

143. On the Haiphong bomb halt, see Johnson, p. 578; on the Rumanian visit to Hanoi, see Packers, pp. 12–13.

144. On these points, see IV Gravel, p. 236; Killy, pp. 1–2; and Robert C. Doty, "Fanfani Saw Two Hanoi Aides," New York Times, February 15, 1968, p. 2.

But before that meeting took place, a far more dramatic undertaking was set in motion by the DRV/VC forces in South Vietnam. On January 31, those forces launched the so-called "Tet Offensive," involving simultaneous attacks on thirty-six of forty provincial capitals, sixty-four district capitals, and five of six autonomous cities. In Saigon alone, as Fitzgerald notes, elements of eleven Viet Cong battalions managed to enter the city, attacking, among other things, the presidential palace, the government radio station, and, most shocking of all from the U.S. point of view, the American Embassy.[145]

Back in Washington, the effect of the offensive was threefold. First, as the Pentagon analyst notes, "the Tet assault appeared only as a massive repudiation of U.S. peace overtures." While Administration spokesmen complained publicly that the offensive clearly demonstrated DRV disinterest in negotiations, privately they were even more caustic in their assessments. Oberdorfer, for example, quotes incoming Secretary of Defense Clark Clifford as telling a visitor: "We have been suckers and we are going to quit being suckers. There is no point in this kind of negotiations. The next time, they come to us, and they had better mean it! San Antonio is the final formula—the furthest we can go."[146]

Second, although U.S. military commanders would later claim that the offensive had been anticipated and that the heavy casualties suffered by the attackers had resulted in a great victory for the Allies, the offensive was in fact a military setback for the American side. To meet the threat in the northern provinces and forestall a Dien Bien Phu-type defeat at Khe Sanh, half of all U.S. maneuver battalions in South Vietnam were deployed in I Corps; the rest, along with the bulk of the combat-ready ARVN units, were tied down defending the cities against the possibility of a second wave of attacks. As a result, the countryside went by default to the NLF, the pacification program was left in a shambles, and whatever losses the DRV/VC forces did suffer in the initial assaults were largely offset by the unimpeded recruiting that they conducted in the rural areas in the weeks that followed.[147]

145. On these points, see Oberdorfer (1971), pp. 133–253; Fitzgerald, pp. 519–534; Robert Shaplen, *Time Out of Hand* (New York: Harper & Row, 1970), pp. 406–422; and Herbert Schandler, *The Unmaking of a President* (Princeton, N.J.: Princeton University Press, 1977), pp. 74–91.

146. For the Pentagon analyst's comment, see IV Gravel, p. 236. For an example of the complaints about the offensive, see Secretary Rusk's comments on "Meet the Press" on February 4, 1968, quoted in IV Gravel, pp. 236–237. For Clifford's comment, see Oberdorfer (1971), p. 191.

147. For MACV's view of the offensive, see Westmoreland, pp. 310–334; Sharp and Westmoreland, pp. 157–169; and Oberdorfer (1971), pp. 182–183. For a harsher view, see Oberdorfer (1971), pp. 203–209; Hoopes (1969), pp. 139–158; Fitzgerald, pp. 523–525; and IV Gravel, p. 547. See also NSSM-1 (produced in early 1969 for the incoming Nixon Administration), p. 190, which reports

Third, as Fitzgerald notes, the offensive "had an electric effect on popular opinion in the United States. . . . Those who had long held doubts and reservations now felt their doubts confirmed." Nowhere was this effect more pronounced than in the ranks of the Pentagon civilians. The Tet offensive, as Hoopes notes, "performed the curious service of fully revealing the doubters and dissenters to each other, in a lightning flash."[148] This effect, as we shall see, played an important role in steering the focus of attention within the Administration back to negotiations, despite the initial feelings of betrayal engendered by the offensive.

This renewed interest in negotiations, however, would take some time to surface, since Administration officials were preoccupied at first with military responses to the offensive. On February 3, the JCS renewed their request to shrink the restricted zones around Hanoi and Haiphong to 3 and 1.5 nautical miles, respectively, with field commanders being given authority to strike targets outside the circles as required. This recommendation was vigorously disputed by ISA at the Pentagon, and the President in response typically sought a compromise. While he rejected the JCS proposal, he did relax the Haiphong prohibition long enough to allow for some strikes on the city, which took place on February 10.[149]

In addition, the Administration moved cautiously to shore up the situation in the South. On February 9, Secretary McNamara queried the JCS concerning General Westmoreland's troop needs and how to meet them. In response, the JCS examined a number of plans for emergency augmentation but then took the somewhat unusual step of recommending that reinforcements be deferred until certain Reserve units could be called up to reconstitute the Strategic Reserve in the United States. McNamara, however, ignored this recommendation and on February 13 ordered a 10,500-man emergency force airlifted to South Vietnam. As the situation there began to settle down somewhat, the U.S. military command in Saigon undertook a comprehensive review of troop requirements. On February 23, General Wheeler (CJCS) arrived in Saigon to participate in the review.[150]

---

that Viet Cong recruiting during the first quarter of 1968 spurted to a level at least double the average for 1967. A xeroxed copy of this study was obtained by the author while doing research in Washington; it can also be found in the *Congressional Record*, starting on May 10, 1972 (p. E4975) and continuing into the Record for May 11 (starting at p. E5008). Page numbers used here are from the author's copy.

148. Fitzgerald, pp. 525–526; Hoopes (1969), p. 145. See also Oberdorfer (1971), pp. 191–192.

149. On these points, see IV Gravel, pp. 235–236.

150. The maneuvering that took place in Washington and Saigon over future troop needs is a fascinating story in its own right but far too complex to be covered here. On this episode, see IV

Despite the initial preoccupation with military matters, diplomatic concerns could not be pushed aside entirely, especially since some of the most intriguing DRV diplomatic maneuvers took place just as the Tet Offensive was building to a peak. On February 4, Ambassador Su and another DRV diplomat met with Fanfani and D'Orlandi in Rome "for talks about the Vietnam conflict and about possible hypotheses of a start [sic] of negotiations to settle it." Four days later, Radio Hanoi broadcast another interview with Foreign Minister Trinh, in which Trinh took a position somewhat similar to that communicated privately to the Rumanians in January—a position that hinted at some softening in the DRV stance (the Rumanian report, however, as mentioned earlier, did not reach Washington until February 12). When asked what issues could be discussed during U.S.-DRV talks, Trinh made no mention of the Four Points but said only that "they are questions related to a settlement on the basis of the 1954 Geneva Agreements on Vietnam. They are also other questions which could be raised by either side." On the question of the gap between the bombing cessation and the opening of talks, Trinh took the ambiguous but seemingly forthcoming position that "the talks will begin *as soon as* the U.S. has proved that it has really stopped unconditionally the bombings and all other acts of war against the DRV." Meanwhile, back in Peking, Algard received the long-awaited invitation to Hanoi.[151]

These diplomatic soundings did not go unnoticed in Washington, but the response was again a cautious one. In mid-February, both the Swedes and the Norwegians were given identical explanations of the "no advantage" formula, which they were asked to pass on to their DRV contacts. Although the explanation claimed that the U.S. was not setting "conditions" by "assuming" that the DRV would not "take advantage" of a bombing halt, the message virtually pleaded for an assurance of some form of reciprocity:

If Hanoi, by taking advantage, forces the U.S. to resume bombing the possibilities of a negotiated solution would drastically recede. Under such circumstances calls for intensified U.S. military action would increase and the probability of another halt in the bombing would be low. The U.S. is trying to

Gravel, pp. 238–239, 539–546; Oberdorfer (1971), pp. 207–209, 275–283; Johnson, pp. 385–388; Westmoreland, pp. 350–362; Schandler, pp. 92–104; and John B. Henry, "February 1968," *Foreign Policy*, 4 (Fall 1971), 3–33.

151. On the Su/Fanfani meeting, see Killy, pp. 3–5. The quoted excerpt is from an Italian Foreign Ministry communique of February 14, quoted in Kraslow and Loory, p. 232. For Trinh's comments, see Conditions for Talks, p. 24. For the DRV message conveyed via the Rumanians, see Packers, p. 14. For Algard's invitation to Peking, see Ohio, pp. 20–21.

ascertain whether Hanoi appreciates this vital fact and fully understands the importance the U.S. attaches to the no-advantage assumption.

In addition, the message once again called attention to the necessity of a cessation being followed by "prompt" and "productive" discussions.[152]

More importantly, on February 23, Daniel Davidson (Special Assistant to Averill Harriman) and Francis E. Meloy, Jr. (DCM of the U.S. Embassy in Rome) met with Fanfani and D'Orlandi in Rome to discuss the most recent Italian contacts with the North Vietnamese. In retrospect, the meeting was apparently a pivotal one in terms of eliciting a DRV pledge of sorts not to "take advantage" of a bombing cessation. In response to Fanfani's mentioning that there had been no discussion of the "no advantage" formula with Su, Davidson gave the Italians the same explanation that had already been provided to the Swedes and Norwegians. In addition, Davidson suggested that

it might repeat might be sufficient if Hanoi stated that it recognized that during a period when the U.S. was not bombing and while talks were continuing that such acts as attacks on U.S. positions in the area of the DMZ, massive terror against the cities such as the Tet campaign or increased infiltration, would show bad faith on its part and that it, of course, would never do anything that smacked of bad faith. Hanoi could then discuss with us at the first meeting more precise definition of actions which would constitute bad faith.[153]

In the days that followed, Davidson undertook to persuade Washington to follow up on the Italian channel, arguing that since Su had sought out D'Orlandi, had traveled to Rome, and had invited D'Orlandi to continue their meetings in Prague, the channel was a serious one and merited attention. Washington, however, was reluctant to provide the Italians with any new formulations. Instead, it simply encouraged D'Orlandi to meet again with Su and, using Davidson's explanation of the "no advantage" formula as the basis for the discussion, explore any ideas the DRV might have.[154]

As things turned out, no new American formulation was needed. On

152. Conditions for Talks, pp. 24–25; Aspen, pp. 59–60; and Ohio, pp. 22–23. The message was passed to the Swedes on February 17, apparently for use during the visit to Stockholm of DRV Ambassador (to Moscow) Nguyen Tho Chanh, which began on February 19. The Norwegians were given the message on February 20 because Loan had told Algard that a DRV representative might visit Oslo (Ohio, p. 22; and Interview Data).

153. Killy, pp. 3–5.

154. On these points, see Killy, pp. 6–8. Interestingly, Su told Fanfani on February 4 that he (Su) did not consider any of the East European channels to be serious ones; when Fanfani asked specifically about Rumanian Prime Minister Maurer, Su "laughed as if to say that he could not rpt not conceivably be a serious channel" (Killy, p. 6).

March 1, D'Orlandi met with Su in Prague, at which time he warned that

if bombing stopped and talks began, assaulting Khe Sanh, invading or trying to detach the two northern provinces of South Vietnam, launching a second wave of attacks against one or more cities or creating a sensation with something else like an assault on Camp Carroll, would sink the whole thing.

In response, Su gave his "personal" view that "from the moment the two sides meet, it was obvious no such thing could happen" (although it is highly unlikely he would have said this without instructions).[155]

Back in Washington, meanwhile, events were building to a climax. Just as the air war had at last reached the end of the line by December 1967, so too did the buildup of American forces in South Vietnam begin grinding to a halt during February and March 1968. On February 26, General Wheeler cabled his report on the situation in the South to Washington; the report, however, proved to be a shocker, to say the least. Wheeler painted a bleak picture, calling attention to the lack of logistic support north of DaNang, the loss of the countryside to the NLF, and the heavy concentration of U.S. troops in I Corps. "Under these circumstances," Wheeler concluded, "we must be prepared to accept some reverses." To deal with the situation, Wheeler and Westmoreland proposed a new troop commitment of 206,756 men over and above the Program #5 ceiling of 525,000, with all of the additional forces to be deployed by the end of 1968. To meet these requirements and also to reconstitute the Strategic Reserve and training base in the U.S., Wheeler recommended calling up some 280,000 reservists.[156]

The Wheeler/Westmoreland troop request was clearly "the fork in the road." The President was faced squarely with a choice between a total commitment to driving the DRV/VC forces out of South Vietnam or placing a ceiling on the U.S. war effort. To aid him in making this choice, he asked incoming Secretary of Defense Clifford to

155. On this meeting, see Killy, pp. 8–9 (the quoted excerpts are from Davidson's summary of D'Orlandi's report on his meeting with Su, cabled to Washington on March 4). See also Conditions for Talks, pp. 1, 28.

156. On the Wheeler report, see IV Gravel, pp. 546–549; Schandler, pp. 105–120; Hoopes (1969), pp. 159 ff.; Oberdorfer (1971), pp. 282–283; and Henry, pp. 20 ff. It appears that Westmoreland was more optimistic than Wheeler about the situation in the South and intended to use the additional troops to seize the initiative (or so he hoped) by executing maneuvers such as an invasion of DRV/VC sanctuaries in Laos and Cambodia and an amphibious landing north of the DMZ. Wheeler, however, apparently felt that painting a bleak picture stood a better chance of getting the troops (and also the Reserve call-up) from the President. On this point, see Westmoreland, pp. 354–359; Schandler, pp. 96–111; Henry, passim.; Hoopes (1969), pp. 159 ff.; Oberdorfer (1971), pp. 276 ff.; and Fitzgerald, pp. 532–533.

convene a group of senior advisers and conduct a thorough review of American strategy in the war.[157]

The work of the Clifford Group, as it came to be known, has been described in exhaustive detail elsewhere and need not be recounted here.[158] What is important for our purposes is to note that the Group's recommendations, as developed in a DPM given to the President on March 4, sidestepped the crucial question of what should be American strategy in the war. In an earlier version of the DPM, the ISA staff had argued for a sweeping change in policy—i.e., rejecting the Wheeler/Westmoreland troop request, rejecting JCS proposals for escalating the air war, and scrapping the Westmoreland emphasis on "search and destroy" operations in favor of an emphasis on protecting the population by deploying U.S. troops along a "demographic frontier."[159] While the senior members of the Clifford Group rejected this approach as too negative, they had little in the way of innovative suggestions to substitute for the ISA approach. As a result, the final version of the DPM was nothing more than another in a long line of papers recommending "more of the same."

On the crucial issue of negotiations, for example, an annex to the DPM prepared by William Bundy argued that the "San Antonio formula" was the "rock bottom" and that it should not be revised downward.[160] Similarly, on the troop issue, the DPM recommended the immediate deployment of 22,000 more troops and three fighter squadrons, early approval of a Reserve call-up sufficient to meet the balance of the Wheeler/Westmoreland request, and deferral of a decision to meet the request in full pending further study.[161] On the air war, the DPM

157. There has been some controversy over the assignment given the Clifford Group. Clifford, for example, writes that the group was "not instructed to assess the need for substantial increases in men and materiel; we were to devise the means by which they could be provided." The President, in contrast, has claimed that the Clifford Group was to examine alternatives and not just the means of implementing the troop request. On this point, see Clark Clifford, "A Viet Nam Reappraisal," *Foreign Affairs*, 47:4 (July 1969), 609; "Crucial Vietnam Decisions of Johnson Administration Discussed by Former President in Second TV Interview," *Congressional Quarterly Weekly Report*, February 6, 1970, pp. 334–335; Schandler, pp. 133–138; Johnson, pp. 390 ff.; IV Gravel, pp. 239, 549; Hoopes (1969), p. 172; Henry, pp. 24–25; and Townsend Hoopes, "LBJ's Account of March 1968," *The New Republic*, March 14, 1970, pp. 17–19. Whatever the task assigned to it, the Clifford Group did in fact undertake a comprehensive review of all aspects of the American war effort.

158. See, for example, IV Gravel, pp. 239–258, 549–584; Schandler, pp. 121–176; Oberdorfer (1971), pp. 297–308; Taylor (1972), pp. 386–390; as well as the sources listed in note 157, above.

159. For the ISA draft, see IV Gravel, pp. 250–252, 561–568.

160. IV Gravel, p. 253.

161. See IV Gravel, pp. 573–576. This recommendation was made despite the pungent comment from the Systems Analysis Office that: "While we have raised the price to North Vietnam of

recommended a "general decision on bombing policy," although it provided little guidance to the President, noting only that

here your advisers are divided: (a) General Wheeler and others would advocate a substantial extension of targets and authority in and near Hanoi and Haiphong, mining of Haiphong, and naval gunfire up to a Chinese Buffer Zone; (b) others would advocate a seasonal step-up through the Spring but without these added elements.[162]

Despite the inadequacies of the DPM, Hoopes probably goes too far in characterizing it as "mindless folly, confirming once more the depressing truth that the inner core of the Administration was frozen solid in misconceptions as to the nature of the war, as to what our military power could accomplish, as to how our real interests in Asia should be served." For one thing, Clifford was still feeling his way on Vietnam, and, while he later "fought ferociously to turn the tide, to limit the number of troops and to reduce the bombing," it is possible the DPM reflected the tentative judgments of an adviser who was just beginning to see, as Clifford himself later put it, "how little one knows if he had been on the periphery of a problem and not truly in it."[163] More importantly, it is also possible that the DPM reflected a conscious decision by Clifford to fight one bureaucratic battle at a time. On the question of a partial bombing halt, which had been a leading alternative considered by the Clifford Group but which was not mentioned in the DPM,

Clifford may well have decided that fully countering the JCS recommendations for escalation was sufficient for the formal DPM. To have raised the idea of constricting the bombing below the 19th or 20th Parallel in the memo to the President would have generalized the knowledge of such a suggestion and invited its sharp, full, and formal criticism by the JCS and other opponents of a bombing halt.[164]

In any event, the idea of a partial bombing halt very quickly came to the fore during the March strategy review. On March 4, Secretary Rusk

aggression and support of the Viet Cong, it shows no lack of capability or will to match each new U.S. escalation. Our strategy of attrition has not worked. Adding 206,000 more U.S. men to a force of 525,000, gaining only 27 additional maneuver battalions and 270 tactical fighters at an added cost to the U.S. of $10 billion per year raises the question of who is making it costly for whom" (IV Gravel, p. 557).

162. IV Gravel, p. 576; see also IV Gravel, pp. 254–258.

163. On these points, see Hoopes (1969), p. 178; Halberstam, p. 793 (for the "fought ferociously" comment); and Clifford, p. 609. On Clifford's later opposition to the troop increase, see Hoopes (1969), pp. 181, 224; Clifford, p. 613; and Schandler, pp. 210–217.

164. IV Gravel, p. 258. See also Cooper's (1972, p. 467) characterization of the DPM as a "delaying action"; Hoopes (1970), p. 18; and Schandler, pp. 165, 175–176.

suggested a temporary suspension of the bombing north of the 20th Parallel, and, while the President would later credit Rusk with starting the process that culminated in the President's dramatic gesture of March 31, it would appear that what Rusk really had in mind was a short-term cutback (on the order of one month) that would not seriously affect the U.S. war effort (since the winter monsoon restricted the bombing north of the 20th Parallel to a few days per month) and that could be used to good effect with world opinion.[165]

On March 11, a much more serious effort to place restrictions on the air war was launched by the ISA Policy Planning Staff. In a memo to Clifford discussing the DRV position on negotiations, the staff concluded that Hanoi had, in the recent contacts through the Italians, indicated "acceptance of the operative portion of the San Antonio formula." On this basis, the staff recommended testing North Vietnamese acceptance by asking them to repeat the assurances transmitted by Su via D'Orlandi. This memo was signed by Warnke and sent to Clifford and Nitze (Clifford's deputy) on March 12. Four days later, the ISA office completed work on a DPM that urged concentrating the bombing on the southern DRV and targeting only enough strikes in the Hanoi/Haiphong area to prevent the relocation of DRV air defenses.[166]

It is difficult to tell, however, just how much influence these proposals had—neither Clifford's nor Nitze's reactions to the March 12 memo are available, and the March 16 DPM was never signed by Clifford.[167] The one thing that is clear is that the President was wavering. On March 8, by his own account, he told his senior advisers he would never approve 205,000 more troops for Vietnam, although on March 13 he approved 30,000 more (later expanded to 43,500) to go along with the 10,500-man emergency force. On March 16, he angrily denounced suggestions for a bombing halt, followed on March 17 and 19 by two of the more bellicose speeches of his Administration. And yet, on March 19, he rejected JCS proposals for hitting new targets in Hanoi and Haiphong,

165. On the Rusk proposal, see Johnson, pp. 399–401; Schandler, pp. 182–188, 237–240; CQ *Weekly Report*, February 6, 1970, pp. 334–335; Oberdorfer (1971), pp. 306–308; and IV Gravel, pp. 258–259. For the argument that the Rusk proposal was more a propaganda ploy than anything else, see Hoopes (1970), pp. 17–18. See also the comments by Clark Clifford and William Bundy, cited in Schandler, pp. 241–242, 250–251.

166. On these points, see IV Gravel, pp. 263–266; and Schandler, p. 242. On March 15, Ambassador Goldberg sent the President a memo proposing a complete bombing halt over North Vietnam. On this, see Johnson, p. 408; Oberdorfer (1971), pp. 311–312; CQ *Weekly Report*, February 6, 1970, p. 334; Hoopes (1970), p. 19; and Schandler, pp. 237–240.

167. On this point, see IV Gravel, p. 264. See also Schandler (pp. 247–248), who suggests that Clifford's views were sympathetic to the arguments being made by Warnke and the ISA staff.

followed on March 22 by a decision to move Westmoreland upstairs to Army Chief of Staff. On March 23, again by his own account, he decided in principle to go ahead with a partial bombing halt; and on March 28, he decided that the troop increase would be only 13,500 rather than 43,500.[168]

And then, on March 31, the President went on national television to make his dramatic announcement of a bombing cutback coupled with a plea for negotiations. Judging from the cable that went out to six American embassies in the Far East on March 30 announcing the contents of the President's speech, relatively little was expected in return for the bombing cutback: reciprocity from Hanoi was viewed as "unlikely," and the cable noted that "Hanoi is most likely to denounce the project and thus free our hand after a short period." This time, however, American policymakers were in for a pleasant surprise (for a change). On April 3, Radio Hanoi announced that:

It is clear that the U.S. Government has not correctly and fully responded to the just demand of the DRV Government, of U.S. progressive opinion, and of world opinion. However, on its part, the DRV Government declares its readiness to send its representatives to make contact with U.S. representatives to decide with the U.S. side the unconditional cessation of bombing and all other war acts against the DRV so that talks could begin.[169]

After some cautious deliberation in Washington, the President decided to accept the offer, and the DRV Embassy in Vientiane, Laos, was duly informed of this on April 4. There would still be another month of at times bitter haggling over the site for the talks; but on May 10, U.S. and DRV representatives finally did sit down together in Paris for formal talks.[170] With that, the Johnson Administration would seek to win at the conference table what it had not been able to win on the ground in South Vietnam and in the air over North Vietnam.

168. On these points, see IV Gravel, pp. 268, 589–595; Schandler, pp. 231–232; Johnson, pp. 402, 405; Hoopes (1969), pp. 185, 205–206; Oberdorfer (1971), pp. 310–311; and Halberstam, pp. 794–795.

169. On the President's speech, see IV Gravel, pp. 271–275, 596–602; and Schandler, pp. 250–289. For the March 30 cable, see IV Gravel, pp. 270, 594–595. For the DRV announcement, see Johnson, p. 495. For a discussion of the DRV reaction to the speech, see Ashmore and Baggs (who were in Hanoi at the time), pp. 112–158.

170. On the haggling over the site for talks, see Johnson, pp. 495–507; Ashmore and Baggs, pp. 138 ff.; Oberdorfer (1971), pp. 338–339; and Kraslow and Loory, pp. 236–239.

Part II

When Governments Clash

The opening of the Paris peace talks in May 1968 was in many respects not the end but rather the beginning of a new chapter of the Vietnam story. Those talks would drag on into 1973 before a settlement of sorts was reached, and even that proved nothing more than a flimsy device allowing the U.S. to extricate itself from the war while the Vietnamese fought on. The peace talks, though, would require a book-length study in their own right, and for our purposes May 1968 is an appropriate stopping point, since it marks the Johnson Administration's abandonment of incremental escalation in favor of an attempt to secure its goals by means of formal negotiations.

Having completed our review of the evolution of the Administration's strategy over the period 1964–1968, we now turn to an evaluation and assessment of that strategy. As we saw in Chapter 1, the Administration's strategy for coercing North Vietnam rested on three main assumptions:

1. That a program of gradually rising military pressures would induce the government in Hanoi to end its support for the insurgency in South Vietnam.
2. That the leadership would be able to "fine-tune" the Administration's actions so as to enable it to "orchestrate" words and deeds and "signal" by deed as well as by word.
3. That the use of force would be controllable—i.e., that the pressures against the North could be turned on or off, up or down, at will.

And yet, as we saw in Chapters 2 to 4, each of these assumptions proved to be of rather dubious validity. The problem for us now is to explain why this was the case, a task that we take up in Chapters 5 to 7.

In the latter chapters, moreover, our discussion will be conducted on two levels. As we saw in Chapter 1, the assumptions listed above were by no means confined to officials in the Johnson Administration; rather, they were also widely held among academic theorists interested in "limited" and/or coercive war. Our discussion, therefore, will focus both on the specific case of Vietnam and also on the more general subject of "limited/coercive" war, in an attempt to use the American experience in Vietnam to suggest modifications and revisions to the theoretical perspectives developed by analysts such as Kaufmann, Brodie, Schelling, Kahn, and George.

5

Coercing Governments

On December 21, 1963, as we saw in Chapter 2, President Johnson made one of the more fateful decisions of his Administration when he directed that an interdepartmental committee should undertake a study of possible covert pressures against North Vietnam. The committee's report, which recommended a variety of covert operations (code-named OPLAN 34A), was approved by the President on January 16, 1964, with implementation to begin on February 1. Throughout the remainder of 1964, the Administration experimented with a variety of other activities such as Presidential statements of American resolve to defend South Vietnam, warnings conveyed directly to Hanoi via diplomatic channels, and well-publicized transfers of American troops and equipment to the Far East, all of which were intended to intimidate the North Vietnamese and persuade them to end their support for the insurgency in the South. When these activities proved inadequate, the Administration moved to step up the pressures on the North, first through retaliatory air strikes and then through a continuous, gradually escalating bombing campaign, code-named ROLLING THUNDER. On March 8, 1965, six days after the first ROLLING THUNDER strikes, U.S. ground combat units were committed for the first time in the war as two battalions of Marines came ashore at DaNang.

From then on, the American role in the war expanded rapidly in a way that few members of the Administration had anticipated. By September 1966, U.S. aircraft were flying as many as 12,000 attack sorties *per month* over North Vietnam (compared to only a few hundred in February and March 1965); in the meantime, the U.S. troop commitment in the South climbed steadily, eventually reaching 549,500.[1] Although a

1. For data on the number of sorties flown by American planes over North Vietnam, which fluctuated from month to month depending on weather conditions, see III Gravel, pp. 284–286; IV

few officials, such as George Ball, had warned that "once on the tiger's back we cannot be sure of picking the place to dismount," the prevailing mood in early 1965 was one of cautious optimism.[2] Even at the time of the Honolulu Conference of April 20, 1965, when it was clear that a much greater commitment would be required, senior Administration officials remained relatively optimistic. Although Secretary McNamara's report to the President noted that it would now take "more than six months, perhaps a year or two, to demonstrate Viet Cong failure in the South," there was no doubt as to whether the U.S. would succeed in Vietnam, only as to how long it would take.[3]

With the benefit of hindsight, it is easy to criticize these expectations as being overly optimistic and totally unwarranted. Yet, at the time, they seemed plausible enough. Not only were key members of the Administration convinced that the North Vietnamese were obsessed with protecting their meager yet hard-won industrial base; in addition, still fresh in their minds was the memory of Kennedy's triumph during the Cuban missile crisis, and it was Cuba II that served as the precedent for what they were planning for Vietnam.[4] Given those beliefs, it was but a short step to the conclusion that a bombing campaign that started in the southern part of North Vietnam and gradually moved north in the direction of Hanoi and Haiphong, all the while building to a crescendo in terms of the frequency and intensity of strikes, would suffice to erode the will of the DRV leadership to continue their support for the insurgency in the South.[5]

Gravel, pp. 109, 125, 134, 136, 208, 229–230, 382; Littauer and Uphoff (eds.), p. 274; and Neil Sheehan, "August Air Raids Heaviest in Vietnam," New York Times, September 2, 1965, p. 4.

2. For Ball's comment, see "Top Secret: The Prophecy the President Rejected," The Atlantic, July 1972, p. 41. For a discussion of other Administration doubters and the way in which they were eased out of Vietnam policymaking, see Halberstam, pp. 449–461. One must be careful in trying to generalize about Administration expectations concerning the bombing, since, as Halberstam notes, many members of the Administration expressed doubts at one time or another about the wisdom of the bombing. Still, by February 1965, when the consensus on bombing crystalized in the aftermath of Pleiku, it seems fair to say that it was generally believed that the bombing (plus a modest troop commitment in the South) would lead the North Vietnamese to accept a settlement favorable to the U.S. On these points, see the discussion in Chapters 1–3, above, especially note 6 in Chapter 1 and note 32 in Chapter 3.

3. On these points, see Document no. 256 in III Gravel, p. 706; Halberstam, pp. 700–701; and Chapter 3, above.

4. On the Administration's view of the importance of DRV industry to the Hanoi leadership, see III Gravel, pp. 153, 155, 212–215; IV Gravel, pp. 57–58; and Halberstam, pp. 431 ff. See also the sources cited by Simons, "The Vietnam Intervention, 1964–1965," in George, Hall, and Simons, p. 201, note 9. On the influence of the Cuban precedent, see Halberstam, p. 625; and the essays by Simons ("The Vietnam Intervention, 1964–1965") and George ("Comparisons and Lessons") in George, Hall, and Simons, pp. 148–149, 211.

5. Again, one must be careful in making categorical statements about how the bombing was

And yet, however plausible the scenario may have seemed at the time, the Administration's optimism did prove unwarranted—coercing Hanoi turned out to be much more difficult than coercing Moscow. How can we account for the failure of the Administration's plans to work out as expected? Why didn't the North Vietnamese back down? What was it that went wrong?

There has been, to be sure, no shortage of answers to questions such as these. One of the more popular preoccupations in recent years for academics and journalists, as well as members of Congress and the military, has been precisely to deal with the question of where the U.S. went astray in Vietnam. In the process, three main schools of thought have emerged, which can perhaps best be labeled the "left-wing," "right-wing," and "pragmatic" critiques of American policy in Vietnam.

The characteristic feature of the left-wing critique has been its tendency to argue that the strategy of "graduated pressures" was inherently flawed and thus doomed to failure from the start. In its most polemical form, Richard Barnet has condemned the "rat psychology premises" underlying the strategy and accused the Johnson Administration of planning a "fantasy" that overlooked all of the evidence from the World War II Strategic Bombing Survey "demonstrating that strategic bombing would not compel surrender." A similar argument was developed, although in a more restrained fashion, by a group of American scientists working through the Institute for Defense Analyses' JASON Division, who reported to Secretary McNamara in December 1967 that the failure of the bombing

> reflects a general failure to appreciate the fact . . . that a direct, frontal attack on a society tends to strengthen the social fabric of the nation, to increase popular support of the existing government, to improve the determination of both the leadership and the populace to fight back, to induce a variety of protective measures that reduce the society's vulnerability to future attack and to develop an increased capability for quick repairs and restoration of essential functions.[6]

---

supposed to work. As we saw in Chapters 2–3, the military wanted to use the bombing to destroy DRV *capabilities* and in that way make it impossible for them to continue supporting the Southern insurgency, while civilian policymakers wanted to use the bombing to influence DRV *will*. In addition, other objectives that were pursued through the bombing were: (1) to improve South Vietnamese morale; (2) to impede infiltration; (3) to make the North "pay a price" for its role in the war; (4) to show the world the lengths to which the U.S. would go for a friend; and (5) to provide a "bargaining chip" in negotiations. On these points, see Chapters 2–4, above; see also III Gravel, pp. 349, 385, 668–669; and IV Gravel, pp. 43, 171, 200.

6. Richard Barnet, "The Men Who Made the War," in Ralph Stavins, Richard Barnet, and Marcus Raskin, *Washington Plans an Aggressive War* (New York: Vintage, 1971), pp. 212–214; and IV Gravel, p. 224 (for the JASON Division Report). See also the comments by Theodore Draper

Right-wing critics, in contrast, argue that, while the Administration's strategy was basically sound, it was the incompetent and irresolute way in which it was implemented that was at the heart of the Administration's failure to achieve its objectives in Vietnam. Walt Rostow, for example, one of the principal advocates of the bombing, later deplored "our tendency to use air power in ways that dissipated its effects through attacks on too many target systems." Similarly, Maxwell Taylor, another architect of the air war, has argued that "there was a certain logic" in the Administration's strategy of "gradualism," but only "if not carried to excess":

While this carefully controlled violence may have had some justification at the start, it ended by defeating its own purposes. Designed to limit the dangers of expanded war, it ended by assuring a prolonged war which carried with it the dangers of expansion. The restrained use of our air power suggested to the enemy a lack of decisiveness. The repeated bombing pauses . . . were taken by the enemy as an indication that our leaders were not sure of themselves and were unlikely to continue the bombing in the face of domestic and international pressures. So gradualism encouraged the enemy to hang on until his hopes were fulfilled in 1968 by a collapse of the American will to persist in the bombing.[7]

Standing in the middle are those analysts who have criticized American policy on what might be called "pragmatic" grounds. These analysts argue that, while the strategy of "graduated pressures" may be valid under certain circumstances, Vietnam was the wrong place to apply it. David Halberstam, for example, in noting the Administration's reliance on the Cuban precedent, argues that such reliance

was fine, except that they made one fatal mistake; they forgot that in the Cuban missile crisis it was the *Russians*, not the Cubans who backed down. The

---

and Stanley Hoffmann in Richard Pfeffer (ed.), *No More Vietnams?* (New York: Harper & Row, 1968), pp. 26–30, 34–35, 122–131, 201–202; David Marr's comments in Patricia Krause (ed.), *Anatomy of an Undeclared War* (New York: International Universities Press, 1972), pp. 95–96; Aron, pp. 8–11; and Ralph K. White, *Nobody Wanted War* (Garden City, N.Y.: Doubleday, 1970), pp. 134–140.

7. See Walt Rostow, *The Diffusion of Power* (New York: Macmillan, 1972), p. 509; and Taylor (1972), pp. 403–404. See also Westmoreland, pp. 112–113, 118–121; John McDermott's comments on the thinking of "right-wing members of Congress" in Pfeffer (ed.), p. 30; the 1967 report of the Stennis Committee, cited in IV Gravel, pp. 203–204; Task Force on National Security, "Gradualism—Fuel of Wars," for the Republican National Committee, March 1968, cited in George, Hall, and Simons, p. 215; Hanson Baldwin, "After Vietnam—What Military Strategy in the Far East?" *New York Times Magazine*, June 9, 1968; and William Safire, "What Went Wrong," *New York Times*, April 24, 1975, p. 35.

threat of American power had had an impact on the Soviets, who were a comparable society with comparable targets, and little effect on a new agrarian society still involved in its own revolution. Thus, though they were following the same pattern as they had in the missile crisis, they lacked a sense of history and what had seemed so judicious before became injudicious in Vietnam. The bluff of power would not work and we would be impaled in a futile bombing of a small, underdeveloped country. . . .

In somewhat different fashion, Alexander George identifies eight preconditions that favor the successful implementation of "coercive diplomacy." "To the extent that the eight conditions are absent," he argues, "and perhaps as many as six were missing in 1965 when Johnson attempted to coerce Hanoi . . . , then it is difficult and imprudent for American leaders to adopt the strong form of coercive diplomacy."[8]

Unfortunately for our understanding of the utility of coercive pressures for pursuing foreign policy goals, it appears that each of these critiques has captured only a portion of the truth. The right-wing critique, while correct in calling attention to the Administration's inept implementation of its strategy for coercing North Vietnam,[9] is nonetheless gravely flawed in that it rests on the unproven premise that the DRV would have backed down had the Administration escalated rapidly and forcefully and kept on escalating until the North Vietnamese agreed to end their role in the war. This premise is open to question in two respects. First, there is evidence (to be examined in more detail below) that by early 1965 the North Vietnamese had made considerable preparations in anticipation of an American decision to escalate the war. As a result, while the Administration's strategy may have violated the "military principles of surprise and mass as means to gain prompt success with minimum loss,"[10] it seems unlikely that, given DRV preparedness combined with the relative invulnerability of an underdeveloped agrarian economy, a more forceful bombing campaign would have led to a different outcome.

Second and more importantly, despite the slow start to the air war, the bombing gathered momentum rapidly during the summer and fall of

8. See Halberstam, p. 625 (emphasis in original); and Alexander George, "Comparisons and Lessons," in George, Hall, and Simons, p. 216. See also Roger Hilsman, *To Move a Nation* (New York: Dell, 1967), pp. 526–536; Wicker, pp. 264–276; Hoopes (1969), pp. 126–130; Shaplen (1970), p. 444; Osgood (1969), pp. 48–53; Pierre, pp. 170–176; Gray, p. 123; and Paul Kattenburg, "Vietnam and U.S. Diplomacy, 1940–1970," *Orbis*, 15:3 (Fall 1971), 830–831, 838.

9. The Administration's problems in this respect will be discussed in more detail in Chapter 6, below.

10. Taylor (1972), p. 404. See also Westmoreland, pp. 112–113.

1965. Attack sorties over North Vietnam rose from roughly 2,000 per month in mid-1965 to 4,000 per month by the end of 1965 to 6,000 per month in early 1966 and then up to 12,000 per month by September 1966. During 1966 alone, American planes flew a total of 148,000 sorties over North Vietnam. By any criteria, this was a huge bombing program—so huge that, after allowance is made for diminishing returns, it seems highly unlikely that an additional 1,000 or even 5,000 sorties per month would have sufficed to tip the scale.[11]

Left-wing and pragmatic critics, on the other hand, while correct in emphasizing the difficulties inherent in any attempt to coerce an impoverished opponent that is totally committed to achieving its goal in the conflict (as North Vietnam apparently was), are likewise guilty of overlooking some important points. For one thing, the evidence from the Strategic Bombing Survey, which virtually all of these critics cite, is not, strictly speaking, relevant to the case of Vietnam. As the Pentagon analyst notes, the bombing was never intended to terrorize the DRV population; instead, it was aimed at the leadership in an attempt to influence their hopes and fears with respect to the DRV's long-sought goals of industrialization and economic growth.[12] And in this respect, it appears that the bombing was effective to a degree, although nowhere near as effective as the Administration had hoped. By July 1967, as we saw in Chapter 4, Pham Van Dong, at least, was seriously concerned about the bombing, as indicated by his comments during his first meeting with Aubrac and Marcovich. In addition, as Oberdorfer notes, by late 1967

the war policies of the regime were under substantial attack . . . within the Party, and both arrests and exhortations were necessary to quiet the dissent. Beginning in September, more than 200 officials of the Party and government

11. For sortie data, see the references in note 1 of this chapter, above. The diminishing returns argument was originally made by Secretary McNamara, cited in IV Gravel, pp. 126, 134. Ironically, as a Systems Analysis study reported in late 1967, the North Vietnamese showed a "substantial net gain" in military equipment from the bombing. While the bombing had inflicted roughly $400 million worth of damage on the DRV economy (at a cost to the U.S. of roughly three times that figure), the DRV had received (as of late 1967) $1.6 billion in aid from the Soviet Union and China. On this, see Halberstam, p. 782; IV Gravel, pp. 225–227; Hoopes (1969), pp. 106, 153; and Oberdorfer (1971), pp. 113–114. For a highly detailed treatment of the limitations of bombing as an instrument of coercion, see the material prepared by the CIA and the Office of the Secretary of Defense for inclusion in NSSM-1, pp. 217 ff., 527 ff.

12. See IV Gravel, pp. 57–58. It must be conceded that the bombing did have the effect of causing severe hardship for the population in the North (see, for example, Shaplen [1970], pp. 401, 403). This was the result of an indiscriminate policy of shooting at anything and everything that moved on DRV highways and waterways, combined with the inherent inaccuracy of bombing (on this latter point, see Hoopes [1969], pp. 75–78).

were taken into custody because of their opposition to the direction of the war, according to a North Vietnamese intelligence officer who later defected. Among those reported arrested were Hoang Minh Chinh, director of the Party's foremost school of theoretical political studies and a leader in the wave of internal dissent; Colonel Le Trung Nghia, director of Central Intelligence for North Vietnam; Bui Cong Trung, deputy chairman of the State Science Committee and a member of the Party Central Committee; and Nguyen Viet, chief of the Finance Section of the Ministry of Light Industry.[13]

Most importantly, though, the leadership's concern over the bombing is best illustrated by its willingness to "pay a price" (albeit a modest one) to get the bombing stopped (after nearly three years of insisting that it would never make such a move) in the form of the assurances conveyed privately by Ambassador Su to D'Orlandi.[14]

If, then, the three main critiques of American policy are all defective, how can we account for the failure of the Administration's efforts to induce the North Vietnamese to end their role in the war in the South? In dealing with this question, a starting point can be found in our discussion of the left-wing and pragmatic critiques. As we saw there, the bombing of the North was intended to influence the DRV leadership, and yet, what is perhaps most remarkable about the Administration's strategy is *how little* it knew about the targets of its strategy. General Taylor, for example, candidly admitted that

in 1965 we knew very little about the Hanoi leaders other than Ho Chi Minh and General Giap and virtually nothing about their individual or collective intentions. We were inclined to assume, however, that they would behave about like the North Koreans and the Red Chinese a decade before; that is, they would seek an accommodation with us when the cost of pursuing a losing course became excessive.[15]

13. Oberdorfer (1971), p. 83. Oberdorfer's report is corroborated by intelligence sources cited in the State Department's assessment of the bombing in NSSM-1, pp. 166–170.

14. The Su/D'Orlandi meetings are discussed in Chapter 4, above. In addition, as Gareth Porter notes (*A Peace Denied* [Bloomington: Indiana University Press, 1975], p. 92): "By late September [1968] revolutionary forces in the South were beginning a significant withdrawal of main force units. Five divisions of North Vietnamese troops—from 40,000 to 60,000 men—were withdrawn into North Vietnam and Laos, half of them going as far north as the twentieth parallel. This may have been due in part to the difficulty of supplying troops in that area, but it was also clear that the DRV was interested in [completely] ending the bombing of the North and getting negotiations started. They were willing to signal to the United States that a tacit understanding on the Demilitarized Zone was possible."

15. Taylor (1972), p. 401. Chester Cooper makes the same point in "The Complexities of Negotiations," *Foreign Affairs*, 46:3 (April 1968), 459. Even as late as 1969, the authors of the summary section of NSSM-1 admitted that "our knowledge of possible political factions among the North Vietnamese leaders is extremely imprecise," while the authors of the Pentagon's contribution to

Surely this must stand as one of the more amazing aspects of an amazing war—an American Administration attempting to coerce a group of foreign leaders about which it knew "virtually nothing."

Upon reflection, however, this lack of knowledge is perhaps not so surprising. After all, Taylor and his colleagues were not the only ones to assume that an opponent "would seek an accommodation with us when the cost of pursuing a losing course became excessive." Rather, as we saw in Chapter 1, this was a theme that ran through much of the literature on "limited" and "coercive" war produced in the U.S. during the 1950s and 1960s. William Kaufmann's famous essay on "Limited Warfare," for example, noted that underlying the traditional American view of war was a "picture of [a] fanatically determined individual [as the enemy] who will battle on until the weapons are dashed from his hands." That view, however, while applicable to a Hitler, was no longer relevant to the situation facing the United States:

> The Soviet Union, Red China, and their satellites have been notorious as practitioners of violence. . . . They have used it in limited quantities for limited objectives both offensive and defensive. . . . Bold in their reliance on military action they have proved cautious, cool, and calculating in its application. Although ready to take risks, they have shown a keen awareness of costs and a related ability to retreat as well as advance.

Consequently, a more appropriate basis for American military strategy was one in which the enemy was viewed as a "calculating individual with a multiplicity of values, aware of cost and risk as well as of advantage, and capable of drawing significant inferences from symbolic acts."[16]

In short, then, both the Johnson Administration and the theorists of limited/coercive war had a rather special view of the opponent facing the U.S.—specifically, a view based on an analogy between a government and a unitary actor capable of calculating the costs and gains at stake in any conflict and ready to back off whenever the cost-benefit calculus turned negative. Given this perspective, it wasn't necessary to know much about an opponent; instead, American policymakers could concentrate on what the U.S. was doing and in particular on conveying to the opponent "the prospect of cumulative losses that were more than

---

NSSM-1 stated that "as far as our knowledge of how Hanoi thinks and feels, we see through the glass darkly if at all." See NSSM-1, pp. 3 (Summary); 93 ff. (State Department material); 247 ff. (Saigon Embassy material); 337 ff. (Defense Department material).

16. Kaufmann, "Limited Warfare," in Kaufmann (ed.), pp. 102–103, 117. Similar views are presented in Osgood (1957), pp. 5, 51–52; and Schelling (1966), p. 167. See also Gurtov and Kellen, p. 14.

the local war was worth, more unattractive than concession, compromise, or limited capitulation."[17]

Of course, at least some theorists recognized that there might be more to it than this. Schelling, for example, included a paragraph in *Arms and Influence* in which he noted that

> to coerce an individual it may be enough to persuade him to change his mind; to coerce a government it may not be necessary, but it also may not be sufficient to cause individuals to change their minds. What may be required is some change in the complexion of the government itself, in the authority, prestige, or bargaining power of particular individuals or factions or parties, some shift in executive or legislative leadership. . . . The victims of coercion, or the individuals most sensitive to coercive threats, may not be directly in authority; or they may be hopelessly committed to noncompliant policies. They may have to bring bureaucratic skill or political pressure to bear on individuals who do exercise authority, or go through processes that shift authority or blame to others. In the extreme case governing authorities may be wholly unsusceptible to coercion—may, as a party or individuals, have everything to lose and little to save by yielding to coercive threats. . . . For working out the incentive structure of a threat, its communication requirements and its mechanism, analogies with individuals are helpful; but they are counterproductive if they make us forget that a government does not reach a decision in the same way as an individual in a government.

Later on, Schelling went even further: "I have often said that if I were to write the book again, I would write a whole chapter on the general subject of that paragraph, and I feel pretty sure that the main motivation for wanting to do that came from reflecting on the war in Vietnam."[18]

Unfortunately, however, these caveats were never picked up by other theorists and incorporated into the literature on limited/coercive war. Nor is there much evidence that officials in the Johnson Administration were sensitive to the problems suggested by Schelling. Instead, in those instances in which Administration officials did try to anticipate their opponent's reaction to the pressures they were planning, they invariably referred to the actor to be coerced as simply "Hanoi."[19] Maxwell

17. Schelling (1966), p. 167. For a specific example of this approach, see the discussion of "persuasive deterrence" by General Thomas Power (former commander of the Strategic Air Command), quoted in Dudman, pp. 92–93.

18. Schelling (1966), pp. 85–86; and personal communication, December 16, 1974.

19. While it is admittedly true that the Pentagon Papers are not the only repository for documents on the war and that certain categories of documents were systematically omitted from them (e.g., records of daily intelligence briefings), one cannot help being struck by the paucity of references in the available documents and memoirs to the problems likely to arise when coercive

Taylor, for example, explicitly admitted the importance of the "Hanoi-as-unitary-rational-actor" model underlying Administration planning when he noted that he

> was left wondering about the soundness of judgment of the decision-makers in Hanoi, whose imprudent actions [during the Gulf of Tonkin affair] reminded me of Khrushchev's rashness in introducing missiles into Cuba and worried me for similar reasons. One likes to feel able to count on the rationality and good sense of a dangerous opponent.[20]

But is this analogy between a government and a calculating individual valid for purposes of coercion? What kinds of problems might arise in trying to coerce a government? Are there any special pitfalls that the coercer should be aware of? In trying to answer these questions, it will be helpful to review the evidence from the Vietnam conflict, but this time from the perspective of the DRV. In this way, we should be able to gain some important insights into the difficulties likely to arise when one government attempts to coerce another.

I. Coercing Governments: The View from Hanoi

A. DRV Policy from the Geneva Conference to the Formation of the NLF

On July 20, 1954, representatives of France and the Viet Minh meeting in Geneva reached an agreement ending the long and bitter struggle known as the "first Indochina war." In addition to a cease-fire, the agreement provided for the division of Vietnam into two "regrouping zones" with the "military demarcation line" between them set at the 17th Parallel, called for the regroupment of each side's forces into its respective zone, and, "pending the general elections which will bring about the unification of Vietnam," assigned the "conduct of civil administration in each regrouping zone" to "the party whose forces are to be regrouped there." On July 21, the Final Declaration of the Geneva Conference was issued, which noted that

---

pressures are directed against a government, as opposed to a unitary, calculating actor (e.g., "Hanoi").

20. Taylor (1972), p. 319. At another point, Taylor noted that "the purpose of rational war is to break the will of the adversary and cause *him* to adjust *his* behavior to our purposes, not necessarily to destroy *him*" (1972, p. 403, emphasis added). For examples of the tendency to speak of "Hanoi" doing something in response to American moves, see III Gravel, pp. 214–215, 327–328, 346, 525–526, 542, 615, 645–647, 653–654; IV Gravel, p. 170, 236–237; Taylor (1972), passim.; and Johnson, passim.

the military demarcation line is provisional and should not in any way be interpreted as constituting a political or territorial boundary. . . . In order to insure that sufficient progress in the restoration of peace has been made, and that all the necessary conditions obtain for free expression of the national will, general elections shall be held in July 1956. . . . Consultations will be held on this subject between the competent representative authorities of the two zones from 20 July 1955 onwards.[21]

Although the Geneva Agreements in effect sanctioned the rule of Ho Chi Minh's Democratic Republic of Vietnam over Vietnam north of the 17th Parallel, the settlement was nonetheless greeted with something less than enthusiasm by many of the Viet Minh. This lack of enthusiasm was especially apparent among Southern cadres. Jeffrey Race, for example, quotes a "high ranking defector" as stating that: "When the Geneva Accords were signed, there was already much ill will against the Central Committee and Ho Chi Minh, because people felt that the South was always to be treated as a sacrificial animal when it came to reunification."[22]

Still, the anger felt by Southern cadres was probably mitigated to some extent by a belief that the Geneva Accords represented only a temporary setback and that the South would soon fall under Viet Minh control. Not only was the feeling widespread that the Viet Minh would easily win the elections prescribed by the Accords, but there was also the possibility of coming to power in the South by other means—for example, by filling the vacuum that would result if the Diem government collapsed or by a coup d'etat.[23] Consequently, although 87,000 armed Viet Minh were regrouped from the South to the North (accompanied by 43,000 administrative cadres, liberated POW's, and families),

21. On these points, see I Gravel, pp. 270–285. The quoted excerpts are from p. 284. See also Franklin B. Weinstein, "Vietnam's Unheld Elections," Data Paper no. 60, Southeast Asia Program, Cornell University, July 1966, pp. 10–14.

22. Jeffrey Race, interview with "Le Van Chan" (pseudonym), in Race, *War Comes to Long An* (Berkeley: University of California Press, 1972), p. 74. Chan was the former deputy secretary for the Lao Dong Party's Interprovince Committee for Western Nam Bo (South Vietnam). See also the *New York Times'* report for July 25, 1954, quoted by Weinstein, p. 9n; and Bernard Fall, *Last Reflections On a War* (New York: Schocken, 1972), pp. 187–188. For an analysis of Viet Minh motives in accepting the partition of Vietnam, see Porter, pp. 7–8.

23. On the expected Viet Minh electoral success, see President Eisenhower's famous remark (cited by Weinstein, p. 15) that he did not know a single person knowledgeable about Vietnam who denied that Ho Chi Minh might well win 80 percent of the vote in an all-Vietnam election in 1954. Even with the provision for delaying the elections until 1956, the consensus among Western observers was that Ho and the Viet Minh would still win easily. On this point, see Weinstein's summary of the relevant literature, pp. 14–15; and Porter, pp. 37–38. On the chaotic conditions in the South and the likelihood of a GVN collapse, see I Gravel, pp. 291–305; Fitzgerald, pp. 102–135; and Shaplen (1966), pp. 113–132.

an estimated 8,000–10,000 cadres were left behind, of whom approximately 5,000 were armed.[24] While their primary mission was to engage in "political struggle" aimed at forcing the Diem government to agree to hold elections and building support for the Viet Minh cause, the Party leadership was taking no chances:

The overall goal of those remaining behind was to develop a readily available force to carry out the Geneva Accords, i.e., to propagandize for the general elections. In reality, they were to develop both political and military forces, the latter being absolutely secret, to provide against any developments in the revolutionary situation in the coming years. Thus the slogan "to remain is to bring success" meant that they were to develop political and military forces to take advantage of any situation to gain power in the South—if by general elections, fine, but if not, then by whatever means were necessary.[25]

As things turned out, not only did Diem's government not collapse, but it set about consolidating its hold on the South in a way that "far exceeded the Party's worst expectations." Even though the Geneva Accords prohibited reprisals against former Viet Minh for their pre-1954 antigovernment activities, "the government proceeded unhindered with an extensive manhunt in the cities and the countryside, ultimately destroying almost the entire political apparatus that the Party had concealed in the South."[26] Still, the Party leadership continued to emphasize "political struggle" as the means for achieving reunification,

24. For details on the regroupment, see *U.S.-Vietnam Relations*, IV. A. 5., Tab 1, pp. 16–17. See also the Pentagon analyst's estimate that the cadres left behind constituted only a small fraction of the Viet Minh apparatus—cadre, local workers, and sympathizers—in the countryside; I Gravel, p. 328.

25. Jeffrey Race, interview with "Vo Van An" (pseudonym), in Race, p. 33. An was a Party member for nineteen years and a former alternate member of the Tay Ninh Province Committee. For additional details on the mission of these cadres, see "Forty Years of Party Activity," a history of the Lao Dong Party published in 1970 by the Historical Department of the VWP Central Committee, reprinted in *Vietnam Documents and Research Notes*, no. 76, pp. 51–52; Race, p. 32; *U.S.-Vietnam Relations*, IV. A. 5., Tab 3, pp. 45–47; I Gravel, pp. 328–329; and Weinstein, pp. 24 ff. See also the CRIMP Document, pp. 8–9. The CRIMP Document was Item no. 301 in a set of intelligence reports, prisoner interrogation reports, and captured documents included as appendices to the Working Paper. Items included in the Working Paper appendices will hereafter be referred to as "Working Paper, Item _____." One must, of course, exercise great caution in using captured documents, since there is always the possibility that the document was "planted" in order to "spoof" U.S. intelligence agencies. The Working Paper appendices, however, have been widely cited in the scholarly literature on Vietnam, and the author is not aware of any challenge to their validity. This is especially true with respect to the CRIMP Document, which has been universally accepted as authentic.

26. Race, p. 37. See also Fitzgerald, pp. 197–198; and Porter, p. 12. On the American role in the anti-Viet Minh witch-hunt, see Porter, p. 39.

even though there began to appear appeals from Southern cadres that "political struggle" be abandoned in favor of "armed struggle":

Prisoners and documents attest that Le Duan, the Lao Dong chieftain in South Vietnam, had lost faith in "political struggle" as early as 1955; one source reported that it was Le Duan's view that Hanoi was "wasting time," and that the Diem government should be "forcibly overthrown" as soon as possible if the DRV were to expect to "succeed in gaining control of South Vietnam." In February 1956, Le Duan is reported to have conferred with southern leaders on tactics and concluded that "military pressure" was essential for reunification.[27]

These appeals, however, were rejected on the grounds that "the contradictions had not yet developed to a high degree and the hatred had not yet developed to a point where the use of armed struggle could become an essential and popular struggle tactic."[28] Still, there was a need for the leadership to do something: the Party in the South was under severe strain as a result of the Diemist repression; more importantly, with the passing of the July 1956 deadline for elections, Party cadres in the South were desperately in need of guidance as to what their activities should be aimed at, now that the goal of reunification-via-elections had proved illusory. This need was met by a document authored by Le Duan and widely circulated among southern cadres in late 1956. Entitled "The Path of the Revolution in the South," the document undertook to outline a new long-range strategy for achieving reunification.[29]

27. *U.S.-Vietnam Relations*, IV. A. 5., Tab 3, pp. 48–49. According to the Working Paper (p. 7): "There are reports of Party meetings in 1956–1957 to discuss a change of tactics and Le Duan is represented as urging increased military action. 'Our political struggle in the South will sometimes have to be backed up with military action to show the strength of [our] forces,' he told a Party conference in the South on March 18, 1956. 'Therefore we should increase our forces in the South and develop military action.'" On Le Duan's views, see also Working Paper, Items 18, 19, 204.

28. The CRIMP Document, Working Paper, Item 301, p. 9 (see also p. 8). Carlyle Thayer ("Southern Vietnamese Revolutionary Organizations and the Vietnam Workers' Party: Continuity and Change, 1954–1974," in Joseph Zasloff and MacAlister Brown [eds.], *Communism in Indochina* [Lexington, Mass.: D.C. Heath, 1975], p. 36), attributes the continued emphasis on "political struggle" to the Central Committee's deep involvement in the problems of socialist construction and land reform in the North.

29. On the difficulties encountered by the Party at this time, the CRIMP Document notes that: "Particularly after 20 July 1956, the key cadres and Party members in South Vietnam asked questions which demanded answers: 'Can we still continue the struggle to demand the implementation of [the] Geneva Agreement given the existing regime in South Vietnam? If not, then what must be done?' A mood of skepticism and nonconfidence in the orientation of the struggle began to seep into the party apparatus and among some of the masses" (Working Paper, Item 301, p. 2). See also the remarks by Le Van Chan, quoted by Race, p. 74; and Thayer's essay in Zasloff and Brown (eds.), pp. 36–38. On "The Path of the Revolution in the South," see Race (p. 75n), who notes that

As described by Jeffrey Race:

The introductory passage to "The Path of the Revolution" ascribed failure to reunify the country under the Geneva Accords to "the American imperialist invaders and the feudalist dictator Ngo Dinh Diem, who have employed every means to sabotage the execution of the Geneva Accords in the hopes of prolonging the division of our country and turning the South into a colony and military base of the imperialists in order to renew the war and take over our country."

To cope with this situation, the document continued, "the Central Committee has put forth three principal goals as the general line for the overall revolutionary effort of the entire country at the present time." These were: (1) "firmly consolidate the North" (necessary since "the North must be developed into a firm base of support for the revolutionary movement to liberate the South"); (2) "strongly push the revolutionary movement to the South"; and (3) "win the sympathy and support of the democratic, nationalist, and peace-loving peoples of the world."[30]

The order in which the movement's priorities were listed was instructive because, after discussing the second objective in detail, "the document then drew a conclusion which nevertheless proved to be a great disappointment to large numbers of cadres in the South. It abandoned the option of armed activity . . . and directed that the conflict was to be carried on by means of political activity. . . ."[31] In justifying this decision, the document paid homage to the judgment of the 20th Congress of the Communist Party of the Soviet Union that "all current international conflicts can be resolved by means of peaceful negotiations" and that "the revolutionary movement in various countries can develop peacefully." More importantly, the document noted that the revolutionary movement in the South had been seriously weakened, making this an inopportune moment to launch an armed struggle: "Without an internal force, it is impossible to take advantage of the [favorable] international situation."[32]

"this document . . . was the foundation of Party policy in the South from 1956 to 1959, and is constantly referred to by Party cadres in their discussions of this period. The original document was captured in the Tan Buu area of Long An province in 1957; a copy was located by the author [Race] in the Cong An archives in Long An. It is #1002 in the collection of materials deposited [by Race] with the Center for Research Libraries. . . ." On the authorship of this document, see Race, p. 75n; and the CRIMP Document, Working Paper, Item 301, p. 3.

30. Quoted in Race, pp. 75–76.
31. Race, p. 77. See also Porter, p. 11.
32. Quoted in Race, pp. 77–79.

But while the CRIMP Document claimed that "The Path of the Revolution" was of "great significance" because it "solved" the "ideological crisis" facing the Party, the debate over strategy was in fact just beginning. Le Duan himself apparently was less than enthusiastic about the way in which the "political struggle" line had been implemented, as indicated by his comment that

at the present time a number of comrades in the South . . . look only at the international situation and see only international solutions. These comrades make a serious mistake by failing to understand the course of revolutionary development. As a consequence, the revolutionary movement has not only failed to develop but has moved into passivism.[33]

More importantly, while the essence of the new strategy was contained in the slogan "To lie patiently in ambush, gathering one's forces, waiting to strike at the right moment," "The Path of the Revolution" was ambiguous on the key issue of *when* the Party would strike. How long the period of "political struggle" might be was left unanswered; instead, the document noted only that "we are determined to follow explicitly the Party line until the development of the situation permits us to act."[34]

In view of his criticism of the "political struggle" line during 1955–1956 and his chiding of "a number of comrades" for their tendency toward "passivism," it seems reasonable to infer that Le Duan's preference would have been to begin "armed struggle" sooner rather than later.[35] Similarly, Race reports that

the southern branch of the Party had never been content with the political line. Thus "The Path of the Revolution in the South" had to devote so many pages to justifying it. From conversations with individuals who were in the movement at this time, it becomes clear that southern Party members had found armed activity congenial and effective during the Resistance, and were now anxious to resolve their difficulties in the same way.[36]

33. For the CRIMP author's comments, see Working Paper, Item 301, p. 3. Le Duan's comment is from "The Path of the Revolution," quoted in Race, p. 79.

34. On these points, see Race, pp. 39, 80.

35. On Le Duan's views, see Latimer, pp. 43–44. As we shall see, Le Duan was consistently "hawkish" on the subject of the Southern revolution. Given his views, and the Southern cadres' well-known fears of betrayal, it is not surprising that he was chosen to author "The Path of the Revolution in the South." Who could better reassure Southern cadres that the renewed emphasis on "political struggle" was not another sellout à la Geneva?

36. Race, p. 103. See also the CRIMP Document, Working Paper, Item 301, p. 4; and *U.S.-Vietnam Relations*, IV. A. 5., Tab 3, p. 55, which cites reports captured while being forwarded from the South to Hanoi as indicating an intra-Party debate over whether to continue with political struggle or turn to armed struggle.

Yet it was precisely on the question of when to launch the armed struggle that the interests of those advocating violent revolution in the South and those concerned with consolidating the Party's hold on the North collided head-on. Although "The Path of the Revolution" did not say so explicitly, the revolutionary movement in the South was not alone in needing a respite: 1956 was also a time of troubles for the North as a result of the overzealous implementation of the land reform campaign. This campaign, during which several thousand Northerners died, was obviously out of hand by the summer of 1956, leading Ho Chi Minh to announce on August 18 the "successful completion" of the campaign, while simultaneously admitting that "errors had been committed."[37] In October, Truong Chinh (who had been closely identified with the campaign) was replaced as General Secretary of the Party by Ho himself, while Vo Nguyen Giap made a major speech denouncing the errors involved. These measures, however, were followed by an even graver crisis—an armed revolt, which erupted in Nghe An province in November 1956.[38] While the rebellion was quickly crushed, it seems likely that one effect of the uprising was to convince those in the leadership responsible for governing the North that the task of "consolidating" North Vietnam required their urgent attention and that reunification would have to wait. "From this time onwards," Devillers reports,

it would seem that Hanoi became painfully resigned to the situation. It was recognized in the course of the sixth session of the [DRV] National Assembly (January 1957) that "the struggle for unity would be long and difficult" and that a prerequisite would be the "consolidation" of the already-liberated North: to disguise the failure of the compaign for unification, they fell back on the building of "socialism within one country."[39]

37. A thorough and dispassionate account of the land reform campaign can be found in Edwin E. Moise, "Land Reform and Land Reform Errors in North Vietnam," *Pacific Affairs*, 49:1 (Spring 1976), 70–92. I am indebted to William S. Turley, personal communication, September 12, 1977, for calling the Moise article to my attention.

38. This is not to imply that the land reform campaign was the immediate cause of the Nghe An revolt. As William Turley notes (personal communication, April 30, 1979): "The uprising, which began on 7 November, originated in several Catholic hamlets of a largely Catholic district. These populations long had felt themselves to be fundamentally at odds with the Communists and had grown increasingly restive as efforts to migrate to the South met with official obstacles and signs of future curbs on communal (and therefore religious) autonomy appeared. Excesses associated with land reform only intensified their fear and hostility. Elsewhere, land reform was more directly the focus of popular unrest, although it should be noted that protest was directed more against the methods of implementation than against the objectives." For additional details on the agricultural crisis and the Nghe An revolt, see William Kaye, "A Bowl of Rice Divided: The Economy of North Vietnam," in P. J. Honey (ed.), *North Vietnam Today* (New York: Praeger, 1962), pp. 107–108.

39. Philippe Devillers, "The Struggle for the Unification of Vietnam," *China Quarterly*, 9

Despite these setbacks, the Party did not simply write off the South and concentrate solely on "consolidating" the North. Instead, it appears that during 1957–1958, the Party leadership, not unlike the Johnson Administration in its dealings with Vietnam, pursued several lines of policy at once. First, the leadership in fact gave first priority to "consolidating" the North. A number of observers have noted that 1957 marked a distinct shift in DRV foreign policy toward closer ties with Moscow, and it appears that this shift was linked to a desire for increased Soviet aid that was of critical importance if the DRV economy was to be modernized. The Soviets, for their part, were eager to strengthen their ties with Hanoi: within a year of Marshall Voroshilov's May 1957 visit to Hanoi, the Soviet Union had replaced China as the DRV's principal source of economic aid.[40]

Second, during 1957–1958 the Party in the South also undertook to "consolidate" its forces. As explained by a former high-ranking Southern cadre:

We can say with absolute certainty that by 1956 the Party was weakened. Yet from the Party viewpoint this was an opportunity to get rid of the passive, undependable elements, and to consolidate the reliable elements. Thus the Party considered that it lost in quantity but gained in quality. In 1957 the Party began to recover because of a number of not very intelligent actions and policies on the part of the government, which the Party exploited. Among these actions and policies the most deserving of attention were Ordinances 2 and 57 of the land-reform program, which automatically restored to the landlords who had followed the French all the lands granted to the peasants during the Resistance. . . .[41]

In addition, the Party in the South attempted to strengthen its support

---

(January–March 1962), 10–11. See also Zagoria, p. 102; and Ho Chi Minh's statement of February 15, 1957, in which the "consolidation" of the North was made a prerequisite for unification: "To achieve national reunification, all our people must unite closely, make further efforts to consolidate the North and make it a base for national liberation" (quoted in U.S.-Vietnam Relations, IV. A. 5., Tab 3, p. 49).

40. On these points, see Zagoria, pp. 102–103; P. J. Honey, Communism in North Vietnam (Cambridge, Mass.: MIT Press, 1963), pp. 48–51; Kaye, pp. 111–113; and U.S.-Vietnam Relations, IV. A. 5., Tab 3, p. 52.

41. Jeffrey Race, interview with Le Van Chan, in Race, p. 97. Chan's account corresponds closely with that given by the CRIMP Document, Working Paper, Item 301, pp. 9–10. Closely related to this process of "consolidation" was the Party's attempt to build up agent networks along the South Vietnam–Cambodia border, in preparation for securing base areas in Cambodia immediately adjacent to the border. On these activities, see Race, pp. 84–85; and "Hanoi's Role in the Support of the Present War in South Vietnam," unpublished State Department paper filed with the Working Paper and its appendices at the Bureau of Intelligence and Research, pp. 1–2. See also the Pentagon analyst's discussion of the key role assigned to careful preparatory work in Vietnamese Communist doctrine, in U.S.-Vietnam Relations, IV. A. 5., Tab 3, pp. 53–55.

among the people while simultaneously weakening the government in Saigon. On the one hand, Party cadres during 1957–1958 mounted a strenuous propaganda campaign based on the themes of "peace and reunification," "freedom and democracy," and "popular livelihood"; on the other hand, the Party also engaged in a campaign of assassinations aimed at government officials, teachers, and members of the Cong An (the Diemist secret police) in an effort to destroy the government apparatus in the countryside:

At the same time that the possibility of armed activity by Party military units was disappearing, another type of armed activity was on the rise, which the Party called *tru gian*, "the extermination of traitors." Although the period after the circulation of "The Path of the Revolution in the South" was supposedly one of purely political activity, "extermination" activities were considered essential to the survival of the Party's apparatus.[42]

Finally, perhaps the most significant gain made by the Southern movement during this period came not in the South but rather in Hanoi. Sometime in 1957, Le Duan and Pham Hung were recalled from the South to Hanoi, where they both took up important positions in the leadership—Le Duan as de facto General Secretary of the Party (although the position was still formally held by Ho), and Pham Hung as a Deputy Premier. With their election to the Politburo in 1957, Southern cadres gained two important and strategically located allies in the North.[43]

The third line of policy undertaken by the DRV was essentially diplomatic and was itself pursued on two fronts simultaneously. On the one hand, Ho Chi Minh made two trips out of the country during 1957, apparently soliciting aid for the DRV. Significantly, he was accompanied on his second trip, during which he visited Moscow for the 40th anniversary celebration of the Bolshevik Revolution, by the two veteran

42. Race, p. 82. For additional details on the terrorist campaign, see Race, pp. 83–84; Devillers, pp. 13–14; and Porter (p. 11), who argues that the *tru gian* campaign was actually quite limited in scope. For details on the Party's propaganda campaign, see Race, pp. 86–97.

43. On the return of Le Duan and Pham Hung, see Latimer, p. 50; Thayer's essay in Zasloff and Brown (eds.), p. 40; Working Paper, p. 9; *U.S.-Vietnam Relations*, IV. A. 5., Tab 3, pp. 39, 49–50; and Albert Palmerlee, "The Central Office of South Vietnam," *Vietnam Documents and Research Notes*, no. 40, pp. 4, 8. Between 1951 and 1954, the Lao Dong Party's Central Office for South Vietnam (COSVN) had been headed by a six-man committee, which was itself headed by Le Duan, with Pham Hung a committee member. In 1954, COSVN was dissolved and its functions split between the Nam Bo Regional Committee (headed by Le Duan, with Pham Hung as his deputy) and the Trung Bo Inter-region Committee. On these points, see Palmerlee, p. 4; and Working Paper, Item 19, p. 1. See also Latimer (p. 30), who suggests that Pham Hung's real duty as a Deputy Premier was to monitor the progress of the Southern revolution.

leaders of the Southern movement just recently returned to Hanoi—Le Duan and Pham Hung. In this respect, Latimer has speculated, plausibly enough, that Ho had begun to look favorably upon Le Duan's advocacy of "armed struggle" as early as 1957; hence the recall of Le Duan and Pham Hung to Hanoi. But, having been sold out once before at Geneva, he would certainly want to nail down as firmly as possible the kind of support the DRV could expect in any future conflict. As a result, one suspects that at least part of the two months Ho spent in Moscow in late 1957 was devoted to introducing Le Duan and Pham Hung to the world Communist leadership and lobbying for support for their ideas on armed struggle.[44]

On the other hand, Pham Van Dong was also conducting a diplomatic campaign of his own during this period, aimed at reaching an accommodation with the Diem government in the South:

In June 1957 Dong wrote to the Geneva Conference Co-Chairmen again calling on them to take steps to facilitate the holding of elections. In July 1957, March and December 1958, July 1959 and July 1960, Dong addressed notes to Diem urging that he agree to the holding of a consultative conference to discuss reunification elections. The DRV also sought to institute at least a normalization of relations with the South, which would permit Hanoi to trade for southern rice. Diem rejected all of Hanoi's offers, condemning them as "false propaganda."[45]

As things turned out, in late 1958 all of these lines of policy came together, with consequences that were of the greatest importance. By then, the DRV had secured substantial Soviet aid, thus enabling steady progress in "consolidating" the North.[46] Moreover, by the end of 1958, the Party in the South had completed two years of rebuilding, during which it "was able to recover its apparatus and its mass organizations." Significantly, this recovery coincided with an apparent surge in demands for the launching of an armed struggle to complement the Party's political struggle in the South. As the CRIMP Document notes:

Faced with the fact that the enemy was using guns, assassinations and imprisonment to oppose the people in their political struggle, many voices among the masses appealed to the Party to establish a program of armed resistance against the enemy. Within the Party, on the one hand, the members were

44. On these points, see Latimer, pp. 50–55. Honey (1963, pp. 52–58) attaches a somewhat different interpretation to Ho's trip to Moscow; see also Honey, "North Vietnam's Party Congress," *China Quarterly*, 4 (October–December 1960), 32–33.

45. Weinstein, p. 54; see also Porter, p. 12.

46. On this point, see *U.S.-Vietnam Relations*, IV. A. 5., Tab 3, p. 56; and Honey (1963), p. 66.

saturated with the responsibility to lead the revolution to a successful overthrow of the enemy, but on the other hand the majority of party members and cadres felt that it was necessary to immediately launch an armed struggle in order to preserve the movement and protect the forces. In several areas, the party members on their own initiative had organized armed struggle against the enemy.[47]

Third, Pham Van Dong's diplomatic efforts were making no progress whatsoever—his initiative of December 1958 was rejected by Diem just like all the others. Finally and most importantly, in late 1958, Le Duan made an extensive visit to the South to survey the situation there; and it appears that this visit was the catalyst for an intensification of the intra-Party debate over strategy for the Southern revolution.[48]

On returning to Hanoi, Le Duan most likely presented his report to the 15th Plenum of the Central Committee, which met in Hanoi in January 1959.[49] Based on his past views, it seems reasonable to infer that

47. On these points, see Jeffrey Race, interview with Le Van Chan, in Race, p. 110; Working Paper, Item 301, p. 10; and Thayer's essay in Zasloff and Brown (eds.), pp. 41–42.

48. On the Le Duan visit, see King C. Chen, "Hanoi's Three Decisions and the Escalation of the Vietnam War," *Political Science Quarterly*, 90:2 (Summer 1975), 245; and *U.S.-Vietnam Relations*, IV. A. 5., Tab 3, p. 56. The most extensive report on Le Duan's visit was provided by George Carver ("The Faceless Viet Cong," *Foreign Affairs*, 44:3 [April 1966], 359–360): "Several VC cadre members who were subsequently captured have reported that in late 1958 Le Duan himself was sent on an extensive inspection trip in the South, and that upon his return to Hanoi in early 1959 he presented a list of recommendations subsequently adopted by the Lao Dong Central Committee and referred to in Viet Cong cadre training sessions as 'Resolution 15.' These recommendations laid out the whole future course of the southern insurgency, including the establishment of a National Liberation Front to be controlled by the Central Committee of the South Vietnamese branch of the Lao Dong Party and supported by a South Vietnamese 'liberation army.'" However, one must be careful in using Carver's essays, not only because he slants his interpetation to support the official U.S. Government view of the war (he was, after all, a CIA official) but also because he is careless at points: witness his reference to the Central Committee of the southern branch of the Lao Dong Party. There was and is only one Central Committee, headquartered in Hanoi, although several Central Committee members were usually present in the South to direct Party operations there.

49. There has been considerable confusion over the date of this Plenum, with Race, Honey, Carver, and the Pentagon analyst assigning the meeting to May 1959. The source of the confusion can probably be traced to the fact that the communique from the Plenum was not broadcast until May 1959, even though, as indicated by subsequent Party documents, the Plenum was actually held in January. For the correct date of the Plenum (i.e., January 1959), see "Forty Years of Party Activity," reprinted in *Vietnam Documents and Research Notes*, no. 76, p. 126; "A Brief Chronology of Momentous Facts and Events in the History of the Democratic Republic of Vietnam," reprinted in *Vietnam Documents and Research Notes*, no. 84, p. 57; and the resolution of the 9th Plenum of the Central Committee (December 1963), "Strive to Struggle, Rush Forward to Win New Victories in the South," reprinted in *Vietnam Documents and Research Notes*, no. 96, p. 3. See also Chen (1975), p. 246n; Latimer, pp. 62–65; Porter, p. 13; and Thayer's essay in Zasloff and Brown (eds.), p. 43, all of which provide the correct date for the Plenum.

he argued that the time had come to begin the armed struggle in the South. If this was the case, then Le Duan got at least part of what he wanted—the evidence available suggests that the 15th Plenum resulted in two main decisions: (1) a decision to create a limited number of armed units in the South according to the slogan "political struggle mixed to the right degree with armed struggle"; and (2) a decision in principle to begin the armed struggle at some future date.[50] However, the evidence available also suggests that these decisions were not easily reached; in fact, it appears that Le Duan's views were sharply disputed by those in the leadership responsible for governing North Vietnam. Jeffrey Race, for example, argues that the policies approved by the 15th Plenum "must have been born of a sharp conflict within the Central Committee, in which the proponents of change overcame the backers of the political struggle line," a conclusion he bases on "the tone of subsequent Party commentaries."[51] Similarly, the existence of conflict within the Party at this time was tacitly admitted by a Party history published in 1970 which noted that, during 1958-1960, "the Party also struggled to overcome confused notions about the interlocking relationship between the socialist revolutionary task in North Vietnam and the task of liberating South Vietnam and worries to the effect that the progress to socialism in North Vietnam would impede the struggle to unify the country."[52]

Furthermore, the evidence available suggests that the 15th Plenum by no means resolved completely the dispute within the Party. As the

50. On the decision to create armed units in the South, see Race, pp. 105-106. The principal evidence for concluding that the decision to launch the armed struggle did not include a specific date for beginning the struggle is the fact that it was not until May 1959 that the Politburo issued a directive ordering the armed struggle to begin (see below).

51. Race, p. 105. See also Latimer, pp. 58-65.

52. "Forty Years of Party Activity," reprinted in *Vietnam Documents and Research Notes*, no. 76, p. 56. See also the CRIMP Document, which notes that the launching of the armed struggle was a "very important problem" on which there were "many opinions and many hesitancies" (Working Paper, Item 301, p. 11). This is not to imply, however, that there was any disagreement within the VWP leadership concerning the desirability of the goal of reunification under the aegis of the VWP: no member of the leadership could have renounced reunification and expected to retain his position and the respect of his colleagues. What disagreement there was (and there was plenty of it) centered exclusively on questions of timing and tactics. For example, when to begin the armed struggle? How much emphasis should be placed on political struggle as opposed to armed struggle? To what degree should resources be diverted from construction in the North (an especially important task if the North was to field a modern army that could deter or, if necessary, defeat the Americans) to the task of revolution in the South? This fundamental agreement on the legitimacy of the goal of reunification, as we shall see, would have important implications for the American effort to "convince" the North Vietnamese to content themselves with the territory assigned them by the 1954 Geneva Accords.

CRIMP Document notes, in the aftermath of the Plenum the dispute focused on the way in which the Central Committee's decisions were to be implemented:

> The Resolution of the 15th Conference of the Central Committee officially and concisely specified the responsibilities and strategic aims of the South Vietnam revolution.
>
> But problems still existed: how were these responsibilities, aims, and progress of the South Vietnam revolution to be implemented? What must the main forms and procedures of the struggle be? Although the Resolution outlined some of these factors, at the time of the Conference, the details of the South Vietnam movement as well as revolutionary experiences of friendly nations were not sufficient enough for the conference to formulate a precise program.[53]

In the months following the 15th Plenum, it appears that the Party leadership devoted considerable time and effort to the question of what kind of conflict it should prepare for in the South ("the main forms and procedures of the struggle"). In dealing with this question, the Party had two main "models" to choose between: a general uprising along the lines of the Party's August 1945 seizure of power, and a prolonged military conflict like the Resistance War against the French. In the case of the former, the emphasis would be on political struggle in an attempt to win over the people and lay the groundwork for a successful uprising. While some armed forces would be required, principally for the purpose of weakening the government apparatus by means of assassinations and terrorist activities, thus creating a political vacuum for the Party to fill, they would be relatively small compared to the forces needed to fight a prolonged Resistance-type conflict; furthermore, those forces could probably be supplied by recruitment in the South supplemented by the pool of Southern "regroupees" available in the North. If, however, the war in the South should evolve into a Resistance-type conflict, sizable armed forces would be required, thus raising the very real possibility that Northerners would have to be committed to the battle (especially if the U.S. intervened). In the aftermath of the 15th Plenum, then, it appears that those in the leadership who did not want to see resources diverted from the North to the South counseled against moving too quickly to all-out warfare in the South, urging instead that the Southern movement concentrate on political struggle in order to build the necessary base of support for a successful general uprising. In contrast, those who had been skeptical of the political struggle line all along apparently

53. Working Paper, Item 301, p. 5.

urged greater reliance on armed struggle, including, if necessary, the injection of Northern men and materiel into the conflict in the South.[54]

The evidence available, however, suggests that the leadership was unable to resolve this dispute over the type of conflict to prepare for. On the one hand, a March 1960 "Message From the Regional Committee to All Comrades at Village Level" noted that:

Our struggle movement is headed toward an armed uprising and seizure of power. To succeed, we must rely on a seething mass political struggle movement, progressing from lower to higher forms, from limited to widespread, from scattered to conventional, extremely vigorous and strong.

Armed activities only fulfill a supporting role for the political struggle movement. It is impossible to substitute armed forces and armed struggle for political forces and political struggle. Formerly we erred in slighting the role of armed activity. Today we must push armed activity to the right degree, but at the same time we must not abuse or rely excessively on armed activity.[55]

Similarly, documents cited by Jeffrey Race combined exhortations to rely primarily on political struggle with veiled hints not to expect too much help from the North:

At the present time armed struggle proceeds in the direction of an uprising and seizure of power, and not, as in the Resistance, according to the concept of seizing the rural areas in order to surround and finally to liberate the cities. At the present time the armed struggle is not guerrilla warfare, nor is it continuous prolonged conflict, liberating large areas and establishing a government as during the Resistance.

At the present time the armed struggle consists of arming the entire people for self-defense and propaganda. To accomplish this it is necessary to build upon the organized political forces of the masses. *The people must arm themselves,* both for self-defense and also to strike back and to destroy the village and hamlet officials, Dan Ve, Cong An, informers, landlords, and other cruel hard-core elements, to defend their own interests, to protect their lands, and to preserve their country. *The people must not sit passively and wait for others: they must rise up and liberate themselves.*[56]

And yet, at the same time that Southern cadres were being told to fight and win their own revolution and to rely primarily on political

---

54. On these points, see Latimer, pp. 63–77; and Race, pp. 105–112. See also the CRIMP Document, Working Paper, Item 301, pp. 15–16.

55. Quoted in Race, p. 119. See also Working Paper, Item 34, p. 5.

56. Quoted in Race, p. 108 (emphasis added). See also the October 1960 article by Minh Tranh (summarized by Latimer, pp. 96–97), which argued that "the people in South Vietnam" had the responsibility for overthrowing the Diem government.

struggle, others in the leadership were apparently preparing for a conflict in which armed struggle would play a much greater role and to which Northern manpower might well be committed. The Pentagon analyst cites POW reports that

in early 1959 they [the POW's] were chosen to man "special border crossing teams" for moving drugs, food, and other materiel across the DMZ into Quang Tri and Thua Thien. In April 1959, a prisoner reported that the Lao Dong Party Central Committee directed the forming of a headquarters to control this effort, which came into being on May 5, 1959 as the 559th Transportation Group, directly subordinate to Party headquarters. Another prisoner served with the 70th Battalion of the 559th Group, which was formed in 1959 and sent into southern Laos. The 70th Battalion received weapons, ammunition, mail, and supplies from Hanoi and transported them to another organization in charge of distribution to insurgent units. The 70th Battalion was in charge of 20 way-stations, furnished escorts for infiltrating groups from North to South Vietnam, and transported sick and wounded personnel from Thua Thien Province back to North Vietnam. While the 559th Group was being deployed on land, other prisoners reported that the 603d Battalion was formed in June 1959 to manage maritime infiltration into South Vietnam. According to prisoners, the 603d Battalion had 250 men upon formation, and by December 1959, had 11 infiltration "cells" and supporting bases in operation. Still other POW's stated that in January 1960, a training center for infiltrators was in operation at Son Tay, northwest of Hanoi, and that in early 1960, the NVA 324th Division in Nghe An was directed to begin infiltrator training. About the same time the Xuan Mai Infiltration Center was established southwest of Hanoi, a school which by 1961 could accommodate several 1000-man classes simultaneously.[57]

Judging from the scale of these preparations, it appears that whoever was in charge of them was anticipating a very sizable conflict indeed.

Perhaps the most important indicator of the disagreements within the Party leadership was the fact that the decision to *begin* the armed struggle was not made until May 1959. As mentioned earlier, the Central Committee's 15th Plenum decided in principle to launch the armed struggle at some future date. Significantly, though, the communique from the Plenum was not broadcast until May 13, four months after the Plenum itself, thus suggesting that the opponents of the new policy had kept up the fight even after the Plenum and that it took four

---

57. *U.S.-Vietnam Relations*, IV. A. 5., Tab 3, pp. 34-35. See also Working Paper, pp. 9-10; and U.S. Department of State, "Hanoi's Role in the Support of the Present War in South Vietnam," pp. 3-7. It should be noted that the NVA 324th Division was composed mainly of Southern regroupees (see Working Paper, p. 7). On the Party's difficulties in deciding what kind of struggle to conduct, see the CRIMP Document, Working Paper, Item 301, pp. 29-30.

months to resolve the issue. Sometime in May, though, the Politburo met to deal with the issue, and at that meeting it was the proponents of armed struggle who came out on top. As the CRIMP Document notes: "The directive of the Politburo in May 1959 stated that the time had come to push the armed struggle against the enemy."[58]

What tipped the balance in favor of going ahead? In retrospect, it appears that the Party simply had no choice—"it was then or never," as Race puts it. After the rebuilding of 1957–1958, the Party in the South entered what has often been called "the darkest days in Party history" in early 1959. The Diem government had itself been increasing its strength during 1957–1958, and in 1959 it launched an all-out attack on the Party apparatus:

This period was the darkest because of Law 10/59 [promulgated on May 6, 1959], because of the various political organizations such as the National Revolutionary Movement and the rural youth organizations, and because of the constant military campaigns. There was no place where Party members could find rest and security. Almost all were imprisoned or shot. A number were forced to surrender. . . . In the face of such fierce activity by the Diem government, the demand for armed activity by Party members increased daily, particularly in [Western South Vietnam] and particularly after the proclamation of Law 10/59. Party members felt it was no longer possible to talk of political struggle while looking down the gun barrels of the government.[59]

Even after the Politburo directive, however, the revolutionary movement gained momentum only very slowly. The CRIMP Document, for example, claimed that the armed struggle was "launched" in October 1959 (five months after the Politburo directive), but even this seems an exaggeration. As Race notes, the Politburo directive did not arrive at district and village level in the South until November 1959, "because of the Party practice of requiring a complete discussion of a new policy at each committee level before the decision is passed to the next subordinate level." Consequently, the main accomplishment during the

58. Working Paper, Item 301, p. 10. For excerpts from the Central Committee's communique, see *U.S.-Vietnam Relations*, IV. A. 5., Tab 3, pp. 57–59. See also Chen (1975), pp. 246–247; and Race, pp. 112–113.

59. For the "then or never" comment, see Race, p. 110. On the "darkest days in Party history," see Race, pp. 99–104; and I Gravel, p. 332. The description of conditions in the South at this time is provided by Jeffrey Race, interview with Le Van Chan, in Race, p. 79. Chan's assessment is corroborated by the CRIMP Document, Working Paper, Item 301, p. 12; and by a Party history cited by Thayer in his essay in Zasloff and Brown (eds.), pp. 42–43. See also Chen (1975), p. 246; and Porter (p. 13), who notes that "Le Duan himself later told a cadre conference that by 1959 Party branches in the South had been up to 70 or 80 percent destroyed."

remainder of 1959 appears to have been stepped-up preparations for the armed struggle:

As a result of the Party's new policy events began to move more rapidly in Long An and the surrounding areas. During the last six months of 1959 the Party reorganized and rearmed a number of province main force battalions and began to rebuild traditional base areas such as the Plain of Reeds and the Rung Sat.[60]

By January 1960, though, these preparations were largely complete, and in that month the armed struggle erupted across South Vietnam with a vengeance. In Long An province, for example, Viet Cong cadres used the Tet holidays to spread a wave of terror among the population. During all of 1959, as Race notes, "only three individuals had been assassinated in the whole province. Now within one week—the most solemn week of the year—26 people were killed: hamlet and village chiefs, youth leaders, Cong An, etc."[61] More ominously, this was also the time when the conflict in the South "escalated" significantly, as Viet Cong forces began launching large-scale attacks directly on ARVN bases as well as Government-held towns. On January 25, 1960, a Viet Cong battalion

launched an attack coordinated with four guerrilla companies . . . which penetrated the compound of the 32nd Regiment, 21st ARVN Division at Tay Ninh, killed 23 ARVN soldiers and netted a large haul of arms and ammunition. On 29 January an insurgent band seized the town of Dong Xoai, some 60 miles north of Saigon, held the place for several hours, and robbed a French citizen of 200,000 piasters. In the same month, large VC forces opened operations in the Camau peninsula and the Mekong Delta. In Kien Hoa province VC units numbering hundreds effectively isolated the province capital from six of its eight districts.[62]

60. On these points, see the CRIMP Document, Working Paper, Item 301, p. 10; Race, pp. 107n and 113. The Pentagon analyst, however, suggests that the upsurge in VC activity began in mid-1959. See I Gravel, pp. 337–338; and *U.S.-Vietnam Relations*, IV. A. 5., Tab 3, p. 60. See also Thayer's essay in Zasloff and Brown (eds.), p. 44.

61. Race, pp. 113–115. Other indicators also showed the step-up in VC activity. In 1959, the average number of contacts per month between revolutionary and government forces in Long An province in which fire was exchanged was 3.2; in 1960, the average climbed to 12.0. The average number of incidents per month in Long An (any reported appearance of revolutionary forces in which fire was not exchanged) climbed from 7.8 in 1959 to 88.4 in 1960. For this data, see Race, pp. 113–115; see also Sharp and Westmoreland, p. 78.

62. I Gravel, p. 338. See also Race, pp. 106–107. Further evidence that the armed struggle did not begin in earnest until 1960 can be found in a report by one of Race's interviewees (Vo Van An) that "cadres from the Regional Committee explained that the purpose of the [Tay Ninh] attack was to launch the new phase of the conflict with a resounding victory . . ." (Race, p. 107). We should note that this was also the time when the Party moved to strengthen its forces in the South through

Despite the successful launching of the armed struggle in the South, critics of the new policy in Hanoi apparently remained unconvinced. On April 20, 1960, for example, Le Duan felt it necessary to deliver a lengthy speech defending the new policy toward the South, which he portrayed as the direct result of the application of Lenin's teachings to Vietnam. Significantly, in contrast to the warning cited above that the South Vietnamese people "must not sit passively and wait for others: they must rise up and liberate themselves," Le Duan asserted that the liberation of the South was "not only a task of southern people but also of the entire people, of the South as well as of the North." In addition, as Latimer notes, in this speech

Le Duan threw off all pretension of sticking to the old line of peaceful political struggle. He stated flatly that "in a colony such as our country, where the imperialists resorted to violence for their domination, our people had no other road than to carry out an armed insurrection and utilize revolutionary force." In that passage he was referring to the party's past struggle against France but the relevance of his remarks to the current situation in the South could not have been lost on his audience. To make his point clear, Le Duan asserted that "the road to liberate the people from the imperialist plight cannot be other than the road of revolution."[63]

Similarly, the August and September issues of *Hoc Tap* (the Party's theoretical journal) carried a lengthy article by the recently promoted Nguyen Chi Thanh (who, in September 1959, became North Vietnam's second Senior General, Giap being the first) in which Thanh openly identified himself with Le Duan and the proponents of armed struggle. Thanh insisted that the correct way to solve the "contradiction"

---

a significant increase in the rate of infiltration into South Vietnam of soldiers and cadres drawn from the pool of "regroupees." On the sharp increase in infiltration that took place in late 1959 and early 1960, see *U.S.-Vietnam Relations*, IV. A. 5., Tab 3, .pp. 35–36; and Working Paper, p. 10.

63. On these points, see Le Duan, "Leninism and Vietnam's Revolution," quoted by Chen (1975), p. 249; and Latimer, pp. 80–81. Zagoria (p. 105) attaches a considerably different interpretation to this speech, arguing that "Duan stressed the problems of industrializing the North and building up its agriculture and then went on to make a frank plea for 'restricting' the Southern resistance movement so that it would not interfere with world peace. . . ." However, as the excerpt from this speech quoted by Zagoria clearly shows, Le Duan was not talking about "restricting" the Southern revolution in the sense of *restraining* it; instead, after noting that "the Northern people will never neglect their task with regard to one-half of their country which is not yet liberated," Le Duan went on to state that "we can and must guide and *restrict within the South* the solving of the contradiction between imperialism and the colonies of our country." Viewed in this light, Latimer's interpretation (pp. 78–83) seems much more plausible—i.e., Le Duan was not attempting to stifle the Southern revolution; instead, it appears that he was trying to reassure those within the Party (and perhaps in Moscow) who feared an expansion of the war outside the borders of South Vietnam by claiming that the revolution could be confined to the South despite a more active role by the North.

between the Party and its enemies was to use "revolutionary violence." More importantly, Thanh's claim that the new policy toward the South was irrevocable suggests that some elements within the Party were hoping to have that policy changed, probably at the Party's Third National Congress, scheduled for September 1960.[64]

If there were some Party members who hoped that the Congress would reverse the decisions of January and May 1959, they were to be disappointed, although probably not terribly so. In retrospect, the decisions ratified at the Congress appear to have been a bundle of compromises containing something for everyone. On the one hand, the Congress approved, albeit in guarded language, the decisions of January and May 1959 by calling for the "liberation" of the South:

In the present stage, the Vietnamese revolution has two strategic tasks: first, to carry out the socialist revolution in North Vietnam; second, to liberate South Vietnam from the ruling yoke of the U.S. imperialists and their henchmen in order to achieve national unity and complete independence and freedom throughout the country. . . .

The resolution passed by the Congress, however, carefully skirted the issue of tactics, such as the relative importance of political and armed struggle; instead, the main guidance offered by the Congress dealt with the problem of creating a "broad national united front":

This front must rally all the patriotic classes and sections of the people, the majority and minority nationalities, all patriotic parties and religious groupings, together with all individuals inclined to oppose the U.S.-Diem clique. The aims of its struggle are peace, national independence, democratic freedoms, improvement of the people's living conditions, and peaceful national reunification.

This front must carry out its work in a very flexible manner in order to rally all forces that can be rallied, win over all forces that can be won over, neutralize all forces that should be neutralized, and draw the broad masses into the general struggle against the U.S.-Diem clique for the liberation of the South and the peaceful reunification of the fatherland.[65]

On the other hand, the Congress also ratified decisions that contained significant concessions to those who opposed diverting resources from the North to the struggle in the South. Not only did the resolution passed by the Congress note that it was "our compatriots in the South"

---

64. On Thanh's articles, see Chen (1975), p. 249; and Latimer, pp. 84–85. On Thanh's promotion, see Honey (1963), pp. 96–97.

65. The text of the resolution is reprinted in *Vietnam Documents and Research Notes*, no. 91, pp. 32–56.

who "have the task of directly overthrowing the rule of the American imperialists and their agents in order to liberate South Vietnam," but it also endorsed the argument that "consolidation" of the North remained the highest priority:

> To take the North towards socialism and make it more and more powerful in every field will benefit the revolutionary movement for the liberation of the South, the development of the revolution throughout the country and the preservation and consolidation of peace in Indochina, Southeast Asia, and the world. Therefore, to carry out the socialist revolution in the North is the most decisive task for the development of the whole Vietnamese revolution, for the cause of national reunification.[66]

In addition, the Congress approved an extraordinarily ambitious 5-Year Plan, calling for average annual increases in the value of industrial and agricultural output over 1961–1965 of 20 percent and 10 percent, respectively. Under the plan, by 1965 industry would provide 51 percent and agriculture 49 percent of the total value of industrial and agricultural output, truly a "staggering target for industrialization," given the backward nature of the DRV's economy.[67]

However, one must be careful not to overstate the extent of the concessions to those primarily concerned with "consolidating" the North. In addition to the decisions already mentioned, the Congress took two additional steps that insured that those favoring an increased effort in the South would play a significant role in policymaking. First, the Congress confirmed Le Duan in his (newly retitled) post as First Secretary of the Party; second, the Congress created a new executive body, the Secretariat, intended to run the business of the Central Committee between sessions. Significantly, of the eight Central Committee

66. Quoted in *Vietnam Documents and Research Notes*, no. 91, pp. 35, 34. See also Porter, p. 15; and Thayer's essay in Zasloff and Brown (eds.), pp. 44–46.

67. Honey (1960), pp. 69–70; see also Kaye, p. 111; and Latimer, p. 91. The evidence available suggests that the decision to embark on such an ambitious program was linked to a secret visit to Moscow by Ho in August 1960. As Honey (1960, p. 73) notes: "Ho made no public appearances in Vietnam between August 3 and 24, and the Hungarian Party daily, *Nepsabadzag*, reported that he was present in Moscow on August 15. On August 31, immediately after his arrival in Hanoi [for the Party's Congress], the chief Soviet delegate, Mukhitdinov, paid a visit to Ho and handed him a personal letter from Khrushchev. This, coupled with the staggering program of industrial development envisaged in the Five-Year Plan, points to the following explanation. Ho Chi Minh visited Moscow without the knowledge of the Chinese and bargained with Khrushchev, offering Vietnamese support of the Soviet line and closer links with Russia in the future in exchange for greatly increased aid from Russia in the industrial sphere." Honey's explanation, which seems plausible enough, suggests that Ho's primary concern was to preserve a consensus of sorts by trying to arrange a "package deal" involving both greater support for the war in the South and greater efforts in developing the North. On these points, see also Honey (1963), pp. 76–82.

members named to the Secretariat, the four most senior (all Politburo members) were all closely identified with the struggle in the South: Le Duan, Nguyen Chi Thanh, Pham Hung, and Le Duc Tho.[68]

Most importantly, though, the long-sought goal of "liberating" South Vietnam had now been endorsed by the highest authority in North Vietnam—a Party Congress. And before the year had ended, the Congress's call for the creation of a "broad national united front" would be answered by the formation in December 1960 of the National Front for the Liberation of South Vietnam. As 1960 came to a close, then, not only were the proponents of armed struggle entrenched in the Party bureaucracy, but they had helped create an important new organization that could, if necessary, appeal to friendly governments for assistance.[69]

B. DRV Policy from the Formation of the NLF to the 9th Plenum of the Central Committee

Despite the leadership's ability to fashion a "package deal" at the Third Party Congress, the apparent consensus produced by the Congress proved to be short-lived. Less than a year after the Congress had ended, the debate over strategy had erupted anew. Ironically, the attack on the policies espoused by Le Duan and Nguyen Chi Thanh was led by Truong Chinh and General Giap, both of whom had earlier stressed their "complete agreement" with the Political Report read by Le Duan at the Party Congress.[70]

In particular, in April 1961, Truong Chinh published an article in *Hoc Tap* which stressed, in contrast to Le Duan's claim that the revolution in the South was the duty of Northerners and Southerners alike, the separate duties of Northerners (building socialism) and Southerners (completing the national, democratic revolution). Southerners, Truong Ching asserted, "must not rely on the Northern

68. On these points, see Latimer, pp. 86–87; Zagoria, pp. 162–163; and Jean Lacouture, *Vietnam: Between Two Truces* (New York: Vintage, 1966), p. 49–50. Le Duc Tho had previously 'served in the South as Deputy Secretary of COSVN between 1951 and 1954 (see Palmerlee, p. 8). The other four members of the Secretariat were Hoang Anh, To Huu, Nguyen Van Tran, and Le Van Luong.

69. The possibility of the Front's appealing for aid was raised in a December 21, 1961 note from the Front to foreign governments (see Latimer, p. 109; and Honey [1963], pp. 111–112). Some scholars (e.g., Devillers, pp. 15–20) have suggested that the Front was an autonomous organization created by Southerners opposed to Diem; however, using captured Party documents, Pike, Chen, and Race have shown conclusively that the Front was in fact Hanoi's creation. On this, see Douglas Pike, *Viet Cong* (Cambridge, Mass.: MIT Press, 1966), pp. 74–84; Race, pp. 121–123; Chen (1975), pp. 250–251; and I Gravel, pp. 339–346.

70. Their statements during the Congress can be found in *Vietnam Documents and Research Notes*, no. 98, pp. 14, 37.

forces"; instead, the revolution in the South had to be carried out "by the southern people themselves." Furthermore, Chinh argued that the proper way to further the revolution in the South was by placing primary emphasis on political rather than armed struggle. Such an approach, it should be emphasized, was absolutely essential if the separation of tasks between North and South was to be preserved, since it was only by stressing political struggle that the southern revolutionary movement would be able to develop sufficient support among the masses to build an army strong enough to defeat Diem and ARVN (backed by the U.S.) without drawing on Northern manpower.[71]

Like Truong Chinh, Giap too was dissatisfied with the conduct of the war in the South, and he also favored greater reliance on political struggle, although for different reasons. In 1961, Giap published *People's War, People's Army*, and, as Latimer notes, it would seem to be not by chance that Giap chose that particular time to publish a book rehashing the experience of the Resistance War against the French. In retrospect, it appears that Giap was lecturing Le Duan and the southern command on how the war in the South should be conducted. In particular, Giap appears to have been especially worried that Le Duan and his supporters planned to move too quickly to full-scale warfare in the South, a move that carried with it an increased risk of American intervention. Noting that during the Resistance, "the shifting from political struggle to armed struggle was a very great change that required a long period of preparation," Giap suggested that the Party focus on setting up bases in the rural areas and defending them until the political struggle in the more populous areas had won over sufficient followers to warrant expanding the conflict to those areas.[72]

71. On these points, see Latimer, pp. 97–100.
72. On these points, see Latimer, pp. 98–105. See also the CRIMP Document (Working Paper, Item 301, p. 30), which noted that fears were expressed that launching the armed struggle "would cause imperialist America to help Ngo Dinh Diem destroy the movement and the revolution." Although both Giap and Truong Chinh were critical of the conduct of the Southern revolution, this is not to imply that their views were identical. While Truong Chinh consistently maintained that the revolution in the South was the responsibility of the Southern people, Giap's dissent centered on the *timing* of Northern intervention. As William Turley notes (personal communication, September 12, 1977): "Actually, Giap, as one might expect of a party leader who had come to perceive himself as the party's leading military specialist, wanted continued economic development of the North if necessary at [the] cost of a go-slow approach in the south in order to build an industrial base capable of sustaining the army in combat against the south at some later time. What better way to deter the Americans from intervening on a large scale than to build a strong conventional army that would not be abjectly dependent on the Soviet Union and China for support? In the meanwhile, the revolutionary movement in the south could keep itself viable, perhaps even win, by relying on guerrilla warfare occasionally reinforced by small main force action that would

Judging from what was actually being done, though, it appears that the arguments of Chinh and Giap were falling largely on deaf ears. For one thing, as noted earlier, during 1960 and 1961, preparations were under way in the North for a sizable infiltration effort. In addition, it appears that the Chinh/Giap argument that armed struggle should be deferred until the political struggle could win over more adherents was rejected by the leadership of the southern revolution. The CRIMP Document noted that

some people wish to restrict the uprising in the rural areas, only construct bases and large armed forces in a number of mountain areas while the compatriots in the rural delta areas only push the political struggle with armed propaganda support, keeping the situation normal and the areas under enemy control intact. . . .

These views, however, were not shared by the Southern command. Instead, as the CRIMP Document also noted, the leadership of the Southern movement intended to combine armed struggle with political struggle right from the start. In addition, the leadership intended to pursue an ambitious plan involving operations both in the mountains and in the heavily populated Delta (in contrast to Giap's conservative emphasis on first securing and defending bases in the sparsely populated areas and then only gradually extending the war to the more populous areas). In the mountains, the plan called for using main-force units to engage ARVN units and also to probe into the heavily populated coastal regions whenever possible. In the Delta, the Party would also develop main-force units, although in those areas it would rely more heavily on guerrilla and local forces and on political struggle.[73]

But while this ambitious strategy worked quite well during 1961, the movement's successes served only to trigger a greatly expanded American aid program; and by 1962 the effects of this increased aid were becoming apparent. Not only did the number of American advisers in South Vietnam climb from 685 in April 1961 to approximately 3,400 by April 1962, but the U.S. also began to supply helicopter

---

not provoke massive American intervention. But there is no question Giap envisioned a major war in the event guerrilla warfare failed, by which time he hoped economic development of the North would permit the army to hit the Americans hard on their own terms." Also on Giap's views, see his speech at the Third Congress, reprinted in *Vietnam Documents and Research Notes*, no. 98, pp. 37–54.

73. On these points, see the CRIMP Document, Working Paper, Item 301, pp. 30–37. The quoted excerpt is from p. 30. The Party's strategy was also described in the Resolution passed by the 9th Plenum of the Central Committee in December 1963, reprinted in *Vietnam Documents and Research Notes*, no. 96, especially pp. 18–20. See also Latimer, pp. 106–108.

companies to improve ARVN mobility and new automatic weapons along with air and artillery support to increase ARVN firepower. As a result, Viet Cong units in the South were pushed back on the defensive; about all the Southern command could claim was that events during 1962 proved "that the forces and the struggle movement of the Southern compatriots can be maintained . . . under very difficult circumstances." To make matters worse, these setbacks occurred at roughly the same time that the North was encountering difficulties in meeting the ambitious targets mapped out in the 5-Year Plan approved at the Third Party Congress. As a result, by early 1963, the debate over strategy had flared up anew and was being hotly contested in the pages of the Party press.[74]

In understanding this debate, it must be kept in mind that, from the Party's point of view, 1963 was a year of both great opportunity and great peril. On the one hand, the setbacks of 1962 notwithstanding, the year began with a resounding Viet Cong victory at Ap Bac, in which VC forces defeated a multi-battalion ARVN force backed by American helicopters. In May, the Buddhist crisis erupted throughout South Vietnam, and, with the Diem government preoccupied with the crisis in the cities, Viet Cong forces took advantage of the situation to tighten their grip on the countryside, including the seizure of hundreds of Strategic Hamlets.[75]

On the other hand, however, 1963 was also the year in which the Sino-Soviet dispute moved into its bitterest and most polemical phase, a development that apparently caused no end of worry for the Party leadership. On February 10, 1963, the Politburo issued an extraordinary public appeal for bloc unity. On February 21, General Giap published an important article commenting on the Politburo's appeal which frankly admitted that the unity of the Lao Dong Party itself had been threatened and which called once more for unity both within the Party and the socialist camp.[76]

74. On Viet Cong successes during 1961, see II Gravel, pp. 31–32, 35–36, 70–72, 134–135, 439. On increased U.S. aid during 1961–1962, see II Gravel, pp. 37–39, 114–117, 438–439, 451–457. On Viet Cong setbacks during 1962, see Lieutenant General Nguyen Van Vinh's assessment over Radio Hanoi, December 27, 1962, quoted by Pike (1966), p. 160. See also II Gravel, pp. 155–157, 173–174; Race, p. 123; and Latimer, p. 110. See also the CRIMP Document (Working Paper, Item 301, pp. 12–13), which noted that some people thought that "by 1962 the revolutionary warfare had not developed correctly and had to be re-examined."

75. On the battle of Ap Bac, see Latimer, pp. 112–113; Fitzgerald, p. 200; and Document no. 120 in II Gravel, p. 718. On the Buddhist crisis and Viet Cong successes during the summer and fall of 1963, see II Gravel, pp. 158, 183–184, 189–190, 225–274; and Latimer, p. 114.

76. The text of the Politburo's statement is reprinted in Honey (1963), pp. 181–185. It was apparently intended to suggest that the South Vietnamese movement would have achieved even

The source of the Party's problems was not difficult to identify: it seems clear in retrospect that the American buildup in the South had given rise to considerable doubts concerning the wisdom of adhering to the ambitious strategy mapped out by Le Duan and the Southern command. These doubts were prominently displayed in a February 1963 *Hoc Tap* article by Minh Tranh, an author and historian.[77] Arguing that the American buildup meant that the Southern revolution was faced with "new circumstances," Minh Tranh claimed that the Party would have to abandon its hopes for a quick victory, since, as the article noted repeatedly, the struggle against the Americans was likely to be long and difficult. To deal with the new situation, the article continued, the Southern revolutionary movement would have to adopt a new long-range strategy placing primary emphasis on political struggle in order to broaden the movement's base.

In addition, Minh Tranh had the audacity to suggest that the success of the Southern revolution would depend not just on the situation in the South but also on the international situation. The most urgent task facing the Party, he asserted, was to avoid provoking a disastrous nuclear war.[78]

Coming, as it did, on the heels of Giap's unity appeal, Minh Tranh's article suggests that the Party was facing a serious internal split over strategy for the war in the South. Not only did the article, as Latimer notes, give the impression that it was intended to refute the arguments of someone urging a stepped-up effort in the South, but its raising of the polemical issue of avoiding nuclear war suggests that at least some elements in the Party were thinking of drastically curtailing the Southern revolution in favor of "peaceful coexistence" and "peaceful transition to socialism." Furthermore, it seems likely that the dispute extended to the Party's highest levels, since it is doubtful that someone like Minh Tranh would have lectured the Party's First Secretary on the conduct of the Southern revolution without high-level support.[79]

---

greater success in 1962 if bloc unity had been maintained, since the U.S. would not have dared to put so many troops into South Vietnam if it had not been for the Sino-Soviet split. On this point and also in Giap's article, see Latimer, pp. 114–117; and Honey (1963), pp. 148–149. As Latimer notes, it may have been that Giap was chosen by Ho to make the unity appeal precisely because of his past opposition to the policies espoused by Le Duan.

77. This was not the first time that Minh Tranh had served as a spokesman for those primarily concerned with developing North Vietnam. For a summary of his earlier articles, see Latimer, pp. 96–97, 107–108.

78. On this article, see Latimer, pp. 118–127.

79. On these points, see Latimer, pp. 120–127. Latimer (pp. 96–97) suggests that, based on similarities in their published works, Minh Tranh's patron may have been none other than Truong Chinh.

But while Minh Tranh's high-level support was strong enough to see that his views were published, it was not strong enough to save him: the February 1963 *Hoc Tap* article was his last.[80] Nor were his opponents slow in delivering their replies. On March 13, both Le Duan and Nguyen Chi Thanh delivered speeches rejecting the views expressed by Minh Tranh. While the thrust of their counterattack was cast in terms of the Sino-Soviet dispute (both backed China), it appears that this was the result of their belief that the only path open to them lay in complete support for China for fear that any encouragement of Khrushchev's "peaceful coexistence" line would undercut the revolutionary zeal of the Party's southern cadres. Thus, Le Duan noted that "the proletariat has no alternative but to use violence to demolish the bourgeois state apparatus and establish one of its own." At another point, he argued that, while Marxist-Leninist parties could seek to make revolution by peaceful means, they must also "make active preparations for the seizure of power by violence."[81]

By the summer of 1963, the star of the advocates of violent revolution in the South was clearly on the rise in Hanoi. In July, for example, Nguyen Chi Thanh published a major article in *Hoc Tap* that directly countered the views of Minh Tranh. Although Thanh conceded that "the South Vietnam revolution will have to go through a protracted and hard struggle before winning final victory," he nonetheless claimed that "the victory is already in our hands . . . because the South Vietnam revolution has gone through nine years of terrific trial and recorded undeniable successes." Similarly, Thanh rejected the claim that American intervention necessitated a slow and cautious approach:

The U.S. imperialists are not invincible. If the proletarian revolution and the peoples of the world resolutely struggle against the American imperialists, they can repel them step by step. . . . If one is afraid of the United States and thinks that to touch it would bring bitter failures and that any stiff opposition to the U.S. imperialists would bring about nuclear bomb blasts, then the only alternative would be to conciliate with and surrender to them.

In addition, Thanh rejected the position taken in the resolution passed by the Third Party Congress, which had stated that strengthening the North was the "most decisive task for the development of the whole Vietnamese revolution, for the cause of national reunification." Instead, Thanh asserted that:

---

80. Latimer (pp. 127–128) concludes that Minh Tranh was "almost certainly" purged.
81. Quoted in Honey (1963), pp. 155–156. See also Latimer, pp. 128–131; and Zagoria, p. 108.

A powerful North Vietnam will be a factor playing a decisive role in the development of the entire Vietnamese society. Such an assertion is by no means one-sided and does not mean that if North Vietnam becomes strong, the South Vietnam revolution will automatically succeed. . . . The building of the North itself cannot in any way replace the settlement of inner contradictions in the South Vietnam society. This correct view helps avoid opportunistic mistakes. On the other hand, if one fears the United States and does not believe in successfully opposing it, and calls on the South Vietnamese people to wait and to "coexist peacefully" with the U.S.-Diemists, one will be committing an irreparable mistake.[82]

More importantly, the evidence available suggests that Le Duan and Nguyen Chi Thanh were not only successful in vanquishing opponents such as Minh Tranh but that they were also able to influence the development of policy toward the war in the South in accordance with their views on stepping up the armed struggle. Pike, for example, reports that "increasingly and perhaps inevitably after mid-1963, the armed struggle moved to the forefront, tending to dominate the scene and push the political struggle into the background." In addition, Pike cites "reliable GVN intelligence reports" as indicating that "in August and September 1963, at least two generals from Hanoi arrived in the highlands of the South to act as advisers, or possibly commanders, in the NLF's armed struggle movement." In early September, they allegedly convened a "military conference," at which

NLF military units were reorganized and their development accelerated. The conference was followed in October by a series of two-week special training courses throughout the liberated area at which guerrilla units received retraining in conventional small-military-unit tactics, antiaircraft defenses, and techniques of sabotage.[83]

Despite the ascendance of Le Duan and Nguyen Chi Thanh in the Party's councils, it appears that not everyone in the leadership shared their enthusiasm for using violence to overthrow the Diem government. Significantly, 1963 was also the year in which Pham Van Dong's diplomatic campaign was resurrected, ostensibly for the purpose of reaching an agreement with Diem on neutralizing South Vietnam and normalizing relations between the two Vietnams. As described by the Polish diplomat who served as the liaison between Diem and Hanoi:

82. Nguyen Chi Thanh, "Who Will Win in South Vietnam," quoted in Latimer, pp. 133–139. See also Zagoria, p. 109.

83. On these points, see Pike (1966), pp. 101–102, 162. See also II Gravel, pp. 183–184, for reports of increased Viet Cong armed activity during the summer of 1963.

Under the plans, North and South Vietnam could slowly develop postal, economic and cultural relations. Northern industrial goods would be paid for by the South with its rice.

Also, the North would not press for a speedy unification, but instead a coalition government would be set up in the South. I asked if such a government could be headed by Mr. Diem. In the summer of 1963 the answer was finally yes.[84]

By December 1963, however, the Party had come to another critical juncture in its history. Not only had Diem been overthrown and replaced by a military junta which disavowed any interest in negotiations, but the coup that ousted Diem also had the effect of forcing the Party to confront squarely the issue of the North's role in the Southern revolution. "After the coup," as Pike notes,

the country went on an emotional binge. The government went on a political holiday. Governmental administration broke down as three-fourths of the country's 41 province chiefs were fired. Whole areas of the country were without any GVN officials. The Vietnamese felt that a long nightmare was over, that they were coming up from the depths. It was an exhilarating feeling for them, and they reveled in it. The military were the heroes of the day, and the new government, the liberating generals, would rule but would not govern; they would enforce no unpopular edicts, exert no governmental discipline. The resulting government was weak, but it was popular.[85]

In the past, the Party leadership had attempted to resolve internal disputes over the relative importance of building socialism in the North as opposed to aiding the revolution in the South by attempting to pursue both goals at once. Now, however, the leadership was forced to choose between (1) increasing the flow of men and materiel from the North to the South (a flow that would have to include significant numbers of native-born Northerners, since the pool of Southern "regroupees" was by now nearly exhausted), in the hopes of achieving a decisive victory before the new government in Saigon could consolidate its hold on the South, or (2) continuing with the cautious approach that had been followed since 1959, relying largely on recruitment in the South to supply the manpower needed. This was the choice facing the leadership as the

84. Mieczyslaw Maneli, "Vietnam, '63 and Now," *New York Times*, January 27, 1975, p. 25. Maneli at the time was the head of the Polish ICC delegation. See also Chen (1975), pp. 254–255; and Porter, pp. 17–19.

85. Pike (1966), p. 163. On the junta's decision to break off contacts with the North, see Chen (1975), pp. 254–255.

Central Committee met in Hanoi in December 1963 for its ninth Plenum since the 1960 Congress.[86]

With the benefit of hindsight, the 9th Plenum stands as one of the crucial turning points for the entire Vietnam conflict. And yet, what has often been overlooked is the fact that the 9th Plenum was important not only for the decisions that were made but also for the way in which those decisions were reached. For one thing, as Le Duan noted in a speech delivered near the end of the Plenum, at the time the speech was delivered the Central Committee had been in session "for over 10 days" discussing "extremely important problems . . . thoroughly and carefully," thus suggesting that the sessions had been marked by considerable debate rather than a mere rubber-stamping of the top leadership's proposals. Furthermore, it appears that the debate was an acrimonious one and that Le Duan's views in particular had been subjected to considerable sniping either before or during the Plenum, since, after noting (in his final speech) that "the people in our entire country are presently in an enthusiastic and acute revolutionary situation," he launched a scathing attack on "certain communists" who, in his view,

have become modern revisionists because they are afraid of perilous revolutionary struggle and of making sacrifices. They only want to lead a carefree and happy life and therefore, they cherish bourgeois habits, modes of living and ideology. For them the lofty and beautiful ideals of communism have vanished. They only think of the western bourgeoisie's way of living and consider it a model and the highest objective of their struggle. They tremble before, reconcile themselves with, and gradually surrender ideologically to the imperialists and their lackeys.[87]

Finally and most importantly, a careful comparison of Le Duan's concluding speech with the resolution passed by the Central Committee indicates that he did not get everything he wanted, suggesting that he had been forced to compromise with his opponents within the leader-

86. On the depletion of the pool of "regroupees," see *U.S.-Vietnam Relations*, IV. A. 5., Tab 3, p. 35. On the decisions facing the Party at this time, see Latimer, pp. 145–147.

87. Le Duan's speech at the 9th Plenum is reprinted in full in *Vietnam Documents and Research Notes*, no. 96, pp. 49–91. The quoted excerpts are from pp. 49, 86–87. On these points, see also Latimer, pp. 150–155. In addition, King C. Chen has noted that "the 'peace men' in Hanoi, who were [a] minority in the Vietnamese leadership, were not silent. As Le Duc Tho revealed in February 1966 ["Let Us Change the Trend and Step Up the Party Building Task in Order to Insure Successful Execution of the Anti-U.S. Struggle for National Salvation," *Nhan Dan*, February 3, 1966, and *Hoc Tap*, February 1966], they questioned the wisdom of the war strategy at the showdown meeting of the 9th Plenary in December 1963, and were pessimistic after the escalation of the war." On this point, see King C. Chen, "Hanoi versus Peking: Policies and Relations—A Survey," *Asian Survey*, 12:9 (September 1972), 812.

ship.[88] For example, while Le Duan argued that "he who speaks of compromising with imperialism to build economy and regards this as the number one requirement, willingly or unwillingly only hinders the progress of revolution," the resolution stated that "we must understand that the favorable development of the Revolution in the South depends on our unceasing efforts to strengthen North Vietnam. Therefore, we must increase our economic and defensive strength in North Vietnam."[89]

Similarly, Le Duan claimed that

> a number of comrades assess the world situation erroneously because they inaccurately analyze and appraise our forces and imperialist forces. . . . After casting an overall glance at the world situation, . . . we find that revolutionary, socialist, and pacifist forces are obviously superior to the imperialist reactionary and warlike force. We are stronger than the enemy. Therefore, the revolution is not on the defensive and revolutionary strategy must not be a defensive strategy. On the contrary, the revolution is on the offensive and revolutionary strategy must be an offensive one. . . . Because [the imperialists] want war and not peace, peace cannot be obtained by making concessions to them. Nor can negotiations be considered the most fundamental means for protecting peace, although negotiations are necessary during the process of the struggle for peace.

Despite Le Duan's rejection of a "defensive" strategy, the resolution called for caution:

> The war waged by the people in South Vietnam is a protracted one because we are a small people having to fight an imperialist ringleader which is the USA. We are using our political and moral strength with our military and material weakness to oppose an enemy who is weak politically and morally but strong militarily and materially.

> We need time and efforts to overcome many difficulties in order to tip the balance of power between the enemy and us in our favor: we become stronger while the enemy becomes weaker, only in this way can we gain the final victory. We should try to contain the enemy in the special war, but at the same time we must be ready to cope with him in case he wages the war on a larger scale or brings in troops from the Southeast Asia aggressive bloc to fight us.[90]

88. In fact, the 9th Plenum passed two resolutions, one on the Sino-Soviet dispute ("World Situation and Our Party's International Mission," reprinted in *Vietnam Documents and Research Notes*, no. 98, pp. 68–134), and the other on the war in the South ("Strive to Struggle, Rush Forward to Win New Victories in the South," reprinted in *Vietnam Documents and Research Notes*, no. 96, pp. 1–41). A copy of the latter, which was never published or referred to in the media, was later captured in the South. Significantly, the fact that Le Duan felt it necessary to make one last appeal "before comrade Truong Chinh recapitulates the debates and presents the draft resolution" (*Vietnam Documents and Research Notes*, no. 96, p. 49) suggests that many Central Committee members remained skeptical of his views.

89. *Vietnam Documents and Research Notes*, no. 96, pp. 63–64 and 40.

90. *Vietnam Documents and Research Notes*, no. 96, pp. 79–80 and 13.

Still, the resolution of the 9th Plenum must be considered a victory for Le Duan and his allies, since on several key points the resolution went far toward recognizing their positions as Party policy. For example, the resolution rejected Minh Tranh's claim that victory was far away and implied that an increased effort now would prove decisive:

Since early 1963, the South Vietnamese people have gained significant successes and changed the situation in our favor. Our forces are being strongly developed while the enemy forces are weakening. . . . We have sufficient conditions to quickly change the balance of forces in our favor.[91]

Furthermore, while the resolution recognized that "political struggle plays a decisive and fundamental role," it accorded somewhat greater weight to armed struggle by noting that

the key point at the present time is to make outstanding efforts to rapidly strengthen our military forces in order to create a basic change in the balance of forces between the enemy and us in South Vietnam. . . . If we do not defeat the enemy's military forces, we cannot overthrow his domination and bring the Revolution to victory. To destroy the enemy's military forces, we should use armed struggle. For this reason, armed struggle plays a direct and decisive role.[92]

Most importantly, the resolution endorsed what Le Duan had been advocating all along—namely, that the time had come for the North to increase its role in the war, even if this meant diverting resources from the North to the South:

Not only the Party and the people in the South must make outstanding efforts but the Party and people in the North must make outstanding efforts as well. The role of the two "mien" [parts: North and South Vietnam] in the revolutionary undertaking of the country, as defined by the Party's Third National Congress, is unchanged; however it is time for the North to increase aid to the South, the North must bring into fuller play its role as the revolutionary base for the whole nation. . . . We should plan to aid the South to meet the requirements of the Revolution, and because of this aid we must revise properly our plan for building North Vietnam.[93]

With that, the die was cast: the Central Committee was now on record as favoring a greater role for the North in the war in the South, a

91. *Vietnam Documents and Research Notes*, no. 96, pp. 1, 9. At another point (p. 5), the resolution dismissed Minh Tranh's fears of American intervention, arguing that American forces were scattered throughout the world, thus making the balance of forces in Southeast Asia favorable to the revolution. The likelihood of an American decision to expand the war was judged "remote," although the resolution did urge preparations for such a contingency, just in case.

92. *Vietnam Documents and Research Notes*, no. 96, pp. 15–16 (emphasis in original).

93. *Vietnam Documents and Research Notes*, no. 96, pp. 39–40 (emphasis added).

war in which armed struggle would play the decisive role. But the Central Committee's decision left many questions unanswered—in particular, would the new policy suffice to topple the government in Saigon? What if the U.S. stepped up its role in the war? This latter question, moreover, was soon to take on special significance, since, as we know from the start of this chapter, the Central Committee's decision coincided roughly with President Johnson's approval of a study of possible covert pressures against the North.[94] Within a month, the U.S., too, would be committed to a greater role in the war—specifically, to carrying the war to the North through OPLAN 34A. How would the North react to this new development? Would Le Duan and his supporters be willing to return to political struggle and protracted conflict? Or would they press on, despite the risks involved?

C. DRV Policy, January-December 1964

It did not take long for the answers to the questions posed above to become apparent. As Latimer notes, the 9th Plenum had scarcely ended when speculation began to appear in the American press concerning possible U.S. intervention. Meanwhile, in Hanoi, the communique from the Plenum was not released until January 20, 1964, suggesting that opponents of the new policy had kept up their fight, possibly on the grounds that it was too risky, since it might provoke American intervention.[95] As we saw earlier, such worries were exactly what Washington hoped to create in Hanoi, both through the covert war and also through the other activities described in Chapter 2, above.

It appears, however, that these activities had relatively little impact on DRV policy. As we saw in Chapter 2, the covert war got off to what the JCS called a "slow beginning," making it doubtful that the small number of operations carried out during Phase I (February–May), most of which failed anyway, accomplished much in the way of striking fear into the hearts of Le Duan and his supporters. Even if the covert war

94. On the timing of the 9th Plenum, see "A Brief Chronology of Momentous Facts and Events in the History of the DRV" (broadcast by Hanoi Radio on August 9, 1970 and reprinted in *Vietnam Documents and Research Notes*, no. 84, p. 34), which reports that the resolution on "World Situation and our Party's International Mission" was passed on December 20, 1963. It seems reasonable to assume that the resolution on South Vietnam was also passed on or around that date.

95. On these points, see Latimer, p. 163; Hedrick Smith, "Cruiser Ordered to Saigon by U.S.," *New York Times*, January 13, 1964, p. 1; and P. J. Honey, "North Vietnam Quarterly Survey no. 11," *China News Analysis*, 508 (March 13, 1964), 4. The fact that Le Duan in his final talk before the 9th Plenum and the resolution on South Vietnam passed by the Plenum both disparaged the chances of American escalation suggests that someone had raised this argument. On this point, see note 91, above; and *Vietnam Documents and Research Notes*, no. 96, pp. 78-80.

had gotten off to a more forceful start, it is still doubtful that this would have had much effect in Hanoi, since, as we saw in Chapter 2, political stability in the South during early 1964 remained as elusive as ever. The Khanh coup of January 1964, in particular, touched off a new round of upheavals in Saigon, such that the Hanoi leadership could hardly have been expected not to believe that victory was near.

More importantly, though, the evidence suggests that those in the leadership who were most sensitive to the threat of American attacks on the North—for example, Giap, Truong Chinh, and Pham Van Dong—were not in a position to influence the conduct of the war in the South. Instead, control over the Southern revolution apparently centered in the Secretariat (dominated by Le Duan, Nguyen Chi Thanh, Pham Hung, and Le Duc Tho) and the Central Committee's Reunification Department, headed by another veteran of the Southern resistance, Lieutenant General Nguyen Van Vinh.[96] And, in the months following the 9th Plenum, it was the latter group that moved decisively to insure that this time there would be no turning back.

On the one hand, on January 27, 1964, Le Duan, Le Duc Tho, and Hoang Van Hoan (Politburo member and foreign affairs specialist) left Hanoi for Peking and Moscow in an apparent effort to line up support for the new policy. Not surprisingly, they apparently found a more receptive audience in Peking than in Moscow. On February 11, the day after their departure from Moscow, *Nhan Dan* (the Party daily) warned that if the U.S. attacked the North, it would have to fight "not only with North Vietnam but also with China, or eventually with the Socialist camp as a whole." Interestingly, February 11 was also the day that Hanoi Radio broadcast an article from the January *Hoc Tap* which explicitly rejected the idea of a cautious approach toward the war in the South:

The people in the South should not pin their hope on the "sincere desire for peace" of the U.S. aggressor, nor should they wait for 15 or 20 more years for the defeat of the imperialist camp by the socialist camp in their economic competition before they can bring about a peaceful reunification of Vietnam. On the contrary, they should rise up and integrate their political struggle with armed struggle to uphold their right to existence. The road of struggle now taken by the people in South Vietnam is the only correct road to liberation.[97]

96. See Latimer, pp. 69–70, 86–87. Vinh had served as Secretary of the Trung Bo Inter-region Committee and as political commissar of the Committee's military units during the mid-1950s. See Palmerlee, p. 4.

97. Both of these are quoted in King C. Chen, "North Vietnam in the Sino-Soviet Dispute, 1962–1964," *Asian Survey*, 4:9 (September 1964), 1034–1035.

On the other hand, early 1964 was also the time during which Le Duan and his allies moved to squelch dissent over the new policy toward the South once and for all. The communique from the 9th Plenum, though couched in the language of the Sino-Soviet dispute, made "unanimity" within the Party an "extremely important precondition" for the success of the Southern revolution and strongly implied that dissent would no longer be tolerated:

rightist ideologies exist among a number of our cadres and Party members. We must overcome these rightist ideologies, prevent the influence of modern revisionism, strengthen the cohesion and unity of the Party. . . . Unanimity within our Party on the line of the Vietnamese revolution and the international communist movement is an extremely important precondition for the strengthening of the militant forces of our Party in the struggle for socialism in the North and for the peaceful reunification of our fatherland. Every member of our Party must constantly stand firmly on the revolutionary position of the working class, . . . study the revolutionary theories of Marxism-Leninism, thoroughly imbue himself with the line and policies of the Party, bravely correct his shortcomings and mistakes, and struggle irreconcilably against erroneous opportunist ideologies.[98]

To insure that "unanimity" was achieved, there appeared in *Nhan Dan* on February 3–4 an article authored by Le Duc Tho which announced the start of a rectification campaign. As summarized by Latimer:

[Le Duc Tho] warned that it was "absolutely necessary to compel each and every comrade to submit himself to party discipline." He further directed that it was essential that all party resolutions become the course of action for all party members. . . . Le Duc Tho also charged "an extreme minority" of cadres and Party members with being guilty of assuming the attitude of an "on-looker" on the issue of revolution in the South, "hardly aware of their own responsibilities."[99]

Still, one suspects that the rectification campaign achieved something less than total success, since, in late March 1964, Ho Chi Minh took the unprecedented step of convening a Special Political Conference. As

98. Quoted by P. J. Honey, *China News Analysis*, 508 (March 13, 1964), 4–5. See also the *Nhan Dan* editorial on the communique, January 21, 1964, reprinted in *Vietnam Documents and Research Notes*, no. 96, pp. 42–48, especially p. 46.

99. Latimer, pp. 163–164. As head of the Central Committee's Organization Department, Le Duc Tho would naturally be in charge of such a campaign. In addition, the January 1964 *Hoc Tap* article quoted above mentioned that an indoctrination campaign had begun to bring about "vigorous changes" in the feelings of Northerners toward the "South Vietnamese revolution" (see Latimer, p. 166; and Honey, *China News Analysis*, 508 [March 13, 1964], 3–4).

Latimer notes, the theme of the Conference, which was attended by representatives of virtually every major group in the North,

> was unity with a strong element of support for the Party's policy in the South. It is interesting that the emphasis was on North Vietnamese pledging support to Ho and his policies. Those chiefly identified with the war in the South were conspicuously spared from making the public obeisance to Ho. . . . If there was any doubt that the purpose of the Conference was to rally the people of North Vietnam behind the war, a resolution adopted by the North Vietnamese National Assembly in April 1964 ended it. That resolution hailed "the brilliant success of the Special Political Conference" and it called upon the people to "develop their tradition of heroism and to be ready to give all for the supreme interests of the nation." Their "all," it soon was learned, was to send native northerners to fight in the South.[100]

Although some analysts dismissed the Special Political Conference as an "elaborate charade," in retrospect it appears that the Conference confirmed the primacy of Le Duan and the proponents of armed struggle and heavy Northern involvement in the Southern revolution. While there were some isolated expressions of dissent in the following months—Giap, for example, published articles in July and December 1964 containing pointed references to the need for the Southern revolutionaries to rely mainly on their own strength and also to carefully balance political and armed struggle—these were few and far between.[101] More importantly, a comparison of Giap's writings with what was actually being done in the South suggests that Le Duan's critics were able to exert relatively little influence over the course of the war. Throughout the remainder of 1964, those in favor of stepping up the armed struggle and increasing the North's role in the war pushed ahead with their plans in the hope of achieving a decisive victory as quickly as possible.

In the South, for example, 1964 was the year in which the combat capabilities of Viet Cong units were significantly upgraded. As General Westmoreland reports: "The Viet Cong continued their military tactic of building their forces from the lowest level upward. Additional companies were formed at district level, thus permitting the formation of new battalions in many provinces. This increase, in turn, allowed battalions of the main forces to expand into regiments." By early 1965, there were reports of at least five Viet Cong regiments in operation in

---

100. Latimer, pp. 169–172. See also P. J. Honey, "North Vietnam Quarterly Survey no. 12," *China News Analysis*, 520 (June 12, 1964), 4 ff.

101. On the Conference, see Honey, *China News Analysis*, 520 (June 12, 1964), 4. On Giap's articles, see Latimer, pp. 173–174, 191–198.

the South, each with three battalions and a regimental heavy weapons unit, along with at least thirty other battalions, many of which had their own heavy weapons platoon.[102] Larger units, in turn, required a better logistics system to keep them adequately supplied. Significantly, in this respect, the New York Times reported on June 26, 1964, that U.S. reconnaissance flights over Laos showed that Communist forces there were improving the road network and increasing the pace of their supply convoys. By the end of the year, as Dommen reports, this activity had apparently been stepped up even further:

Aerial reconnaissance photos taken in September 1964 by carrier-based aircraft under Operation Yankee Team had revealed large sheds, trucks, personnel, and concrete bunkers under construction in the Mu Gia Pass near the Laos border. With the end of the rainy season in November and December, the North Vietnamese undertook a massive effort to improve the network of trails known collectively as the Ho Chi Minh Trail. Existing paths were widened, river crossings strengthened, and new sections of road constructed so that trucks and other heavy vehicles could ply many parts of the Trail system from the Mu Gia Pass to the tri-border junction of Laos, Cambodia, and South Vietnam.[103]

The improved logistics system, moreover, made possible yet another significant improvement—i.e., equipping Viet Cong main force units with new Soviet-style weapons manufactured in China. This process, which was largely completed by early 1965, not only ended their dependence on captured weapons and ammunition but also, by increasing their firepower, greatly improved their already formidable fighting ability.[104]

Second and more importantly, it was in the aftermath of the Special Political Conference that preparations began for the infiltration of regular units of the North Vietnamese Army (NVA) into South Vietnam:

Some regular NVA units are known to have begun preparing for infiltration as early as April 1964. Several prisoner from the 95th Regiment of the 325th

102. On these points, see Sharp and Westmoreland, p. 84; and Hanson Baldwin, "VC Forming Bigger Units, Hinting War Is Near 'Third Phase,'" New York Times, April 2, 1965, p. 6.
103. On these points, see Hedrick Smith, "Hanoi Improves Supply Line to South Vietnam," New York Times, June 26, 1964, p. 6; Dommen, p. 280; Working Paper, p. 12; Working Paper, Items 100 and 101; Latimer, pp. 172–173; the AP dispatch, "Reds Add Roads in Laos," New York Times, March 2, 1965, p. 3; and U.S. Department of State, "Hanoi's Role in the Support of the Present War in South Vietnam," p. 22.
104. See Dommen, p. 281; Sharp and Westmoreland, pp. 84, 87–88; and the articles by Baldwin and the AP cited in notes 102 and 103, above.

Division have reported that their unit was recalled in that month from duty in Laos. Back in North Vietnam, the 95th underwent special military and political training for operations in the South. Hanoi also began to form new regimental-sized units for dispatch to the South. One of these, the 32nd Regiment, was activated sometime in the Spring of 1964, with personnel drawn from a number of established units. Trained draftees were added from the Son Tay and Xuan Mai infiltration centers which were in operation by 1961.

Nor were NVA personnel held back to defend the North, as Giap apparently would have preferred: July 1964 saw the first reports of individual NVA officers serving with VC units in the South; while in October 1964, the 95th Regiment left the North for the South, the first complete NVA unit to be deployed in the South. The 95th, which arrived in Kontum Province, South Vietnam, in December 1964, was followed shortly by the 32nd and 101st Regiments, both of which arrived in the South in early 1965. Significantly, the departure of these regiments came shortly after Seaborn's August 1964 visit to Hanoi, during which, as we saw in Chapter 2, he warned that the U.S. had "ways and means of measuring the DRV's participation in, and direction and control of, the war in South Vietnam and Laos" and would be "carefully watching" the DRV's actions in response to his message.[105]

The dispatching of NVA units to the South, however, did not mean that the regime was neglecting preparations to defend the North. Instead, the third line of policy followed during this period centered on strengthening the North's defenses in anticipation of an American invasion. As Turley notes, beginning in December 1964, the regime organized the first in an annual series of "Military-Civilian Unity Days," aimed at "preparing the population for greater cooperation with the military, increasing 'revolutionary awareness' of the coming danger, and reassimilating the regular army to society." More importantly, the Party set about in late 1964 organizing "combat villages" through which the entire population would be mobilized in support of the war effort:

Some of these villages were fortified strongpoints, similar to the "strategic hamlets" that flourished briefly in South Vietnam under the GVN; this type of combat village was constructed most frequently along the DMZ and the southern coastline. But generally the term "combat village" referred to organizing the entire village for a wide variety of war-related tasks. Able-bodied men received intensive training to form a stronger militia; local arsenals were established to produce weapons in case fighting severed links with national supply

105. On these points, see Working Paper, p. 12; Working Paper, Item 91, p. 1; Latimer, pp. 179–180, 190; and Rostow, p. 447.

depots; trenches were dug around and throughout the village; every villager was given a specific task to perform if an attack occurred; and everyone was expected to participate in the labor brigades which would assist the main force when it passed through the region. By these means, all of North Vietnam was to be transformed into a guerrilla base, the "rear base" for the war in the South, and the regular forces of the PAVN were to be freed from dependency on long lines of supply and troop-consuming maintenance and support tasks and from stationary defense roles.[106]

Fourth, the aftermath of the Special Political Conference was also the period during which Le Duan and his allies strengthened their grip on the Party machinery for controlling the war in the South. Nguyen Chi Thanh was dispatched to the South, where he took charge of the Party's military and political assets there. In addition, Dommen reports that in early 1965,

North Vietnam's command structure of its forces along the [Ho Chi Minh] Trail underwent a significant change. The frontier guard battalions posted along the border of southern Laos, which had previously been attached to regional military headquarters in North Vietnam, were for the first time placed under a unified independent command. The new command, named *Doan* (Group) 559, controlled all frontier guard, Trail security, engineer, communications, and liaison troops, porters, and guides, as well as units of troops on the move down the Trail from its headquarters at Tchepone, and reflected the increased size and complexity of the Trail operations.[107]

Since, as we saw earlier, the 559th Group had originally been placed directly under the Central Committee (whose business between sessions was run by the Secretariat, which was itself dominated by Le Duan and his allies), it appears that this move was an attempt by the proponents of armed struggle to gain complete control over the infiltration effort by transferring out of the regular army chain of command (headed by Giap) not only the battalions guarding the Trail but also "units of troops on the move down the Trail" (which, when they arrived in the South, would be commanded by Nguyen Chi Thanh).

Thus, by early 1965, the "victory" of Le Duan and his supporters was

106. William S. Turley, "Army, Party and Society in the DRV: Civil-Military Relations in a Mass-Mobilization System," Unpublished Ph.D. thesis, University of Washington, 1972, pp. 171–174. See also Nguyen Hoang, "Combat Villages," *Quan Doi Nhan Dan* (People's Army), November 14, 1964. In addition, Seaborn reported observing precautionary measures being taken (i.e., air raid drills, slit trenches, brick bunkers) in anticipation of additional American air strikes during his August 1964 visit to Hanoi (see Seaborn Discussion, p. 2).

107. On these points, see Latimer, pp. 181–182; Palmerlee, p. 8; Dommen, p. 281; and Working Paper, pp. 9–10.

largely complete. Not only had they become the dominant force in policymaking for the war in the South, but more importantly, it looked very much at the time as if they had correctly identified the route to victory in the South. Not only was the armed struggle going very well indeed, as evidenced by the disastrous ARVN defeat at Binh Gia (see Chapter 3, above), but political stability in Saigon was no closer in December 1964 than it had been in December 1963. In addition, the failure of the Administration to carry out its threat (conveyed by Seaborn) to retaliate in response to Viet Cong "spectaculars" like the attacks on Bien Hoa and the Brink BOQ very likely suggested that even the Americans could be attacked with impunity.

Still, from the perspective of Le Duan and the proponents of heavy Northern involvement in the Southern revolution, there were at least a few clouds on the horizon. For one thing, despite Le Duan's evident distaste for negotiations, Pham Van Dong was still keeping alive the option of settling for less than complete control over the South by means of a coalition government, which he had proposed to Seaborn during their first meeting in June 1964 (see Chapter 2, above).[108] While the negotiated settlement route, which the Premier continued to pursue during his August meeting with Seaborn and also through the DRV's acceptance of U Thant's August 1964 initiative, would have avoided the need for a potentially costly struggle in the South (thus minimizing the drain on DRV resources and conciliating those who had opposed Le Duan all along), it would have required still more delay in achieving reunification, and for that reason alone would have been a bitter pill for the proponents of armed struggle to swallow.

In addition, despite the successes enjoyed by Viet Cong forces in the South, it appears that Le Duan and his allies were still encountering resistance within the Party from opponents of their policies. One of the more intriguing aspects of the entire war centers on the relatively slow pace of infiltration during 1964 and early 1965. In particular, why were only three PAVN regiments sent South in late 1964 when, considering the dismal state of the Saigon government and its armed forces, a few more might have provided a knockout blow? Was this a case of overconfidence on the part of Nguyen Chi Thanh, or was it a case of Giap

---

108. P. J. Honey reports that, after his return to the North in 1957, Le Duan criticized Ho's decision to participate in the Geneva Conference, arguing that continued fighting would have resulted in the complete conquest of Vietnam. See Honey, "Vietnam: To the Bitter End?" *The Spectator*, December 17, 1965, reprinted in *Survival*, 8:2 (February 1966), 55. See also Le Duan's critique of negotiations at the 9th Plenum, cited in note 90, above. For additional details on DRV diplomatic initiatives during 1964, see Porter, pp. 20–22.

successfully arguing that additional regiments could not be spared from the defense of the North? Although the evidence on this point is sketchy, Latimer has noted that, in a 1966 letter to Southern cadres,

Le Duan implied that the party leadership had made a miscalculation in 1964. "It was obvious that the situation of the war developed more rapidly than we had anticipated. At that time we had not yet acquired adequate conditions to cope with the rapid development of the situation." Le Duan may have been honestly admitting to a shortcoming in the leadership's direction of the war but the thrust of his remarks suggested that he was trying to lay the blame for the failure to "acquire adequate conditions" on Giap's refusal to dispatch northern troops in time to give the final coup to the tottering Saigon government.[109]

Perhaps the biggest cloud on the horizon, though, was the possibility that the U.S. would greatly increase its role in the war. The Johnson Administration, as we saw in Chapter 2, had rejected Pham Van Dong's offers of a negotiated settlement, not only because it feared that the kind of settlement the Premier had in mind would have led eventually to a Communist takeover but also because of a belief that the North Vietnamese could be dissuaded from continuing their support for the Viet Cong. During 1964, as we saw, the Administration attempted to accomplish this "on the cheap"—i.e., by threats, shows of force, bombing in Laos, etc.—while simultaneously trying to stabilize the situation in Saigon. By early 1965, however, it was obvious that more drastic measures would be required, thus leading the Administration to embark on the path of troops and bombing described in Chapters 3 and 4. As we saw there, the Administration was confident that once the U.S. proved that it really was committed to defending South Vietnam, the North Vietnamese would choose to negotiate a settlement acceptable to the United States. But was this confidence justified? Would actions succeed where verbal threats had failed? Was there much chance that coercive pressures would "work" in the way that the Administration expected? As we know only too well, the answers to these questions all proved to be "no."

109. Latimer, pp. 181–182. At another point in this letter, Le Duan noted that: "In the past, some comrades had mistakenly believed that, once the revolution was started, it would develop itself. They failed to realize that the movement should be promoted and then could make great strides. For this reason, efforts were not appropriately made to give strong impetus to the movement so that the war situation could be rapidly changed" (quoted in Latimer, p. 152). While it is difficult to say for sure, this again sounds like an oblique criticism of Giap for failing to release the necessary NVA troops to give "strong impetus" to the revolution. For background information on the Le Duan letter, a copy of which was captured by U.S. troops in the South in January 1967 and which is Item 302 in the Working Paper Appendices, see Working Paper, p. 5.

II. Coercing Governments—The Case of Vietnam

As the preceding section has suggested, the Administration's hope that a short period of bombing (combined with a modest troop commitment in the South) would suffice to persuade the North Vietnamese to end their role in the war was totally unwarranted. By 1965, DRV policy toward the war in the South was effectively controlled by Le Duan, Nguyen Chi Thanh, and the other advocates of armed struggle and heavy Northern involvement in the Southern revolution. By then, not only had these men (and, indeed, the entire DRV leadership) invested a quarter-century or more in the struggle for national independence and reunification,[110] but they had also engaged in a 10-year effort to promote the cause of armed struggle in the South and increase the North's role in the war. This latter effort, moreover, was one in which careers and professional reputations had been staked on the argument that a quick victory in the South was possible and that the Americans could be defeated if they intervened. To have reversed themselves in the face of the bombing would not only have constituted a tacit admission that they had been wrong all along (surely not an easy thing to do under any circumstances) but would possibly have jeopardized their positions in the Party hierarchy. Truong Chinh, after all, had been "sacrificed" in the aftermath of the land reform campaign (not to mention Minh Tranh); who could say for sure what would happen to those who promoted violent revolution in the South and failed?

Considering how deeply committed Le Duan, Nguyen Chi Thanh, and their supporters were to the policies of armed struggle and heavy Northern involvement in the Southern revolution, it does not seem unreasonable to ask if there was *any* possibility that the American effort to coerce North Vietnam could have "persuaded" them to change their minds on the question of DRV policy toward the war in the South. As Ernest May's study of seven cases in which bombing was used in an effort to induce changes in an opposing government's policies suggests, it is extraordinarily difficult to coerce government officials into abandoning their deeply held attitudes and beliefs. "What stands out in all these cases," May notes, "is the fact that bombing worked relatively

110. "Forty Years of Party Activity" mentioned that Le Duan attended the 6th Conference of the Central Committee in November 1939 (*Vietnam Documents and Research Notes*, no. 76, p. 18); in 1940, he was arrested and imprisoned for his activities on behalf of the Party in the South (William S. Turley, personal communication, September 12, 1977). Similarly, Latimer (pp. 30–31) notes that Nguyen Chi Thanh had been active during the 1930s in Party activities in central Vietnam.

little change in the positions or attitudes of individuals. Haile Selassie, the Spanish Republicans, Chiang, and Churchill became, if anything, more resolute."[111] Similarly, as Allison and Halperin note, "no major figure in Japanese ruling circles changed his mind about the desirability of war with the United States from the beginning of the war to the end. Those who wanted to begin the war remained opposed to surrender."[112]

Nor did the attitudes of the leadership in Hanoi constitute an exception to the pattern identified by May, Allison, and Halperin. As we saw earlier and will see again in Chapter 6 when we discuss DRV decision-making between 1965 and 1968, Le Duan, Nguyen Chi Thanh, Pham Hung, and Le Duc Tho remained deeply committed to armed struggle and to a major Northern effort in the Southern revolution (as well as being opposed to any negotiated settlement that did not ratify a DRV/VC victory in the South), while Truong Chinh and General Giap consistently emphasized the importance of political struggle and guerrilla warfare as well as the need for Southerners to make greater efforts on their own behalf.[113] In addition, Pham Van Dong (apparently supported by Ho Chi Minh[114]) consistently sought to pursue a path

111. May, p. 130. The cases studied by May were Italy-Ethiopia, the Spanish Civil War, Japan-China, Germany-Britain (World War II), the Allied bombing of Italy (World War II), the U.S. and Japan, and the U.S. and North Korea/China. The first four were examined only briefly; the last three were discussed in more detail. In the three cases in which bombing did appear connected with a change in the target state's policy (i.e., Italy in World War II, Japan in World War II, and North Korea/China during the Korean War), there occurred changes in the target state's government: "What was crucial in each case was not changes of heart but the fact that events brought into power men not committed to the earlier course of action" (May, p. 131). This possibility will be discussed in more detail below.

112. Graham Allison and Morton Halperin, "Bureaucratic Politics: A Paradigm and Some Policy Implications," *World Politics*, 24 (Spring 1972), 66.

113. As suggested in note 72, above, Giap is a partial exception to this statement in that he apparently envisioned a major Northern effort in the South once a fully modernized army had been created in the North, along with the industrial base needed to support it. Further, as we shall see in Chapter 6, Giap's views apparently changed somewhat in the direction of a willingness to pursue a quick victory in the South after the July 1967 death of Nguyen Chi Thanh, an event which apparently resulted in an enhanced role for Giap with respect to the war effort. I am indebted to William S. Turley (personal communication, September 12, 1977) for his thoughtful comments on this point.

114. As should be evident by now, Ho has played a distinctly secondary role in our analysis, which is surprising in view of his preeminent position within the VWP hierarchy. The reason for this is that Ho rarely descended into the polemical pits, preferring to keep himself above the battle, so that it is inevitable that he would appear in the background in a study as heavily dependent on published articles and speeches as this one is. What evidence there is suggests that Ho was preoccupied with two problems: (1) completing the Vietnamese revolution by achieving reunification and Communist control over the South; and (2) maintaining unity within the VWP. Further, the evidence suggests that Ho never pursued the former at the expense of the latter; instead, he apparently atempted to make progress toward both at once. This he did by using North Vietnam's

between the proponents of armed struggle in the South and those primarily concerned with the "consolidation" of the North—i.e., a path that would placate both groups by achieving reunification by means of negotiations, thus avoiding a long and costly struggle that would drain the North's resources.

Furthermore, the evidence available suggests that these attitudinal rigidities are likely to persist well beyond the point at which an "objective" appraisal of the information available would seem to suggest that the attitudes being maintained are no longer valid. As we saw earlier, Le Duan and Nguyen Chi Thanh consistently denigrated the likelihood of American intervention and insisted that, even if the U.S. did intervene, it could be defeated militarily. Significantly, they adhered to these positions even as more and more evidence accumulated during 1964 and 1965 indicating that the U.S. was in fact committed to massive intervention and that American troops were inflicting heavy casualties on DRV/VC units in the South. And, as Jervis has shown, it would seem to be not by chance that the positions taken by Le Duan, Nguyen Chi Thanh, and their supporters were so resistant to change.

For one thing, as Jervis notes: "While . . . there is no way to specify exactly how open or closed-minded a person should be, actors are more apt to err on the side of being too wedded to an established view and too quick to reject discrepant information than to make the opposite error of too quickly altering their theories." This tendency to undergo "premature cognitive closure," in turn, has important implications for a strategy that attempts to use low-level pressures to communicate the threat of greater pressures to come. The problem for the coercer, as Jervis notes, is that

the initial organization of the stimuli strongly structures later perceptions. Some cognitive processes can be reversed only with great difficulty. Once a belief has taken hold, new information will not have the same impact it would have had at an earlier stage. Earlier, when the person is trying to make sense out of the evidence, he will experiment with different interpretations of incoming information. Later, when he thinks he understands the stimulus, he will automatically perceive new information as having a certain meaning.[115]

position in the Sino-Soviet dispute to lobby for substantial Soviet aid with which to "buy off" the proponents of "consolidation" and by supporting Pham Van Dong (who is universally regarded as Ho's closest associate) in his efforts to progress toward reunification via negotiations. For background on Ho's role as the guardian of Party unity, see William J. Duiker, "Building the United Front: The Rise of Communism in Vietnam, 1925–1954, " in Zasloff and Brown (eds.), pp. 3–26; and Robert F. Turner, *Vietnamese Communism: Its Origins and Development* (Stanford, Calif.: Hoover Institution Press, 1975), chaps. 1–4.

115. Robert Jervis, *Perception and Misperception in International Politics* (Princeton, N.J.: Princeton

Consequently, in situations in which members of the target state's government have been arguing that the coercer will not intervene in strength, a coercive strategy based upon "graduated pressures" may serve only to "convince" the opponent that low-level pressures are all that will be attempted.[116]

This danger that a strategy based upon "graduated pressures" may backfire becomes especially acute when a second factor is added to the analysis, namely that

a person is less apt to recognize evidence into a new theory or image if he is deeply committed to the established view. Commitment here means not only the degree to which the person's power and prestige are involved but also—and more importantly—the degree to which this way of seeing the world has proved satisfactory and become internalized.[117]

In the Vietnam case, not only had Le Duan and Nguyen Chi Thanh staked their prestige and indeed their careers on the argument that the Southern revolution could be brought to a successful conclusion by means of armed struggle and heavy Northern involvement, but it looked very much as if their view of the world had been correct all along: by early 1965, DRV/VC forces stood on the verge of victory in the South. Under these circumstances, it should not be surprising that Le Duan and his supporters sought to press ahead, despite the mounting evidence that the U.S. was determined to resist a Communist takeover in the South.

Third and finally, as Jervis has noted:

In everyday life, in the interpretation of other states' behavior, and in the scientific laboratory, expectations create predispositions that lead actors to notice certain things and to neglect others, to immediately and often unconsciously draw certain inferences from what is noticed, and to find it difficult to consider alternatives.

Since Le Duan and his supporters had argued all along that the U.S. would not intervene in force, we would expect that the U.S. would have great difficulty convincing them that it was determined to prevent a

---

University Press, 1976), pp. 187–188. See also Jervis's discussion of "perceptual satisficing" on pp. 191–193.

116. This seems to have been the case in the Vietnam conflict. As we saw in Chapters 2–3, Seaborn consistently reported that the North Vietnamese were not convinced that the U.S. meant to bomb them, or if it did, that it would continue the bombing for any length of time. Instead, they viewed American attempts to increase the pressures on them (e.g., OPLAN 34A, the Tonkin Gulf reprisals, and ROLLING THUNDER) as limited attempts to improve the American bargaining position prior to seeking a face-saving exit from the war.

117. Jervis (1976), p. 196.

Communist victory in the South, on the grounds that "when a states-
man has developed a certain image of another country he will maintain
that view in the face of large amounts of discrepant information. . . ."[118]
Significantly, in this respect, the "signals" transmitted by the U.S. were
anything but consistent and unambiguous.[119] Instead, as we saw in
Chapters 2 and 3, the Administration's behavior during 1964 and early
1965 was quite erratic, thus providing Le Duan and Nguyen Chi Thanh
with considerable evidence to draw on for their argument that the
Americans would not intervene in force.

But even if it was unlikely that Le Duan and Nguyen Chi Thanh
could be "persuaded" to change their views, they could still be outvoted
in the Politburo;[120] conceivably, if the war had gone badly, they might
even have been replaced.[121] There were, as we have seen, at least some
high-ranking leaders (e.g., Giap and Truong Chinh) who strongly
opposed the policies espoused by Le Duan and his allies, while others in
the leadership (Pham Van Dong and probably Ho Chi Minh) were sufficiently concerned about the risks inherent in a major military effort in
the South to have pursued reunification by means of negotiations.
Furthermore, we can infer from the frequent disparaging comments by
Le Duan and Nguyen Chi Thanh on the likelihood of an American
intervention that at least some in the leadership were using this argument against them. Finally, there is the evidence from the Japanese case,
which suggests that it is possible (albeit very difficult) for a state engaged
in coercion to take actions that mobilize officials in the target state to
respond as desired by the coercer. As Allison and Halperin note:

118. Ibid., pp. 145–146 (see also p. 410). This line of argument assumes that the speeches and
articles of Le Duan and Nguyen Chi Thanh were an accurate index of their expectations; but it is
difficult to believe that after making the case so often and so vehemently that the U.S. would not
intervene, they would not have come to believe their own words.

119. This point will be discussed in more detail in Chapter 6, below.

120. Issues of war and peace were apparently decided by the Politburo on the basis of a majority
vote; on this point, see Allan Goodman, "Fighting While Negotiating: The View from Hanoi," in
Zasloff and Brown (eds.), p. 90. Within the 11-man Politburo, four slots were held by the propo-
nents of armed struggle and heavy Northern involvement in the Southern revolution (Le Duan,
Nguyen Chi Thanh, Pham Hung, and Le Duc Tho), two were held by vocal opponents of Le Duan
and his allies (Giap and Truong Chinh), and two were held by a "centrist" group (Ho and Pham
Van Dong). It is difficult to state with certainty the views of the other three members—Le Thanh
Nghi, Nguyen Duy Trinh, and Hoang Van Hoan—although Trinh has often been linked with
Pham Van Dong as a proponent of negotiations.

121. This was, after all, what happened to Truong Chinh in the aftermath of the land reform
excesses. Changes in the composition of the target state's government also occurred in the three
cases in which May found bombing to have had some effect in inducing acceptance of a political
settlement (see note 111, above; and May, pp. 128–139).

The American effort to get the Japanese government to surrender without invasion of Japan succeeded only because (1) the United States sent Japan some of the clearest signals in history, including dropping two atomic bombs, destroying Tokyo with fire bombing, destroying the Japanese fleet, and assembling an invasion force; (2) there was a strong group within the Japanese government, including the Emperor, his principal adviser, and the Foreign Minister who had opposed the war from the start and wanted to surrender; and (3) the American signals increased this group's sense of determination and willingness to run risks while discrediting and demoralizing their opponents.[122]

But while the Japanese case suggests the possibility of inducing officials in another government to respond in the desired fashion, the Vietnamese case reinforces the conclusion that it will be extraordinarily difficult to do this in practice, especially if the coercer relies on a strategy of "graduated pressures." In the Vietnamese case, there was, as we saw earlier, no disagreement in Hanoi over the *legitimacy* of the goal of unifying Vietnam under the control of the Lao Dong Party.[123] Instead, the disputes that took place were exclusively over the means to be used in attaining that goal—e.g., the relative emphasis on political versus armed struggle, the share of the burden to be borne by Northerners and Southerners, and so on. Furthermore, as Pike notes, the goal of a unified Vietnam

was within DRV grasp in 1954. The Viet Minh had defeated the French, at least psychologically, and all of Vietnam was theirs for the taking; they had achieved victory, only to be deprived of its fruit by their erstwhile allies; "sold out" perhaps would not be too strong a term. The Soviets, as part of a deal to scuttle the European Defense Community, and the Chinese, then pressing Nehru's *panch shila* (coexistence) and what was soon to be called the "Spirit of Bandung in Asia," convinced Ho Chi Minh and his fellow Politburo members to settle for partition, using the argument that all the country would soon be theirs.[124]

These hopes, however, proved to be illusory. The Diem Government refused to have any dealings whatsoever with the North, even to the point of spurning DRV appeals for a normalization of relations between the two Vietnams. The effect of all this, however, was to create a legacy of bitterness in Hanoi and specifically a feeling that the legitimate goal of reunification had been snatched away by the machinations of the

122. Allison and Halperin, p. 66.

123. This point was conceded in the State Department's contribution to NSSM-1 (p. 94): "It would seem highly unlikely that any Politburo member would ever believe (much less say) that the Communist Party should give up its efforts to unite all of Vietnam under its control."

124. Douglas Pike, *War, Peace, and the Viet Cong* (Cambridge, Mass.: MIT Press, 1969), p. 34 (see also p. 32).

Americans and their puppets in Saigon. As a result, even Pham Van Dong, generally counted as one of the less "hawkish" members of the leadership, could tell Aubrac and Marcovich (apparently with some feeling) that "we should have had unification in 1956" (see Appendix V).

In addition, far from advocating policies that "failed," by early 1965 it looked very much as if Le Duan and Nguyen Chi Thanh had been correct in their assessment of how best to pursue the goal of victory in the South. The Saigon government, as we saw in Chapter 3, was on the brink of disintegration: the dissolution of the High National Council in December 1964 had been followed in January by a new round of Buddhist-led riots and demonstrations. These, in turn, were followed by yet another coup attempt on February 19, 1965 (the eve of what was supposed to be the first ROLLING THUNDER strike). The continuing turmoil in Saigon, as the authors of NSSM-1 subsequently conceded,

presented an opportunity for rapid progress by the National Liberation Front in recruiting, arming, and influencing the South Vietnamese population. The series of governments following Diem was characterized by starting their tenure with the highest level of support they were ever to achieve and rapidly losing this support until they fell or were overthrown. By the fall of 1964, in the judgment of nonaligned Vietnamese, U.S. and other foreign missionaries and numbers of the Viet Minh [sic], the National Liberation Front enjoyed the active, willing cooperation of more than 50% of the population in South Vietnam and a belief among the majority of the population in the inevitability of a Communist takeover. Scarcely 4,000 hamlets could be regarded as relatively secure [compared to 7,000–8,000 in early 1963].[125]

Taken together, these last two points suggest that it was highly unlikely that the start of the air war would have resulted in an abrupt reversal of DRV policy toward the war in the South. Not only were the opponents of that policy in the minority to begin with, but even the opponents shared the desire of Le Duan and Nguyen Chi Thanh for a Communist victory in the South. Furthermore, the apparent success of the policies advocated by Le Duan and his allies would have made it difficult, to say the least, for their opponents to dislodge them from their position as the dominant group in the Politburo. As Jervis notes:

Success is apt to consolidate the power of those who advocated the policy, defeat to undermine it and strengthen the hand of those who had different views. Thus Japan's initial success in World War II reinforced the position of the dominant group in that country, which believed that she could win a

125. NSSM-1, pp. 416–417.

limited victory, and made it even more difficult for dissenters to ask what Japan would do if the Allies refused to accept the verdict of a short struggle.[126]

But even if the opponents of a major Northern role in the Southern revolution had wanted to abandon the effort to gain control over the South, their cause would have been seriously hampered by the arguments that they would have had to overcome in order to make their views prevail. By March 1965, when the first ROLLING THUNDER strikes were launched, DRV preparations for wider war had been under way for more than six years (ever since January 1959). In the process, as we saw in the preceding section, regimental-size units had been created in the South and equipped with modern Soviet-style weapons; an extensive and highly effective logistical system had been set up; a sizable apparatus for training men and infiltrating them from the North to the South was in place; and preparations had been made in anticipation of an American invasion of the North. Even considered separately, each of these was no small undertaking; considered together, they represented an enormous investment in human and material resources. Needless to say, when large organizations are created and thousands of military and civilian personnel mobilized to staff them, the momentum built up is not easily reversed. To have expected, as the Johnson Administration apparently did, that elements of the DRV leadership would argue (successfully) that the fruits of six years of hard labor should be thrown away, *especially when victory in the South was so near,* simply because of a few air strikes (which did relatively little damage during February, March, and April 1965) appears in retrospect to have been the height of folly.[127]

Furthermore, the very act of suggesting that the North should yield in the face of American pressures would itself have entailed significant risks—risks that, from the Party's point of view, might well have exceeded the risks being run by refusing to submit to American demands. A decision to yield would surely have split the Party and possibly have resulted in the outright secession of the Southern branch. After having been abandoned once at Geneva and left to the tender mercies of the Diem regime, Southern cadres were almost certainly watching carefully

126. Jervis (1976), pp. 238–239.

127. For a strikingly similar case, see Russett's description of the situation of the Japanese government in 1941, in "Pearl Harbor: Deterrence Theory and Decision Theory," reprinted in Russett, *Power and Community in World Politics* (San Francisco: W. H. Freeman, 1974), p. 227. See also Allison's discussion (p. 234) of the difficulty of reversing a government decision once a complex process has been set in motion.

to see what the North would do in response to the American escalation. Southern cadres, moreover, had persistently been out in front of their Northern comrades on the question of when to launch the armed struggle: the CRIMP Document, for example, reports that "in several areas [in 1958] the [Southern] party members on their own initiative had organized armed struggle against the enemy." As a result, if the North had attempted to call off the insurgency, it seems likely that Southern party members would have refused to obey. They were, after all, fighting to protect *their* homes and way of life, and it is difficult to envision the veteran cadres who had survived the worst of the Diemist repression meekly laying down their arms and accepting permanent exile in the North. (Given the Diem regime's disregard for the provisions in the Geneva Accords prohibiting reprisals against former members of the Viet Minh residing in the South, accepting "amnesty" in the South would have been tantamount to signing their death warrants.) Nor was the North unaware of the danger of appearing to yield to American pressure. As Turley notes, "instructions from Hanoi repeatedly sought to assure the Southern command that the North would never abandon the war, regardless of cost or scope of American intervention."[128]

Finally, the nature of the pressures being applied by the Administration did little to strengthen the hand of those who were primarily concerned with "consolidation" in the North and who may have feared the effect of an air war on the hard-won gains of the preceding decade. The "signals" transmitted to Hanoi during 1964 were erratic, to say the least; in addition, the President's unwillingness to respond to the attacks on Bien Hoa and the Brink BOQ very likely contributed to a belief in Hanoi that the Administration's policy was one of bluff and bluster and nothing more.[129] Even when the Administration resorted to more forceful actions against the North, in the form of the reprisals of February 1965 and the start of the ROLLING THUNDER program, the initial air strikes, as we saw in Chapter 3, were relatively infrequent and were aimed at targets far removed from Hanoi and Haiphong. Furthermore, the relatively slow pace of escalation during the first few months of the air war very likely suggested not only that serious damage might not be incurred for some time but also that serious damage might not be incurred at all, provided the war in the South could be won quickly enough and the Americans presented with a *fait accompli*. As a result,

---

128. The CRIMP Document, Working Paper, Item 301, p. 10; Turley (1972), p. 184. See also Fall, pp. 187–189.

129. This was, as we saw in Chapter 2, Seaborn's impression of the thinking in Hanoi during his June 1964 visit there.

one suspects that, if anything, the Administration's policy of gradually increasing the pressures on the North actually had the effect of spurring the North Vietnamese to *increase* their efforts in the South in the hope of achieving a quick victory there or, at the least, strengthening their own bargaining position prior to an international conference (which, as we know, *they* thought the U.S. was seeking in order to extricate *itself* from the war).[130]

Although there is insufficient evidence to permit us to confidently assert the existence of a causal relationship here, the evidence that is available (see Table 2) is consistent with the interpretation that the Administration's efforts were counterproductive, in that they only spurred the North Vietnamese to do more.[131] Thus, the first explicit Presidential warning to Hanoi (the President's February 1964 UCLA speech—see Chapter 2, above) was followed shortly by preparations to infiltrate two PAVN regiments into South Vietnam. Similarly, the Tonkin reprisals and the explicit threats of further retaliation conveyed by Seaborn in August 1964 were followed in September and October by the departure for South Vietnam of the 32nd and 95th PAVN regiments.[132] Furthermore, it was in February 1965 (coinciding with the reprisals for Pleiku and Qui Nhon) that a fourth PAVN regiment departed for South Vietnam, followed in March by an assortment of service units: transportation battalions, as well as medical, security, signal, and engineer companies.[133] The gradual intensification of the air war, culminating in the "bridge raids" of April 3–4, 1965 (see Chapter 3, above), was followed on April 8–10 by a series of steps taken by the

130. On this point, see Seaborn's report on his March 1965 visit to Hanoi, discussed in Chapter 3, above.

131. The point is of more than particular significance, since several analysts (e.g., Schelling [1966], pp. 68–69; Young, p. 360; and Snyder, "Crisis Bargaining," in Hermann [ed.], pp. 249–251) have stressed the advantages of starting with relatively low levels of pressure in any attempt at coercion in order to minimize the risk of an uncontrollable escalatory spiral. The Administration's experience in the Vietnam case thus suggests an important qualification to their argument.

132. A third PAVN regiment, the 101st, left in December 1964. The State Department paper, "Hanoi's Role in the Support of the Present War in South Vietnam" (p. 14), mentions that the 808th PAVN battalion left the North in August 1964, which would further strengthen the inference that U.S. threats and military moves (i.e., the Tonkin reprisals and Seaborn's second meeting with Pham Van Dong) only spurred the North Vietnamese on. It is, however, the only source mentioning the 808th Battalion; all others refer to either the 32nd or 95th regiments as the first complete tactical units of the North Vietnamese Army to leave for South Vietnam.

133. On these points, see Working Paper, p. 21; and U.S. Department of State, "Hanoi's Role in the Support of the Present War in South Vietnam," p. 16. In addition, the authors of NSSM-1 (p. 177) point out that "after February 7, 1965 (the beginning of the bombing) intensified civil defense measures were undertaken. On February 7, AFP reported that trenches were being dug, air raid shelters constructed, and vehicles and important installations camouflaged in Hanoi."

Table 2

U.S. "Graduated Pressures" and DRV Counterescalation, February 1964–May 1965

Date	U.S. Move	DRV Move
February 1964	Phase I, OPLAN 34A, begins (February 1) President's UCLA speech (February 21) Stories planted with newsmen appear (February 23)	
April 1964		95th PAVN regiment recalled from Laos for infiltration training 32d PAVN regiment formed for infiltration training 98th PAVN support regiment leaves for duty along supply trails in Laos
May 1964	YANKEE TEAM missions begin over Laos (May 21)	PAVN reinforcements sent to VC units in South Vietnam
June 1964	U.S. air attacks on Pathet Lao installations (June 9) First Seaborn meeting with Pham Van Dong (June 18)	*New York Times* reports stepped-up road-building in Laos (June 26) First reports appear of PAVN officers serving with VC units
July 1964	OPLAN 34A PT-boat raids begin (July 31) DE SOTO patrol in Gulf of Tonkin begins (July 31)	
August 1964	Presidential warning to Hanoi (August 3) OPLAN 34A PT-boat raid (August 4) Tonkin reprisal strikes (August 5)	First attack on *Maddox* (August 2) Second incident in Gulf of Tonkin (August 4)

Date		
September 1964	U.S. military forces transferred to South Vietnam, Thailand, and Western Pacific (early August)	32d PAVN regiment leaves for South Vietnam (arrives January 1965)
	Second Seaborn–Pham Van Dong meeting (August 13)	
	DE SOTO patrols resumed in Gulf of Tonkin (September 12)	
October 1964		95th PAVN regiment leaves for South Vietnam (arrives December 1964)
November 1964		VC attack on Bien Hoa (November 1)
December 1964	Third Seaborn mission to Hanoi (December 10–18)	101st PAVN regiment leaves for South Vietnam (arrives February 1965)
	BARRELL ROLL missions begin over Laos (December 14)	"Military-Civilian Unity Days" begin in North Vietnam
		Work on combat villages begins in North Vietnam
January 1965		National Defense Council issues directives on preparations for air attacks
February 1965		VC attack on Pleiku (February 6)
	Pleiku reprisal strike (February 7)	VC attack on Qui Nhon (February 10)
	Qui Nhon reprisal strike (February 11)	18th PAVN regiment leaves for South Vietnam (arrives April 1965)
		Second PAVN support regiment leaves for Laos
	Leaks to press on planning for air strikes (late February)	First urban evacuation order issued (February 28)

Table 2 (Continued)

Date	U.S. Move	DRV Move
March 1965	First ROLLING THUNDER strike (March 2) Marines land at DaNang (March 8) Second ROLLING THUNDER strike (March 14–15) ROLLING THUNDER strikes launched on daily basis (late March)	PAVN support units leave for South Vietnam
April 1965	"Bridge raids" near Hanoi (April 3–4)	DRV National Assembly orders partial mobilization (April 8–10)
May 1965		VC summer offensive begins with attack on Song Be (May 11)

Sources: For additional details on U.S. activities, see Chapters 2–3, above. For details on DRV activities, see Chapters 2–3 and Section II-C of Chapter 5, above. See also Working Paper, pp. 12, 13, 21; Working Paper, Items 91, 100, 101–1; U.S. Department of State, "Hanoi's Role in the Support of the Present War in South Vietnam," p. 16; NSSM-1, p. 177; and William S. Turley, "Urbanization in War: Hanoi, 1946–1973," *Pacific Affairs*, 48:3 (Fall 1975), 380.

DRV National Assembly to put the economy on a war footing.[134] Last but not least, it was in the summer of 1965, after the air war had been under way for several months, that DRV/VC forces in the South launched the offensive that the authors of NSSM-1 would later term an attempt for a "knockout blow." Even more ominous were DRV moves to strengthen the capabilities of DRV/VC forces in the South: four more PAVN regiments departed for South Vietnam in July 1965 (to join the four already there), followed by two more in August. Overall, by the end of 1965, there were thirty-three PAVN battalions in the South, while the rate of infiltration nearly tripled—from 12,000+ in 1964 to 33,000+ in 1965.[135]

There is, however, one important question still unanswered. If gradual escalation only spurred the North Vietnamese on, would rapid escalation have proved any more successful? In this respect, one advantage of rapid escalation is its greater potential for inducing attitudinal change among the leaders of the target state, who may not initially be convinced of the coercer's intent to use sufficient force to attain his objectives:

Greater change will result when discrepant information arrives in a large batch than when it is considered bit by bit. In the former case, the contradictions between it and the prevailing view will be relatively obvious. But when discrepant information arrives gradually, the conflict between each bit and what the person believes will be small enough to go unnoticed, be dismissed as unimportant, or necessitate at most slight modifications (e.g., addition of exceptions to the rule).[136]

Still, one should not make too much of this "advantage." Even if Le Duan and Nguyen Chi Thanh had been convinced that the U.S. was determined to prevent a Communist victory in the South, they might well have persevered in their advocacy of armed struggle and heavy Northern involvement in the Southern revolution. While the entire DRV leadership was committed to the goal of completing the revolution

134. As summarized by P.J. Honey ("North Vietnam Quarterly Survey no. 16," *China News Analysis*, 568 [June 11, 1965], 4), the Assembly ordered "an extension of military service laws and approved a number of urgent measures designed to strengthen the economic and defense potential of North Vietnam. . . . Briefly, these are the strengthening of the armed forces by extending military service and carrying out a partial mobilization, the consolidation of regional and para-military forces, the development of the economy in line with the new situation, and the redeployment of manpower to meet both economic and military requirements."
135. On these points, see NSSM-1, p. 417; III Gravel, p. 438; and Working Paper, pp. 12, 19, 21.
136. Jervis (1976), p. 308.

in the South and achieving reunification, this commitment seems to
have been especially strong in the case of Nguyen Chi Thanh and Le
Duan (the latter often referred to as the "Flame of the South").[137] In
view of the strength of their commitment—a Communist victory in the
South would, after all, have been the culmination of their life's work—it
seems highly unlikely that they would have acquiesced in a decision to
yield, no matter how rapidly the U.S. escalated.

Second and more importantly, the Vietnam case suggests the overwhelming importance of *timing* in determining whether coercion is
likely to succeed. Between 1956 and 1965, both the Americans in
Washington and the North Vietnamese in Hanoi were engaged in a
lengthy and continuous debate over what should be the role of their
respective governments in the South Vietnamese revolution. And while
it appears that American actions during 1964 and early 1965 had the
unintended effect of spurring the North Vietnamese to increase their
efforts in the South, a broader perspective reveals a considerably more
complex pattern of relationships. Specifically, at each critical point
along the way, a DRV decision to "escalate," in the sense of a decision
committing the Party and the government to a new course of action in
the South, *preceded* a similar decision in Washington. Thus, the decision to launch the armed struggle in the South came nearly two years
before the major increase in the American effort under Kennedy; the
9th Plenum's December 1963 decision to step up the North's role in the
war came one month before Johnson's decision to begin the covert war;
and the decision to commit PAVN units to the war in the South preceded by several months the President's decision to begin the air war. It
was only after the governments in Hanoi and Washington had committed themselves to much greater efforts in the war in the South in
December 1963 and early 1964, respectively, that the escalatory spiral
identified in Table 2 began to operate.[138]

137. William S. Turley, personal communication, September 12, 1977.

138. This is not to suggest that there was a simple and direct causal relationship between North
Vietnamese decisions to step up their role in the war in the South and Washington's decisions to
step up the American role (as U.S. officials often suggested). In fact, the question of causality is
much more complex than the time sequence presented in this paragraph might suggest. In this
respect, the initial impetus for the escalatory spiral appears to have come from Saigon (encouraged
by the U.S.) in the form of the anti-Viet Minh witch-hunt of 1955–1956. This, in turn, resulted in
Hanoi's decision to couple the political struggle in the South with the rebuilding of the Party's
political and military apparatus in the South. In 1959, the Saigon government apparently intensified its efforts against Communists in the South (e.g., Public Law 10/59), which in turn appears to
have tipped the balance within the Politburo, leading it to decide in May 1959 that the time had
come to launch the armed struggle in the South (however, it is not clear whether the Central

With the benefit of hindsight, the timing of these various government decisions appears to be absolutely crucial. As we saw earlier, Administration planners (along with the theorists of limited/coercive war) assumed that the North Vietnamese, to borrow Taylor's phrase, "would seek an accommodation with us when the cost of pursuing a losing course became excessive." This line of reasoning, however, was flawed on two counts: not only were the North Vietnamese *not* losing during 1965, but it is questionable whether another *government* would perceive costs in the same way that the Administration did. While there was no disagreement in Hanoi over the legitimacy of the goal of reunification, there was, as we have seen, considerable disagreement over how best to pursue that goal. As a result, DRV decisions to "escalate" came only after lengthy and acrimonious debates—debates that, as we saw, spanned nearly a decade and included occasional threats of a purge against those opposing a greater role for the North in the war (Minh Tranh's disappearance suggests that these were not idle threats). What this meant, though, was that a decision to yield would itself have involved significant "costs"—costs that American planners never took into account. Not only would there have been severe psychic costs for Le Duan, Nguyen Chi Thanh, and their supporters, who would have had to admit that they had been wrong and that the goal of completing the Southern revolution was now beyond reach (at least temporarily); more importantly, since everyone in Hanoi agreed on the desirability of reunification, a decision to yield would have confronted the leadership with the question of "Since we have abandoned the option of armed struggle, what do we do *now* in terms of attaining reunification?" Confronting that question, however, would have required reopening old issues that had tentatively been settled (e.g., the proper role of political

---

Committee's January 1959 decision—i.e., a decision in principle to launch the armed struggle at some future date—was a response to some act of "escalation" by the GVN or to the rebuilding of the Party apparatus in the South during 1957–1958 combined with Le Duan's forceful advocacy). In fairness to the South Vietnamese, it would appear that the December 1963 decision by the 9th Plenum of the VWP Central Committee (i.e., to step up the armed struggle in the South) was a response not to any "provocation" by the GVN but rather to the chaotic conditions in the South in the aftermath of the Diem coup—conditions which, as we saw earlier, presented an opportunity for a quick Communist victory in the South. Significantly, with respect to the question of who was provoking whom, the documents available suggest that the Johnson Administration was unaware of the decisions at the 9th Plenum when it was considering whether to launch the covert war (OPLAN 34A). At the very least, if the Administration had realized how deeply committed the North Vietnamese were by that point, it would also have realized how inadequate were the harassing actions envisioned by OPLAN 34A (most of which failed, anyway) with respect to influencing DRV decision-making. I am indebted to Professors H. Bradford Westerfield and King C. Chen for their thoughtful comments and suggestions on these points.

versus armed struggle) and tearing open old wounds that had presumably healed somewhat in the months since the 9th Plenum (e.g., Le Duan's scathing denunciation at the 9th Plenum of "certain communists," an attack that almost certainly would have been hurled back at him if he were to acquiesce in a decision to yield). In a sense, then, for the Hanoi leadership, going back would have been almost as "painful" as continuing their role in the war despite American pressures.[139]

Third, one cannot stress too highly the importance of the favorable (from the DRV's point of view) situation in the South. As we have seen, DRV/VC forces in the South stood on the verge of victory by early 1965, with the result that a decision to yield would have meant not only the loss of the all-important goal of reunification (which now seemed to be almost in their grasp) but would also have very likely resulted in bitter recriminations over "Who lost South Vietnam?" What this suggests is that when a government is the target of coercive pressures, the "costs" involved cannot be measured solely in terms of buildings destroyed and bridges bombed out. Instead, government officials in the target state must take care not to furnish their political opponents with ammunition—ammunition that could conceivably ruin many a career. Such officials would undoubtedly think twice before opening themselves to the charge of being "capitulationists" who snatched defeat from the jaws of victory.

Taken together, these last two points suggest a fourth reason why the North Vietnamese might not have backed down even if the U.S. had escalated rapidly and forcefully. In much of the theorizing on coercive war, it was implicitly assumed that weakness on one front could be off-set by strength on another—for example, if an opponent attempted to seize some piece of territory, possible responses were not confined to blocking physically the attempted seizure; instead, one could implement coercive measures (bombing, blockade, etc.) in other theaters in order to "make the enemy behave."[140] Similarly, as American officials despaired of ever rooting the Viet Cong out of the South Vietnamese countryside, their attention focused more and more on a theater of battle for which American power seemed more suited—namely, bombing the North in

139. On this point, see Alexander George and Richard Smoke, *Deterrence in American Foreign Policy* (New York: Columbia University Press, 1974), p. 574; see also Jervis (1976), pp. 388–395, for a discussion of "post-decision spreading apart of the alternatives."

140. For examples of this approach, see Schelling (1966), pp. 170–184; Alexander George, "The Development of Doctrine and Strategy," in George, Hall, and Simons, pp. 20–32; and Williams, pp. 147–148.

the hope of persuading the North Vietnamese to "call off" the Viet Cong. Our discussion, however, suggests that this line of reasoning was gravely flawed. An opponent who stands on the verge of victory in one theater of battle (e.g., South Vietnam) is unlikely to be coerced into giving up all that his efforts have accomplished, regardless of the severity of the pressures imposed upon him. Instead, the attempted coercion is likely to spur the target state to try even harder, in the hope of achieving a quick victory, thus presenting the coercer with a *fait accompli*. In the process, moreover, officials in the target state are likely to become even more deeply committed to securing their objectives, regardless of what the coercing state does.[141]

Fifth and finally, it is important to notice that rapid escalation carries with it its own special dangers. Rapid escalation, that is, not only runs the risk of getting completely out of hand, perhaps triggering a conflict bigger than either of the participants wanted, but in addition, as Schelling himself recognized: "Coercion depends more on the threat of what is yet to come than on damage already done. . . . To use the threat of further violence against somebody requires that you keep something in reserve—that the enemy still have something to lose."[142] Since an opponent with nothing to lose is also an opponent with no incentive to comply, rapid escalation is unlikely to be much more successful than the slower-paced approach, although it will be considerably more dangerous.

If this is the case, however, are there any circumstances under which coercion might succeed? To put this another way, our discussion of the timing of DRV and American decisions would seem to imply that coercion will almost always fail, at least as a response to hostile action. Since the "aggressor" government would, by definition, be the one that fought out its bureaucratic battles first, this analysis would seem to suggest that coercive pressures would have little chance of success so long as the proponents of hostile action in the "aggressor" government were able to maintain themselves in power. This conclusion, however, seems a bit extreme. In the Cuban case, at least, coercive pressures

141. The evidence from the Cuban missile crisis would seem to support this line of argument. Because the U.S. could credibly threaten the Soviets with a defeat in the "local theater" (i.e., Cuba) by means of air strikes on the Soviet missile bases and possibly an invasion of Cuba, the imposition of coercive pressures "worked" in the sense of inducing a Soviet withdrawal of the missiles. If the crisis had taken place in a different location, closer to the sources of Soviet power, the outcome might well have been different. For example, would coercive pressures have had much chance of inducing the Soviets to call off their invasions of Hungary in 1956 and Czechoslovakia in 1968? The answer in both cases would seem to be an unequivocal "no."

142. Schelling (1966), pp. 172–173.

apparently "worked," in the sense of inducing a Soviet withdrawal of their missiles from Cuba. How, then, can we explain the differing outcomes in the Cuban and Vietnamese cases? The answer, it appears, is not that coercion will never work but rather that the chances of success depend on the context in which coercion is attempted. A brief comparison of the Cuban and Vietnamese cases should be helpful in clarifying this last point.

In the Cuban case, the Soviet decision to install missiles in Cuba was apparently made no earlier than the spring of 1962—at most, roughly six months before the actual crisis.[143] In the Vietnamese case, in contrast, the intra-Party debate over strategy stretched over a period of close to a decade, a difference that appears to have been significant in determining the differing Soviet and Vietnamese responses to American pressures. We can hypothesize that the longer the bureaucratic battles involved, the more rigid the positions of the participants will become and the greater the stake each participant will have in insuring that his preferred course of action is adopted. Both of these factors—the rigidity of the participants' positions and the importance of the stakes involved —decrease the likelihood that a government will yield to coercive pressures.

Furthermore, a careful comparison of the Vietnamese case with the Cuban missile crisis suggests that the relationship between the coercer's actions and the *expectations* of officials in the target state's government is also critically important. In the Vietnamese case, while Le Duan and his supporters denigrated the chances of American intervention, the North Vietnamese nonetheless were taking no chances, as evidenced by their preparations both for an American invasion of the North and for an aerial assault on their major cities—preparations that to some extent predated the start of the air war (see Table 2, above). As a result, it appears that in the Vietnamese case, the U.S. ended up with the worst of all possible worlds. Not only did the erratic signals conveyed by the Administration, along with the relatively restrained nature of the bombing during the early months of the air war, appear to confirm the arguments of Le Duan and his supporters that the U.S. would not intervene massively, but in addition, compared to the contingency for which the DRV had prepared (i.e., an invasion of the North along with air attacks on Hanoi), the early months of the air war probably did not seem particularly burdensome. As a result, the North Vietnamese continued to pour resources into the conflict in the South in the hope of

---

143. Adam Ulam suggests that the Soviet decision came sometime around July 1962, while Allison assigns it to April 1962. See Ulam, pp. 667-669; and Allison, pp. 230-244.

achieving a quick victory there before the pressures on the North became too onerous. By the time the air war reached a level of intensity commensurate with initial DRV expectations, the positions of both sides had hardened considerably.

In the Cuban case, in contrast, it appears that the Soviets were as surprised by the firmness of the American response as the Kennedy Administration had been by the discovery of the missiles in the first place. Soviet behavior during the first forty-eight hours after the U.S. announced its discovery of the missiles gave

every indication of unanticipated surprise. Dobrynin, dumbfounded when Secretary Rusk informed him of the crisis, left the State Department visibly shaken. For several days he insisted that there were no Soviet missiles in Cuba, as did Soviet Ambassador Zorin at the United Nations. Khrushchev's refusal to accept the quarantine proclamation, public replies to U Thant and Bertrand Russell, his two secret letters to the President, and finally the harangue to which he subjected William Knox [President of Westinghouse International and a visitor to Moscow] suggest the thrashing about of a surprised and uncertain man. . . . Moreover, . . . more than fifteen hours after the U.S. had informed the Soviets of discovery of the missiles, "There had been no general alert of the Soviet forces in Cuba or around the globe."[144]

As a result, it is perhaps not so surprising that when the American response became known (i.e., blockade, preparations for an invasion of Cuba, and a threat to respond to any nuclear missile launched from Cuba with a full retaliatory strike against the Soviet Union), the Soviets quickly reversed themselves. A limited war in the Caribbean and a possible nuclear war with the United States were not what they had bargained for.[145]

Finally, in the Cuban case, not only did the U.S. possess overwhelming strategic superiority, but it also possessed vastly superior local forces with which it could credibly threaten an invasion of Cuba. In addition, the U.S. was able to provide the Soviets with tangible incentives to yield in the form of the no-invasion promise coupled with Kennedy's tacit pledge to withdraw the Turkish missiles.[146] In the Vietnam case, in contrast, all three of these elements were missing. While the Administration

144. Allison, pp. 134–135 (the internal quote is from Robert F. Kennedy, *Thirteen Days: A Memoir of the Cuban Missile Crisis* [New York: Signet, 1969], p. 58). See also Ulam, pp. 670–671; and Young, pp. 209–210.

145. Similarly, when U.S. involvement in the Vietnam conflict did reach a level far beyond that initially predicted by the DRV leadership, the DRV position became somewhat more flexible, as evidenced by the PINTA (Rangoon) and MARIGOLD contacts. (On this point, see the discussion in Chapter 6, below.)

146. On the missile swap, see Allison, pp. 218–230, especially pp. 229–230.

attempted to threaten the destruction of DRV industry, these threats, as we saw earlier, were continually undercut as a result of foul-ups in the field and/or failures to follow through. More importantly, there appears to have been considerable doubt (at least in Hanoi) as to whether the Administration possessed the capability or the will to introduce sufficient numbers of American troops into the "local theater" (i.e., South Vietnam) in time to thwart a DRV victory there.[147] Finally, the Administration offered little in the way of concessions intended to make it easier for the North Vietnamese to yield. For all the talk of "carrots," the Administration's idea of a "compromise" solution, as we saw in Chapters 2–4, was essentially a demand for unconditional surrender—i.e., a withdrawal of DRV forces and an end to infiltration, compensated only by "amnesty" for the Viet Cong and an offer of financial aid for the North.[148]

What this line of argument suggests, then, is that there is no simple and direct relationship between the rate of escalation and the coercer's chances of success.[149] Instead, it appears that the coercer's chances of success are greatest when the attempted coercion occurs before the target state's government has become too firmly committed to whatever course of action the coercer seeks to prevent, and when the coercer utilizes pressures greater than those anticipated by officials in the target state.[150] If the U.S. had intervened forcefully (or threatened to do so) much earlier than it did in the Vietnamese case—e.g., prior to the May 1959 Politburo decision to begin the armed struggle in the South—so that the attempted coercion had come at a time when the North's role in the war in the South was still unsettled and the question of the relative importance of political versus armed struggle was still being thrashed out, the U.S. might well have "succeeded," in the sense of persuading the North Vietnamese not to increase their role in the war at that time, thus buying a few more years of "stability" for South Vietnam.[151] On the other hand, if coercion is not attempted until well after

147. As we saw in Chapter 2, the President himself repeatedly stated during his election campaign that he had no intention of sending American boys to do a job that Asian boys should do for themselves.

148. On the importance of "carrots," see Alexander George, "The Cuban Missile Crisis, 1962," in George, Hall, and Simons, p. 132.

149. This same conclusion, although based on different reasoning, is reached by Alexander George, "The Cuban Missile Crisis, 1962," in George, Hall, and Simons, pp. 131–132.

150. This is not to imply that the coercer should always "play it safe" by using a great deal of force. As suggested earlier, rapid escalation not only runs the risk of getting completely out of hand but may also prove counterproductive, since an opponent with nothing left to lose is also an opponent with no incentives to comply.

151. In the Vietnamese case, it appears that "buying time" was about all that coercive pressures could have accomplished. Considering how deeply committed the North Vietnamese were to the

the opponent's government has committed itself to the course of action the coercer seeks to prevent, our analysis suggests that there will be no "cheap" way to defeat a determined and resourceful opponent who has already gained the upper hand on the local field of battle. By 1965, the only circumstances in which coercion might have succeeded in the Vietnamese case (in the sense of persuading the North Vietnamese to end their support for the Viet Cong) would have been if the Americans and their South Vietnamese allies had first made substantial progress in uprooting and destroying the Viet Cong infrastructure in the South. As long as the Viet Cong were winning, the North Vietnamese had strong incentives *not* to comply with American demands. Only if the situation were reversed—i.e., the Viet Cong were clearly losing—would the attempted coercion have had any chance of success. Needless to say, in the latter situation one could legitimately question both the necessity and the desirability of resorting to coercion in the first place.

Interestingly enough, Administration officials did indicate an awareness of the importance of winning in the South. At the Honolulu Conference of April 20, 1965, as we saw in Chapter 3, it was recognized that "a settlement will come as much or more from VC failure in the South as from DRV pain in the North." Consequently, additional U.S. forces were to be committed to the South (the war in the South was also to have first call on U.S. air assets in the area), while the air war in the North was to be plateaued at about the "present tempo" with "increasing pressure" to be provided by "repetition and continuation."

This "new" approach, however, proved to be no more successful than its predecessors (OPLAN 34A, ROLLING THUNDER, etc.). Or did it? While it would still take nearly three more years of war to achieve formal negotiations with the North Vietnamese, there was some ambiguous evidence that perhaps the DRV was looking for an exit in the face of American pressures—specifically, the apparent DRV willingness to negotiate even while the bombing continued, as evidenced by the XYZ, PINTA, MARIGOLD, and SUNFLOWER contacts (see Chapters 3–4, above). Did those cases represent tacit DRV acceptance of the bombing as an American "blue chip" that could be traded for some concession on their part? Did DRV willingness to yield on their procedural demand of no talks without a bombing cessation signify willingness to yield on substantive issues? Or is there some other explanation for these actions? It is to these questions that we now turn.

---

cause of reunification, they could at best have been persuaded to defer temporarily an increased effort in the South. Nor would coercion have resolved the problem of what to do with native-born Southern Communists. As we shall suggest in Chapter 8, coercive pressures are no substitute for more imaginative policies designed to alleviate the causes of the behavior that coercion seeks to prevent.

6

The Government as Coercer:
Idioms and Orchestration

I. Intimidating the North: December 1963-February 1965

As the Johnson Administration prepared to launch the air war against
North Vietnam, a central theme in its planning, as we saw in Chapters
1-3, focused on the importance of carefully coordinating military pressures with diplomatic communications to Hanoi. Most Administration
officials believed the war would end through some type of negotiated
settlement; consequently, as John McNaughton put it: "To change
DRV behavior (change can be tacit), [the] U.S. should 'negotiate' by an
optimum combination of words and deeds. Words across any conference table should be orchestrated with continuing military pressures."[1]

Similar concerns, as we saw in Chapter 1, also motivated the academic theorists who dealt with the problems of "limited" and/or
"coercive" war. Preoccupied with enabling the U.S. to resist Soviet and
Chinese expansionism while minimizing the risks of escalation, these
theorists repeatedly stressed the importance of finding the right combination of actions and communications so as to convince an opponent
not just of American resolve to resist but also of American readiness to
limit the conflict and to settle once the opponent had had enough.
While the enemy, as William Kaufmann put it,

> must be fixed and hit hard on the battlefield, and if possible deterred from
> expanding the scope and intensity of the conflict, he must also be allowed to
> extricate himself from his adventure without a serious loss of prestige or
> substance. The conditions of limited war require the maintenance of a delicate
> balance between firmness and tolerance in the conduct of American policy.

---

1. McNaughton's memo is Document no. 209 in III Gravel, p. 581. For other examples of this
type of thinking, see the references listed in Chapter 1, note 8, above; and III Gravel, pp. 149–268,
287–321.

Firmness can be achieved by carefully circumscribed military measures and a program of deterrence. The tolerance necessary to persuade the enemy that there are alternatives more attractive than a continuation and expansion of the war must be a principal function of diplomacy both before and during the conflict.[2]

Policy prescriptions such as these, however, raise serious questions, especially with respect to the ability of a government to put them into practice. One of the more intriguing aspects of both the Administration's plans for "orchestrating" words and deeds and the theorists' stress on coordinating military moves with diplomacy was the feeling of confidence implicit in much of this work. Rarely if ever did these analysts ask themselves whether a government would be able to put their prescriptions into action; instead, there was a tendency to focus on what should be done and to neglect problems of implementation.[3] But was this confidence justified? Are the actions of a government really capable of being "orchestrated"? As we shall see, there are at least four reasons for questioning the ability of a government to perform in the desired manner.

First, the top leadership of any government speaks to many different audiences—e.g., the legislature, the press and other "opinion leaders," foreign governments, and the mass public, whose votes and/or willingness to fight and die in the armed forces can be crucial to the success of a policy involving the risk of armed conflict with another state. But because these audiences may have different policy preferences, the leadership may find it politically expedient to say different things to different audiences, depending on what it thinks the audience wants to hear. Such a tendency, however, may greatly complicate the task of "orchestrating" words and deeds in an optimum fashion, especially since government leaders cannot tell an opponent to stop listening when they speak for domestic consumption only. Thus, for example, President Johnson's speech at UCLA on February 21, 1964 (see Chapter 2, above) warning that "those engaged in external direction and supply [of the war in the South] would do well to be reminded that this type of aggression is a deeply dangerous game" (a statement that the President's press secretary later told newsmen constituted a deliberate warning that

2. William Kaufmann, "Limited Warfare," in Kaufmann (ed.), p. 127. See also Kissinger (1958), pp. 140-142, 189; Osgood (1957), pp. 24, 239; Halperin (1963), pp. 126-128; Kahn, p. 55; and Schelling (1966), pp. 142-151.

3. This judgment was based both on the documents presented in *The Pentagon Papers* and on interviews with former government officials; see also Halberstam, pp. 624-625. The academic theorists cited in note 2, above, did, from time to time, concede that there might be difficulties in finding the right mix of words and deeds, but it seems fair to say that these difficulties were downplayed in their work.

the U.S. might feel compelled to carry the war to the North) resulted in sufficient protest from those opposed to this suggestion that, in their news conferences on February 27 and 29, Secretary Rusk and the President, respectively, denied that there were plans to carry the war to the North. On March 14, the President himself not only denied that there were plans to carry the war to the North but also claimed that his UCLA speech had not been intended to suggest that the war might be expanded.

A second and closely related problem is that the leadership of any government is by no means a monolithic group. Instead, the leadership itself speaks with many voices at once, and there is no guarantee that every voice will convey the same message.[4] As suggested in Chapter 2, the Administration's words and deeds with respect to Vietnam during 1964 were by no means consistent. Instead, Administration policy oscillated between phases of aggressive activism (including "hawkish" warnings of wider war, threatening deployments in the Far East, and increases in covert operations) and phases of hesitant inaction, usually accompanied by "dovish" pronouncements that the Administration sought only "peace" for Southeast Asia (see Table 3). While one cannot make too much of the cyclical nature of Administration policy (some "hawkish" moves did occur during predominantly "dovish" phases), the differences between the phases were sufficiently well-defined to be apparent to newsmen at the time, and, since the North Vietnamese were known to be careful watchers of the American press, one must conclude that they, too, were well aware of the inconsistencies in Administration policy.[5] Consequently, it should not be surprising that the North Vietnamese were not intimidated by the Administration's threats and warnings. Far from creating an image of firmness and resolve to defend South Vietnam, the frequent shifts in Administration policy very likely resulted in an image of a government that was at best unsure of what it wanted to do and at worst looking for a face-saving exit. What is surprising is that Administration officials continued to speak and write of the importance of projecting an image of firmness and resolve even as their own conduct demonstrated the Administration's inability to do anything of the sort.

Third, the leaders of any government are fallible, just like everyone else—they, too, can make mistakes, and they, too, can change their

4. Both Schelling (1966, p. 150) and Halperin (1963, pp. 126–127) indicated an awareness of this problem.

5. On the inconsistency in Administration policy, see Max Frankel's perceptive article, "Confusion Over Asia," *New York Times*, July 3, 1964, p. 3.

Table 3

Alternation of "Hawkish" and "Dovish" Phases in Administration Policy, December 1963–March 1965

Phase	Begins*	Ends*	Main events	For additional details:
Hawk	December 19, 1963	February 22, 1964	Plans for covert pressures forwarded to White House—December 19. President approves study of covert pressures—December 21. Krulak Committee Report approved by President—January 16. Phase I of OPLAN 34A begins—February 1. President directs stepped-up planning for pressuring North Vietnam—February 20. President's UCLA speech—February 21. Stories planted with newsmen—February 22.	See Chapter 2, Section I, above.
Dove	February 23, 1964	March 14, 1964	Rusk news conference—February 27. President denies approving plans for pressuring North Vietnam—February 29. President denies UCLA speech threatened anyone—March 14.	See Chapter 2, Section I, above.
Hawk	March 15, 1964	May 24, 1964	McNamara reports to NSC on South Vietnam trip—March 16. NSAM-288—March 17. Lodge/Johnson cables on "carrot/stick" pressures—March 15-20. Planning begins on NSAM-288 recommendations.	See Chapter 2, Sections I-II, above.

Table 3 (Continued)

Phase	Begins*	Ends*	Main events	For additional details:
			Saigon policy conference—April 18–20. Reconnaissance flights begin over Laos—May 21. ExComm meetings review Laotian crisis—May 24–25.	
Dove	May 25, 1964	June 17, 1964	ExComm abandons scenario approach—May 25. ExComm recommendations deferred by President. Honolulu Conference recommends delay—June 1–2. White House meeting defers decision on further pressures—June 15.	See Chapter 2, Section II, above.
Hawk	June 18, 1964	June 30, 1964	Seaborn meeting with Pham Van Dong—June 18. Release of William Bundy testimony—June 18. Rusk "backgrounder" on U.S. commitment to South Vietnam—June 19. Pentagon briefings on U.S. buildup in Asia—June 20–21. Johnson says U.S. willing to fight—June 28.	See Chapter 2, Section II, above.
Dove	July 1, 1964	July 9, 1964	Rusk press conference on U.S. desire for peace—July 1.	See Chapter 2, Section II, above.
Hawk	July 10, 1964	July 22, 1964	Air power display at DaNang—July 10. William Bundy warning on possible measures against the North—July 13.	See Chapter 2, Section III, above.

Dove	July 23, 1964	July 30, 1964	Taylor says extending war to North Vietnam is contrary to U.S. policy—July 23. Administration officials claim U.S. opposes expanding war—July 27.	See Chapter 2, Section III, above.
Hawk	July 31, 1964	August 13, 1964	OPLAN 34A PT-boat raids begin—July 31. DE SOTO patrol begins—July 31. Tonkin Gulf reprisal strikes—August 5. U.S. forces moved to Western Pacific. Second Seaborn-Pham Van Dong meeting—August 13.	See Chapter 2, Section III, above.
Dove	August 14, 1964	September 3, 1964	"Holding phase" begins—August 14. Matthias paper on neutralizing South Vietnam—August 22. South Vietnamese political crisis—Khanh resigns and is reinstated.	See Chapter 2, Section III, above.
Hawk	September 4, 1964	September 18, 1964	Washington announces buildup will continue—September 4. Washington policy review hints at increased pressures—September 7-8. DE SOTO patrols resumed—September 12.	See Chapter 2, Section IV, above.
Dove	September 19, 1964	November 1, 1964	DE SOTO patrols suspended—September 19. Washington temporizes on air and ground operations in Laos.	See Chapter 2, Section IV, above.

Table 3 (Continued)

Phase	Begins*	Ends*	Main events	For additional details:
			Johnson speech on "not going North"—September 28. Bien Hoa attacked; U.S. does not retaliate—November 1.	
Hawk	November 2, 1964	November 23, 1964	Bundy Working Group convenes—November 2. Intensive planning for wider war.	See Chapter 2, Sections IV–V, above.
Dove	November 24, 1964	January 3, 1965	Principals tone down Working Group proposals—November 24, 27, 28. President defers decision on "Phase II"—December 1. OPLAN 34A proposals softened—December 12–19. Johnson rejects expanding war to North Vietnam—December 15. Third Seaborn mission—U.S. position softens noticeably. South Vietnamese political crisis. Attack on Brink BOQ; U.S. does not retaliate—December 24.	See Chapter 2, Section V, above.
Hawk	January 4, 1965		Planning for overt pressures intensifies. McNaughton memo on intensified pressures—January 4.	See Chapter 3, Section I, above.

William Bundy memo on intensified pressures—
  January 6.
Taylor/Johnson cable on Phase II pressures.
McGeorge Bundy/McNamara memo on intensi-
  fied pressures—January 27.
Contingency planning for reprisals in connection
  with DE SOTO patrols.
Reprisals for Pleiku and Qui Nhon attacks.
ROLLING THUNDER begins—March 2.

---

*Dates listed here should be considered as the approximate starting and ending points of each phase.

minds. Government leaders, for example, may commit themselves to carrying out a course of action but then fail to follow through when the time comes to "put up or shut up." As we saw in Chapter 2, Seaborn was instructed to talk tough during his August 1964 visit to Hanoi, warning that the U.S. was determined to resist not only "any further attacks on U.S. military forces" but also continued DRV efforts to take over the South. This commitment, moreover, was reaffirmed during the September 1964 policy review in Washington and written into NSAM-314, which noted that "we should be prepared to respond as appropriate against the DRV in the event of any attack on U.S. units or any special DRV/VC action against South Vietnam."[6] And yet, when the crunch came, in the form of the Viet Cong attacks on Bien Hoa and the Brink BOQ, the President decided against retaliation—hardly the sort of approach designed to convince Hanoi that the Administration meant what it said.

Fourth, even though government leaders may consider themselves committed to an "orchestrated" effort against an opponent, it is one thing to approve such plans on paper and quite another to get them implemented properly. As a former NSC staff member put it when asked if anyone had questioned the U.S. Government's ability to "orchestrate" words and deeds:

To my knowledge people did not raise that point and I think it was not raised because of the continuing self-deception throughout the process, particularly when you sit fairly high up that you have virtually unlimited control and coordination of power available to you. It feels that way as you sit on the seventh floor of State or in the basement of the White House and it's very remote from reality. I think if you sit around Saigon for an extended period as opposed to a series of military briefings in which everything is painted so "orchestratedly," you get a sense of the total fragmentation that we face in trying to coordinate efforts. But the illusion persists or used to persist and I'm sure it was never challenged. . . .[7]

As the comment quoted above suggests, the reality in the field may be far different from the illusion of "orchestratedness" presented in briefings to high-level officials. Governments, as Allison notes, are really coalitions of large bureaucratic organizations, each of which has its own set of organizational goals (e.g., "proving" the effectiveness of some weapon or program, maintaining or increasing the organization's bud-

6. NSAM-314 is reprinted as Document no. 195 in III Gravel, p. 565. See also Document no. 191, p. 562 in III Gravel; and Chapter 2, above.

7. Interview data.

get, etc.) as well as its own set of organizational activities.[8] As a result, plans to develop an "orchestrated" effort against an opponent are not made in a vacuum. Instead, the "new" effort must be sandwiched in among all of the on-going activities already being conducted by the organizations that comprise the government. What this means, however, is that the "new" effort must be implemented by officials who are already busy with on-going activities and who may be reluctant to divert resources (time, money, manpower) away from the pursuit of organizational goals that will probably determine their prospects for promotion within the organization.[9] In addition, standard operating procedures (SOPs) constrain the choices made by government leaders attempting to "orchestrate" words and deeds in an "optimum" fashion:

At any given time, a government consists of *existing* organizations, each with a *fixed* set of SOP's and programs. The behavior of these organizations—and consequently of the government—relevant to an issue in any particular instance is, therefore, determined primarily by routines established prior to that instance.

To be sure, as Allison himself notes, government leaders can "trim the edges" of organizational outputs and can "exercise some choice in combining outputs"; still, even the most carefully conceived plans can be thwarted by factors as mundane as foul-ups in the field or bad weather.[10]

What this means, in short, is that a truly "orchestrated" effort is likely to be beyond the reach of a government like the one in Washington. To develop a powerful case in support of this proposition, one need only review the record of the Johnson Administration's efforts to coerce North Vietnam. As we saw in Chapters 2–3, the start of the air war in March 1965 was preceded by a 15-month-long effort by the Administration to intimidate the North Vietnamese by means of a campaign of covert pressures and threatening deployments in the Far East, along with a steady stream of threats and warnings aimed at Hanoi. Although Administration officials repeatedly called for an "orchestrated" effort that would provide "the maximum credible deterrent effect on Hanoi," what was actually done differed significantly from what was envisioned

8. On this point, see Allison, Chapter 3. For an excellent discussion of organizational goals in the context of the Vietnam conflict, see Gallucci, pp. 71–86.

9. At the same time, however, subordinate officials have strong incentives to paint a picture of "orchestratedness" in the reports that they pass to their superiors, both to enhance the reputation of their organization as a "can-do" outfit and to enhance their own reputations and career prospects as well. This point is discussed further in Chapter 8, below.

10. On these points, see Allison, pp. 68 (emphasis in original), 78–79.

in the planning papers circulating in Washington.[11] Instead of engaging in a single "orchestrated" effort, the Administration pursued three lines of policy at once—i.e., the covert war (OPLAN 34A), planning for (and warnings of) overt pressures against the North, and Lodge's "carrot and stick" approach—no one of which was implemented effectively. For example, despite the Krulak Committee's call for a covert program involving "substantial destruction, economic loss, and harassment" in North Vietnam (see Chapter 2, above), OPLAN 34A actually got off to a "slow beginning" resulting in few successful operations during Phase I (February–May). Thereafter, the program was hampered by a combination of incompetence in the field, indecision in Washington, and bad weather. Not only did most of the sabotage missions result in failure (witness the Saigon Embassy's admission that 80 percent of the sabotage teams were captured before they could make any progress on their mission—see Chapter 2, above), but proposed intensifications of the program were often rejected by Administration officials concerned about the possibility of escalation (which was ironic, since the purpose of the program was ostensibly to raise fears in Hanoi about American escalation). Thus, as a result of the mid-August "holding phase" and the mid-September incident in the Tonkin Gulf, most 34A operations were suspended, so that "little was accomplished during the remainder of August and the month of September 1964."[12] Similarly, while GVN maritime operations were supposed to be intensified in December 1964, the only new element in the program—"fire sweeps" along the DRV coast—was not approved by Washington; as a result, "the 34A program was, in effect, not intensified at all." Furthermore, as a result of bad weather, no maritime operations were successfully completed during the first three weeks of December 1964.[13]

In similar fashion, planning for overt pressures against the North ran afoul of the Administration's inability to agree on the kinds of pressures to be included in the program. Beginning with the squabbles between the JCS and State/ISA over how to implement the recommendations in NSAM-288 (see Chapter 2, above), the record throughout 1964 is one

11. The phrase "maximum credible deterrent effect" is taken from a Presidential directive dated February 20, 1964, quoted in III Gravel, p. 154. Only at one point during the 15-month-long effort to intimidate Hanoi did the Administration come close to developing an "orchestrated" campaign of words and deeds, i.e., during the week preceding the initial ROLLING THUNDER strike (see Chapter 3, above). The Administration's success, however, proved to be temporary at best; within a short period of time, the "orchestrated" effort had by and large collapsed. On this last point, see the discussion in Section II, below.

12. Document no. 225 in III Gravel, p. 606. See also III Gravel, p. 195; and Chapter 2, above.

13. On these points, see III Gravel, p. 253; and Chapter 2, above.

of an Administration unable to reach an internal consensus on virtually every major issue involved in a program of overt pressures—e.g., fast- versus slow-paced pressures, whether the program should be aimed at eroding DRV will or destroying DRV capabilities, and the targets to be struck (i.e., infiltration-related targets or industrial facilities and air fields). That senior Administration officials expected to be able to "orchestrate" a campaign of overt pressures against the North when they and their subordinates could not even agree on the kinds of pres- sures to be included in the campaign illustrates only too well the remoteness from reality that can blur the vision of those who inhabit the upper reaches of the foreign policy bureaucracy.

Finally, the Administration also tried its hand at Lodge's "carrot and stick" approach, although the Administration's implementation was notably lacking in both "carrots" and "sticks." Despite Lodge's call for a "salable package" involving the withdrawal of some American person- nel from South Vietnam, Lodge himself cynically observed that such a move "would not be a real concession on our part" (see Chapter 2, above). More importantly, Lodge's suggestion of providing aid to the DRV to help cope with food shortages could hardly have held much attraction to a leader like Le Duan, who, as we saw in Chapter 5, had scornfully attacked "certain communists" for their "fear of perilous revolutionary struggle" and for craving the comforts enjoyed by the Western bourgeoisie. Nor was there much "stick" in the Administra- tion's efforts. Not only did the Administration fail to retaliate in response to the attacks on Bien Hoa and the Brink BOQ, but it also quietly removed the remaining B-57 bombers from Bien Hoa during early November, after they had ostentatiously been brought in as a symbol of American power (see Chapter 2, above). One cannot help wondering who was intimidating whom.

But in addition to questioning the ability of governments to "orche- strate" words and deeds in an "optimum" fashion, there is a second and perhaps more important issue that merits our attention. That is, it was recognized by both the Johnson Administration's planners and the theorists of limited/coercive war that not all of the "messages" to be exchanged between the U.S. and an opponent like the DRV would take the form of oral communications, diplomatic notes, and the like. Instead, some of the most important "messages" would be conveyed through the *actions* taken by the United States. Schelling, for example, in discussing "The Idiom of Reprisal," noted that:

It seems that governments do feel obliged to make a pattern of their actions, to communicate with the deed as well as with words. In fact, there is probably no characteristic of limited war more striking than this, that one communicates by deed rather than words, or by deed in addition to words, and makes the actions form a pattern of communication in spite of the fact that each side is literate enough to understand what the other is saying. There is something here in the psychology of communication—in people's sense of proportion, of justice, of appropriateness, in the symbolic relation of a response to a provocation, in the pattern that is formed by a coherent set of actions—that goes beyond the abstract military relation between enemies, beyond the economics of cost and damage, beyond the words that are used to rationalize a set of actions. . . . There is an *idiom* in this interaction, a tendency to keep things in the same currency, to respond in the same language, to make the punishment fit the character of the crime, to impose a coherent pattern on relations.[14]

In similar fashion, Walt Rostow argued that "the threat that is implicit in initial U.S. actions would be more important than the military effect of the actions themselves."[15]

Suggestions such as these, however, much like proposals for "orchestrating" pressures against the North, raise serious questions, especially with respect to the ability of a government to do these sorts of things. Can governments really communicate by deed as well as by word? Can governments make their actions "form a *pattern* of communication"? Is there really an "idiom" of military action?[16] As we shall see, there are again good reasons for questioning the ability of a government to perform in the prescribed fashion.

One problem that governments are likely to encounter in attempting to communicate by deed as well as by word is that of simple foul-ups in the field. As we saw in Chapter 2, after one of the aircraft escorting a low-level reconnaissance mission over Laos was shot down by the Pathet Lao, U.S. jets were sent to attack the offending battery in an attempt to silence the Pathet Lao guns by demonstrating what the U.S. did when one of its planes was shot down. The only problem was that the retaliatory force, flying in bad weather, attacked the wrong installa-

14. Schelling (1966), pp. 146–147 (emphasis in original). See also Kaufmann, "Limited Warfare," in Kaufmann (ed.), pp. 113–114, 116; and Kahn (passim), whose whole book is about the way in which nations can use actions (e.g., escalation) to convey messages to an opponent.

15. Quoted in V Gravel, pp. 336–337. For other examples of this approach, see III Gravel, pp. 547, 562, 645–646.

16. Schelling (1966, p. 151) was aware of the possibility that governments might not be able to act in the desired fashion, but these potential problems were, again, downplayed in his work.

tion, thus necessitating a second attack in order to hit the "correct" target.

A second and closely related problem is that of unplanned coincidences. The Tonkin Gulf reprisal strikes, for example, were described by the Administration as a clear signal of what the U.S. would do if its ships were attacked in international waters, and later on were described by Schelling as an "expressive bit of repartee . . . an extreme case of articulate action."[17] And yet, as we saw in Chapter 2, the incidents in the Tonkin Gulf were considerably more complicated than either the Administration's explanations or Schelling's account would have us believe. The fact that the initial incident was *preceded* by an OPLAN 34A raid on two DRV coastal targets and by attacks on North Vietnamese border posts by Laotian aircraft (which were supplied and serviced by the U.S.), not to mention the fact that the second incident was also preceded by another OPLAN 34A raid on two DRV coastal targets (an attack in which the North Vietnamese assumed the U.S. destroyers were somehow involved), raises the very real question of who was responding to whom. Far from constituting an unprovoked attack on American ships on the high seas, it appears that the incidents in the Gulf of Tonkin constituted a North Vietnamese attempt to demonstrate what *they* would do if their territory was attacked.

Third, the sheer size of the government apparatus involved in an operation on the scale of the American attempt to intimidate Hanoi can easily result in breakdowns in coordination that may greatly complicate efforts to communicate by deed as well as by word. There are, after all, only so many hours in the day, and it would be unreasonable to expect the busy officials who sit at the top of the government hierarchy to monitor each and every act by subordinate officials. Unfortunately, however, failure to monitor can, in the extreme, result in an inadvertent "signal" that may undercut completely whatever message the leadership is trying to get across. Thus, for example, one suspects that, in the eyes of the North Vietnamese, the decision to withdraw the B-57s from Bien Hoa (see Chapter 2, above) spoke far more eloquently about what the U.S. would do when its forces were attacked than all the Administration's verbal threats and forward deployments combined.

Finally, the fact that governments are comprised of many large organizations, each of which is typically engaged in many activities at once, poses yet another problem for government leaders who wish to

---

17. Schelling (1966), pp. 140, 151.

communicate by deed as well as by word. Very simply, the sheer multitude of activities under way at any one point in time is likely to make it difficult, if not impossible, for the sender to draw the receiver's attention to whatever message the sender wants to emphasize. As Jervis notes:

> When people spend a great deal of time drawing up a plan or making a decision, they tend to think that the message about it they wish to convey will be clear to the receiver. Since they are aware of what to them is the important pattern in their actions, they often feel that the pattern will be equally obvious to others, and they overlook the degree to which the message is apparent to them only because they know what to look for.[18]

Thus, for example, when high-level Administration officials asked why the DRV had apparently failed to notice the start of a new program of bombing in Laos code-named BARREL ROLL, the DIA replied that the North Vietnamese apparently made no distinction between

> BARREL ROLL missions on the one hand and the Laotian T-28 strikes and YANKEE TEAM missions on the other. . . . It would be most difficult to distinguish between YANKEE TEAM with its flak suppression aircraft and BARREL ROLL missions. . . . While the Communists are apparently aware of some increased use of U.S. aircraft, they probably have not considered the BARREL ROLL strikes to date as a significant change in the pattern or representing a new threat to their activities.[19]

Similarly, the start of OPLAN 34A apparently was not seen by Hanoi as a new or threatening development for the simple reason that the CIA had been infiltrating sabotage teams into the North ever since 1961, so that Phase I of OPLAN 34A was probably viewed as a continuation of the older program (see Chapter 2, above).

On the basis of what we have seen so far, one conclusion seems obvious: senior officials should be wary, to say the least, of plans that call for "orchestrating" the activities of many agencies or that hinge on the ability to embody precise and specific messages in the actions taken by their government. And yet, there is one final point that needs to be made here. All of the examples used to this point were taken from 1964, *before* the start of the air war (when the ability to "orchestrate" and "signal" by deed as well as by word would presumably be crucial to the effort to negotiate the best possible settlement). Despite the errors and

18. Robert Jervis, "Hypotheses on Misperception," *World Politics*, 20 (1968), 474. See also Charles Hermann and Linda Brady, "Alternative Models of International Crisis Behavior," in Hermann (ed.), p. 286.

19. Quoted in III Gravel, p. 254. See also Westmoreland, p. 110; and Chapter 2, above.

breakdowns catalogued above, Administration officials continued to speak and write of the need to "orchestrate" words and deeds and to use actions to communicate specific messages to Hanoi. Nowhere were these tendencies better illustrated than in the post-Pleiku recommendations by Maxwell Taylor and McGeorge Bundy. Taylor, for example, advocated a

gradual, *orchestrated* acceleration of tempo measured in terms of frequency, size, number, and/or geographical location of the reprisal strikes and of related activities such as BARREL ROLL and 34A. An upward trend in any or all of these forms of intensity will convey *signals* which, in combination, should present to the DRV leaders a *vision* of inevitable, ultimate destruction if they do not change their ways.

Similarly, Bundy argued that

it is of great importance that the level of reprisal be adjusted rapidly and visibly to both upward and downward shifts in the level of Viet Cong offenses. We want to keep before Hanoi the carrot of our desisting as well as the stick of continued pressure. We also need to conduct the application of the force so that there is always a prospect of worse to come.[20]

One should not underestimate the capability of high-level officials for self-delusion.

But perhaps this is too pessimistic a view. There was, as mentioned at the end of Chapter 5, some ambiguous evidence that the DRV might have been seeking an exit from the war in the face of mounting American pressures. Specifically, there were those four instances of apparent DRV readiness to negotiate—namely, the XYZ, PINTA, MARIGOLD, and SUNFLOWER contacts—as well as the eventual DRV decision to "pay a price" (albeit a modest one) for a bombing cessation and to engage in the Paris peace talks. How should we interpret these episodes? Should they be viewed as evidence that the Administration's policies were having the desired effect? Or, since none of them resulted in the kind of settlement envisioned by the Administration in 1964–1965, do they signify the failure of the Administration's policies?

II. "Negotiating" by Word and Deed:
March 1965–May 1968

While the problems encountered by the Administration during its 15-month-long effort to intimidate Hanoi were not the sort to be taken

20. Quoted in III Gravel, pp. 316 (emphasis added), 314.

lightly, their significance would almost certainly have declined in the eyes of historians if the Administration had succeeded in achieving its goals once the air war began. In this respect, though, the start of the air war did *not* result in any magical transformation with respect to the Administration's ability to "orchestrate" words and deeds and to "signal" by deed as well as by word. Instead, the Administration continued to encounter problems much like those described in the preceding section.

Nowhere were these problems more apparent than in the conduct of the air war. As we saw in Chapter 3 and also in the preceding section, there was no shortage of suggestions on how the air war should be conducted; indeed, the memos and cables prepared by Taylor, McNaughton, McGeorge and William Bundy, and the JCS were filled with prescriptive statements concerning the nature and timing of the air strikes. While there were significant differences of opinion between civilian and military officials and also among civilians concerning the targets to be struck and the objectives to be pursued, civilian officials were virtually unanimous in the belief that the air war should be based on the concept of "graduated pressures," whereby the frequency and intensity of the air strikes, as well as the importance of the targets struck, would be gradually increased for each week that the North Vietnamese refused to negotiate an acceptable settlement. It was hoped by Administration planners that the North Vietnamese would realize what was happening to them relatively early in the process and would thus agree to negotiate (on the Administration's terms) before the pressures became too intense, so as to preserve their meager industrial base.

As things turned out, however, the bombing program conducted by the Administration differed significantly from the program envisioned in the cables and planning papers drafted by officials in Washington and Saigon. Despite suggestions to reporters that the attacks would be "intensified geographically by a choice of targets progressively closer to the North Vietnamese capital,"[21] the first two months of ROLLING THUNDER very likely conveyed confusing and misleading "signals" to officials in Hanoi (see Table 4). Instead of a relentless progression northward in the direction of Hanoi and Haiphong, the air strikes jumped around in seemingly random fashion from strikes against targets relatively close to Hanoi to strikes against targets quite close to the DMZ. Nor was there a consistent upward pattern in the intensity of the strikes, measured either by the number of sorties flown on a given day or by the sensitivity of the targets struck. And, while the frequency of

21. See Max Frankel, "Administration Steps Up Pressure to Force Aid Cut to Guerrillas," *New York Times*, March 16, 1965, pp. 1, 3.

Table 4
The Air War Begins: ROLLING THUNDER 5–12 [a]

Series	Targets	Approximate location [b]	Date struck	Approximate number of sorties
ROLLING THUNDER 5	Xom Bang ammo depot Quang Khe naval base	35 miles north of DMZ [c] 235 miles south of Hanoi	March 2, 1965	104 U.S. aircraft 19 VNAF A-1s [d] plus U.S. flak suppression [e]
ROLLING THUNDER 6	Tiger Island barracks Phu Qui ammo depot	20 miles off DRV coast, 290 miles south of Hanoi 100 miles SW of Hanoi	March 14 March 15	24 VNAF A-1s plus U.S. flak suppression More than 100 U.S. aircraft
ROLLING THUNDER 7	Phuvan and Vinhson ammo and supply depots Vu Con barracks	155 and 220 miles south of Hanoi 15 miles north of DMZ	March 19 March 21	More than 120 U.S. aircraft VNAF A-1s plus U.S. flak suppression
	Armed reconnaissance plus Vinhson radar	60 miles north of DMZ	March 22	8 U.S. F-105s
	Armed reconnaissance plus Bubinh radar	10 miles north of DMZ	March 23	8 VNAF A-1s
	Armed reconnaissance (Quang Khe harbor plus Phuxa radar)	235 miles south of Hanoi	March 24	8 VNAF A-1s plus U.S. flak suppression
ROLLING THUNDER 8	Bachlong Island radar Ha Tinh radar Cap Mui Ron radar Vinhson radar	120 miles SE of Hanoi 185 miles south of Hanoi 205 miles south of Hanoi 220 miles south of Hanoi	March 26	Unknown

Table 4 (Continued)

Series	Targets	Approximate location[b]	Date struck	Approximate number of sorties
	Bachlong Island radar	120 miles SE of Hanoi	March 29	42 U.S. Navy jets plus 12 flak suppression
	Donghoi airfield	250 miles south of Hanoi	March 30	24 VNAF A-1s plus 15 U.S. flak suppression
	Radar sites at:			
	Hon Matt	155 miles south of Hanoi		30 U.S. F-105s
	Chu Lao	160 miles south of Hanoi		12 U.S. F-100s
	Hon Nieu	155 miles south of Hanoi	March 31	20 VNAF A-1s
	Ha Tinh	185 miles south of Hanoi		
	Vinhson	220 miles south of Hanoi		More than 50 U.S. Navy jets
	Cap Mui Ron	205 miles south of Hanoi		
ROLLING THUNDER 9	Dong Phuong bridge	65 miles south of Hanoi	April 3	30 U.S. Navy jets—morning, 30 U.S. Navy jets—afternoon
	Thanh Hoa bridge	72 miles south of Hanoi		50 USAF jets[f]
	Thanh Hoa bridge and power plant	72 miles south of Hanoi		Unknown
	Dong Hoi bridge	250 miles south of Hanoi	April 4	23 VNAF A-1s plus 16 U.S. flak suppression
	Two armed reconnaissance missions near Thanh Hoa	85 miles south of Hanoi		45 U.S. Navy A-1s and A-4s

Target/Mission	Date	Location	Forces
Armed reconnaissance		Central North Vietnam	10 U.S. F-105s plus 6 flak suppression and CAP
Vinh Linh radar	April 5	250 miles south of Hanoi	30 U.S. Navy jets plus 20 F-8 and F-4 flak suppression and CAP
Armed reconnaissance (Rte. 1 from DMZ to Vinh)	April 7	Roughly 165 miles south of Hanoi at point of closest approach	35 U.S. Navy jets
ROLLING THUNDER 10 — Tamda highway bridge	April 9	120 miles south of Hanoi	70 U.S. Navy A-1s and A-4s (morning); 70 U.S. Navy aircraft plus flak suppression and CAP (afternoon) 50 USAF F-105s
Qui Vinh RR bridge / Khe Khien highway bridge / Kim Chuong bridge		110 miles south of Hanoi / 150 miles south of Hanoi	35 U.S. Navy A-1s, A-4s, 40 F-4s, F-8s, 40 USAF F-105s
Two armed reconnaissance missions	April 10	Rtes. 7 and 8, 120 miles north of DMZ	
Thanhyen highway bridge	April 13	235 miles south of Hanoi	8 VNAF A-1s, 8 U.S. F-100s; 12 F-100s and F-101s for flak suppression and CAP
Hon Matt radar and Cualo River radar		155 and 130 miles south of Hanoi	15 F-105s plus 25 F-100s, F-101s flak suppression and CAP
Hon Matt radar and Cualo River radar	April 14[g]	155 and 130 miles south of Hanoi	30 USAF jets
Night armed reconnaissance[h]		Not specified	6 A-4s and 6 F-8s
Night armed reconnaissance		Not specified	VNAF A-1s

Table 4 (Continued)

Series	Targets	Approximate location[b]	Date struck	Approximate number of sorties
	Armed reconnaissance[i]	Rtes. 7 and 8, 120 miles SW of Hanoi	April 15	6 F-105s plus 15 flak suppression and CAP
	Night armed reconnaissance	DRV coast and Rte. 1 from DMZ to Vinh (165 miles south of Hanoi)		4 VNAF A-1s
ROLLING THUNDER 11	Road and RR bridges near Phudienchau	150 miles south of Hanoi	April 16	35 F-105s plus 35 flak suppression and CAP
	Xomcatrang bridge and Baiduethon bridge	185 and 170 miles south of Hanoi (both hit twice on same day)		U.S. Navy jets
	Armed reconnaissance—Mugia Pass	Near Laotian border, roughly 185 miles from Hanoi	April 17[j]	12 USAF F-105s and 30 flak suppression and CAP
	Armed reconnaissance—railroad boxcars	Not specified		More than 20 U.S. Navy jets
	Armed reconnaissance[k]	To within 60 miles of Hanoi		2 U.S. Navy A-1s
	Armed reconnaissance	Rte. 1 to 60 miles north of DMZ	April 18	4 A-4s plus 10 F-8s and A-1s
	Armed reconnaissance	Rte. 1 to 60 miles north of DMZ		3 A-4s
	Armed reconnaissance	Not specified		4 A-4s
	Armed reconnaissance	145 miles south of Hanoi	April 19[l]	A-4s
	Armed reconnaissance	165–185 miles south of Hanoi		8 VNAF A-1s
	Armed reconnaissance	Rte. 1 to 65 miles north of DMZ		4 VNAF A-1s
	Armed reconnaissance	Rtes. 8 and 12		Not specified
	Armed reconnaissance	Rte. 1	April 20	U.S. Navy A-1s
	Armed reconnaissance	Rte. 1, Vinh to 20th Parallel		5 U.S. Navy planes
	My Duc highway bridge	270 miles south of Hanoi		15 USAF and VNAF

Mission/Target	Location	Date	Aircraft
Night armed reconnaissance	Rte. 1 south of Donghoi (250 miles south of Hanoi)		2 U.S. Navy A-4s
Night armed reconnaissance	Rte. 1 south of Donghoi		4 U.S. jets
Armed reconnaissance	Rte. 1 south of Donghoi	April 21	4 VNAF A-1s plus 10 USAF planes
Armed reconnaissance	Not specified		4 VNAF A-1s
Armed reconnaissance	Rtes. 8 and 12 near Mugia Pass (185 miles from Hanoi)		15 USAF jets plus 20 flak suppression and CAP
Night armed reconnaissance	Rte. 15, 135 miles south of Hanoi		2 U.S. Navy A-1s
Night reconnaissance	Rtes. 15 and 1		U.S. Navy A-1s and A-4s
My Duc highway bridge	270 miles south of Hanoi		VNAF A-1s
Baiduethon bridge	180 miles south of Hanoi	April 22	8 USAF F-105s
Vinh antiaircraft	165 miles south of Hanoi		Not specified
Barracks near Mugia Pass	185 miles from Hanoi		Not specified
Armed reconnaissance	165 miles from Hanoi		10 U.S. Navy A-4s and 8 F-8s
ROLLING THUNDER 12 — Xuanson ferry	270 miles south of Hanoi		VNAF A-1s
Phu Qui ferry	90 miles SW of Hanoi		40 USAF F-105s, 4 A-1s[m]
Phucthiem bridge	120 miles south of Hanoi		
Ly Nhan bridge	110 miles south of Hanoi		
Phoson bridge	150 miles south of Hanoi	April 23	
Xomphuong bridges (2)	245 miles south of Hanoi		
Xomgia bridge	150 miles south of Hanoi		
Sondinh highway bridge	across Kiem River		
Armed reconnaissance	Rtes. 7, 8, 12		
Komthaixa highway bridge, Vinhson ferry	135 miles south of Hanoi	April 24	6 U.S. B-57s; 35 USAF F-105s plus 25 flak suppression and CAP
Antiaircraft sites and bridges (4 raids)	Not specified	April 25	Not specified

Table 4 (Continued)

Series	Targets	Approximate location[b]	Date struck	Approximate number of sorties
	Songgiang River patrol boat	160 miles south of Hanoi	April 26	Not specified[n]
	Highway bridge	100 miles south of Hanoi		
	Baiduethon bridge	180 miles south of Hanoi		
	Armed reconnaissance (4 missions)	Not specified		
	Huu Hung ferry	270 miles south of Hanoi	April 27	4 VNAF A-1s
	Baiduethon bridge	180 miles south of Hanoi		8 U.S. jets plus 25 flak suppression and CAP
	Quang Khe naval base	235 miles south of Hanoi	April 28	U.S. Navy A-4s
	Bridges, ferries, boats	Not specified		Not specified
	Ron ferry	220 miles south of Hanoi	April 29	VNAF A-1s
	Phovin and Phuongcan bridges	200 miles south of Hanoi		2 U.S. Navy A-4s and 2 F-8s

Sources: The data presented in Table 4 were drawn primarily from the *New York Times'* coverage of the air war, supplemented by III Gravel (especially pp. 284–286); Simons, "The Vietnam Intervention, 1964–1965," in George, Hall, and Simons; and Baggs.

a. ROLLING THUNDER 1 was aborted because of the February 19 coup attempt in Saigon; ROLLING THUNDER 2–4 were aborted because of bad weather over North Vietnam.

b. Distances expressed in statute miles.

c. Distance between DMZ and Hanoi is roughly 300 statute miles.

d. Propeller-driven aircraft.

e. The *New York Times,* March 3, 1965, reported that a total of 160 U.S. and VNAF planes were involved in these raids.

f. The *New York Times,* April 4, 1965, reported that at least 130 U.S. aircraft were over North Vietnam at some time on April 3.

g. Missions on this date also included a drop of propaganda leaflets over Donghoi, Hatinh, Vinh, and Thanh Hoa by 4 U.S. F-100s.

h. No targets were spotted and no bombs dropped.

i. U.S. Navy carrier aircraft were diverted to strikes in South Vietnam.

j. Also included on this date was a VNAF leaflet mission over Donghoi.

k. No targets spotted.

l. Also included was a leaflet mission by 8 U.S. F-8s over Vinh, Hatien, and Thanh Hoa.

m. The *New York Times,* April 24, 1965, reported that more than 200 U.S. and VNAF planes were involved in the bridge and ferry raids of April 23.

n. The *New York Times,* April 27, 1965, reported that many of these missions were flown by flights of 2–4 aircraft unaccompanied by supporting aircraft.

the air strikes gradually increased until, beginning with ROLLING THUNDER 11, strikes were launched on a 7-day per week basis, the effect of the increase was almost certainly diluted by the practice of bunching each week's fixed target strikes near the start of the week, leaving the rest of the week to the more mundane (and widely scattered) armed reconnaissance missions flown usually by flights of two-to-four planes each.[22] In view of the erratic fashion in which the air war was begun, is it any wonder, as an Army brigadier general noted in explaining why *The Pentagon Papers* should not have been declassified, that "one of the aspects of the bombing war with which the North Vietnamese seemed particularly puzzled was the tempo, the why, why things came the way they did, when they did"?[23]

Although, as we saw in Chapter 3, the anti-infiltration program that began with ROLLING THUNDER 9 very likely had the effect of "signalling" Hanoi that the bombing would be confined (at least for a while) to the southern DRV, a strong case could nonetheless be made for marshaling the available air assets for an attack on the infiltration routes despite the unfortunate "signals" that resulted from such a campaign.[24] The Administration, as we saw, was deeply concerned with the rapidly deteriorating situation in the South and with the possibility of a GVN/ARVN collapse before the air war could "persuade" officials in Hanoi that the costs of continuing their role in the war would exceed any benefits they might derive. Further, if the decision should be to introduce large numbers of American troops into South Vietnam in an attempt to stem the tide (an issue that the Administration was clearly grappling with in April 1965), it would make a great deal of sense to concentrate the air strikes on the infiltration routes in an attempt to reduce

22. On the practice of "bunching" fixed target strikes near the start of each new ROLLING THUNDER series, see Table 4; and Gallucci, p. 83. The result of this tendency was very likely to muddle even further any efforts to transmit "signals" to Hanoi. On April 30, 1965, for example, ROLLING THUNDER 13 began with an attack by thirty-nine U.S. Navy planes on the Thien-linhdung army depot, only 85 miles south of Hanoi. The effect of this attack, however, was almost certainly diminished by the events of the next two days: no strikes were launched on May 1, and the strikes on May 2 consisted of an attack on a railroad siding 100 miles south of Hanoi by four Navy jets (these points are based on the *New York Times*' coverage of the air war).

23. Brigadier General Paul Gorman, Ellsberg Trial Transcript, p. 11,512. Gorman's argument was that access to the Pentagon study would have helped the North Vietnamese understand why the bombing was being conducted as it was, certainly an ironic position since the whole strategy of "graduated pressures" constituted an elaborate effort to make the North Vietnamese understand what they were in for if they did not comply with American demands.

24. In this respect, it should be kept in mind that confining the air strikes to the southern DRV very likely reinforced the belief in Hanoi, reported by Seaborn (see Chapter 3, above), that the bombing was a limited measure intended to strengthen the U.S. bargaining position prior to an international conference which the U.S. was seeking in order to gain a face-saving exit from the war.

the flow of men and supplies to DRV/VC forces in the South, thus hopefully reducing the casualties they could inflict on American forces.

And yet, the coincidence between the Administration's deepening concern over the situation in the South and the anti-infiltration campaign that began with ROLLING THUNDER 9 should not be taken as proof that the Administration had finally been able to overcome the problems that had plagued the 15-month-long effort to intimidate Hanoi (see Section I, above). Instead, disagreements over the goals to be pursued through the bombing, breakdowns of coordination, and foul-ups in the field continued to exert a significant influence over the conduct of the air war. For example, as we saw in Chapter 3, NSAM-328 (the product of a Washington policy review on April 1-2, 1965) had specified that, to minimize the risks of escalation, "target systems should continue to avoid the effective GCI (Ground Controlled Intercept) range of MIGs," which in effect meant that the air strikes should be confined to the southern DRV, since the DRV's few MIG aircraft and associated radar facilities were based mainly in the northern part of the country.[25] And yet, less than seventy-two hours after this decision was made, DRV MIGs operating under radar guidance scored their first two "kills" of the war, surprising two bomb-laden F-105s involved in the "bridge raids" of early April (see Chapter 3, above).[26] Less than a week after that incident, U.S. jets on a combat air patrol mission clashed with unidentified MIGs while flying over what the U.S. mission in Saigon labeled the coastal waters of Hainan Island. Although Pentagon spokesmen insisted that the MIGs were unidentified, press reports from Peking, Saigon, and Washington strongly suggested that the MIGs were

25. NSAM-328, which was not circulated until April 6 although the decisions that it records were made on April 1, is reprinted as Document no. 254 in III Gravel, pp. 702-703. The emphasis on avoiding air combat with DRV MIGs stemmed from a desire to minimize the pressures to "take out" the MIG airfields, an action that, it was feared, would result in the stationing of DRV MIGs in China, which, in turn, would greatly increase the risk of war with China. Curiously, though, Administration officials had explained to reporters that the March 15 attack on Phuqui, which was roughly 100 miles from Hanoi and thus within the range of DRV MIGs, had been intended to signal a willingness to take on the MIGs if necessary. On this point, see Max Frankel, "Administration Steps Up Pressure to Force Aid Cut to Guerrillas," New York Times, March 16, 1965, pp. 1, 3.

26. There was a combat air patrol, which was supposed to guard against attacks from hostile MIGs, accompanying U.S. fighter-bombers on these raids, but for some unexplained reason the CAP aircraft were too far to the north to be of any help. Similarly, as explained by officials in Washington, the "bridge raids" took place in an area beyond U.S. radar control, thus requiring U.S. pilots to rely on visual observation of enemy planes; the MIGs, in contrast, operating under radar guidance, were able to operate through heavy cloud banks, thus enabling them to surprise the F-105s. On these points, see Jack Langguth, "Hanoi MIGs Down Two American Jets in First Air Clash," and the AP dispatch, "Bomb Loads Slowed F-105s," both in the New York Times, April 5, 1965, pp. 1, 15.

Chinese and that the clash took place over Hainan rather than near it.[27]

It is difficult to imagine an outcome more at variance with the wishes of high-ranking officials than the Hainan Island air battle. Having specified that they wished U.S. aircraft to avoid combat with DRV MIGs so as to reduce the risks of escalation, not only were U.S. jets quickly embroiled in clashes with the very planes they were supposed to avoid but also with the aircraft of an opponent the Administration was very much fearful of provoking—i.e., China. But while one might hope that the Hainan incident would have sensitized high-level officials to the problems inherent in seeking to control the activities of large organizations by means of generalized directives, additional evidence suggesting that the lesson had not been learned emerged less than a month after the clash over Hainan. At the Honolulu Conference on April 20, as we saw in Chapter 3, it was decided that the DRV was unlikely to be "persuaded" by the bombing until DRV/VC forces in the South had been stymied in their drive to overwhelm the GVN and ARVN. In line with that judgment, the conferees agreed that the air war over the North should be plateaued at its current level and that missions in the South should have first call on U.S. air assets in the area. Furthermore, in the aftermath of the Honolulu Conference, both Secretary Rusk and Secretary McNamara stated publicly that the primary objective of the air war was to interdict the flow of men and supplies to DRV/VC forces in the South.[28]

And yet, there are reasons for doubting that the decisions made at Honolulu had much influence over the conduct of the war. For one thing, there is no evidence that the air war over the North was "plateaued" in line with the consensus at Honolulu; instead, it was in the second and third quarters of 1965 that the air war over the North rapidly gathered momentum as the restraints that inhibited the air strikes during February and March were discarded.[29] Furthermore,

27. On the Hainan Island clash, see the Reuters dispatch from Peking, "Peking Reports Hainan Airfight with U.S. Planes"; Jack Langguth, "One MIG Seen on Fire"; and John W. Finney, "U.S. Unsure on MIGs," all in the *New York Times*, April 10, 1965, pp. 1, 3. See also Jack Langguth, "U.S. Jets Wreck Bridge in North," *New York Times*, April 11, 1965, pp. 1, 6; and "Two on Navy Jet Lost in Friday MIG Clash," *New York Times*, April 12, 1965, p. 2.

28. In this respect, see the statements by Rusk and McNamara quoted in III Gravel, p. 360; and IV Gravel, pp. 31–32.

29. The Pentagon analyst, for example, noted that "combined U.S.-VNAF combat sorties [over the North] totalled about 3600 in April, 4000 in May, and 4800 in June" (III Gravel, p. 384); see also the quarterly figures on U.S. fighter-bomber sorties over the North presented in Littauer and Uphoff (eds.), p. 274.

there is very little evidence that planes and pilots were diverted to targets in South Vietnam. Instead, the major outcome of the decision to attach more importance to strikes against targets in South Vietnam appears to have been a decision to use B-52 aircraft against Viet Cong strongholds in the South.[30] Finally, despite the importance attached by Administration officials to impeding infiltration, it was in the aftermath of the Honolulu Conference that the interdiction rationale began to crumble. Rather than directing that an all-out effort be made to hit the infiltration routes, the President, as we saw in Chapter 3, moved instead to lay the groundwork for much more extensive air strikes against the North by scheduling a brief bombing pause during May 1965, followed by a persistent pattern of doling out "lucrative" targets to the military at a rate of one or two per new ROLLING THUNDER series.[31]

The events of the first three months of the air war, in short, provide additional support for the assertion in the preceding section that a truly "orchestrated" effort is likely to be beyond the reach of a government such as the one in Washington. But there are still two important questions that our discussion has so far left unanswered. In particular, if the Administration was unable to devise a coherent strategy linking the air strikes against the North with its efforts to contain the spread of the insurgency in the South, how well would it cope with the potentially more complex issue of the proper relationship between military moves and diplomatic initiatives? And, if the Administration was to encounter problems in attempting to "'negotiate' by an optimum combination of words and deeds," what would their consequences be for the effort to arrange an acceptable settlement? In order to answer questions such as these, we need to look more closely at the problems that arose once the air war was under way.

For example, during the 37-day bombing pause that began on December 24, 1965, even though the Administration let it be known that it was watching carefully for signs of DRV reciprocity in the ground war (a fact conveyed to the North Vietnamese both by Byroade in Rangoon

30. On these points, see Jack Langguth, "U.S. Navy Planes Sent Out on Raids Against Vietcong," New York Times, May 3, 1965, p. 1 (which reports that U.S. Navy A-1s and A-4s flew thirty-eight sorties against targets in South Vietnam on May 1, 1965); and III Gravel, pp. 383–384. In fairness, though, it should be noted that ROLLING THUNDER missions constituted only 30 percent of the U.S. air effort in Southeast Asia in 1965, thus suggesting that substantial numbers of aircraft were employed against targets in the South (see IV Gravel, p. 30).

31. The documents available are admittedly vague concerning the President's reaction to the recommendations agreed on by his chief advisers at Honolulu, although there is no evidence whatsoever of Presidential disagreement with the recommendations concerning the air war.

and by stories planted with journalists in Washington), the American military command was aggressively pushing ahead with search and destroy operations in the South, not to mention the 8,500 additional U.S. troops that entered South Vietnam during this period—developments that Vu Huu Binh was quick to point to as evidence of American "insincerity."[32] Similarly, in December 1966, at a time when the U.S. was engaged in a delicate effort to open direct talks with the DRV in Warsaw, the military commands responsible for the air war took advantage of a clearing in the weather over Hanoi to launch some of the fiercest attacks of the war on that city, a move that effectively destroyed whatever chance there might have been for the Warsaw talks to materialize (see Chapter 4, above). In similar fashion, an April 1967 State Department proposal to restore and enlarge the DMZ coincided with (and was effectively negated by) attacks on the Haiphong power plant, while an August 1967 appeal for visas to Hanoi by Aubrac and Marcovich coincided with an all-out aerial assault first on Hanoi and then on Haiphong, a move that provided the North Vietnamese with a convenient excuse for denying the desired visas. In assessing the outcome of the April 1967 fiasco, Chester Cooper noted that:

The American bombing during the same 24-hour period in which we launched a major new negotiations approach did not stem from a conscious high-level decision to sabotage the efforts of the peacemakers. Nor was it a "carrot/stick" attempt to signal Hanoi that, even though we were making a new diplomatic initiative, the pressure was still on. Either of these would at least have had the merit of reflecting some thinking on the subject at high levels of the government. But there was none at this point in time; instead, there was inertia, lethargy, and a reluctance "to upset the President." There was just no interest or effort expended in orchestrating military and diplomatic moves; everyone was just doing his own thing.[33]

What these four cases suggest is that, just as in the cases of the 15-month-long effort to intimidate Hanoi and the start of the air war, there was relatively little in the way of careful coordination of military moves with diplomatic initiatives. Significantly, though, in contrast to the Administration's efforts to step up the pressures on North Vietnam during 1964 and the first half of 1965, a situation in which there was serious disagreement both over the ends to be pursued and the means to

32. On these points, see Pinta Chronology, p. 9; and Chapter 3, above.
33. Cooper (1972), p. 447. For background on the April and August 1967 fiascoes, see Chapter 4, above.

be used in pressuring the North, everyone in the Administration was agreed on the importance of coordinating military moves with diplomatic initiatives once the air war had begun in earnest. And yet, what was notable in the four cases described above was the apparent absence of central control over the agencies charged with implementing the decisions of high-level officials. How can we account for this outcome? Where were the Secretaries and Undersecretaries, who were supposedly responsible for the task of "orchestration"? More importantly, what was the role of the President in the instances described above? In light of the repeated emphasis on "orchestrating" words and deeds, surely there must have been someone running the show.

In actuality, someone *was* running the show, although not in the fashion envisioned during the planning of 1964. Part of the problem, it must be conceded, was simply bad judgment. In the case of the MARIGOLD fiasco, as we saw in Chapter 4, the President, after meeting with his senior military advisers on December 6, 1966, decided to leave ROLLING THUNDER 52 unchanged despite Polish warnings that the Hanoi-area bombings of December 2 and 4 had jeopardized the contact, thus clearing the way for the renewed bombings of December 13–14 and the breakdown of the contact. Similarly, in the case of the coincidence between the 37-day bombing pause and the stepped-up ground operations in South Vietnam, no one familiar with the workings of large bureaucratic organizations would be surprised that responsibility for military moves and diplomatic initiatives was in the hands of separate groups of officials. As Allison notes, the parceling out of different aspects of a problem to different organizational subunits "permits more specialized attention to particular facets of problems than would be possible if government leaders tried to cope with the problems by themselves."[34]

But to call attention to factors such as bad judgment and breakdowns of coordination is really to raise a deeper and more important issue. Was the Administration's failure to do a better job of "orchestrating" words and deeds exclusively or even largely the result of insensitivity on the part of the President to the requirements of successful "orchestration" and/or insufficient efforts by senior officials to insure that the left hand of government did not undermine whatever the right hand was doing? Or was there a deeper, more intractable problem underlying the absence of meaningful "orchestration"? A careful examination of three of the cases cited above suggests the latter conclusion.

34. Allison, p. 80.

In the case of the 37-day bombing pause, the evidence available is devoid of any indication that high-ranking officials were seriously concerned about the impact that events in the ground war in the South might have on the Administration's diplomatic initiatives in Rangoon and elsewhere. Instead, just as in the period from December 1963 to February 1965, when the Administration pursued three lines of policy at once (i.e., the covert war, planning for overt pressures against the North, and Lodge's "carrot and stick" approach), the 37-day bombing pause suggests that the Administration had come to regard the military and diplomatic aspects of the conflict as separate and distinct policy tracks with little or no coordination between them. Responsibility for the military aspects of the war and for the handling of diplomatic initiatives was entrusted to separate groups of officials: the military commands in Washington (the JCS), Honolulu (CINCPAC), and Southeast Asia (MACV, the 7th Air Force, and Naval Task Force 77) on the one hand, and a small group of officials drawn primarily from the State Department and the White House staff on the other—with each group so preoccupied with its own aspect of the conflict that there was little in the way of meaningful communication between them.[35]

Similarly, consider the sequence of events immediately preceding the Aubrac/Marcovich appeal for visas. As we saw in Chapter 4, the President approved on August 9, 1967 an addendum to ROLLING THUNDER 57 authorizing attacks on sixteen additional fixed targets (six of which were in the 10-mile circle around Hanoi) as well as an expansion of armed reconnaissance—a move intended to steal the thunder from the Stennis Committee hearings on the air war. With that decision out of the way, the President then turned to problems of diplomacy, approving on August 11 the message that was to be carried to Hanoi by Aubrac and Marcovich. While the evidence is by no means conclusive, it at least gives the appearance of a President dealing separately with different aspects of the same problem rather than attempting to deal with both at once.

The inference that military and diplomatic aspects of the war were dealt with separately rather than simultaneously is strengthened if we reexamine the pattern of decision-making on the war during early 1967 (see Table 5). On the basis of the data in Table 5, it appears that, during early 1967 at least, senior officials (especially the President) did not attempt to "orchestrate" words and deeds by focusing on both military

35. On this division of labor, see Cooper (1972), pp. 343–485 (especially p. 447); and Kraslow and Loory, pp. 43–54.

Table 5
Alternation of Phases in Administration Decision-Making, December 1966–April 1967

Phase	Begins*	Ends*	Main events	For additional details**:
Diplomacy	December 22, 1966	February 12, 1967	Hanoi-area prohibited zone established—December 22. Salisbury interview with Pham Van Dong—January 2 Guthrie-Le Chang contacts begin in Moscow—January 10. Tet truce; Wilson-Kosygin meetings in London—February 6–12. Johnson letter to Ho Chi Minh—February 8.	See Chapter 4, Sections I-A, I-B, above.
Escalation	February 13, 1967	March 10, 1967	Bombing of North Vietnam resumed—February 13. Ho's reply to Johnson—February 15. "Shopping list" of military options sent to President—February 21. President approves limited escalation of U.S. effort—February 22. U.S. artillery begins firing over DMZ into North Vietnam—February 24. Mining of some DRV internal waterways begins—February 27. Thai Nguyen Iron and Steel Mill bombed—March 10.	See Chapter 4, Sections I-B, I-C, above.

Diplomacy	March 11, 1967	March 17, 1967	Ambassador Thompson instructed to seek appointment with DRV counterpart—March 11. Thompson demurs—March 13. U.S. Embassy contacts DRV Embassy—March 16.	See Chapter 4, Section I-C, above.
Escalation	March 18, 1967	April 4, 1967	Westmoreland requests 200,000 more troops—March 18. North Vietnamese refuse to see Thompson—March 21. Haiphong power plants added to authorized list—March 22.	See Chapter 4, Section I-C, above.
Diplomacy	April 5, 1967	April 7, 1967	Embassy Moscow told to deliver new Johnson letter to Ho—April 5. Letter returned—April 6.	See Chapter 4, Section I-C, above.
Escalation	April 8, 1967	April 9, 1967	ROLLING THUNDER 55 approved; Hanoi/Haiphong targets added—April 8.	See Chapter 4, Section I-C, above.
Diplomacy	April 10, 1967		Embassy Moscow told to express interest in meeting with Pham Van Dong—April 10. State Department DMZ proposal—April 19. Haiphong power plants hit—April 20. DMZ proposal rejected—April 22.	See Chapter 4, Section I-C, above.

*Dates listed should be considered as the approximate starting and ending points of each phase.

**See also IV Gravel, pp. 8–10, 285–286.

and diplomatic activities at the same time. Instead, it appears that these officials dealt with military and diplomatic activities in sequential fashion—i.e., making decisions first on escalation and then on diplomacy, then back to escalation, and so on. Not only are the data in Table 5 consistent with the interpretation placed above on the Administration's handling of decisions on war and peace during the 37-day bombing pause and during early August 1967, but they also present a pattern of decision-making remarkably similar to the alternation of "hawkish" and "dovish" phases identified in Table 3. Viewed from this perspective, the data in Table 3 also suggest a pattern of sequential attention to different aspects of the same problem—i.e., intimidating Hanoi while attempting to present an image of moderation and restraint to the electorate. The fact that so much of our evidence points in the same direction, moreover, suggests the existence of a persistent and fundamental pattern of decision-making.[36]

But while this process of breaking problems down into their component parts may ease the difficulties that senior officials face in dealing with a complex environment, such a style of decision-making inevitably carries with it serious risks, principally because of the time lags involved in implementing Presidential decisions. To put this another way, while the military and diplomatic aspects of wartime policy could be dealt with separately by the President, no such disaggregation was possible when it came to implementing his decisions. Instead, what apparently happened was that, as each decision or set of decisions was made by the President, it would be passed to organizational subunits for implementation (e.g., the military commands in the Far East, the U.S. embassies in Moscow, London, Rangoon, etc.). These organizational subunits, however, had considerable discretion as to the timing of implementation—e.g., once a target was added to the ROLLING THUNDER authorized list, field commanders were by and large free to strike that target at any time, depending on weather conditions, the availability of planes and pilots, etc. But while granting this kind of leeway to subordinate

36. On this phenomenon of sequential attention to goals, see Richard M. Cyert and James G. March, *A Behavioral Theory of the Firm* (Englewood Cliffs, N.J.: Prentice-Hall, 1963), p. 118; and John Steinbruner, *The Cybernetic Theory of Decision* (Princeton, N.J.: Princeton University Press, 1974), p. 72. See also Charles Lindblom's argument that decision-makers deal with issues in incremental, serial, and remedial fashion (*The Intelligence of Democracy* [New York: Free Press, 1965], pp. 144–148). While it would have been interesting to attempt to trace out this pattern of sequential attention to the problems of escalation and diplomacy for the entire period March 1965–April 1968, the enormity of the problems of data collection, combined with the fact that some sections of *The Pentagon Papers* are not as richly detailed as others, put such an undertaking beyond the reach of the present study.

officials relieved the President and his top advisers of the need to pay attention to burdensome details, such an approach also had the effect of greatly complicating the problem of striking a deal with Hanoi, the reason being that the implementation of many of the President's escalatory decisions coincided with a number of the Administration's diplomatic initiatives. Thus, for example, while the Haiphong power plants were added to the authorized list on March 22, 1967, bad weather prevented their being hit until April 20, the day after the State Department had put forward its initiative on restoring and enlarging the DMZ (see Chapter 4, above). Similarly, while the President's decision of August 9, 1967 was followed by attacks on the Doumer bridge near the center of Hanoi on August 11-12, bad weather diverted attacks to the China buffer zone and the southern DRV for a week, so that it was not until August 20-23 (coinciding with Aubrac and Marcovich's appeal for visas) that most of the new Hanoi-area targets were hit, resulting in Hanoi receiving its heaviest pounding of the war to that date.[37] Even if the Administration had not been particularly interested in either of those diplomatic initiatives, it still should have had an interest in preventing the kinds of coincidences described above, if for no other reason than to avoid a legacy of bitterness and mistrust that would make it all the more difficult to arrange a settlement at some later date. In this respect, it should be recalled that the August 1967 pounding of Hanoi followed shortly after Algard's second meeting with Loan in Peking and had the (hopefully unintended) effect of confirming Loan's assertion that whenever Hanoi had shown interest in negotiations, the U.S. had responded with escalation (see Chapter 4, above).

Furthermore, the logic of the argument being developed here suggests that the obstacles to successful "orchestration" are of such a kind that they are unlikely to be overcome, no matter how much officials may claim to be committed to an "orchestrated" approach. In this respect, perhaps the most significant conclusion suggested by our review of the Administration's policies is that there does not appear to have been a

37. Since the President had also decided on August 19 that Hanoi would be off-limits to American planes beginning on August 24 (both to insure the safety of Aubrac and Marcovich and also as a gesture of good will), a decision that was almost certainly communicated to field commanders sometime before August 24, one suspects that military commanders were determined to squeeze in as many strikes as possible on the Hanoi targets before August 24, thus explaining the severity of the attacks on Hanoi during August 20-23 (see Chapter 4, above; and IV Gravel, p. 205). See also Gallucci (p. 83), who notes that "when a new group of formerly restricted targets was released as part of a new ROLLING THUNDER series, there was an unhealthy eagerness on the part of the military to strike rapidly lest political considerations cause targets to be lost in any civilian reconsideration."

learning process present. As we noted at the close of the preceding section, Administration officials continued to speak and write of the need for an "orchestrated" approach even as their conduct suggested they were incapable of any such thing. Similarly, we find in the August 1967 fiasco over the Aubrac/Marcovich appeal for visas the same lack of concern over the dangers inherent in allowing attacks on sensitive targets to coincide with diplomatic initiatives that characterized the Administration's handling of the MARIGOLD and DMZ initiatives. Nor does it seem to be by chance that the ability of Administration officials to "orchestrate" words and deeds did not improve over time.

At the very least, the requirements for successful "orchestration" would seem to be three in number: (1) a willingness on the part of officials to integrate separate lines of policy into a coherent whole in order to consider how each might affect the other(s); (2) a willingness to project the consequences of current policy choices reasonably far into the future, so that policy will be more than a series of disjointed initiatives having little or no bearing on each other; and (3) a willingness on the part of subordinate agencies and officials to cooperate in the implementation of an "orchestrated" effort. The available evidence, however, suggests that each of these requirements is likely to be beyond the reach of government officials caught up in the business of coercion.

For one thing, not only are high-level officials likely to respond to complex policy problems by breaking them down into their component parts and dealing with each part separately, but they are also likely to deny that trade-offs may exist between the different values being pursued (e.g., pressuring "Hanoi" and beginning formal negotiations)—a phenomenon that Steinbruner labels the "assumption of value separation":

According to this assumption, the two values of a complex problem will not be related to one another in the mind of the decision maker, but divided and pursued separately, as if they were independent considerations. The information-processing operations of the human mind strain to set up single-value decision problems.[38]

Steinbruner's argument is an important one because of what it implies for the way in which officials "learn" (or fail to learn) from the past. If

---

38. Steinbruner, p. 108. Although Steinbruner uses the term "assumption of value separation," there is considerable empirical evidence suggesting that the mind is likely to operate in this fashion, particularly under conditions of uncertainty. Under conditions of uncertainty, that is, decision-makers are likely to deny that trade-offs exist, because to recognize their existence would be to violate the principle of cognitive consistency. On these points, see Steinbruner, pp. 103–109.

the different values involved in a complex policy problem are divided and pursued separately, then one would expect that there would be very little in the way of "learning" from past failures of "orchestration." Rather than conceding that attacks on sensitive targets might have jeopardized efforts to open formal negotiations, Steinbruner's argument suggests that high-level officials would be likely to deny that there was any connection between the two, thus clearing the way for repeated instances in which delicate diplomatic contacts were undercut by ill-timed bombing raids. And this is exactly what appears to have happened in the Vietnam case—President Johnson, for example, insisted that there was no connection between the bombing raids on Hanoi and the breakdown of the MARIGOLD contact:

> The Poles claimed that the North Vietnamese had failed to appear because we had bombed targets near Hanoi two days before the suggested meeting date. That made little sense, for Lewandowski and Lodge had agreed that one of the items to be discussed in the proposed secret talks was a mutual deescalation formula, including a bombing halt. This was what we called the Phase A–Phase B plan. . . . If Lewandowski had reported accurately to Hanoi, the North Vietnamese knew perfectly well that the bombing would not end before the talks began. Knowing that, they could hardly give our bombing as the excuse for not entering negotiations.

Similarly, a former high-ranking official asserted that he and others in the State Department interpreted a "cable reporting what Rapacki said on December 13, *before* any news of the bombing" as "in effect our turndown," when in fact all Rapacki did was to inform Gronouski that "we should realize that leadership of DRNVN does not want to and cannot yield under pressure; every step from our side that evokes impression that NVN is acting under pressure would be interpreted as sign of weakness and be utilized by all those who have a different vision of this peace move than we have here in Warsaw."[39]

Second, the sheer number and complexity of the problems that high-level officials must deal with would seem to make it highly unlikely that they would be able to adopt the kind of time perspective required for successful "orchestration." As Cyert and March and others have noted, long-range planning is a luxury to which few busy executives can afford to devote much time; of necessity, they seek to solve pressing problems first.[40] Just as the press of business in the months before the attack on

---

39. On these points, see Johnson, pp. 251–252; Interview Data; and Marigold Chronology, pp. 60–61.

40. On this point, see Cyert and March, pp. 118–120; and Allison, pp. 76–77, 92.

Pearl Harbor meant that senior U.S. officials scanned each new group of messages intercepted and broken by American cryptanalysts on a day-to-day basis and never bothered to consider the totality (or even a month's worth) of "signals" pointing toward the likelihood that hostilities would be initiated by Japan, so too did officials in the Johnson Administration become so immersed in the business of picking the targets for the next week's ROLLING THUNDER series or pondering the next message to be carried by an intermediary to Hanoi that rarely was serious consideration given to the "pattern" (or lack of one) that was emerging from the Administration's decisions taken as a whole. To make matters worse, studies of crisis decision-making have suggested that "the individual's time perspective collapses under stress so that he becomes almost exclusively concerned with what happens in the present or very immediate future." As a result, it seems reasonable to conclude that as coercive conflicts become more acute, government officials are likely to be least able to provide effective "orchestration" at precisely the moment when it is most needed.[41]

Finally, even though an "orchestrated" effort involving military and diplomatic components would seem to require at least a minimal degree of cooperation between subordinate agencies and officials, the fact that most decisions made by high-level officials must be implemented by quasi-autonomous organizations means that the requisite cooperation is often not forthcoming. Organizations, as Halperin notes, seek "total operational control over the forces required to carry out a mission and are reluctant to undertake shared operations involving forces of other organizations."[42] Thus, for example, when General Westmoreland chose to stand at Khe Sanh and to use U.S. air power to compensate for the numerical superiority the North Vietnamese had achieved by massing 20,000 troops around the outpost, his decision had the unintended effect of touching off a prolonged struggle involving MACV, the Air Force, the Marine Corps, CINCPAC and the JCS. Even though air strikes in support of the base were often flown by U.S. Marine Corps aircraft, Westmoreland sought to invest control over all air operations involving Khe Sanh in a "single manager"—Air Force Lt. General William Momyer, who was Westmoreland's deputy for air operations. The resultant struggle was not resolved until it had reached the level of

41. On the Pearl Harbor case, see Roberta Wohlstetter, *Pearl Harbor: Warning and Decision* (Stanford, Calif.: Stanford University Press, 1962), chap. 3, especially pp. 180, 197. On the effect of stress, see Hermann and Brady, "Alternative Models of International Crisis Behavior," in Hermann (ed.), p. 285.

42. Halperin (1974), p. 52.

the Deputy Secretary of Defense.[43] No matter how astute they might be, senior officials can hardly be expected to supply brilliant "orchestration" if they are continually distracted by the need to resolve jurisdictional disputes among their subordinates.

By referring once again to organizational impediments to successful "orchestration," we have in a sense come full circle. In the preceding section, we suggested that the goal of meaningful "orchestration" was likely to be beyond the reach of high-level officials, largely as a result of the difficulties they would encounter in attempting to control a bureaucratic apparatus as immense and far-flung as the one centered in Washington. While this section continues the analysis of organizational and bureaucratic factors, it also places considerable weight on an additional set of obstacles to effective "orchestration"—i.e., obstacles stemming from the way in which high-level officials structure the issues they confront ("sequential attention to goals") and conceptualize the goals they seek to achieve ("value separation"). Significantly, however, these two sets of obstacles do not exist independently of each other; if anything, it appears that they both reinforce and help perpetuate each other. The very existence of separate organizational entities invested with special responsibility for certain types of activities and operating largely independently of each other would seem to provide powerful reinforcement for the inclination on the part of high-level officials to disaggregate complex policy problems into their component parts and to deny the existence of trade-offs between the values being pursued. Conversely, the continued reliance by policymakers on techniques such as "sequential attention to goals" and "value separation" both insures that meaningful "orchestration" will be, almost by definition, virtually impossible and that policy decisions will continue to be parceled out to separate organizational subunits for implementation, thereby increasing the likelihood of breakdowns in coordination, unanticipated coincidences, and foul-ups in the field.

Furthermore, since the existence of specialized organizational subunits and tendencies such as sequential attention to goals and value separation are merely symptomatic of the inordinate complexity of the issues that high-level officials are called upon to deal with, those officials are unlikely to be able to escape from this web of constraints on their

43. For details on the struggle over the control of U.S. airpower during the seige of Khe Sanh, see Bernard Nalty, *Air Power and the Fight for Khe Sanh* (Washington, D.C.: U.S. Government Printing Office, 1973), pp. 68–81; and Westmoreland, pp. 342–345. The dispute was so heated that Westmoreland (p. 344) later labeled it "the one issue that arose during my service in Vietnam to prompt me to consider resigning."

ability to "orchestrate" words and deeds. Any attempt, for example, to circumvent those constraints by keeping subordinates on as short a leash as possible would very likely result in senior officials being overwhelmed by the sheer scope of the problems involved—i.e., troop movements, military operations, keeping up with the daily cable traffic, etc.— when one government attempts to coerce another. That being the case, the conclusion seems inescapable: coercion, at least when practiced by twentieth-century governments, is an activity fraught with perils. Regardless of the number of memos that they may write advocating an "orchestrated" approach, such an outcome is likely to be beyond the reach of the overburdened officials to whom responsibility for policy is entrusted.

III. Signals and Messages: Knowing What to Say and When to Say It

It should not be assumed on the basis of our discussion to this point that if the Johnson Administration had been able to overcome the technical and conceptual problems involved in "orchestrating" and "signalling" described above, it would have been more successful in convincing the North Vietnamese to "leave their neighbors alone." As things turned out, perhaps the most serious problem facing the Administration was that it did not know what to look for in terms of signals from Hanoi during the bargaining over a settlement of the conflict. As a result, one suspects that even a brilliantly "orchestrated" campaign would still have resulted in failure (i.e., in the sense of being unable to achieve an acceptable settlement) for the simple reason that the Administration had very little understanding of what it was that motivated the North Vietnamese or what they could realistically be expected to settle for.

As for the causes of this misunderstanding, Administration officials had no one but themselves to blame. As we saw in Chapter 5, Administration plans for pressuring North Vietnam were based on a relatively crude model of decision-making in which "Hanoi" was conceptualized as a unitary rational actor intent on taking over the South at relatively low cost to itself. Given that premise, the task confronting the Administration was fairly straightforward—i.e., to demonstrate to "Hanoi" that the costs of attempting to take over the South would exceed any potential gains the DRV might realize. This the Administration hoped to accomplish by blocking the attempted takeover by inserting American forces into the South and by imposing ever-increasing costs on the DRV itself by means of the air war, while simultaneously providing the North

Vietnamese with a face-saving exit by means of high-sounding phrases such as "self-determination," "eventual reunification," and "economic development."

However, as we know from Chapter 5, the model underlying the Administration's plans bore little relationship to the reality in Hanoi. Not only was the DRV leadership unanimous in viewing the goal of reunification as a legitimate one (sanctioned, in their view, by the Geneva Conference in 1954), but, more importantly, policymaking in Hanoi was dominated by a group of senior Party officials who had fought long and hard to commit the North to a greater role in the war in the South and who, with victory close at hand (as it was in 1965), had nothing to gain and much to lose by backing down under pressure from the United States. As a result, the only viable alternative to the policy espoused by Le Duan and his supporters was Pham Van Dong's diplomatic approach, although even that option was restricted in terms of the concessions that could be made to the U.S. in pursuit of a negotiated settlement. By 1965, the only kind of settlement for which Pham Van Dong would have been able to win Politburo approval involved, at the very least, an American withdrawal, neutralization of the South, normalization of relations between the two Vietnams, and a role for the NLF in a coalition government (although there may well have been room for bargaining on the precise terms of the settlement, such as the timing of the American withdrawal, the number of ministries to be given to the NLF, etc.). Washington, however, interpreted the DRV's minimum goals as a maximum staked out for bargaining purposes. As a result, Washington and Hanoi consistently spoke on different wavelengths, with the Americans never fully understanding the negotiating tactics of their DRV counterparts and the North Vietnamese, one suspects, persistently puzzled by the failure of the Americans to respond meaningfully to the hints occasionally dropped by DRV diplomats. In Chapter 5, we suggested that Washington's failure to understand the nature of Hanoi's internal politics resulted in the U.S. taking steps that, far from leading the North Vietnamese to abandon their support for the insurgency in the South, very likely encouraged them to take the very steps the U.S. sought to prevent. In similar fashion, precisely because the Administration did not understand the subtleties of DRV decision-making, its handling of the various diplomatic contacts with Hanoi between 1965 and 1968 was marked by considerable clumsiness.

In particular, while the Administration publicly argued that it was the DRV and not the U.S. that was uninterested in negotiating (a position

Table 6
Mai Van Bo Contacts in Paris

Date	Nature of contact	For additional details:
December 1964–January 1965	Bo discusses with French officials the possibility of neutralizing South Vietnam along with new international control mechanism to replace ICC.	Chapter 3, note 6, above.
February 1965	French urged to press for new Geneva Conference.	*New York Times,* February 23, 1965.
March 3, 1965	Bo tells French that, as a result of American actions (i.e., bombing North Vietnam), negotiations could not be considered at that time.	Seaborn Discussion, p. 3.
May 18, 1965	Bo contacts French to hint at possible softening in DRV position.	Chapter 3, Section III, above.
June 14, 1965	Bo asks French if U.S. has replied to May 18 message.	Chapter 3, Section III, above.
July 16, 1965	First Bo-Duntov meeting in Paris.	Chapter 3, Section IV, above.
August 5, 1965	Second Bo-Duntov meeting.	Chapter 3, Section IV, above.
August 6, 1965	First Bo-Gullion meeting.	Chapter 3, Section IV, above.

that was quite close to the Administration's private assessments of DRV interest in negotiations), there appears to have been considerable interest in a negotiated settlement on the DRV side. For example, between December 1964 and August 1965, Mai Van Bo, the ranking DRV diplomat in Paris, met several times with French officials to discuss a possible negotiated settlement (see Table 6). Time and again, Bo stressed not only that the DRV was ready to negotiate but also that it was prepared to be "flexible," provided, of course, that the U.S. "recognized" the Four Points as the "basis" for negotiations.[44]

For the first half of 1965, however, Bo's efforts proved all for naught, primarily because at that time the Administration was not so much concerned with starting negotiations as with stalling them off until the bombing and the influx of American troops had strengthened the American bargaining position.[45] In mid-July, though, as we saw in Chapter 3, the President committed himself to going ahead with a major American buildup in the South, a decision made public by the President himself during his July 28 news conference. Once that decision had been made, the Administration felt itself ready for talks with Hanoi on the grounds that it would now be able to talk from a position of strength. As a result, the Administration seized on the opening provided by the Bo-Duntov contact in mid-July, dispatching Edmund Gullion to Paris for direct talks with Mai Van Bo.

Gullion and Bo, however, were speaking on different wavelengths, which helps explain both why the initial meetings seemed to proceed so smoothly and why the contact eventually broke down. Gullion, as we saw in Chapter 3, was to seek peace from a position of strength while at the same time giving the appearance of flexibility.[46] What the Administration failed to realize, however, was that Bo, too, had been instructed to seek peace from a position of strength (based on the undeniable Viet Cong successes in 1964 and 1965) while giving the appearance of flexibility. As a result, as we saw in Chapter 3, Bo took a very forthcoming stance during his early meetings with Gullion, even to the point of

44. Nowhere was the DRV position better illustrated than in Lucet's version of Bo's message of May 18, 1965 (see Chapter 3, above): "If there were agreement on the 'basis,' then a 'ways and means' of application of 'principles' would be found and in a peaceful manner. . . . 'Our suggestion humiliates no one'" (see also XYZ Summary and Analysis, p. 3). The only exception here was Bo's March 3, 1965 contact with the French (the day after the first ROLLING THUNDER strike). On that date, Bo told the French that while the DRV had previously been willing to negotiate, American actions had changed the situation so that negotiations would be inappropriate at that time. Even that statement implied a willingness to negotiate, provided the situation returned to normal—i.e., the bombing stopped.

45. Interview Data. See also the references listed in Chapter 1, note 7, above.

46. See XYZ Chronology, pp. 7–8; and Chapter 3, above.

apparently agreeing with Gullion's demand that any troop withdrawals from the South be mutual and balanced. When it became clear, though, that the U.S. was not about to concede on the crux of the issue—i.e., NLF participation in a coalition government—Bo abruptly broke off the talks.

This analysis, however, still leaves a number of questions unanswered, especially with respect to why the North Vietnamese agreed to participate in the talks with Gullion in the first place. It must be kept in mind that this was *not* a situation in which the DRV had "nothing to lose" by probing the American position. Given that the Johnson Administration was eagerly seeking signs that Hanoi's will was cracking, any decision to engage in negotiations could have been construed by Washington as a sign of weakness, so that "the enemy will press forward and create more difficulties and damage to the revolution," as General (and Politburo Alternate) Van Tien Dung put it in a *Nhan Dan* article, published on August 5–6, 1965, counseling *against* negotiations.[47] In addition, an equally intriguing question centers on the use and deployment of the PAVN regiments infiltrated into the South in late 1964 and early 1965. Upon arriving in the South, those regiments apparently were not committed to battle immediately but instead were held in a reserve role in the Central Highlands while the brunt of the fighting continued to be borne by native southerners.[48] Given the strength of the DRV/VC position in early 1965, along with the strong desire on the part of Le Duan and Nguyen Chi Thanh to press for a quick victory, one wonders why the North Vietnamese bothered to negotiate at all, especially since a quick commitment of the available PAVN regiments might have resulted in the decisive victory that they apparently were seeking.

Although there is much less information available on DRV decision-making for the period 1965–1968 than for the period 1954–1964, we can still attempt some informed speculation on the questions posed above. In particular, while the strategy espoused by Le Duan and Nguyen Chi Thanh had brought the DRV to the verge of victory by mid-1965, there apparently were some in Hanoi who still did not share their view on the question of the North's role in the war in the South. As Latimer notes,

---

47. Quoted in Latimer, p. 213. Significantly, Dung's article coincided with the first Bo-Gullion meeting, held on August 6. That, plus Dung's comment that the Americans' "good will for peace can deceive only those who do not have a revolutionary spirit," suggests that there was a group in Hanoi that adamantly opposed the idea of a negotiated settlement.

48. On this point, see Max Frankel, "U.S. Urging Hanoi to Join in Showing Wish to Ease War," *New York Times*, August 27, 1965, pp. 1, 3. At their September 3 meeting, Bo, when pressed by Gullion, did not deny that the NVA 325th Division was in South Vietnam but claimed that it was not engaged in combat operations at that time (XYZ Chronology, p. 18).

in the August 1965 article cited above, Van Tien Dung made the point that

"a new development has occurred in the relationship between the revolution-ary tasks of North and South Vietnam." In the new situation, the duty of North Vietnam was to "wholeheartedly support" the war in the South. No longer, in his view, was the primary task to develop North Vietnam's economy [as specified at the 1960 Party Congress]. The primary task was to support the war in the South.[49]

The fact that Dung found it necessary to make such a claim suggests that at least some elements in the Party were dissatisfied with the burden being imposed on the North in connection with the war and sought to revise the allocation of resources between North and South. Significantly, within a month of Dung's article,

Truong Chinh offered his assessment that the new developments had not changed the old agreement on the relative tasks of the revolution in the North and in the South. In Truong Chinh's view, although the situation might change during each phase of the revolution, "the task and objective . . . will remain unchanged." In the South, according to Truong Chinh, the national people's democratic revolution was still the main task while in the North, the socialist revolution remained the primary task.[50]

More importantly, it was probably not by chance that the Central Committee convened for its 11th Plenum (since the 1960 Congress) in August 1965, a meeting that coincided both with the rapid increase in the deployment of American troops in the South and the Bo-Gullion meetings in Paris. Although there is no information available which sheds light directly on what was discussed at the Plenum, we can infer from subsequent speeches and commentaries that there were probably at least three distinct viewpoints expressed. One group within the lead-ership apparently argued in favor of a serious effort to negotiate a settlement with the U.S., as evidenced by Le Duc Tho's comment in a February 1966 *Hoc Tap* article that "a small number of comrades" had developed "erroneous thoughts and views":

Concerning the combat task, they have made an incorrect assessment of the balance of power between the enemy and us and of the enemy's ruses. Now, they entertain subjectivism and pacifism, slacken their vigilance, and fail to get ideologically ready for combat. Now, they see only difficulties and do not see opportunities; display pessimism, perplexity, and a reluctance to protracted

49. Latimer, p. 213.
50. Ibid., p. 214.

resistance; fail to realize clearly the deceptive peace negotiation plot of the enemy; and rely on outside aid.[51]

Two other groups were more willing to continue with the struggle in the South, although they apparently disagreed as to how best to fight the war, with one group apparently urging a conservative strategy emphasizing guerrilla warfare and the avoidance of set-piece battles in which the Americans could chew up PAVN units by means of their superior firepower, and a second group urging an ambitious offensive strategy with heavy emphasis on committing main force units against the Americans. Hints of these disagreements can be inferred from various speeches and articles by Nguyen Chi Thanh, such as a July 1966 article by Thanh in *Hoc Tap*, which asserted that some in the Party had been guilty of "ideological wavering" in the face of the American buildup, desiring "to stop when the revolution required that one continue to progress, overcoming all difficulties."[52] Similarly, as Latimer notes,

a speech by Nguyen Chi Thanh, under the pseudonym Anh Sau, . . . indicated fairly clearly that there was considerable hesitation over just what to do in the summer of 1965 about the new American combat troops. He said that "*since July 1965 we have advocated the line of launching big battles and winning victories*." He noted that between July and October, U.S. strength in South Vietnam had increased from 70,000 to 100,000 and he admitted that "we, then, had to think about how to fight. . . . We believed in our ideology but we were not yet firmly resolute to fight." Thanh heaped ridicule, however, on those who advocated a pullback from the offensive strategy saying, "if we want to take the defensive position, we should withdraw to India."[53]

When viewed in conjunction with what the DRV was actually doing at this time, these points suggest that the dispute within the Party was resolved, typically, by a compromise that involved pursuing several lines of policy at once. Specifically, the DRV/VC buildup in the South would continue (although at a somewhat reduced rate)[54] while Bo

51. Quoted in Latimer, p. 244. See also Max Frankel, "Hanoi Discloses Faction in Party Opposes Long War," *New York Times*, February 13, 1966, pp. 1, 4. P. J. Honey ("North Vietnam Quarterly Survey no. 20," *China News Analysis*, 604 [March 18, 1966], 4) also concluded that there was a "peace faction" in Hanoi at this time.

52. Quoted in Latimer, p. 216.

53. Ibid., pp. 223–224 (emphasis added). For the full text of Anh Sau's speech, see Working Paper, Item 65. See also Latimer's summary (pp.224–226) of various articles in the DRV publication *Current Events*, which hinted at discontent with Nguyen Chi Thanh's emphasis on an ambitious offensive strategy.

54. According to the Working Paper, p. 21, four PAVN regiments departed for South Vietnam over the period September 1964–February 1965. These were followed by four more in July 1965 and two more in August 1965. Thereafter, the next PAVN regiment to be infiltrated into the South as a unit did not depart until December 1965.

pursued the possibility of a negotiated settlement in Paris. In addition, as already noted, those PAVN regiments that had been infiltrated into the South were not immediately committed to battle but were instead held in reserve pending the outcome of the Paris contact. While such a "compromise" was probably distasteful to Nguyen Chi Thanh and the other advocates of "launching big battles," it probably served to conciliate those in the leadership (like Truong Chinh) who had never been happy over the dispatching of native northerners to the South.[55]

With the breakdown of the Paris contact, however, the issue of how and when to use the PAVN units deployed in the South could be avoided no longer. As a result, it appears that Nguyen Chi Thanh was given the go-ahead to proceed with the ambitious offensive strategy that he had advocated all along. As General Westmoreland notes:

In October the North Vietnamese Army began a major operation in the Central Highlands. By this time the enemy had asembled three North Vietnamese Army regiments in western Pleiku Province and in adjacent Cambodia —the 32d, 33d, and 66th. We believed this action to be part of his plan to cut South Vietnam in two. In addition, there is reason to believe that he welcomed the opportunity to spoil the debut of the U.S. ground forces in this area; the 1st Cavalry Division, which now stood in his path, was as yet untested in battle.[56]

With the North Vietnamese attack on the Special Forces camp at Plei Me on October 19, the battle was joined and would continue into November, culminating in the bloody fighting in the region of the Ia Drang valley.

Although Halberstam has suggested that Ia Drang constituted a North Vietnamese success,[57] in the sense that they used the battle to perfect close-in tactics that enabled them to neutralize the American advantage in air power and artillery, there is reason to believe that there was some dissatisfaction in Hanoi over the outcome of this first extended clash between American and PAVN units. In his March 1966 letter to southern cadres, Le Duan argued that

U.S. troops are not only strategically but also technically and tactically deadlocked, because they are forced to fight the tactics of our people's war and because . . . the southern people's armed forces have taken the initiative. . . . Accordingly, U.S. troops must passively cope with our attack and cannot fight in their own way.

---

55. Latimer (pp. 220–222) reaches a similar conclusion about the decisions made at the 11th Plenum.

56. Westmoreland, in Sharp and Westmoreland, p. 110 (see also p. 99).

57. Halberstam, pp. 744–745.

Similarly, Le Duan cited the August 1965 battle at Van Tuong as a

turning point testifying . . . that the *southern liberation army is fully capable of defeating U.S. troops under any circumstances, even though they have absolute superiority of their firepower compared with that of the liberation army.* . . . U.S. troops took the initiative in choosing Van Tuong, a coastal battleground in their favor. They mobilized 8000 troops with the coordination and support of Air and Navy units in an attempt to destroy one force of the southern liberation army seven or eight times smaller than their force. But just as in Ap Bac, the helicopter-supported tactics and armored-car supported tactics of the U.S. imperialists were defeated and more than 900 Americans were buried together with the bulk of the iron and steel which the U.S. military used to brag about.[58]

The fact that Le Duan found it necessary to take such an upbeat stance suggests that there may have been considerable dismay within the Party over the prospect of full-scale warfare against an opponent as powerful as the United States.

In addition, it appears that the continuing American buildup was itself contributing to second thoughts in Hanoi. Although the resolution of the 9th Plenum in December 1963 had generally downplayed the threat of a massive American troop commitment, the resolution warned nonetheless that "we should be careful about the possibility that the Americans may bring in from 50,000 to 100,000 additional troops to South Vietnam to expand the war and turn it into a limited war."[59] As we know, this was exactly what happened in 1965, and the fact that Lieutenant General Nguyen Van Vinh found it necessary to address the rhetorical question of what would happen "if the aggressive forces of the Americans and their satellites reach up to 400,000 or 500,000 men" again suggests that some elements in Hanoi were uncertain and/or discouraged over the course of the war. Considering how wrong Le Duan and his supporters had been in discounting the chances of American intervention in the earlier strategy debates, one wonders how reassured Vinh's audience was by his confident stand on the question cited above:

An eventual 400,000 to 500,000 men from the American expeditionary corps would be powerless, even to bar the rising tide of the revolutionary movement.

58. Working Paper, Item 302, p. 16 (emphasis in original). In this passage, Le Duan cited the "turning point" at Van Tuong as comparable to the "turning point" at Stalingrad in World War II. Similarly, in an April 1966 "talk" before the 4th COSVN Congress in South Vietnam, General Nguyen Van Vinh noted that: "Some individuals have asserted that since the Americans have introduced their troops we cannot defeat them and that the Americans have caused us heavy casualties. These assertions are obviously belied by recent realities" (Working Paper, Item 303, p. 11).

59. *Vietnam Documents and Research Notes*, no. 96, p. 21. See also Chapter 5, above.

How could the Yankees envisage a massive concentration of forces on a front aimed at North Vietnam and Laos to try and encircle and isolate the patriotic war of our compatriots on the South? If we consider the possibility of the American imperialists launching a ground war of aggression against North Vietnam, we see that the relation of forces will be completely different. North Vietnam has solid defences at its disposal and the socialist countries are ready to come to its aid. If the American imperialists undertake aggression against North Vietnam, under these conditions and at a time when their reserves are piling up in South Vietnam, no matter what size the forces thrown into the bottomless abyss of such a conflict, they could not avoid final defeat by the immense forces of their adversaries in this region.[60]

A third souce of possible discouragement in Hanoi during this period was the less than overwhelming support that the DRV was receiving from its erstwhile allies in Moscow and Peking. In September 1965, Lin Piao unveiled his famous treatise on the conduct of people's wars, which, with its emphasis on self-reliance and protracted warfare, very likely heightened the doubts of those in Hanoi who had questioned all along the wisdom of the DRV taking on the United States. Significantly, in late 1965, Ho reportedly appealed personally to Mao to reconsider China's rejection of a Soviet proposal for "united action" in support of Hanoi, only to be turned down.[61] In addition, the nature of the aid contributed by Moscow and Peking could hardly have inspired feelings of deep gratitude in Hanoi. On December 5, 1965, for example, Deputy Premier (and Politburo member) Le Thanh Nghi signed an agreement in Peking whereby the Chinese agreed to provide the DRV with *loans*. Similarly, on December 21, 1965, Nghi signed an agreement in Moscow whereby the Soviets agreed to provide additional military and economic aid (the latter providing for a *loan*, postponed payments on earlier *loans*, and a trade agreement guaranteeing no price *increases* on Soviet goods during 1966).[62] The fact that Nghi had to travel to

60. Quoted in Zagoria, p. 253. Vinh's remarks originally appeared in the February 1966 issue of *Hoc Tap*. In similar fashion, Le Duan noted, somewhat defensively, in his March 1966 letter, that while "we cannot give a 100 per cent accurate prophecy of the situation . . . we had correctly estimated the situation and set forth correct lines and policies. Therefore, we were neither caught by surprise nor passive in the face of the U.S. imperialists' escalation of the war in the South during the past. On the contrary, we have still mastered the situation and held the initiative in directing the war according to our strategic intentions in the new situation." Working Paper, Item 302, p. 4 (see also pp. 15, 18).

61. Chen (1972), p. 813. Chen's source is a Radio Paris report, Domestic Service in French, December 6, 1965, 1300 GMT.

62. On these points, see "Hanoi to Get Peking Loan," *New York Times*, December 6, 1965, p. 1; and the AP dispatch, "Soviet Accord Gives More Help to Hanoi," *New York Times*, December 22, 1965, p. 1.

Peking and Moscow to bargain for loans (at a time when the Americans were virtually throwing money at their allies in Saigon) must surely have grated on the Hanoi leadership, especially those who had resented all along the sacrificing of economic development in the North for the sake of the war in the South.

These accumulated frustrations apparently resulted in a showdown at the Central Committee's 12th Plenum, held in Hanoi in December 1965. On the one hand, there was the question of whether to continue with the ambitious offensive strategy espoused by Nguyen Chi Thanh despite the casualties involved; on the other hand, the American press had been filled with rumors that the end of the year would witness some new American peace bid, and the Central Committee may well have discussed plans on how to handle the new bid, if one should come.[63] The available evidence, however, suggests that the North Vietnamese were no more able to resolve their internal disputes than were the contending groups of "hawks" and "doves" in Washington. Instead, it appears that the 12th Plenum resulted in a decision to continue with the two-track policy followed in the past—i.e., escalation while seeking negotiations. As described in a COSVN resolution based on the decisions at the 12th Plenum:

> The objective that we have in view in the immediate future is to achieve a decisive victory within a relatively short period of time [defined elsewhere as "a few years"]. That objective can only be achieved if we coordinate very closely the armed struggle with the political struggle and the psychological struggle. . . .
>
> *We have the capability of coordinating the armed struggle with the popular uprising to liberate the cities and towns*, and of coordinating our offensive with the mass revolt in preparation for a *general attack and uprising which will take place when the opportunity avails itself and the situation ripens.*[64]

On the diplomatic front, as Oberdorfer notes,

> the resolution declared that the war could never be settled through negotiations until the "aggressive will" of the Americans is crushed. It added, however: "At a certain time we can apply the strategy of fighting and negotiating at the same time, in order to support the armed struggle, and thus accelerate the dis-

63. Apparently in anticipation of such a move, the DRV Foreign Ministry, on December 10, 1965, released the text of the note that the U.S. had attempted to pass to Hanoi during the May 1965 bombing pause; the release was accompanied by a stiff denunciation of the possibility of a renewed pause. On these points, see Pinta Chronology, pp. 1–1a. On the timing and content of the decisions at the 12th Plenum, see Working Paper, p. 14; Latimer, pp. 223–236; Oberdorfer (1971), pp. 68–70; and Melvin Gurtov, "Hanoi on War and Peace," P-3696, The RAND Corporation, December 1967, pp. 11–12.

64. Quoted in Oberdorfer (1971), p. 69 (emphasis in original).

integration of the puppet army and regime, and create more conditions favorable for our people to win a decisive victory."[65]

Despite the "more of the same" quality evident in the decisions reached at the 12th Plenum, it appears that significant changes were taking place in the way in which the leadership in Hanoi viewed the conflict in the South. For one thing, the decisions made at the 12th Plenum apparently marked the abandoning of earlier beliefs in the possibility of a quick victory in the South. Instead, it was now agreed that victory would not be achieved for at least a "few years"; moreover, even hawks such as Le Duan and Nguyen Van Vinh conceded that negotiations would probably be necessary at some point, as evidenced by Vinh's comment that "after defeating a greater bulk of the puppet army and an important part of the American troops, we can push the Americans out of South Vietnam by coordinating the political struggle with diplomacy."[66] Still, the "consensus" produced at the 12th Plenum was at best a tenuous one, as different members of the leadership differed on the relative importance of the military and diplomatic tracks. Le Duan, for example, while conceding that "heavy emphasis is to be placed on the political struggle which includes the diplomatic struggle, which is of prime importance," nonetheless stressed that the

basic problem is to defeat the imperialists on the battlefield, to foil their political and military plan, to destroy as much of their potential as possible, and undermine the puppet army. Only when we comply with the above requirements can we break up their plan of aggression.[67]

As a result of the decisions reached at the 12th Plenum, then, the North Vietnamese continued to pursue two lines of policy in the

65. Ibid.

66. From an April 1966 "talk" by General Nguyen Van Vinh before the 4th COSVN Congress in South Vietnam, Working Paper, Item 303, p. 5. On Hanoi's changing perceptions concerning the length of the war, see Giap's article in *Nhan Dan*, January 16–18, 1966, which stressed that the war would be "long and arduous" (discussed in Latimer, pp. 230–231; and in P. J. Honey, "North Vietnam Quarterly Survey no. 20," *China News Analysis*, 604 [March 18, 1966], 4 ff.).

67. Working Paper, Item 302, pp. 25, 26. Significantly, Le Duan also described the problem of "war and negotiation" as "very complicated considering that, at present, the views are quite divergent. The U.S. views hold that negotiation is to be conducted from a strong position. Some countries . . . sincerely support our struggle but, in view of diplomatic reasons and their domestic administration and misunderstanding of the situation in our country, want to see us at the conference table in order to forestall aimless sacrifice on our part. There are those who hold the view that the political struggle is of major importance, but such a view is different from ours as to degree and time to use this strategy" (Working Paper, Item 302, p. 26). See also General Vinh's comments on the importance of fighting vigorously while negotiating (Working Paper, Item 303, pp. 14–16).

months that followed. On the one hand, military strategy dictated pursuit of a "decisive victory in a relatively short period of time"; this, as Gurtov notes,

required that as many American and "puppet" (GVN) forces as possible be put out of action; the goal was set between 30,000 and 40,000 U.S. soldiers, plus about 200,000 "puppet" troops. To achieve these ambitious aims, all three types of forces—guerrillas, regional units, and regular units—would be required as before; but guerrilla warfare was said to have the greatest potentiality "in both causing the attrition of and the destruction of the American and puppet forces."[68]

Toward this end, the DRV embarked on a major new effort to infiltrate additional PAVN units into the South: during December 1965, two additional PAVN regiments began the march to the South, followed by three more in January, two more in February, and two more in March.[69]

At the same time, however, as we saw in Chapter 3, the DRV was also engaged in a renewed effort to begin negotiations with the U.S., an effort that coincided with the Johnson Administration's 37-day bombing pause and attempted contact in Rangoon. In this respect, it was probably not by chance that the DRV Foreign Ministry released its statement on January 4, 1966 hinting that "recognition" of the Four Points did not constitute a precondition for negotiations (see Chapter 3, above). Similarly, Vu Huu Binh's performance during his January 21 and 31 meetings with Byroade strongly hinted at a readiness to begin substantive negotiations with the United States. Unfortunately, however, neither Byroade in Rangoon nor Administration officials in Washington were attuned to this apparent DRV interest in negotiations. Instead, Administration officials apparently assumed that, since infiltration into the South was continuing and even increasing, the DRV was not ready to "negotiate" seriously (i.e., agree to "leave their neighbors alone").[70]

More importantly, though, the Administration apparently had very

68. Gurtov, p. 11 (the internal quote is apparently taken from the COSVN resolution cited above). See also Gurtov, pp. 15 ff.; General Vinh's "talk," Working Paper, Item 303, pp. 11–12; and the speech by Nguyen Chi Thanh, Working Paper, Item 65, p. 3.

69. Working Paper, p. 21.

70. On these points, see Washington's instructions to Byroade (especially Deptel 227 to Rangoon, January 20, 1966) and Byroade's subsequent comments to Vu Huu Binh, in Pinta Chronology, pp. 7–14. Significantly, despite the apparent DRV effort during the Rangoon contact to signal that "recognition" of the Four Points was no longer a precondition for negotiations, as late as January 1967 Administration officials were still discussing the possibility of a link between acceptance of the Four Points and the start of negotiations (see Sunflower Chronology, p. 17).

little understanding of the maximum and minimum goals being pursued by the DRV. As suggested earlier, it appears that the bare minimum that would have been acceptable in Hanoi was a negotiated settlement that resulted in some type of coalition government in the South. The Administration, however, apparently viewed this as a maximum bid made for bargaining purposes which it adamantly refused to consider.[71] With the benefit of hindsight, this refusal stands as one of the Administration's more serious errors. Given the doubts and disagreements in Hanoi described above, an American offer to discuss a coalition arrangement for the South might well have seriously undercut the position of Le Duan and the "hawks" and strengthened the position of those who had opposed his policies all along. Nor would such an offer necessarily have led to the collapse of the anti-Communist position in the South, as Administration officials feared. The Administration would have been free to go ahead both with military operations in the South and with the bombing of the North—the DRV had no monopoly on a strategy of "fighting and negotiating."[72] In addition, a coalition arrangement and de facto partition of the South (e.g., along the lines of the "leopard spot" solution eventually accepted by the Nixon Administration) might well have strengthened the position of the GVN by entrenching it in a smaller and more defensible territorial base. However, not only did the Administration refuse to negotiate along these lines, but the chance of even talking about a coalition arrangement was effectively lost by the holding of the Honolulu Conference in February 1966, during which Administration and GVN spokesmen condemned the idea of coalition in no uncertain terms (see Chapter 3, above). In short, it appears that a chance to, at best, negotiate a settlement and, at least,

71. See, for example, the Administration's formal reply to the DRV message of January 31, 1966, discussed in Chapter 3, above; see also the discussion of the DRV negotiating position in the cables exchanged between Washington and the U.S. Embassy in Moscow in January 1967, in Sunflower Chronology, pp. 13-15.

72. The Administration, however, would have been well advised to avoid striking sensitive targets in the North if it appeared that serious negotiations were under way. It might also be helpful to distinguish this point from an earlier criticism directed at the Administration. During the bombing pause, as we saw earlier, the Administration called on the DRV/VC side to reduce (and preferably end) the infiltration into the South as well as the level of fighting in the South while the pause was under way. However, not only was the U.S. building up its own forces in the South while pushing ahead with its own side of the ground war, but, more importantly, its emphasis on mutual de-escalation, if accepted by the DRV, would have had the *political* side effect of leaving the GVN in place in Saigon. It seems hypocritical to call on one's opponent to match some de-escalatory move in a way that has disastrous military and political consequences for the opponent, while it seems only realistic for both sides to continue (or even escalate) their military efforts in an attempt to influence negotiations then under way on the political issues involved (i.e., a strategy of fighting-and-negotiating).

raise havoc among the contending factions in Hanoi was thrown away for the sake of what was essentially a public relations exercise.[73]

This failure to understand what it was that motivated the North Vietnamese also characterized the Administration's handling of subsequent diplomatic initiatives, especially the MARIGOLD contact, which was supposed to result in direct U.S.-DRV talks in Warsaw. Despite the collapse of the Rangoon channel (not to mention the abortive effort by the Canadian intermediary, Chester Ronning), it appears that by the summer of 1966 there was more interest in negotiations than ever before in Hanoi, a development that was almost certainly related to a rising tide of discontent over the course of the war in the South. Indicative of this discontent were two articles published in the summer of 1966—one by Truong Son (a pseudonym) and the other by Nguyen Chi Thanh.[74] Since the two articles constituted a resounding defense of Nguyen Chi Thanh's leadership of the war in the South, it seems reasonable to infer that there must have been considerable criticism aimed at the Southern command during early 1966; furthermore, the argumentative tone of both articles suggests that the dispute was a heated one. For example, as Latimer notes,

on the vital question of whether the communists' forces should have gone on the defensive when faced with the American dry season offensive, Truong Son stated flatly that "if we had hesitated even for a minute and busied ourselves with finding fighting methods against the Americans before firmly asserting our determination to fight them, disastrous consequences would have resulted." The article belittled those who "trembled" in the face of American military strength and boasted that the "liberation" forces would "defeat the Americans politically and even militarily."[75]

In similar fashion,

Nguyen Chi Thanh lashed out at those who opposed his offensive strategy, accusing them of having "feeble revolutionary determination," of using "empty arguments in illogical reasoning," of refusing to study theory and reality, of

---

73. As Cooper (1972, pp. 362–363) notes, the Honolulu Conference was timed to coincide with (and thus steal the headlines from) the Senate Foreign Relations Committee hearings on Vietnam. See also Evans and Novak, pp. 592–595.

74. As Latimer (p. 252) notes: "Throughout the article by Truong Son, the word 'we' was used to connote the leadership of the southern command, making it almost certain that Truong Son was Nguyen Chi Thanh himself or one of his top lieutenants at the Central Office for South Vietnam." Honey ("North Vietnam Quarterly Survey no. 22," China News Analysis, 628 [September 9, 1966], 4) also concludes that Truong Son was a very high-ranking official. Truong Son's article appeared in the June 14, 1966 issue of Nhan Dan; Thanh's article appeared in the July 1966 issue of Hoc Tap.

75. Latimer, pp. 256–257.

making "vague statements" in order to win others over to their viewpoint, of pointing to difficulties but not to overcome them, of pointing to the enemy's strength, not to cope with it but to threaten others, thus spreading pessimism, of arousing "non-revolutionary feelings" which undercut other people's determination, of citing problems but without offering solutions, and of throwing in a lot of "but's" whenever mentioning that the war would be successful.[76]

The bitterest rejoinders, though, were reserved for Giap and Truong Chinh, both of whom had continually stressed the importance of following the path blazed during the Resistance War against the French, with its heavy emphasis on guerrilla war and political struggle. In a particularly scathing passage, Thanh noted that:

Firstly, one may have a conservative spirit and fail to identify and discover the new factors. As a result, one would devote oneself to working according to the "old methods." Secondly, one may be incapable of analyzing the new concrete situation so as to formulate correct and creative opinions. As a result, one turns one's attention to finding the new factors in the formulas that already exist in the books and, copying in a mechanical manner one's past experiences or the experiences of foreign countries, then apply to the live revolutionary realities a "forced marriage" in accordance with a dogmatic tendency.

For instance, upon learning that the enemy has just increased his troop strength, and without conducting a prior inquiry and studying the situation, one hastily jumps to such conclusions as: the number of phases in our revolutionary war and the phase which we are now in; to annihilate one puppet battalion we must have a troop superiority of two to one and, therefore, to fight and annihilate one American battalion—which is better equipped, and whose American officers are better than puppet officers—we must have a superiority in strength of at least seven to one or nine to one; and so forth. In fact, this is nothing but a kind of "divination" and not a scientific calculation, and usually the "diviners" are inclined to take retrogressive steps. . . . To repeat exactly what belongs to history in the context of a new reality is an adventurous act.[77]

As should be evident from the passage just cited, at least some in the leadership apparently questioned the wisdom of attempting to stay on the offensive against as formidable an opponent as the Americans. As a result, it was probably not by chance that Lewandowski returned to

76. Ibid., pp. 262–263.

77. Quoted in P. J. Honey, *China News Analysis*, 628 (September 9, 1966), 4–5. See also Zagoria, pp. 85–86. On the roles of Giap and Truong Chinh and on Nguyen Chi Thanh's critique of their views, see Latimer, pp. 264–266. Both Truong Chinh (*The Resistance Will Win*) and Giap (*People's War, People's Army*) had authored well-known books, which suggests that Thanh's comment on "finding new factors in the formulas that already exist in the books" was aimed directly at them.

Saigon from Hanoi in late June 1966 with what he called a "very specific peace offer" (see Chapter 3, above). Significantly, it appears that this time the North Vietnamese went much further than ever before in attempting to whet Washington's appetite for talks. In this respect, it might be worthwhile to recount Lewandowski's list of items *not* being demanded by Hanoi: immediate reunification, socialism in the South, neutralization of the South, immediate U.S. withdrawal, and the right to interfere with the GVN. In addition, it appears that the North Vietnamese were no longer demanding that the NLF be considered the sole legitimate representative of the South Vietnamese people. Instead, they insisted only that the NLF "take part" in the negotiations, a position later amplified by Lewandowski's comment to D'Orlandi that the North Vietnamese envisioned a "coalition government" consisting mainly of "sensible South Vietnamese politicians" with one or two men each from the "right" and the NLF in "unimportant ministries" (see Chapter 3, above).

Assuming that Lewandowski was reporting accurately, this new DRV stance represented a considerable softening from previous positions. More importantly, the softening in the DRV stance came *before* the actual negotiations, thus suggesting that further concessions might have been forthcoming once direct U.S.-DRV talks were under way. Furthermore, it appears that the shift in the DRV position was itself the subject of bitter controversy in Hanoi.[78] As we saw in Chapter 3, the contact bogged down in August and September 1966, a development that Lewandowski attributed to the absence from Hanoi of Pham Van Dong and Giap. Interestingly, both Pham Van Dong and Giap were reported to be in Moscow in August 1966 for secret negotiations with the Soviets (during which the Soviets apparently urged them to seek a settlement with the U.S.), which suggests that, in their absence, other DRV officials were unwilling and/or unable to move the contact forward.[79] In

78. As Latimer (pp. 262–263) notes: in the July 1966 *Hoc Tap* article cited in note 74, above, Nguyen Chi Thanh "suggested that there was some inclination to accept President Johnson's negotiation offer. Thanh noted that the American 'carrot and stick' approach was one of the factors putting a strain on the 'ideological stand' of the party." See also the list of conditions for entering negotiations posed by General Nguyen Van Vinh during his April 1966 "talk" before the 4th COSVN Congress (Working Paper, Item 303, p. 16). A comparison of the conditions posed by Vinh with the list of items that the DRV was *not* demanding as part of the MARIGOLD contact suggests that Pham Van Dong's handling of the contact provoked bitter opposition from the hard-liners in the leadership.

79. On the Pham Van Dong/Giap visit to Moscow, see Zagoria (p. 155), who cites "unconfirmed reports" that Pham Van Dong (Zagoria does not mention Giap) was in Moscow during August 1966; and P. J. Honey (*China News Analysis*, 628 [September 9, 1966], 6), who reports that both Pham Van Dong and Giap went to Moscow in August. On the possibility that the Soviets urged

addition, by October 1966, the intra-Party dispute over strategy had broken out again in full force. As Latimer notes:

Despite Nguyen Chi Thanh's vigorous defense of his command in the South, critics continued to snipe at him. An unsigned article in the October 23, 1966 issue of *Quan Doi Nhan Dan* (People's Army), for example, praised the guerrilla war in the South but noted that it was not strong in the northern two provinces of South Vietnam, the delta or the coastal areas of central Vietnam and in the delta provinces around and south of Saigon. In short, guerrilla warfare under Nguyen Chi Thanh was doing fine except where it counted, namely where the people were. A major article, written in November 1966 under the pseudonym Cuu Long (the Vietnamese name for the Mekong River), took basic issue with Nguyen Chi Thanh's thesis that the situation was ripe for main force warfare to play the primary role in South Vietnam. According to Cuu Long . . . guerrilla warfare is a "basic form of warfare." Guerrilla units, said Cuu Long, were capable of striking and defeating battalion-sized units of the U.S. and ARVN. He emphasized the need for coordination between guerrilla and main force operations, a significant point in light of the unsigned article's notation that guerrilla warfare was weak in certain areas where the communists were trying to wage regular warfare on a fairly large scale.[80]

Most importantly, on October 25, 1966, Pham Van Dong pledged publicly that there would be no sellout peace in Vietnam: "Never Munich again, in whatever form."[81] The Premier's reference to "Munich," at a time when he was engaged in a delicate effort to open negotiations with the U.S., suggests that the proponents of main force warfare in the South (who were themselves the target of increasing criticism in Hanoi) may have responded to their critics by attempting to discredit the main alternative to their preferred approach—namely, Pham Van Dong's diplomatic track.

Once again, though, the Administration was not attuned to the subtleties of DRV decision-making, and this lack of understanding would ultimately prove fatal for the MARIGOLD contact. By the end of November 1966, as we saw in Chapter 4, the North Vietnamese were sufficiently interested in Lewandowski's formulation of the American position that Lewandowski was authorized to tell Lodge that "if the U.S. are really of the view which I have presented, it would be advisable

---

the DRV to begin negotiations, see Marigold Discussion, pp. 11–12; and P.J. Honey, "North Vietnam Quarterly Survey no. 23," *China News Analysis*, 641 (December 16, 1966), 5.

80. Latimer, pp. 267–268. Cuu Long's article was broadcast over Liberation Radio on November 13, 1966. Latimer also suggests that, based on the authoritative tone of his articles, Cuu Long was probably a leading Party official in the South.

81. Quoted by Fall, p. 161.

to confirm them directly by conversation with the North Vietnamese Ambassador in Warsaw."[82] At this point, however, everything that could have gone wrong did so, with results that can only be characterized as disastrous. As suggested in Chapter 4, it appears that the one factor that enabled Pham Van Dong to win Politburo support for the Warsaw talks was the thinly veiled reference in the second of Lewandowski's 10 Points (see Appendix IV) to the formation of a coalition government in the South. And yet, within a few days of Lewandowski's return to Saigon, not only were Hanoi-area targets bombed twice (on December 2 and 4), using considerably more ordnance than in earlier raids, but the U.S. also informed the Poles that Lewandowski's 10 Points, while broadly reflecting the U.S. position, contained "several specific points" that were "subject to important differences of interpretation." Taken together, these two moves could easily have appeared to Hanoi not just as an American attempt to renege on the coalition government issue but as a tacit ultimatum to allow the U.S. to modify the terms of the 10 Points or else risk the devastation of Hanoi.

Still, the contact was not yet dead—in fact, if Burchett's information[83] is correct and the North Vietnamese had an official en route to Warsaw at the time of the renewed bombing of Hanoi on December 13–14, then it would appear that they were willing to proceed with the talks despite the ill-timed bombings of December 2 and 4 and the apparent attempt to renege on the 10 Points.[84] However, it also appears that there was considerable sensitivity in Hanoi on both of these issues, as evidenced by the frequent Polish warnings (which the Poles claimed were based on

82. It is tempting to speculate on the possible links between the MARIGOLD contact and the travel plans of various Politburo members. In early December 1966, DRV Foreign Minister Trinh, who has often been identified as a proponent of negotiations with the West, was scheduled to visit Hungary. Trinh, however, was unable to make the visit because of "urgent problems at home," so Le Duan went instead. Le Duan, according to Foreign Minister Peter of Hungary (who told U Thant, who passed the information to Arthur Goldberg), "took a very hard line about settlement of Vietnamese conflict—a harder line than [Hungarians] believe would have been taken by Trinh." Was it by chance that Trinh stayed in Hanoi while Le Duan (a consistent opponent of negotiations) visited Hungary, thus conveniently removing him from the scene while the Warsaw talks were being considered in Hanoi? Unfortunately, the data available do not permit us to answer this question with any certainty. On this point, see Marigold Chronology, p. 87.

83. On December 6, 1967, Wilfred Burchett told officials at the American Embassy in Paris that a DRV official had been en route to Warsaw to take over the talks at the time of the December 13–14 attacks on Hanoi (see Marigold Chronology, p. 134). Burchett's claim, however, should be treated with skepticism, since he was obviously not an impartial observer. In an interview with the author (March 4, 1977), William Bundy stated that he was not aware of any information supporting the validity of Burchett's claim.

84. This line of argument was suggested by the Pentagon analyst in Marigold Discussion, pp. 4–5.

what Hanoi was telling them) to Washington to clarify its position on the 10 Points and refrain from *escalating* the bombing.

These Polish warnings, however, were not taken at face value in Washington. Not only did the Administration not wish to clarify its position on the coalition government issue (not surprising since the Administration adamantly opposed any coalition arrangement), but the President refused to delete the Hanoi-area targets authorized as part of ROLLING THUNDER 52. Given the decision-making "model" underlying Administration policy, in which a DRV decision to end its role in the war was seen as a function of increasing American pressures (i.e., when costs exceed expected gains, the DRV will quit), the President's decision was hardly surprising. The ensuing raids on Hanoi, however, on December 13–14, during which more than one hundred tons of ordnance were dropped (compared to approximately fifty tons on December 2 and 4) and residential areas of the city were hit, apparently shattered the fragile consensus in Hanoi and resulted in the breakdown of the contact. As described in Michalowski's postmortem (see Chapter 4, above), the bombings of December 13–14 had provided those in the leadership in Hanoi who had been skeptical of negotiations all along with a powerful argument to support their case. Once again, the Administration's actions had resulted in exactly the opposite of what they were intended to accomplish.

With the benefit of hindsight, it appears that the MARIGOLD contact offered the best opportunity for the Johnson Administration to negotiate a settlement of the conflict. At that time (November–December 1966), public support for the war within the U.S. was still relatively high;[85] in addition, with close to 400,000 American troops in South Vietnam (and more on the way), it appears that this was the point at which the balance of forces was most favorable to the U.S./GVN side.[86] Most importantly, late 1966 was probably the point at which the position of the "hawks" in Hanoi was weakest, largely as a result of the failure of their ambitious strategy to result in victory.[87] In retrospect, it

85. As of November 1966, only 31 percent of a national sample responded "yes" to the question, "In view of the developments since we entered the fighting in Vietnam, do you think the U.S. made a mistake sending troops to fight in Vietnam?" Fifty-one percent answered "no," and 18 percent had no opinion. It was not until October 1967 that opposition to the war exceeded support as measured by the "mistake" question. On these points, see John E. Mueller, *War, Presidents, and Public Opinion* (New York: John Wiley, 1973), pp. 52–58.

86. On this point, see IV Gravel, pp. 387–388.

87. In addition P.J. Honey (*China News Analysis*, 641 [December 16, 1966], 4) cited reports that during late 1966, more than half of the military aid dispatched to North Vietnam by the Soviet

appears that Lewandowski was correct when he claimed that Pham Van Dong had "the Praesidium behind him."

With the breakdown of the MARIGOLD contact, though, two crucial developments took place in Hanoi. First, it appears that the proponents of negotiations were somewhat discredited, as Michalowski claimed, by the ill-timed bombings of December 2, 4, 13, and 14, which, when viewed from Hanoi, must have appeared as a heavy-handed attempt to squeeze additional concessions from Hanoi (this, after the North Vietnamese had apparently gone further than ever before in attempting to appear reasonable).[88] As a result, while DRV representatives continued to probe the U.S. position for evidence of willingness to discuss coalition arrangements for the South, those representatives would evince a much more cautious attitude throughout 1967 on the question of beginning substantive talks. In contrast to their readiness to discuss substantive issues during the Paris and Rangoon contacts and the proposed Warsaw talks, the North Vietnamese now insisted that if the Americans wanted talks, they would have to take the first step by stopping the bombing—only then would it be possible to discuss substantive issues.[89]

Second, it appears that the breakdown of the MARIGOLD contact signalled the renewed ascendance of the "hawks" in Hanoi. During the last week of January and the first week of February 1967, as we saw in Chapter 4, an additional PAVN division moved into position just north of the DMZ (joining two others already in the area). In addition,

With the Tet truce, the movement of supplies southward between the 19th and 17th parallels in the DRV increased sharply, to a rate about double that of the Christmas truce and several times that of non-truce. Thus throughout the first

---

Union and Eastern Europe was being held up in China, which could well have been a further cause for discouragement in Hanoi.

88. Ambassador Dobrynin and the Soviet Chargé in Washington, Alexander Zinchuk, insisted that the bombings of Hanoi had been interpreted by the North Vietnamese as an attempt to pressure them into making additional concessions, thus leading the North Vietnamese to instruct the Poles to break off the contact. On this point, see Marigold Chronology, pp. 78–79; Sunflower Discussion, p. 24; and Sunflower Chronology, pp. 75, 87.

89. One possible exception to this statement is the January 17, 1967 meeting between Guthrie and Le Chang in Moscow (see Chapter 4, above), during which Le Chang asked for clarification of the U.S. message of January 10, especially with respect to the kind of settlement envisioned by the U.S. It appears, however, that this was simply a request for additional information rather than a signal of willingness to negotiate, for when the U.S. reply indicated that the U.S. still sought a settlement based on mutual de-escalation, Le Chang rejected the American proposal for immediate talks and demanded a bombing halt as the price for talks.

weeks of [1967], the Communists seemed increasingly to be positioning themselves to undertake combat operations at a substantially increased level.[90]

Furthermore, it appears that the early months of 1967 witnessed an emerging consensus in Hanoi that the time was ripe to launch the all-out offensive in the South that had been foreshadowed in the Resolution passed at the Central Committee's 12th Plenum in December 1965. Indicative of this emerging consensus was the resolution passed by the Central Committee's 13th Plenum, which convened in Hanoi sometime in early 1967, calling for a "spontaneous uprising" in order to win "a decisive victory in the shortest time possible" (in contrast to the resolution of the 12th Plenum, which, as we saw, mandated a "decisive victory within a relatively short period of time"—i.e., a "few years").[91] Such an offensive, moreover, was probably intended to be combined with a well-timed offer of negotiations leading to a settlement that would provide for an American withdrawal and a coalition government for the South.[92]

This is not to suggest, however, that the consensus that emerged was easily reached. Instead, it appears that there was still considerable disagreement during early 1967 over how best to fight the Americans, especially with respect to the question of which forces—i.e., the main forces or the guerrilla and regional units—should bear the brunt of the fighting.[93] In addition, there appears to have been considerable disagreement over how far the Party should go in attempting to negotiate the Americans out of the South, as evidenced by a July 22, 1967, article by General Le Quang Dao, which argued that "If one deviates from the path of revolution through violence, he will enter the path of reform and compromise," which would "inevitably lead toward the loss of independence, freedom, and the right to be master of one's destiny."[94] Le

90. Sunflower Discussion, p. 12. See also Sunflower Discussion, p. 13; and IV Gravel, pp. 143–144.

91. The resolution of the 13th Plenum is quoted in Shaplen (1970), p. 400. There is no consensus in the literature on the date of the 13th Plenum: Shaplen says that it occurred in early 1967, although he also cites an April 1967 meeting in the South at which high-level cadres were informed of the Plenum's decisions. P.J. Honey ("North Vietnam Quarterly Survey no. 28," *China News Analysis*, 701 [March 22, 1968], 4–6) assigns the 13th Plenum to April 1967; while Oberdorfer (1971, p. 63) states that the Politburo's (not the Plenum's) decision on the Tet Offensive was not made until July 1967. Oberdorfer's account is not necessarily inconsistent with those of Shaplen and Honey, since the Central Committee's decision may have been limited to a call for a "spontaneous uprising," leaving the details to be worked out by the Politburo. That was, after all, the pattern used in the 1959 decision to launch the armed struggle in the South (see Chapter 5 above).

92. On this point, see Shaplen (1970), p. 400; and Oberdorfer (1971), pp. 67–82, especially p. 79.

93. This debate is summarized in Latimer, pp. 278–288, 294–297.

94. Quoted in Latimer, p. 300. See also Chapter 4, above.

Quang Dao's denunciation of the "path of reform and compromise" takes on special significance when viewed in the context of Pham Van Dong's statement to Aubrac and Marcovich on July 25 (see Chapter 4, above, and Appendix V) that the NLF sought a "broad coalition government" for the South, which could include members of the GVN and ARVN.

By the late summer of 1967, however, these disputes had apparently been resolved sufficiently to permit a firm decision to go ahead with a General Offensive and Uprising in the South, a development that may have been facilitated by the death of Nguyen Chi Thanh in June or July of 1967.[95] Thanh was replaced in the South by several senior officials. Pham Hung, as Latimer notes, dropped from sight in Hanoi at about this time and later turned up directing DRV/VC political operations in the South, while the military aspects of Thanh's position were assigned to a number of DRV generals in the South. Meanwhile, in Hanoi, over-all direction of the Southern military effort was apparently given to Giap, who until then had been largely excluded from military planning.[96]

Giap's emergence as over-all commander, in turn, signalled the start of a DRV offensive in the South which apparently was to have three phases and was probably intended to culminate in both the toppling of the Saigon government and an American withdrawal.[97] The first phase (October–December 1967) involved a number of set-piece battles below the DMZ and in the Central Highlands and was apparently intended to draw large numbers of American troops away from the heavily populated areas. Once that had been accomplished, the way was clear for launching the second phase—i.e., an assault on the cities and towns which was carried out during the 1968 Tet holidays. The third phase, which never really got off the ground due to the severe losses suffered by DRV/VC units during the first two phases, was apparently intended to involve a second wave of assaults on the cities along with set-piece battles with American units.

95. Thanh's death was announced by Hanoi on July 7, 1967. On his death, see Latimer, pp. 320 ff.; Shaplen (1970), p. 402; Oberdorfer (1971), pp. 60 ff.; and Turley (1972), p. 189. Oberdorfer's book, especially Chapter 2, contains indispensable background material on the Vietnamese view of the General Offensive and Uprising.

96. On these points, see Latimer, p. 302; Shaplen (1970), p. 402; and Oberdorfer (1971), pp. 73–74. Giap's "signing on" was symbolized by his September 1967 article on "The Big Victory, The Great Task" (summarized in Latimer, pp. 304–308), in which he endorsed both the idea of an all-out offensive and heavy Northern involvement in the war.

97. This discussion of the DRV "Winter–Spring Offensive" is based heavily on Shaplen (1970), pp. 402 ff.; and Pike (1969), pp. 126 ff.

While the first phase of the "Winter–Spring Offensive" was under way in the South, DRV representatives were still participating in various diplomatic contacts, but it appears that whatever interest there had been earlier in a settlement had by and large disappeared during late 1967. It was probably no accident that October 1967 witnessed the breakdown of both the Paris and Peking channels (involving Aubrac/Marcovich and the Norwegians, respectively). Furthermore, as we saw in Chapter 4, Harriman's November 1967 meeting with Maurer in Bucharest revealed, if anything, a stiffening of the DRV position. Viewed in this light, it appears that DRV diplomacy during the period October 1967–January 1968 was aimed not so much at arranging a genuine "compromise" (à la MARIGOLD) as at probing for weaknesses in the American position and sowing discord in the West. If this was the case, it was a remarkably successful policy, as evidenced by the furor aroused in the West by Foreign Minister Trinh's statement on December 29, 1967 that talks "will" take place if the bombing ended.[98]

Hanoi's best-laid plans, however, were just as prone to foul-ups and breakdowns as were Washington's. Not only did the first phase of the Winter–Spring Offensive generate enormous casualties, but the second phase—i.e., the Tet attacks—did not work out as planned either. Not only were the attackers unable to seize and hold (with the temporary exception of Hue) any of the cities and towns hit in the onslaught, but the expected popular uprisings did not take place either. Worst of all, thousands of veteran Southern cadres—an irreplaceable asset from the DRV/VC point of view—were lost in the fighting. As a result, DRV policymaking during the rest of 1968 can only be characterized as an abrupt about-face. On the one hand, the semi-secret contacts involving Ambassadors Su and D'Orlandi (see Chapter 4, above) suddenly bore fruit, with Su providing his "personal" view that if the bombing stopped and talks began, DRV/VC "spectaculars" such as an assault on Khe Sanh, an invasion of the two northern provinces of South Vietnam, or a second wave of attacks on the cities would not take place.

On the other hand, it appears that the "hawks" in Hanoi were again somewhat discredited by the failure of the all-out offensive to produce the desired results. Indicative of the resurgence of the proponents of a more cautious strategy in the South was a report delivered by Truong Chinh in May 1968 which argued for a return to a more conservative strategy and even went so far as to note that "at times, under certain

98. On this point, see Oberdorfer (1971), pp. 85–86.

circumstances, we must shift to the defensive to gain time, dishearten the enemy, and build up our forces for a new offensive."[99] This is not to suggest, however, that the turnabout was easily achieved. Truong Chinh's report generated "several sessions of heated debate," which suggests that the intra-Party struggle must have been especially tumultuous.[100] Further evidence of the existence of a serious rift within the Party can be found in the fact that Truong Chinh's report, while delivered in May, was not mentioned publicly in the North until August and was not broadcast until mid-September. By then, though, it was clear that Truong Chinh and his supporters had in fact won the intra-Party struggle. As Latimer notes, the Radio Hanoi announcement cited above noted that Truong Chinh's report had been delivered on behalf of the Politburo, while an October 1968 *Nhan Dan* article described the report as a "new contribution to the treasury of theoretical works on the Vietnamese revolution."[101] With that, Hanoi, like Washington, had come full circle on questions of war and peace. The way was now clear for both sides to pursue at the negotiating table in Paris what they had not been able to win on the battlefields of South Vietnam.

IV. Summary and Conclusions

At this point it might be helpful to review briefly the main themes of this chapter. The record is certainly a disturbing one. Not only did the Administration have great difficulty with what might be called the "technical" aspects of "orchestrating" words and deeds and "signalling" by deed as well as by word, but in addition it appears that an awareness of these technical problems never did make its way to the highest levels of the Administration. As a result, senior officials continued to speak and write of the need for an "orchestrated" effort that would convey certain messages to Hanoi even as their own actions and the actions of their subordinates demonstrated their inability to act in conformity with their own prescriptive statements.

More importantly, though, even if the Administration had been able to overcome these technical problems, it remains doubtful that its policies would have proven more successful, for the simple reason that the

99. See *Vietnam Documents and Research Notes*, no. 51, which contains the complete text of Chinh's report; the quoted excerpt is from p. 26.

100. Radio Hanoi, August 23, 1968; quoted in *Vietnam Documents and Research Notes*, no. 51, p. 2.

101. Radio Hanoi, August 23, 1968, and *Nhan Dan*, October 12, 1968; both quoted in *Vietnam Documents and Research Notes*, no. 51, p. 2. See also Latimer, p. 323.

Administration had so little understanding of what was going on in Hanoi. It is not enough to "orchestrate" words and deeds or to arrange the actions taken by a government into a "pattern" that supposedly communicates certain messages to an opponent; instead, those actions must be meaningful to the audience at which they are aimed. Even the most brilliant "orchestration" will count for nothing if the targets of that effort cannot or will not grasp the significance of the actions taken for their benefit. Consequently, before one can engage in coercion by orchestration or in communication by deed as well as by word, one must know what it is that motivates an opponent, the goals the opponent seeks, and the price the opponent is willing to pay to achieve those goals. Furthermore, since the "opponent" is not a single individual but rather a government comprised of numerous individuals, each of whom will have his or her own goals and aspirations (not the least of which is the desire to save one's political neck by avoiding any admission of error in past policy recommendations), government leaders about to engage in coercion would at the very least require substantial amounts of information about their opposite numbers along with the willingness and the ability to interpret that information correctly.

One may legitimately question, however, whether the leaders of any government—even the "best and the brightest"—would be capable of performing those tasks successfully. As we saw earlier in this chapter, it was difficult, if not impossible, for the top leaders of the Johnson Administration to monitor continuously all of the activities that their subordinates were engaging in, much less pay close attention to what the various actors in Hanoi were saying or doing. In addition, as Neustadt's study of the Suez and Skybolt crises has shown, even when American officials were dealing with a foreign capital as familiar as London, they still had great difficulty understanding what it was that motivated their opposite numbers.[102] How much more difficult it must have been in dealing with a capital as inscrutable as Hanoi. Is it any wonder that Administration officials took refuge in simplistic analogies such as the "Hanoi-as-unitary-rational-actor" approach discussed earlier? And yet, it was precisely this misleading analogy, with its consequent blurring of the subtleties and nuances of decision-making in Hanoi, that led the Administration time and again to take steps that ultimately proved counterproductive.

Still, one must take care not to go further than the evidence allows in drawing conclusions about the ability of governments to pursue foreign

102. Richard Neustadt, *Alliance Politics* (New York: Columbia University Press, 1970).

policy objectives by means of coercive pressures directed at other governments. Although the Administration encountered numerous problems in attempting to shape its actions in a way that would communicate meaningful messages to Hanoi, one cannot conclude that all such efforts would inevitably be doomed to fail. In this respect, it appears that the blockade and military buildup initiated by the Kennedy Administration in October 1962 was at least somewhat successful in convincing the Soviets that an air strike and possibly an invasion of Cuba would follow if their missiles were not withdrawn from the island. Furthermore, despite the very real problems that they encountered, officials of the Johnson Administration probably came closer to succeeding than they realized at the time—i.e., if only the weather had stayed bad over Hanoi for a few days longer in mid-December 1966, the Warsaw talks just might have gotten under way with consequences that could have been of incalculable importance. And yet, a "success" of that sort would hardly have been grounds for self-congratulation in Washington. If there is one conclusion that the evidence does permit us to draw, it is that it is inordinately difficult for one government to influence another in the way that the influencer intended. While Washington's actions admittedly had an effect on those taken by officials in Hanoi, the gap between what Washington hoped Hanoi would do and what Hanoi actually did was so great that one can legitimately question whether an Administration "success," had one been achieved, would have been accomplished because of or in spite of the Administration's efforts. Similarly, the moral of Allison's study of the Cuban crisis is really that the Kennedy Administration succeeded in forcing the Soviets to withdraw their missiles despite the ExComm's inability to control tightly the activities of the agencies charged with implementing its directives.[103] What this means, in short, is that a certain amount of humility is indispensable for the conduct of foreign policy. Statesmen should not delude themselves into believing that the actions of their opponents or allies are solely a function of what they themselves do, nor should they delude themselves into believing that they are in control of events when in fact it is events that are controlling them.

---

103. This seems especially true with respect to the activities of the U.S. Navy. On this point, see Allison, pp. 127–132, 259–261; see also the discussion in Chapter 8, below.

7

Coercive Violence:
"Controllability" and Consensus

In EARLIER CHAPTERS, we saw how the Johnson Administration was generally optimistic concerning the eventual outcome of the air war over North Vietnam and the influx of American troops into South Vietnam. That is, by using military force in a carefully controlled, "orchestrated" fashion, Administration officials expected to achieve a negotiated settlement on terms acceptable to the United States. At the same time, though, senior Administration officials believed that at least the bombing was not an irrevocable step, that it could be turned on or off, up or down at will, and that if it did not "work" it could always be stopped. Indeed, the belief that the bombing would be "controllable" was implicit in everything U.S. officials wrote and said on the subject of "orchestrating" words and deeds: what could be started ("orchestrated") could also be stopped, or at least that was what Administration officials apparently believed. Thus, for example, Maxwell Taylor, in a post-Pleiku cable to Washington, recommended a "measured, *controlled* sequence of actions against the DRV taken in reprisal for DRV-inspired actions in South Vietnam." Similarly, William Bundy's November 24, 1964 "Draft Position Paper on Southeast Asia" noted that the "whole sequence of actions [against the DRV] should be designed to give the impression of a steady, deliberate approach, and to give the U.S. the option at any time (subject to enemy reaction) to proceed or not, to escalate or not, and to quicken the pace or not." Even the JCS climbed on board the "controllability" bandwagon, as evidenced by Admiral Mustin's (their representative on the Bundy Working Group) comment that "while the JCS offer the capability for pursuing Option B [the "fast/full squeeze"] as defined, they have not explicitly recommended that the operations be conducted on a basis necessarily that inflexible. All implementing plans . . . would permit suspension whenever desired by national authority."[1] While these officials were admittedly more skeptical about their ability to control the level of violence once American ground troops entered the war —Taylor, for example, cabled Washington on February 22, 1965 that, once the policy of "avoiding commitment of ground combat forces in South Vietnam . . . is breached, it will be very difficult to hold the line" —those doubts were apparently offset by a belief that once American troops were brought in, it would all be over relatively quickly.[2]

In similar fashion, a belief in the "controllability" of violence was widely held among academic theorists interested in the problem of limited/coercive war. With the exception of Herman Kahn, who recognized that going up the escalation "ladder" might prove easier than coming down, most of these theorists assumed, at least implicitly, that limits could be set during wartime and that it would be possible to escape from a losing cause. William Kaufmann, for example, argued that:

> Whether attempting to deter or beat back the enemy, we will be acting, not on an all-or-nothing basis, but within the context of a continuing competition. Whatever the nature of the particular situation, we shall therefore want to ensure our ability to go on playing the game. To do so, however, means far more than the adoption of limited objectives. It implies a willingness to bargain, to avoid fixed positions, and on occasions even to cut losses and bow out as gracefully as possible from difficult and unprofitable conflicts.[3]

Once again, however, just as in the case of beliefs about DRV susceptibility to American pressures and the "orchestratability" of American actions, these expectations proved to be unwarranted. It is one of the more tragic ironies of the Vietnam conflict that Secretary

1. Taylor's cable is quoted in III Gravel, p. 315. Bundy's memo is Document no. 246 in III Gravel, p. 678. For Mustin's comments, see III Gravel, p. 221, and Document no. 231 in III Gravel, pp. 630–632; see also III Gravel, pp. 233–234, for additional JCS comments on this point. See also President Johnson's comments on the "controllability" of the air war, quoted in Doris Kearns, *Lyndon Johnson and the American Dream* (New York: Signet, 1977), p. 277; the McGeorge Bundy memo cited in Chapter 6, note 20, above; and the references cited in Chapter 1, note 11, above.

2. For Taylor's cable, see III Gravel, p. 418. See also the reservations expressed by Alex Johnson, cited in III Gravel, p. 472; and the Pentagon analyst's discussion of John McNaughton's attempt to substitute the 173rd Airborne Brigade for the Marines at DaNang (III Gravel, pp. 421–422). On the belief that the introduction of U.S. troops would lead to a speedy settlement, see Halberstam, pp. 696, 717.

3. William Kaufmann, "Force and Foreign Policy," in Kaufmann (ed.), pp. 247–248. See also Kaufmann, "Limited Warfare," in Kaufmann (ed.), p. 116; Kissinger (1958), pp. 188–189; Schelling (1960), chap. 3; Halperin (1963), p. 122; Schelling (1966), chap. 4; and Kahn, pp. 231–234. See also the comment by Brodie, cited in Chapter 1, note 31, above.

McNamara, who had been a forceful proponent of the view that the Administration was not foreclosing any options by going ahead with the air war,[4] should have spent his last two years in office in a futile attempt to stabilize and eventually end the air war and also to place a ceiling on the number of American troops in South Vietnam, only to be rewarded for his efforts by the loss of his job. How could McNamara have been so wrong? Why should it have proven so hard to control the escalatory process? Why were the Administration's expectations so mistaken?

Closely related to questions such as these is the problem of accounting for the persistent "sameness" in American policy toward Vietnam between March 1965 and March 1968. As we saw in Chapters 3–4, the President repeatedly opted for choices involving "more of the same" (i.e., a few more troops and/or a little more bombing, along with a constant repetition of the same peace terms) even as it was becoming abundantly clear that "more of the same" was not good enough. As suggested by the starkly pessimistic memos produced by civilian officials at the Pentagon and in the CIA in 1966 and 1967, such a policy was not only *not* having the desired effect on Hanoi but was very likely proving to be counterproductive.[5] Even General Westmoreland, when asked by the President on April 27, 1967 what would happen if the U.S. increased its forces in the South, conceded that "this war is action and counteraction. Any time we take an action we expect a reaction. . . . If we add 2½ divisions, it is likely the enemy will react by adding more troops."[6] Still, the President refused to be budged, despite the depressing "sameness" in the results of his choices—i.e., more planes lost over the North, more casualties in the South, and a growing feeling at home that the "light at the end of the tunnel" was proving more elusive with each passing day.

This proclivity for choices involving "more of the same" ranks as one of the more perplexing aspects of Administration policy, standing in stark contrast to the belief that the bombing would be "controllable" and that it could be turned off if it did not lead to an acceptable settlement. Why should there have been this rigidity in Administration policy? This was not, after all, a situation in which no alternatives were

4. For McNamara's views, see Halberstam, pp. 624–626.

5. See, for example, the May 5, 1967 DPM prepared by John McNaughton, quoted in IV Gravel, p. 161; and the March 1967 memo by the Systems Analysis Office, quoted in IV Gravel, p. 457. See also the CIA reports on the failure of the air war, quoted in IV Gravel, pp. 56, 137, 168, 184; and the 1966 and 1967 JASON studies of the air war, quoted in IV Gravel, pp. 111–112, 115–123, 222–225.

6. Quoted in IV Gravel, p. 442.

available. As we saw in Chapters 3–4, civilian officials at the Pentagon (with some help from the Bundy brothers) argued strenuously during 1966 and 1967 for a reorientation of the bombing that would shift the weight of the air war away from the Hanoi-Haiphong area and concentrate it instead on the infiltration routes in the southern DRV (with a further alternative being to eliminate the bombing completely and substitute instead an anti-infiltration barrier along the 17th Parallel).[7] These suggestions, however, were uniformly rejected by the President (at least up until March 31, 1968). Why? Why this unwillingness to abandon a policy that was clearly not accomplishing what its architects had expected?

In attempting to answer questions such as these, it might be helpful to review both the strategy underlying the Administration's policies and also the style of decision-making utilized by the President in the course of implementing that strategy. The Administration's strategy, as we saw earlier, was based on the concept of "graduated pressures," the idea being that by applying progressively more severe pressures on the North (while using American troops to block a DRV/VC takeover in the South), "Hanoi" would be led to calculate that the costs of continuing its role in the war would exceed any possible gains, thus causing it to negotiate a settlement acceptable to the United States.

The strategy, however, was flawed in that it generated considerable criticism both from inside and outside the Administration. On the one hand, the strategy was denounced by "hawks" (in the military and the Congress) who wanted the Administration to do much more to end the insurgency in South Vietnam, while, on the other hand, the strategy was also criticized by "doves" who opposed the Administration's policies in Southeast Asia, arguing that it should do less militarily and more with respect to seeking a negotiated settlement. By late 1966, "dovish" critics (most of whom were outside the Administration) were joined increasingly by Pentagon civilians who opposed the military's requests for more troops and bombing and who sought instead to stabilize and eventually end the American role in the war.

As a result, as Gelb notes, President Johnson, much like his predecessors, was pressured from all sides, both by "hawks" who wanted to do more and by "doves" who wanted to do less. In response, the President, again like his predecessors, played the role of "brakeman," "pulling the switch against both the advocates of 'decisive escalation' and the advocates of disengagement."[8] The key was to stake out the middle ground.

7. On the barrier proposal, see IV Gravel, pp. 112–124.

8. Leslie Gelb, "Vietnam: The System Worked," *Foreign Policy*, 3 (Summer 1971), 147–148.

As we saw in Chapters 3-4, prior to each Presidential decision on a revision of the ROLLING THUNDER program or the deployment of additional American troops to South Vietnam, the military would prepare a list of targets that they wished to strike (often involving sensitive targets such as the Haiphong docks or targets in or around Hanoi) or a list of the units that they wanted to send to South Vietnam; civilian officials would vigorously dispute the wisdom of those proposals; and the President would invariably respond by seeking a compromise—i.e., by authorizing the military to strike some but not all of the targets on their list or to deploy some but not all of the troops they wished to send to South Vietnam. At the same time, the President did many things that the "hawks" opposed but which were reassuring to and applauded by the "doves," such as publicly announcing the Administration's readiness for "unconditional discussions" and pursuing (albeit unenthusiastically) numerous diplomatic contacts with Hanoi.[9]

But in order to understand fully the reasons underlying the Administration's inability to achieve better control over the use of force in Vietnam, there are three additional questions that must be raised. First, why was there this deep concern on the part of the President for maintaining at least the appearance of a consensus on Vietnam within his Administration? Second, what were the consequences of the President's style of decision-making? Third and most importantly, was "consensus politics" really compatible with "graduated pressures"? Would a policy that satisfied the dictates of the former also meet the requirements of the latter?

Concerning the first question, whatever its faults (and these will be discussed in more detail below), the Johnsonian tactic of capturing the middle did have the virtue of maintaining at least the appearance of unity within his Administration. Although the JCS grumbled repeatedly in private about not being able to fight the war in the way they thought best, publicly the Administration was able to present a more or less united front to its critics (the Stennis Committee hearings on the air war were a prominent exception here). There were no senior military resignations over the conduct of the war, as there might well have been had the President accepted McNamara's arguments to stabilize and eventually halt the bombing.[10] At the same time, the periodic peace initiatives and the standing offer of "unconditional discussions" sufficed to keep the "doves" within the Administration "on board,"

9. On this pattern of decision-making, see Gelb, pp. 162-165; and Ralph Stavins, "Washington Determines the Fate of Vietnam: 1954-1965," in Stavins, Barnet, and Raskin, pp. 180-185.

10. On this point, see Halberstam, p. 782. On the Stennis Committee hearings, see IV Gravel, pp. 199-205; and Chapter 4, above.

although they, too, grumbled privately about the course the Administration was following. Keeping people "on board," moreover, was politically important to a President who, at least up until March 1968, gave every appearance of seeking reelection and who could hardly afford a public split within his official family at a time when his policies were being subjected to increasing criticism by opponents outside the Administration. More importantly, the appearance of consensus was critically important to a President who, upon discovering that the expected quick victory had not materialized, sought to persevere in the hope that tenacity and force of will would eventually persuade "Hanoi" to negotiate a settlement acceptable to the United States.[11]

Second, with respect to the consequences of the President's style of decision-making, three points come readily to mind. One consequence, obviously, was incremental escalation, as the President continually doled out bits and pieces of escalatory authority to the military. A second consequence stemmed from the President's desire to pacify the "doves" as well as the "hawks." As James Reston noted:

Everything in the Johnson strategy seems to be done in twos—something for the hawks and something for the doves; bomb North Vietnam and go to the UN Security Council; step up the military forces and increase the pacification program and send Hubert Humphrey to Saigon at the same time; criticize the Saigon government in private and commit American prestige to it in public; assert that America cannot police the world but proclaim simultaneously that tyranny and subjugation in the jungles of continental Asia is just as much America's concern as tyranny and subjugation of the peoples in Europe.[12]

Third and perhaps most importantly, to the extent that the President sought to keep everyone on board, not only was he forced to turn time and again to the tactic of staking out the middle ground and doling out additional bits of escalatory authority to the military (along with the dramatic, but ineffective, peace overtures), but, in addition, this Presidential preoccupation with consensus introduced an element of rigidity into Administration policy that greatly complicated the task of striking a deal with Hanoi, thus ensuring that the President would have to continue doling out bits and pieces of escalatory authority. For example, one suspects that at least one reason behind the President's December 6, 1966 decision to leave ROLLING THUNDER 52 unchanged (a decision that led to the renewed bombing of Hanoi on December 13–14 and the breakdown of the MARIGOLD contact) was a desire not to offend the

11. On the importance of perseverance, see Gelb, p. 152.
12. James Reston, "Washington: Ships Passing in the Night," *New York Times*, February 9, 1966, p. 38.

JCS. As we saw in Chapter 3, the Chiefs had been incensed by an October 1966 suggestion by Secretary McNamara that the U.S. stabilize the air war over the North and possibly shift the bombing away from the Hanoi/Haiphong area in an attempt to smooth the way to negotiations. In response, the Chiefs argued that any further overt actions in search of negotiations would not only be "nonproductive" but "counterproductive," in that they would cast doubt on the Administration's resolve to finish the job, and they went on to urge a "sharp knock" against DRV capabilities (defined specifically as Presidential authorization for the JCS-approved program for ROLLING THUNDER 52).[13] In light of this proposal, a Presidential decision to suspend the Hanoi-area targets authorized in November as part of ROLLING THUNDER 52 would very likely have been regarded as a direct slap at the JCS (they were, after all, present at the December 6, 1966 meeting at which the critical decision was made).[14] Consequently, the President decided to leave ROLLING THUNDER 52 unchanged, with results that can only be characterized as disastrous. What these examples suggest, in short, is that there was virtually a direct trade-off between the President's ability to sustain a Vietnam consensus and the President's ability to exert close control over the conduct of the air war—i.e., to the extent that the President sought to keep everyone "on board," he was unable to turn the bombing up or down in accordance with the goal of "negotiating" by word and deed in an optimal fashion. Furthermore, because he was unable and/or unwilling to "negotiate" in the desired fashion, he had little choice but to turn repeatedly to policies designed to preserve at least the appearance of consensus, which in turn restricted his ability to "negotiate," and so on.

This suggestion that there was a trade-off between consensus and "controllability" leads directly to the third of the three questions posed above—namely, the compatibility (or lack of it) between "consensus politics" and "graduated pressures." As we saw earlier, the strategy of "graduated pressures" assumed that the Administration could coerce Hanoi into negotiating a settlement acceptable to the U.S. by means of an "orchestration" of military moves and communications to Hanoi. If that didn't work, Administration planners reasoned, the Administration could always stop the air war and try something else. Unfortunately, however, the desire for consensus not only foreclosed the option of

13. For the JCS memo, which they requested be brought to the attention of the President, see IV Gravel, pp. 127–129.

14. In addition, as we saw in Chapter 4, efforts by civilians in the State Department to delete some of the JCS-proposed targets from ROLLING THUNDER 52 resulted in the military attaching unusual importance to striking the remaining targets.

quitting and trying something else, but it also greatly complicated the task of "negotiating" by word and deed by introducing an element of rigidity into the Administration's policies. Furthermore, while "consensus politics" was played out for the benefit of "hawks" and "doves" in Washington, the strategy of "graduated pressures" was aimed at an entirely different audience—namely, officials in Hanoi. How would such a combination appear when viewed from Hanoi? Would an Administration that did everything "in twos" really be capable of "orchestrating" words and deeds in the desired fashion? Consider, for example, the following three cases, all drawn from our survey of U.S.-DRV relations between 1966 and 1968.

The MARIGOLD contact, as we saw in Chapters 3–4, resulted from the efforts of the Polish ICC Commissioner, Janusz Lewandowski, to arrange for direct talks between Washington and Hanoi. In the course of a Lewandowski visit to Hanoi that began on November 16, 1966, the North Vietnamese apparently concluded that "the U.S. was . . . attempting to send a definite, albeit subtle, message. The fact that bombing attacks on Hanoi and Haiphong had practically ceased from mid-November apparently led some North Vietnamese officials to believe that the U.S. was signalling its support of Lewandowski's efforts. . . ."[15] But when Hanoi was bombed on December 2 (shortly after Lewandowski met with Lodge in Saigon to seek American approval for the Warsaw talks) and again on December 4, those same officials "might well have concluded that we were waiting for Lewandowski to return from Hanoi and were dissatisfied with his report. Perhaps the North Vietnamese concluded that the Americans as a consequence had decided to resume attacks on the North Vietnamese capital and major port."[16] In the aftermath of those raids, moreover, both Rapacki in Warsaw and D'Orlandi in Saigon suggested that the U.S. was guilty of deliberate bad faith as a result of the timing of the attacks on Hanoi. In addition, as Michalowski

15. Cooper (1972), p. 405. Cooper's interpretation is supported by the Pentagon analyst, who notes that "Lewandowski told D'Orlandi (who in turn told the U.S. on December 9) that he believed Hanoi had attached significance to the fact that during the two weeks he had been in Hanoi (approximately November 16–30) the bombing had appeared to be at a reduced level. Lewandowski thought Hanoi had interpreted this as a tacit signal of U.S. support for his mission" (Marigold Discussion, p. 16). Similarly, the Soviet Chargé in Washington, Alexander Zinchuk, told William Bundy on December 22, 1966 that "he himself had been in Moscow in late November and had gained the impression that Hanoi (or elements in it) were seriously interested in starting something [i.e., negotiations]. They had been encouraged by the apparent slackening in the pace of our bombing during this period. I [Bundy] at once asked whether this was just a general impression or whether it had something more specific behind it. He replied that it was 'more than a general sense'" (Marigold Chronology, p. 79).

16. Cooper (1972), p. 405.

later told Gronouski, the bombings of early December "had given a weapon to those in Hanoi who had not wanted to agree to negotiations in the first place," while the subsequent attacks on December 13–14 "undercut our [the Poles] whole argument, destroyed that little bit of confidence that existed in Hanoi about [the] intentions of [the] U.S., and left us wide open to charges of being completely naive."[17]

A second example is provided by the efforts of the two French intermediaries, Aubrac and Marcovich, to obtain visas to Hanoi in August 1967. As we saw in Chapters 4 and 6, the President on August 9 approved an addendum to the ROLLING THUNDER authorized list, which included several targets in or near Hanoi, in an attempt to preempt criticism likely to surface at the Stennis Committee hearings on the air war. Two days later, the President approved the text of a message to be carried to Hanoi by Aubrac and Marcovich; while on August 19, the day after their first appeal for visas, the President ordered that all bombing within a 10-mile circle around Hanoi should halt for a 10-day period beginning on August 24 (both to guarantee the safety of Aubrac and Marcovich and as a gesture of good will). Military commanders in the field, however, in an apparent attempt to ensure that the new Hanoi-area targets were hit prior to the August 24 deadline (bad weather between August 13 and August 20 had diverted attacks away from Hanoi), launched some of the fiercest attacks of the war on Hanoi during the period August 21–23, a move that coincided with an August 21 cable to Hanoi by Aubrac and Marcovich urgently requesting visas to Hanoi. On August 25, after the visa request had been turned down, Aubrac and Marcovich passed the American message to Mai Van Bo in Paris for transmission to Hanoi. Unfortunately, however, the "coincidence of heavy bombing attacks on Hanoi on August 21–23, just prior to the transmission of the message, coupled with the fact that the Hanoi suspension was to be of limited duration must have left the DRV leadership with the strong impression that they were being squeezed by Johnsonian pressure tactics and presented with an ultimatum."[18] Consistent with this interpretation, Bo told Aubrac and Marcovich on August 31 that "his government noted unfavorably that the receipt of the August 21 message [requesting visas to Hanoi] coincided with the escalation of the bombing of the North with Hanoi as its objective. Under these

17. The accusations of American bad faith are discussed in Marigold Discussion, p. 18. For the comments by Rapacki and D'Orlandi, see Marigold Chronology, pp. 72–74. For Michalowski's remarks, see Marigold Chronology, pp. 94–95. See also the discussion of the MARIGOLD case in Chapters 4 and 6, above.

18. IV Gravel, p. 205.

conditions it is impossible for the DRV to grant visas to permit Marco-vich and Aubrac to carry the August 25 message to Hanoi."[19] On September 11, Bo gave Aubrac and Marcovich the text of the official DRV reply to the American message of August 25, which noted that "the American message has been communicated after an escalation of the attacks against Hanoi and under the threat of continuation of the attacks against Hanoi. It is clear that this constitutes an ultimatum to the Vietnamese people."[20]

Third, despite the President's attempt to defuse criticism of his policies by means of the August 1967 addendum to ROLLING THUNDER, the Stennis Committee nonetheless released a report that was bitterly critical of the Administration's handling of the air war. As a result,

the President called an unscheduled news conference on September 1 to deny differences among his advisers and to generally overrule his Secretary of Defense on the bombing. More stinging for McNamara, however, than this oral repudiation must have been the subsequent escalatory decisions against his advice. On September 10, for instance, North Vietnam's third port at Campha, a target he had specifically counseled against in his testimony [before the Stennis Committee] was struck for the first time.[21]

Furthermore, on September 11 and 12, U.S. planes struck previously untouched targets in Haiphong.[22] These raids, however, coincided with a new effort by Aubrac and Marcovich, this time to arrange for a Bo-Kissinger meeting in Paris. On September 13 and 14, Marcovich saw Bo to discuss the possibility of such a meeting to allow Kissinger to present the U.S. response to the DRV message of September 11. On September 16, Aubrac and Marcovich met with Bo to pass a written version of the American reply to the DRV message of September 11. Thereafter, Aubrac and Marcovich continued to press Bo on the subject of a meeting with Kissinger. Bo, however, resisted their entreaties, telling them on September 21 that "the Americans are playing a double game—on

19. Pennsylvania, p. 17.
20. Ibid., p. 23.
21. IV Gravel, p. 205. The Stennis Committee's report is summarized in IV Gravel, pp. 203–204.
22. On these attacks, see Don Oberdorfer, "Kissinger Played Major Role in 1967 Dialogue," *Washington Post*, June 27, 1972, p. A-12. See also the UPI dispatch, "U.S. Jets Attack Third Largest Port in North Vietnam," *New York Times*, September 11, 1967, pp. 1, 2; and "Haiphong Bridges Hit by U.S. Bombs; Rail Yards Struck," *New York Times*, September 13, 1967, pp. 1, 3. It is not clear from the available documents when these new targets were authorized, although the Pentagon analyst's comment (note 21, above) would seem to imply that the decision was reached sometime between September 1 and 10.

the one hand they are offering us peace; on the other they increase their bombing."[23]

What is noteworthy about these three examples is the apparent readiness in each case of the North Vietnamese to interpret American actions as the result of a conscious design. Because these events happened that way, someone in Washington must have intended for them to happen that way, or so the North Vietnamese appear to have reasoned.[24] As a result, DRV officials concluded that the U.S. was playing a "double game" or that it was presenting the DRV with an ultimatum (as in the case of the August 1967 bombing of Hanoi), even though, in each case, the motives governing the conduct of American officials appear to have been somewhat less sinister than the motives attributed to them by their counterparts in Hanoi.

Thus, as Cooper notes, "the relationship between major bombing raids and American political decisions was by no means as intimate as the North Vietnamese, or even more sophisticated observers, might have assumed."[25] In the MARIGOLD case, the decline in the level of bombing during the last two weeks in November was not the result of an effort to signal support for Lewandowski, nor were the raids of December 2 and 4 intended to signal dissatisfaction with the message he carried to Saigon—"such a rationale," in Cooper's words, "would have done American policy-makers too much credit." Instead, "the weather became unfavorable for high-level precision bombing just as Lewandowski was leaving for Hanoi with his message, and it remained bad during the entire period he was there. Shortly after he returned to Saigon the skies cleared and the bombing was resumed."[26]

Similarly, the coincidence between the Aubrac/Marcovich appeal for visas and the pounding of Hanoi on August 21–23 resulted not from any conscious scheme but rather from the interaction of three factors:

23. Pennsylvania, p. 33. In a message conveyed orally to Marcovich on September 23, Bo accused the U.S. of following a "two-faced policy" (Pennsylvania, p. 34).

24. On this point, see Jervis (1976, p. 350), who notes that "research on how we form impressions of others has found 'a tendency for perceivers to assume that people always intend to do what they do and intend it to have the effect it has.' In international relations this is especially pronounced when the other's behavior is undesired. Rather than seeing any injuries as a by-product of a policy that was pursued with little regard for him, the actor puts himself at the center of the other's attentions." The portion quoted by Jervis is from Mark Cook, *Interpersonal Perception* (Baltimore: Penguin, 1971), p. 53.

25. Cooper (1972), pp. 405–406.

26. Ibid., p. 405. Cooper's account is supported by the Pentagon analyst (Marigold Discussion, p. 16); and by the *New York Times'* coverage of the air war during November 1966, which confirms that bad weather did in fact hamper the bombing during the last two weeks in November. See also Chapter 4, above.

(1) the President's desire to mollify his critics in the Senate by adding targets to the ROLLING THUNDER authorized list; (2) bad weather over Hanoi between August 13 and August 20, which diverted attacks to the China buffer zone and the southern DRV; and (3) an apparent desire on the part of field commanders to "plaster" the Hanoi-area targets prior to the August 24 ban on attacks within a 10-mile radius of Hanoi. In like manner, the coincidence between the September 1967 attacks on Campha and Haiphong and the attempt to arrange for a Bo-Kissinger meeting in Paris resulted not from any calculated design but rather from the President's desire to pacify his Senatorial critics by adding to the ROLLING THUNDER authorized list.

What we have here, in short, are three cases in which officials in Hanoi apparently assumed that "governmental behavior can be most satisfactorily understood by analogy with the purposive acts of individuals"—i.e., they viewed decision-making in Washington through the "conceptual lenses" of a unitary rational actor model, to borrow Allison's terminology.[27] Nor do these three cases represent isolated instances of such a tendency. As we saw earlier, the military strategy underlying the Johnson Administration's policy toward Vietnam was to a large extent based on a similar model in which "Hanoi" was seen as a unitary actor capable of calculating the expected costs and gains involved in continuing its role in the war and ready to yield as soon as the cost-benefit calculus turned negative. Furthermore, this tendency to perceive the actions of other governments as the product of a single calculating intelligence has been widely noted both by theorists of misperception such as Jervis, Bauer, and White and by theorists of "bureaucratic politics" such as Allison and Halperin. As described by Jervis:

Actors see others as more internally united than they in fact are and generally overestimate the degree to which others are following a coherent policy. The degree to which the other side's policies are the product of internal bargaining, internal misunderstandings, or subordinates' not following instructions is underestimated. This is the case partly because actors tend to be unfamiliar with the details of another state's policy-making processes. Seeing only the finished product, they find it simpler to try to construct a rational explanation for the policies, even though they know that such a rationale could not explain their own policies.[28]

27. Allison, pp. 2–3.
28. Jervis (1968), pp. 475–476. See also Jervis (1976), chap. 8; Raymond A. Bauer, "Problems of Perception and the Relations between the United States and the Soviet Union," *Journal of Conflict Resolution*, 5 (1961), 223–229; Raymond A. Bauer, "Accuracy of Perception in International Relations," *Teachers College Record*, 64 (1963), 291–299; White, chaps. 9–10; Allison and Halperin, pp. 61–64; and Allison, pp. 146–147, 251.

But while the existence of these perceptual tendencies should come as no surprise, their influence on the activities of policymakers in both Washington and Hanoi was striking nonetheless. For one thing, as we have seen repeatedly, officials in Washington were deeply aware of the splits within the Johnson Administration on the subject of Vietnam policy; furthermore, those officials were not only ready but willing and eager to jump into the fray in an attempt to influence Administration policy in accordance with their own views. Most important of all in this respect was the role of the President, who sought both to stand above the fray and also to manipulate it so as to maintain at least the appearance of unity within his Administration.

And yet, while officials in Washington were fully aware of the cleavages within the Administration and also of the fact that the content of policy could be influenced, perhaps decisively, by influencing the "who" and "how" of policymaking, those same officials were apparently unaware, for all practical purposes, that similar cleavages and factional struggles existed in Hanoi.[29] Furthermore, as our discussion of DRV policymaking in Chapters 5 and 6 combined with the three examples presented earlier in this chapter should suggest, this tendency to be aware of factionalism and infighting at home but to overlook the possibility that the same phenomena might be present in an opposing capital was also a characteristic of officials in Hanoi. While DRV officials were fully aware of the ongoing struggle between the contending factions in the Party and constantly seeking to influence DRV policy in accordance with their own views (e.g., by speeches, articles, and efforts to secure strategic appointments or promotions for "allies" within the Party and the Government), they do not appear to have given much thought to the possibility that official Washington might have been involved in a similar struggle between "hawks" and "doves" and that the skill and determination of the members of each group might have had a great deal to do with the content of "American" policy.

Second and more importantly, not only were officials in Washington and Hanoi not particularly sensitive to the existence of factionalism and infighting in the other's capital, but, in addition, neither side appears to have been especially concerned with the way in which the *output* of the struggles at home—i.e., the DRV's pursuit of a dual-track policy involving main force warfare in the South coupled with efforts to negotiate the U.S. out of Vietnam, and the Johnson Administration's tendency to do

29. On this tendency, see Allison, pp. 146-147, 251; and Allison and Halperin, pp. 61-64.

everything "in twos"—would appear to the other side. Instead, each appears to have either ignored this problem or assumed that the other side would be able to perceive correctly the motives underlying the first side's policies.[30] Thus, in the case of the MARIGOLD contact discussed above, American officials apparently believed that their DRV (and Polish) counterparts would understand that the bombing raids of December 2 and 4 had been scheduled before the contact blossomed (which was true) and thus could not be taken as an index of the American view of the message carried by Lewandowski from Hanoi to Saigon. This explanation, however, was rejected by the Poles, and presumably by Hanoi, as "unconvincing."[31] Similarly, in the aftermath of the bombings of Campha and Haiphong on September 10–12, 1967, Kissinger passed a message to Bo (via Marcovich) which argued that "Bo should remember that the number of officials in Washington aware of the current exchange of views is very small. This makes it difficult to send the message of August 25 and maintain secrecy." Bo, however, rejected this line of argument, telling Marcovich on September 23 that "Washington's explanation about the bombing of Haiphong cannot be received."[32] In each case, an attempt to explain American actions as the unintended consequence of SOP's and/or coincidence collided head-on with the DRV belief that American policy was in fact the product of a government that was far more internally united and centrally controlled than it really was. Given this belief, explanations emphasizing coincidence or lack of coordination were at best inconceivable and at worst a conscious attempt by Washington to deceive. To make matters worse, DRV rejections of these explanations were interpreted by American officials as further evidence of DRV perfidy—i.e., they (the North Vietnamese) *knew* why we acted as we did, and yet they deliberately chose to be obstinate.[33] President Johnson's recollections of the MARIGOLD

30. On this point, see Jervis (1976), p. 354.

31. See Marigold Chronology, pp. 44–46.

32. See Pennsylvania, pp. 25, 34. It seems highly unlikely that the decision to bomb Haiphong was taken prior to August 25, as Kissinger claimed. Instead, the decision was probably taken sometime between September 1 and 10 (see note 22, above). It should also be noted that even if the North Vietnamese were aware of the cleavages within the Johnson Administration, they would still have found it convenient to take the position expressed by Bo, in an effort to extract concessions from Washington on the bombing. There is, however, no evidence that Hanoi's private view of policy-making in Washington diverged from the "Washington-as-unitary-rational-actor" model implicit in Bo's remarks to Aubrac and Marcovich.

33. As Jervis (1968, p. 477) notes: "When actors have intentions that they do not try to conceal from others, they tend to assume that others accurately perceive these intentions. Only rarely do they believe that others may be reacting to a much less favorable image of themselves than they think they are projecting." See also Jervis (1976), pp. 67–75.

contact are worth quoting in this respect: "If Lewandowski had reported accurately to Hanoi, the North Vietnamese knew perfectly well that the bombing would not end before the talks began. Knowing that, they could hardly give our bombing as the excuse for not entering negotiations."[34]

But why should these perceptual tendencies have been present at all? How could the supposedly sophisticated officials in Washington and Hanoi have been so attuned to the factionalism and infighting at home and yet so ignorant of the existence of those elements on the other side? Three factors would seem to be relevant here. First, as Jervis notes, experimental evidence from psychology suggests that perceivers "resist explanations that involve several independent elements" and instead seek to link as many events as possible to a minimum number of causes. As a result, "most people are slow to perceive accidents, unintended consequences, coincidences, and small causes leading to large effects. Instead, coordinated actions, plans, and conspiracies are seen."[35]

Second, as Jervis notes:

The context of international politics shapes the content of the perceptions of unity and planning. An awareness of the implications of anarchy leads decision-makers to be alert for dangerous plots. If another's behavior seems innocuous, they will look for a hidden and menacing significance. They see not only plans, but sinister ones. Within society, this perspective characterizes the paranoid. But since threats and plots are common in international relations, the perception that others are Machiavellian cannot be easily labelled pathological. It may have been extreme of Metternich, when he heard that the Russian ambassador had died, to ask "I wonder why he did that," but the search for the devious plan believed to lurk behind even the most seemingly spontaneous behavior is neither uncommon nor totally unwarranted.[36]

Third, as Jervis's comments suggest, the anarchic nature of the international system makes it critically important for government officials to have some understanding of both the motives underlying other states' policies and the intentions that determine what other states will do in the future. This task of discerning another state's motives and intentions is extraordinarily difficult, especially since officials on one side cannot simply ask officials in a foreign capital why they are doing something or what they intend to do next and expect to receive a truthful response.[37] How, then, do government officials deal with questions of

34. Johnson, pp. 251–252. See also Cooper (1972), p. 409.
35. Jervis (1976), pp. 319–320. See also Bauer (1961), p. 225.
36. Jervis (1976), p. 320. See also Bauer (1963), p. 294.
37. See Jervis (1970), who argues persuasively that, in some situations, states may have strong

motivation and intention? A clue in this respect is provided by the three examples discussed earlier. As we saw, the North Vietnamese, in attempting to discern the motives underlying American actions, discounted the explanations presented by or on behalf of the Johnson Administration and looked instead at the actions themselves, attempting to draw inferences about American motives on the basis of what the U.S. was actually doing. Nor were the North Vietnamese alone in relying on their opponent's actions as a guide to motives and intentions, as illustrated by Secretary Rusk's comments on the meaning of the Tet Offensive:

they've also known that the Tet cease-fire was coming up. And they've known from earlier years that we've been interested in converting something like a Tet cease-fire into a more productive dialogue, into some opportunity to move toward peace. Now in the face of all these elements they participated in laying on this major offensive. Now I think it would be foolish not to draw a political conclusion from this that they are not seriously interested at the present time in talking about peaceful settlement. . . . Well, they have rejected the San Antonio formula publicly, simply on the political level. And I think it would be foolish for us not to take into account what they're doing on the ground when we try to analyze what their political position is. You remember the old saying that what you do speaks so loud I can't hear what you say.[38]

To say that government officials use their opponent's actions as the basis for drawing inferences about motives and intentions is not to suggest that the task is an easy one. As we saw in Chapter 6, governments are typically engaged in a multitude of activities at any one point in time; furthermore, foreign policy moves are not decided on and implemented in discrete lumps that can be dealt with swiftly and tidily. Instead, as Allison notes:

most "issues" . . . emerge piecemeal over time, one lump in one context, a second in another. Hundreds of issues compete for players' attention every day. Each player is forced to fix upon his issues for that day, deal with them on their own terms, and rush on to the next. Thus the character of emerging issues and the pace at which the game is played converge to yield government "decisions" and "actions" as collages. Choices by one player (e.g., to authorize action by his

---

incentives to project false images of their intentions so as to secure important objectives "on the cheap."

38. Quoted in IV Gravel, p. 237. See also President Johnson's interpretation of the 1965 Viet Cong attack on Qui Nhon and his view of the 1968 DRV proposal to hold peace talks in Warsaw or Phnom Penh for additional examples of this tendency to draw inferences about an opponent's intentions on the basis of the opponent's actions (Johnson, pp. 129, 499, 503).

department, to make a speech, or to refrain from acquiring certain information), resultants of minor games (e.g., the wording of a cable or the decision on departmental action worked out among lower-level players), resultants of central games (e.g., decisions, actions, and speeches bargained out among central players), and "foul-ups" (e.g., choices that are not made because they are not recognized or are raised too late, misunderstandings, etc.)—these pieces, when stuck to the same canvas, constitute government behavior relevant to an issue.[39]

Since it is often difficult for analysts and historians blessed with hindsight and ample research time to puzzle out the motives underlying this "collage" of activities on any one issue, how much more difficult it must be for the harried officials who seek to comprehend their opponent's motives and intentions but who must grapple with the "collage" (along with dozens of other problems) as their opponents construct it.

As a result, then, it should not be surprising that officials in Washington and Hanoi fell back on simplistic formulae such as the "opponent-as-unitary-rational-actor" model in attempting to comprehend their opponent's motives and intentions. Precisely because other governments are engaged in a multitude of activities at any one point in time, officials need some way of organizing the mass of data with which they are confronted into a coherent whole, of deciding how the pieces of the "collage" fit together, and of judging which of their opponent's activities are important and which can be safely ignored. Given the time constraints under which they operate, the great advantage of the "opponent-as-unitary-rational-actor" model is that it provides a convenient framework within which to incorporate a host of data about an opponent's actions and intentions—certainly an easier framework than trying to fathom the complexities of another state's "bureaucratic politics." No special expertise is required; the official simply takes note of whatever activities the opponent is currently engaged in and then asks himself, "If I was in their position, why would I do those things?"[40] In this way, busy officials can, without too much difficulty, deduce the motives that link their opponent's actions into a comprehensive and comprehensible pattern.[41]

39. Allison, pp. 145–146.

40. See Allison and Halperin, pp. 41–42. The list of activities being undertaken by an opponent will of course be determined partly by the SOP's of the intelligence agencies that compile such information and by the decisions of subordinate officials as to what information to pass up to superiors and what to withhold.

41. This is not to imply that all officials think in this way at all times. Although military men, with their habit of personifying the enemy as "he," would seem to be especially susceptible to this

If, as our discussion to this point has suggested, government officials are likely to reason in the manner described above, what would be the consequences of this mode of thought, especially in situations in which one government was attempting to coerce another? How would these perceptual tendencies affect the coercer's chances of success? In attempting to answer questions such as these, four potential problems come readily to mind.

First, to the extent that government officials rely on the "opponent-as-unitary-rational-actor" model in attempting to evaluate their opponent's motives and intentions, phenomena such as mistakes, foul-ups, and unplanned coincidences will be perceived as intentional rather than accidental. As Schelling notes in discussing the "idiom of reprisal":

verbal messages come from different parts of the government, with different nuances, supplemented by "leaks" from various sources and can be contradicted by later verbal messages, while actions tend to be irrevocable, *and the fact that action occurred proves that authority is behind it.*[42]

Thus, for example, even though the DE SOTO patrol by the *Maddox* and the OPLAN 34A raids by the South Vietnamese on the DRV coastline were separate operations planned and controlled by different agencies of the U.S. Government, the North Vietnamese assumed that the *Maddox* (later joined by the *Turner Joy*) was somehow connected with the raids on their coastline, with the result that the DRV response was directed at the U.S. ships rather than at targets in South Vietnam. Similarly, the North Vietnamese assumed that the timing of the raids on Hanoi on December 2, 4, 13, and 14, 1966 was deliberate and in some way connected with the MARIGOLD contact. Such beliefs, moreover, can have an important effect on efforts to bring a coercive conflict to a conclusion. As Jervis notes:

Directly relevant are the experiments that have shown that people react less to the actual punishment that another person has inflicted on them than they do to what they believe the other sought to do to them. "People will become less angry (and retaliate less) when they believe that their partner intended them little harm—regardless of how much they were harmed. Conversely, people

---

style of thinking (see White, pp. 256–257), President Kennedy, in contrast, appears to have been sensitive to the delicate position of Khrushchev within the Soviet government during the Cuban missile crisis (see Allison, pp. 210–215). Was this solely the result of some personal trait of Kennedy's, or was it also due (at least in part) to the presence within the ExComm of Lewellyn Thompson, a bona fide Soviet specialist? We can hypothesize in this respect that "country specialists" would be less susceptible to this type of thinking. On this question, see Jervis (1976, pp. 327–329) for a discussion of "Variables Encouraging the Perception of Unity and Planning."

42. Schelling (1966), p. 150 (emphasis added).

become very angry (and retaliate to a greater extent) when they believe that their partner intended them harm—regardless of how much they were harmed."[43]

Is it any wonder, then, that the North Vietnamese reacted to the December 1966 raids on Hanoi by canceling the Warsaw talks? It was bad enough to be treated in such a fashion after they had gone further than ever before in an attempt to appear reasonable, but then for the Americans to insult their intelligence with flimsy explanations claiming that the timing of the bombing depended solely on the weather! One suspects that Polish Foreign Minister Rapacki was voicing sentiments widely shared in Hanoi when he told Gronouski on December 7, 1966 that "policy is more important than weather."[44]

Second, if government officials do exaggerate the extent to which their opponents are internally united and overestimate the degree to which others are following a coherent policy, those officials may be led to exaggerate their opponent's capabilities with respect to deciphering incoming signals and responding quickly.[45] In February 1967, as we saw in Chapter 4, British Prime Minister Wilson sought to arrange for an extension of the Tet bombing pause in exchange for a halt in the southward movement of several PAVN divisions deployed just north of the DMZ. Since Wilson's proposal did not reach Washington until shortly before the bombing was to resume, he requested that the pause be extended to give the North Vietnamese time to reply. President Johnson responded (grudgingly) by extending the pause for ten hours, on the grounds that

it does not take all that long to cable "yes" or "no" or "We are giving it serious study," even from as far away as Hanoi. As a matter of fact, Hanoi did not have to send a cable at all. . . . If the leaders in Hanoi wanted to move toward peace, they knew that all they had to do was take some visible step to cut back their half of the war.[46]

During this period, however, U.S. officials and assorted intermediaries had made more than a dozen separate offers to "Hanoi," with significant differences between them with respect to the Administration's

43. Jervis (1976), p. 33. The quoted excerpt is from Ted Nickel, "The Attribution of Intention as a Critical Factor in the Relation Between Frustration and Aggression," *Journal of Personality*, 42 (1974), 489.

44. For Rapacki's comment, see Marigold Chronology, p. 46.

45. On this point, see Jervis (1976), p. 338.

46. Johnson, p. 254.

conditions for beginning negotiations (see Table 7). And yet, as evidenced by the President's comments quoted above, officials in Washington were not at all disposed to believe that "Hanoi" could have been confused by this array of proposals. Instead, those officials were preoccupied with a much more ominous-looking development—namely, the possibility that the North Vietnamese would take advantage of a "loophole" in the original version of the Phase A–Phase B plan by using the lull between the bombing halt (Phase A) and the end of infiltration (Phase B) for an all-out effort to move the divisions poised just north of the DMZ into South Vietnam.[47] Obsessed with the possibility that they were about to be conned, officials in Washington were in no mood to admit that their counterparts in Hanoi might have been as confused and worried about their intentions as they were about the intentions of the men in Hanoi.

Third, the tendency to rely on a formula like the "opponent-as-unitary-rational-actor" model may easily result in unwarranted policy judgments.[48] As we saw in Chapter 6, given the model of DRV decision-making utilized by American officials, "Hanoi's" refusal to negotiate on American terms could mean only one thing—namely, that "Hanoi" remained unpersuaded of the futility of its efforts to take over the South and that additional pressure was required to bring it to see the error of its ways. As a result, Administration officials remained unaware that there was considerable interest in a negotiated settlement among at least some officials in Hanoi, as evidenced by DRV willingness to participate in the Paris (XYZ), Rangoon, and MARIGOLD contacts. In the MARI-GOLD case in particular, the model utilized by American officials contributed to a disastrous policy decision—i.e., to go ahead with additional raids on Hanoi (carried out on December 13–14, 1966) in an attempt to force "Hanoi" to negotiate on American terms. Unfortunately, that decision produced exactly the opposite of the desired effect, namely the collapse of the MARIGOLD contact.

Finally, the tendency to perceive an opponent as more internally united than it really is has important implications for the ability of governments to communicate by deed as well as by word. If officials do perceive their opponents as more internally united than they really are and capable of following a coherent, centrally controlled policy, then the "signal" that they read into the actions of their opponent may differ

47. President Johnson cited this possibility as the reason for his reversal of the phases in his February 1967 letter to Ho. On this point, see Johnson, pp. 253–254; Sunflower Chronology, pp. 54–56; and Chapter 4, above.

48. On this point, see also Jervis (1976), pp. 338–342.

Table 7

U.S. Proposals for De-escalation and/or Beginning Talks with the DRV, November 1966–February 1967

Date of proposal	Channel	Nature of proposal	For additional details, see:
November 13, 1966	Polish ICC Commissioner Lewandowski	"Phase A–Phase B" proposal—a bombing suspension (Phase A) followed by other de-escalatory acts by both sides.	Marigold Chronology, p. 28; Chapter 3, Section VII, above.
November 16, 1966	British Foreign Secretary Brown	"Phase A–Phase B" proposal (same version as given to Lewandowski).	Marigold Chronology, p. 34; Sunflower Discussion, p. 7.
November 30, 1966 December 3, 1966	Lewandowski	U.S. agrees to participate in Warsaw talks based on Lewandowski's 10 Points "subject to important differences in interpretation."	Marigold Chronology, pp. 35–38; Chapter 4, Section I-A, above.
December 22, 1966	Polish Foreign Ministry	Gronouski tells Rapacki that U.S. has stopped bombing within 10 nm of Hanoi and would be impressed by reciprocal de-escalatory activity by Communist side.	Marigold Chronology, pp. 76–81; Chapter 4, Section I-A, above.
December 31, 1966	Goldberg letter to U Thant	U.S. is ready to order a "prior end to all bombing of North Vietnam the moment there is an assurance, private or otherwise, that there would be a reciprocal response toward peace from North Vietnam. . . ."	Sunflower Discussion, p. 7; Sunflower Chronology, p. 1.
January 10, 1967	Guthrie–Le Chang meeting in Moscow	U.S. wishes to exchange with the DRV communications about possibilities of achieving a peaceful settlement.	Sunflower Chronology, pp. 6–7; Chapter 4, Section I-B, above.
January 20, 1967	Guthrie–Le Chang	Guthrie presents agenda of topics that U.S. is prepared to discuss.	Sunflower Chronology, pp. 6–7; Chapter 4, Section I-B, above.

Table 7 (Continued)

Date of proposal	Channel	Nature of proposal	For additional details, see:
February 2, 1967	Guthrie–Le Chang	U.S. has continued bombing suspension near Hanoi, is prepared to implement "additional measures to deescalate the bombing of the North" and would be "impressed with similar acts of restraint" by the DRV; Guthrie also presents Phase A–Phase B plan as given to Lewandowski and Brown.	Sunflower Chronology, pp. 18–21; Chapter 4, Section I-B, above.
February 3, 1967	Presidential news conference	Johnson says that reciprocity for a bombing suspension could consist of "just almost any step."	Sunflower Discussion, p. 8.
February 5, 1967	Ashmore letter to Ho Chi Minh	U.S. is interested in beginning talks after a bombing halt and end to U.S. troop buildup, provided there is "some reciprocal restraint to indicate that neither side intended to use the occasion of the talks for military advantage. . . ."	Sunflower Discussion, p. 8; Sunflower Chronology, pp. 25–26.
February 6– February 9, 1967*	Wilson-Kosygin meetings in London	Wilson passes written version of Phase A–Phase B plan (drafted by British) on February 7 and written proposal for reconvening Geneva Conference combined with mutual de-escalation along the lines of the original version of the Phase A–Phase B plan on February 9.	Sunflower Chronology, pp. 27–40; Chapter 4, Section I-B, above.
February 8, 1967	Johnson's letter to Ho Chi Minh	U.S. will halt bombing of North Vietnam and troop buildup in South Vietnam "as soon as [it] is assured that infiltration into South Vietnam by land and by sea *has stopped*" (emphasis added).	Sunflower Chronology, pp. 33–35; Chapter 4, Section I-B, above.

February 9, 1967	Rusk's news conference	Updated version of "14 Points": #14—"We are prepared to order a cessation of all bombing of North Vietnam, the moment we are assured—privately or otherwise—that this step *will be* answered promptly by a corresponding and appropriate deescalation of the other side" (emphasis added).	Sunflower Chronology, pp. 41–43.
February 10, 1967	Goldberg speech at Howard University	"The U.S. remains prepared to take the first step and order a cessation of all bombing of North Vietnam the moment we are assured, privately or otherwise, that this step *will be* answered promptly by a tangible response toward peace by North Vietnam" (emphasis added).	Sunflower Chronology, p. 44.
February 10, 1967	Wilson-Kosygin	Wilson says he is authorized to state that the U.S. will halt bombing if assured infiltration will stop; Kosygin asks for and later receives a written version he can cable to Moscow (for relay to Hanoi).	Sunflower Chronology, pp. 46–47; Chapter 4, Section I-B, above.
February 10, 1967 (late evening)	Wilson-Kosygin	Kosygin is given revised version of the Phase A–Phase B plan, stating that bombing will stop when U.S. is assured that infiltration "has stopped."	Sunflower Chronology, pp. 46 ff.; Chapter 4, Section I-B, above.
February 12, 1967	Wilson-Kosygin	U.S. will continue Tet bombing suspension, provided infiltration stops within 10 hours (later extended by 6 hours).	Sunflower Chronology, p. 60; Chapter 4, Section I-B, above.

*Kosygin asserted that he was in continuous contact with Hanoi, although it is unclear how many of the proposals passed through the British were actually relayed to Hanoi.

drastically from the "signal" the sender is actually attempting to communicate.[49] As we saw earlier in this chapter, DRV officials consistently read into the timing of attacks on Hanoi and Haiphong "messages" that U.S. officials never intended to be sent. Similarly, because U.S. officials assumed that DRV policy could best be understood as a single-minded attempt to conquer the South, those officials were unable to recognize genuine signals of DRV interest in negotiations, even though the Administration was supposedly watching carefully for such signs. Thus, William Bundy dismissed the DRV Foreign Ministry memo of January 4, 1966 as just another "fairly straightforward reiteration of the Four Points,"[50] even though, as we saw in Chapter 3, that statement was apparently intended to signal DRV readiness to negotiate without prior American "recognition" of the Four Points.

Summary and Conclusions

At this point, it might be helpful to take stock of the material covered in this chapter, as there are a number of points that merit special attention. For one thing, as we saw earlier in this chapter, when a government like the one in Washington engages in coercion, it is by no means free to escalate or de-escalate or do whatever seems necessary to bring the conflict to some kind of conclusion. One problem, as Allison notes, is that

the nature of foreign policy problems permits fundamental disagreement among reasonable men about how to solve them. Analyses yield conflicting recommendations. Separate responsibilities laid on the shoulders of distinct individuals encourage differences in what each sees and judges to be important. But the nation's actions really matter. A wrong choice could mean irreparable damage. Thus responsible men are obliged to fight for what they are convinced is right.[51]

Furthermore, a President is by no means free to pick and choose from among the conflicting recommendations thrust upon him by subordinate officials. Not only do the officials who sit at or near the top of the foreign policy bureaucracy come into the government (usually) with some independent standing (and therefore power), but there will always be political opponents ready to criticize a President's policies and capitalize upon his errors. As a result, a President by necessity treads warily among the different interests represented in his Administration. While

49. The implications of this tendency are considered in more detail in Chapter 8, below.
50. See Pinta Chronology, p. 23.
51. Allison, p. 145.

outright defection to the opposition party is rare, there are less spectacular but still damaging ways in which disgruntled subordinates can "fight for what they are convinced is right"—for example, by "leaking" unfavorable information to outsiders, testifying before Congressional committees in ways that undercut whatever policy the President espouses (e.g., the Stennis Committee hearings on the air war), or even by resigning in protest (or threatening to). To avoid political pitfalls such as these, a President will find it advantageous to keep as many members of his Administration as possible reasonably satisfied with the course the Administration is following. That goal, however, cannot be accomplished if the President consistently ignores the suggestions put forward by one or more groups of advisers. As a result, U.S. policy often has something of a "smorgasbord" quality to it, as a President seeks to placate some or all of the interests represented in his Administration by adopting at least some of their proposals. Unfortunately, however, this preoccupation with consensus will, by definition, severely restrict a President's freedom of action, especially when it comes to bringing an attempt at coercion to a close. There will always be those who will believe that better terms will be forthcoming from an opponent if only more pressure is applied, just as there will always be those who will believe that too much pressure has already been used.

Second, however, the way in which a President goes about making this trade-off between consensus and "controllability" will be critically important with respect to his ability to "negotiate" in the desired fashion. In this regard the Johnsonian obsession with capturing the middle provides an almost perfect lesson in how *not* to engage in coercion. This is not to say that doing things "in twos" will always be inappropriate. Such a tactic may at times be useful to a President who seeks to gain flexibility for the future by neutralizing one or more opponents of his policies. What *is* inappropriate, however, is to delude oneself into believing that doing things "in twos" is the same as "orchestrating" words and deeds, as well as to engage in such a tactic without carefully considering how such an approach will appear to foreign audiences (such as the all-important audience in Hanoi). In the Vietnamese case, not only did officials in Hanoi have little understanding of the intricacies of decision-making in Washington, but, in addition, officials in Washington appear to have been largely unaware of Hanoi's lack of understanding (the same would be true if we substituted "Washington" for "Hanoi"). As a result, when the Administration did things "in twos," officials in Hanoi saw only plots and trickery rather than a President trying to strike a balance between "hawks" and "doves" at home.

Nor did officials in Washington ever really understand why their "explanations" were never accepted in Hanoi. The effect of all this, as we suggested earlier in this chapter, was to complicate greatly the task of striking a deal between Washington and Hanoi.

This is not to suggest, though, that these perceptual errors and mis-understandings were the only, or even the most important, source of conflict between Washington and Hanoi. On the contrary, that conflict was first and foremost a dispute over who would rule in South Vietnam. As a result, even if the errors and misunderstanding identified above had been nonexistent, it would still have been difficult for Washington and Hanoi to strike a deal, primarily because the principal issue at stake —who would rule in the South—was, or was perceived to be, essentially zero-sum. South Vietnam would either be Communist or not—there was no middle way. Even a "compromise" solution involving some type of coalition in the South was perceived (correctly) by both sides as little more than a facade behind which the life-or-death struggle between Communists and non-Communists would continue.[52] Still, however, the errors and misunderstandings identified above *did* exist, and their effect was to make an already difficult problem virtually insoluble.

52. This is not to suggest that there was nothing the Administration could have done with respect to seeking a solution that would have been both feasible and an improvement over the policy it actually followed. As suggested earlier, an imaginative policy might well have identified a "compromise" solution involving a coalition government and de facto partition of South Vietnam. While such a compromise would by no means have ended the struggle between Communist and non-Communist forces, it would have had several advantages: (1) by holding out the "carrot" of an American withdrawal, it would have strengthened the position of those in Hanoi who wanted to do less for the Southern revolution, on the ground that the Southerners should have been left to fight and win their own revolution while the North concentrated on building socialism; (2) by entrenching the GVN in a smaller and more defensible territorial base, it could well have enabled the anti-Communist forces to hold out for years; (3) the ensuing struggle would very likely have involved much less destruction and loss of life; and (4) the eventual Communist takeover would very likely have been much more of a "slow motion" process, in which the damage to U.S. prestige would have been greatly reduced, since the DRV role ("aggression from the North") would have been smaller, and since the blame could have been more easily pinned on the South Vietnamese (for their ineptness and unwillingness to fight to save themselves).

8

Coercive Warfare: An Appraisal

A T A 1968 conference at the Adlai
Stevenson Institute, Samuel Huntington suggested that

If the legacy of misplaced analogies which the past has bequeathed to the Vietnam debates is even half equaled by the misplaced analogies which Vietnam
bequeaths to the future, error will compound error in positively horrifying
manner. It is conceivable that policy-makers may best meet future crises and
dilemmas if they simply blot out of their minds any recollection of this one.
The right lesson, in short, may be an unlesson.[1]

Despite the risks inherent in drawing lessons from a single case, the significance of the American experience in Vietnam is such that it cannot
be disregarded. As suggested by the claims of former Secretaries
Kissinger and Schlesinger that the Ford Administration's "rescue" of
the containership *Mayaguez* and its crew was the "result of what is presumed to be the decision of the Cambodians to deliver them up in order
to terminate combat activities directed primarily at the mainland"[2]
(when there is evidence that both the offer to release the crew and the
release itself *preceded* the air strikes against the mainland),[3] the same

---

1. Huntington, in Pfeffer (ed.), pp. 1–2. See also Albert Wohlstetter's comment (in Pfeffer [ed.],
p. 4) that "I am painfully aware that, of all the disasters of Vietnam, the worst may be the 'lessons'
that we'll draw from it."

2. Secretary of Defense Schlesinger, quoted in R. W. Apple, Jr., "Timing of Attack Raises Questions," *New York Times*, May 16, 1975, p. 14. See also Secretary Kissinger's comments, quoted in
David Binder, "Second Cambodia Raid Disclosed by U.S.," *New York Times*, May 17, 1975, p. 11.

3. According to news accounts (see the references in note 2, above), at 7:07 P.M. on May 14,
Washington time (6:07 A.M. on May 15, Cambodia time), Phnom Penh Radio broadcast a statement offering to release the ship and crew. At 10:15 P.M. (Washington time), the carrier *Coral Sea*
began launching aircraft for an attack on the Ream airfield, which began around 11:00 P.M.
(Washington time). At 10:45 P.M. (Washington time), however, a fishing boat with the *Mayaguez*
crew was sighted by the destroyer *Wilson* (word of this was flashed to the Pentagon at approximately 10:53 P.M., Washington time). In order to have reached the *Wilson*, the boat must have set
out from the mainland (thirty miles away) several hours *before* the air strikes began.

kinds of attitudes concerning the efficacy of coercive violence that contributed to the Vietnam tragedy are still prevalent among American officials. As a result, a careful review of the Vietnamese case should provide an invaluable corrective for this unwarranted confidence in the ease with which one government can coerce another. That review, as we know, has been the subject of the preceding chapters. Consequently, it might be helpful at this point to pull together some of the main themes in those chapters in order to identify the attitudes and beliefs most urgently in need of change.

I. Coercion and Diplomacy: Lessons from Vietnam

By far the two most important lessons that can be drawn from the Vietnamese case center on the nature of governmental interaction in situations involving the use of coercive pressures and on the difficulties that government officials are likely to encounter when they seek to influence the choices of their counterparts in another government.

A. The Nature of Governmental Interaction

Plans for exerting coercive pressures, as we suggested in Chapter 6, are not drawn up in a vacuum; instead, they are typically prepared by officials drawn from several government departments. The governmental framework, in turn, influences both the process by which decisions are made and, more importantly, the way in which those decisions are translated into action. In the U.S. at least, the top positions in the executive departments are reserved for Presidential appointees whose tenure of office is likely to be relatively brief; furthermore, the higher the individual's rank, the greater will be the duties and responsibilities assigned to him, resulting in a diminished ability to devote time and effort to any one issue. But since meaningful coercive pressures will almost certainly require either the actual or threatened use of military force,[4] the lower ranks of the departments most likely to be involved in an attempt at coercion will be staffed almost entirely by members of career services—the military, the Foreign Service, or the CIA—each with its own largely autonomous promotion machinery. While these

---

4. Although nonmilitary moves such as economic sanctions or boycotts may be used for coercive purposes, such efforts have proven notably unsuccessful to date (Rhodesia being an obvious case in point). Even the 1973 Arab oil embargo is an ambiguous case in that it is extremely difficult to establish a direct causal relationship between the use of the "oil weapon" (as opposed to the worldwide shortage of oil due to the OAPEC production cutback) and changes in U.S. policy toward the Middle East. On this point, see Hans Maull, "Oil and Influence: The Oil Weapon Examined," *Adelphi Papers*, no. 117 (1975).

lower-ranking officials are legally charged with carrying out the directives of the President and his appointees, their prospects for advancement will be determined largely by the loyalty they exhibit to their service, in terms of supporting its programs, roles, and missions.[5]

In addition, because the officials involved in any attempt at coercion are likely to be drawn from several different departments (and also to hold different positions within the same department), they are likely to hold rather different views on how to go about coercing another government. Although it need not always be the case that "where you stand depends on where you sit," differing organizational perspectives combined with differing responsibilities within each organization (plus the fact that no two individuals are alike) make it almost certain that there will not be an identity of views within the government, regardless of the issue under consideration.[6]

Taken together, the factors cited above—i.e., hierarchical structure, severe time constraints, separation of responsibility for policy from control over promotions, and divergent views on policy choices—combine to produce a decision-making process in which there are numerous points at which "slippage" can occur, in the sense that the activities undertaken by the government diverge from those envisioned by senior officials at the time of decision. More specifically, when senior officials meet to consider whether and what kinds of coercive pressures should be attempted against another government, they are likely to come away from their deliberations with a mental image of the decisions that were made and thus of the activities to be undertaken by their government in the days and weeks that follow.[7] These decisions are generally followed by two types of implementing activities: activities undertaken by senior officials personally, such as speeches, press conferences, and background briefings; and activities that must be delegated to subordinates, such as troop movements, military operations, intelligence-gathering activities, and so on. In both cases, there are numerous ways in which the activities undertaken by the government can diverge from those envisioned by senior officials at the time of decision.

5. On the promotion policies of the career services within the U.S. Government, see Halperin (1974), pp. 85–89, 261–268.

6. For evidence in support of this assertion, one need only recall the sharp and persistent differences of opinion in both Washington and Hanoi over the proper role of the U.S. and the DRV in the insurgency in South Vietnam. See also Allison, chaps. 4 and 6, for an analysis of how differing organizational perspectives and differing job responsibilities influenced policy disputes in Washington during the Cuban missile crisis.

7. On this point, see Halperin (1974), p. 244.

1. *Senior officials may fail to follow through on decisions that they themselves have made.* As we saw in Chapter 2, even though it was agreed at the September 1964 Washington policy review (and recorded in NSAM-314) that the U.S. should retaliate for any further attacks on U.S. forces or for any VC "spectaculars" in South Vietnam (a threat that had been conveyed directly to Pham Van Dong by Seaborn during the latter's August 1964 visit to Hanoi), the President was unwilling to retaliate for the attack on Bien Hoa, because it occurred just before the Presidential election, or for the bombing of the Brink BOQ, because it occurred during the Christmas holidays.

2. *Senior officials may take actions that, knowingly or unknowingly, undercut policy decisions made earlier.* As we saw in Chapter 2, while the President had directed on February 20, 1964 that planning for overt pressures against North Vietnam give particular attention to producing the "maximum credible deterrent effect on Hanoi"—a directive that was followed the next day by a Presidential warning to Hanoi in the form of the President's UCLA speech along with a background briefing for newsmen highlighting the threatening nature of the President's remarks —the President himself, in an effort to mollify critics of his Southeast Asia policies, later denied that there were plans to carry the war to the North or that his UCLA speech had been intended as a warning to Hanoi.

3. *Senior officials may attempt to control policy by means of generalized directives, while neglecting the details of organizational implementation.* Because of the demands on their time, senior officials can rarely give sustained attention to the myriad details involved when one government attempts to coerce another. Instead, they are likely to focus on the broad outlines of policy, leaving lesser issues to subordinates. But while such an approach allows them to focus on more issues than would be possible if they examined each proposal put before them in minute detail, such a practice necessarily entails certain costs. The generalized directives trigger organizational routines that are at best imperfectly understood by senior officials and which often result in actions that, while reasonable from the perspective of subordinates, conflict with or even undercut the preferences of senior officials. For example, in the aftermath of the Gulf of Tonkin incidents, senior officials in Washington sought to intimidate the North Vietnamese by transferring additional American forces to Southeast Asia and the Western Pacific, including a squadron of B-57 bombers to the air base at Bien Hoa.[8] But

8. The B-57s played a central role in the effort to intimidate Hanoi, since, as was carefully

while senior officials chose the objective to be pursued (i.e., intimidating Hanoi) and set in motion the process of transferring military units in pursuit of that goal, details such as aircraft storage and base security were left to the discretion of officials in the field. Preoccupied with the danger of sabotage, those officials packed the aircraft close together at Bien Hoa, to ease the task of guarding them. That decision, however, made it possible for a small group of VC guerrillas to launch a devastating mortar attack on the B-57s, which, when combined with the President's refusal to retaliate for the attack on Bien Hoa, very likely strengthened the position of those in Hanoi urging a greater Northern role in the war in the South by suggesting that the Americans could be attacked with impunity.[9]

Furthermore, senior officials cannot constantly watch over the shoulders of their subordinates to ensure that their directives are implemented faithfully. Instead, some authority must be delegated to officials in the field, who are presumably more familiar with the problem at hand and who can hopefully tailor the government's response to the particular demands of the situation. What senior officials want and what subordinates actually do, however, may be entirely different things. As we saw in Chapter 3, senior officials meeting in Washington on April 1, 1965 concluded that U.S. military forces should continue with the "slowly ascending" tempo of the ROLLING THUNDER program, taking care to avoid clashes with DRV MIGs and putting primary emphasis on interdicting infiltration into the South. The task of translating this directive into a specific plan of action, however, was delegated to military commanders. In the process, the wishes of senior officials were effectively ignored as a result of standard operating procedures that dictated attacking the northernmost bridges first, so as to trap the maximum amount of rolling stock in the southern DRV, where it could be destroyed at will. As a result, not only did U.S. planes become quickly embroiled in air combat with DRV and Chinese MIGs, but the conduct of the air war in the aftermath of the "bridge raids" of early April 1965 very likely generated confusing and misleading "signals" to Hanoi (see Chapter 6, above).

---

pointed out to reporters at the time, they had sufficient range and payload to strike targets in the North. On this point, see V Gravel, p. 330; and Chapter 2, above, especially note 84.

9. On the aircraft storage arrangements at Bien Hoa, see Westmoreland, p. 88. This was not the first time that a seemingly insignificant detail had contributed to a serious setback for American forces. Westmoreland himself draws the obvious parallel with Pearl Harbor; in addition, see Allison's discussion (p. 139) of President Kennedy's efforts to ensure that U.S. aircraft would not be caught wing-to-wing during the Cuban missile crisis.

Even if senior officials attempted to control the activities of their sub-ordinates by means of highly detailed directives, no directive can anti-cipate all possible contingencies, with the result that a certain amount of discretion must always be granted to field commanders. Nor can one assume that their judgments will always faithfully reflect the preferences of their superiors—a problem that can be exacerbated by the need for quick decisions based on intelligence data that cannot always be for-warded to superiors for analysis and interpretation. In the case of the first incident in the Gulf of Tonkin, for example, it was the *Maddox* that fired first, a decision based on the appearance of hostile intent on the part of the DRV torpedo boats (see Chapter 2, above). One can only speculate as to the outcome of the Cuban missile crisis if a Soviet sub-marine commander had reacted like the commander of the *Maddox* and fired a torpedo at an American destroyer attempting to force his vessel to the surface.[10]

4. *Subordinate officials, not being fully informed of the considerations on which a policy decision has been based, may take actions that conflict with the intent of their superiors.*[11] During the diplomatic contact code-named PENNSYLVANIA, the President decided that Hanoi would be off-limits to American aircraft for ten days beginning August 24, 1967, both to ensure the safety of Aubrac and Marcovich during their ex-pected second visit there and, more importantly, as a gesture of good will. Military commanders in the field, however, not being informed of the diplomatic basis for the President's decision and fearing that the ges-ture might result in a permanent loss of authority to strike Hanoi, scheduled extremely fierce attacks on Hanoi for August 21–23, a move that very likely negated the value of the President's good will gesture and greatly complicated the Administration's diplomatic efforts.

5. *Because responsibility for implementing the decisions of senior officials is fragmented among numerous organizational subunits, subordinate officials may unwittingly schedule implementing activities in a way that results in em-barrassing coincidences.* As we saw in Chapter 2, the fragmentation of responsibility for covert operations in Southeast Asia inadvertently resulted in the coincidence of three separate operations in early August 1964: the start of OPLAN 34A raids on DRV coastal targets, attacks by Laotian T-28s on DRV border villages, and the DE SOTO patrol along the DRV coast by the *Maddox* (later joined by the *Turner Joy*). Would senior U.S. officials have responded as they did to the alleged attack on

10. On the activities of U.S. destroyers during the Cuban crisis, see Allison, p. 138.
11. For a fuller discussion of this phenomenon, see Halperin (1974), pp. 239–242, 265–266.

the night of August 4 if they had known there had been an OPLAN 34A raid less than twenty-four hours earlier? In this respect, it should be recalled that senior officials in Washington did not learn of the OPLAN 34A raid in question until sometime after August 6—i.e., at least forty-eight hours after the President's decision to launch the reprisal strikes.[12]

6. *Foul-ups in the field may result in subordinates taking actions that diverge from those intended by senior officials.* Although President Johnson boasted about the close control he maintained over targets selected for the ROLLING THUNDER authorized list, the targets struck did not always correspond to those on the list. Since U.S. fighter-bombers could not fly supersonically while carrying externally mounted bomb loads, the approach of DRV MIGs forced U.S. pilots to jettison ordnance in order to defend themselves, regardless of where they were at the time. On at least one occasion, this practice resulted in the inadvertent bombing of an area that had been designated as off-limits to U.S. aircraft.[13]

7. *Pursuit of promotion by members of career services may lead them to take actions that conflict with or undercut the wishes of senior officials.* In the Vietnamese case, the goals being pursued by senior American officials were essentially three in number: (1) to prevent a DRV/VC takeover in the South, which in turn was to be accomplished (2) by eroding DRV will to continue and (3) by impeding the flow of men and materiel to DRV/VC forces in the South. Success in achieving the latter two goals, however, depended to a large extent on the performance of the planes and pilots of the 7th Air Force and Task Force 77 (the 7th Fleet carriers stationed off Vietnam), which were responsible for the bombing of North Vietnam and Laos. Career military officers, however, viewed the air war as a means for pursuing both personal and organizational goals —i.e., promotions, bigger budgets, more planes and pilots, etc.—which they attempted to do by maximizing the number of sorties flown over North Vietnam. For the pilots, as Stavins notes,

the number of sorties flown determined length of duty and rapidity of promotion. The more missions a pilot could run, the sooner he would leave Vietnam and the more quickly he would be promoted. But there was no incentive to hit the target, especially if it was surrounded by missiles. Hence the pilot was solely interested in receiving credit for a sortie. . . . For the services, the sortie rates determined their budgetary allocations for the following year. The reality for

12. On this point, see Goulden, pp. 220, 260; Austin, p. 310; and Chapter 2, above.

13. See Col. Jack Broughton, USAF (ret.), *Thud Ridge* (Philadelphia: J. B. Lippincott, 1969), p. 76. For additional corroboration on this point, see Sharp and Westmoreland, p. 27.

the services was to compete with each other to see who could fly the most sorties.[14]

While it might appear that there would be a high correlation between the number of sorties flown and the amount of damage caused by the bombing (which hopefully would be directly related to the goals of impeding infiltration and eroding DRV will), such was not the case:

Responding to the need to maximize sorties, the pilots were forced to fly two per day. To accomplish this, they had to fly the shortest route to the target so they could get back to the base in time to refuel and fly another mission. Forced to take the shortest route, the planes departed at the same time each morning and were forced into what the pilots referred to as "milk runs"—fixed routes saturated with enemy antiaircraft guns and SAM missiles. . . . The results were disastrous; planes were shot out of the air at a brutally high rate.

Once this loss pattern developed, pilots decided to avoid their primary targets and proceed instead to secondary targets, where there was less chance of being shot out of the sky. Each pilot was assigned three targets: North Vietnam, Route Pack One (the Ho Chi Minh Trail along the Laotian border), and Laos proper. The pilots would continue to fly the milk run, but they would drop their bombs short of the primary target or in the sea, receive credit for a sortie, return to base for refueling, and head to Route Pack One. Hanoi, meanwhile, would observe the planes failing to enter their primary target zone, then time their return back to the base and their second mission to Route Pack One. Hanoi would then notify the trucks moving along the infiltration corridor; fifteen minutes before the planes arrived at their secondary target, the trucks would get off the road, wait in the bush, watch the bombs drop, then continue on their way. The net result of the air war against the North was an extremely high sortie rate, a waste of ordnance, an appallingly high percentage of U.S. planes lost, and few targets hit with any degree of accuracy.[15]

Furthermore, as Gallucci notes, the fact that a plane flew one sortie did

14. Stavins, "Washington Determines the Fate of Vietnam: 1954–1965," in Stavins, Barnet, and Raskin, p. 190. See also Morris J. Blachman, "The Stupidity of Intelligence," in Charles Peters and Timothy Adams (eds.), *Inside the System* (New York: Praeger, 1970), p. 275. Note also the strong parallels with the Cuban missile crisis, which Navy officers viewed as an opportunity to prove the efficacy of Navy antisubmarine warfare techniques by tracking Soviet submarines (and even forcing some to surface), even though President Kennedy and his advisers sought to minimize provocative actions during the crisis (see Allison, p. 138).

15. Stavins, "Washington Determines the Fate of Vietnam: 1954–1965," in Stavins, Barnet, and Raskin, pp. 185–186. While Stavins overstates his case (not all bombs were dropped in the sea), his conclusions on the net results of the air war are supported by a former DIA analyst; see Blachman, pp. 273–276. See also Gallucci (pp. 117, 143–144), who argues that when senior officials seek to monitor the performance of subordinates by means of quantitative measures, the subordinates will seek to excel in the monitored area regardless of the effect on the organization's total performance.

not necessarily mean that it was carrying a full bomb load when it took off:

It appears that in the spring and summer of 1966, an insufficient number of whole bombs of the desired variety were to be found at the necessary points— the body of the bomb, its fuse, and its tail turning up at different locations. In response to this situation, in the words of a special military study of logistics in Vietnam, "CINCPAC established monthly allocations of critical air munitions and specified maximum ordnance loads for air munitions." In other words, the military continued to fly the same number of planes, cutting down not on sorties but on the effectiveness of each aircraft. . . . Referring to this period an air force colonel said, "Our planes were flying with one-half a load, but bombs or no bombs, you've got to have more Air Force over the target than Navy."[16]

*　　*　　*

Although there is likely to be a divergence between the activities envisioned by senior officials at the time of decision and the activities actually undertaken by the government, few analysts would be surprised by such a conclusion. What *is* perhaps surprising is that, despite the often considerable discrepancies between what senior officials intended to be done and what actually was done, the mental image formed by senior officials of what was supposed to be done has considerable staying power. What appears to have stuck in the minds of senior officials, in Washington at least, was the dramatic incident, or the far-reaching decision, or the hard-fought battle to fashion an internal consensus on some new line of policy. In the process, however, what was lost sight of was the far more complex and often muddled and confusing reality that emerged as a composite of the implementing activities undertaken (or neglected) by both senior officials and their subordinates. For example, it appears that far more attention was given by senior officials, especially the President, to the supposedly clear-cut signal transmitted by the Tonkin Gulf reprisal strikes (i.e., attack our ships and we will retaliate against the offending PT-boat bases)[17] than to

16. Gallucci, p. 84. The existence of the bomb shortage is confirmed by Admiral Sharp, in Sharp and Westmoreland, p. 55; and by Broughton, p. 79. Broughton, a former F-105 pilot, also reports (p. 79) that as a result of the bomb shortage and an Air Force "race with the Navy to see which could record the most flying hours, . . . we were at one time sending kids out to attack a cement and steel bridge with nothing but 20-millimeter cannon, which is like trying to knock down the Golden Gate Bridge with a slingshot."

17. See, for example, the statements by the President and Secretary Rusk immediately after the incidents, stressing the clear-cut nature of the reprisals (Johnson Papers, 1963–1964, pp. 927–932; and DOSB, August 24, 1964, p. 269).

the much more equivocal picture that was very likely conveyed to Hanoi as a result of the coincidence of OPLAN 34A raids, Laotian T-28 strikes, DE SOTO patrols in the Gulf of Tonkin, the reprisals themselves, and the cacophony of "hawkish" and "dovish" statements emerging from Washington in the aftermath of the incidents. Similarly, it appears that senior officials were so impressed by the fact that the U.S. had at last explicitly committed itself to a program of pressures against the North, in the form of the President's December 1, 1964 decision to go ahead with "Phase 1" pressures (see Chapter 2, above) that they never did notice that "Phase 1" actually resulted in little in the way of increased pressures on the North.[18] Finally, as the behavior of senior American officials during the U.S.-U.K. "battle of the tenses" (see Chapter 4, above) would seem to suggest, those officials were far more impressed by the fact that the U.S. was offering to halt the bombing in return for some quid pro quo than they were by the very high level of "noise" that was very likely generated by the blizzard of conflicting proposals offered to Hanoi in late 1966 and early 1967 (see Chapter 7, above, especially Table 7).

Contributing to the persistence of the mental image held by senior officials are the work loads those officials must bear. With a calendar crowded with issues that demand their attention (and with new issues arising every day), senior officials have little choice but to resolve each day's problems as they arise, pass the bulk of their decisions to subordinates for implementation, and move on to the next problem or issue area. From this flow of issues there is no respite, nor is there much opportunity for a glance back to see how last week's decisions are being handled by subordinates in the field.

Finally, the persistence of the mental image held by senior officials of what the government is supposed to be doing is very likely enhanced both by the reactions of their subordinates and by the briefings they receive. On the one hand, as McGarvey notes, there is a "'can-do' attitude that prevails among the officer corps. It is unthinkable for an officer to tell his superior that he cannot complete a task. It is a form of

18. At the very least, the argument being developed here would seem to be the only way to account for the ease with which senior U.S. officials accepted the extraordinarily tough negotiating positions being discussed in Washington during late 1964 and early 1965, such as the one presented by Ambassdor Taylor to the Principals in late November 1964 (see Document no. 242 in III Gravel, p. 673). In similar fashion, as we saw in Chapters 3 and 6, above, senior officials in Washington were apparently much more impressed by the decision to begin the ROLLING THUNDER program than by the confusing and misleading signals that resulted from the way in which the initial air strikes were carried out.

heresy."[19] On the other hand, as the name suggests, briefing officers are not expected to describe the complexities of troop movements, bombing missions, covert operations, and intelligence-gathering activities in minute detail. Instead, it is their job to present information in the kind of neat and orderly package that makes it appear as if everything is being "orchestrated" according to plan.[20] Nor are briefing officers, particularly if they are cognizant of the color of their uniform, likely to recount for their audiences the kinds of foul-ups in the field that can significantly influence the success or failure of an attempt to "orchestrate" words and deeds or "signal" by deed as well as by word. How many career military officers, for example, would be likely to call the attention of senior officials to the fact that pilots are not always successful in finding the target assigned to them?[21]

*   *   *

Having specified some of the ways in which the activities envisioned by senior officials may differ from the activities actually undertaken by their government, it remains to be seen how these discrepancies can affect the interaction between governments involved in a competitive process like an attempt at coercion. In particular, how might these discrepancies affect efforts by senior officials to "orchestrate" words and deeds and "signal" by deed as well as by word? Conversely, how might they appear when viewed from a foreign capital?

Perhaps the most obvious point to be made in this respect is that officials in a foreign capital (Side B) observe and thus react to *not* the set of activities intended by senior officials on Side A but rather the activities actually undertaken by A's government. Furthermore, not being privy to the deliberations preceding a decision by senior officials on Side A, B's leaders will necessarily be at least somewhat uncertain of A's intentions and will thus be forced, as suggested in Chapter 7, to draw inferences about A's intentions on the basis of what A is actually doing. In

19. Patrick McGarvey, "DIA: Intelligence to Please," *The Washington Monthly*, July 1970, p. 74. See also Jervis (1976, p. 330) for a discussion of the tendency to assume that one's orders are being carried out as intended.

20. In this respect, see the comments of the former NSC staff member cited in Chapter 6, above (at note 7). See also McGarvey's description of "dog and pony shows" in *CIA: The Myth and the Madness* (Baltimore: Penguin, 1972), pp. 152–154. This problem is compounded by the use of misleading statistical indices such as sortie rates and body counts. On this point, see the comments by Stavins, Blachman, and Gallucci, cited in notes 15 and 16, above.

21. It might be helpful, in this respect, to recall the attack by USAF planes on the "wrong" Pathet Lao target, described in Chapter 2, note 71, above.

such a situation, there are four possible outcomes concerning A's efforts to "orchestrate" words and deeds and "signal" by deed as well as by word.

1. *There is no significant divergence between the activities envisioned by senior officials on Side A and the activities actually undertaken by A; furthermore, there is no significant divergence between the "message" intended for transmission to B by A's leaders and the "message" read into A's actions by senior officials on Side B.*

Although such an outcome is theoretically possible, it seems highly unlikely that it would occur in practice. On the one hand, as suggested by the discussion earlier in this chapter and also in Chapter 6, the discrepancies between what senior officials intend to be done and what the government actually does do not occur by chance. Instead, those discrepancies would seem to be inherent in any governmental structure requiring collaboration by many officials, drawn from different departments, guided by differing views of what is required to satisfy the national as well as organizational interests, and responding to different promotion systems.

On the other hand, as we shall see, it is also unlikely that there will be no discrepancy between the "message" intended by senior officials on Side A and the "message" read into A's actions by senior officials on Side B.

2. *There is no significant divergence between the activities envisioned by senior officials on Side A and the activities actually undertaken by A, but there is nonetheless a divergence between the "message" intended by A's leaders and the message read into A's actions by senior officials on Side B.*

Although, as suggested earlier, it is unlikely that there would be no significant divergence between what is intended by senior officials on Side A and what is actually done by A's government, it is useful to consider this case nonetheless because of what it can tell us about the way in which efforts to "orchestrate" words and deeds and "signal" by deed as well as by word may be perceived by officials in a foreign capital. In this respect, it is essential to bear in mind that officials on Side B can hardly be considered impartial observers of A's activities. Instead, as we stressed in Chapter 5, those officials are likely to be deeply enmeshed in the complexities of moving their own government to adopt certain courses of action. As a result, they may be strongly tempted to assign to A's signals an interpretation that promises the least inconvenience for them as they interact with their colleagues in making policy for their own government.[22] Nor will yielding to such a temptation require them

22. On this point, see the discussion of British and American perceptions of each other during the Suez and Skybolt crises, in Neustadt, pp. 61–62.

to engage in chicanery or conscious distortion of incoming signals (although they might). Instead, there are a number of reasons why A's actions, even if they correspond perfectly to the intent of senior officials on Side A, are likely to be ambiguous and thus open to multiple interpretations.

First, in any competitive situation, officials on Side B will be observing and thus reacting to not just those activities that officials on Side A *want* officials on Side B to notice but rather to all of A's actions that are visible to B, even though many may be the product of ongoing routines or directed at other problem areas and thus, in the minds of officials on Side A, quite irrelevant to the dispute with B. The U-2 on the "routine air-sampling mission" that strayed into Soviet airspace during the Cuban missile crisis comes readily to mind; similarly, one suspects that President Johnson's frequent campaign speeches denying any intent to carry the war to the North or to send American troops to fight in the South had a much greater effect on officials in Hanoi, particularly those pressing for a greater Northern role in the war in the South, than American officials (who probably dismissed them as the normal hyperbole of a political campaign) realized. Conversely, the sheer number and scope of the activities being undertaken by a foreign policy bureaucracy as large as the one centered in Washington may result in officials on Side B failing to notice a signal that to officials on Side A seems crystal clear, as in the cases of the apparent DRV failure to notice the start of OPLAN 34A in early 1964 or the start of BARREL ROLL strikes in Laos in December 1964 (see Chapter 2, above).

Second, as we saw in Chapter 6, senior officials on Side A may attempt to ease the burdens that they bear by factoring complex policy problems into their component parts and then dealing with each part separately. But while such a style of decision-making may result in an orderly and comprehensible flow of decisions from superiors to subordinates, what is produced as a result of organizational implementation may be anything but orderly and comprehensible. Depending on the latitude given organizational subunits with respect to the nature and timing of implementing activities and the time lags that result as orders are transmitted down organizational chains of command, what may result in the field is a confusing jumble of activities in which escalatory moves coincide with or precede or follow diplomatic initiatives in seemingly random fashion. Furthermore, the divergence between the "message" intended by senior officials on Side A and the "message" read into A's actions by senior officials on Side B will very likely be increased by the tendency, noted in Chapter 7, of officials to assume that whatever was done by an opponent must have been intended by its leaders, regardless of any denials or disclaimers that might accompany the action in question.

Third, as we saw in Chapter 7, there was a noticeable tendency on the part of both American and DRV officials to rely on analogies between governments and unified calculating actors when attempting to comprehend their opponent's motives in undertaking some action or actions. As a result, however, officials on both sides were singularly ill-equipped to understand the dual-track strategy (involving both military and diplomatic components) that each side pursued throughout the war. Significantly, in this respect, while officials in both Washington and Hanoi apparently viewed it as only natural that responsibility for their own side's military and diplomatic activities should be assigned to separate groups of officials, with senior officials alternating between decisions on military moves and decisions on diplomatic initiatives, neither side seemed willing to concede that that same kind of compartmentalization of authority might be characteristic of their opponents. Instead, officials on both sides repeatedly assumed that their opponent's military activities provided a reliable guide to his diplomatic intentions, even though, as we saw in Chapters 6 and 7, decisions on military issues were very often made separately from decisions on diplomatic initiatives, with little or no consideration of how each track in one side's strategy would affect the other.

Fourth, just as there can be "slippage" in the implementation of the decisions by senior officials on Side A as a result of organizational routines and the preferences of subordinate officials, so can there be "perceptual slippage" as a result of the standard operating procedures of intelligence agencies and the preferences of officials on Side B. For example, just as intelligence officers associated with the U.S. military command in Saigon sought to manipulate estimates of the rate of infiltration and of the DRV/VC order of battle in accordance with the policies advocated by senior U.S. military commanders (i.e., seeking at first to inflate estimates of enemy strength so as to justify the U.S. troop buildup and then to hold down those estimates in order to support the view that the war was "winnable"),[23] one suspects that DRV officials such as Le Duan and Nguyen Chi Thanh eagerly sought out information confirming their belief that the U.S. would not intervene forcefully and that it could be defeated if it did. To the extent that they and their allies were able to influence the promotion prospects of officials in the

---

23. On these manipulations, see McGarvey (1970), pp. 69–70; Sam Adams, "Vietnam Cover-Up: Playing War with Numbers," *Harpers*, May 1975; and Adams's testimony in Ellsberg Trial Transcript, pp. 14,592 ff.

DRV intelligence agencies, one suspects that the latter would have strong incentives to seek out and disseminate information that supported the arguments that Le Duan and Nguyen Chi Thanh were pressing on their colleagues in the Politburo. Although there are limits to the extent to which intelligence officers can overlook or ignore information that their superiors would prefer not to hear, so long as the sender's signals are ambiguous (as they are likely to be when numerous agencies and officials are involved in making and implementing policy on the side of the sender) and the amount of "noise" in the signalling system is high (as it is likely to be in a world of many major actors, each of which is engaged in many activities at once), intelligence officers will inevitably have great leeway in choosing which signals to pay attention to and which to ignore.

Fifth and finally, even if officials on Side B were not influenced by the problems cited above, they could still fail to grasp the significance of the message intended for them by A's leaders—e.g., by dismissing it (incorrectly) as a bluff. As Jervis notes, the receiver of a message must draw inferences on two levels: "First he must determine what message the sender is trying to convey. Second, the receiver must estimate whether this accurately reflects what the sender will do in the future."[24] In the Vietnamese case, while DRV officials were certainly aware of the threats aimed at them by the Johnson Administration (some of which were conveyed directly to Pham Van Dong by Seaborn), they apparently underestimated the lengths to which the U.S. would go in defending South Vietnam. As a result, they viewed U.S. activities such as the Tonkin Gulf reprisal strikes not as an index of U.S. determination to resist but rather as an attempt by President Johnson to outbid the Republican candidate in the Presidential election.[25]

3. *There are significant discrepancies between what is intended by senior officials on Side A and what is actually done by A, but there is nonetheless little or no divergence between the "message" intended by A's leaders and the "message" read into A's actions by senior officials on Side B.*

Although, as suggested earlier, the "message" intended for transmission to B's leaders by senior officials on Side A may be subject to distortion both as a result of "slippage" in the process of implementation on Side A and of the difficulties that B's leaders are likely to encounter in seeking to discern the meaning of A's signals, one can nonetheless conceive of situations in which these potential distorting influences

---

24. Jervis (1970), p. 24.

25. This point was made by Pham Van Dong to Seaborn during their August 1964 meeting (Interview Data).

would have relatively little impact on the transmission of messages between the two sides. In the Cuban missile crisis, for example, senior officials in Washington sought to convince the Soviets of their determination to see the missiles removed from Cuba, by force if necessary, while at the same time avoiding actions that might provoke the Soviets into doing something rash. But despite extraordinary efforts by the ExComm to control the activities of organizational subunits, there were nonetheless significant discrepancies between the actions intended by senior American officials and the actions undertaken by the U.S. Government during the crisis.[26] Whereas members of the ExComm desired the Air Force to prepare plans for a "surgical" strike aimed only at the Soviet missiles, Air Force planners presented a proposal for strikes against the missiles, SAM sites, airports, and military bases involving as many as 500 sorties and significant collateral damage. Whereas the President sought to have the blockade moved closer to Cuba so as to provide the Soviets with additional time to deliberate, the Navy apparently stuck to its original plan to intercept Soviet ships out of range of aircraft based in Cuba. Whereas the ExComm sought to minimize provocations during the crisis, Navy ships tracked Soviet submarines and forced several to surface; in addition, there was the U-2 that strayed into Soviet airspace at the height of the crisis. Whereas Secretary McNamara's "no cities" doctrine sought to minimize civilian casualties in the event of a nuclear exchange, the Strategic Air Command dispersed its aircraft to civilian airports, some of which were in range of the Soviet MRBMs in Cuba. Whereas President Kennedy sought to ensure that U.S. aircraft in Florida would not present a tempting target, the Air Force nonetheless parked the aircraft wing-to-wing.[27]

And yet, despite the potential for disaster inherent in the discrepancies cited above, the Kennedy Administration was nonetheless successful in convincing the Soviets of its determination to see the missiles removed; and in this respect, the buildup of conventional forces begun by the Administration in anticipation of an invasion of Cuba appears to have been of overwhelming importance. Despite the discordant and distracting signals generated by activities such as the Navy's overzealous implementation of the blockade, the attention of both the Soviets and the Cubans was apparently riveted on the buildup in Florida and on the prospect that an invasion would be launched.[28]

26. On this point, see the discussion of the efforts of ExComm members, particularly Secretary McNamara, to maintain control over the blockade, in Allison, pp. 128–132.

27. On these points, see Allison, pp. 125, 129–130, 138–139, 141. See also Halperin (1974), pp. 279–280.

28. On the importance of the U.S. military buildup, see Allison, pp. 64–66; and Young, p. 209.

It is difficult to state with certainty why the Kennedy Administration was so successful in convincing the Soviets of its determination to see the missiles removed (but without provoking them) despite the existence of the discrepancies cited above between what senior officials intended and what the government actually did. It is conceivable, for example, that compared to the central issue in the crisis—i.e., would the Soviets remove the missiles voluntarily or attempt to keep them in place, with the attendant risks of nuclear war—the discrepancies cited above were simply not significant in the eyes of the Soviet leadership and therefore not considered carefully (perhaps not even noticed). Or it may have been the case that U.S. conventional and nuclear superiority was so great that the Soviets felt compelled to proceed cautiously despite the more provocative moves by certain agencies of the U.S. Government. Perhaps most importantly of all, it may have been that the structure of the situation—i.e., the dispatching of the missiles to an island only 90 miles from the United States, followed by the announcement of the blockade and the assembling of an invasion force in Florida, poised to strike at Cuba if the missiles were not withdrawn[29]—was such that the signal conveyed by the Administration's actions was so compelling that there was no question of the Soviets not recognizing it and taking it seriously. Or it may have been a combination of all of these factors. In any case, the Cuban crisis suggests that the kinds of discrepancies cited above need not prove fatal to efforts to "signal" by deed as well as by word.

And yet, it may also be the case that the Cuban crisis is the exception that proves the rule with respect to the difficulties that senior officials are likely to encounter when they attempt to take actions that convey unambiguous "messages" to officials in a foreign capital. It must surely be significant that the Cuban crisis is the only clear-cut example of a successful attempt by one government to coerce another in the post-1945 international system.[30] Geographical proximity and local conventional superiority did not result in Chinese Communist successes during

On the Soviet/Cuban concern over the possibility of an invasion, see Khrushchev's remarks on the imminence of an invasion, cited in Allison, pp. 65–66.

29. "Connectedness" is the term used by Schelling (1966, pp. 86 ff.) to describe situations in which the structure of the situation contributes to the clarity of a threat (e.g., cross this well-defined boundary, behind which our troops are entrenched, and we will fight) and thus enhances the credibility of the threat.

30. David Hall ("The Laos Crisis, 1960–1961") and Alexander George ("Comparisons and Lessons"; both in George, Hall, and Simons) argue that the Kennedy Administration successfully used "coercive diplomacy" to resolve the 1961 Laotian crisis; yet it is not at all clear who was coerced into doing what by the Administration's threats. All the U.S. achieved was the reestablishment of a neutralist coalition government (which the U.S. had been instrumental in overthrowing to begin with) and a renewed (albeit temporary) cease-fire (which the U.S. had been

the Taiwan Strait crises of 1954–1955 and 1958, nor did they allow the Soviets to push the West out of Berlin during the crises of 1948–1949 and 1958–1961 (although the advantages enjoyed by the Communist side in all of these cases were admittedly offset by U.S. nuclear superiority and the presence of strong U.S. conventional forces in the general vicinity of each clash). Nor did overwhelming superiority in weapons and firepower enable the Johnson Administration to coerce the North Vietnamese into halting their efforts to gain control of South Vietnam.[31] And, while the governments resisting the imposition of coercive pressures in the cases cited above were at times able to take actions that convincingly communicated their determination to resist (e.g., the American decision to supply naval escorts to Nationalist convoys, combined with the American military buildup in the Far East during the 1958 Taiwan Strait crisis),[32] such efforts were not always successful. As Young notes in discussing the Berlin crisis of 1961:

The actions of the principals in the crisis were frequently ambiguous, contradictory, or inconsistent over time. And there were several occasions on which actions were more nearly a source of confusion than a procedure for improving understanding. Despite the very striking communications success in coordinating actions in the aftermath of the actual closing of the sector boundary in Berlin, therefore, the 1961 crisis as a whole was characterized by a number of communications failures between East and West. As a result, there were serious deficiencies of understanding between the parties at a number of points in the crisis, a factor leading to several dangerous developments.[33]

4. *There may be significant discrepancies both between the actions intended by senior officials on Side A and the actions undertaken by A and between the message intended for transmission to B by A's leaders and the message read into A's actions by senior officials on Side B.*

Because B's leaders observe and thus react to *not* the set of activities intended by senior officials on Side A but rather the totality of A's

---

partly responsible for breaking by its encouragement of the Laotian rightists). The Pathet Lao were not dislodged from their bases in northeastern Laos, nor were they and their North Vietnamese allies dissuaded from continuing their efforts to gain control of all of Laos. Similarly, some officials and analysts have claimed that the Eisenhower Administration successfully coerced the Chinese Communists during the Korean armistice negotiations by threatening nuclear attacks on China itself; however, in light of the paucity of evidence available on Chinese Communist decision-making, a careful analyst would hesitate before arguing that this case proves the utility of coercive pressures.

31. Similarly, the massive bombing of Hanoi and Haiphong during December 1972 failed to compel the North Vietnamese to agree to major changes in the peace agreement that had been tentatively accepted by both sides in October 1972. On this point, see Porter, pp. 125–173.

32. On this point, see Young, pp. 127–129, 191–192.

33. Young, p. 136; see also p. 198.

activities that are visible to B (regardless of whether they were aimed at B or some other audience), there may well be a significant discrepancy between the "message" that senior officials on Side A think is being communicated to B and the "message" that B's leaders read into A's actions—a discrepancy, moreover, *that senior officials on both sides are likely to be unaware of.* For example, if senior officials on Side A adopt what to them appears as a relatively conciliatory stance on some point at issue between A and B, their intent may nonetheless be obscured both by "slippage" in the process of implementation on Side A and by the problems that B's leaders face in attempting to discern the true meaning of A's signals. As a result, B's leaders may conclude that A is taking a much harder line than was intended by senior officials on Side A. If, in response, B's leaders choose to stiffen their own position (a stance that may itself appear all the more inflexible because of "slippage" in the process of implementing the decisions taken by B's leaders and/or distorted perceptions on Side A), the stage will be set for a significant hardening of positions on both sides. Senior officials on Side A, recalling their original conciliatory intent and being largely unaware, for the reasons described earlier, of the factors that can distort the meaning of "messages" exchanged between A and B, will assume not only that B's actions indicate intransigence but also that their own conciliatory gesture was treated with contempt, thus leading them to stiffen their own position and possibly increase their efforts to gain the upper hand in their dispute with B. Seeing Side A stiffen its position and/or escalate its efforts, B's leaders may assume they have no choice but to follow suit.

Thus, for example, in the MARIGOLD case, senior officials in Washington apparently believed that the U.S. was making two conciliatory gestures: (1) offering the Phase A–Phase B plan, which backed away somewhat from earlier U.S. demands for reciprocity for a bombing halt; and (2) agreeing to conduct the proposed talks in Warsaw on the basis of Lewandowski's 10-point formulation of the U.S. position, thus tacitly committing the U.S. to consider some change in the South Vietnamese status quo. These gestures, however, were effectively obscured both by the ill-timed bombing raids on Hanoi in early December 1966, which, as we saw, used considerably more ordnance than previous attacks on the Hanoi area, and by the confusion generated by Lodge's "differences of interpretation" statement to Lewandowski. Furthermore, senior U.S. officials were not in possession at the time (i.e., the first two weeks of December 1966) of two key pieces of information: (1) that the North Vietnamese were apparently watching the pattern of the air strikes very

carefully and drawing inferences about Washington's diplomatic intentions on the basis of the conduct of the air war; and (2) that the Poles
apparently jumped the gun in reporting Washington's "acceptance" of
Lewandowski's proposal to Hanoi without conveying, at least at first,
Washington's reservations over Lewandowski's text.[34] As a result,
officials in Washington and Hanoi were viewing the same events from
strikingly different perspectives, with officials in Hanoi apparently reading into Washington's actions "messages" that officials in Washington
never intended to be sent—i.e., a tacit ultimatum to make additional
concessions or else risk further attacks on Hanoi, and an attempt to
renege on the "commitment" to consider a coalition government for the
South. To make matters worse, when the North Vietnamese broke off
the contact, senior officials in Washington apparently concluded that
they had been suckered by the Poles, that the North Vietnamese had
never intended to go through with the talks at all, and that the whole
exercise had been a Polish/North Vietnamese attempt to win concessions on the conduct of the air war—an attitude that very likely contributed to the general loosening of restraints on the air war in early
1967 and the stiffening of the American position during the subsequent
contacts in Moscow and London.[35] Significantly, as we saw in Chapter
4, this escalation of the air war coincided with a greatly stepped-up
effort by the North Vietnamese, which included the positioning of three
PAVN divisions just north of the DMZ, a move that itself greatly complicated the search for a diplomatic breakthrough that occurred in
Moscow and London in January and February of 1967.

Although it is tempting to conclude that the MARIGOLD case constitutes an isolated instance of such distorted perceptions and that the
normal process of sending and receiving "messages" is much less prone
to "noise" and interference, we can infer from the available evidence
that the fourth of our four possible outcomes is the one most likely to
occur when governments clash.[36] Although one might expect that

34. For background on these points, see the discussion in Chapters 4 and 6, above.
35. On the American reaction to the breakdown of MARIGOLD, see Cooper (1972), p. 409;
Johnson, pp. 251–252; and the discussion in Chapters 6 and 7, above. The escalation of the air war
in early 1967 is described in Section I-C of Chapter 4, above.
36. This point is conceded by Schelling (1966, p. 151), who notes that "the process of diplomacy
by maneuver is typically a good deal clumsier, with actions less subject to careful control for the
message they embody, subject to background noise from uncontrollable events, and subject to misinterpretation" than the Gulf of Tonkin incidents, which, as we saw earlier, themselves constituted
an extremely muddled and confusing situation. Interestingly, though, Schelling devotes virtually
all of his analysis to situations in which the exchange of unambiguous messages is supposedly
possible, rather than pondering the problems that might arise to confuse the communications
process.

senior American officials with lengthy experience in government would be aware that their wishes are not always faithfully translated into action, the list of cases in which those officials were apparently not attuned to the divergence between what they thought their government was doing and what it actually did is too long to be overlooked or dismissed as inconsequential. The "slow beginning" to OPLAN 34A, the incidents in the Gulf of Tonkin, the shift to "Phase 1" pressures in December 1964, the uncertain beginning of the ROLLING THUNDER program, the confusing signals emanating from the conduct of the air war in April and May 1965, the embarrassing coincidences that dogged the Administration's handling of diplomatic contacts with Hanoi—all these suggest that senior officials in Washington acted as if their directives were being faithfully implemented both by themselves and by their subordinates.[37] Nor should we assume that the North Vietnamese were any less prone to the kind of "slippage" in the process of implementing the decisions of senior officials that so often obscured the intent of senior officials in Washington. Although the data available on decision-making in Hanoi are admittedly less than adequate, the existence of continuing (and often heated) policy disputes in Hanoi, reliance on generalized directives (i.e., Central Committee and COSVN resolutions) to control the war effort, and the need to delegate a certain amount of authority to dispersed military units operating in a hostile environment all suggest that what "Hanoi" did was not necessarily a perfect reflection of the wishes of the members of the Politburo.

Similarly, although the evidence concerning North Vietnamese perceptions of U.S. signals is not sufficient to permit us to trace out other cases in as much detail as the MARIGOLD case, there is enough evidence to permit us to conclude that the existence of significant discrepancies between the signal intended by the sender and the signal perceived by the receiver is more common than earlier accounts, such as Schelling's, would lead us to believe. In both the MARIGOLD and PENNSYLVANIA (Aubrac/Marcovich) cases, DRV officials read into American actions threats and tacit ultimatums that do not appear to have been intended by senior American officials. Conversely, as we saw in Chapters 2–3, DRV officials apparently did not conclude, as U.S. officials hoped they would, that the start of the covert war and then later the ROLLING THUNDER program constituted a determined American effort to thwart a DRV/VC takeover in the South, viewing them instead as a limited effort to improve the U.S. bargaining position

37. For a useful discussion of "Being Misinformed about One's Own Behavior," see Jervis (1976), pp. 329–338.

prior to an international conference that the U.S. was seeking in order to disengage from a losing cause.[38]

*   *   *

Governmental interaction in the Vietnamese case was thus characterized by three critical assumptions, each of which proved to be incorrect at key points in the war:

1. Senior officials on both sides appear to have assumed that their own decisions would be implemented faithfully, either by themselves or by their subordinates.

2. Senior officials on both sides appear to have assumed that the "message" that they intended to be transmitted to their opponents would be the same as the "message" read into their actions by their opponents.

3. Senior officials on both sides appear to have assumed that what their opponents did was done because senior officials on the other side wanted it done.[39]

Precisely because these assumptions proved incorrect, the process of interaction between Washington and Hanoi was one in which the possibilities for distorted communications and mistaken perceptions were legion. Because officials on both sides were apparently unaware that their decisions were not always implemented faithfully (although their opponents assumed that they were) and also because they were unaware that their opponents might be noticing actions not aimed at them or failing to notice actions that were aimed at them, they do not appear to have been concerned that the "messages" received might not be the

---

38. Ironically, as we saw in Chapters 1-3, at the very time that DRV officials apparently believed that the U.S. was seeking a diplomatic exit from the war, U.S. officials were in fact preoccupied with the task of stalling off negotiations until the pressures being applied to North Vietnam could strengthen the U.S. bargaining position.

39. In the case of the first two of these assertions, to state that senior officials on *both* sides felt this way is admittedly to stretch the evidence. We simply do not know enough about decision-making in Hanoi to state with certainty that the characteristics that prevailed in Washington also prevailed in Hanoi, although there were the exaggerated claims of the prowess of DRV/VC forces in the South made by Le Duan and his supporters (see Chapter 6, above) as well as the inflated claims of numbers of U.S. planes shot down over the North, both of which suggest that senior officials in Hanoi might have been at least somewhat misinformed concerning the activities of their subordinates and the "message" that their actions were conveying to Washington. Concerning the third of these assertions, there is evidence that DRV officials assumed that what the U.S. did was done because senior officials in Washington wanted it done, in the form of the DRV's reaction to the attacks on Hanoi during the MARIGOLD and PENNSYLVANIA contacts (see Chapter 7, above).

same as the "messages" sent. In scrutinizing their opponent's response, moreover, officials on both sides appear to have interpreted that response in light of what they *thought* their own side had done rather than what had actually been done. What was salient for senior officials, in Washington at least and quite possibly in Hanoi, were the decisions that *they* had made and not what was actually done. Senior officials had neither the time nor the inclination to monitor continuously the activities of their subordinates—their "in baskets" were too full, the press of business too great. Of necessity, they focused on the present, leaving the past to take care of itself. Nor did their subordinates alert them to the divergences between what they thought had been done and what actually was done.

Viewed from this perspective, it should not be surprising that U.S. officials viewed their DRV counterparts as at best inscrutable and at worst engaged in a calculated effort to score propaganda points or wrest some unreciprocated concession from the United States. It was almost as if the two sides existed in different political universes. What U.S. officials saw as politically risky steps toward a settlement, DRV officials saw as a heavy-handed effort to bludgeon them into making further concessions (e.g., MARIGOLD). What U.S. officials saw as gestures of good will, DRV officials saw as a tacit ultimatum to accept a settlement on American terms or else risk the destruction of Hanoi (e.g., PENNSYLVANIA).

What all this suggests, in short, is that governmental interaction in competitive situations such as an attempt at coercion is likely to be far more complex than the relatively simple action-reaction models favored by many social scientists would lead us to believe. Indeed, on the basis of our review of the Johnson Administration's efforts to coerce North Vietnam, one can legitimately question the extent to which the concepts of "action" and "reaction" are applicable to clashes between governments. At the very least, those concepts would seem to imply a single reality, a set of moves and countermoves, that is known to and understood by both participants and observers. But while the analyst, armed with the benefit of hindsight, may be able to reconstruct what to him appears as an intelligible sequence of thrust and parry, of "messages" sent and received, such a reconstruction may bear relatively little resemblance to the flow of events as experienced by the officials involved in making and implementing policy. As our discussion of the MARIGOLD case suggests, the same set of events may be viewed quite differently by officials in different capitals. What may be one official's ongoing routine may be another's tacit ultimatum.

Furthermore, implicit in the concept of an action-reaction sequence is the notion of governmental interaction as an alternating series of discrete moves, in which each participant responds to what the other has already done (analogies with the game of chess come readily to mind). But while there is a certain validity in conceptualizing clashes between governments in terms of moves and countermoves, as evidenced by the frequent high-level policy reviews in both Washington and Hanoi at which wartime strategy was thrashed out, decision-making within governments is typically far more fluid and continuous than the chess-game analogy would suggest. As we saw in earlier chapters, in between the high-level policy reviews, senior officials (in Washington at least) served largely as "firemen," responding to problems as they percolated up to the top as a result of the failure of past policies and/or subordinates lobbying for permission to undertake some new course of action. In response, the President and his advisers almost always selected an option representing a marginal adjustment to past policies—e.g., an increase in the number of bombing sorties or targets on the ROLLING THUNDER authorized list, or in the number of troops that could be sent to South Vietnam, or a reformulation of the U.S. demand for "mutual deescalation."[40] Then, having dealt with whatever issue was before them, they would pass their decisions to subordinates for implementation and move on to the next issue on their list. The result, as we saw in Chapter 6, was a policymaking process in which complex policy problems (i.e., coercing North Vietnam) were factored into their component parts (i.e., military moves and diplomatic initiatives), which were dealt with sequentially, with the sequence being repeated as additional marginal adjustments to past policy decisions were required.

As a result, what has often been conceptualized as government "action" and "reaction" would be more appropriately viewed as a continuous stream of decisions from superiors to subordinates, which may or may not be implemented faithfully and which may or may not be interpreted by opponents in the way that senior officials intended. Furthermore, the organizational outputs triggered by the decisions of senior officials are themselves lumped together with the hundreds of actions that are routinely performed each day by the officials who collectively comprise each government's foreign policy bureaucracy. In such a milieu, with senior officials considering problems sequentially rather than simultaneously, with decisions confined largely to marginal

40. Even the high-level policy reviews, as we saw in earlier chapters, could hardly be considered fundamental reappraisals of wartime strategy. Instead, they too produced decisions that almost always called for little more than marginal adjustments to past policies.

adjustments to past policies, with subordinates not always fully informed of what it is that their superiors desire, with superiors not always aware of what their subordinates are doing, with the intent of each side's leaders distorted both by "slippage" in the process of implementation and by the difficulty of discerning the true meaning of incoming signals, and with each side reading into the actions of the other "messages" that the other did not always intend to be sent, the concepts of "orchestrating" words and deeds and "signalling" by deed as well as by word begin to lose all meaning.

The "lesson" to be drawn here should be at once both obvious and compelling. Coercion is an inherently risky business. The statesmen whose decisions trigger such an attempt will be starting a process over which they will have only imperfect control (although, as suggested earlier, it may be relatively easy for them to delude themselves into believing otherwise). Senior officials cannot do everything by themselves, nor can they constantly look over the shoulders of their subordinates to ensure that their decisions are promptly and faithfully executed. Indeed, they are likely to be largely unaware of the great mass of routine activities that daily constitute the actions of their government. Most importantly, however, even if they could exert total control over the actions of their government, they still could not ensure that their opponents would notice what they wanted them to notice or draw the inferences that they wanted them to draw. Success, if it is achieved (and it rarely is), is thus likely to be as much the product of accident and good fortune as of design and skill. In a world filled with weapons of mass destruction, senior officials should at the very least think long and hard before starting down a path that is so fraught with peril.

B. Influencing Governments

In addition to highlighting the complex nature of governmental interaction, the Vietnamese case can also be used to illustrate the inordinate difficulties that officials are likely to encounter when they attempt to influence the choices of officials in another government. As we saw in Chapters 5–7, underlying much of the theorizing done in this country on the problems of coercive war was a "model" in which the target of the coercive pressures was conceptualized as a single, calculating actor endowed with a high degree of control over the actions of "his" government. Given that perspective, the task facing the coercer was relatively straightforward—namely, to take actions that threatened to impose on the target state costs in excess of any potential gains the target state might realize by continuing with the policies that triggered the coercive response in the first place. And yet, as we saw earlier, coercing "Hanoi" proved to be far more difficult than might be expected on the basis of the "model" utilized by Administration planners.

One problem, as we saw in Chapter 5, was that the "model" envisioned as the target of coercive pressures not just a unitary actor but an actor endowed with a coldly calculating intelligence: witness Taylor's belief that the North Vietnamese would back down "when the cost of pursuing a losing course became excessive" and Kaufmann's suggestion that the "enemy" could be best understood as a "calculating individual with a multiplicity of values, aware of cost and risk as well as of advantage, and capable of drawing significant inferences from symbolic acts."[41] And yet, it may well be both misleading and dangerous to expect an opposing government to base its policies on the kind of careful, cost-benefit calculations that the Johnson Administration apparently imputed to "Hanoi." As Russett has noted:

When General Hideki Tojo was Japanese Minister of War in September 1941 he advised Premier Konoye that at some point during a man's lifetime he might find it necessary to jump, with eyes closed, from the temple of Kiyomizudera on the heights of Kyoto into the ravine below. Other Japanese officials used less colorful words invoking the necessity to take great risks, or to plunge with faith into the sea of the unknown.[42]

In similar fashion, DRV leaders such as Le Duan and Nguyen Chi Thanh were deeply and passionately committed to the goal of completing the revolution in South Vietnam. It was a goal they had been pursuing for virtually all of their adult lives, and it hardly seems likely that the start of the air war would have resulted in a reordering of their priorities. Indeed, at a number of points along the way, Le Duan and Nguyen Chi Thanh had contemptuously dismissed the kind of "rational" calculations that seemingly suggested that their preferred approach to the problem of reunification (i.e., main force warfare in the South with heavy Northern involvement) was inappropriate. Thus, as we saw earlier, Le Duan, in his concluding speech at the 9th Plenum, heaped scorn on "certain communists" for their fear of "perilous revolutionary struggle," while Nguyen Chi Thanh vilified his opponents for their "feeble revolutionary determination." It was that kind of reasoning, Latimer notes, that was perhaps

the key to understanding why Le Duan, Nguyen Chi Thanh, and finally, Ho Chi Minh himself, chose an offensive strategy for the southern revolution and

41. Taylor (1972), p. 401; and Kaufmann, "Limited Warfare," in Kaufmann (ed.), p. 117.

42. Bruce Russett, "Pearl Harbor: Deterrence Theory and Decision Theory," in Russett, *Power and Community*, p. 217. See also Wohlstetter, pp. 351–357.

why they remained determined to push ahead toward their goal despite the threat of American intervention. The key is their revolutionary spirit. Those men were in every sense of the word, revolutionaries. They cast aside cold calculations of material strength and insisted that a properly motivated people, even in a small, undeveloped nation such as Vietnam, could successfully challenge the world's mightiest military power.[43]

Furthermore, as we stressed in Chapter 5, there is an enormous difference between coercing an individual and coercing the individuals who collectively comprise an opposing government. Not only is it likely that at least some of them will have fought long and hard to persuade their colleagues and/or superiors to go along with them in undertaking whatever action(s) necessitated a coercive response, but, in addition, for an opposing government to yield under pressure, it will be necessary for those officials either to admit (tacitly or explicitly) that they were in error or leave the government (or be forced out of it). Particularly if the crisis has been brewing for some time and the opponent has invested considerable resources in creating or expanding the organizational subunits charged with securing the objectives that the coercer seeks to defend, it may be highly unlikely that the target state will yield in the face of coercive pressures. Whenever "sunk costs" (not the least of which are the reputations and careers of both the officials who lobbied for going ahead with whatever policy brought on the coercive pressures and the officials staffing the organizations charged with implementing that policy) are high, an opposing government may easily be led to raise the ante rather than yield, especially if victory seems near or the pressures being applied are not very severe at the outset.[44] Thus, as we saw in Chapter 5, the initial American pressures against North Vietnam during 1964 very likely spurred Le Duan and his supporters to redouble their efforts to secure a quick victory in the South by means of armed struggle and heavy Northern involvement so as to win in the South before the American pressures on the North became too severe, thus presenting the U.S. with a *fait accompli* and vindicating themselves in the process.

To suggest that analogies between governments and unified, calculating actors obscure far more than they reveal is *not*, however, to suggest that officials who make use of more sophisticated approaches will necessarily be more successful in influencing the activities of officials in a foreign capital. While preferable to the kind of crude decision-making calculus imputed by officials of the Johnson Administration to "Hanoi,"

43. Latimer, pp. 138–139.
44. On the importance of "sunk costs," see Jervis (1976), pp. 397–398.

approaches that seek to comprehend an opposing government's policies as the product of "internal bargaining among the bureaucratic elements and political personalities who collectively comprise its working apparatus"[45] may nonetheless founder, not only as a result of limits on the available information but more importantly as a result of the unwillingness and/or inability of senior officers to make proper use of the information that is available to them. In this respect, the ease with which American officials gravitated to approaches such as the "Hanoi-as-unitary-calculating-actor" formula is perhaps best understood as symptomatic of a deeper and more pernicious problem—namely, a search for convenient forms of shorthand that could be used to provide a comprehensive framework for describing and explaining DRV activities and motivation.[46]

For example, on those occasions when U.S. officials sought to go beyond simplistic approaches such as the analogy between "Hanoi" and a single, calculating actor, they consistently identified the driving force behind DRV decision-making with one or the other of two key personalities: Ho Chi Minh or Vo Nguyen Giap. Not surprisingly, President Johnson appears to have conceived of the conflict as essentially a test of wills between Ho and himself, while General Westmoreland often described his efforts as a response to initiatives taken by the person he presumed was his opposite number in Hanoi, namely, General Giap.[47] Or, to take a second example, in their descriptions of DRV activity during and after the rapid escalation of the war in 1964 and 1965, U.S. officials often spoke of their opponent as shifting ahead or reverting back to one of the three stages of guerrilla war described in the writings of Mao Tse-tung.[48]

But while Ho and Giap were admittedly prominent personalities, and while there is a certain amount of understanding to be derived from describing DRV policy in terms of Mao's stages, these shorthand formulations are perhaps most revealing of how little American policymakers actually understood about decision-making in Hanoi. On the one hand, as we saw in Chapters 5 and 6, throughout the period 1954–1965, Ho apparently functioned primarily as "Chairman of the Board," keeping himself above the polemical disputes that recurred throughout that

---

45. Neustadt, p. ix.

46. On this search for shortcuts to understanding, see Neustadt, p. 69.

47. Their memoirs are indicative of their feelings in this respect, especially Johnson, pp. 252–256. See also Halberstam, p. 532; and Sharp and Westmoreland, p. 84.

48. See, for example, Robert Komer, "Bureaucracy Does Its Thing: Institutional Constraints on U.S.-GVN Performance in Vietnam," The RAND Corp., R-967-ARPA, August 1972, p. 40; Sharp and Westmoreland, p. 84; and Westmoreland, passim.

period and concerning himself primarily with maintaining unity within the Politburo. By 1967, as Aubrac and Marcovich's meeting with him demonstrated (see Chapter 4, above), Ho was apparently in semi-retirement, with the day-to-day business of governing relegated to Pham Van Dong. Giap, meanwhile, at least up until the mid-1967 death of Nguyen Chi Thanh, was apparently largely excluded from control over the war in the South, which was instead the province of Le Duan, Nguyen Chi Thanh, Pham Hung, Le Duc Tho, and their supporters on the Central Committee and in the military. And yet, assuming that their memoirs are a reliable guide to their perceptions of the conflict, American officials were by and large ignorant of who was really in control of DRV policy toward the war in the South. As the data in Table 8 indicate, those memoirs were practically devoid of references to Pham Van Dong, even though he was the Party's chief negotiator and the official apparently most interested in arranging a negotiated settlement of the conflict, while references to Le Duan, Nguyen Chi Thanh, Pham Hung, and Le Duc Tho were virtually nonexistent. On the other hand, as we saw in Chapters 5 and 6, DRV policy toward the war in the South was determined entirely by developments in the South along with the persistence and skill of the proponents of an increased Northern role in the Southern revolution, and *not* by any slavish adherence to Mao's theories.

In view of the attraction exerted by the "Hanoi-as-unitary-calculating-actor" approach on the thinking of American officials, it is perhaps not surprising that those officials were not well informed concerning decision-making in Hanoi. The line of argument being developed here is important, nonetheless, since it illustrates two elementary dangers that those who seek to influence the workings of another government may fall prey to—dangers so elementary that they have often been overlooked. On the one hand, officials seeking to influence the policies of another government may not know or may be misinformed as to who is in control on the other side and thus at whom to direct their efforts. On the other hand, even if they know who is in charge, they may not be aware of the goals that their targets are pursuing. In the Vietnamese case, officials in Washington assumed that the North Vietnamese would attach more importance to protecting their meager industrial base than to gaining control of the South.[49] Such an assumption, however, was simply incorrect. As we saw in Chapter 5, for Le Duan, Nguyen Chi Thanh, and their supporters, completing the Southern revolution was

49. See, for example, Walt Rostow's comment to Secretary Rusk that "Ho has an industrial complex: he is no longer a guerrilla fighter with nothing to lose" (quoted in III Gravel, p. 153).

Table 8
References to DRV Officials* in Memoirs** by:

	President Johnson	Walt Rostow	Maxwell Taylor	General Westmoreland	Chester Cooper	Townsend Hoopes	The Pentagon Papers Narrative	The Pentagon Papers Documents	Total
Ho Chi Minh	26	10	10	4	16	10	5	0	81
Vo Nguyen Giap	1	4	1	9	0	5	0	1	21
Pham Van Dong	4	1	0	0	3	0	6	0	14
Le Duan	0	3	0	0	0	0	0	1	4
Nguyen Chi Thanh	0	0	0	2	0	0	0	0	2
Pham Hung	0	0	0	0	0	0	0	0	0
Le Duc Tho	0	0	0	2	0	0	0	0	2

*Number of pages on which their names appear (names may appear more than once on the same page).
**Lyndon B. Johnson, *The Vantage Point* (excluding appendices)
    Walt Rostow, *The Diffusion of Power*
    Maxwell Taylor, *Swords and Ploughshares*
    William Westmoreland, *A Soldier Reports*
    Chester Cooper, *The Lost Crusade*, rev. ed. (chapters on Johnson Administration only)
    Townsend Hoopes, *The Limits of Intervention*
    The Pentagon Papers, The Senator Gravel edition (sections on Johnson Administration only)

the most important task facing the North, and certainly more important than "building socialism" in the North.[50]

Furthermore, even if officials attempting to influence the activities of another government should know who is in charge and what those officials are pursuing, they still could be uncertain or misinformed as to what actions to take so as to move their opponents to act in the desired fashion. As we suggested in Chapter 6, the one U.S. move that appears to have contained the greatest potential for undercutting the arguments of Le Duan and his supporters and strengthening the position of the proponents of a diplomatic solution such as Pham Van Dong was an American offer to discuss some kind of coalition arrangement for South Vietnam. And yet, this was precisely the kind of move that U.S. officials were most reluctant to make, primarily because of their fears concerning the effects such a move would have on their South Vietnamese allies.

Finally, even if officials attempting to exert influence over officials in another government were fully informed as to who is in charge on the other side, what those opposing officials were seeking, and what actions to take in order to move their opponents in the desired direction, their efforts could nonetheless come to naught because of an inability to ensure that their own government acted in the required manner. As we saw in the preceding section, the control that senior officials have over the actions of their own government is at best imperfect; furthermore, there are numerous points at which their intent could be frustrated, either by "slippage" in the process of implementing their decisions or by the difficulties their opponents will encounter in attempting to discern the meaning of incoming signals. In the MARIGOLD case, albeit more by accident than by design, the Johnson Administration did begin to move in the direction necessary to strengthen the proponents of a negotiated settlement in Hanoi and discredit the opponents of such an outcome, in the form of the Administration's tentative acceptance of Lewandowski's formulation of the American position as the basis for the proposed Warsaw talks. Despite the promising beginning, however,

50. This point is also relevant to our earlier discussion of the problems with analogies between governments and calculating individuals—i.e., even if an opponent should engage in the kind of "rational" calculations predicted by the opponent-as-unitary-rational-actor "model," an American Administration could still fail to grasp the value attached to a certain goal by the opponent and hence the risks that the opponent was willing to run in pursuit of that goal. Ironically, the report by the Johnson Study Group argued that the North would attach more importance to completing the Southern revolution than to protecting its industrial base (see Chapter 2, above); Rostow, however, attempted to suppress the report, and it was ignored by senior officials (see Halberstam, p. 437).

the Administration was nonetheless unable to follow through effectively, first because of the ill-timed bombing raids on Hanoi and the President's unwillingness to order a cancellation of further attacks, and also
as a result of the confusion generated by Lodge's "differences of interpretation" statement to Lewandowski (see Chapter 6, above).

II. Prospects for the Future

Having said this much, however, there are still two questions that
remain unanswered. First, despite the very serious risks inherent in
efforts by one government to coerce another, there may still arise, as in
the case of the Cuban missile crisis, situations in which the vital interests of the U.S. are challenged in a way that seemingly necessitates
coercive pressures in response. With that possibility in mind, are there
any suggestions that we can offer that will improve the ability of policymakers to cope with the difficulties that invariably accompany attempts
at coercion? Second, since there are likely to be sharp differences of
opinion, even in the direst of situations, over the necessity and/or
advisability of resorting to coercive pressures,[51] are there any suggestions that we can offer that will help policymakers in differentiating
those situations in which coercion would be necessary and appropriate
from those in which it would be unnecessary and/or doomed to fail?

A. Improving Chances for Success

With respect to the first of the two questions posed above, our discussion to this point has identified two general categories of problems that
invariably arise when one government attempts to coerce another: (1)
"technical" problems associated with "orchestrating" words and deeds
and "signalling" by deed as well as by word (e.g., avoiding inadvertent
"signals," embarrassing coincidences, and foul-ups in the field); and (2)
"perceptual" problems that stem from each side's inability to understand the motives and intentions underlying an opponent's activities.
Each of these will be addressed in turn.

Concerning the first category—i.e., coping with the technical problems inherent in attempts at coercion—there are a number of ways in
which senior officials might seek to minimize these kinds of difficulties.
First, the President and his advisers could attempt to improve their control over the activities of subordinate agencies and officials. There are

---

51. It should be recalled that Robert McNamara initially disagreed with proposals for a forceful
response to the Soviet emplacement of missiles in Cuba, while Adlai Stevenson argued against the
blockade and in favor of a diplomatic response. On these points, see Allison, pp. 195–196, 202, 209.

several ways in which this might be done, none of which, however, is wholly satisfactory. One possibility would be for high officials to seek to minimize the number of agencies and officials involved in any attempt at coercion, since only by reducing the number of actors involved could they hope to approximate the kind of close personal control that would seem to be required for success at "orchestrating" and "signalling." One problem with this suggestion, however, is that it would be extraordinarily difficult to implement, since any attempt to delegate responsibility in this fashion would be strenuously resisted by organizations eager to secure a "piece of the action" so as to "prove" their effectiveness and justify their claims for maintaining or increasing their budgets and manpower. In addition, while reducing the number of actors involved might result in senior officials achieving better control over the remaining agencies, the price of such control would necessarily be a reduction in the options available with respect to transmitting "messages" to an opponent—i.e., the fewer the agencies involved, the fewer the "messages" that could be sent by ordering an agency to do something (e.g., move troops or planes to forward positions, etc.). Furthermore, as Rourke has noted:

The most pathological possibility presented by the ability of bureaucratic organizations to define the options open to policy-makers is that organizational interests will come in time to transcend national interests, and that executive agencies will force the adoption of policies which reflect, not the needs and interests of the country, but their own appetite for power, prestige, or security. . . . Allowing agencies to acquire a monopoly in the performance of a foreign policy function heightens the danger that organizational interests will become confused with national interests in the conduct of foreign affairs.[52]

Finally, this approach would do little to remedy the problems created by inadvertent signals resulting from routine activities, which, as suggested earlier, can be particularly troublesome during attempts at coercion.

Alternatively, if reducing the number of actors involved is likely to be impractical, a President seeking to improve his control over attempts to coerce another government might undertake to concentrate as much power as possible for foreign policy decision-making at one point in the government (e.g., the White House) in an effort to convince foreign audiences that only the signals emanating from that point were authoritative and that all others could be ignored. Again, however, not only are there likely to be serious problems with respect to the practicality of

52. Francis E. Rourke, *Bureaucracy and Foreign Policy* (Baltimore: Johns Hopkins University Press, 1972), p. 47.

such an approach, but, in addition, the question can legitimately be raised as to whether the cure would not be worse than the disease. On the one hand, the foreign policy bureaucracy is too large and the issues too complex for a President to retain sole control over all aspects of policymaking. Even a President who seeks to circumvent this problem by focusing his attention on one or a few aspects of policymaking (such as an attempt at coercion) while allowing the bureaucracy to handle the day-to-day business of relations with other governments is likely to be overwhelmed by the enormous demands on his time that would result from an attempt to keep track of all aspects of an attempt at coercion—i.e., troop movements, signals to an opposing government, diplomatic communications with allies and third parties, and so on.[53] Furthermore, as the U-2 incident cited earlier suggests, potentially disastrous surprises may still arise where a President least expects them—i.e., in the routine business that is of necessity supervised by career officials.

On the other hand, as the Johnson and Nixon presidencies have demonstrated only too well, a President powerful enough to do great and good deeds (e.g., pursue the Great Society, negotiate a rapprochement with China) is also a President powerful enough to do horrendously bad deeds (e.g., lead his country into a land war in Asia while deceiving Congress and the public about his intentions and the cost of the war; conduct "secret wars" in Laos and Cambodia; etc.). In fact, as Rourke has noted, it may be desirable to have the President encumbered to some extent by the inertia imposed by organizational routines:

In 1969 an American reconnaissance plane was shot down over North Korea, and Nixon decided to launch a retaliatory air strike against North Korean airfields. He could not do so immediately, however, since it took considerable time for the American military apparatus to deploy the forces necessary to conduct such a mission. As it turned out, Nixon changed his mind during this delay. "As the military slowly moved air and sea reinforcements toward Korea, his anger cooled and he decided against retaliatory raids." In this case, the

---

53. At the very least, the President would have to find some way of dealing with the enormous amounts of paper churned out by the foreign policy bureaucracy in Washington. Charles Hermann, for example, cites the substantial increases in State Department cable traffic during the Lebanese (1958) and Cuban missile crises ("Threat, Time, and Surprise: A Simulation of International Crisis," in Hermann [ed.], p. 201); while Ole Holsti suggests that decision-makers during the crisis preceding the outbreak of World War I were snowed under by an information overload ("Time, Alternatives, and Communications: The 1914 and Cuban Missile Crises," in Hermann [ed.], pp. 73–74). See also Daniel Ellsberg's testimony concerning the very sizable Vietnam cable traffic that flowed through the Pentagon's ISA office in 1964 and 1965, in Ellsberg Trial Transcript, pp. 19,501–19,502.

cumbersome nature of bureaucratic routines forced Nixon to reverse a major decision, perhaps in the long run to his own and the country's advantage.[54]

Finally, even though neither of the approaches suggested above seems especially promising, it might be possible for senior officials, by means of an intensive effort on their part, to approximate for short periods (perhaps as long as a week) the kind of close control over subordinate agencies and officials required for successful "orchestration" and "signalling."[55] As a result, it would seem highly desirable for those officials to resort to coercion only if they were reasonably certain that the affair could be brought to a quick conclusion. Unfortunately, however, as suggested at the start of this section, senior officials may not always have the luxury of choice in these matters: there may arise situations which necessitate coercive pressures of some sort even though there may be no certainty that the pressures will "work" quickly. Even in extended conflicts, however, the logic of our argument should still be applicable. Senior officials concerned about the technical problems associated with "orchestrating" and "signalling" would be well advised to make strenuous efforts to end the attempted coercion as quickly as possible. Not only will each passing day be likely to diminish their ability to exert the kind of control required for successful "orchestrating" and "signalling"—other problems, after all, can be put off only for so long—but, in addition, there are the all too real problems of stress and fatigue, which are likely to diminish significantly both the will and the ability of busy officials to supervise closely the activities of subordinates. In this respect, we can hypothesize that the longer the attempted coercion drags on, the more likely busy officials will find it convenient to deal with the military and diplomatic aspects of coercion separately rather than simultaneously; the more tempted senior officials will be to delegate decisions on the timing of military and diplomatic moves to subordinates, thus freeing themselves to deal with other problems; and the more likely a President will be to resort to tactics such as doing things "in twos" (with the attendant restrictions on his ability to "negotiate" in an "optimal" fashion) so as to maintain support for his policies.[56] Each of these

54. Francis Rourke, in Robert Osgood et al., *Retreat from Empire?* (Baltimore: Johns Hopkins University Press, 1973), p. 101. The internal quote is from the *New York Times*, January 21, 1971, p. 12.

55. On this point, see Glenn Paige, *The Korean Decision* (New York: Free Press, 1968), p. 290, Proposition 1.7: "The greater the crisis, the greater the interdepartmental collaboration."

56. On these points, see Williams (pp. 75–76), who, drawing on evidence from the Cuban missile crisis, argues that under conditions of "fairly intense stress" (which would seem to be characteristic

tendencies, in turn, as we saw in earlier chapters, increases the probability of undesirable outcomes such as breakdowns in coordination, unplanned coincidences, and inadvertent "signals" to the other side.

In short, then, no matter how hard they try, there is always likely to be some discrepancy between the "orchestrated" set of actions that senior officials think their government is undertaking and the set of organizational outputs actually being produced, just as there is likely to be a discrepancy between the "message" that senior officials think is being communicated to an opponent and the "message" that the opponent reads into the actions of the first side. As a result, senior officials should not only be aware of these discrepancies but should make an effort to allow for them in their planning. Not only should those officials be skeptical of proposals calling for the "orchestration" of the activities of many agencies over relatively long periods of time (e.g., the 30-day scenarios developed in conjunction with the Laotian crisis of May 1964),[57] but, in addition, if it should be necessary to resort to coercion, perhaps the worst mistake that senior officials could make would be to delude themselves into believing that coercion will be easy. If anything, senior officials should *expect* the kind of mistakes and foul-ups described in earlier chapters to occur (despite the illusion of "orchestratedness" likely to be presented in briefings by subordinates). In addition, it would probably be a wise investment to assign some staff members to monitor the situation and report as best they could on a regular basis on how the *totality* of actions being undertaken by their government would appear to an opponent. While there is no guarantee that such reports will be taken seriously,[58] such an effort certainly would not hurt and might do a great deal of good by sensitizing top officials to the difficulties involved in conveying precise and specific "messages" to an opponent.

---

of an attempt at coercion), "there is probably an upper time-limit within which decision-makers can operate efficiently." For a fuller discussion of the effects of fatigue and stress on government officials, see the essays by Thomas Milburn ("The Management of Crisis") and Charles Hermann and Linda Brady ("Alternative Models of International Crisis Behavior"), in Hermann (ed.), pp. 259–277, 281–303.

57. On these, see III Gravel, pp. 165–169; and Chapter 2, above.

58. As part of the Johnson Administration's conduct of the Vietnam conflict, the State Department published a one-page sheet on a weekly basis for inclusion in the President's Evening Reading Items showing how American moves might appear to Hanoi. The sheet, however, irritated Walt Rostow, who felt that it was too pessimistic, and he attempted to suppress it (see Halberstam, p. 775). In any event, a one-page sheet published weekly is hardly the sort of sustained attention to the details of government activity that is being proposed here.

Closely related to this last point is the final suggestion that we wish to offer with respect to the technical problems associated with "orchestrating" and "signalling." As we saw in Chapters 6 and 7, not only was the Johnson Administration plagued by a tendency to speak with many voices at once, but, in addition, at several critical points the Administration had great difficulty "explaining" certain embarrassing coincidences to the North Vietnamese. These difficulties suggest that if another Administration should find itself embroiled in a prolonged coercive conflict in the future, it might be advantageous to have available a formal communications channel that could not only convey authoritative explanations of American policy but that, more importantly, would have a reputation for truthfulness. To put this another way, while Jervis and others have shown that great advantages can accrue to states that successfully engage in deception, the Johnson Administration's experiences suggest that there might well be advantages to being able to claim convincingly that one is telling the truth.[59] In this respect, an incoming President might be well advised to appoint a senior member of the foreign policy "establishment" to the post of Ambassador-at-large and then hold the Ambassador in reserve, so to speak, for those situations in which a high-credibility channel might be of great importance (semi-retired status might make such a role more palatable). To be most effective, such a channel would have to be used both discreetly and infrequently, since any reluctance to use the high-credibility channel could be construed as indicating that the U.S. was using some other channel for deception. To avoid this pitfall, it would be best to reserve such a channel for the direst of circumstances, like the imminent collapse of the MARIGOLD contact in December 1966 (thus preserving the option of claiming that the high-credibility channel was not being used because the situation was not grave enough to warrant it).[60] In addition, rather than informing other governments of the Ambassador's role (since that information in itself would automatically "debase" other channels), it would seem best simply to include along with any messages conveyed through this channel a quiet suggestion that the recipient check the veracity of previous messages conveyed through the channel—a check that presumably would confirm the

59. On the role of deception, see Jervis (1970); Schelling (1960), chaps. 2–3; and Schelling (1966), chaps. 2–3. See also Halperin (1963), pp. 126–127, on the importance of maintaining formal channels of communication.

60. In addition, the Ambassador's semi-retired status or full-time work in business or law would provide a plausible basis for claiming that the channel could not be used because the Ambassador was busy with other things.

channel's reputation for truthfulness. While there is no guarantee that messages conveyed in this way would always be believed (especially by a government that was the target of coercive pressures), it should be possible to increase over time the credibility of the channel by appointing Ambassadors with a reputation for candor, and, more importantly, by never using the channel for an attempt to deceive. While the temptation to misuse the channel would very likely increase in direct proportion to its credibility (other governments would of course be aware of this), such a temptation would have to be resisted at all costs so as to preserve the channel for some future crisis when an Administration might be seeking desperately to explain American policy in a way that would be believed by an opponent.

With respect to the second category of problems to be considered here —i.e., "perceptual" problems resulting from each side's inability to understand the motives and intentions underlying an opponent's activities—there are several points that need to be made. As we stressed in Chapter 7, it is critically important in any conflict situation for officials on both sides to have some understanding both of the motives underlying their opponent's current activities and of the intentions that will guide their opponent's actions in the future. In this respect, perhaps the most important step that officials in the government doing the coercing could take to improve their understanding of the situation and minimize the harmful effects of the perceptual problems identified earlier (i.e., assuming that everything the opponent does is part of a carefully designed scheme, assuming that any injuries inflicted by the opponent were done so intentionally, etc.) would be to realize just how misleading the opponent-as-unitary-rational-actor "model" can be and to seek to develop some sensitivity to the bureaucratic and organizational constraints under which their opponents must operate. To some extent, this kind of sensitivity should be a welcome by-product of the implementation of the suggestions put forward above as part of our discussion of the technical problems associated with "orchestrating" and "signalling." That is, to the extent that senior officials realize how tenuous is their control over their own government, and to the extent that they attempt to monitor how the totality of their own government's activities would appear to an opponent, they should also come to appreciate the difficulties that their opponents are likely to be encountering. Still, one should not make too much of this point. As we saw in Chapter 7, officials in Washington at least, while cognizant of the splits within their own government, were nonetheless quick to assume that no such cleavages existed in Hanoi. As a result, what is needed more than anything else is a conscious effort on the part of senior officials to change the way they view an opponent's decision-making processes. In particular, officials should realize that what their opponents do is not solely a function of the coercer's actions; furthermore, they should realize that it almost always takes time to fashion an intragovernmental consensus (particularly in cases requiring the abandonment or modification of a previously approved policy). As a result, officials should not expect the imposition of coercive pressures to produce an immediate change in their opponent's policies, nor should they assume that the absence of an immediate reaction by their opponent is a sign of treachery or perfidy. Finally and most importantly, officials in the state doing the coercing should realize that their opponents will very likely be encountering problems analogous to their own with respect to "orchestrating" and "signalling." Consequently, officials on both sides should realize that the "messages" that they read into their opponent's actions may differ significantly from the "messages" actually being communicated, and they should at least be willing to consider the possibility that their initial reading of incoming signals is inaccurate.

While such a reorientation in the thinking of high-level officials will admittedly increase the already formidable burdens upon them, the dangers associated with an inadequate understanding of an opponent's decision-making processes make such a reorientation imperative. As we saw in Chapter 7, officials in both Washington and Hanoi were quick to view injuries or rebuffs that were actually the result of factors such as breakdowns in coordination, unplanned coincidences, or overzealous subordinates as the product of plots and schemes concocted by a calculating opponent that never did anything unintentionally. Attitudes such as these, moreover, while not the basic cause of the dispute between Washington and Hanoi, nonetheless greatly complicated efforts to resolve a conflict that would have been difficult enough to settle even in the absence of the extreme distrust and suspicion that gripped officials on both sides. When one government attempts to coerce another, the risks involved (particularly that of uncontrolled escalation) are simply too great to permit such an effort to be conducted on a basis as flimsy as that provided by the opponent-as-unitary-rational-actor "model." While it will never be possible to eliminate completely the foul-ups and breakdowns that invariably occur when instruments as blunt as government bureaucracies are used to pursue foreign policy goals, we can at least make a start toward eliminating the unwarranted and exaggerated fears that inevitably accompany a lack of understanding.

As a final point, however, suppose the Johnson Administration had been more successful in overcoming the various technical and perceptual problems identified earlier and that, as a result, the strategy of "graduated pressures" had "worked" and the North Vietnamese had agreed to end their role in the war in the South. What then? What would the Administration have gained besides a temporary respite? As we saw earlier, there was no disagreement in Hanoi over the legitimacy of the goal of reunifying Vietnam under Communist control. Furthermore, since Le Duan and Nguyen Chi Thanh had devoted virtually the whole of their careers to bringing the Southern revolution to fruition, it seems highly unlikely that they would have accepted a DRV "defeat" as final and contented themselves with "building socialism" in the North. Instead, they would very likely have simply resumed the effort to promote the cause of "armed struggle" in the South along with a high degree of Northern involvement in the Southern revolution. Nor would an American "success" in coercing the North have eliminated the problem of the Viet Cong guerrillas in the South: given that their homes and families were in the South, it seems quite unlikely that they would have accepted permanent exile in the North. Furthermore, considering their experiences with the Diem regime, Southern Communists could hardly have been expected to accept amnesty and live peacefully under the GVN. In short, then, any "success" that the Administration could have achieved would have been temporary at best. Sooner or later, the insurgency would have broken out anew (assuming it could have been ended in the first place); sooner or later, the North would have become involved in aiding the insurgents (considering the degree of their involvement with the Southern revolution, Le Duan and Nguyen Chi Thanh could hardly have been expected to sit on their hands while their compatriots fought and died in the South); sooner or later, an American President would have had to face once again the question of how to avoid the "loss" of South Vietnam.[61] What George and Smoke have said about deterrence theory could also be usefully applied to the theory of coercive war: "As many deterrence theorists have realized it needs to be supplemented with attempts to *reduce the motivation* underlying that

61. In this respect, NSSM-1 (p. 340) included a "report on new Viet Cong policy from a highly reliable agent [received] just four days prior to the bombing halt [of October 31, 1968]. In describing the new policy, he said that in the near future the VC may approve negotiations with the GVN and the Americans in order to bring about a cease fire and a coalition government. But it must be emphasized from the beginning that a coalition government is only temporary. The parallel was drawn with someone on a long journey. One must stop and rest before continuing. The ultimate goal is still a communist South Vietnam. There might be a cease fire, but after a period of time there would be another general uprising."

[aggressive] intention, and/or to *provide alternative goals* that may be relatively satisfactory to the deterred power."[62]

What this line of analysis suggests, then, is that a mastery of the techniques of coercion is no substitute for an effective foreign policy.[63] Policymakers should realize that not all situations can be dealt with satisfactorily by means of coercion, and they should strive to develop a capacity for distinguishing situations in which coercive pressures can "work" (i.e., induce an opponent to stop what it is doing and/or undo whatever it has done with a reasonably high probability that the distasteful activity will not be repeated in the foreseeable future) from those situations in which they would inevitably fail. In the Vietnamese case, it was subsequently conceded by the authors of NSSM-1 that "frequent references by Hanoi spokesmen to helping the U.S. find a face-saving formula for withdrawal suggest that there may be some in Hanoi who believe that this essentially is what the U.S. really desires and would eventually settle for."[64] Similarly, it was also conceded in NSSM-1 that DRV/VC forces in the South as of June 1965 had been significantly underestimated by American officials. Whereas intelligence estimates at the time set the enemy order of battle in South Vietnam (as of June 1965) at 92.8–98.8 thousand, retrospectively adjusted estimates made at the end of 1968 set the enemy order of battle (as of June 1965) at 200.6 thousand.[65] Would the Johnson Administration have plunged ahead had it known it faced a tenacious and determined opponent with formidable military capabilities at its disposal? Should it have plunged ahead? At the very least, these are questions that should have been raised *before* the Administration attempted to coerce the DRV, not after.

B. Coercion—Where and When?

While, as suggested earlier, there may arise situations in which the vital interests of the United States are challenged in a way that seemingly necessitates a coercive response, it should also be clear that not every challenge faced by this country in the future will be as serious as that posed by the introduction of Soviet missiles into Cuba in 1962. Similarly, as suggested in the preceding section, there may also arise situations in the future in which, because of the nature of the circumstances

62. George and Smoke, p. 63 (emphasis in original).
63. On this point, see George and Smoke, pp. 507–508.
64. NSSM-1, p. 78; see also p. 94.
65. Ibid., p. 368.

involved, coercive pressures would inevitably fail, thus suggesting that, in those cases at least, the U.S. would be better off not attempting coercion at all.[66] As a result, in order to minimize the chances of another fiasco similar to that produced by the Johnson Administration's mishandling of the Vietnamese conflict, policymakers must first be able to distinguish those situations in which coercive pressures are both necessary and appropriate (in the sense of having a reasonable chance of "working" as intended) from those in which they are unnecessary and/or doomed to fail.[67]

But while the desirability of this kind of analytical capability should be self-evident, it should also be apparent that the institutionalization of such a capability within the foreign policy bureaucracy is easier said than done. By the mid-1960s, the conflict in Vietnam was for all practical purposes a situation in which coercion was both unnecessary and inevitably doomed to fail. On the one hand, as we saw in earlier chapters, there were other options besides coercing the North that were available to the U.S. (although American officials steadfastly refused to consider them), the most prominent of which involved the establishment of a coalition government in Saigon and de facto partition of

66. It was argued at one point by officials in the Johnson Administration that the U.S. should go ahead with the bombing of North Vietnam even though the bombing would probably fail to prevent a Communist takeover in the South. At the very least, it was argued, the Communists would pay a price for their success and therefore would think twice about inaugurating future insurgencies. This argument, however, was defective in two respects. First, as we saw in Chapter 7, the "controllability" of coercive violence appears to be very low—i.e., once an attempt at coercion is begun, it may prove very difficult to bring it to an end. As a result, the danger is very great that the coercer will be entrapped in a much more costly conflict than originally envisioned and still fail to attain its objectives. Second, the fact that the U.S. did pay an enormous price in Vietnam and still failed to attain its goals has hardly set the kind of precedent designed to discourage future insurgencies. If anything, the effect of the U.S. failure was probably to convince Communist states that the U.S. will not intervene in future Vietnam-type insurgencies. As a result, officials must take care in choosing when and where to attempt coercive pressures. An attempt at coercion that fails may only convince potential opponents that coercion will not be used against them. In that way, attempts at coercion that fail may only increase the risk of contingencies that the coercer seeks to prevent, rather than vice versa.

67. It is important to notice the distinction being drawn in this paragraph. It is conceivable that future challenges to American interests may come as such a complete surprise that there simply is no time to conduct a detailed analysis of the prospects for the success or failure of coercive pressures; instead, the situation may be so grave that policymakers feel compelled to do something immediately (examples of this type of crisis would be the invasion of South Korea in 1950 or the Cuban missile crisis). It was primarily for situations of that type that the suggestions in Section II-A above were intended. Nonetheless, we can also conceive of challenges to American interests that develop in more leisurely fashion, thus giving policymakers time to consider whether to embark on an attempt at coercion. It is this latter situation that concerns us in Section II-B. (Needless to say, however, if policymakers should decide to attempt to coerce another government, the suggestions presented in Section II-A would still be relevant.)

South Vietnam. While such an approach would almost certainly have resulted in an eventual Communist takeover in the South, the circumstances of the case—i.e., the determination of the Communist leadership to achieve reunification, the strength of the NLF within South Vietnamese society, the extensiveness of DRV/VC preparations for wider war, and the closeness to victory on the part of DRV/VC forces by early 1965—were such that it seems highly unlikely that any policy adopted by the U.S., including rapid escalation, would have done more than postpone inevitable defeat (this despite the enormous costs in lives, money, and American prestige involved in the attempt to coerce the North—costs that would have been avoided by the coalition government/partition approach). And yet, despite the unfavorable circumstances, the Johnson Administration plunged ahead.

Still, it has to be conceded that all of this is clear only with the benefit of hindsight; one cannot condemn policymakers too harshly for failing to perceive options with the same degree of clarity that the passage of time conveys to the analyst. This does not mean, however, that officials cannot be held accountable for their choices. There were and are steps that policymakers can take to improve both their understanding of the options open to them and their ability to distinguish those situations in which coercive pressures have a reasonable chance of succeeding from those in which the chances of success are virtually nonexistent. In a nutshell, both the ability to perceive options and the ability to identify situations in which coercive pressures can "work" depend to a large extent on the ability of officials in the government doing the coercing to understand the "political realities" within the target state's government and to shape their policies in a way that maximizes the influence of those in the target state's government whose hopes and fears are most compatible with the coercer's objectives. While creativity of this sort in policymaking is admittedly difficult to achieve in practice, it need not be an impossibility, provided officials in the government doing the coercing are willing to ask themselves the right questions, encourage subordinates to research those questions thoroughly, and act on the basis of the answers obtained, no matter how unpleasant they might be. At the very least, policymakers contemplating an attempt to coerce another government should ask themselves the following: *What* is it that we are demanding of the other side? *Who* on the other side will have to do *what* in order to comply with our demands? What are the backgrounds, interests, and career stakes of the leaders on the other side, and how will these factors influence their willingness to act as we desire? Which agencies and individuals will be involved on our side? Do the repertoires of the relevant organizational subunits on our side contain routines that will enable them to act so as to induce actors on the other side to act in accordance with our wishes? What capabilities do our opponents possess, and how might these be used to thwart our efforts to achieve our goals?

While the data required to answer questions such as these will place a formidable burden on the intelligence agencies of any government, such a requirement still should not prove to be an insurmountable obstacle. In the Vietnamese case, for example, a thorough and realistic analysis of these kinds of questions would in all probability have indicated that no one in the DRV leadership could have advocated abandoning the struggle for reunification (and expected to remain in the leadership).[68] Furthermore, it does not seem unrealistic to assume that a serious research effort during 1964 could have discovered that the Politburo in Hanoi was increasingly dominated by a group of leaders (Le Duan, Nguyen Chi Thanh, Pham Hung, and Le Duc Tho) whose early careers had been devoted to furthering the Communist cause in the South, whose published articles and speeches had indicated that they attached the highest priority to completing the revolution in the South (even if that meant sacrificing economic development in the North), and whose influence within the Party and the Government was steadily increasing. In addition, it should have been apparent that the North Vietnamese and their Viet Cong allies possessed very formidable military capabilities, which, considering the chaotic situation in the South plus the fact that it was *their* country that was to be the battlefield, suggested that it would have been virtually impossible to compel them to give up the gains they had already won in the South. Most importantly, though, the claim that it is not unrealistic to assume that this type of analysis could and should have been available to American officials during 1964 is perhaps best supported by the fact that such analyses *were* to some extent available, in the form of the report prepared by the Johnson Study Group and the results of the Sigma Games (see Chapter 2, above). It is one of the great tragedies of the Johnson Administration that the information contained in the Study Group's report and in the results of the Sigma Games should have been either suppressed or ignored by high-level officials.

By the same token, a thorough understanding of the political realities in an opposing government will be essential to identifying the options

---

68. In this respect, note the conclusion drawn by NSSM-1 (p. 94): "It would seem highly unlikely that any Politburo member would ever believe (much less say) that the Communist Party should give up its efforts to unite all of Vietnam under its control."

open to the coercer. In the Vietnamese case, as we saw in earlier chapters, the coalition government approach advocated by Pham Van Dong was in fact the only viable alternative to the policies advocated by the more "hawkish" members of the leadership such as Le Duan and Nguyen Chi Thanh. And yet, officials in Washington persistently failed to realize that a coalition government in Saigon was the minimum that "Hanoi" could settle for. Consequently, expressions of apparent DRV interest in negotiations, as in the case of the XYZ (Paris), PINTA (Rangoon), and MARIGOLD contacts, went unnoticed in Washington, with the result that several opportunities to bring the war to some sort of conclusion were lost by an Administration that never really understood what it was that motivated its opponents or what its opponents could realistically settle for. Lest we be too harsh in our condemnation of Washington officialdom, it must be conceded that officials in Hanoi had very little grasp of the political realities in Washington. With the exception of Pham Van Dong, officials in Hanoi were by and large just as prone as their opposite numbers in Washington to put forward proposals that could have been accepted only if their opponents were willing to risk the gravest political consequences.

To the suggestions presented to this point there are two more that must be added. First, taken as a whole, the argument developed in this section constitutes more than anything else a plea for realism on the part of officials contemplating an attempt to coerce another government. Foreign policy in general and coercion in particular cannot and must not be based on the hope that officials in another government would willingly commit political suicide. Nor should officials expect their opponents to readily abandon positions that they may have been advocating for years and which they may have only with great difficulty imposed upon colleagues and/or superiors.

Second, while our suggestions to this point have highlighted the value of thoroughly researching all aspects of an attempt to coerce another government prior to deciding whether to go ahead, it cannot be emphasized too highly that no amount of staff work will save from disaster policymakers who are unwilling and/or unable to make proper use of the information they receive from subordinates. As we saw earlier, there were available within the Johnson Administration studies that could have alerted policymakers to the pitfalls inherent in attempting to coerce North Vietnam. And yet, not only did high-level officials not make use of this information but they apparently made no serious effort to answer the kinds of questions suggested above. Those documents that are available are devoid of any expression of concern on the part of the

President and his advisers as to *who* in Hanoi would have to do *what* in order to comply with their demands. Instead of a searching appraisal of the interests and career stakes of their opponents in Hanoi, senior Administration officials were content to rely on bromides such as Taylor's observation that the North Vietnamese would probably behave "about like the North Koreans and the Red Chinese a decade before; that is, they would seek an accommodation with us when the cost of pursuing a losing course became excessive."[69] And, as we saw in Chapters 5 and 6, it was largely as a result of their ignorance of the reality in Hanoi that Administration officials were led time and again to take steps that resulted in exactly the opposite of what they were supposed to produce. For this, senior officials in the Johnson Administration have no one to blame but themselves. While staff members and outside consultants can do their research for them and write their speeches for them, no one can force senior officials to ask the right questions. No one can force them to confront realistically the choices that they face. Most importantly, in this respect, no one can help them except as they help themselves.

69. Taylor (1972), p. 401.

APPENDIX I

The "Four Points": Pham Van Dong Speech to DRV National Assembly, April 8, 1965

It is the unswerving policy of the Government of the Democratic Republic of Vietnam to strictly respect the 1954 Geneva Agreements on Vietnam, and to correctly implement their basic provisions as embodied in the following points:

1. Recognition of the basic national rights of the Vietnamese people: peace, independence, sovereignty, unity and territorial integrity. According to the Geneva Agreements, the U.S. government must withdraw from South Vietnam all U.S. troops, military personnel and weapons of all kinds, dismantle all U.S. military bases there, cancel its "military alliance" with South Vietnam. It must end its policy of intervention and aggression in South Vietnam. According to the Geneva Agreements, the U.S. government must stop its acts of war against North Vietnam, completely cease all encroachments on the territory and sovereignty of the Democratic Republic of Vietnam.

2. Pending the peaceful reunification of Vietnam, while Vietnam is still temporarily divided into two zones, the military provisions of the 1954 Geneva Agreements on Vietnam must be strictly respected: the two zones must refrain from joining any military alliance with foreign countries, there must be no foreign military bases, troops and military personnel in their respective territory.

3. The internal affairs of South Vietnam must be settled by the South Vietnamese people themselves, in accordance with the program of the South Vietnam National Front for Liberation, without any foreign interference.

4. The peaceful reunification of Vietnam is to be settled by the Vietnamese people in both zones, without any foreign interference.

This stand unquestionably enjoys the approval and support of all peace- and justice-loving Governments and peoples in the world.

The Government of the Democratic Republic of Vietnam is of the view that the above-expounded stand is the basis for the soundest political settlement of the Vietnam problem. If this basis is recognized, favorable conditions will be created for the peaceful settlement of the Vietnam problem and it will be possible to consider the reconvening of an international conference along the pattern of the 1954 Geneva Conference on Vietnam.

Source: Vietnam News Agency, reprinted in "Recent Exchanges Concerning Attempts to Promote a Negotiated Settlement of the Conflict in Vietnam" (London: Her Majesty's Stationery Office, 1965), Cmnd. 2756, p. 51.

APPENDIX II

The U.S. Version of the "Four Points," presented to Mai Van Bo by Edmund Gullion, August 6, 1965

Point I—The basic rights of the Vietnamese people to peace, independence, sovereignty, unity and territorial integrity are recognized as set forth in the Geneva Accords of 1954. Obtaining compliance with the essential principles in the Accords is an appropriate subject for immediate, international discussions without preconditions and subsequent negotiations. Such discussions and negotiations should consider, among other things, appropriate means, including agreed stages, for the withdrawal of foreign military and quasi-military personnel and weapons from South and North Vietnam; the dismantling of foreign military bases in both areas; the cancellation of military alliances in contravention of the Accords; and the regrouping and redeployment of indigenous forces.

Point II—Strict compliance with the military provisions of the Geneva Accords must be achieved in accordance with schedules and appropriate safeguards to be agreed upon in the said discussions and subsequent negotiations.

Point III—The internal affairs of South and North Vietnam must be settled by the South and North Vietnamese peoples themselves in conformity with the principles of self-determination without any foreign interference.

Point IV—The issue of reunification of Vietnam must be decided peacefully, on the basis of free determination by the peoples of South and North Vietnam without foreign interference.

Source: XYZ Chronology, p. 9.

APPENDIX III

"Fourteen Points for Peace in Southeast Asia"
(White House press release, January 7, 1966)

1. The Geneva Agreements of 1954 and 1962 are an adequate basis for peace in Southeast Asia;

2. We would welcome a conference on Southeast Asia or on any part thereof;

3. We would welcome "negotiations without preconditions" as the 17 nations put it;

4. We would welcome unconditional discussions as President Johnson put it;

5. A cessation of hostilities could be the first order of business at a conference or could be the subject of preliminary discussions;

6. Hanoi's four points could be discussed along with other points which others might wish to propose;

7. We want no U.S. bases in Southeast Asia;

8. We do not desire to retain U.S. troops in South Viet Nam after peace is assured;

9. We support free elections in South Viet Nam to give the South Vietnamese a government of their own choice;

10. The question of reunification of Viet Nam should be determined by the Vietnamese through their own free decision;

11. The countries of Southeast Asia can be non-aligned or neutral if that be their option;

12. We would much prefer to use our resources for the economic reconstruction of Southeast Asia than in war. If there is peace, North Viet Nam could participate in a regional effort to which we would be prepared to contribute at least one billion dollars;

13. The President has said "The Viet Cong would not have difficulty being represented and having their views represented if for a moment Hanoi decided she wanted to cease aggression. I don't think that would be a problem."

14. We have said publicly and privately that we could stop the bomb-

ing of North Viet Nam as a step toward peace although there has not been the slightest hint or suggestion from the other side as to what they would do if the bombing stopped.

Source: DOSB, February 14, 1966, p. 225.

APPENDIX IV

The Lewandowski 10 Points

1. The U.S. is interested in a peaceful solution through negotiations.

2. Negotiations should not be interpreted as a way to negotiated surrender by those opposing the U.S. in Vietnam. A political negotiation would be aimed at finding an acceptable solution to all the problems, having in mind that the present status quo in South Vietnam must be changed in order to take into account the interests of the parties presently opposing the policy of the U.S. in South Vietnam.

3. The U.S. does not desire a permanent or a long-term military presence in South Vietnam.

4. The U.S. is willing to discuss all problems with respect to the settlement.

5. The U.S. is willing to accept the participation of "all" in elections and the supervision of these elections by an appropriate international body.

6. The U.S. believes that reunification should be settled by the Vietnamese themselves after peace and proper representative organs are established in South Vietnam.

7. The U.S. is prepared to abide by a neutral South Vietnam.

8. The U.S. is prepared to stop bombing "if this will facilitate such a peaceful solution." In this regard the U.S. is prepared to accept DRV modalities on the cessation and not require the DRV to admit infiltration into South Vietnam.

9. The U.S. will not agree to "reunification under military pressure."

10. The U.S. "will not declare now or in the future its acceptance of North Vietnam's 4 or 5 points."

Source: Ambassador Lodge's summary, Saigon Embassy cable #12247, November 30, 1966, in Marigold Chronology, pp. 36–37.

APPENDIX V

Pham Van Dong's Remarks to Aubrac and Marcovich, July 25, 1967

"Dear Friends. Our conversation yesterday was very useful. If you want to understand the problem in Vietnam, I advise you to read the book by Morris West called *The Ambassador.* We are facing a problem which is at the same time very simple, very complex and of great importance for the world. It is simple because it concerns the freedom of a people. It is complex because many considerations are involved. It is of great importance because it has involved so many peoples. We have come to the opinion that the U.S. government is trying to solve the problem within its present limits. We also think that the U.S. government is trying to get a clear picture of the present position. Our view is this: U.S. power is enormous and the U.S. government wants to win the war. President Johnson is suffering from a pain and this pain is called South Vietnam. We agree that the situation on the battlefield is decisive; the game is being played in South Vietnam. From the newspapers we see that some people want to confine the war to the South. However, the White House and Pentagon seem determined to continue the war against the North. Therefore we think that attacks on the North are likely to increase. We have made provisions for attacks on our dikes; we are ready to accept war on our soil. Our military potential is growing because of aid from the USSR and other Socialist countries.

"As for the situation on the battlefield, it is improving all the time. The dry season was good and the wet season will be better. The Marines are in difficulty. The United States is forced to replace its well-trained troops by ever-younger soldiers. We fight only when we choose; we economize on our resources; we fight only for political purposes.

"For example, news from Saigon suggests that Ky is considering moving his capital because it is no longer safe. This is true. We could easily step up our actions inside the city. But we take only those actions which have political meaning and which economize human lives.

"Now I shall talk to you about negotiations and solutions. We have been fighting for our independence for four thousand years. We have defeated the Mongols three times. The United States Army, strong as it is, is not as terrifying as Genghis Khan. We fight to have peace at home; we have no wider aims. We have made clear our position in our four points and in the interview of January 28, 1967. We are ready to talk at any time provided that actions against the North are unconditionally ended. I want to repeat what I said yesterday: we are willing to settle for a de facto stoppage.

"Ending the war for us has two meanings: (1) An end of bombing which is permanent and unconditional; (2) A withdrawal of United States forces. We like the formula of President de Gaulle." Marcovich interrupted to say that it was not realistic. Pham Van Dong agreed and said that he realized that some U.S. troops would have to stay until the end of the process of political settlement. He added: "We do not want to humiliate the U.S. Lenin did not like war but fought when necessary. As Lenin we are Communists.

"Now let me speak of U.S. policy and the NLF. We should have had unification in 1956. The period 1956-59 was a political fight. It saw the mutual assistance pact between the U.S. and Saigon and the introduction of U.S. staffs. This led to the formation of the NLF. The second period, 1960-1964, saw a disintegration of the U.S. position to which the U.S. responded by 'special' war. In 1965, the United States started a 'limited' war which lasts until today. At the same time the NLF has expanded its activities from the country into the cities and from inside Vietnam to the outside. Our position is: North Vietnam is socialist and wants to remain so. As for the South, our goals are national independence, democracy, peace and neutrality. Some people think we want to impose Socialism on the South. We are convinced that the NLF will not make such an error. The NLF envisages a broad coalition government, including *all* significant groups and religions *without consideration of past activities including members du gouvernement fantoche et cadres d'armes fantoche.* [He repeated the underlined words.] The essential thing is to forget the past.

"As for unification, we recognize that the important first step is a political settlement of the South. We agree not to push things toward unification. Once the war in the South is settled, we shall discuss with the South and find the best means. Our people are magnificent.

"Peace would have been easy for the U.S. three years ago. But with every year the political situation worsens. We do not like secret negotiations, but we recognize their necessity in this situation. As long as the issues do not concern South Vietnam, the NLF need not participate. However, we do not believe that the United States is ready for a settlement." Then turning to Aubrac he asked: "Que veulent les Americains?"

Source: Aubrac's report to Kissinger; Pennsylvania, pp. 6-9.

APPENDIX VI

Text of U.S. Message Passed to Mai Van Bo by Aubrac and Marcovich, August 25, 1967

The United States is willing to stop the aerial and naval bombardment of North Vietnam with the understanding that this will lead promptly to productive discussions between representatives of the United States and the Democratic Republic of Vietnam looking toward a resolution of the issues between them. While discussions proceed either with public knowledge or secretly, the United States would assume that the Democratic Republic of Vietnam would not take advantage of the bombing cessation. Any such move on the part of the Democratic Republic of Vietnam would obviously be inconsistent with the movement toward resolution of the issues between the United States and the Democratic Republic of Vietnam which the discussions are intended to achieve.

The United States is prepared to enter into discussions either openly or secretly. It would seem, however, that a total cessation of the bombing is inconsistent with keeping secret the fact that discussions are taking place. Accordingly, the Democratic Republic of Vietnam may prefer to consider the alternative of a cutback in the magnitude or scope of the bombing while secret discussions are in progress.

The United States is ready to have immediate private contact with the Democratic Republic of Vietnam to explore the above approach or any suggestions the Democratic Republic of Vietnam might wish to propose in the same direction.

Source: Pennsylvania, p. 15.

Bibliography

Adams, Sam. "Vietnam Cover-Up: Playing War With Numbers." *Harper's,* May 1975.

Allison, Graham. *Essence of Decision.* Boston: Little, Brown, 1971.

———, and Halperin, Morton. "Bureaucratic Politics: A Paradigm and Some Policy Implications." *World Politics,* 24 (Spring 1972).

Aron, Raymond. "The Evolution of Modern Strategic Thought." *The Adelphi Papers,* 54 (February 1969).

Art, Robert. "Bureaucratic Politics and Foreign Policy: A Critique." *Policy Sciences,* 4:4 (December 1973).

Ashmore, Harry, and Baggs, William. *Mission to Hanoi.* New York: G. P. Putnam's Sons, 1968.

Austin, Anthony. *The President's War.* Philadelphia: J. B. Lippincott, 1971.

Baggs, Andrew. "Bombing, Bargaining, and Limited War: North Vietnam, 1965–1968." Unpublished Ph.D. thesis, University of North Carolina, Chapel Hill, 1972.

Baldwin, Hanson. "After Vietnam—What Military Strategy in the Far East?" *New York Times Magazine,* June 9, 1968.

Ball, George. "Top Secret: The Prophecy the President Rejected." *The Atlantic,* July 1972.

Barnet, Richard. "The Men Who Made the War," in Stavins, Barnet, and Raskin.

Bauer, Raymond. "Problems of Perception and the Relations Between the United States and the Soviet Union." *Journal of Conflict Resolution,* 5 (1961).

———. "Accuracy of Perception in International Relations." *Teachers College Record,* 64 (1963).

Blachman, Morris. "The Stupidity of Intelligence," in Peters and Adams (eds.).

Brandon, Henry. *Anatomy of Error.* Boston: Gambit, 1969.

Brodie, Bernard. "Unlimited Weapons and Limited War." *The Reporter,* November 18, 1954.

———. *Strategy in the Missile Age.* Princeton, N.J.: Princeton University Press, 1959.

————. *Escalation and the Nuclear Option*. Princeton, N.J.: Princeton University Press, 1966.

————. "Learning to Fight a Limited War," in William Gerberding and Bernard Brodie, *The Political Dimension in National Strategy: Five Papers*. UCLA Security Studies Project, 1968.

Broughton, Col. Jack. *Thud Ridge*. Philadephia: J. B. Lippincott, 1969.

Carver, George. "The Faceless Viet Cong." *Foreign Affairs*, 44:3 (April 1966).

Chen, King C. "North Vietnam in the Sino-Soviet Dispute, 1962–1964." *Asian Survey*, 4:9 (September 1964).

————. "Hanoi versus Peking: Policies and Relations—A Survey." *Asian Survey*, 12:9 (September 1972).

————. "Hanoi's Three Decisions and the Escalation of the Vietnam War." *Political Science Quarterly*, 90:2 (Summer 1975).

Clifford, Clark. "A Viet Nam Reappraisal." *Foreign Affairs*, 47:4 (July 1969).

Cook, Mark. *Interpersonal Perception*. Baltimore: Penguin, 1971.

Cooper, Chester. "The Complexities of Negotiations." *Foreign Affairs*, 46:3 (April 1968).

————. *The Lost Crusade*, rev. ed. Greenwich, Conn.: Fawcett, 1972.

Cousins, Norman. "Vietnam: The Spurned Peace." *Saturday Review*, July 26, 1969.

"Crucial Vietnam Decisions of Johnson Administration Discussed by Former President in Second TV Interview." *Congressional Quarterly Weekly Report*, February 6, 1970.

Cyert, Richard, and March; James. *A Behavioral Theory of the Firm*. Englewood Cliffs, N.J.: Prentice-Hall, 1963.

Devillers, Philippe. "The Struggle for the Unification of Vietnam." *China Quarterly*, 9 (January–March 1962).

Dommen, Arthur. *Conflict in Laos*, rev. ed. New York: Praeger, 1971.

Dudman, Richard. "Military Policy in Vietnam." *Current History*, 50:294 (February 1966).

Duiker, William J. "Building the United Front: The Rise of Communism in Vietnam," in Zasloff and Brown (eds.).

Ellsberg, Daniel. *Papers on the War*. New York: Pocket Books, 1972.

————. "The Theory and Practice of Blackmail," in Young (ed.).

Evans, Rowland, and Novak, Robert. *Lyndon B. Johnson: The Exercise of Power*. New York: Signet Books, 1966.

"Experiences of the South Vietnam Revolutionary Movement During the Past Several Years" (The CRIMP Document), in U.S. Department of State, "Working Paper on the North Vietnamese Role in the War in South Vietnam," Appendices, Item 301.

Fall, Bernard. *Last Reflections on a War*. New York: Schocken, 1972.

Fitzgerald, Frances. *Fire in the Lake*. New York: Vintage, 1972.

Galloway, John. *The Gulf of Tonkin Resolution*. Rutherford, N.J.: Fairleigh-Dickenson University Press, 1970.

Gallucci, Robert. *Neither Peace Nor Honor*. Baltimore: Johns Hopkins University Press, 1975.

Gelb, Leslie. "Vietnam: The System Worked." *Foreign Policy*, 3 (Summer 1971).

George, Alexander. "The Development of Doctrine and Strategy," "The Cuban Missile Crisis, 1962," and "Comparisons and Lessons," in George, Hall, and Simons.

———; Hall, David; and Simons, William. *The Limits of Coercive Diplomacy*. Boston: Little, Brown, 1971.

———, and Smoke, Richard. *Deterrence in American Foreign Policy*. New York: Columbia University Press, 1974.

Geyelin, Philip. *Lyndon B. Johnson and the World*. New York: Praeger, 1966.

Goodman, Allan. "Fighting While Negotiating: The View from Hanoi," in Zasloff and Brown (eds.).

Goulden, Joseph C. *Truth Is the First Casualty*. Chicago: Rand, McNally, 1969.

Gray, Colin, "What RAND Hath Wrought." *Foreign Policy*, 4 (Fall 1971).

Gurtov, Melvin. "Hanoi on War and Peace." P-3696, The RAND Corp., 1967.

———, and Kellen, Konrad. "Vietnam: Lessons and Mislessons." P-4084, The RAND Corp., 1969.

Halberstam, David. *The Best and the Brightest*. Greenwich, Conn.: Fawcett, 1972.

Hall, David. "The Laos Crisis, 1960–1961," in George, Hall, and Simons.

Halperin, Morton. *Limited War in the Nuclear Age*. New York: John Wiley, 1963.

———. *Bureaucratic Politics and Foreign Policy*. Washington, D.C.: The Brookings Institution, 1974.

Hanoi VNA International Service in English, 9 August 1970. "A Brief Chronology of Momentous Facts and Events in the History of the Democratic Republic of Vietnam," in *Vietnam Documents and Research Notes*, no. 84 (September 1970).

Henry, John B. "February 1968." *Foreign Policy*, 4 (Fall 1971).

Hermann, Charles, "Threat, Time, and Surprise: A Simulation of International Crisis," in Hermann (ed.).

——— (ed.). *International Crises: Insights from Behavioral Research*. New York: Free Press, 1972.

———, and Brady, Linda. "Alternative Models of International Crisis Behavior," in Hermann (ed.).

Hilsman, Roger. *To Move a Nation*. New York: Dell, 1967.

Holsti, Ole. "Time, Alternatives, and Communications: The 1914 and Cuban Missile Crises," in Hermann (ed.).

Honey, P. J. "North Vietnam's Party Congress." *The China Quarterly*, 4 (October–December 1960).

———— (ed.). *North Vietnam Today.* New York: Praeger, 1962.

————. *Communism in North Vietnam.* Cambridge, Mass.: MIT Press, 1963.

————. "Vietnam: To the Bitter End?" *The Spectator*, December 17, 1965; reprinted in *Survival*, 8:2 (February 1966).

————. "North Vietnam Quarterly Survey." *China News Analysis*, 1962–1968.

Hoopes, Townsend. *The Limits of Intervention.* New York: David McKay, 1969.

————. "LBJ's Account of March 1968." *The New Republic*, March 14, 1970.

Huntington, Samuel. *The Common Defense.* New York: Columbia University Press, 1961.

Jervis, Robert. "Hypotheses on Misperception." *World Politics*, 20 (1968).

————. *The Logic of Images in International Relations.* Princeton, N.J.: Princeton University Press, 1970.

————. *Perception and Misperception in International Politics.* Princeton, N.J.: Princeton University Press, 1976.

Johnson, Lyndon. *The Vantage Point.* New York: Popular Library, 1971.

Kahn, Herman. *On Escalation.* Baltimore: Penguin, 1965.

Kattenburg, Paul. "Vietnam and U.S. Diplomacy, 1940–1970." *Orbis*, 15:3 (Fall 1971).

Kaufmann, William. "The Requirements of Deterrence," "Limited Warfare," and "Force and Foreign Policy," in Kaufmann (ed.), *Military Policy and National Security.* Princeton, N.J.: Princeton University Press, 1956.

Kaye, William. "A Bowl of Rice Divided: The Economy of North Vietnam," in Honey (ed.).

Kearns, Doris, *Lyndon Johnson and the American Dream.* New York: Signet, 1977.

Kennedy, Robert. *Thirteen Days: A Memoir of the Cuban Missile Crisis.* New York: Signet, 1969.

Kissinger, Henry. *Nuclear Weapons and Foreign Policy.* Garden City, N.Y.: Doubleday, 1958.

————. *The Necessity for Choice.* New York: Harper & Bros., 1960.

Knorr, Klaus and Read, Thornton (eds.). *Limited Strategic War.* New York: Praeger, 1962.

Komer, Robert. "Bureaucracy Does Its Thing: Institutional Constraints on U.S.–GVN Performance in Vietnam." R-967-ARPA, The RAND Corp., 1972.

Kraslow, David, and Loory, Stuart. *The Secret Search for Peace in Vietnam.* New York: Vintage, 1968.

Krasner, Stephen. "Are Bureaucracies Important?" *Foreign Policy*, 7 (Summer 1972).

Krause, Patricia (ed.). *Anatomy of an Undeclared War.* New York: International Universities Press, 1972.

Lacouture, Jean. *Vietnam: Between Two Truces.* New York: Vintage, 1966.

Latimer, Thomas. "Hanoi's Leaders and Their South Vietnam Policies, 1954–1968." Unpublished Ph.D. thesis, Georgetown University, 1972.

Lindblom, Charles. *The Intelligence of Democracy.* New York: Free Press, 1965.

Littauer, Raphael, and Uphoff, Norman (eds.). *The Air War in Indochina,* rev. ed. Boston: Beacon Press, 1972.

McGarvey, Patrick. "DIA: Intelligence to Please." *The Washington Monthly,* July 1970.

———. *CIA: The Myth and the Madness.* Baltimore: Penguin, 1972.

Maneli, Mieczylaw. "Vietnam: '63 and Now." *New York Times,* January 27, 1975, p. 25.

Martin, John Bartlow. *Adlai Stevenson and the World.* Garden City, N.Y.: Doubleday, 1977.

Maull, Hans. "Oil and Influence: The Oil Weapon Examined." *Adelphi Papers,* 117 (1975).

May, Ernest. *"Lessons" of the Past.* New York: Oxford University Press, 1973.

Mecklin, John. *Mission in Torment.* Garden City, N.Y.: Doubleday, 1965.

Milburn, Thomas. "The Management of Crisis," in Hermann (ed.).

Moise, Edwin. "Land Reform and Land Reform Errors in North Vietnam." *Pacific Affairs,* 49:1 (Spring 1976).

[Moyers, Bill.] "Bill Moyers Talks About LBJ, Power, Poverty, War, and the Young." *The Atlantic,* July 1968.

Mueller, John. *War, Presidents, and Public Opinion.* New York: John Wiley, 1973.

Nalty, Bernard. *Air Power and the Fight for Khe Sanh.* Washington, D.C.: U.S. Government Printing Office, 1973.

National Security Study Memorandum-1, 1969, xeroxed. (Also available in the *Congressional Record,* May 10, 1972, pp. E3975 ff.; May 11, 1972, pp. E5008 ff.)

Neustadt, Richard. *Alliance Politics.* New York: Columbia University Press, 1970.

New York Times. Selected articles, 1964–1975.

Nickel, Ted. "The Attribution of Intention as a Critical Factor in the Relation Between Frustration and Aggression." *Journal of Personality,* 42 (1974).

Oberdorfer, Don. *Tet!* New York: Avon, 1971.

———. "Kissinger Played Major Role in 1967 Dialogue." *Washington Post,* June 27, 1972, pp. A1, A12.

Osgood, Robert. *Limited War: The Challenge to American Strategy.* Chicago: University of Chicago Press, 1957.

———. "The Reappraisal of Limited War." *The Adelphi Papers,* 54 (February 1969).

——— et al. *Retreat From Empire?* Baltimore: Johns Hopkins University Press, 1973.

Paige, Glenn. *The Korean Decision.* New York: Free Press, 1968.

Palmerlee, Albert. "The Central Office of South Vietnam." *Vietnam Documents and Research Notes,* no. 40 (August 1968).

Pennock, J. Roland, and Chapman, John (eds.). *Coercion-Nomos XIV.* Chicago: Aldine Atherton, 1972.

The Pentagon Papers. The Senator Gravel Edition. 5 vols. Boston: Beacon Press, 1971.

Peters, Charles, and Adams, Timothy (eds.). *Inside the System.* New York: Praeger, 1970.

Pfeffer, Richard (ed.). *No More Vietnams?* New York: Harper & Row, 1968.

Pierre, Andrew. "American Down, Russia Up: The Changing Political Role of Military Power." *Foreign Policy,* 4 (Fall 1971).

Pike, Douglas. *Viet Cong.* Cambridge, Mass.: MIT Press, 1966.

———. *War, Peace, and the Viet Cong.* Cambridge, Mass.: MIT Press, 1969.

Porter, Gareth. *A Peace Denied.* Bloomington: Indiana University Press, 1975.

Race, Jeffrey. *War Comes to Long An.* Berkeley: University of California Press, 1972.

"Recent Exchanges Concerning Attempts to Promote a Negotiated Settlement of the Conflict in Vietnam." Cmnd. 2756. London: Her Majesty's Stationery Office, 1965.

Ronning, Chester. *A Memoir of China in Revolution.* New York: Pantheon, 1974.

Rossi, Mario. "U Thant and Vietnam: The Untold Story." *New York Review of Books,* November 17, 1966.

Rostow, Walt. *The Diffusion of Power.* New York: Macmillan, 1972.

Rourke, Francis. *Bureaucracy and Foreign Policy.* Baltimore: Johns Hopkins University Press, 1972.

Russett, Bruce. "Pearl Harbor: Deterrence Theory and Decision Theory." Reprinted in Russett, *Power and Community in World Politics.* San Francisco: W. H. Freeman, 1974.

Safire, William. "What Went Wrong." *New York Times,* April 24, 1975, p. 35.

Salisbury, Harrison. *Behind the Lines—Hanoi.* New York: Harper & Row, 1967.

Schandler, Herbert. *The Unmaking of a President.* Princeton, N.J.: Princeton University Press, 1977.

Schelling, Thomas. *The Strategy of Conflict.* Cambridge, Mass.: Harvard University Press, 1960.

———. *Arms and Influence.* New Haven, Conn.: Yale University Press, 1966.

Schurmann, Franz; Scott, Peter Dale; and Zelnik, Reginald. *The Politics of Escalation in Vietnam.* Greenwich, Conn.: Fawcett, 1966.

Scott, Peter Dale. *The War Conspiracy.* Indianapolis, Ind.: Bobbs-Merrill, 1972.

Sevareid, Eric. "The Final Troubled Hours of Adlai Stevenson." *Look,* November 30, 1965.

Shaplen, Robert. *The Lost Revolution,* rev. ed. New York: Harper & Row, 1966.

———. *Time Out of Hand.* New York: Harper & Row, 1970.

Sharp, Mitchell. Report on Seaborn missions, Canadian House of Commons, *Proceedings,* June 17, 1971.

Sharp, Adm. U. S. G., and Westmoreland, Gen. William. *Report on the War in Vietnam.* Washington, D.C.: U.S. Government Printing Office, 1968.

Simons, William. "The Vietnam Intervention, 1964–1965," in George, Hall, and Simons.

Snyder, Glenn. "The New Look," in Warner Schilling, Paul Hammond, and Glenn Snyder, *Strategy, Politics and Defense Budgets*. New York: Columbia University Press, 1962.

———. "Crisis Bargaining," in Hermann (ed.).

Stavins, Ralph. "Washington Determines the Fate of Vietnam, 1954-1965," in Stavins, Barnet, and Raskin.

———; Barnet, Richard; and Raskin, Marcus. *Washington Plans an Aggressive War*. New York: Vintage, 1971.

Steinbruner, John. *The Cybernetic Theory of Decision*. Princeton, N.J.: Princeton University Press, 1974.

Taylor, Maxwell. *The Uncertain Trumpet*. New York: Harper & Bros., 1960.

———. *Swords and Ploughshares*. New York: W. W. Norton, 1972.

Thayer, Carlyle. "Southern Vietnamese Revolutionary Organizations and the Vietnam Workers' Party: Continuity and Change, 1954-1974," in Zasloff and Brown (eds.).

Thomson, James. "How Could Vietnam Happen?" *The Atlantic*, April 1968.

Truong Chinh. "Let Us Be Grateful to Karl Marx and Follow the Path Traced by Him." *Vietnam Documents and Research Notes*, no. 51 (February 1968).

Turley, William. "Army, Party, and Society in the DRV: Civil-Military Relations in a Mass-Mobilization System." Unpublished Ph.D. thesis, University of Washington, 1972.

———. "Urbanization in War: Hanoi, 1946-1973." *Pacific Affairs*, 48:3 (Fall 1975).

Turner, Robert. *Vietnamese Communism: Its Origins and Development*. Stanford, Calif.: Hoover Institution Press, 1975.

Ulam, Adam. *Expansion and Coexistence*. New York: Praeger, 1968.

U.S. Department of Defense. *U.S.-Vietnam Relations, 1945-1967*. 12 vols. Washington, D.C.: U.S. Government Printing Office, 1971.

U.S. Department of State. "Hanoi's Role in the Support of the Present War in South Vietnam," (xeroxed, no date).

———. "Working Paper on the North Vietnamese Role in the War in South Vietnam." Reprinted in *Vietnam Documents and Research Notes*, no. 37 (June 1968).

U.S. Mission, Saigon. "The Nineteenth Plenary Session of the Central Committee of the Vietnam Workers' Party and its Reference Documents." *Vietnam Documents and Research Notes*, no. 91 (March 1971).

———. "The Vietnam Workers' Party's 1963 Decision to Escalate the War in the South." *Vietnam Documents and Research Notes*, no. 96 (July 1971).

———. "World Situation and Our Party's International Mission." *Vietnam Documents and Research Notes*, no. 98 (September 1971).

U.S. Senate, Committee on Foreign Relations. *Background Information Relating to Southeast Asia and Vietnam*. 6th rev. ed. Washington, D.C.: U.S. Government Printing Office, 1970.

U.S. vs. Ellsberg and Russo. U.S. District Court, Los Angeles, 1971 (Ellsberg Trial Transcript).

Vietnam Workers' Party, Central Committee Historical Department. "Forty Years of Party Activity." *Vietnam Documents and Research Notes*, no. 76 (April 1970).

The Washington Post. Selected articles, 1964–1972.

Weinstein, Franklin. "Vietnam's Unheld Elections." Data Paper no. 60, Southeast Asia Program, Cornell University, July 1966.

Westmoreland, William. *A Soldier Reports*. Garden City, N.Y.: Doubleday, 1976.

White, Ralph. *Nobody Wanted War*. Garden City, N.Y.: Doubleday, 1970.

Whiting, Allen. "The Scholar and the Policy-Maker." *World Politics*, 24 (Spring 1972).

Wicker, Tom. *JFK and LBJ*. Baltimore: Penguin, 1968.

Williams, Phil. *Crisis Management*. London: Martin Robertson, 1976.

Wilson, Harold. *A Personal Record: The Labour Government, 1964-1970*. Boston: Little, Brown, 1971.

Windchy, Eugene. *Tonkin Gulf*. Garden City, N.Y.: Doubleday, 1971.

Wohlstetter, Albert, and Wohlstetter, Roberta. "Controlling the Risks in Cuba." *The Adelphi Papers*, 17 (April 1965).

Wohlstetter, Roberta. *Pearl Harbor: Warning and Decision*. Stanford, Calif.: Stanford University Press, 1962.

Young, Oran. *The Politics of Force*. Princeton, N.J.: Princeton University Press, 1968.

——— (ed.). *Bargaining: Formal Theories of Negotiation*. Urbana: University of Illinois Press, 1975.

Zagoria, Donald. *Vietnam Triangle*. New York: Pegasus, 1967.

Zasloff, Joseph, and Brown, MacAlister (eds.). *Communism in Indochina*. Lexington, Mass.: D.C. Heath, 1975.

Index

439